THE VIOLENT IMAGE

NEVILLE BOLT

The Violent Image

*Insurgent Propaganda
and the New Revolutionaries*

Columbia University Press
New York

Columbia University Press
Publishers Since 1893
New York
cup.columbia.edu
© Neville Bolt, 2012

Library of Congress Cataloging-in-Publication Data

Bolt, Neville.
  The violent image : insurgent propaganda and the new revolutionaries/
Neville Bolt.
    p. cm.
  Includes bibliographical references and index.
  ISBN: 978-0-231-70316-1 (alk. paper)
  ISBN: 978-0-231-80088-4 (e-book)
  1. Insurgency—Public relations—History. 2. Revolutionaries—Public
relations—History. 3. Communication in politics—Technological
innovations. 4. Mass media and propaganda. 5. Political violence
in mass media. 6. Terrorism in mass media. 7. Public relations
and politics. I. Title.

JC328.5.B65 2012
303.3'75—dc23

                    2012003349

∞

Columbia University Press books are printed on permanent and durable acid-
free paper. This book is printed on paper with recycled content.
Printed in India

c 10 9 8 7 6 5 4 3 2 1

References to Internet Web sites (URLs) were accurate at the time of writing.
Neither the author nor Columbia University Press is responsible for URLs that
may have expired or changed since the manuscript was prepared.

To victims of political violence

CONTENTS

CONTENTS

CONTENTS

LIST OF PHOTOGRAPHS

LIST OF FIGURES

GLOSSARY

Digital Revolution

The shift from analogue to digital technologies allowing increased miniaturisation, storage, and ease of diffusion, and creating changes in the social relations of societies adopting these new technologies.

Framing

Interpretive schemata that allow people to simplify and understand events and problems in their lives, conceptualise the 'world out there', and formulate action-oriented beliefs that underpin collective action.

Information War

A contest of ideas, messages and images conducted inter-state, and intra-state between state and state challengers in the global mediaspace.

Insurgency

A political spectrum that embraces both rebellion and revolution. Its defining aspect is that of a political uprising born of a social movement, namely a community united around a particular value system or set of ideals or grievances aimed at changing the government and sometimes the very structure of society. It can emanate from a majority or minority in the population. To rebel is to strike out violently against the government; revolution is to seek to overthrow it. Insurgency is a political not a military process; the mood and attitudes of the population are paramount. Since populations vary, so insurgencies are context specific.

Memory   Memory is a process of constructing historical continuity from discontinuity and where a worldview derives from this process of constructed recollection.

Metaphor   The means to understand and experience one thing in terms of another, where one element simplifies or elucidates the meaning of the other.

Narrative   A medium-free representation, a cognitive construct, a semiological way of communicating shared reality. Social life is storied and individuals experience it as an ontological condition constructing meaning through a repertoire of 'emplotted' stories. Thus people make sense of what is happening to them by absorbing experiences into episodic narratives and producing discursive meaning by which they live.

Opportunity Space   The opportunity space can be a state of mind, a collective reaction following a brutal interruption to daily equilibrium. It also arises when new social reforms allow greater freedom to assemble or organise, when liberalised rules increase participation in elections, or even when violent conflict occurs, levels of support and opposition to challengers fluctuate. This causes an ebb and flow in political oppo-

Political Marketing

Political Terrorism

Propaganda

Propaganda of the Deed

tunity and activity, unsettling the status quo.

An iterative, mutual exchange of values between producers and heterogeneous audiences or consumers where divergent messages target segmented groups, creating different effects.

The rational assault on state targets of operational and symbolic significance, and/or the deliberate dissemination of fear among, or indiscriminate injuring or killing of civilian or non-combatant targets through extreme acts of violence aimed at government overthrow or state transformation.

A devalued currency in the public realm, a linguistic shorthand popularly called 'spin', lies, dark arts and dirty tricks. In academe it remains a source of contention, speaking variously to 'deceit and corruption'; 'manufacture of consent' and control of public opinion; managerial and scientific direction; 'control of attitudes by the manipulation of symbols'; and 'thought control'. It is usually identified with modern, atomised mass populations.

An act of political terrorism, thus a technique inter alia employed by insurgents with kinetic, symbolic and strategic objectives. Formerly violent acts of terror were deployed against state institutions and representatives with the objective of goading states into over-reacting with excessive force; by responding disproportionately, governments would lose legitimacy in the eyes of the population. This was the judo-throw principle: use the weight of the state against itself. Today POTD is a terrorist act of political violence aimed against state targets, sometimes populations, with the objective of creating a media event capable of energising populations to bring about state revolution or social transformation. Today's revolutionary uses the weight of the media against the media.

Public Diplomacy

A state-initiated messaging strategy where governments speak publicly to populations of foreign governments with the aim of winning over their sympathy and support.

Semiotics

A theory of signs and symbols that generate messages and meanings.

Social Movement

Groups of actors who adopt the same symbols, values, and beliefs creating 'networks of shared meaning' with the intention of changing some aspect of the social structure.

Social Network

Collections of individuals or organisations (nodes) that are connected by relationships (links) of friendship, family, interest, business or common values. They are neither new nor dependent on technology. Intersecting all societies, traditional, agricultural and industrial, they are not contingent on Western notions of economic development.

Strategic Communications

A state-initiated messaging strategy directed at other states, aimed at unsettling and/or winning over their populations and political elites. More broadly, the harmonising of tiered messages within a hierarchy of communications aimed at changing external and internal audience behaviour.

Strategic Operating Concept   The positioning and application of kinetic (military) and political (non-military) uses of power to achieve national (strategic) aims. In the insurgent project this means recognising the advantage of employing kinetic but more significantly and increasingly symbolic means to contest state-constructed discourses when challenging states for control of the population.

PREFACE

July 2011 proved a busy month for terrorism. In separate incidents in distinct areas of the world dramatic scenes of violence and chaos were played out to the increasing bewilderment of onlookers. Despite Norway's reputation as a placid, conciliatory society, its capital and a wooded island barely a stone's throw away witnessed the mass slaughter of 76 young people, victims of a far-right fanatic who felt this was the best way to draw attention to what he saw as the Muslim colonisation of Western Europe. That a bomb placed under government offices and a variety of assault weapons trained on the unsuspecting should be the means to achieve Anders Behring Breivik's ideological aims only brought out the irony in his mirroring methods already employed by the very extremists he feared most. His convoluted response to a government purportedly 'soft on Islam' was to gun down a host of Nordic youth. According to his 1,500-page manifesto released on the web only hours before his murderous rampage, the government of this inclusive democracy deserved to be brought down because it had caved into misguided multicultural policies and overweening tolerance. And he was not alone, he claimed at his court hearing. There were other cells across Europe ready to rise to the same challenge. His message to the uninitiated, however, seemed surprising though revealing: 'We are selling the promise of a better future for our people and our children. Resistance fighters are in many ways sales representatives. They are marketers and ambassadors to not only their specific organisations and movements but to the future we wish to create. As such, it is important that all resistance fighters learn the basics of sales and marketing'.[1] The insurgent as marketer will become a recurrent theme throughout this book.

Half a world away, in the badlands that span much of Afghanistan and North West Pakistan, similar political killings had long since become routine. But in July three deaths in particular stood out. The mayor of Kandahar, the former governor of Uruzgan, and the Afghan president's half-brother fell victim to two suicide bombers and a gunman respectively. All had been allies of President Hamid Karzai. And although suspicions of internecine killing surrounded the murder of Mayor Haidar Hamidi, the Taliban were quick to claim responsibility, suggesting that no one was beyond their reach, that no transgressor was safe. Whether any of them had been sacrificed to factionalism among competing warlords remains uncertain, but the assassinations sent an unmistakeable message in the ongoing war of images and ideas with Western forces mired in a decade-long struggle with the Taliban.

Meanwhile in the Arab states inflamed by popular uprisings, bombs and bullets gradually replaced stolid defiance as the persuader-of-choice for revolutionaries intent on changing society. From Tunisia, Egypt and Mauritania to Syria and Yemen, people were not only setting fire to their country but to their own bodies. Acts of self-immolation were to be the trigger for historic uprisings, capturing in one incident, in a single photographic frame, the pent-up anger and grievance of successive generations of the economically marginalised, the politically suppressed, the tortured.

Their grievances differed: for some it was political participation—the right to be free and active actors determining their own futures; for others it was a different kind of freedom—the desire to throw off the Western and American yoke. If anything connected these disparate events, it was the way they were caught on camera and disseminated to the rest of the world. Such incidents acted locally but spoke globally. Yet it was not down to the street protesters to drive this process, nor merely regular press and television. Paralleling their efforts were the more immediate and widespread communications of millions of activists, sympathisers and simply curious onlookers linked via the new, interconnected media ecology which hummed feverishly twenty-four hours a day. This was a far cry from the way insurgents had gone about their business only a generation before when I was a television producer covering many of the world's conflict zones.

This book traces its origins to the deep winter of President Ronald Reagan's Cold War more than a generation ago. It was a time and a world where bipolar ideologies seemed set for the long haul while geopolitics fused with a host of particular dynamics and local causes: a time of proxy conflicts when journalists enjoyed no dearth of opportunity to ply their trade, picking their way through the carnage and detritus of human suffering. Then, as now, attention shifted from one theatre to the next as interest waned or a hotter story emerged a continent away. In that sense, things have changed little, except that fads and fashions move much faster today. As a television producer I moved seamlessly between trouble spots in Central America, Africa, the Middle East and the Indian sub-continent. However, the seeds of doubt were already sown: doubts that questioned the default mode of analysing civil wars according to an enlightened cookie-cutter model forced on the journalist by the demands of delivering a story on budget and on time, but equally by the expectations of a consensus of professional understanding of what made these places tick. Not that journalists were welcomed as enthusiastically as their self-image as custodians of the truth might have craved. Dictators and their uniformed goons and death squads shared a common need with their enemies, those guerrillas and so-called freedom fighters who pursued their cause in the hills and urban slums. Overcoming their suspicion of the outsider, all protagonists felt a need to get their story out. And in that early cross-over era of terrestrial and satellite television, the journalist remained the primary conduit: states and insurgents had no direct route to market, no way of locking into global audiences other than to pass the test of editorial gatekeepers and take their chances with a version of events that would inevitably remain beyond their control. Despite the threats, few reporters and their crews were murdered: the name of the game was to kill with kindness. Repeated tours of the same theatres would eventually erode our hosts' indulgence as public relations dividends visibly failed to emerge. Yet it was such absurdities as the head of El Salvador's Treasury Police death squad pleading that the International Rotary Club would willingly offer a character reference to counter my accusations of torture and systematic murder on his part that would soon become redundant.

Thirty years on, the world is a different place. Not simply because the Cold War has given way to multi-polar global politics and that much misunderstood phenomenon—globalisation. Rather, the media environment has been completely transformed in an unprecedented manner not witnessed for five hundred years. The more the Digital Revolution has made inroads into our lives, the less pivotal the journalist has become. Political actors can now talk directly to the audiences of their choice, at a time of their choosing. The web, mobile telephony and satellite television, all interacting and feeding off each other, amplify the reach and penetration of their messages, skirting varying degrees of editorial intervention and often pre-empting them entirely. Admittedly, not all populations share the same access to information technologies. Yet the interconnection of all media in today's paradoxically co-operative and competitive ecology means messages and their condensed form—images—increasingly find a way to their targets. Add to that the deregulation of media markets—even while · many states still exert firm control over their domestic communications space—and the concentration of over half of mankind in urban spaces where the advance of technologies is felt most acutely, and one begins to understand why message proliferation is now a different proposition from any moment in human history.

Yet with the advent of this apparently liberal utopia of communication has emerged a fresh challenge. Not only do digital technologies offer ways for ordinary citizens to communicate with their counterparts unimpeded by media entrepreneurs and their editors and, broadly speaking, state censors, but those very populations now also incubate the political actors and insurgents who wish to contest the sovereignty and legitimacy of governments by employing these selfsame technologies. At the same time state agencies, corporations and a host of individuals and organisations are producing competing outputs. The result presents a new obstacle course to be negotiated, a cacophony of ideas, images and messages—the deliberate and accidental; the considered and rash; the enduring and ephemeral; the strategic and tactical. *The Violent Image* explores how newly empowered insurgents resolve this dilemma. It offers a new conceptualisation of the terrorist act. By privileging the disseminated image of the Propaganda of the Deed, that is the representation of political violence as a still or moving picture, over the local, military effect of slaughtering combatants and non-combatants, it speaks to a world where visual communications now dominate our lives, not just in the West but in metropolitan centres and in many rural communities across the globe. Thus we should speak of *homo communicator* rather than *homo economicus*. This fresh way of considering political violence should neither trivialise the sheer horror of terrorism, nor circumscribe that 'imagination of disaster' described by Henry James a century ago. Today the electronic image threatens the advance of the written word among mass populations, something that has been achieved relatively recently within the unifying projects of nation-states. In our time, screens in cinemas, offices, homes, billboards, and even on portable devices have become the new theatres of shock and awe. As another James, the critic Clive James, once wrote of a dandy monologuist: his skill was to 'condense pictures into an information beam of words which the reader's eye converts back into pictures'.[2] It is my contention that the Propaganda of the Deed translates messages into dramatic images only to be converted back into ideas. For this to happen, the viewer must be enveloped in the same all-consuming bright, white light that survivors of London's 7/7 terrorist explosions recalled—the moment of shock and awe. To seize the political agenda is to be the first to exploit that hiatus. Consequently, in the pages that follow I set out to show how insurgents treat the images of their violence no longer as peripheral to their objectives but as a new strategic operating concept.

ACKNOWLEDGEMENTS

Please allow me one brief intercession. While I accept sole responsibility for its content, *The Violent Image* has been a collaborative effort: the author is but the sum total of his influences. It draws on the inspiration and love of my son Max and daughter Olivia—their academic excellence has served as my guiding light and they remain my most valued critics. Its appearance is a product of my wife Lisa's unwavering encouragement which allowed me to explore to the full a varied career; my mother Alexa whose irresistible spirit has driven me forward from cradle to maturity; and my father Fred who sadly did not live to see its publication. It is indebted to the extraordinary Dr John Mackinlay, soldier-scholar of King's College London who enticed me into the maze and led me safely out again; to Dr David Betz who enthusiastically promoted this project and repeatedly stretched my thinking; as well as Professors Mervyn Frost, Sir Lawrence Freedman, Mats Berdal, Yezid Sayigh and Dr Peter Busch of that same department of War Studies and from whose ideas and support I have variously benefited; and Professor Nicholas Jackson O'Shaughnessy of Queen Mary, University of London and Dr Paul Baines of Cranfield University for their wise advice. It also reflects the faith shown me by my friends and former BBC and CBC colleagues Glynn Jones, Gavin Hewitt, and Angus Margerison, the time and patience invested in me by my publisher Michael Dwyer and his editorial team, and the painstaking copy-editing of Nathanael Jarrett and my former Masters students Oliver Mains and Andrea Berger. Professor George Brock and Sir Peter Stothard, both formerly of the *Times*, also gave generously of their time and unique insights.

To all these I extend my deepest gratitude.

Neville Bolt, London, December 2011

New York, 11th September 2001.
© Press Association / Naomi Stock/Landov.

INTRODUCTION

In reappraising the terrorist act, the 'Propaganda of the Deed' (POTD),[1] I wish to update a late nineteenth-century theory of insurgent violence and place it at the heart of the contemporary Information Age.[2] My aim is to show how it developed from a kinetic and symbolic technique to a strategic communications tool;[3] indeed, to argue that in today's transformed digital media environment it has become a strategic operating concept for some national, but particularly global insurgents.[4] What was once peripheral has become central to modern insurrectionists in the 'war of ideas and images' played out between insurgent and state. What they have won with one hand, they have lost with the other. Put more explicitly, in the digital era, information networks— the 'new nervous system for our globe'[5]—now empower insurgents, allowing them to bypass the editorial mediators of traditional media (television, press and radio) who historically censored or reinterpreted insurrectionist messages. But once released into the 'digital commons' (namely the internet and mobile-phone universe), ideas and messages can evade mediation and resist control; they take on a life of their own in real time. Fast-moving, self-propelled violent imagery is transforming insurgency.[6]

Long forgotten amid the horrors of twentieth-century revolutions and industrial warfare was a phenomenon that briefly flourished in the late 1800s known as 'Propaganda of the Deed', which emerged as an anarchist revolutionary tactic aimed at bringing down Western states. It was commonly understood as violent acts of terror deployed against state institutions and representatives with the objective of goading states into over-reacting with excessive force; by responding disproportionately governments would lose legitimacy in the eyes of the people.

1

Thus by means of a judo throw the anarchist would use the weight of the state against itself;[7] popular outrage would be mobilised to overturn the political and social system. In this manner POTD presaged Maoist theory, identifying the population as the centre of gravity in any insurgency,[8] but for all its high-profile successes—and many heads of state were assassinated—POTD never once overthrew a single government. Subsequently it was eclipsed by the October Revolution and two World Wars, and slipped into the footnotes of history. Its failure was compounded by the insurgent's inability to manage the process of message control and media diffusion.

With the 1960s consumer boom in television POTD re-emerged as a systematic tactic. Several revolutionaries saw the attractions of 'armed propaganda', abandoning Mao's doctrine of strategic patience and political preparation of the population. For theorists like Marcuse and Fanon, rural focoists Debray and Guevara, but particularly urban guerrillas Marighella and Guillén, security forces and foreign multinational employees became the 'audience'.[9] But the Provisional IRA (PIRA), with their sensational bombings, and the Palestinian Liberation Organisation (PLO), through its hijackings and kidnappings, such as that which marred the 1972 Munich Olympics, were probably the first to realise the political value of connecting violent acts with global television audiences. The last twenty-five years witnessed a revolution in digital technologies and POTD has increasingly become almost a quotidian feature on our televisions, computers, and mobile phones. When New York's Twin Towers collapsed after the terrorist strike of 11 September 2001, Western governments talked of an historic paradigm shift. Not till then had audiences grasped the full potential of the new media landscape, yet insurgents were already ahead of the curve, famously claiming:

'we are in a battle and that more than half of this battle is taking place in the battlefield of the media. And that we are in a media battle in the race for the hearts and minds of our *ummah*'.[10]

What is Propaganda of the Deed (POTD)?

POTD has evolved into an act of political violence with the objective of creating a media event capable of energising populations to bring about state revolution or social transformation. POTD is a terrorist act; but not all terrorist acts are POTD and nor is terrorism intrinsically political. While many contemporary observers see indiscriminate targeting of non-combatants as its defining characteristic, even this criterion remains highly contested.[11] Fifty years ago when Nelson Mandela and the ANC created a military wing, MK, they pondered a course between four types of violence. Terrorism was just one alongside open revolution, guerrilla warfare, and sabotage.[12] The same holds good today; terrorism is but one tool in the insurgent's armoury. So POTD is a technique of either a peaceful or violent insurgency propelled by a bottom-up social movement[13] rooted in a minority, sometimes majority, population; it is born usually of grievance and injustice with the aim of replacing government and achieving social change, although insurgency may be understood through contested theoretical frameworks of political violence and revolution.[14] These question the causes of spontaneous and collective forms of political violent action within states, and increasingly beyond sovereign borders, both of which feature in this book.[15] POTD is also political terrorism understood as the rational assault on targets of operational and symbolic significance, and/or the deliberate dissemination of fear among, or indiscriminate injuring or killing of civilian targets through extreme acts of violence aimed at state overthrow. Today POTD stands for political violence irrespective of whether it uses bombs, bullets or hunger strikes.

On the surface, POTD is a military, tactical act that does not flinch from destroying human or material assets. Counter-intuitively, at its best, it is political since it seeks to influence individuals and communities, and change the government, state or society. But as it triggers, it becomes a communicative act by intent and/or by effect. The violent deed may be planned in the first instance for military, destructive gain, but only secondly for the added benefit of producing a persuasive effect on readers and viewers in and beyond the immediate operations theatre. Frequently, it is planned dramaturgically with precision, rendering it primarily strategic. For POTD to become a fully fledged act of communication requires viewers. A tank that explodes under insurgent fire is a military tactical strike. But place a camera before it, and it becomes strategic POTD. That camera may anticipate the event, or its presence may be fortuitous. A journalistic film crew happens to take a wrong turn and unexpectedly records the event before broadcasting it; a passer-by accidentally captures it on a mobile phone, and then sends it to a friend or unseen viewers on the web. So POTD is strategic, opportune and/or serendipitous. Crucially, I propose, in the digital era the line between the strategic and opportune is so fine, the global dissemination so immediate that a planned kinetic attack instantly transforms into a communications strike.

Contemporary media are dominated by images. The visual is increasingly privileged over the written word where attention spans are brief and visual sophistication high. This favours the impact of violent imagery on audiences, thus benefiting insurgents. Perhaps we are returning electronically to the stained glass window which could shock and awe the mediaeval populace. Indeed an unusual convergence of factors in the late twentieth century has compounded this visual process while revitalising POTD: 'globalisation', mass migration, social networks, digital mass media, and mediated politics.

(i) 'Globalisation', that much trumpeted, misunderstood phenomenon is a new phase of internationalisation characterised in its various cultural, economic, political, and technological forms by instantaneous connectivity. While the global invades local spaces, the local is imported into the global. Yet just as it homogenises cultures globally, paradoxically it fragments communities, rejuvenating parochial identities. Its effect, when harnessed to 1980s neoliberal economic policies and structural conditionality between donor-states and international institutions, and their supplicants, has been to sharpen the divide between winners and losers. Grievance has grown, fuelling identity politics of ethnicity and faith.[16] (ii) Although mass migration has been a feature in the West over the last two centuries, successive waves following World War II have seen populations move to littoral cities and megacities. In 2006 some 200 million people migrated throughout the world, twice as many as in 1980. Those populations carry with them personal kith-and-kin structures and ties to the homeland. Some of these *patries* are today's theatres of conflict. What happens to those homelands and families still matters to migrant populations. (iii) Cutting across these populations are social networks. They are collections of individuals or organisations connected by relationships of friendship, family, interest, business or common values. Such networks are not new. They exist in all societies pre-modern, modern, and post-modern. What is new is how they link disparate populations globally, then map onto virtual, technological networks of the web and mobile telephony. Digital technologies now allow faster, greater, and more complex linkages between stable and fluid networks, thus accelerating communication.

(iv) Newspapers, radio, and analogue/terrestrial television each enjoyed their heyday in the twentieth century. By the 1980s however, digital technologies that could capture, compress, store, and transmit in split seconds unprecedented volumes of data through national and global networks had brought about a revolution. A so-called Information Age was born, likened in its impact to the print revolution that propelled Europe's Protestant Reformation 500 years before.[17] But what actually drove dramatic changes in the digital era were consumers and audiences. Once offered easy and cheap access to satellite television, computers, digi-cameras, laptops, and mobile phones, they revelled in new-found ways of communicating directly with family, friends and colleagues using miniaturised, fast processing, adaptable and mobile devices. Persistently though unevenly, such innovations penetrated urban and even rural communities globally.

Significantly, what the digital era has introduced are ways around gatekeepers and the editorial controls safeguarded by traditional media. Many-to-many communications could supplement, even replace one-to-many traditional media. Not only could millions of people transmit ideas and information between themselves uninterrupted, but insurgents could connect directly to their target constituencies. (v) Media have penetrated societies, both urban and rural, to such an extent that it is difficult to find large populations cut off from some technology whether radio, print, satellite television, mobile telephony, or the web. Information transmits around-the-clock, leading Castells to conclude 'outside the sphere of the media there is only political marginality': in our times politics have become media politics. In Western societies, at least, media shapes politics according to its own requirements. POTD plays to this transformation.

There have been numerous attempts to understand the changing face of insurgency emerging from the 'certainties' of Cold War embracing Fukuyama's prematurely heralded 'end of history', Huntington's 'clash of civilisations', and Kaplan's 'coming anarchy'.[18] For decades bipolar geopolitics had promoted proxy wars that disguised various conflicts in the shape of nationalist and liberation struggles. The political economy of war however is rarely simple, nor are its protagonists. Indeed Kilcullen confides 'we have yet to stumble on some kind of unified field theory that fully explains current conflicts'.[19] Few typologies adequately capture the battlespace where POTD exerts a growing influence. Nor do they centralise the role of information and communications. The

United Nations sees groups as 'reactionary', 'opportunistic' or 'ideological'.[20] O'Neil categorises insurgencies by organisational goals and means; Weinstein by economic endowments; British Army doctrine by historical evolution. Mackinlay, in his evolutionary approach, appropriately highlights POTD's importance. While Kilcullen offers informational conditions that support insurrectionist ambitions.[21] I assume the population to be the insurgent's centre of gravity, adopting Mackinlay's maxim, namely insurgents backed by the population will overcome the combined strength of the state and security forces, albeit in the long term. I further propose information and communications technologies (ICTs) which fighters employ, and how they use them to capture, stage-manage and transmit pictures of politically inspired violence be mapped onto American military and British Army doctrine's models of irregular warfare. The latter distinguishes between: 1) disembodied terrorism; 2) global insurgency; 3) popular insurgency; 4) feral militias including tribal clans and feral insurgents; 5) road bandits, organised crime.[22] All these categories employ various communications media operationally. Most, except bandits, use media to promote their parochial or global aims, whether for resource capture or ideology. Information campaigns and technology adoption vary widely and are specific to local context. Most groups can call on laptops and mobile phones freely available to the general consumer population quite simply because they are members of that selfsame population. Very quickly conventional typologies break down. However whom insurgents choose to target with ICTs becomes the defining criterion. Insurgent political economies today draw on diverse resources involving rogue or porous states, criminal syndicates, and business corporations to exploit natural resources, criminal arms, narcotics, and human trafficking. Significantly it is global insurgents who have most enthusiastically embraced POTD, exploiting social networks and dispersed populations where communities with common grievances and identities can be linked through digital technologies. The first global insurgents effectively to seize this new opportunity currently promote the politics of Salafi jihadism. Although, to adopt Jason Burke's depiction of them as a 'nebuleuse', or enhanced complex web, is to accept a movement with a hitherto novel appearance.[23] This is a view endorsed by former British Army chief General Sir Mike Jackson who notes: 'Possession of terrain is a vital matter in inter-state war…However 9/11—and, indeed Madrid and 7/7 in this country—represent a very different struggle where the battleground is people's attitudes, allegiances, values—their very identities'.[24] Notwithstanding, I favour the term global insurgents over global insurgency since many groups with supra-national ambitions may co-operate pragmatically but are driven by diverse political economic, ideological or cosmological beliefs. Equally to be a national insurgent does not preclude looking beyond sovereign borders for strategic purposes. This does not assume a unified global uprising.

As a media event POTD attempts to turn each opportunity into a spectacle that plays to global media's appetite for dramatic images and craving for audience attention. But it depends what is meant by an event. It may unfold in minutes (London 2005), hours (Mumbai 2008) or days (Dublin 1916). The local act or event kills and destroys. However the true event is the aftershock that resonates across the mediascape and triggers associations with memories of multiple acts, recent and historic in an archipelago of violence.[25] Only by stepping back does a holistic meaning take shape. Only members or sympathisers of aggrieved communities truly read the full picture. And increasingly it is pictures, images triggering crystallised messages that resonate with popular memories of grievance and injustice. In today's overcrowded marketplace of ideas and communications, they offer clarity. Hence POTD acts as a lightning rod for collective memory.[26]

But collective memory is a constructed act. Insurgents actively contest state memory as society's official account of events past. States invest in institutions of parenthood, education, employment and governance to propagate 'the story so far'.[27] States own history; insurgents want to change it. Insurgents fight for control of the past in order to legitimise their role in the present, and stake their claim to the future. Since insurgency is a political not military process, the mood and attitudes of the population are paramount. Equally since populations vary, so insurgencies are context specific. Such is the power of media today that insurgents find themselves in a three-way struggle contesting hegemonic memory they see diffused through a state-media concord.[28] This belies the iterative relationship between governments and publicly and privately owned media organisations. POTD becomes a communications tool that unlocks a set of assumptions in the population. It is akin to political marketing[29] in the way it employs techniques of resonance and symbolic association with different constituencies; it resembles state-level strategic communications in the way it speaks to governments and their populations. No longer is it propaganda as George Orwell once understood it.[30]

So what has changed to at least promise insurgents an even chance of getting their ideas past government or corporate mediators? For years insurgents were beholden to the intervention of journalists in conflict theatres. Reporters became the purveyor, thus the intermediary for revolutionary messages: recording, editing, broadcasting but above all interfering with the purity of the intended communication. Today's mediascape is dominated by fast-moving images. In the digital domain insurgents enter a new era, where web-based or mobile phone images and messages once triggered find their own way into and between populations. Images spread virally, exponentially like self-generating epidemics. For insurgents this promises maximum return for minimum investment. Integral to the Maoist theory of insurgency is the notion of space which buys insurrectionist forces time to out-run the enemy. Space and time were traditionally confined to the terrestrial domain. Now the virtual offers post-Maoist fighters a new cognitive space which is as wide as the internet is infinite. Crucially it can be crossed in split seconds. Message control, however, so vital to earlier revolutionaries, is weakened as audiences receive and transmit emotive images between themselves, investing them with enthusiasm, inciting shared values, inviting collective action. But what today's insurgent gains by immediate connection to the population, it sacrifices on command-and-control. Thousands, perhaps millions take up the struggle as political outriders, but the movement becomes subject to the lurches of ephemeral enthusiasm. Virtual space in 2012 is given to sudden surges of communication beyond the reach or restraint of both states and insurgent. For reasons not present in POTD 1880, POTD 2012 cannot control its message dissemination. However it now has a direct route to the population. And where there is a way, there is a will.

Overview

In the early stages of this inquiry, it was proposed that I conduct field research in Afghanistan. That conflict theatre and the insurgencies that spilled over neighbouring Pakistan's ill-defined border seemed to represent the paradigm of complexity that could best offer a nuanced understanding of how violent political communications interact locally, nationally, regionally and globally in today's insurgent landscape. As both countries were beset by near daily IED attacks and suicide bombings, this seemed ideal POTD terrain. However the sheer volume of state and anti-state voices intersecting the battlespace would soon undermine any scientific attempt to arrive at reliable evidence. With some forty ISAF/NATO coalition partners facing a similar number of loosely allied Taliban groups, not to mention the weak voice of Kabul's government and other ethnic populations speaking out beyond the Pashtun heartland, the confusion of messages on the ground was mirrored by a similar fog at the strategic level. My familiarity with the region had been gained while filming during the Afghan-Soviet war, in apparently simpler times. The Digital Revolution had not yet arrived, and the binary messages of Cold War geopolitics were readily propagated and embraced.[31] The frames of the debate addressed an Afghan nationalist uprising against a foreign invader; the truth was somewhat different. The problems of obtaining reliable information in the midst of a brutal conflict, verifying the true intent of messages intersecting the conflict-theatre, and measuring their actual effect in a variety of populations with cultural codes and institutions remote from Western understandings are more pertinent today than ever before. Two decades later, upon closer reflection, the new conflict now demanded an anthropological sensitivity exceeding any previous journalistic or academic experience. Moreover, the exhortations of colleagues in the Department of War Studies at King's College London suggested that even fine-tuned ethnographic experience would fall short of delivering a satisfactory outcome.

Notwithstanding, the need to deepen our understanding of POTD has grown more pressing as insurgent violence has evolved over the last two decades, escalating in recent years in the context of 'globalised' change, the Digital Revolution and 'hybrid warfare'. Consequently, *The Violent Image* represents an attempt to fashion a conceptual, theoretical framework around the terrorist act in today's image-driven media ecology. My objective is to rescue POTD from late-night television news programmes where it has become a fashionable label, a journalistic short-hand for any terror outrage, and furthermore, where it remains divorced from its historical legacy while lacking contemporary insight.

By applying the strengths of various disciplines and perspectives, this book is methodologically pluralist, employing qualitative methods of inquiry. It remains possible to reflect the inclinations of Paul Feyerabend without necessarily embracing his 'anarchic', 'anything goes' extremes.[32] Nor should bricolage be viewed as a 'science of the concrete', employing 'the means at hand' simply from the perspective of Claude Lévi-Strauss' characterisation of the 'savage mind'.[33]

I have also drawn upon the lessons of many years spent as a television documentary producer in conflict zones. Film-makers are subjective narrators but by trade collectors, assemblers, bricoleurs. Since this book is concerned with the production and reception of mediated images and messages, it invites pluralist approaches of analysis common to media practice and divergent academic disciplines. What must be emphasised here is the conviction that social science research and theorising take place in open systems where reality has ontological depth.[34] Chris Blackmore describes the pluralist approach as the 'capacity to develop and utilise a diversity of methodologies that may range from highly reductionist basic scientific research at one extreme, through to creative artistic expression as a means of developing community understanding at the other'.[35] Pre-empting the charge of eclecticism, Della Porta and Keating highlight the benefits of pluralism in its ability first to escape 'non-communicating silos' and encourage interdisciplinary learning, and second, to combine new methods and approaches within research. For them, the nature of the research challenge should dictate the methodology, not vice versa.[36] At the same time, however, at the individual level of research this should not lead to a mix-and-match approach without order or reason.[37] Yet the historic dichotomy of *Verstehen* (understanding) versus *Erklärung* (explanation) within the social sciences, each broadly favouring the study of case histories or generalisations respectively, need not be a hindrance to a cross-informed methodology.[38] Indeed it has been observed that even in pure science, laboratory discoveries frequently result from initial 'concrete' approaches before being re-positioned within formalist modes of inquiry.[39] In their *Synthesis Account* Fay and Moon promote synthesis as a way of overcoming the innate weaknesses of any dominant, individual point of view. They recognise that interpretation and causal analysis can work in harmony in the pursuit of critical social science.[40] Meanwhile, Paul Roth's *Pragmatic Account* proposes that 'one proper set of rules' occludes understanding. For him *Verstehen* represents a 'moral decision—a question of how one chooses to view one's fellow humans, or a question for which one is studying them'. Thus, which methodology is adopted should depend on contextual purpose and line of inquiry.[41] There remain, nevertheless, scholars who argue for methodological 'exclusivism' in the face of pluralists who see complimentary approaches able to promote 'cumulative knowledge building'.[42] Without denying its kinetic dimension, POTD is considered in this book to be a communications tool, a form of political marketing—understood as an iterative mutual exchange of values between producers (insurgents) and different consumers or audiences (political and social population groups), while employing different messages to different effect. This echoes Stephan Henneberg who sees political marketing as a 'way of knowing politics [that] has to be seen as part of a methodological pluralism'.[43]

This book engages critically with theories of communications (POTD involves various producers speaking to divergent populations through different channels), political marketing (POTD mutually exchanges values and desires), memory (POTD plays into cognitive spaces, manipulating individuals' and groups' conceptions of time), narrative (POTD triggers socially constructed identity stories of the past) and semiotics (POTD works through metaphor and symbols that carry meaning).[44] It then applies these to the more realist and kinetic terrain of strategic and insurgency analysis (POTD employs extreme force against states and between belligerents). Thus it seeks to inflect with an inter-subjective and culturally sensitive understanding those evaluations commonly made by military and strategic thinkers who privilege the use of force and prescription of political economy in conflict analysis and resolution. Consequently, such a pluralist approach must be interpretative, drawing on thick data and inter alia original interviews, archival documents, public statements, feature films, newspapers, advertisements, photographs, radio and television programming, and social media websites and blogs. Furthermore, it must interpret the intentions and ambitions of insurgents often with a paucity of first-hand information that derives from individuals and groups who strive to stay under the radar of state security agencies, at least while planning their activities and evading capture. Thus this requires 'immersing ourselves in information about the actors in question, and using both empathy and imagination to construct credible accounts of their senses of identity'.[45] Interpretation, however, has two aspects: first, there are sets of interpretations which social actors have of themselves and others; second, social scientists further interpret those interpretations. Moreover Anthony Giddens highlights a 'double hermeneutic' where those same actors in today's complex media ecology reflexively absorb the latter's interpretations back into their lives.[46]

The advantage of enjoying 'power without responsibility' means many insurgents and terrorists offer post hoc rationalisations of perpetrated acts, making their contributions less than reliable witnesses to history. *The Violent Image* also attempts to interpret the effects on diverse audiences, often too traumatised to reflect dispassionately on their experience or too frightened (or hostile) to respond to conventional opinion-polling and quantitative analysis; indeed, on populations whose interests are best served when not too publicly identified with anti-state challengers, even if their apparent desire for change might straddle the line between sympathy and active support. This hermeneutic dimension is important to establishing POTD as a form of political marketing or strategic communications which try to rouse populations to articulate latent, passive or sometimes active desires. At the same time, the author must remain self-aware and self-critical, cognisant of being a subject grounded in the Western liberal tradition. 'Globalisation's' most salient feature is instantaneous interconnectivity, promoting cultural overlap and fragmentation. While analysing multiple insurgencies that emerge from or occur in conflict regions there is a risk, commonly ignored, of unconsciously viewing foreign wars from the perspective of Western state forces intent on promoting the Western liberal project, whether through human rights or political economy development, and within a discourse prescribed by Western political and media elites.

Critical self-awareness and methodological pluralism define this approach to addressing a gap in the academic literature. Moreover this book's conceptual framework of what constitutes POTD in contemporary insurgency examines how terror acts shock and trigger sedimented meaning, first by shattering, then reassembling memory of grievance in the populace.

Different Ways of Reading POTD

Terrorism is a bestseller in popular and academic publishing. POTD meanwhile receives uneven attention from scholars, many of whom all too readily dismiss it for its naïve failures, yet it sits 'at the heart of terrorism'.[47] Attempts to position it within strategic thinking condemn it to a passing phase in evolutionary political violence. Many discuss terrorism through the lens of particular events or as a phenomenon. Fewer examine POTD theoretically or even in its historico-anarchist context. That said, writers have frequently conflated anarchism[48] and political violence generically, and unjustifiably according to Wood-cock.[49] So POTD is under-researched, judged from the perspective of insurgency theory. Occasional overlap notwithstanding, interpretations divide broadly four ways: 1) provenance; 2) innovation; 3) utility; and 4) semiotics.

POTD is commonly viewed as a late-nineteenth century episode, rooted in an anti-state tradition born some centuries before.[50] Hence it emerges from the schism between statist, authoritarian socialists (Marxists) and anti-authoritarian communists (Anarchists) personified by Karl Marx and Mikhail Bakunin.[51] Anarchists are portrayed as divided by a paradox between two temperaments, the religious and rationalist, the apocalyptic and humanist.[52] The German Max Stirner championed freedom from all institutional control: a form of individualist not collective anarchism.[53] And the Frenchman Pierre-Joseph Proudhon, 'father of nineteenth-century anarchism' declared '(w)hoever lays his hand on me to govern me is a usurper and tyrant, I declare him my enemy'.[54] But for Fleming POTD arises as the Anarchist solution to the paradox which Engels had identified: how to achieve revolution without an organised structure of authority.[55]

Almost contrapuntally to Russia, the literature acknowledges different geographical centres of action from Kiev to Chicago embracing the uprising engineered by Carlo Cafiero and Errico Malatesta in Italy (1877);[56] the Frenchman Paul Brousse's now landmark article for the Jura Federation amid the Berne troubles (1877);[57] Paris-based Peter Kropotkin's and Elisée Reclus' incitement to violent action following the noble but failed Paris Commune;[58] the grass-roots actions of Emma Goldman in America;[59] and Johann Most's agitations in Germany, Austria, and eventually America, espousing, according to Laqueur, 'the philosophy of using weapons of mass destruction'.[60] The 'year of attempted assassinations' (1878) and the following decade witnessed numerous individual attacks throughout Western Europe.[61] Russia's model however was comparatively one of collective organisation, albeit insufficient to satisfy the aversion to individual, spontaneous action shared by Marx, Engels, Lenin and Trotsky.[62] Its début (Vera Zasulich's strike) was the exception that proved the rule.[63] This was critical for Lenin who held violent actions undertaken by individuals in the name of the people to be counter-productive. Whereas actions 'together with the people', namely consistent with Bolshevik practice, underpinned long-term organisation and propaganda.[64] All of which countered the peripatetic Russian Mikhail Bakunin's more ominous declaration that '(t)he desire for destruction is at the same time a creative desire'.[65] Generally, Russia's POTD activists formed movements striking at strategic targets, constituting 'tactics of war'. More than violent acts of protest, these positioned Russian revolutionaries 'half way between partisan warfare and the coup of the anarchist'. Conversely, Europeans appeared more as inspired individuals with vague notions of ideology.[66] Albeit, a 'sense of collective responsibility' bound many French proponents 'into a self-conscious movement'.[67] Outbreaks of violence in France's industrial centres grew spontaneously responding to escalating hardship of pay and working conditions.[68] If Russian organisations were better structured, more systematic in decision-making, targeting and execution, did this mean they were more effective? DeNardo's answer lies in strategy. *Zemlya I Volya*'s (Land and Liberty) party rules stated 'the end justifies the means, excluding those cases in which the use of certain means may harm the organisation itself'.[69] Their doctrine was key. They taught recruits to use, adapt and transmit it.[70] But this strategy was not solely imparted within clandestine cells. Their campaigns envisaged committing atrocities that broke conventions. Activists would die by their own dynamite, or face their day in court, grandstanding the cause and condemning the state. Whichever path was chosen there should be no cult of martyrs. Subsequently the 'first terrorist group in Russian history'[71] *Narodnaya Volya* (People's Will) represented the 'first systematic attempt to implement a strategy based on the belief that an entire nation's political discourse could be transformed through a series of acts of violence'.[72] Measured by outcome, they failed because they were too respectful of avoiding civilian casualties. Compared with recent insurgents, exploiting the twentieth-century's breakdown in the combatant-non-combatant distinction, their response was inadequate.[73]

Rapoport argues that of the first of 'four waves of modern terrorism'—the anarchist—was the first 'global or truly international terrorist experience in history'.[74] But what does 'international terrorist' actually mean? Inside Russia terrorism was a strategy for attacking the state. Outside Russia rapid improvements in transport and communications offered Russian activists opportunities to travel and disseminate their doctrine. Why the 'philosophy of the bomb' originated here is less researched. Much observation is personality-driven, attributed to the exiled Bakunin graduating from committed revolutionary (1840s) to terror architect (1860s),[75] and his 'revolutionary prototype' Nechaev, a 'believer(s) without God, hero(es) without rhetoric',[76] who became too hot for even Bakunin to handle. Yet these are but two innovators of POTD. And Wilkinson suggests not only was Bakunin more influential in western Europe than in his homeland, but his and Kropotkin's theories failed to impact Russia significantly until between 1905 and 1914.[77] Why particularly Russian autocracy should engender a unique anarchist threat attracts some critical analysis that centres on the stop-go policies of successive administrations.[78] A nascent intelligentsia receptive to Western ideas was thwarted by failed attempts at democratisation during limited periods of political relaxation and freedom of expression, but radicalised during successive phases of retrenchment and repression.[79] Alternative solutions were called for: ideas on strategy and revolutionary tactics were sought[80] in a context the father of populism Alexander Herzen labelled 'arrested modernisation'.[81] But for Boym the 'vicious circles' between state oppression and radical opposition, secret services and revolutionary cells, and messianism and utopianism have been underplayed, particularly in Laqueur's analysis of the rise of Russian terrorism.[82]

There is another way of looking at Propaganda of the Deed. Recent POTD discourse addresses operational tactics. Clutterbuck sees the Irish as the true progenitors of terrorism, predominantly for their operational superiority in creating a 'blueprint for the conduct of terrorism' that endured for a century.[83] This assertion invites a mixed response: no paper is wasted on the Irish dimension;[84] they are minor players;[85] inconsequential;[86] 'almost always bungled their operations';[87] 1867's Fenian Rising was an 'unmitigated disaster';[88] 1916's Irish Republican Brotherhood (IRB) Rising represented a 'triumphant self-immolation';[89] perpetrated by 'deadly serious revolutionaries'.[90] In mitigation, the innovation of operational bridgeheads among the American diaspora is noteworthy; it capitalised on Irish-American veterans from the American Civil War who exported military training, finance and weapons to Ireland's struggle.[91] Operationally, the Republican Skirmishers' bomb attack on Salford Barracks (1881) signalled three distinct innovations: 1) symbolism; 2) sustained campaigning; 3) weaponry. First, targets became symbolic. Three Irishmen were caught and hanged after violently rescuing Irish-American Fenian leaders. Their gallows would be erected on the site of the attack. Hence the Manchester Martyrs were born. Secondly, between 1883–87 the IRB bombed economic and mass-transport targets in a 'dynamite campaign' extending from London to Glasgow and Liverpool—'the first major example of early Irish Republican strategy and tactics'.[92] By establishing foreign safe-havens for repeated strikes, publicising and fund-raising domestically and across global diasporas, a systematic strategy could underpin the deed. Insurgency therefore moved from single events to sustained campaigning. It further drove the need for more sophisticated propaganda campaigns.[93] Thirdly, weapons, gunpowder and time-delay fuses to deliver POTD, supported sustained campaigning. Perpetrators could hit and run, maintaining control over timing and campaign tempo. Russians by contrast used electrical charges, command wire, and home-made dynamite, requiring visual contact risking bombers' deaths. The Provisional IRA would imaginatively develop POTD by introducing car-bombs, labelled 'the nuclear weapon of guerrilla warfare', as well as 'ANNIE' or 'Donegal mix', blending ammonium nitrate, nitrobenzene and diesel oil with a booster charge. By 1972 they were committing over 1,300 bombings in a single year.[94]

What motivates individual or group protagonists? Richardson investigates behavioural aspects she characterises as the 3 Rs: revenge, renown, reaction. Insurgents 'want to exact revenge, they want to acquire glory and they want to force their adversary into a reaction'.[95] Such repertoire partially undermines strategic conceptions of POTD rooted in the over-extension of state force. Normally, utility theory studies how and why legitimacy collapses when states are pushed too far. Rational-utility models are inspired by established theories of collective action and thresholds in collective behaviour.[96] The central premise stands nevertheless. As rational actors, insurgents use violence to goad states into over-reaching their remit of force, thus undermining governmental authority, legitimacy and popular support. But by 'directly reducing the state's repressive capacity or by undermining the forces of repression',[97] rebels draw state force into creating economic externalities and negative effects. Segments of populations are consequently more likely to engage in armed struggle. Of interest are those mechanisms employed by insurgents to mobilise populations, and the way counterinsurgents calculate cost and efficacy in their response. Game theory offers various insights into asymmetric interplay between target-rich states and target-weak terrorists.[98] How do governments use private information to weigh trade-offs between sacrificing community welfare spending versus increased security expenditure against terror threats?[99] One conclusion is that governments recognise counterterrorism as unproductive but are obliged to increase security, particularly where a terrorist vanguard is located inside an aggrieved population, isolated from a pro-government constituency. So populations are mobilised by damage inflicted by counter-terror campaigns and perceptions of government aims.[100] Where state and insurgent compete for public opinion, a trade-off favouring public goods spending predisposes populations more towards government as opposed to counter-terror expenditure that undercuts it.[101]

Shifting from collective to individual will, suicide-bombers invite rational choice analysis. Suicide-deeds are commonly attributed to pathology. But the notion of a 'martyrdom contract'[102] is filtered through utility theory, variously suggesting every society has madmen,[103] suicide-bombers aim for heavenly reward,[104] activists seek rational trade-offs between group solidarity and autonomy, that they aspire to devotion to a leader,[105] or trade life for identity.[106] POTD as 'martyrdom contract' sits within a continuum of risky contracts of revolutionary violence. Along this continuum are ranged 1) state-sponsored suicide (Japanese kamikaze, Assassins, Iranian Pasdaran); 2) group-sponsored (Palestinians, Sri Lankan Black Tigers); and 3) volunteer (early Christians, anarchists). By such analysis what defines traditional, anarchist POTD is how volunteers 'benefit' from contributing to the cult of martyrs, how the 'buzz' of internal culture in the activist cell inspires them, or how significant is the opportunity for self-publicity and ideological rhetoric at public trials if arrested. However, the contemporary contract paradigm is considered quite different. Here the collective offers suicide-bombers a two-part deal with guaranteed benefits in the first period (life), and potential benefits in the second (death). For Palestinians born into the impoverished 'youth bulge' prospects are bleak, so individuals volunteer for terrorist actions and the almost certainty of death. Consequently, social prestige within the context of the wider political struggle attaches to those volunteers and their families during their remaining lifetime. In death, a place in the 'cult of martyrs' further benefits the family.[107] Hamas' social network legitimises the suicide-deed. While regularly providing public services to meet community shortage, it similarly extends the suicide-martyr's self-sacrifice to the common interest. Volunteers, says the political scientist Robert Pape, are reassured their intended purpose in dying will be widely understood within the selfsame 'altruistic' framework.[108] Political suicides 'attract more walk-in volunteers' than conventional or religious suicides, he maintains. Their prevalence among the secular, educated and employed suggest 'no upper bound on the potential number'.[109] Although suicide-terrorism, Michael Horowitz reminds us, needs low financial capital but high organisational capital to succeed.[110]

Individuals are not the sole beneficiaries. Group leaderships gain 'market share' from POTD, argues Mia Bloom. By late 2000 Hamas and Islamic Jihad, low on funds for social welfare expenditure, shifted their emphasis to bombing, particularly suicide missions. As hopes for unlocking the peace process plummeted, opinion polls reflected growing sympathy for groups following martyrdom attacks. Against rising economic hardship and waning peace-dividend, attacks served to increase Hamas and Islamic Jihad prestige at the expense of Yasser Arafat's Palestinian Authority, perceived as corrupt and indolent. Internationally they increased profile and foreign financial support, domestically 'market share'. Subsequently new or revived groups (Marxist DFLP, PFLP, 'Al Aqsa Martyrs' Brigade, An-Nathir) vied to claim ownership of new incidents of violence.[111]

A fourth way of understanding Propaganda of the Deed is to look to its symbolic content. The 9/11 spectacle transmitted POTD's symbolic value across the new global mediascape from America, which Fraim sees as '"the ground zero" of the global battlefield of symbols'.[112] Indeed it went further, reinforcing the primacy of the image 'rich with emotion-laden nonverbal information'.[113] For Altheide, 9/11 was no series of events, rather 'a series of meanings so diverse that it is best conceived as still emergent, still under construction, and varies widely by the situation and the social occasion of its use'.[114] Those who argue direct actions contain symbolic meaning, see 'propaganda endowment' almost everywhere, in war, architecture, music, bureaucracy; POTD and terrorism merely sit at one end of the spectrum. Terrorism is not simply violence but communication.[115] However Laqueur notes a 'millenarian and apocalyptic tone' entered, then constrained the conversation in the 1990s as new 'ecological and quasireligious' forces emerged. Thus it undermines for him the notion of actions as symbolic communication.[116] Nevertheless, meaning depends on contexts of understanding into which deeds are inserted. Those contexts multiply spatially as groups increasingly fragment in Western societies and understandings and identities diverge between groups.[117] But whether in Western or non-Western societies, the more we come to recognise and accept in our worldview the plurality of social groups with complex, multivalent identities, the more those spaces expand to allow POTD to exercise meaning.

Deeds must resolve a tension between, on the one hand, uncertainties arising from societal and globalised fragmentation, and on the other Jacques Ellul's more enduring and all-embracing 'collective sociological presuppositions' (namely beliefs, feelings, images) and 'social myths' fundamental to all societies (myths of 'nation', 'youth', 'heroes') that in the West we associate with the mass.[118] Preconditioning audiences is paramount. Tugwell's 'pre-existing attitudes and fundamental trends' are narrative constructions nurtured over centuries. POTD must trigger them if ordinary people are to take up arms.[119] Today's global media with their affinity for sensation and spectacle ('if it bleeds, it leads'), repeatedly host the deed, in the process benefiting global insurgents.[120] In the digital mediascape, sites of martyrdom and holy war define a new Islamic landscape for contemporary Islamic jihadis. Deeds communicate with audiences predisposed by long-standing grievance and common faith. These offer tangible evidence when history is 'rewritten'. They fuel processes where identity can be radicalised and mobilised within the global *ummah*.[121] A virtual community of Muslims becomes a space in the ether of television and internet where individuals 'belong to a community to whose enactment they contribute, rather than being passive members'.[122] Here terrorists, 'subjectively religious in extreme degree and substantially secular in their aspirations',[123] communicate with the like-minded, venting outrage at near and far enemies. The virtual dimension of imagined community and shared values merges with actions on the operational battlefield. The virtual hosts the war of images, words and ideas in a contest of strategic narratives,[124] whose implications have yet to be recognised by Western states.[125] Successful political communication depends on repetition. Not only major but minor events command media attention. Yet minor face additional obstacles of breaking into the 'triangle of political communication' of mass media. Here government decision-makers, the public, and interest groups shape the news agenda. Moreover the triangular relationship is vulnerable to timing and context, competition from other events, particular locations, and selected targets.[126] What remains unexplored is what individuals and communities read into major and minor acts, and how deeds trigger first sympathy, then action. Where is the tipping-point from minority to majority political engagement? In search of an answer, recent research has begun to interrogate class, gender, and age to gauge the effects of POTD on target Muslim constituencies.[127]

The Violent Image acknowledges different perspectives and emphases applied to investigating the Deed, but locates itself in symbolic analysis. It draws on the symbiosis between Propaganda of the Deed and global media, that near ubiquitous and instantaneous space where narratives and myths have become the insurgent's weapon of choice in a politico-military strategy.

Vietnam: directing the eye.
© Press Association/Nick Ut.

1

THE TERRORIST ACT AS COMMUNICATOR

'For all of our languages we can't communicate,
For all our native tongues we're all natives here,
The scars of the past are slow to disappear,
The cries of the dead are always in our ears'

Christy Moore 'Natives'[1]

In the twenty-first century POTD acts as a unifier, a lightning rod amid fragmenting media output. Yet over a century earlier a wave of leftist insurrection similarly confronted a proliferating media landscape amid social turmoil born of rapid economic expansion, but to less effect. Heads of state were killed in high-profile attacks. Ultimately, no government fell.

This chapter offers the background to why nineteenth-century models of POTD faltered when revolutionaries failed to control strategic communications. Part 1 examines the nineteenth-century 'historical context' to an emergent form of political violence, theorised as popular communication, and notes its eventual failure. Part 2 re-positions POTD as the 'twenty-first century communicator' in our insurgency landscape by placing it within a discussion of propaganda, political marketing and strategic communications. It concludes that rather than propaganda as commonly understood, it has become a form of political marketing.

Historical Context

Part 1 offers two definitions of POTD: one appropriate for 1878, the other 2012. Initially the deed was an act of political violence aimed against state targets with the objective of goading the state into over-reacting and using excessive force, thus losing its legitimacy in the eyes of the population, and securing revolution. The rationale is what Rupert Smith calls the judo-throw principle: use the weight of the state against itself.[2] Today's revolutionary, I argue, looks to use the weight of the media against the media. Thus POTD is an act of political violence aimed against state targets with the objective of creating a media event capable of energising populations to bring about state revolution or social transformation. The result may be the same but the means has shifted emphasis. Nineteenth-century POTD failed because it was unable to reach mass audiences with its message. For the twenty-first century digital era it is too early to call. Why? We should note the complexity of communications captured in Harold Lasswell's 'convenient' aphorism:

'Who
Says What
In Which Channel
To Whom
With What Effect?'[3]

Were he writing today, he might add a sixth lens: at what speed? A century ago, across the insurgent spectrum many had much to say to many. Revolutionary words found no shortage of sympathetic listeners. But the channels of communication which expanded as technological innovation and capitalist markets grew, remained one-to-many.[4] Insurgent messages placed in the public domain were editorially skewed if not censored by the political and entrepreneurial few. Reported in mass circulation newspapers, deeds would be cast as heinous crimes. Yet even when promoted in revolutionary pamphlets and journals, activist messages were overwhelmed by outlets controlled by states and elites who gripped tight the reins of popular media.[5] Since insurgency reflects particular contexts from which it arises, POTD was a political tool that captured the frustrations and dynamics of the time.[6] It did not appear overnight; rather, it grew slowly at the heart of a reactive, strategic campaign. Its death-cull was rooted in fertile, intellectual soil, but nurtured by popular ferment. Oversimplifying the complexities of competing capitalist models during the rise of the nation-state is misleading. Nevertheless, five interacting developments broadly underlie the appearance of POTD.

First, international migration flowed consistently westwards from Russia's Steppes and Europe's homelands to the welcoming territories of the United States, which busily extended its frontiers to the Pacific, reinforcing the 'crucial founding fiction' of continental emptiness.[7] Between 1846–1875 mass migration of the working poor saw 9 million people, four times the population of London, abandon Europe mainly for America.[8] Some 25 million Europeans would migrate there during the last quarter century, millions more to other countries. Those last three decades in Europe experienced agrarian decline as workers flocked to the cities from the countryside, which itself was undergoing modernisation.[9] Vibrant stock markets financed dynamic expansion in communications, enabling railways to transport the migrant poor across countries.[10] Steamships ferried them between continents, often to rapidly expanding industrial centres.[11]

Second, centralising manufacturing and capital, as Marx and Engels observed, leads to population concentration and poverty creation.[12] Rapid urbanisation and industrialisation that accompanied economic turbulence drew immigrant (international) and migrant (domestic) labour forces to live in cramped ghettoes, typified by squalor and disease. In Glasgow's tenements it was not unusual for letters to be addressed to 'Bridgegate, No. 29 back land, stair first left, three up, right lobby, door facing'.[13] Multiple occupancy in single rooms across Britain's cities and starving unemployment were prevalent.[14] By mid-century Friedrich Engels would pillory a middle class 'ashamed to lay the sore spot of England bare before the world'.[15] Boom-and-bust capital and commodity markets, periodic wage-reductions and redundancy underpinned the rise of European nation-states competing for imperial power and global resource extraction.[16] Yet this was a complex era of economic and social transformation. What many see as the Great Depression of the 1870s and 1880s was overshadowed by the fastest growth rate in living standards, however unevenly between economies. Despite financial instability and monetary crises (1873, 1882, 1890, 1893) heightened by Europe's long agricultural depressions,[17] international trade expanded. European middle classes preserved their 'margin of consumption' for cheap manufactures and commodities, enjoying a standard of living which as the twentieth century approached showed no signs of waning.

Third, against this background, the failure of successive European revolutions (1789, 1830, 1848, 1870) persuaded ideologues and activists that the bourgeois class was no longer a reliable partner in the struggle for social transformation.[18] On another level two revolutions had already transformed the nineteenth century: the economic British Industrial Revolution and political French Revolution. Against their enduring legacy the struggle of proletarian movements would emerge. For some groups on the Left the idea of 'permanent revolution'[19] had already entered their lexicon earlier in the century.[20] Consequently, the impetus would transfer from bourgeois to popular struggle, stalked by the shadow of political violence.[21] Equally, the notion of violence as prerequisite to revolution gradually gained traction in certain quarters.[22] Yet it would cause widespread misunderstanding too. Bertrand Russell later noted a tendency to equate the anarchist with pathological bomb-throwing: 'either because he is more or less insane, or because he uses the pretence of extreme political opinions as a cloak for criminal proclivities'.[23] The anarchist utopia of emancipating labourer-producers from capital's yoke, of the individual from government oppression and religious morality and authority,[24] was too often lost amid the sensationalism of the popular press.[25] Robert Graham observes it is wrong to equate POTD with terrorism, when 'it really means nothing more than leading by example, on the basis that actions speak louder than words'.[26] Technically that may be true, but practice would show otherwise. By the 1890s Jean Grave was urging anarchists to be leaderless skirmishers engaged in scattered groups targeting institutions. He meant destroying property deeds and tax records. Crucially, regular 'warfare of army against army, battles arrayed on fields, struggles laid out by strategists and tacticians' was not for him.[27] Nor was it for POTD's proponents. Nevertheless skirmishing that chose to attack state representatives rather than mere property became central to their modus operandi.

Fourth, use of violence was understandably controversial. It impacted ideological splits on the revolutionary Left, polarising around big personalities in the shape of the socialist Karl Marx and anarchist Mikhail Bakunin. The schism in the Socialist ferment centred on whether to embrace or destroy the state, and whether to employ terrorism to achieve this. The tangible personality clash between the German and Russian barely masked fundamental ideological differences between authoritarian socialists and anti-authoritarian, libertarian anarchists.[28] But the essential conflict resided in the question of the state. Lenin would later underline its centrality to Marxian doctrine:

'All the revolutions which have occurred up to now have helped to perfect the state machine, whereas it must be smashed, broken'.[29]

Yet Marxist revolutionaries advocated first seizing political power then destroying the bourgeois state-machine. For Engels 'the state is not "abolished", it withers away'.[30]

Anarchists wanted state destruction now, albeit not through authoritarian means. Lenin, on the other hand, saw revolution as intrinsically authoritarian because

'one part of the population imposes its will upon the other part by means of rifles, bayonets and cannon, which are authoritarian means if ever there were any'.[31]

Marxists believed centralised, hierarchical party discipline would manage the historic process of dialectical materialism. Thus the proletariat would free itself from despotism of an entrepreneurial class that resided in ownership of the means of production, distribution and exchange. The proletariat would subsume the state into the mass before it withered away into a non-state. Conversely anarchists saw in the state the means of oppression and cause of human ills; its destruction should be the immediate priority. Anarchism was rooted in spontaneity, mutuality, and decentralisation. It advocated innovative political and economic forms of administration free of constitution, political party or government with its inevitable authoritarianism.[32] Political parties, like the state, denied individuals the ability to negotiate free and ad hoc contracts. For populations to act freely meant rejecting the state's fixed laws and inherent propensity to foster partisanship and conflict in society. This was a touchstone of the anarchist creed, reaching back to William Godwin's condemnation of France's revolutionary Terror: '(g)overnment lays its hands upon the spring that is in society and puts a stop to its motion'.[33] This same drive to decentralisation and individualism would impact the deed as an operational tool. First, violent action was carried out inconsistently, uncoordinated on a local, national or international scale. Second, party organisation and discipline proved anathema to its proponents.

There is a further dimension to the schism of the Left: the use of terrorism. James Joll notes much anarchist doctrine appears contradictory, embodying a clash between two temperaments: the religious and the rationalist, the apocalyptic and the humanist. Its intellectual legacy in the Enlightenment must therefore be balanced against the psychology of religious beliefs.[34] In short, across the anarchist and parts of the socialist fabric, the rational and apocalyptic were finely interwoven threads. Some would occasionally manifest themselves in collective violence. Again this impacted the deed in two ways. First, a nihilist tendency led to acts of self-sacrifice and attempted suicide-bombings. Second, those selfsame acts would become public statements of intent. Vera Zasulich's strike against St Petersburg's head of security, the first acknowledged POTD, did not kill its target. Nor did she resist arrest, pleading in mitigation that she was a 'terrorist' not a murderer. Her trial jury agreed, acquitting her since her actions had not been pursued for self-interest. Rather she was, as one witness put it, 'the selfless slave of her idea, in the name of which she raised the bloody hand'.[35]

Although POTD was born of utopianism, its defining characteristic was violence. Alexander Herzen, Mikhail Bakunin, and their spiritual successor Peter Kropotkin shared an antipathy to Russian autocracy with its stop-go policies of social reform and repression. The failed uprising of Russian officers, the Decembrists in 1825, fuelled their enmity. Bakunin's doctrine of 'direct action' grew out-and-out messianic. Activism, he believed, should celebrate violent state overthrow.[36] Significantly he would find his true voice in doctrinal collaboration with Sergei Nechaev, nihilist and charismatic activist.[37] *The Revolutionary Catechism* (1869), a doctrine of 26 articles proclaimed '(t)he object remains always the same: the quickest and surest way of destroying this filthy order'.[38] Which amplified Bakunin's earlier maxim: '(t)he desire for destruction is at the same time a creative desire'.[39] Their mission was uncompromising: their task 'terrible, inexorable, and universal destruction'.[40] Revolutionaries henceforth would be judged 'not by words but by deeds'[41] and singled out by their adherence to unbending selflessness:

'The revolutionary...lives in this world for the purpose of bringing about its speedy and total destruction'.[42]

So POTD gradually took shape. The radical Italian nationalist Carlo Pisacane felt:

'The propaganda of the idea is a chimera. Ideas result from deeds, not the latter from the former...'[43]

That doctrine would fix its cross-hairs on Marx and his supporters, manœuvring to dominate the floor of the International: 'Communists believe that they must organise the working class in order to seize power in states', Bakunin accused, whereas '(r)evolutionary socialists (meaning anarchists) organise in order to destroy states'.[44] But the error of anarchist ways, claimed Marx, rested in embracing subjectivism in politics at the expense of objective conditions in society. Thus activists were seduced 'to pre-empt the developing revolutionary process, drive it artificially to crisis, to create a revolution *ex nihilo*, to make a revolution without the conditions of a revolution'. Subjectivism was likened to impatient self-indulgence, otherwise considered the preserve of the bourgeois class.[45] Terror tactics, concluded Engels, were 'mostly useless cruelties perpetrated by frightened people in order to reassure themselves'.[46] Furthermore they represented the interests of a particular group imposed on all society.[47]

Internecine conflict spread from the centre of the primary discursive forum of the Left, infecting local branches of activists. Bakunin's ejection by Marxists following the 1872 International Congress and the rival, short-lived anarchist International became cues for his supporters to choose violent direct over political action. Thus POTD became intricately rooted in fierce competition between revolutionaries over the optimum path to attaining state and societal transformation, not merely operational utility of asymmetric insurgent versus government force.

Fifth, information and communications technologies accompanied political and economic change in the most dramatic advance for four hundred years. Luther had used newly available printing presses to kick-start a revolution, namely the Protestant Reformation.[48] With the same means the Catholic Church launched its counter-revolution, the Counter-Reformation, supplementing monastic scribes with mass production techniques. Amid the breakdown of centralised, royal censorship, the advent of civil war in England witnessed a dramatic increase in the printing of political pamphlets. In 1642 London's presses turned out 4,038 titles compared with an output of 848 in 1640 and 2,042 in 1641.[49] 'There is nothing more congruent to the nourishment of division in a State or Commonwealth, then diversity of Rumours mixt with Falsity and Scandalisme [sic]' wrote one concerned observer.[50] France's 1789 Revolution would also spawn an explosion in print materials—newspapers, pamphlets, books, and engravings. One Jacobin advocate for a free press had celebrated 'teach(ing) the same truth at the same moment to millions of men'.[51] But by 1886, Ely's survey of anarchist press in America was recording urgent appeals for an 'Educational Campaign' to accompany the Propaganda of the Deed, concluding 'some even of the Anarchists think [the campaign] ought to precede it, though the tendency now is strongly in the direction of immediate action'.[52] Such was the race to connect with the populace, '(i)t was urged that tracts be published, existing journals encouraged, new ones founded, and teachers sent out into the four quarters of the earth to spread the doctrines of socialism far and near'. For nineteenth-century revolutionaries not to exploit a new generation of media was unthinkable. Insurgents are nothing if not products of their environment. Nobel may have patented dynamite (1867) before easing the path to insurrection by inventing the more stable gelignite (1875). But their century would witness such startling ICT innovations as the telegraph (1830s), photography (1830s), rotary printing presses industrialising popular newspapers (1840s), typewriter (1860s), transatlantic cables (1866), telephone (1876), motion picture cinema (1894), wireless telegraphy (1896), magnetic tape recording (1899), and eventually radio (1906).[53]

Information became a commodity like any other in the capitalist market place. Anarchist publications in America and Western Europe such as *Truth*, *Alarm*, *Liberty*, *Freiheit*, *Fackel*, *Vorbote*, *Le Revolté*, *La Révolte*, *Le Réveil*, *Le Droit Social*, *L'Avant-Garde* found themselves competing for readership and veracity with mass-newspapers owned by magnates like Joseph Pulitzer, William Randolph Hearst, and Alfred Harmsworth (Viscount Northcliffe).[54] Newspaper pages became entertaining mosaics of hard and soft news, interspersed with drawings and engravings,[55] supported by eye-catching advertising. Soon readers were gradually educated into linking discontinuous photographs, then composing them into scenes in the new age of fast-turnaround press photography.[56] 'News' increasingly drove circulation where 'fact' came to replace 'opinion'.[57] The ground was laid for Roger Burlingame's eventual claim 'thought is served to us pre-digested like a baby's breakfast food'.[58] Control of information proved to be a source of struggle between state and entrepreneur, and this tension diverged over time between countries. The press industry fought for freedom of expression through financial independence.[59] For revolutionaries the fight was different: they needed to win public backing to challenge the state. So the anarchist press was part of the explosion in consumable information as well as competitor to an industry dominated by the 'penny press' with its appetite for sensationalism. Revolutionaries were not just competing in circulation-battles they could not win. They were contesting whose version of reported events readers would accept as authoritative. Insurgents faced not only asymmetry of state force but of media power.

Information was central to changes governments were introducing to secure greater controls over populations. Regulatory climates highlighted a tension between liberal constitutionalism and promoting the nation-state.[60] These variously impacted free-flowing information. Its collection and dissemination assumed fresh importance. Electricity replaced steam-power in factories. Firms adopted new methods for organising management and labour. Speed and efficiency were sought via Taylor's scientific techniques and time-and-motion studies.[61] Rationality and expediency would be delivered by professional, white-collar elites skilled in information management. These were considered necessary to run industrial societies growing ever more complex as capitalist states embraced hierarchical bureaucracy in firms and government. This new centralising process Hegel, Marx and Weber variously identified as an inevitable harbinger.[62] By introducing primary and secondary schooling, literacy for the masses provided props for nationalist and modernising projects.[63] New information technologies and management processes kept step with, Beniger asserts, a 'crisis of control' arising from unprecedented, run-away demand in global markets for manufactured goods from America, Britain, Germany and France. They could now co-ordinate supply processes which in their exuberance to perform had proved chaotic and out of control. Consumer demand had to be tracked, interpreted, organised: market signals had to be improved. A 'control revolution' was afoot; at its heart was information.[64]

Against this bewildering backdrop of change, revolutionaries projected their information in pamphlets and journals. More significantly, they did so via spectacular acts with shock appeal for the popular press.[65] In this respect, few could deny their success. Prussia's Kaiser Wilhelm I narrowly survived the assassin's bullet (1878). Less fortunate high-profile victims included Russia's Tsar Alexander II (1881), French President Carnot (1894), Spain's Prime Minister Cánovas (1897), Empress Elisabeth of Austria (1898), King Umberto of Italy (1900), US President McKinley (1901), King Carlos I of Portugal (1908), Spanish Prime Minister Canalejas (1912), Greece's King George I (1913), Austro-Hungarian Archduke Franz Ferdinand (1914). All died. Nonetheless POTD failed.

Three factors contributed to this failure: asymmetrical force exercised by states; insurrectionists' inability to control messages in a mediaspace influenced by entrepreneurs whose interests lay in preserving the status quo; and powerlessness to co-ordinate activists operationally within and between countries. Most important, a disconnect emerged between a strategy of communications focused on violence as a catalyst to change, and well-publicised campaigns needed to explain how populations might seize control of the new order, whenever and whatever it might prove to be. Kropotkin's prognosis was sincere, if ambiguous: '(i) it is impossible to legislate for the future. All we can do is to guess vaguely its essential tendencies and clear the road for it'.[66] So POTD remained kinetic, partially symbolic, nevertheless marginalised.

POTD: Twenty-First Century Communicator

Margaret Thatcher contended that effective political communication demands twin imperatives: definition and repetition.[67] Insurgent communicators know this too well: state your terms; tirelessly restate them. Bomb your way onto media and public agendas; keep bombing to command them. The question is: what kind of communication is POTD? Is it a technique of political marketing, strategic communications or as the name might suggest, propaganda? A clearer framework of analysis might identify insurgent intentions. Meanwhile we should caution against insurgents' post hoc rationalisations of violent acts: the path from intent to effect looks smoother in hindsight.

Violent acts are more ambitious than kinetic, richer than passive symbolism. Rather they are subversive marketing tools, metaphors with sedimented meaning. They resonate; they are intertextual. At the moment of violent impact, an 'opportunity space' appears: a temporary shock or hiatus insurgents wish to fill with their own values.[68] Violent deeds trigger latent rhetorical messages using iconic images. Recognising pictures is more emotive than words, while perhaps acknowledging the ambiguity of imagery, insurgents nevertheless wish to make their values as unambiguous as possible. Indeed

'(a)ll fields of communication (including advertising) seek messages that resonate with values. Yet values, like objectives, are typically multiple and conflicting, their ranking constantly altering with changes in circumstances'.[69]

Oppositional politics thrive on ambiguity, hence there remains an intrinsic tension.

POTD is not propaganda as conventionally understood but a form of political marketing arising from the incursion of the private into the public sector, of commercial techniques of persuasion into political discourse and language. It is a form of strategic communications, aping modes of ideological exchange between states and other states, and their populations.

Propaganda

Propaganda is a devalued currency in the public realm, a linguistic shorthand popularly called 'spin', lies, dark arts and dirty tricks. In academe it remains a source of contention, speaking variously to 'deceit and corruption';[70] 'manufacture of consent' and control of public opinion;[71] managerial and scientific direction;[72] 'control of attitudes by the manipulation of symbols';[73] and 'thought control'.[74] As a communications process, it means 'the deliberate, systematic attempt to shape perceptions, manipulate cognitions, and direct behaviour to achieve a response that furthers the desired attempt'.[75] So the catchment area is wide. Advertising shares traits with propaganda; it is deliberate and systematic. As mass 'suggestion' or 'influence', propaganda's aim is for audiences to embrace 'voluntarily' the viewpoint being propagated.[76] This may sound like persuasion, 'a complex, continuing, interactive process in which a sender and receiver are linked by symbols, verbal and nonverbal'.[77] But it is not. Persuaders do not seek to be what they are not: they promote change in attitudes by making 'the purpose as clear as possible'. Propagandists however, conceal their true intentions, if not occasionally their identity. They go further still. Controversially, propagandists need not believe in the message nor care for the audience.[78]

Propaganda comes in different shades: 1) white, where the producer is freely disclosed and boasts accurate information; 2) grey, where source and veracity of content are ambiguous; 3) black, which deliberately fabricates and distorts: the bigger the lie, the greater the chance of it being believed.[79] Moreover some observers differentiate between propaganda as 4) 'direct incitement' where democratic leaders identify with a campaign belief, and 5) 'indirect' where authoritarian politicians perform to a passive populace in a coercive atmosphere.[80] Others separate 6) the 'political', namely top-down imposed by government, from 7) the 'social' that grows bottom-up from socio-economic systems in which audiences are located.[81] Today any of these approaches may be employed side by side in this indistinct arena of definitions.

Crucially, at its most efficient, propaganda seeks 'unambiguous transmission of message'[82] constraining any space for discussion. In this last respect, POTD qualifies as propaganda.

Once propaganda graduated from the Catholic Counter-Reformation, American Civil War and two World Wars, any neutral association with the process of *propagare* (closer to the notion of nineteenth-century POTD) was lost. 'Propaganda and censorship were religious long before they were political', argues Asa Briggs.[83] Consciously directing information to serve political self-interest, however, is nothing new. The American Civil War and two World Wars were intricately bound to the expansion of mass newspapers, cinema and radio.[84] States quickly learnt to manufacture and distribute partisan information on an industrial scale, matching negative accounts of the enemy with progressive reports of their own forces, thus sustaining popular home support. Britain's press barons, Northcliffe and Beaverbrook, assigned the Ministries of Enemy Propaganda and Information respectively,[85] undertook to 'direct the thought of most of the world'.[86] Soon British popular misgivings would be compounded by the practices of Germany's National Socialists and their Propaganda Minister Joseph Goebbels.[87] He understood from the emergent advertising industry the necessity of systematically segmenting audiences but also immersing whole populations in an atmosphere of information control. His approach was indirect. Politicising audiences meant entertainment; films avoided showing the Nazi salute. Indeed 1,150 feature films were made during the Third Reich; only one-sixth contained overt political propaganda. Nevertheless all had a political purpose.[88] Significantly, unlike the business world of ads and brands, propaganda denied consumers any means to influence the sales process or product on offer. Successful political communications, Goebbels argued, required understanding populations without canvassing their unruly demands. Borrowing from the branding industry, he emphasised imposing messages through centralised control. Speed, that fundamental component in the theatre of war, was imported into the competitive marketplace of ideas. Reaching audiences first was paramount: '(w)hoever speaks the first word to the world is always right'.[89] Furthermore audiences would most readily assist the propagandist if catchy slogans were attached to events and protagonists. Messages succeeded where they offered a means of displacing popular aggression to an object of hatred defined by the message. Crucially, says Nicholas O'Shaughnessy, propaganda need not be entirely believed to be successful: a suspension of disbelief within a climate of threat and permanent campaigning are sufficient to achieve desired ends.[90] Through global communications today's POTD spans pre-modern, modern and post-modern societies. A propagandised society is a modern society, according to the philosopher Jacques Ellul, where individual and mass co-exist. Individuals must first break traditional bonds of small, local social groups to discover a sense of isolation and alienation. Hence Goebbels and Lenin were equally disdainful of peasant communities for their inherent conservatism,[91] wedded to preserving *Gemeinschaft* over *Gesellschaft*.[92] Atomised individuals become 'exposed to the influence of mass currents, to the influence of the state, and direct integration into mass society'. In dense, urban populations social structures are more fluid, and contact increases. There Ellul sees shared 'interest in technical matters, the same mythical beliefs, the same prejudices'. Thus propaganda draws on psychological bonds flowing from this change. In modernity symbols and stereotypes are more flexible, more abstracted than in traditional societies where they are fewer and more fixed in their usage. Modern mass communications manipulate these.[93] Nevertheless, most insurgent movements remain rural. Mexico's Zapatista uprising in Chiapas celebrates its village roots, its Mayan tribal identity integral to its anti-globalisation political platform. Colombia's FARC, India's Naxalites, Indonesia's GAM in Aceh, the Philippines' Abu Sayyaf, Afghan Taliban are rural guerrilla movements tied into traditional, ethnographic structures.[94] Locally, they link to modern urban and diasporic support populations, offering entry into post-modern insurgency. But their core constituencies fall short of qualifying for Ellul's criteria of mass psychology.

Two points stand out here: the nature of the population, and the ability to control the information space. Few states today engage in totalitarian or industrial propagandising: North Korea and Myanmar are exceptions whose hermetic seal is seldom broken. This begs the question: which producer or regime retains the ability to control the information environment? China, with perhaps 'the best-honed system for monitoring and censoring the internet for suppressing dissidence',[95] has centralised its internet structure reducing the number of service providers through which traffic passes.[96] Notwithstanding, it recently discovered the difficulties states face in excluding competitive messages, monopolising media outlets, while attempting to centralise and harmonise internal communications.[97] Only exceptional circumstances such as industrial warfare, national emergency and mass mobilisation in democracies, or coercive control under autocratic dictatorships favour such outcomes. However full information control lies beyond insurgents, even for secessionists enjoying some territorial autonomy, such as Nigeria's Movement for Emancipation of the Niger Delta (MEND), Colombia's Fuerzas Armadas Revolucionarios de Colombia (FARC) or latterly Sri Lanka's Liberation Tigers of Tamil Eelam (LTTE, Tamil Tigers). In sum, POTD is not strictly propaganda.

Political Marketing

POTD draws on more subversive principles of commercial and political marketing to chart ways through an overcrowded media-world of information and symbols.[98] Today's insurgents play into a marketplace of ideas where consumer understandings are inflected by the language and principles of advertising. Even political ideas and values require more sophisticated or dramatic packaging: POTD has become a sales tool.

By the 1960s Peter Drucker argued the West had entered an 'age of discontinuity'. New technologies would revolutionise our lives; old economic certainties were waning. The result: a new 'world economy where common information would generate the same economic appetites, aspirations, and demands cutting across national boundaries and languages, and largely disregarding political ideologies'. The world had become a single marketplace, a 'global shopping centre'.[99] Business had traditionally favoured shifting 'our product', when it should have been listening to customers' needs and desires. The change he proposed was 'innovative marketing' that could stretch new horizons, creating new markets.[100] A couple of generations on, that message has been absorbed, although not quite as Drucker anticipated. Today few people are unaffected by marketing language ('sell yourself', 'sell the dream', 'buy into', 'image', 'image makeover') or brand jargon ('brand loyalty', 'brand image', 'brand identity'). Individuals, corporations, and institutions market themselves to anyone willing to listen. Even countries are 'brand states' keen to shape what outsiders think.[101] Google reveals 1,030,000 results for 'Al-Qaeda brand'.[102] We have all become marketers.

Marketing assumes an iterative, reciprocal process between producer and consumer where the latter, far from passive, influences the selling process. However marketing is a contested term. For the American

Marketing Association it has become a loose catch-all: 'the activity, set of institutions, and processes for creating, communicating, delivering, and exchanging offerings that have value for customers, clients, partners, and society at large'.[103] An earlier, product-centric definition demanded four prerequisites: 'the right product backed by the right promotion and put in the right place at the right price'.[104] Nevertheless these '4 Ps' should put the consumer first by segmenting the public and recognising the existence of a 'heterogeneous market as a number of smaller homogenous markets, in response to differing preferences'.[105]

Over decades Western societies, modelled on Keynesian-Fordist principles, have become increasingly inflected with the language of commerce. That offerings might be other than utilitarian objects—consumer durables or services—gained rapid currency. Corporate brands, the outer manifestation of the inner spirit of an organisation's values, could also be marketed. These promised the Rolls Royce of quality assurance; buyers acquired essential meaning with each purchase. Consumers could select any underlying corporate philosophy, value-system or lifestyle choice distilled in the name or product to enhance their own lives. Public sectors were not immune. Gradually they acclimatised to the ethos and logic of market liberalisation, particularly after the late 1970s, when citizens were encouraged to see themselves as customers.[106] Subsequently the persuasion business was not slow to expand its repertoire of 'product'. That it could have social or political content required no great stretch of the imagination. For decades electorates had witnessed a steady ratchet in the 'selling' of political candidates, most notably in US presidential contests. People with short memories could recall the packaging of JFK, Reagan, Clinton, latterly Obama. Those with greater recall might evoke the campaigns of the two Roosevelts and Coolidge which finessed image-making techniques begun by Jackson, Lincoln, Clay, and Grant.[107] Advertising agencies and mass media in the early twentieth century had already demonstrated how to suffuse policy (substance) with ephemera and malleability attached to politicians' identity (style).[108]

It is hardly surprising that social marketing for non-business organisations should eventually find a voice in the increasingly sophisticated marketplace of public life. Awareness campaigns designed to share the benefits of a caring society, from anti-smoking, anti-drink-driving, public health-hygiene, condom-use, to famine and emergency relief would be repackaged alongside adverts for foods, cars and other fast moving consumer goods (FMCGs). It would be captured as 'design, implementation, and control of programmes calculated to influence the acceptability of social ideas and involving considerations of product planning, pricing, communication, distribution, and marketing research'.[109] The social marketer's role was to define the desired change, segment target markets, and design buyable products to motivate audiences.[110] A new breed of political strategist was needed, versed in media methods and demands, and familiar with selling consumer products and services, information campaigns and candidates seeking office.[111]

Political marketing has inherited this legacy. Its focus is 'the relationship between a political organisation's product and the demands of its market'.[112] Jennifer Lees-Marshment's model distinguishes three approaches to political marketing. The product-oriented party offers finished product (policies) on a take-it-or-leave-it basis, resembling the classical view of party politics rooted in ideologies electorates recognise and hopefully support. Second, a sales-oriented party does the same but employs a communications campaign based on market research. It segments the market or constituency, catering specific ways to persuade audiences the offering is right, but without changing the product. Third, the market-oriented party works backwards from market demands, creating products to fit. This is most pragmatic yet not always most successful.[113] Driven by research, politicians amend their positions: electorates turn into political consumers who 'demand persuasion not dogmatism'.[114] This might suggest politicians no longer lead the masses but follow what voters want.[115] However there is disparity within countries and parties on which model delivers effective results. Nevertheless the advance of global consumerism suggests marketing awareness increasingly informs the consciousness and behaviour of politicians and their advisers.[116] This process is far from automatic. Marketing concepts are limited by how far politicians are willing to refashion their product.[117] Meanwhile the consumer remains 'a beast difficult to influence'.[118]

As the market advances into the public sphere, political classes 'not only act out but also "think" in marketing terms; they believe that they do marketing management, and they try to integrate their use of marketing instruments in a coherent marketing strategy'.[119] So much so that focus groups and market research represent 'a new approach to politics'.[120] Furthermore, this approach to the business of politics has progressed from pure communications to capturing processes of administration and government.[121] Increasingly in Western democracies '(p)eople have no time for a style of government that talks down to them or takes them for granted', claims one government communicator.[122] Electorates are regularly conceptualised and courted as consumers, clients, stakeholders (in the popular designation of the United Kingdom as a corporate UK PLC, for example). Britain's former Prime Minister Tony Blair announced: 'as opposed to the old welfare state, government does not dictate: it empowers. It makes the individual... the driver of the system'.[123] More controversial is the emergent phase in governing where packaging, brand, and presentation have moved centre-stage. This tempts the disturbing conclusion that in the symbolic state 'the production of the correct imagery is politically more significant than the creation and execution of policy'.[124] Here the visual campaign switch is permanently set to 'on'.[125]

Insurgents and states have always employed symbolism and imagery to distil messages for sympathisers and subjects of varying degrees of literacy. Mass media further familiarise populations with their meaning through repeated transmission. Yet increasingly 'government by narrative' sees governments conduct affairs through story-telling rather than argument. Management of 'pseudo-events', media events or 'symbol-rich theatrical scenes' reinforces a deliberate merging of symbolism and narrative.[126] Branding, which symbolically attached visual imagery to audience desires, was evident in the 1980s politics of Britain's Labour Party. Attempting to rise from the ashes of successive electoral defeats, while remaining silent on policies, its 'Imagine' television spot depicted gleaming hospitals, healthy babies, hi-tech factories, happy retirement homes. A choir of schoolchildren sang the only words on the soundtrack: John Lennon's 'Imagine'. Its success rested on a purely utopian appeal to 'Join Us'.[127] That same year, President Reagan's re-election campaign created the television ad, 'Morning Again in America' evoking scenes of Americans in their diversity, safe and secure, leaving for work, like on every other day before. Such was the comforting portrait of their country Republicans painted after the demise of the hapless President Carter. Implicitly this state of affairs was thanks to Reagan. His first name-check in the ad could confidently await its closing frame, which read, 'President Reagan'.[128] Marketing techniques, filtered through political specialists[129] reinforced the 'soft-sell'. In political marketing, meaning derives from personal identification on the part of viewers, emotional gratification and social improvement from adopting the product, together with excitement that might be tapped.[130]

How does this discussion impact insurgents? Insurgents project meaning into the same domestic mediaspace as states, although their tools are more limited. Information, manufactured as news (quasi advertising campaigns), is transformed into a political resource, namely power.[131] Familiarity with marketing reshapes the political landscape; citizens become consumers; the public sphere a market for competing products; ideals turn into brand messages. Change affects political elites and challengers alike, although state-challengers may choose violence to project their manifesto. Arenas where insurgents launch attacks comprise neither passive audiences nor even playing-fields. The information space is the new insurgent-counterinsurgent theatre of conflict. Counterinsurgency (COIN) environments become 'more like a violent and competitive market than war in the traditional sense where clear and discrete combatants seek strategic victory'.[132] That media organisations and states are seen as complicit in dominating this competitive field only inspires insurgents. And this is the key point: does using violence disqualify insurgents from being political marketers?[133]

The way insurgent appeals resonate with particular constituencies suggests marketing awareness,[134] though such sensitivity is uneven. Al-Qaeda's ideologue, Ayman al-Zawahiri, criticising insurgent leader Abu Musab al-Zarkawi in Iraq, revealed an attentiveness to the information marketplace, intuitively recognising three of marketing's '4 Ps': namely, a willingness to adapt the product with the right promotion in the right place. Critical of al-Zarkawi showing televised beheadings of hostages, al-Zawahiri identifies first its alienating effect on Muslim support and second a potential backlash from non-Muslims. However far from abandoning violent images, this was a finessing of the right kind of revolutionary image:

Among the things which the feelings of the Muslim populace who love and support you will never find palatable—also—are the scenes of slaughtering the hostages. You shouldn't be deceived by the praise of some of the zealous young men and their description of you as the shaykh of the slaughterers, etc. They do not express the general view of the admirer and the supporter of the resistance in Iraq, and of you in particular by the favour and blessing of God…the general opinion of our supporter does not comprehend that…And we would spare the people from the effect of questions about the usefulness of our actions in the hearts and minds of the general opinion that is essentially sympathetic to us.[135]

This same lesson evaded Pakistan's Taliban during its takeover of the Swat Valley under Maulana Fazlullah. Images revealing ideological conviction may target local audiences but risk rebounding on wider dissemination. Television pictures of a girl aged seventeen suffering a punishment beating by three Taliban reached beyond Pakistan to international viewers, causing widespread controversy.[136] The images had circulated by mobile phone between Swat inhabitants before diffusing globally.[137] By contrast, Afghan Taliban leader Mullah Omar recognised the tension between distinct audiences that could undermine the original intent of communications. His was a sophisticated understanding of the need to segment any potential consumer base. While incorporating them into an overarching theme, his Eid communiqué (2009) addressed nine messages to nine delineated audiences: 1) 'our Mujahid people'; 2) 'heroic protective mujahideen in the trenches'; 3) 'those working in the cooperative administration in Kabul'; 4) 'the Islamic conference and what is referred to as human rights institutions'; 5) 'the educated...the writers...the literary'; 6) 'regional and neighbouring countries'; 7) 'the rulers of the White House, and the America war supporters'; 8) 'supporters of freedom from the people of Europe and the West in general'; 9) 'the entire Islamic Nation'.[138] Compare this with Washington's strategic audience breakdown: (i) Afghan population; (ii) Afghan government; (iii) Pakistani government and military; (iv) Pakistani population; (v) ISAF governments; (vi) ISAF populations; (vii) enemy leaders (AQ, AQAM, Taliban, criminal networks); (viii) Taliban rank-and-file; (ix) Central Asian governments; (x) Central Asian populations; (xi) IGO/NGO community; (xii) US domestic audiences.[139]

In sum, the languages of Western commerce and democratic politics are converging as citizens become consumers. Meanwhile insurgent communications practices resonate with many characteristics of commercial and political marketing.[140] There is a tendency in the West to assume messages, such as those emanating from Islamic political groups, target either a single Western mass audience or a partisan, domestic population. But they identify and segment audiences for whom they cater messages. These are branded and delivered to diverse markets, sometimes locally, sometimes globally. They offer 'products' they consider 'consumer researched' insofar as they supply market demand, addressing underlying grievance. However loosely, some adjust that 'product' to suit changes in demand. Is it so unreasonable, then to think of insurgents as political marketers?

Strategic Communications: The State

Or are insurgents really strategic communicators? If strategic communications (SC) meant governments speaking publicly to other governments, and public diplomacy (PD) described governments speaking publicly to populations of those foreign governments, it would be much easier.[141] Academics, policy-makers, and politicians consistently contest definitions of SC, prompting Barack Obama to highlight the confusion.[142] The problem is exacerbated when judging effect rather than intent. If SC and PD simultaneously reach 'receiving' governments and 'consuming' citizens amid today's explosion of media technologies, does it matter whether communicators think they are propagating SC or PD? If public and private sectors blur when politics adopts the language of business, must SC and PD remain the preserve of the state, or are state-challengers strategic communicators? For Obama SC means the bringing together of words and deeds, and their effect on selected audiences. National interest is its rationale,[143] echoing what POTD's proponents feel they are engaged in; some pursue national, others transnational ambitions. Legitimacy bestowed by sovereignty and legal monopolies of violence should not define who is and who is not a strategic communicator. So if insurgents do not use propaganda, as theorised and defined by many political scientists, is it fair to assume they draw on political marketing or strategic communications? I suggest both.

Fifty years ago Davison and George identified the difficulties facing anyone practising 'international political communication': namely, 'the use by national states of communications to influence the politically relevant behaviour of people in other national states'.[144] Their analysis holds true today for both state and insurgent whose chosen theatres of operation cross international borders and target global populations. Equally, insurgents eying domestic agendas appreciate the importance of communicating on a national level. Predicting, no less measuring, responses of domestic audiences is problematic. Gauging how 'an amorphous audience in another culture' will react to outside communications becomes a thankless task. Davison underscores the complexity—so too Lasswell, witness the variables in Lasswell's formula at the opening of this chapter. But it gets even more complicated. Davison suggests communicators rarely have a clear idea of what they are trying to achieve; they address many audiences simultaneously with many messages; and foreign audiences are not always accessible to measure effect. Additionally political communication is usually an instrument of policy, harnessed to actions rooted in diplomatic, military or economic actions. Any initial clarity is quickly obscured.[145] This critique of metrics aimed at the state dilemma stands the test of time. Today it is equally valid for insurgents since POTD's proponents have for some decades seen communications to some degree as part of offensive campaigns. Although a blunt tool, since the digital watershed POTD has been transformed into a central pillar of insurgent communications strategy. A once peripheral technique now dominates the arsenal of global insurrection.

What is strategic communication(s)[146] and do insurgents employ it (them)? First, it is more illuminating to define the terrain from the state's perspective. Advisers entering politics from advertising, media or business call themselves strategic communicators.[147] In the politico-military domain the term carries a different emphasis. An 'emerging (and important) concept *sans* doctrine',[148] it has always been a tool of warfare in some shape or form. When labelled public diplomacy, it is allied to 'government-sponsored programmes intended to inform or influence public opinion in other countries'.[149] The US Department of Defense (DoD) talks of Strategic Communication: the State Department prefers Public Diplomacy.[150] For some the two are synonymous, for others one has primacy, and vice versa. Some avoid a definition altogether, confessing 'we know it when we see it',[151] so does it matter anyway?[152] Some employ both terms narrowly, others widely.[153] DoD's latest report defines it as 'sharing meaning (i.e., communicating) in support of national objectives (i.e., strategically)'. For Robert Gates, it is a process, a work in progress rather than a set of capabilities, designed to maximise impact.[154]

Fundamentally SC is a state-initiated messaging strategy directed at other states aimed at unsettling and/or winning over their populations and where possible political elites. This may apply to inter-state warfare, or more recently interventions by peacekeeping forces supporting fragile state administrations. More robustly, Americans regard it as combining diplomatic, information, military and economic means (DIME) to realise presidential and national policy and strategy.[155] At its simplest it is 'a way of persuading other people to accept one's ideas, policies, or courses of action'.[156] In that respect it approaches Nye's concept of 'soft power' with its distinct components of influence and attraction. Influence draws on coercion, the carrot-and-stick of military and economic hard power. Attraction co-opts rather than coerces: it seduces and charms.[157] Making it a soft rather than hard sell. For Nye, SC is akin to overarching brand messaging in political or commercial marketing, presenting a set of simple themes. But what prevents it becoming propaganda is its desire for long-term relationships to 'create an enabling environment for government policies'.[158]

SC has only recently re-entered daily discourse in international politics. The industrial character of total war between 1939–45 and the Western anti-Soviet consensus throughout the Cold War saw a communications onslaught against hostile governments. Eisenhower's Total Cold War strategy committed resource and expertise (the Marshall Plan *inter alia*)[159] to back his Great Equation: 'Spiritual force multiplied by economic force, multiplied by military force, is roughly equal to security'.[160] All this was wrapped in coherent and persuasive messaging. Domestic populations, seen as critical to sustaining the continuing war effort, were not spared.[161] As Michael Howard points out: 'It was largely the realisation of their reciprocal vulnerability that prevented the conflict between the West and the Soviet Union from erupting into violence, and made it possible for the Soviet Union to be defeated by American "soft power"'.[162] Notwithstanding, America's experience in Vietnam, reflecting on British counterinsurgency in Malaya (although with different strategies and outcomes), underscored the importance of winning 'hearts and minds' of populations.[163] America, like France, which had suffered defeat in the Algerian conflict in the international and French domestic press rather than in theatre, was reminded that, like charity, 'hearts and minds' begins at home.[164] The North Vietnamese adapted and extended Mao's notion of terrain to include the US domestic population, thus attacking grass-roots political support for Washington's war effort. As the Cold War passed, Public Diplomacy was scaled down. Today the picture has changed. George Kennan's model focused inter-agency effort on containment. Once thought to have functioned 'reasonably well', in the post-9/11 era, it is considered 'completely and wholly inadequate'.[165] In a transformed global information environment, a reinvigorated approach is called for, employing 'more deliberate and well-developed Strategic Communications processes'.[166] Facing unprecedented conditions of insurgency, critics highlight government failure to act strategically; words, deeds and resources seldom match up to intended effect.[167] But inter-agency harmonisation is back on the menu, while 'synchronisation' is a new dish that blends action and deed in equal measure: Obama's notion of 'strategic engagement' goes hand in hand with communication. It recognises that 'what we do is often more important than what we say because actions have communicative value and send messages'.[168] Meanwhile a new approach to SC is discernible, blending social marketing principles and private sector marketing techniques honed in the public sector.[169]

Through this definitional fog, I see SC as the harmonising of tiered messages within a hierarchy of communications aimed at changing external and internal audience behaviour. It is a pyramid of persuasive statements built around a 'big idea', or overarching communications narrative. By any definition it must embody the core values of the communicator. The American thinker Michael Vlahos calls it 'the foundation of all strategy'.[170] In marketing it captures the essence of the core brand. In politics it is the philosophy behind policy statements that roll out to the strategic, then operational, and finally tactical levels. Geopolitically this translates as speaking to global, regional, and national— indeed local—populations. Therein lies the challenge. To be successful, the whole must be coherent: no individual message should conflict with any other, nor undermine brand unity. This should be as true for corporations like Apple and Nike as it is for states such as the United Kingdom and USA, or indeed state-challengers whether the successful ANC or unsuccessful FARC. Tony Blair captures the difficulty of tackling the current 'strain in Islam':

We need the suasion in argument of an Obama (or Clinton) and the simplicity in approach of a Bush (or Reagan). We need an intellectual case, brilliantly marshalled, combined with a hard-headed ability to confront.[171]

Unfortunately, British governments over the last decade have failed to demonstrate such brilliance, suffering a succession of disjointed policy messages directed at influencing the population and political groups in Afghanistan. Globally and regionally, the problem remains that different audiences have different culturally and economically determined priorities whether or not they sympathise with those core values Blair alludes to. This explains why audience segmentation is so important but often elusive for advertisers.[172] Thus, there is a constant tension. High principles must demonstrate consistency if they are to be trusted and inspire. Local ambiguities however are prey to constant flux. In conflict theatres, dynamics of political economies change, attitudes within populations fluctuate. The dilemma remains: how to ensure core values remain relevant to shifting but immediate concerns of ordinary people just trying to make a living? Achieving message continuity and harmony is a further uphill struggle. Particularly in today's Afghanistan, where ISAF/NATO forces and multiple agencies are deployed supporting a centralising state built on the thinnest legitimacy and buy-in from regional power-brokers.[173] Furthermore this mix has 'set well-intentioned partners at cross purposes'.[174] Targeting diverse audiences is even harder. In Afghanistan, NATO's global or top-level narrative—promoting Western liberalism and human rights—sits uneasily with using force and expeditionary warfare. Meanwhile failure to deliver on mid-level promises of nationwide reconstruction in an agrarian economy undermines narrative cohesion. Whereas local-level policy vacillations have the effect that opium production on which many rural communities depend for their livelihoods, and in which all strata of state and non-state actors are economically implicated, is sometimes tolerated, periodically interdicted; when crops are razed by intervention forces, the contradiction is all too apparent.[175] The result is alarming: local farmers join Taliban forces for economic over ideological reasons. 'It's just so damn complicated', confessed former US Special Representative for Afghanistan and Pakistan Richard Holbrooke.[176] Particularly since SC is judged as much by actions as words, an interpretation President Obama is keen to promote. But even in less economically developed areas, these actions are captured in image and reports that can quickly disseminate as negative publicity through television and mobile phones. As if to highlight the underlying tension between audience segmentation and message coherence, Obama's Cairo speech to win over the Arab world in April 2010 fell back on an 'us and them' approach. By seeking to divide the world into moderates and fundamentalist radicals, the simple strategic narrative of 'a new beginning between the United States and Muslims around the world' was duly served. The plaudits flowed. It was undermined by the need to speak over the heads of governments direct to broad populations in order to draw them into the moderate fold and away from the terrorist enemy. The corollary of going straight to the people was the daring move to criticise authoritarian Arab regimes and in the same breath Israel's continued expansion of Jewish settlements in the West Bank. For as many listeners as might be won over, inevitably others would be lost. In the mosaic of narratives that speak to daily global realpolitik, harmonious messaging from the strategic to operational and tactical levels appears to be a bridge too far.[177]

Is this concept of communication so different from political marketing? Not according to RAND, who suggest that SC means more than using marketing language. They propose adopting business practices into the politico-military domain: segmenting, positioning, and branding.[178] Thus indigenous populations should be segmented then targeted. The US military should 'know its customer base and orient its products to those customers' needs and wants'.[179] Thus might they discover the chances of their supporting coalition aims. Positioning creates 'intended identity for each product that is meaningful, salient, and motivating'. And all organisations and products have a brand capturing their essence. So why not state militaries too?[180] Memories of Iraq offer a cautionary note. Before beating a well-publicised retreat, Madison Avenue recruit Charlotte Beers discovered Iraqi populations responded indifferently to the fine-tuned techniques of American advertising.[181]

Strategic Communications: The Insurgent

Can insurgents engage in SC? In an era of 'hybrid warfare' (see the closing chapter),[182] states compete with sub- and supra-state insurgents, sometimes in overlapping conflicts. Insurgents' efforts are directed towards winning over and controlling a variety of locally and sometimes globally dispersed sympathisers and target populations. SC is a two-way street. Insurgents, like other non-state actors, apply strategic thinking to their objectives.[183] In the shift from state-state conflict to state-insurgent, insurgents have grown more adept at creating information strategies. Al-Qaeda 'maintains a network that collects information about the debate in the West and feeds this along with an assessment of Al-Qaeda's propaganda, to its leaders'. The reason, says COIN theorist David Kilcullen, is that 'the "information" side of Al-Qaeda's operation is primary; the physical is merely the tool to achieve a propaganda result'.[184] The means to this end is a clear and simple 'high level narrative' that pleads:[185] everywhere Muslims are under attack from Western economic, military, and cultural forces, and the global *ummah* must unite and resist to protect itself. Such thinking remains contentious in Western political and military circles where Al-Qaeda remains an overarching military threat not an information force. Politicians can explain this tried-and-tested story to electorates;

generals can muster the danger to protect their budgets. Advocates of kinetic primacy over information war cite a lack of organisational cohesion in Al-Qaeda's affiliate structure that militates against unified messaging.[186] Similarly with the Taliban, its heterogeneous make-up of forces undermines consistent and coherent SC. Michael Boyle estimates some forty different groups[187] operate within the loosest of command-and-control structures. Nevertheless Gilles Dorronsoro assesses Taliban 'strategic planning and coordinated action' as 'centralised enough to be efficient, but flexible and diverse enough to adapt to local contexts' with a 'relatively sophisticated propaganda apparatus'.[188]

Despite its inchoate make-up, the change in approach by Afghanistan's neo-Taliban indicates an appreciation of the growing value of multi-tiered communications.[189] Unlike Al-Qaeda, earlier generations of Taliban leaders consistently fought shy of media. Greater engagement, particularly with television, followed earlier shunning of 'living images' where appearances on broadcast channels had been largely didactic. Despite its ambiguous organisation, a new leadership structure[190] soon boasted a 'cultural commission' to supplement an already active 'media unit'.[191] The overarching message from Mullah Omar, as early as 2001, captured the 'big idea'. Far from being about Bin Laden, the conflict was 'an issue of Islam. Islam's prestige is at stake. So is Afghanistan's tradition'.[192] This formed the top-line, brand narrative to which POTD would appeal.

Dramatic images of civilian casualties and destroyed property soon played into a more immediate set of narratives at national level, but with one eye trained on foreign audiences. These pilloried Western invaders whose own corpses would be filmed then disseminated alongside footage of dead Afghan security forces. At local level schools and schoolchildren became narrative targets: 'There was a letter posted on the community's mosque saying that "men who are working with NGOs and girls going to school need to be careful about their safety".' More explicitly: 'If we put acid on their faces or they are murdered, then the blame will be on the parents'.[193]

Allegedly driving this harsh campaign was American cultural manipulation of the Afghan state. Hence responsibility for future atrocities should exonerate insurgents. The bigger narrative would justify local actions:

the present curriculum is influenced by the puppet administration and foreign invaders...The use of the curriculum as a mouthpiece of the state will provoke the people against it. If schools are turned into centres of violence, the government is to blame for it.[194]

One Taliban statement later concluded they were winning the communications war:

US and their friends with such strong publications and propaganda is disappointed that even with that huge expenses the propaganda is not as effective, even in some areas the US propaganda face failure day by day and people lose trust on US claims with the passage of every day.[195]

By comparison, the first sophisticated users of modern, internet-based communications strategies were southern Mexico's Zapatistas (EZLN). A national, rural insurgent movement in Chiapas and Oaxaca 'used arms to make a statement'[196] to 'culturally distinguish themselves within Mexico'[197] as 'entities of public right' rather than subjects of the state.[198] They attacked central government's rewriting of Mexico's Constitution Article 27—guarantor of agrarian rights since the Mexican Revolution—and condemned signature to the NAFTA Agreement, which would liberalise communal lands settled by indigenous peasants. Government policies were clearing the way for privatisation and commercial exploitation of rich resources by logging, energy and agricultural companies. The Zapatistas' sophisticated model responded by speaking to many levels of communication but harmonising them in a coherent ideology.[199] On the local level legitimacy is rooted in an early 1990s referendum which a million people supported, and sustained in consultative processes with indigenous communities.[200] The message is historically rooted in land rights, ethnic identity and freedom from military persecution. It mobilises through myriad 'local and regional grassroots organisations with authentic leadership, and the accumulated wisdom of indigenous struggles throughout Latin America'.[201] An appeal 'for humanity and against neoliberalism' to wider constituencies and solidarity networks brought some 3,000 campaigners to Chiapas in 1996.[202] Their all-embracing message addresses anti-globalisation and anti-neoliberalism at the overarching level, while integrating the local into the global, depicting indigenous groups as disenfranchised and persecuted '"minorities" in the mathematics of power who happen to be the majority population in the world'.[203] For Paul Routledge three interwoven strands formed the politico-media strategy: (1) the physical occupation of space; (2) the media-tion of images (the movement as a form of media); (3) the manipulation of discourse (a war of words).[204] Finally, what differentiates this model is the importance attached to managing tactical media opportunities. That is treating communications events as mediated spectacles.[205]

In sum, insurgents adopt similar approaches to state SC. They repeat branded messages that target various tiers of audience. These may address local problems. They may be national, depicting failures of government, highlighting state agencies' direct or proxy attacks on family and livelihood. Moreover they may appeal to wider global constituencies. Mindful of diaspora communities, united by religion, ethnicity or nationality, higher values of faith, community, and destiny are called on. All are swathed in easily identifiable brand philosophy that captures narratives of historic grievance and suffering.

* * *

Nineteenth-century POTD failed because it was unable to convey a sustained message and explain how using violence could deliver a better society. Scattered high profile acts of assassination by fragmented groups did not connect sufficiently to evoke a coherent understanding in the population. Yet the real failure lay in the lack of control its proponents exerted over the means of disseminating messages to mass populations of industrial and rural poor. Pamphlets and journals remained too parochial when facing the power of press barons. By the late twentieth century that would change as consumer populations around the world gained variable access to, by then, traditional media (television, press, radio, cinema, fixed-line telephones) and new digital media (satellite television, computers, internet, mobile telephony). This allowed insurgents to use violent political acts not just as kinetic or symbolic deeds but as systematic triggers for memory of political-economic grievance and stories that tapped deep into communities' spiritual lives. POTD became not so much propaganda—a notion long since appropriated by the industrial war-machines of the early twentieth century—but a combination of political marketing and strategic communications. It played into a world of media production and consumption where techniques of commercial and latterly political marketing were long internalised by producer and receiver. And it spoke to a world of international politics as insurgents with transnational designs employed communications strategies normally associated with states. Changes in modern media allowed them to reach populations, circumvent media controls, and increasingly subvert state and media hegemony.

London bombings, 7th July 2005.
© Press Association/AP/Jane Mingay.

2

ARCHIPELAGO OF MEMORIES

Memory keeps folding in upon itself like geologic layers of rock, the deeper strata sometimes appearing on top before they slope downwards into the depths again.

Arthur Miller[1]

The year was 1962; the name was Bond, James Bond. What would soon become familiar to cinema-goers, beyond the sardonic manner of MI6's favourite agent, was an accelerated form of story-telling emerging from the cutting-rooms of Pinewood Studios. From the advent of *Dr No*, audiences would be spared the 'boring bits'—uneventful sequences of linear narrative.[2] The new 'crash-cutting' technique meant Connery's Bond would never again park the car, step out, walk the distance to the office, before arriving to indulge flirtatious asides with Miss Moneypenny. Instead the convertible could draw up, a glance in the rear-view mirror, and Bond would be inside Moneypenny's office. It was more than the affections of M's secretary that Bond would toy with; it was the audience's ability to contract and re-arrange narrative order. What was left out, the film editor correctly gauged, viewers would fill in for themselves.

While not the first, Orson Welles was a revolutionary manipulator of time and space in Hollywood's masterpiece *Citizen Kane*, some two decades earlier. Of the picture's nine nominations, it was the screenplay that won its sole Oscar, with its 'flashback' technique triggering almost from the opening titles. From 'rosebud'—the first word spoken and last emitted by the dying newspaper magnate, audiences would elide instantly into the timescale of memory past before being pulled backwards and forwards repeatedly via interposed scenes using 'flashbacks' (analepsis) and 'flash forwards' (prolepsis) between distant past, recent past, and present—a potentially disorienting temporal shift in narrative.[3] That audiences were not confused by such cinematographic devices suggests how we remember time past, and reconfigure it into narratives that suit our present and future purpose. It illuminates how individuals and groups act as storytellers, arranging and repeatedly reordering unreliable fragments of the past via narratives or myths we continually employ. This technique for making movies presages a reappraisal of POTD as a means for making myths.

'Archipelago of Memories' investigates the relationship between memory and narrative that recurs separately and contiguously, at levels of individual, group, and media. Ultimately, any revolutionary cell's memory and narrative must perforce contest hegemonic memories and narratives disseminated by media organisations.

Individual memory is a process of constructing continuity from discontinuity. 'Making sense of the past' helps shape personal identity, from which a worldview derives. Moreover, group memory is a constant process of negotiation between individual memories and group memory. By controlling the past, a group's present actions are validated, its 'ownership' of the future legitimised. Finally, group memories compete in today's busy media landscape, which offers and distorts a confusing array of discontinuous memories. Media rivals unwittingly reinforce this unstable process. Organically, media consensus emerges to thwart the hard-fought memory of insurgent groups. Consequently to counter this, POTD's acts become metaphors. These resonate within an archipelago of violent deeds across time and space. Insurgents connect these acts of violence in the minds of individuals and groups, to carefully crafted memories of grievance. Preparing the population is not simply about reinforcing ideology. It is about fracturing state and media memories—the status quo ante—and rooting violence in freshly constructed narratives, spawning a new revolutionary memory. The question thus becomes, can POTD anchor a stable narrative or myth within this irregular landscape?

This argument hangs on whether a dramatic act of political violence can ever offer more than 'shock and awe', which in itself appears coun-

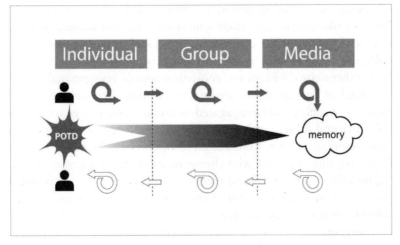

Fig 2.1: How POTD Anchors Memory[4]

terintuitive. How can violent spectacles played out before millions speak to grievance and espouse revolutionary doctrine capable of social transformation?[5] In short, the deed triggers narratives or stories. Actors reinvest old stories with contemporary experience and relevance. These resonate within an archipelago of violence, a mosaic of similar 'remembered' acts in time and space and are justified through appeals to underlying memories and myths. These myths are meta-narratives: deep-seated, primary understandings that define value systems in societies.[6] Insurgent accounts gain traction by tapping into what people take to be the norm—common understandings of the way things have been and ought to be. Their own appeal must find latent or newly emergent consensus in some part of the community. Only then is the insurgent offering likely to meet with success.

Personal memory is constructed from unreliable fragments of the past, some directly experienced, others acquired, pre-dating a person's existence. But memory is repeatedly re-constructed or 'selectively exploited'[7] at different times of an individual's life, drawing on fragments from multiple related and unrelated events. From this editing process of Wellesian 'flashbacks/flashforwards', a story emerges. The individual self is inextricably linked to this new memory. Identity derives from 'fragmentary social faces ...integrated into a visceral sense

55

of a single self...and identified as one person by those around us'.[8] Memory like identity formation is no solitary act, but accomplished by interacting with a wider community. Individual memory engages with collective memory in a 'conversational process in which individuals locate themselves'.[9] From the consensus emerge renegotiated understandings of the way things are and are deemed always to have been. Enduring memories are propagated as myths or narratives within the collective and subsequently may come to represent group identity.[10] A new continuity is born. Constructed stories become the new reality for future recruits to groups who choose to subscribe to a particular collective ethos. But constructed memory remains subject to permanent threat of re-negotiation from internal and external pressures, sometimes leading to group fracture.

Insurgents use narratives to tell the story of a group's past, present and future. A narrative process irons out inconsistencies. Orthodoxy emerges and is gradually but selectively tempered into a coherent account by leaders, an account which progressively becomes the

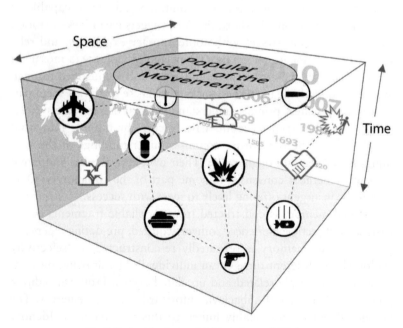

Fig 2.2: Archipelago of Memories and Violence

group's collective memory, locking individuals in while excluding the outside world with its many contradictions. Story as memory is 'essential to a group's notion of itself and thus must continually be made over to fit historical circumstance'.[11] Just as an individual defines his/her own identity by reference to the past (we are each the sum of our pasts), so the insurgent group fuses memory to identity. Without corporate identity or culture and a legitimating history there can be no effective internal command-and-control.[12] Moreover externally, there is no clear 'brand', advertising its unique sales proposition to the wider community.[13]

Memory, Myths and Terror

What connects violent deeds to heroic narratives and collective memory? Through the metaphor of an archipelago of violence, each violent act may be represented by the image of an island. Indonesia's archipelago has 19,000 islands, Greece 1,400. Like archipelagos, islands come in all shapes and sizes. Only inhabitants appreciate the primacy of any single one or cluster, or indeed the networks of understanding between them. Similarly only insurgents and sympathetic communities appreciate the significance of the single deed in a spectrum of violent incidents across time and space. Some carry greater meaning when targeting pre-identified audiences during a campaign of 'political marketing'. Put simply, what connects the archipelago of violence is imagined community and identity shaped through collective memory continually invested with reinforcing narratives.[14]

Constructing Memory[15]

The human brain is complex. Each of a hundred billion nerve cells or neurons shares ten thousand connections to other nerve cells. Neurologically, memory is not a 'small scale model of external reality'; rather it is constructed with 'the ability to re-create an act separated by a certain duration from the original signal set that is characteristic of memory'. Thus it represents 'a form of constructive recategorisation during ongoing experience, rather than a precise replication of a previous sequence of events'.[16] As Israel Rosenfield suggests:

Memories are not fixed but are constantly evolving generalisations—recreations—of the past. Which gives us a sense of continuity, a sense of being, with a past, a present, and a future. They are not discrete units that are linked up over time but a dynamically evolving system.[17]

Individual and by extension, collective memories are not 'fixed' and 'lifeless'.[18] Nor does memory comprise immutable units of called-up events; rather it derives from a continual process where an individual self-referentially reconstructs the past. To fashion continuities from these fragments, the brain utilises procedures to meet complexities in an ever-changing world. Thus the same fragment may have different values depending on each act of creation, in the way that '3' changes in the context of '3', '36' or '391'.[19] As we progress through life our memory of the same event changes. Forgetfulness is rarely the culprit. Rather, events are filtered through perspectives processed through the prism of each particular subsequent stage of our lived life.[20] Each stage exercises a time-specific, distinctive attitude and outlook. Hence the fifty-year old perceives the world differently from the way he or she did as a twenty-year old. This does not preclude the fifty-year old sharing a sympathetic memory of that younger worldview emotionally, intuitively or intellectually. Yet it is incomplete, partially forgotten, and by attempting to refresh and recall it in the present, re-configured. It is simultaneously truthful and distorted, cumulative and particular in an ever-unfolding process. It is the relationship to the present which determines the past and the hypothetical future: 'the past (or some meaningful structure of the past) is as hypothetical as the future'.[21] To view the past requires conjuring up 'memory images'.[22]

We might deduce the past does not exist. Only the short, 'specious present', according to Mead, survives.[23] This dialectic between past and present creates a new dialectic between temporal continuities and discontinuities. Continuity depends on actors organising images of the past into a time continuum. But individuals not only arrange new chronological sequences, they attach meaning to these. Where the mind switches between different forms of present, discontinuities or breaks arise through unexpected occurrences. These jolt our awareness. Without this 'primal break of novelty' the present would appear seamless and could not be experienced as continuous, says Mead.[24] Where a break occurs individuals are forced to reconstitute the present. For some this conceptualisation of time is over-simplistic.

It is argued we move between different stretches of time—durées. Hence time is multi-tiered, beyond being linear and iterative. Alberto Melucci talks of 'cyclical', 'simultaneous', 'multidirectional' time;

Claude Lévi-Strauss of 'reversible time'.[25] For individuals in their daily routinised activities, time is reversible and repetitive. Simultaneously people see their lifetime as irreversible and finite. Whereas institutions occupy the *longue durée*—theirs is reversible and 'supra-individual', institutional time.[26]

Short-term working memory that processes immediate activity differs from long-term historical or autobiographic memory which extends backwards beyond the life-span of the individual. He or she cannot have witnessed events before birth. The subjective narrator comes to the fore: imagined pre-life can only be constructed, not directly experienced. A person's imagined identity is consequently defined by dialectically engaging and negotiating with the past. Similarly the external world of the past becomes an imagined world. This perspective might incline to cultural relativism: that external culture determines the identity of individuals, that different cultures shape different understandings of self. Indeed one anthropologist cautions against overlooking 'how people represent themselves to themselves in history because it is, to a certain extent, in terms of these representations, that they will react to revolutions, migration or colonial conquests'.[27]

How or even whether memory is constructed is contested. Sigmund Freud and Henri Bergson explore divergent paradigms: one psychological, the other philosophical. For the former memories are dredged from the subconscious as *faits accomplis*. They are impressions, imprints on a mind requiring triggers to reawaken them.[28] His theory of memory is informed by the process through which memory acts in dreams. By analogy, a physician through 'post-hypnotic suggestion' may present a stimulus to bridge the conscious and unconscious.[29] However for Freud, the mind is in perpetual conflict: 'a set of organisations in conflict with one another; what one segment of the mind wants, another is likely to reject, often very anxiously'.[30]

Bergson's analysis is philosophically complex and radically different.[31] He overturns the phenomenology of Kantian idealism and representation, where the world exists inside our heads. No longer is perception directed at pursuing knowledge. Rather the body serves action. Meanwhile he shuns the realist assumption that the brain and neurological circuits determine our perceptions.[32] The brain does not act 'as a reservoir of images'[33] and nor are representations and memories stored in a photographic library. They are more than functions of the brain. Instead '(t)he past survives...under two distinct forms: first, in motor mechanisms; secondly, in independent recollections'.[34] Motor or automatic memory is akin to a driver getting into a car and putting the key in the ignition. It is habitual, repetitive. Image memory (*la mémoire qui revoit*) is different: '(p)ure memory is entirely virtual. It operates spontaneously, and its memory image "is necessarily imprinted right away in my memory"'.[35] Memory itself is inextricably a function of time. Wherein lies the paradox: 'The past is "contemporaneous" with the present that it has been...The past and the present do not denote two successive moments, but two elements which co-exist'.[36]

The Outside World of the Self

Collective memory is paramount to insurgent groups: it is the objective of POTD. Yet it highlights the dichotomy between structure and agency. To what extent is group memory socially determined, as the Durkheimian Maurice Halbwachs would have it,[37] or projected from the individual in the way Freud or Bergson had conceived?

Others have latterly expressed concern with an undue haste to homogenise collective memory, choosing to distinguish between collected and collective. Psychological and psychoanalytical tools lend themselves to the collected where individual memories mirror each other in a group context. Collective however evokes a unified dynamic.[38] Attempts to hone the latter methodologically foreground the role of political agency:

while the emanation of individual memory is primarily subject to the laws of the unconscious, public memory—whatever its unconscious vicissitudes—testifies to a will or desire on the part of some social group or disposition of power to select and organise representations of the past so that these will be embraced by individuals as their own.[39]

However for Wulf Kansteiner:

[i]t is a collective phenomenon but it only manifests itself in the actions and statements of individuals. It can take hold of historically and socially remote events but it often privileges the interests of the contemporary. It is as much a result of conscious manipulation as unconscious absorption and it is always mediated.[40]

Structuration and routinisation theories, associated with the sociologist Anthony Giddens, illuminate the two-way process between self and group.[41] Remembered past is not merely the cognitive preserve of the individual. Rather it is continually 'traded' with others in society through daily personal and mediated discourse. Individuals shape their self in the way they write their history leading to the present, and how they find middle-ground between personal memory and multiple memories others bring to groups to whose membership they aspire. In this sense individual memories are negotiated, accommodated or abandoned within the group,[42] with varying results.[43] Beyond a certain point failure to accept hegemonic consensus results in being labelled an 'outsider' or deviant.[44] Consequently, memory and identity are closely bound. Complex interaction between actor and external society is observed in Erving Goffman's seminal studies of behavioural characteristics of communication.[45] The metaphor 'all the world's a stage' portrays the individual simultaneously as performer and character, or actor and role, in a play. But he or she retains critical or 'role distance' between the two, continually adjusting the performance, creating a normative image of the self. However the self derives not from the individual but from a process of interacting with others in an actual scene 'on stage'. This means individuals engage in 'impression management', continually readjusting their normative image of themselves when encountering others.[46] As we shape the past through process externally, internally 'even at the moment of reproducing the past our imagination remains under the influence of the present social milieu'.[47] Thus memories are collective functions arranged in 'social frameworks' which give them meaning.

Memory is a function of both time and group interaction. Like insurgents, societal generations pass down collective memory, transmitting ideas on culture, custom and practice in a 'set of social representations concerning the past which each group produces, institutionalises, guards and transmits through the interaction of its members'.[48] Commemorative practices critical to the construction of national identities through costume, dress, festivals, celebrations, museums, galleries, music, and literature shape collective identity.[49] So if memory is a socially constructed narrative of the past negotiated with the present, how does it relate to collective identity? Identity has been described as:

an individual's cognitive, moral, and emotional connection with a broader community, category, practice or institution. It is a perception of a shared status or relation, which may be imagined rather than experienced directly, and it is distinct from personal identities, although it may form part of a personal identity.[50]

Identity however remains contested, as 'blurred and indispensable',[51] overworked and ambiguous,[52] or 'portentous incoherence'.[53] In short, two broad interpretations of identity cluster around whether it is a) 'located' in a Freudian sense within an individual's psychic make-up, underpinning an 'inner sameness and continuity' despite the rough-and-tumble of being conditioned and moulded by social interaction; or, b) an artefact of individual-societal interaction where the individual accepts a designation and behaves according to the role he or she is assigned. Thus the self is no longer fixed or innate but 'a process continuously re-created in each social situation that one enters, held together by the slender thread of memory'.[54] While continuity is common to both, the former (internal) stresses the endurance of a personality; the latter (external) the repeated adoption of various identities demanded by divergent situations. It is this second interpretation which informs *The Violent Image*, echoing Virginia Woolf:

...a biography is considered complete if it merely accounts for six or seven selves, whereas a person may well have as many thousand. (sic)[55]

Much theory addressing the psychological roots of terrorism diverges over whether internal causes of behaviour, pathology, and personality deficiency should be privileged over external, situational influences. Which drives activists to seek collective identity through violence? 'Ego identity' analysis sees self-awareness developing in contact with others, where a child has to master eight potential stages of 'crisis' before reaching fulfilment as an adult.[56] The most significant of these is early to late adolescence (12–19 years) where failure to negotiate the struggle between identity and role confusion, it is argued, can lead to life-long 'identity crisis'.[57] That need and belonging affect self-esteem is an idea prevalent throughout personality-as-cause literature.[58] It is exemplified in a study of 250 German terrorists:

They found themselves in social and political circumstances that for different reasons were not favourable to the acquisition of a positive identity.[59]

Finding meaning or reconciling past deficiencies is considered significant in terrorist identity which

offers the individual a role in society, albeit a negative, which is commensurate with his or her prior expectations and sufficient to compensate for past losses.[60]

Alternative analyses are found in pathological narcissism where terrorist 'psycho-logic' acquires a new characteristic of 'special logic':

political terrorists are driven to commit acts of violence as a consequence of psychological forces...and their special logic, which is grounded in their psychology and reflected in their rhetoric, becomes the justification for their violent acts.[61]

Early-life loss of a parent, or experience of conflict and failure with school and authority may lead to two types of terrorist: the 'nationalist-separatist' and 'anarchic ideologues'. One, the loyal child, continues the parent's project alienated from the regime. The second rejects established order associated with parent and parental generation.[62]

By contrast, the impact of activists' social situation on shaping identity looks to a person's response and adjustment to others within the corporate group. Social identity theory (SIT) underlines how group cohesion is instilled in the minds of individuals, and value is assigned from belonging to the group so that a threat to the group becomes a threat to the self. Because of the social forces at work in the group, any move towards more extreme rhetorical positions reinforces the group think, and group survival becomes equated with absolutist goals.[63] As one case suggests:

Sean O'Grady was a young lion born in the Irish Republican Army (IRA). He had a reputation as being one of its most daring and violent members, directly responsible for the death of three Protestants in Northern Ireland...O'Grady observed that he did not grow up hating Protestants but had adopted the hatreds of his chosen group. He said: 'They (Protestants) are the enemy of my people, and I was their instrument of death. I carry the hatred of my own group'.[64]

This drive for collective identity means that it 'is not only clear but simplistically clear, it is espoused without even minor variation by every member of the organisation, and it is forward-looking with the promise of better conditions for the group and the individual'.[65]

Whether individuals within the group are driven by psychological motives, or whether they make strategic choices within collective rationality, provide a fresh line of inquiry. This questions why individuals undertake personal risk where costs are high and benefits shared (the free rider principle). One possible answer lies in interaction with the broader community:

Organisations arrive at collective judgments about the relative effectiveness of different strategies of opposition on the basis of observation and experience, as much as on the basis of abstract strategic conceptions derived from ideological assumptions.[66]

'Symbolic interactionists'[67] (the Chicago School of sociologists) drew philosophical inspiration from pragmatist theorists—George Herbert Mead, John Dewey, Charles Sanders Peirce and William James.[68] Their laboratory was early 1900s Chicago, a rapidly urbanising industrial centre with mass-immigration of diverse classes, races, and faiths. For them reality was always 'in-the-making'. A Chicago gangland study concluded 'the ganging process is a continuous flux and flow, and there is little permanence in most of the groups'.[69]

Moreover:

(e)ffective collective action and continued corporate existence require the gang control its members. Hence, the group, both through planned and unreflective methods, attempts to incorporate them, to subordinate each to the demands of the whole, and to discipline the unruly.[70]

The researchers examined how symbolic systems and social interaction mould individual identity.[71] Society and the self, they observed, were reflexive: 'individuals create the world around them just as they are moulded by it, in a continuous process of mutual construction'.[72] Mutuality was central:

(s)ituations are structured by individuals who, in the course of interaction, establish a joint sense of the present, develop a corresponding sense of shared past, open common horizons to the future, and shape their conduct with respect to this collectively-established and situationally-sustained time-frame.[73]

Consequently the self is formed by complex interaction between five key factors: acts; objects; meanings; role-taking; and the emergence of self. The concluded objects can become meaningful symbols, hence terrorists might equate a bank with capitalism. The acts people undertake can provoke common meaning, becoming significant symbols. But the meaning of an act is fluid, open to change. 'Anchored in behaviour', it is contingent upon how individuals act towards objects. Individuals however play roles, attempting to 'get inside' the minds of the other and predict his/her behaviour (Mead's 'generalised other').[74] Ultimately that entails the individual negotiating his or her own experience with reference to others in a tit-for-tat process of second-guessing and accommodating what other parties think.[75] This fuels attacks on interactionists, suggesting their ideas are excessively subjectivist, and neglecting structural effects, inequality, and power.[76]

Any collective seeking legitimacy for future projects in the eyes of the population requires an historic identity that must be intelligible and credible. Past achievements and future aspirations are linked in this temporally negotiated identity. 'Futures arise out of attempts to create forms which can serve as goals for common action in the present'.[77] Any state aims to drive a wedge between the populace and this identity, denying insurgents an acceptable narrative of the past. States build a counter-identity for that organisation attaching meaningless or criminal violence to it. For the insurgent, already operating *de facto* outside the law, it is a small step from being assigned the status of criminal to being vilified as mafia exploiter or pathological killer. Mud sticks and states have the resources to throw it.[78]

People lead lives according to socially inherited institutions—ways of behaving communicated and internalised by the state through hegemonic understandings nurtured in families, schools, employment, and bureaucratic state processes of administration.[79] Hegemonies succeed by remaining unseen by us, imperceptible. They become common sense, the norm, and enter collective memory. For this the family is a working laboratory:

One must radically distinguish...the family from the relationship of beings united by a physiological bond, from which proceed individual psychological feelings that can also be found among animals.[80]

It has been noted '(a)ll families invent their parents and children, give each of them a story, character, fate, and even a language'.[81] Family members' status is conditioned not by feelings so much as 'rules and customs independent of us that existed before us'.[82] Recalling a parental moment or past scene involves not mirror-imaging the original event but investing it with various associations and memory fragments taken from different moments in time. The parental moment becomes a 'landmark' 'pregnant' with all that preceded and follows. Such is the family group's power to inspire.[83] How this influences patterns of collective action, how inclinations to 'insurgency' spread within and between generations of families will be considered in the next chapter's discussion of Irish Republicanism.[84] It 'runs in families and social networks, held together by sustained cultural narratives', proposes the American anthropologist Montgomery McFate.[85] Of six members who founded Republican Sinn Féin in 1986 in a breakaway act of ideological purity, all six had grown up in Republican families with connections dating back to the 1920s' armed conflicts.[86]

The Outside World of the Group

How does small-group memory compete with asymmetric state memories disseminated and mediated by all-pervasive global media? The group's collective memory is in permanent flux. Change may be small or great, but not apparent until organisational schisms occur. In processes of social interaction, the collective confronts the world of the enemy. Identity is defined in opposition to the demonised 'other' and prevailing counter-ideologies. Precarious security is undermined by external threat. Targeted constituencies for revolution or social transformation lie beyond the collective's *cordon sanitaire*. Recidivism stalks group membership. So how can group memory survive on the media battlefield?

Individual and group memory are fragmentary, iterative, and constructed processes. Media memory too is shaped by many providers.[87] Global media represent a Heath-Robinson structure of ill-fitting parts which are heterogeneous, mutually competitive, and dissonant. Perhaps their only commonality is that we attribute to them membership of the same media family. Despite the cultural divergence between national broadcast or publishing organisations, whether publicly or privately owned, niche or mass consumed, overarching characteristics nevertheless emerge. 'Flows' of information lead to confluences of consensus.[88] Output is commoditised and formatted. Content becomes reflexive and self-referential. The outside world is annexed, mediated, reconstituted before being offered back to itself as authentic real life:

the memories TV recalls via constant reruns, remakes, and parody, the past it recreates, rarely summon or echo personal experience.[89]

Processed events shut out alternative understandings. The terms of engagement by which individuals participate become pre-determined, and role-allocated. Memory is no longer individual, but affirmed and authorised as collective. (The complexities of how memory is negotiated in the mediaspace will be discussed below, in Chapter Five).

In sum, collective memory is negotiated and routinised between individual and group. In an iterative flux, some consensus must emerge if the insurgent group is to coalesce as an effective military unit, both ideologically and organisationally. It underscores collective identity reflected in constructed memory. But insurgents have more than one audience: internally, they contribute to a self-reinforcing process; externally, to the immediate support constituency outside must also be revealed a unanimous purpose and consistent memory. What happens when that same memory—an account of the past and reading of the present—ventures further afield to challenge alternative group hegemonies mediated by powerful disseminators in the global mediascape?

Myths Maketh Man

Memory and identity are shaped through narrative devices such as myth and metaphor. Memory mythologises the past in relation to the present and future. However memory and myth are not synonymous. Some conceptualisations of myth identify an *a priori* force.[90] However, they become artefacts. Bound by time and space, some endure more widely and longer than others. Even '(n)ations, like narratives, lose their origins in the myths of time and only fully realise their horizons in the mind's eye'.[91] The myth of nationhood will offer context for much of the following discussion.

One observer proposes refining under-theorised myth. Frieden talks of 'governing myths' that become akin to an ideology, an 'action-oriented thought-structure that, in its endeavour to stifle debate over possible political alternatives tries instead to decontest the essentially contested concepts which structure political discourse'.[92] In effect, myths iron out the politically inconvenient contours of remembered past that mould identity, removing nuance, and stifling competition. Yet this does not prevent subaltern, dissenting myths rivalling them.[93] National identity myths of the nation state cannot deny the space where group memories of the oppressed and marginalised form. Nor can they prevent rival nationalist myths jostling for daylight, without which there would be no insurgencies. However the nature of ideology is to overwhelm all rivals. This notion of myth as ideology resembles propaganda where propaganda is seen as a 'specific form of activated ideology'.[94]

For Ellul, controversially, Western society is predicated on a dialectical opposition between two fundamental myths: Science and History. Contingent on these, he sees secondary, collective myths determining the orientation of society: Work, Happiness, Nation, Youth, Hero.[95] These are complementary and mutually supportive. For example, ideas of *scientific progress* are fundamental to the post-Enlightenment West where they equate to *technological efficiency* and the *route to happiness*. In their need to incorporate all society, state or insurgent communications appeal to these deeply held beliefs, taking advantage of them. 'Men do not have with myth a relationship based on truth but on use'. Today myth is a 'system of communication', a 'message'.[96]

How do we imbibe myths? Narratives resonate with underlying myths permeating society. '(I)t is through narratives and narrativity that we constitute our social identities' argues one commentator, gainsaying traditional social sciences which dismiss narrative as overly hermeneutic, excessively based in the humanities.[97] However we are reminded 'social life is storied and that narrative is an ontological condition of social life' where people construct identity through a limited repertoire of 'emplotted' stories. That means people make sense of what is happening to them by absorbing experiences into episodic narratives which affect them on various levels. That they are also 'public' enables them to form 'traditions', capturing broader social institutions, such as notions of the 'working-class hero', 'every American can become President', or the 'American Dream'. On another level 'meta-narratives' offer plots that form the 'epic dramas of our time' like 'Capitalism vs Communism', 'Individual vs Society', and progressive accounts like 'Marxism and the Triumph of Class Struggle', 'Liberalism and the Triumph of Liberty', or 'the Rise of Islam'. They shape how we think, live and position ourselves inside these unfolding stories.[98] Consequently, they condition how Propaganda of the Deed is perceived once inserted into them.

In constant story-telling each individual seeks the role of story-teller recounting his/her life as subject, while adopting the perspective of the audience. Thus we are subject, object, and agent. But these are not passive texts. 'They are told in being lived and lived in being told'.[99] As much as stories endure, they are characterised by fragility, mutability, even evanescence. In the frenzy of daily life people are told they live in a world that is getting faster all the time. Central to propagating this tried but untested narrative is today's burgeoning mass media. Information technologies were already entrenched by the late Industrial Revolution. But each era believes it is more modern than the last. An earlier generation witnessed the unease of the first rail-passengers riding Stephenson's Rocket. These felt they might die of asphyxiation travelling at 29 miles per hour: such was the pace of modern living.[100]

The primary influence on narratives, myths, and indeed identity is a unified vernacular. For Anderson language before territory sets boundaries between the 'in-group' and the 'other'. It coheres a population, defining its ethnicity, nationalism, and belief-system *vis-à-vis* the outside world. By disseminating a newborn sense of self through common language, publishing media are central to the process of moulding 'imagined political community'.[101] Once established, media hold up a mirror, albeit a contorting looking-glass to the individual and group. Mass media thrive on a diet of self-reference. They operate by interacting with other media as much as with the public. They exchange opinions and 'facts'. But facts quietly assume a life of their own, deserting any claim to scientific veracity. Mass media spawn 'factoids', a term Norman Mailer parenthesised as 'literary smog': 'facts which have no existence before appearing in a magazine or newspaper, creations which are not so much lies as a product to manipulate emotions in the Silent Majority'.[102] For newsprint read television and the net. Facts expand to embrace the visual and symbolic language of television. Today these myths are transmitted faster and more widely than ever.

POTD as Metaphor

Satellite television and computer technologies have much to answer for. The rate and scope of take-up have transformed how insurgents read the insurrectionist landscape.[103] Audiences and users replace populations to become potential subscribers to the revolutionary struggle. Furthermore these technologies have obviated insurgents' requirement for face-to-face contact, at least during early recruitment. However any mass medium is inherently flawed. It is no friction-free conduit along which messages are sent unimpeded. Audio-visual media are 'mediatised'.[104] Individuals, corporations, governments and institutions mould or interpret content as it passes. Taken to extremes this suggests media communications are part-and-parcel of systematic manipulation by ideological elites.[105] For Herbert Marcuse they are precisely that, exercising all-pervasive control over audiences:

> the irresistible output of the entertainment and information industry carry with them the prescribed attitudes and habits, certain intellectual and emotional reactions which bind the consumers…to the producers, and, through the latter to the whole [social system]. The products indoctrinate and manipulate; they promote a false consciousness which is immune against its falsehood… Thus emerges a pattern of one-dimensional thought and behaviour.[106]

But times change. This fear must now be tempered by the unforeseen characteristics of digital media. Yet audio-visual media remain distinctive in another key respect; they are symbolic. Behind the empirical reality of what we see sits a conceptual association. Viewers associate objects with ideas as part of everyday life. For this association to prompt action, a gulf between the concrete act and the abstract idea must first be bridged.

We are concerned here not so much with aggression in the violent act and whether it leads to further aggression.[107] Rather, that element of political violence which engages viewers, triggering them to commit to a political ideal. So what does it mean when we say a violent event 'resonates', is 'symbolic', or functions as 'metaphor'? By proposing violent events be conceived as islands, then as islands within an archipelago, suggests each event has a relative meaning for its neighbours. It implies a greater continuity or bond that harmonises apparently disparate moments within an overarching scheme. As nationhood unifies the Greek archipelago, so revolution aggregates a metaphoric archipelago of diverse explosions and killings. Insurgent groups strengthen this analogy by continually reinvesting in the narrative. Thus subsequent violent events not only contribute to a political campaign, but merge into a process of revolutionary mythmaking.

Is POTD truly a metaphor? Can a terror technique represent a body of ideas? Semiotic study demonstrates that individuals understand signs;[108] that flags, corporate logos, ceremonies, rituals, costumes, road signs, traffic lights, indeed any object can represent concepts. The idiosyncratic Canadian pianist Glenn Gould toyed with the practice of semiotic reading when seeking to mitigate his absent-mindedness:

It's true that I've driven through a lot of red lights on occasion, but on the other hand I've stopped at a lot of green ones but never gotten credit for it.[109]

We denote the concrete object or act but connote the abstracted association.[110] Marlboro cigarettes originally targeted a female market in the 1920s. As sales fell in the 1950s, the company's advertising agency re-positioned the brand into the mythical American West, using real cowboys to embody the spirit of the product. The connotation arose from consumers' identification with the underlying values associated with the Western myth: manliness, ruggedness, the great outdoors, and freedom. The product was inserted into the myth of the 'heroic West', itself a connotation. According to Marlboro's brand manager:

(i)n a world that was becoming increasingly complex and frustrating for the ordinary man...the cowboy represented an antithesis—a man whose environment was simplistic and relatively pressure free. He was his own man in a world he owned.[111]

Umberto Eco concludes: 'semiotics is in principle the discipline studying everything which can be used in order to lie'.[112] So prevalent are metaphors in our language that most are 'dead'. To such an extent we have lost the original poignancy of the relationship between signifier and signified. We fail to notice we are using metaphors. Poetic usage provides clues to how we might interrogate the POTD metaphor:

poetic metaphors differ from everyday metaphors because there's often an element of surprise. Even the sense that a rule's been broken or that a category error has been made, as in the apparently outlandish or extravagant 'Can't lovers be like a pair of compasses'.[113]

But can we build a conceptual bridge between dramatic events as lived (a bomb) and a conceptual body of thought (national self-rule)?[114] This is crucial if POTD is to rise above the purely tactical effects of 'shock and awe'. People associate immediate cause and effect: a bomb with damage, death, and injury without actually witnessing the aftermath. But can they engage in complete abstraction?

Resonance, or association, is nothing new; it is the bedrock of the advertising industry. When President Lyndon Johnson was challenged by Republican Barry Goldwater in the 1964 US Presidential election, Johnson ran a television ad against the Arizona senator mindful of his campaign pledges to escalate the nuclear arms race with Russia. The 'Daisy spot' depicted a young girl pulling the petals off a daisy, one by one. As each petal fell, a mechanical voice counted down a missile launch—10, 9, 8…until the image of the girl dissolved into a full-screen nuclear explosion. To avoid this outcome the nation should vote Johnson, intoned the voiceover. Not once was Goldwater mentioned in sound or picture. However Goldwater's team was first to demand the ad's withdrawal. So controversial was its impact that it only ran once. American audiences knew what was being said without having it spelled out: Goldwater was a warmonger who would bring about the end of the world.[115]

A striking aspect of 9/11 was the commentary of television studio-presenters whose role was to shepherd audiences through the tragedy unfolding in real time. However anchors and reporters were lost for words in 'dead air', long periods of silence. This arose less from respect than the extraordinary nature of the event beyond the scope of com-

71

mentators' experience. Language proved inadequate to process and communicate the intensity of emotion arising from the shock. For once a nation reared on lexical superlatives had 'nothing left in the tank' with which to express its horror. One American novelist, Don De Lillo, wrote: '(o)ur world, parts of our world...have crumbled into theirs, which means we are living in a place of danger and rage'.[116]

How should we translate the metaphor of 9/11? For the revolutionary it reads variously as a strike against a) America; b) capitalism; c) imperialism; d) sponsors of corrupt, Arab political regimes; e) aggressors against Islam; and f) Islamic renaissance. In many societies within and beyond the West, for both the vulnerable and less engaged, it equates to an attack on a) the Bush administration; b) the American nation; c) capitalist Wall Street; d) real estate; e) individual rights and freedoms; and f) unleashing violent forces inherent in Islam. Yet such a response is simplistic. Two questions arise. Which primary association above did viewers make between the act (explosion) and a conceptual framework? Second, where the viewer had a particular pre-existing framework of political violence, was there a marked difference in the response? A further dimension problematises connotations of POTD. Universalists hold we can express any idea in any language to the same effect. On the contrary, argue cultural relativists:

No two languages are ever sufficiently similar to be considered as representing the same social reality. The worlds in which different societies live are distinct worlds, not merely the same world with different labels attached...We see and hear and otherwise experience very largely as we do because the language habits of our community predispose certain choices of interpretation'.[117]

For POTD to be universally accessible, it must cross inter-textual borders. Paradoxically, to reveal more profound levels of meaning, it must mine rich veins of culture and context. The premise of *The Violent Image* is that deeds are constructed as foci of narratives targeted at global and national television populations. They have meaning because they are texts that can be read for their meaning. The difference today is the global reach of information media. Everyone is watching. So does each revolutionary with the distinct provenance of his or her movement read the same image differently? How far does each invest the image with reference to his or her own particular political struggle? Television pictures showed local detail within 9/11's explosion site. Two distinct buildings dominated the New York skyline. These were struck by two aeroplanes and subsequently collapsed.

The assailants' identity was unknown at this stage. So did the streets and high rises, and distinctly American attributes of the scene impact the process of association as semiotic theory would anticipate? If so, what did the Al-Qaeda sympathiser actually see on television: a strike against a military occupier of Arab states, or a supporter of Israel? New York is a notable Jewish centre-of-influence, perhaps more than Washington, a metonym for American culture and power. What did the IRA viewer witness: an imperialist power morally equivalent to the British occupier of Ireland, or the home to a large American-Irish community, where many felt affection for Irish republican separatism? And what of the Zapatista locked in his enduring struggle against the central Mexican state over land and forest rights in Chiapas?[118] Not only cultures, but events are no longer discrete bodies of text. Satellite television and internet have put paid to that. They revolutionise the way information travels. They render discrete bodies of understanding 'soft-edged', their walls porous and repeatedly penetrated by voracious technologies. Information 'flows' characterise today's media.

For a metaphor to perform to the full, behaviour should be universal. But can it ever rise above cultural relativism? Philosophers and psychologists have long discussed the mind's propensity for translating what it sees into abstractions. The Aristotelian canon describes metaphor as a comparison between two things, but as an act of genius. Widely contested and still under-researched, Andrew Ortony views it as more than literary flourish, defining it is 'an essential ingredient of communication'.[119] Images possess a symbolic function. Metaphorical thinking derives from the very 'nature of perception, in abstractive seeing', rather than language.[120] Pictures recall better than words. They lead to efficient ways of storing information.[121] To know how many windows are in your home, you have the capacity to examine the house from various points of view in the mind's eye, then tally up the panes visually. Information can be processed 'free from sequential restraints'.[122] Given that metaphors start somewhere, the question is whether our minds are programmed with schemata that identify and understand them, or whether through language we accumulate them from everyday experience. Since all languages contain metaphor, the former is the likelier. One observer considers metaphor's power vested in its 'relational structure to an abstract domain by importing it (by analogy) from a more concrete domain'.[123]

One study of the metaphorical mind compares two insights into the psychology of reminding: reminding by experience, and reminding by conceptualising. First, by the familiar association through the senses—a smell, taste, or sound triggers the comparison or metaphor.[124] 1980s Hollywood blockbusters were released with a best-selling pop song. The music was more than a marketing tool. It was the trigger which conjured up memory of the film. One London cinema-goer went further: 'It creates an imprint in your mind; as soon as you hear that song, it provokes thoughts of the film'.[125] Conversely, it is a 'shared skeleton of abstract ideas'. One commentator explores 'the inefficiency of waiting a long time to obtain a small quantity':

X described how his wife would never make his steak as rare as he liked it. When this was told to Y, it reminded Y of a time, 30 years earlier, when he tried to get his hair cut in a short style in England, and the barber would not cut it as short as he wanted.[126]

This is no arcane debate. It directly impacts the way we interpret events in today's insurgency landscape. The last two decades have witnessed a market expansion that multiplies the potential use and effect of information, beyond earlier transitions of nineteenth-century mass-media print and twentieth-century broadcast television. The global domination of media leads Faisal Devji to conclude that Islam's *ummah*—the global community of Muslim diasporas—defines itself less by territory than as a landscape of time and space. This imaginary space is occupied by religious sites and landmarks, and historic associations of Muslim heroics and tragedies. In the minds of Muslim audiences, this new landscape becomes real. But what actually holds the imagined political community together is the panoply of satellite television and information technologies.[127] Olivier Roy elaborates:

[the internet] is the perfect place for [Muslim] individuals to express themselves while claiming to belong to a community to whose enactment they contribute, rather than being passive members of it.[128]

Cognitive space of groups merges with global media space. But the abstraction is only possible if some consensus joins the cognitive experiences of individual group members. They must share the same interpretation of the same symbols to identify in a similar manner (see fig 2). Hence a group universe comprising what Faisal Devji calls 'cosmopolitan militants' is not limited to Islamic movements; indeed it may yet emerge more manifestly in other political spheres, particularly environmentalism. The difficulty facing any such scientific investigation is that this discussion occupies an uneasy cusp between cognitive and social psychologies. Some place it in cultural psychology, arguing the mind is:

'content-driven, domain-specific, and constructively stimulus-bound; and it cannot be extricated from the historically variable and culturally diverse intentional worlds in which it plays a constructive part'.[129]

This might suggest different cultures interpret the same event differently. Indeed one philosopher reminds us: 'reflection must find its way among symbols which constitute an opaque language, symbols that belong to the uniqueness and contingency of different cultures and which give rise to equivocal interpretations'.[130] Moreover global insurgents engaged in a war of ideas and images believe deeds are persuasive because they do more than terrorise populations. They carry meaning that speaks beyond immediate pools of potential recruits to irradiating circles of support constituencies.

It is unsatisfactory to argue simply that violent spectacles play favourably into pre-propagandised communities.[131] Otherwise, if we assume individuals within the same family share common grievances and conditions of political economy, why do different family members react differently to extreme violence? By hypothesising POTD as a symbol, more accurately metaphor, we should ask why humans respond to metaphors. As Steven Pinker says: 'TO THINK IS TO GRASP A METAPHOR—the metaphor metaphor' (sic).[132]

We are so in thrall to the attractions of media that individual and group memories are variously conditioned and impacted by the continuous process of creating media-memory. This does not mean, as some have argued, that viewers are mere passive consumers, or that programming is little more than a commoditised culture industry.[133] Rather, audiences are active and passive, caught in a permanent tension between belief and disbelief, persuasion and rejection. Television itself loudly abhors terrorist violence, yet seeks to edge ever closer to the heat of the flame. Visual electronic media present competing agendas of belief and disbelief. Moreover, they host complementary 'factual' and 'fictional' accounts of reality contained in news and drama programming. In the latter, belief further fragments to accommodate 'suspension of disbelief'. Yet so overwhelming is the force of electronic media, so constricting their own consensus of how the outside world should be defined, that freedom of choice is *a priori* compromised and constrained. When television creates memory, metaphors are stretched to a new plane. They become hyperbole. In the process television drains the essence from personally constructed memory, emptying it of what is personal or individual. The old metaphor is hollowed out and replaced unseen by a new heightened one, a simulacrum. The Holocaust is a prime case:

> What no one wants to understand is that Holocaust is primarily (and exclusively) an event, or, rather, a televised object (fundamental rule of McLuhan's which must not be forgotten), that is to say, that one attempts to rekindle a cold historical event, tragic but cold.[134]

Televised memories do not mirror-image historical events and nor are they even an amalgam of memories collected from the public sphere. They take on a life of their own. Memory resides in the surface-layer of the construct; the essence is long abandoned. This same construct is repeated over and over again via multiple broadcasts. The representation of heightened reality is repeatedly updated by producers, continually re-consumed by audiences. In this sense media memory becomes caricature, a distorted version of original events. But media memory increasingly becomes society's memory. Thus the 2001 attack on the Twin Towers some years on is distilled to an iconic image. So too are most deeds reduced to single frames: the story of the suicide bomber is told through the shot of the aftermath of devastation wrought; the IED through the burning armoured vehicle; the assassination through the bloodied corpse. Although television audiences were mesmerised by the slow-motion inevitability of 9/11, the retained image is the snapshot, the 'still-photograph' of the event. Television's distinctive character—its ability to capture attention through moving picture—has been commandeered by the violent spectacle. POTD freeze-frames the moving picture into the older medium of the photograph.[135] As Susan Sontag notes, the photograph's power is unique:

> Photographs may be more memorable than moving images, because they are a neat slice of time, not a flow. Television is a stream of under selected images, each of which cancels its predecessor. Each still photograph is a privileged moment, turned into a slim object that one can keep and look at again.[136]

But this slim object is the property of personal and group memory. What is retained and continually re-examined is the 'insurgent's photograph'.[137] Sontag's analysis seems not far removed from the insurgent project:

> The photographic exploration and duplication of the world fragments continuities and feeds the pieces into an interminable dossier, thereby providing pos-

sibilities of control that could not even be dreamed of under the earlier system of recording information: writing. That photographic recording is always, potentially, a means of control was already recognised when such powers were in their infancy.[138]

While insurgent representation of life seeks to fragment photographically, it aims to overwhelm state and media memory. It fractures the continuities of hegemonic myths and narratives only to assert the continuity of revolutionary narrative constructed from its own discontinuities. POTD resists throwing out the baby with the bathwater. Its spectacle takes advantage of television's 24-hour availability and the multiplier-effect of repeated transmissions. How this is done is developed in later chapters.

So insurgent strikes become simple logos. We recall them as icons, mental photographs depicting two aeroplanes ploughing into two monoliths igniting a ball of flame and smoke. Our mental clutter is intersected by this single caricature. The despair of suffocating office-workers inside buildings, imagined hopelessness of doomed airline passengers, jumping office-workers impacting pavements from a great height, metronomic cries of horror caught on street-level cameras and microphones, even the martyrs' eye-view: all are lost. As iconoclastic as the nomenclature 9/11, so is our memory of the tragedy distilled into a simple logo. Jean Baudrillard argues that beyond the accepted wisdom of semiotics, events are reduced to essential components. Symbols dissimulate: they cover 'truth' leaving it whole. But simulation creates an entirely new order of reality:

...pretending, or dissimulating leaves the principle of reality intact: the difference is always clear, it is simply masked, whereas simulation threatens the difference between the 'true and the 'false, the 'real and the 'imaginary'.[139]

POTD, no longer symbol, becomes simulacrum. The 9/11 icon no longer represents the history of an event unfolding with multiple perspectives and nuanced arguments. Instead it has become the distilled, distorted memory of event. Repeated with reverence on television and the net, it excludes discourse, it ring-fences its own memory.

In today's world the medium and the message merge to the point of creating a 'nebula' of meaning. If television memory is to be challenged, audiences must draw on unprecedented levels of resistance to assert their independent memories. For insurgents the dilemma is clear: whose memory will predominate? Insurgents have no interest in a free market of ideas; they aim to dominate and monopolise discourse, supplanting one hegemony with another. Should insurrectionists reject the iconographic image-making of electronic media? After all there are risks in waging war through ideas whereas fighting with weapons is tried and tested. The impact of words cannot be measured: battlefield casualties can be counted. Like any commercial corporation, exercising 'brand control' is central to any movement's ideological purity. Political or commercial, brands have their commissars. Therefore what do they do when faced with media who present a hyperbole of the state's self-image, similarly distorting the insurgent message? Heightened image-making can be destabilised by erratic surges of public opinion that swarm periodically and unpredictably through societies. Self-generating images surge through the web. In the digital era, they lie beyond the control of any broadcaster, publisher, or insurrectionist. Ever opportunist, insurgents embrace future uncertainty, controlling home-grown narratives where possible. Therein lies the conundrum; having created chaos, insurgents must exploit ensuing uncertainty. Yet at some point, opportunism should give way to systematic organisation and coherence. For this reason Lenin rejected POTD, however useful in the short-term. In revolutions organisation should not be sacrificed to spontaneity.[140] Long-term, POTD lacks control and focus.[141] Its nineteenth-century proponents failed, at least because they proved unable to articulate a route between chaos and the choate. Twenty-first century POTD faces committing to spontaneity and serendipity.

POTD's true role then is to problematise the landscape of competing discourses. Challenging hegemonic memory through the only tool available, extreme insurrectionist violence, stakes its claim to root the struggle in its own primary metaphor. It fights on two fronts, against the state and media. Yet as boundaries between television, internet and mobile telephony blur, and technologies converge, insurgents already recognise one advantage. The web's infinite space will ultimately—governmental controls notwithstanding—favour insurgents more than states. Digital communications space is porous and dynamic. However controlled and targeted, information flows like balls in a pinball machine. Controllable to a degree, very soon the ball ricochets randomly with unintended consequences. Can insurgents tolerate such randomness more than states, and thus become reconciled to memory and images that never die, once released into the digital ether, always capable of being absorbed into the next generation's insurrectionist memory? Besieged by the tabloid press, Julia Roberts explains to a perplexed Hugh Grant in the film *Notting Hill*: once incriminating photographs get out into the public domain, they can never be retrieved. They merely wait for some editor on a quiet news-day to rediscover them.[142] Albert Camus had suspected the same: 'the plague bacillus never dies'. It only lies low, biding its time.[143]

* * *

Memory at the level of individual, group or state is socially constructed. Those who wish to re-engineer society understand that their own political legitimacy emanates from the way their roots in the past lend them authority when seeking support from populations today. But states and political elites that control media, perhaps the most substantial force in moulding our views of the past and present, invest resources and time in shaping a hegemony which insurgents must challenge with their rival revolutionary memory. The narrative grip must be broken and replaced. But so strong is this hold, so commonsensical the official view of historical identity, that insurgents use POTD to detonate the equilibrium. Consequently they use violent acts as a lightning rod to trigger competitive memories that activists place in societies, but which remain overshadowed or criminalised. Today's digital media revolution opens a way for POTD to become a strategic operating concept. A war of ideas and images now becomes possible because this transformation allows more and more people to communicate without passing through the editorial sanctions of media owners and elite gatekeepers.

'Time to Consider' campaign on the London Underground.
© CBS Outdoor.

3

INSURGENT MEMORY AND NARRATIVE

I experienced them at the present moment and at the same time in the context of a distant moment, so that the past was made to encroach upon the present and I was made to doubt whether I was in the one or the other.

Marcel Proust[1]

Insurgents challenge states for control of the past to legitimise their role in the present and lay claim to ownership of the future. To achieve this they manipulate time, creating a narrative of collective identity, a popular group memory.[2] Building on the framework of memory interaction developed in the previous chapter, this chapter examines how both states and opposition groups make long-term investments in that process through the construction of narratives. People remember events as stories. These may be enshrined in rituals, ceremonies, and monuments. However, in order to underpin them, revolutionaries subjugate past suffering and atrocity to remembered acts of pre-emptive and retaliatory violence. Ireland's Republican and nationalist struggle is one such assembly of loosely connected episodes repeatedly honed over two, some would say four, centuries into a cohesive, contiguous account of resistance against a brutal foreign occupier.

Discontinuous historical accounts of the revolutionary struggle are shaped into a self-legitimising continuity. Without a 'social myth', talk of revolt can go on forever. Myths become 'expressions of a determination to act'.[3] These are rooted in a minority's, sometimes majority's tragedy and oppression, not least heroic resistance.[4] For all their geographical differences (Chapter One), insurgents resemble each other in how they demarcate borders between the self and 'other'. They employ schema of vernacular language, symbolic vocabulary, and ethnic or ethical/religious membership. These frequently lead to inwardly directed political messianism, embodying the 'in-group' story. POTD seeks to trigger this story *qua* memory and inspire sympathisers to collective action.

Today some groups choose global struggle that transcends sovereign borders. They appeal to communities of shared ethnic or religious identity, rooting them in a constructed, marginalised history. During the nineteenth-century imperialist era and twentieth-century Cold War, most popular struggles were nationalist or colonial liberationist. In democracies or autocracies, movements for national identity and self-rule did not exclusively turn to political violence, but often more gradual, cultural contests. Narratives shaped by elites but challenged by oppositional forces were and remain a constant process of state-building negotiated at state and sub-state levels. Insurgents contest their own demarcated space through limited means. Beyond territorial, administrative, and fiscal control, their group narratives serve that purpose. War becomes both cognitive and kinetic, but not in the Clausewitzian sense of 'psychological forces exert(ing) decisive influence on the elements involved in war'.[5] Rather in an age of global communications the narrative domain becomes the new, contested battlespace.

A Chinese newspaper photograph adds to China's daily drip-feed of state narrative. It depicts a government tribute to a 'hero', Zhou Bo, a People's Liberation Army (PLA) official who died saving two boys from drowning. The deceased soldier was publicly honoured as a 'revolutionary martyr'; his funeral drew 10,000 people and 400 PLA officials from eight counties.[6] Even the smallest fragment becomes the cement that binds the historical edifice. Some narratives target domestic populations. Others are explicitly aware of the global dimension, as a *Paris Match* eight-page photo-spread, shot in Afghanistan, demonstrates. A Taliban unit had ambushed and killed ten French troops within days of President Sarkozy's pledge to increase military co-operation with NATO. The photographs show a Taliban commander posing in the uniform, and with the weapon and equipment of a deceased French soldier. The commander's accompanying interview declares:

They crossed a line by coming here. Uzbin valley is ours. It's our territory...
With this attack we wanted to show French soldiers they had to stop helping
the Americans...We shall hit French interests everywhere in the world. We easily have the means. We are not alone or isolated in these mountains.[7]

French Defence Minister Hervé Morin attacked *Paris Match* for
publishing the photos:

Should we be doing the Taliban's promotion for them? The Taliban are waging a war of communication with this kind of operation.[8]

The magazine's decision to publish the photographs only helped
reinforce internationally a heroic group identity, which had already
spread locally by word of mouth.

Symbols of Resistance

Insurgents and states exploit periods of perceived existential threat to
reshape community narratives. Against rising tensions in 1989, Slobodan Milošević stood before a crowd of Serbs as their leader on the
600th anniversary of the Battle of Kosovo. It was a conflict widely
recalled for the victory of the Muslim Ottoman Empire over the Serbs.
With Yugoslavia fragmenting, he spoke of Serb national identity,
brushing over historical accuracy. That date for Serbia, he said,

celebrated an event of the distant past which has a great historical and symbolic significance for its future. Today it is difficult to say what is the historical truth about the Battle of Kosovo and what is legend.[9]

Whether Serbs had been defeated was no longer relevant. What mat-
tered was a new Serb sectarian purpose was linking into the 'symbol of
heroism'. To question this disregard for truth, wrote one 'myth-raking'
investigator fearing for more than her career prospects, had become a
'dangerous business'.[10]

One particular epic underscores the value of myth. Masada's defence
is a latter-day act of Israeli historical reclamation. It mutated at different times of political risk, consistent with Mead's theory that communities at moments of rapid change create new pasts to find new
meanings.[11] In 73 AD a siege involving 900 Jewish religious zealots
confronted the Roman forces of Flavius Silva after the fall of Jerusalem. As a final act of resistance, facing inevitable defeat, the mountain
stronghold witnessed mass suicide. Not until a Masada Society was
formed in London around 1900, at which time a tenth-century Greek

text was translated into modern Hebrew, did this POTD acquire its new-found significance.[12] Its heroism echoes the rise of political Zionism, revealing also the insecurity of 1920s Jewish settlers. By 1928 Jewish immigration to Palestine was in crisis: for every immigrant, there was one emigrant. Lamdan's contemporaneous poem 'Masada' captures contradictory moods of 'defiant optimism' and 'morbid pessimism'. In the settlers' imagination it offered meaning of the present gleaned from the past. The past stood for 'the very real prospect that the second Masada would fall in the same manner as did the first—by self-destruction'.[13] Paradoxically, in the pessimism of the historic outcome was to be found hope and conviction for their own future.

Contemporary Afrikaner experience is noteworthy. A community of 2.5 million, once dominant in twentieth-century apartheid South Africa, feels vulnerable faced with the black African National Congress which in 2004's general elections polled 69.7%. Its majority secured not only primacy in a near one-party state, but placed it a hair's breadth from the legitimate right to alter the constitution unilaterally. A song with accompanying video has recently become popular in Afrikaans communities.[14] It evokes the dramatic exploits of guerrilla-leader General De La Rey during the Anglo-Boer War between Afrikaners and British forces (1899–1902). The memory evoked is of a political and economic underclass, marginalised 'children of the soil'. Women and children suffer disease and starvation in British concentration camps, their lands terrorised by Kitchener's 'sweep and scour' strategy. Nevertheless its hero symbolises Boer resistance through the lightning raids of his 'fight and flee' campaign.[15] However this resistance is considered metaphoric:"When they sing about how nasty the British were to the Boer women in the concentration camps and "general come and lead us because we will fall around you", they're not thinking about the British', says one Afrikaans writer, 'they're thinking about blacks. Their enemy is now black'.[16]

The timing coincides with the trial of a member of the Boeremag (Farmers' Force) for an anti-government bombing-campaign. For the government this is a right-wing hijack of 'a "struggle song" that sends out a "call to arms"'.[17]

As Hobsbawm and Ranger remind us, narratives alone do not create identity. Outward symbols of identity are constructed and over time lose their extraordinary character, only to become mundane and commonly accepted. Thus are traditions invented, 'often deliberate and always innovative', most effective when absorbed into daily ritual and national symbolism.[18] So the Highland kilt of tartan, introduced by an English industrialist in 1728, was subsequently romanticised by Walter Scott's novels and Colonel Stewart's nationalist project.[19] Scotland's national myth arose against the backdrop of the 1707 Union, Scottish rebellions in 1715, 1745, and Parliament's 'Disarming Act' of 1747. Highland regiments deployed in British imperial adventures in India and America, like the clan-based Black Watch, formed only in 1745, became distinguished for fighting prowess and their now 'traditional' costume. Kilt production boosted a weaver economy while scattering the martial Scots conveniently to distant frontiers of empire. However the most tangible dimension of any group identity is language, particularly the vernacular, as Anderson reveals in his survey of Philippine literature.[20] Cultural progenitor and repository, it forms a borderline between self and the 'other'. As a vehicle for conscious and unconscious political discourse, it reaches inaccessible corners of doubt and inertia. A *lingua franca* of the oppressed becomes both tool and symbol. Importantly it carries group memory from decade to decade, century to century.

Irish Republicanism

Irish nationalism and Republicanism do not mirror all insurgencies. Rather their longevity across at least two centuries illustrates how discontinuous events can be turned into a harmonious and mobilising story. Between the historical landmarks of Irish nationalism—Wolfe Tone's Rising 1798; Daniel O'Connell's Catholic Emancipation 1823–29;[21] Young Ireland Insurrection 1848; Great Famine 1845–52; Fenian Rising 1867; Land League 1879; Easter Rising 1916; Anglo-Irish War 1919–21; Civil War 1922–23; and Troubles 1969–1997,[22] the context of each interlocking event was ever-changing. To view this trajectory as linear and coherent risks teleological pitfalls or political opportunism. Notwithstanding, this was the intention at particular moments during the last two centuries where different Irish elites wove threads of secession, nationalism, Catholicism, Republicanism, even socialism into a single Irish cloth. Yet the warp and weft of modernisation and romantic nostalgia were often at odds in the insurrectionist struggle.

At the centenary of Wolfe Tone's Rising in 1898, Sinn Fein's founder wrote:

we accept the nationalism of '98, '48, and '67 as the true nationalism and Grattan's cry of "Live Ireland—perish the Empire!" as the watchword of patriotism.[23]

Nearly a century later, Sinn Féin's Martin McGuinness proposed it was time for change. Addressing the annual Wolfe Tone Commemoration, he only underscored the dilemma of his movement:[24]

As republicans we possess a continuity of vision and action that stretches back to 1798 and beyond. But the Ireland Wolfe Tone lived in bears only a historical relationship to the Ireland of today and tomorrow.[25]

What his words revealed was the predicament of insurgents caught in the straitjacket of their collective discourse. Theodore Wolfe Tone was a touchstone of Irish nationalism. But his heroic sacrifice had been ambiguous at best. Court-martialled in the uniform of a French Chef de Brigade, the 'military incompetent'[26] confessed to having acted 'traitorously and hostilely' against George III: 'Under the flag of the French republic I originally engaged with a view to save and liberate my own country'.[27] Condemned to hang, Tone committed suicide, embracing a martyr's death.[28] His naval invasion had sought to create an Irish republic uniting all Irishmen, Presbyterian and Catholic. It would remedy his belief that:

The proximate cause of our disgrace is our evil government, the remote one is our own intestine division, which, if once removed, the former will be instantaneously reformed.[29]

The call was nationalist. However what motivated 1798's unsuccessful naval insurrection were the spirit and ideals of the French Revolution.[30] 'His republicanism, indeed his separatism, was of his time—and was vastly different from that of Davis or Pearse' argues Sean McMahon.[31] Tone's cult as 'father of Irish Republicanism' would not be born until after his death. Nurtured by Young Irelanders (1840s), particularly Thomas Davis writing in *The Nation* and John Mitchel in *The United Irishman*, and against a backdrop of Romantic nationalism sweeping Europe, they 'moulded Irish nationalism and elevated Tone as its central inspiration'.[32] Marianne Elliott concludes:

The tradition of the unfinished, centuries-old struggle against England was skilfully conveyed in the simplistic message of Mitchel's intransigent republicanism, and his interpretation of Tone inspired a succession of young intellectuals from the Fenians onward. Not least influential was his promotion of the Tone cult with the developing Irish-American nationalism.[33]

The flame would be carried by a new generation of independence fighter just before World War I of which Padraig Pearse was its most celebrated publicist. Steeped in Catholic mysticism, ancestral worship, and blood sacrifice, following the failed Easter Rising Pearse likened his own end to Jesus Christ's on the cross. But not before he had welcomed Tone into the hallowed brethren, elevating him to the high altar of militancy and nationalism. Conjuring up Tone's celebrated words, he invited Irish heroes to 'break the connection with England, the never-failing source of all our political evils, and to assert the independence of my country'. He evoked the 'high and sorrowful destiny of the heroes', which should 'follow only the far, faint call that leads them into the battle or to the harder death at the feet of a gibbet'.[34] Yet Garvin suggests '(t)he modern self-contradictory attempted derivations of Irish nationality from Gaelic, Catholic or even Anglo-Irish aristocratic identities would have horrified and bewildered Wolfe Tone'.[35] Later veneration was far from universal. Not only was the Protestant Tone regarded as Popish in Protestant circles but even Catholic bishops in the 1930s attacked his cult of sainthood. Notwithstanding he remains integral to the fabric of continuous myth.

Conor Cruise O'Brien criticised politicians who espouse McGuinness' 'continuity of vision and action':

Mistaken analogies are eagerly clutched at. The fact that the same names— Sinn Féin and IRA—which belonged to those by whom the Anglo-Irish treaty of 1921 was negotiated are also used by the contemporary terrorists and their friends, is one of confusion.[36]

Such accusations draw fire from insurgent publicists. Sinn Féin's Danny Morrison condemned those who concoct:

'distortions of republican history to berate us…(and) to support their contention about just how different the Republican Movement today is supposedly from the Republican Movement of the past'.[37]

When Sinn Féin President Gerry Adams addressed his party conference in 1988, his audience pondered its legacy. By overturning 77 years of history, calling for an end to war, and disavowing 'abstentionism', that touchstone of Republican orthodoxy, a golden thread with the past was cut.[38] He appealed across the sectarian divide saying 'our republicanism grows from the separatist roots of the mainly Presbyterian United Irishmen'. Nonetheless he reasserted '(w)e do not accept the legitimacy of the six county statelet. And we never will'. His appeal to a future of uncertainty but hope required continuity with the past. Adams evoked the fallen socialist hero of the 1916 Easter Rising:

This is the day that James Connolly was executed here in this city eighty two years ago. It is a good day for us to recommit ourselves to our republican ideals and the struggles which lie ahead of us.[39]

Sinn Féin would remain in some way prisoner to its rhetorical heritage.

By excavating the context of milestones, discontinuities within the myth become clearer. Black does not suddenly become white. Strategic narratives are more subtle: they absorb nuanced political positions of allies into the mainstream of successive generations of insurgent messaging. Across 200 years of Republicanism, tangential, overlapping, sometimes discreet themes were diverted into current narratives. These were as distinct as Romantic nationalism, land rights, Republicanism, socialism, sacrificial Catholicism, anti-constitutionalism, and secession from the imperial occupier. For many the creation of the Irish state and de facto acceptance of the British rump of six counties proved one additional obstacle too far.

Young Ireland

The 1848–9 Rising of Young Ireland is valued in Republican ideology for its incendiary idealism. Like many attempts it fell short of its objective, if it ever possessed a clear aim beyond 'stumbling into insurrection, a movement at its weakest in action'.[40] The movement gained momentum through the *The Nation* (with its self-proclaimed 'tone of Wolfe Tone'), and *United Irishman*, proselytising newspapers advocating nationalist policy to unite all faiths and constituencies.[41] Their platform was repeal of the 1801 Union, and a unified Irish nation rooted in Irish tradition; their inspiration was Wolfe Tone. As famine began to bite, the group adopted a sterner nationalism than the politics espoused by moderate septuagenarian Daniel O'Connell. His last 'monster meeting'[42] at Clontarf had been cancelled under government threat of military intervention, and was viewed by Young Irelanders as a constitutionalist climb-down. Their new initiative moved towards physical violence, embracing James Fintan Lalor's doctrine.[43] Yet for Lalor land reform should underpin the appeal:

Adopt this process; create what has never yet existed in Ireland an active and affluent husbandry, a secure and independent agricultural peasantry, able to accumulate as well as to produce—do this, and you raise a thriving and happy community, a solid social economy, a prosperous people, an effective nation.[44]

The implication was by withholding rents, resisting eviction, and striking against poor rates, a social revolution might be born. Hence the Famine revealed a class struggle between peasant and landowner. Fired by France's 1848 Revolution, John Mitchel, a northern Presbyterian returned to Ireland convinced of the prospect of revolution. Mitchel developed Lalor's logic, fanning armed insurrection through his journalism. But before the revolution could gain momentum, the proponents were arrested, Mitchel deported to Tasmania, their newspapers closed down, the Irish Confederation and political clubs banned. Attempts to strike back ended in local skirmishes which armed police brought to an expeditious end. The romantic venture flickered and died, its life less manifest than the revolutions that had spread throughout Europe in 1848, before burning themselves out. However its import for the future was significant.

Mitchel wrote a *Jail Journal*.[45] There he deals with the Famine, equating his life of imprisonment to Ireland's. The Journal adopts the present tense of 1848, where Ireland remains in suspended suffering: 'there is more to Irish history, too, this month...if I could but only get at it'.[46] What Mitchel set in train was a genocidal genealogy. He rails:

these people [peasants] have all been dealt with of late (by those who rule and rob) as 'masses'; a sort of raw material, to be thinned when they think it too thick, to be absorbed or distributed as the interests of society (that is those who rob and rule) may seem to require.[47]

Its influence would affect historians and novelists throughout the next century. In 1903 the Irish-American author DP Conyngham captured the mood of the Famine years:

'this potato blight and consequential famine were powerful engines of state to uproot millions of the peasantry, to prevent law and order...and to clear off surplus population, and to maintain the integrity of the British empire...'[48]

James Joyce's *Ulysses* (1919) picks up the theme:

they drove out the peasants in hordes. Twenty thousand of them died in the coffin shops. But those that came to the land of the free remember the land of bondage.[49]

At each re-telling the narrative gains traction.[50] Witness the Real IRA's words today: 'Then came the Irish Holocaust (aka the Irish Famine) in which between 1845 and 1852 at least a million people died of starvation and a million more emigrated...'[51] Holocaust or no, the mass migration of Famine victims thesis has been challenged, highlighting a cleft between academic and popular understandings.[52] Ireland's population doubled to 8.2 million between 1785–1852. It fell again by 1.5 million during seven years of blight (1845–52). However the earlier population surge obscured complex, external factors impacting migration patterns, and producing self-sustaining outward flows. The Famine coincided with Britain's industrial recession. American diaspora remittances encouraged 'chain migration' while shipping lines cut prices for passage from British ports to America.[53] Other causes existed, including British negligence and inefficiency. The point is not to deny levels of starvation, disease or migration, merely to problematise the debate surrounding accusations of Westminster's deliberate genocide.

A \$4.5 million memorial in New York's Battery Park to the Famine or Great Starvation was unveiled in 2002 by Mayor Bloomberg. Prominent Irish representatives attended. The mood rapidly suffused into post-'9/11' mourning, however, acquiring additional poignancy. The Chairman of the Port Authority signalled:

There were ample funds in England for famine relief. But there were also voices in London proclaiming the potato blight to be the result of "Divine Providence", that God was punishing the Irish for laziness and popery.[54]

For Irish President Mary McAleese, attending the event, the handed-down memory of famine remained vivid:

it is a colossal heart-rending fault line in the story of Ireland: My grandfather told us the stories of the bodies his grandmother had seen piled six deep in the ditch...Wherever in the world our people have gone they carry that memory with them and wherever people suffer famine in our contemporary world you will find the Irish bringing help and hope.[55]

The narrative had not simply endured. It was offered fresh life; a new humanitarianism informed Irish state foreign policy. Her plea was that the Irish understood what it was to have suffered. To summarise, what characterised Young Ireland's rhetoric was the belief in change rooted in land reform and rural peasantry. What survived a public discussion of revolution that barely fired a shot in anger was fuel for nationalist rage; it 'evidenced' foreign oppression.

* * *

Fenians

Irish-American politics would soon make its mark on the long-term shaping of the narrative. After the American Civil War many combatants of Irish birth or descent found themselves jobless but trained in the use of arms. Their politics were romantic, national and radical. From the ashes of the 1848 revolutionary debacle arose a new organisation. On St Patrick's Day 1858, the American Fenian Society[56] was founded, its support-base rooted in a socio-economic underclass of Irish immigrants. Nineteen of thirty-nine recorded Fenian leaders had emigrated to the US, most victims of the Famine. Thus the Great Hunger myth figured large in a movement whose focus shifted between the 1850s and 1920s. Three distinctive Fenian phases have been identified: 1) the insurrectionist (1858–79) led to a failed uprising in 1867; 2) the agrarian which allied with constitutionalists Parnell and Davitt, and the Land Reform movement (1879–91); and 3) 'romantic revolutionism' (1891–1923).[57] The complexities of their political development exceed the scope of this book.

What is of relevance here is the fact that not only were there critical differences of strategy and interpretation between and within American and Irish Fenians, but these changed periodically over six or seven decades. The importance of America's Fenians (*Clan na Gael*)[58] was first, they marked the arrival of revolutionary diasporas on the nineteenth-century political scene, providing remittances, arms, and sanctuary. Second, they incubated nostalgic Irishness which blossomed with spatial and temporal distance. Meanwhile Fenianism spread throughout Ireland and Britain, infiltrating industrial and rural populations, even British army ranks. These discontinuities question the notion of a unified, linear Republican discourse. The movement in its insurrectionary phase was riven with personality and tactical splits between luminaries within American and Irish contingents.[59] 'Should Fenians invade Canada or rise up in Ireland?'[60] This question absorbed and divided the Americans. Armed attempts to cross the Canadian border foundered in 1866,[61] 1870, and 1871. When the 1867 Irish Rising collapsed, one contemporary account records that Americans viewed it as a 'madcap enterprise'[62] that had been conceived 'through rose-tinted glasses, and translated through the imagination'.[63] More noteworthy Devoy would conclude 'Fenianism was not agrarian; but, as it was essentially a movement of the people, its members nearly all held the national creed on the Land Question'.[64]

Of two later Fenian phases, the 'revolutionist' is discussed below. However it should be noted that an urban, socialist strain entered the nationalist debate during this period. James Connolly, executed following 1916's Rising, and James Larkin, led the Irish Transport and General Workers' Union, dominating Ireland's labour movement. At Wolfe Tone's centenary commemoration (1898), the Irish Socialist Republican Party was already in evidence.[65] It was not until 1912 as the Irish Labour Party that it 'nailed its colours to the mast' of Home Rule. In correspondence with Larkin, Connolly identified an historic opportunity:

We are at present in a very critical stage for the whole of Ireland as well as the Labour movement. One result of this is that we have an opportunity of taking the lead of the real Nationalist movement and a certainty of acquiring great prestige among Nationalists outside the Home Rule gang, provided that our own movement is in charge of somebody in whom the Nationalists have confidence.[66]

Yet Larkin resisted committing the Irish Citizen Army of militant workers and trade unionists to the revolutionary Irish Volunteers. Bitterness divided the two forces. Dublin's Metropolitan Police suppressed transport workers' strikes in 1913 and subsequently employers declared lock-outs. This led militant workers to mobilise. Larkin had urged the Volunteers to engage in public debate to 'justify their appeal for the support of the Irish working class'. He exhorted his men:

Now is the time to realise the aspirations of Wolfe Tone...While we see in the Volunteer movement great possibilities, the Irish Citizen Army is the only armed force in Ireland today standing for the rights of the worker and the complete independence of our country.[67]

It was left to Connolly to see the initiative through, mindful of not squandering the opportunity to exploit British weakness afforded by the outbreak of World War. However despite Connolly's engineering a guarded rapprochement between the two groups, Labour's position remained ambiguous. Connolly pledged the Citizen Army to the Irish Republican Brotherhood (Volunteer) insurrection after January 1916. But not before defining their position:

We are out for Ireland for the Irish. But who are the Irish? Not the rack-renting, slum-owning landlords; not the sweating, profit-grinding capitalists...Not these are the Irish upon whom the future depends. Not these, but the Irish working class, the only secure foundation upon which a free nation can be reared. The cause of labour is the cause of Ireland, the cause of Ireland is the cause of labour. They cannot be dissevered.[68]

Yet he allegedly warned his followers on entering the General Post Office from which they would fight, should the Rising be successful they must retain their weapons, fearing the Volunteers had different objectives. Until then his programme remained socialist, dedicated to 'redistributionist and collectivist ideals, as the blueprint for a social reorganisation following a Citizen Army putsch'.[69] It was appropriate while the tricolour flag was run up over the Post Office that the Citizen Army's standard with its starry plough was hoisted over the Imperial Hotel opposite.[70]

Easter Rising 1916

'In every generation the Irish people have asserted their right to national freedom and sovereignty; six times during the past three hundred years they have asserted it in arms'. Provisional Government of the Irish Republic, 1916.[71]

Seven men signed the Proclamation of Independence which would become the 'Magna Carta of all Irish Republicans' throughout the twentieth century.[72] A six-day insurrection followed, engineered by a cell, the Irish Republican Brotherhood (IRB), acting clandestinely within the Irish Volunteers. Its outcome saw fifteen leaders executed, and 2,500 interned.[73] A failed military operation became classic POTD. However, not until its leaders' court-martial and execution did its implications become apparent. So incomplete in planning, so under-resourced its fighting force, so shallow-rooted in popular sympathy its action, that on surrendering 'with waving white banners as if they were banners of victory',[74] ringleaders were jeered by onlookers. Nevertheless Padraig Pearse's contribution to nationalist mythology is unique. Fired by political messianism and Catholic martyrdom, his strength was in communications; he intuitively understood political marketing. Throughout the Rising and immediate aftermath, he forecast the symbolic value of the IRB's blood sacrifice for generations of yet unborn fighters:

If you strike us down now, we shall rise again and renew the fight. You cannot conquer Ireland. You cannot extinguish the Irish passion for freedom. If our deed has not been sufficient to win freedom, then our children will win it by a better deed.[75]

The IRB's POTD was inextricably woven into the Irish cultural renaissance flowering in the late nineteenth and early twentieth centuries. The rediscovery of Gaelic language, literature, history and Irish sports was given voice through schools, publishing, societies, and a radicalising politics. This last blended mystic Catholicism,[76] national-ism, latterly republicanism with an infusion of socialism.[77] At the same time, reviving Irish language rooted nationalist claims to a separatist homeland. Pearse grasped the need for a legitimising past within the continuity of struggle. He offered himself as sacrificial lamb, as had once Jesus Christ. Weeks before the Rising Pearse took leave of his pupils at the school where he was director: 'As it took the blood of the son of God to redeem the world, so it would take the blood of Irish-men to redeem Ireland'.[78]

Later to emerge as a supreme guerrilla tactician during the Civil War, Michael Collins fought inside the GPO. He described that week's events as a 'Greek tragedy', recognising the dichotomy:

They have died nobly at the hands of the firing squads. So much I grant. But I do not think the Rising week was an appropriate time for the issue of memo-randa couched in poetic phrases, nor of actions worked out in a similar vein.[79]

But Collins eschewed the fact that long wars need pragmatists to inspire troops to heroic actions, but visionaries to speak to history. Wars are won as much in the hearts of men, as in their minds.

Significantly, Pearse's 'spin machine' went into overdrive immedi-ately after his cohorts surrendered. Pearse, MacDonagh, and Plunkett were setting the agenda in their death-row correspondence. Within two months of their execution a volume of martyrs' verse was published propagating the myth. Colum's introduction declared the insurrection 'signal days in Irish history'.[80] The IRB was perhaps always likely to fail, but it was an heroic failure.[81] The discontinuous path of republi-canism had never had a spectacle of revolutionary, heroic proportions to sanctify. If victory was to come it could now be with the catharsis of blood sacrifice. Sean MacStiofain, chief of staff and a founder of Provisional IRA (PIRA), would say as much when resisting attempts to follow a constitutional path in the mid-1970s: 'for freedom, to do good, must be gained with difficulty and heroic sacrifice, in the face of perils and death'.[82] But to succeed, blood sacrifice needed to be eulo-gised, internalised in group memory, then replenished with further bloodshed. The poet W.B. Yeats began the process:

I write out in verse–
MacDonagh and MacBride
And Connolly and Pearse
Now and in time to be,

Wherever green is worn,
Are changed, changed utterly:
A terrible beauty is born.[83]

Even in 1957 Diarmuid Lynch, an original member of the pre-1916 IRB Supreme Council, still sought to iron out inconsistencies which revisionist historians had begun to introduce into the unity of the IRB's Easter POTD. He downplayed suggestions of ideological divisions underlying trade unionist James Connolly's motives and his Irish Citizen's Army ('the main purpose of the ICA was an economic one').[84] Did Connolly act out of socialist or separatist reasons? Lynch tries to tie up loose ends:

That Connolly's ideas gradually developed beyond the purely socialistic and took on a more national turn (as the term was usually understood) is of course beyond doubt…The sole purpose for which the IRB existed was the establishment of Ireland's national independence; its succession from the Fenians of 1867 was unbroken.[85]

Writing in 1916, the year of the Rising, Eoin MacNeill illuminates the mobilisation of traditional POTD:

Now the government wants and has always wanted to suppress the Irish Volunteers. It could at any time have used sufficient military force to suppress them if opposed by them in military fashion. Why then has the government not employed force against us? Because the government is convinced that it would lose more than it could gain by moving its military forces against us, unless we create a special opportunity for it.[86]

Which is precisely what happened. However, what marks out 1916 is how it moved the boundaries beyond the operational to the communicative.

This begs several observations. Revolutionary narratives see history driven by their own protagonists. Events and other actors are sideshows to their ideological and military achievements. Hence Ireland's nationalist trajectory is committed to the hands of a chosen few. Witness PS O'Hegarty, member of the IRB Supreme Council (1908–14) writing in 1952:

The Insurrection of 1916 came because the Supreme Council of the Irish Republican Brotherhood decided that it would come…it was the Supreme Council of the I.R.B. which decided the Insurrection, planned it, organised it, led it, and financed it.[87]

This is questionable. Revisionist historians argue that the domestic and foreign contexts reveal how this discourse has been straitjacketed within an orthodoxy of the subsequent Irish state and Republican movement.[88] What alternative dimensions existed? Protestant sectarian politics, World War I, and the fate of Home Rule alone undermine the linear path of the story.[89]

The 1912–14 period was a landmark for Unionists too. An 'Orange Genesis' was moulded by the skilled electoral marketer, James Craig. At its heart was the carefully constructed heroic identity of Edward Carson, 'the saviour of his tribe' from British betrayal.[90] As PIRA would later look back to 1916, so Ulster Unionist Ian Paisley in 1985 evoked Carson's spirit to Unionist fundamentalists when opposing the Anglo-Irish Agreement. One scholar concludes:

Paisley is as much a victim of myth-making as he is an exploiter and perpetuator of myths. His image of 1912–14 is certainly, in part, an image of his own manufacture, but it is also in some respects the creation of older publicists.[91]

'Spin', he continues, is key:

It was the skill of the image-builders, rather than the complexity or elusiveness of their subject which shaped subsequent attitudes towards the events of 1912–14'.[92]

Pearse's and the IRB's action was, if not a direct reaction against Protestant political manoeuvrings, then one heavily influenced by them.[93] Founded in January 1912, the Protestant Ulster Volunteer Force (UVF) became increasingly vocal.[94] Its programme included a draft for provisional government, military hierarchy, and plans for staging a coup guided by senior British army officers.[95] Furthermore in April 1914 militant UVF gun-runners landed 25,000 weapons and 3 million rounds at Larne, County Antrim, supplementing existing stocks. British and European newspapers publicised the widespread celebrations greeting the event, ensuring it became 'one of the defining episodes in the Unionist epic'. Its effect was to further charge the atmosphere.[96] Thus in July 1914 the recently constituted Catholic Irish Volunteers in turn imported 1,500 Mauser rifles and 25,000 rounds at Howth and Kilcoole to equip their expanding membership. What had fuelled Protestant fears was the impending acquiescence to Home Rule by Westminster, a fear of being 'sold out' within a unified Ireland of thirty-two counties.[97]

The First World War provided the critical backdrop. Not only were some 150,000 Irishmen fighting, many dying in Flanders by the time of the Rising, but a shortage of security forces to police an aggrieved

Ireland presented an opportunity. Prime Minister Lloyd George's drive to recruit more Irishmen to the war effort only exacerbated the situation. The opportunity was not lost on the IRB.[98] Since the early Fenians it had been understood that the optimum moment to exploit an overstretched Britain was when she was at war with a third party.[99] But political radicalisation was already growing;[100] Gaelic League membership expanded from 107 branches (1899) to 400 (1902), while Britain's Boer War campaigns (1899–1902) served only to heighten Irish anti-imperialist sentiment.[101]

Thus the idea of a movement inexorably approaching the climax of its ambitions through strategy and popular will was more ambiguous than first meets the Republican eye. The Rising has been characterised as a *coup d'état* against Westminster:

it ran flat counter to the wishes of Redmond and the majority of Irish Nationalists. It was a mutiny against MacNeill and the constitution of the Irish Volunteers, and it usurped the powers of the I.R.B. itself. But Pearse, Clarke and their followers...were what Jacques Maritain calls 'the prophetic shock-minority' who had to rouse a people from national slumber.[102]

Alternatively the Rising was:

a form of politics which may be called 'demonstration politics', the armed propaganda of a self-selected vanguard which claimed the power to interpret the general will. Cathartic action was substituted for methodological debate; ideal types replaced reality; symbols took on real powers.[103]

It is not only the slant placed on successive events that determines revolutionary folklore. Communicators cherry-pick, reconfiguring them into a new discourse to infuse future struggle. Pearse's achievement was to shift POTD from the operational to the communicative. By sleight of hand 'republican separatism had to trick itself out in the garments of linguistic revivalism to appeal to the clergy, and in the clothes of nationalist athleticism to appeal to the young men', says Garvin, '(a) persistent atmosphere of make-believe has surrounded all variants of republican separatism ever since'.[104] The decision to execute 1916's leaders was the over-reaction POTD sought: again the judo-throw principle. The popular climate following the insurrection was febrile and Westminster and Dublin only helped raise the temperature. The shift into a communications war would follow and continue for most of the century. Yet which political programmes defined the Rising of this subversive minority? The mystical martyrdom of Pearse,

MacDonagh and Plunkett sprang from an intellectual, cultural elite. Connolly's socialism ('Ireland's most distinguished labour activist and professional agitator')[105] derived from trade union militancy. Tone's republicanism drew on Napoleonic fervour, but Lalor's was firmly rooted in the peasantry and Irish soil. All were nationalist. All fuse in the subsequent telling.

'Republican separatist ideology was both modernising and nostalgic' observes one commentator. He likens how nationalists identified modernising capitalism with England to how today's insurgents equate capitalism with Americanisation. Thus '(o)pposition to English rule attracted different people for different reasons, and often for opposing sets of reasons': reactionaries hankered after a feudalism the English would reform; Catholics saw themselves defending their faith against English sceptics; centrist Nationalists opposed variously state socialism, big business, trade unions, and English commerce; indeed radicals sought secession to replace imperialism with Irish socialism.[106] Some separatists envisaged a republic, others like Pearse a constitutional monarchy, albeit with independence.[107] Militant Irish separatism and constitutional Irish nationalism had centres of gravity English distinguishes as some distance apart.[108] This ideological multivalence has been attributed to the constraints of there being only two languages in Irish politics—British democratic liberalism and international Catholicism—that forced alliances between unlikely bedfellows.[109]

Anglo-Irish and Civil Wars

The intention here is not to recount the complex events of the IRA war with Britain, or the ten-month internecine conflict that split the IRA in 1922–3. Within Republican ranks the schism afflicting the IRA opened deep wounds, centring on claims to orthodoxy and legitimacy in the eyes of their support constituencies. The period following the failed Rising and World War I proved one of Ireland's most turbulent: it saw anti-imperial war with England, and civil war between Republicans divided over whether to accept a treaty with Westminster. This would grant independence to Ireland for twenty-six counties, leaving six in the north-east dominated by a Protestant population and within the United Kingdom. Irish Republicanism's reflowering in the 1950s and 1970s would draw on 1916 and the events of this era.[110] But the key point is that what would be remembered and how, depended on who was remembering. What would be airbrushed from the official record varied between absolutists committed to unifying Ireland through armed struggle, and gradualists, former brothers-in-arms wedded to partition as either de facto permanent or a stepping-stone, who embarked on state-building.

Context is important. Both conflicts unfolded in the slipstream of propaganda techniques acquired locally after Easter 1916, and internationally from the mass persuasion of industrialised world warfare. All parties engaged on Irish soil actively sought to master the publicity agenda. By the truce of 1921, Britain had not been evicted from Irish soil; the IRA had fought itself to a standstill. The movement's realists admitted military victory was beyond reach; its hardliners rejected such defeatism. But not before the heroic leader Michael Collins had refined the IRA's guerrilla tactics through his 'flying columns', achieving classic POTD. His killing of eleven unarmed, suspected British intelligence operatives met with British Black and Tans opening fire on a football crowd in which twelve civilians died. Yet the lessons of 1916's communicative deed had not been forgotten, but honed into a full-fledged propaganda war. One hardliner Ernie O'Malley wrote:

Every one of our little fights or attacks was significant, they made panoramic pictures of the struggle in the people's eyes and lived on in their minds. Only in our country could the details of an individual fight expand to the generalisations of a pitched battle. What to me was a defeat, such as the destruction of an occupied post without the capture of its arms, would soon be sung of as a victory. Our own critical judgments which adjudged action and made it grow gigantic through memory and distance, were like to folklore.[111]

Gleeson concludes: 'Collins knew the value of the gun "as a propaganda weapon, its power of destruction a headline, its detonation a slogan".'[112] *The Irish Bulletin* of the period captures the ferocity of the publicity war. Daily reports and weekly reviews from the Republican publicity department update readers on names and addresses of Irish civilians and soldiers slain, actions successfully executed, and massacres perpetrated by security forces. Extended articles elucidate point-by-point the strategic road from 1916 to the present.[113] Repeated attempts at forensic autopsy unveil the enemy's propagandist subterfuge detailing specious letters from Republican leaders, proclamations allegedly forged by British propagandists, newspaper articles printed 'at the bayonet's point', and leaflets dropped from aeroplanes purporting to be signed by Catholic bishops.[114]

POTD's ability to resonate with both Irish and English audiences is manifest in O'Malley's account of 1935. Thomas Ashe, a protagonist in the Rising had already died from force-feeding while on hunger-strike in 1917, having been arrested attempting to revive the IRB throughout the country.[115] In 1920 the seventy-four day hunger strike in an English prison of Terence MacSwiney, Sinn Féin's Lord Mayor of Cork presages later events:

Feeling at home seemed to have sent impulses abroad to the European press; it seemed the most important event that had occurred in Ireland. In Washington women picketed the British Embassy, longshoremen walked off British boats. Ireland went into mourning when he died on the seventy-fourth day of his fast. He had become a symbol of part of a new nation; disciplined, hard, clear, unsentimental, uncompromising, a conscious using of vigour to build up strength.[116]

It is echoed in the death of PIRA's Bobby Sands sixty-six days into his hunger strike in 1981. Athens, Antwerp, Milan, Oslo, Brisbane and Chicago witnessed anti-British street-demonstrations; 110,000 American longshoremen refused to man British ships for twenty-four hours. *The New York Times* wrote:

By willing his own death… Bobby Sands has earned a place on Ireland's long role of martyrs and bested an implacable British Prime Minister.

The Boston Globe lamented:

He is myth now, part of an elaborately cultivated contrivance about the past.[117]

Seventy-seven IRA men were executed by Dublin's government during the Civil War. That government contained many erstwhile comrades from the anti-imperialist struggle. Old friends now became interchangeable with the British state. The spirit on death row was 'remembered' by IRA propagandists. Liam Mellows wrote to his mother shortly before his execution:

Though unworthy of the greatest human honour that can be paid to an Irish man or woman, I go to join Tone, Emmet, the Fenians, Tom Clarke, Connolly, Pearse, Kevin Barry, Childers. My last thought will be on God and Ireland and you…It is a hard road, but it is the road…our Saviour followed—the road of sacrifice. The Republic lives; our deaths make that a certainty…Go to Mrs Pearse. She will comfort you.[118]

Pearse and the 1916 leaders on death-row had committed themselves to God, the cause and posterity with a similar *sang-froid*. So would the next generation. One internee, Frank Gallagher recalled:

Every hour of the waking day they heard that this was what Pearse had died for, what Terence MacSwiney had fasted unto death for, what Kevin Barry had desired. From Press, from platform, from pulpit the assurance came incessantly.[119]

While a new generation of fighters sought a common bond with past acts and actors, new fissures were emerging within the movement. The Truce brought Republican division; the later Treaty spurred complete schism and civil war. Enduring fault-lines intersecting the Republican movement date from these years.[120] The old challenge of persuading a population to subscribe to a crafted anti-imperialist myth was one thing. Negotiating a new orthodoxy, squaring competing accounts between moderate and hard-line separatist combatants was something altogether new. The battle for the legend became contested through acts of violence.

Insurgency narratives are fiercely fought over. This struggle is manifest in the IRA rhetoric of abstentionism—a refusal to take up seats in the Dublin or Westminster parliaments if elected. The IRA claimed direct lineage from the first all-Ireland Dail or Republican Parliament of 1919.[121] For absolutists, to recognise the primacy of a foreign government over the Irish people was anathema. Revoking the anti-constitutional principle was considered the thin end of Britain's strategic wedge that would terminate military struggle. Only in 1986 would abstentionism from participating in constitutional politics finally be abandoned by Gerry Adams backed by a majority *Ard Fheis* (party congress) vote. The dual strategy of ballot-box and bullet aimed at delivering a socialist, democratic Irish republic would now isolate militarist hardliners.[122] The issue had divided the movement before in 1969–70. Factions had taken to internecine killing that lasted several years. This time the move forced a further split in Provisional IRA/Sinn Féin ranks. But abstentionism was cemented into Republican narrative. By abandoning Home Rule, by Pearse's declaration of the new Republic, and the Civil War, a new continuity would need to be shaped for those who would carry the myth into the twenty-first century. The break within Republican ranks (1983) and the later disavowal of the Good Friday Agreement (1998) by militant breakaway groups suggest embers may yet ignite in a revisionist myth for future generations.[123] But that myth will have to elide the story of betrayal by their comrades-in-arms and reinforce a purged commitment to the nationalist destiny. The warning to the pragmatist constitutionalists from the hardliner Continuity Army Council (CAC) in 1996 was ominous: 'action will be taken in the future at an appropriate time'.[124] Perhaps one author was right to assert '(t)he Irish revolution has been a long time dying'.[125]

Mitigating Atrocity

It is one thing to construct an insurgency memory within the movement and within the population over a number of years. Yet it is something far more ambitious to centre that memory not only on violence experienced by the aggrieved community at the hands of the state, but around acts of destruction and terror perpetrated by those who proffer themselves as custodians of the moral high ground. POTD as a technique of revolutionary communication must face its critics.

The sheer atrocity of POTD precludes most people from countenancing any justification for it. Pictures and survivor testimonies are all too harrowing. That it should be considered part of a communications strategy or campaign is equally unthinkable, particularly when its non-combatant victims become the 'collateral damage' of attacks on state targets.[126] This is especially so when those 'innocent' victims appear to be the prime objective of the bomber. That combatant groups remain sensitive to this last charge is reflected in the words of one mid-ranking Taliban commander, Malwi Abdul Rahman:

We're doing our best to avoid civilian casualties. When we plant mines for American convoys most of the time we don't do it in civilian areas. We've even stopped using so many suicide bombers to try to reduce so many civilian casualties.[127]

Such conciliatory sentiments do not, however, silence some activists (even within the same movement) whose own message expressed through death and devastation is one of defiance, resilience and shock-and-awe. For these the trigger to grievance resembles more a millenarian celebration of violence. More broadly, because state agencies and their physical assets—buildings, personnel—are so often situated in the midst of population centres, insurgents perpetually face both intentional and unintentional political consequences of their decisions to kill or maim. It is for this reason that the framing of the act must synchronise the popular mood with the preparation of the people by the insurrectionist.[128] So sensitive is the decision to embark on the terrorist path by the 'responsible' insurgent that the framing process continues years after the actual event as the movement or group seeks to justify its actions of the past. By reinvesting in the narrative, a political rationale is sought to underpin just cause and authority, most pertinently in those rare cases where the revolutionary finally attains government but also where the long war endures. In this process there is recognition of the extreme methods adopted, usually under the waiver of 'last resort'. Witness the IRA *Green Book*: 'We do not employ revolutionary violence as our means without being able to illustrate that we have no recourse to any other means'.[129]

O'Brien is one commentator who argues the IRA did not act purely defensively, instead accusing them of committing acts which betrayed the defence of 'last resort'. Rather, bombing was part of a long war with a military campaign at the heart of a political strategy. According to Sinn Féin's Gerry Adams in 1990: 'the onus is on those who claim there is an alternative to the IRA's armed struggle to prove that this is the case'.[130]

From the perspective of the ANC, now the legitimate, constitutional government of South Africa, Nelson Mandela wrote with regret of the Church Street, Pretoria bombing. An ANC Special Operations Unit had carried it out in May 1983. It claimed 19 dead and over 200 injured. Its fallout exceeded its military target. The chief orchestrator Ismael argued later: 'We did not target civilians. However the policy of the ANC at the time was that we could not for the sake of saving a few lives be prevented from striking at the power of State, the apartheid state'.[131]

Mandela was one of those policy-makers:

The killing of civilians was a tragic accident, and I felt a profound horror at the death toll. But disturbed as I was by these casualties, I knew that such accidents were the inevitable consequence of the decision to embark on a military struggle. Human fallibility is always a part of war, and the price of war is always high. It was precisely because we knew that such incidents would occur that our decision to take up arms had been so grave and reluctant. But as Oliver [Tambo] said at the time of the bombing, the armed struggle was imposed upon us by the violence of the apartheid regime.[132]

He is careful to root his apologia and strategy in the 'new birth of popularity' for the ANC among Africans, accompanied by a grassroots coalescence. Opinion polls at the time, he notes, reflected this support despite the party having being banned for a quarter century. Last resort is a central principle of *jus ad bellum*. Although Guthrie would caution it should not be employed in isolation but alongside the complete repertoire of just cause; proportionate cause; right intention; right authority; and reasonable prospect of success.[133] The ANC, however, in its submissions to South Africa's Truth and Reconciliation Commission (TRC) in 1996 and 1997, sought to legitimate its past actions in humanitarian and international law. Here the ANC bases its case on the historical precedence of the American Revolution, namely the right to meet illegitimate state force with popular force; the UN General Assembly Resolution 1514 (XV) 1960 containing the Declaration on the Granting of Independence to Colonial Countries and Peoples; the UN Declaration of International Law Concerning Friendly Relations adopted by the General Assembly Resolution 2625 (XXV) 1970 and promoting the right to self-determination, freedom and independence; and the General Assembly Resolution 2852 (XXV) 1972 on Respect for Human Rights in Armed Conflicts.[134] This is the language of sovereignty. More prosaically, Mandela casts the Church Street bombing in the context of a reprisal for the apartheid government's killing of forty-two men, women and children at an ANC outpost in Maseru, Lesotho in 1982 (the latter a retaliation against the ANC's bombing of a nuclear power plant under construction, and other military and apartheid targets).[135]

However much the insurgent pleads the asymmetry of state-insurgent force and appeals to last resort in redressing civil grievance, popular support for POTD is far from uniform. Sympathy depends on family or community and how these figure in the equation of ongoing struggle. It is contingent on whether the struggle itself is sectarian, ethnic or class-based. Charles King identifies 'hawks' and 'doves' in insurgent groups that must be understood when attempting to resolve civil wars.[136] This simplistic view of organisations is as un-nuanced for fighting movements as it is for the general population, a heterogeneous and dynamic aggregation of individuals and groups, some sympathetic to the cause, some contributing to the means to achieving the cause, others—perhaps the largest body—'floating voters', yet still others committed against but representing a spectrum of potential negotiation and outright rejection. To what extent the terrorist deed is tolerated by the public depends on the nature of the conflict, the 'enemy' being targeted, and the timing of the event within the life cycle of the struggle. Support waxes and wanes. Gauging popular mood for framing issues, and measuring putative outcomes from violent inputs, remains an inexact science. The fact that some civil groups within society continue to support terrorist cells and insurrectionist movements cannot be merely written off to the insurgent use of threat against families, even though this feature is common in the conflict theatre. For segments of the population POTD retains its attraction. Moreover, those segments provide sufficient encouragement for its orchestrators to build on.

* * *

If images of revolutionary struggle are to mobilise populations they must tap into group memories. Such 'histories' have always been carefully constructed, then fiercely defended by insurgents. Long wars require sustained campaigns of violent events to cohere into meaningful schema that connect to the daily lives of sympathetic communities. Ideology alone is not enough: insurrectionist narratives are paramount, communicating viscerally. Today populations consume information continually from diverse media where state and media hegemony rarely favour the insurgent case. Hence stories have become the revolutionary's strategic tool in fighting the asymmetric war of ideas and images.

Image within an image: the killing of Benazir Bhutto.
© Getty/AFP/Carl De Souza.

4

THE INSURGENT IMAGE

Sometimes there is one unique picture whose composition possesses such vigour and richness and whose content so radiates outward from it, that this single picture is a whole story in itself.

Henri Cartier-Bresson[1]

How many people ever witness a terrorist act? Certainly far fewer than observe their chaotic aftermath. Yet while even these numbers remain minimal, everyone has a clear mental picture of a terrorist strike. So commonplace is the television image, so graphic Hollywood's portrayal, that our lasting impression retains the immediacy of any eyewitness. What we perceive as the act is mediated. Furthermore it is conditioned by our ethical response to violence deriving from each individual's cultural circumstances. But that culture is continually shaped by elites who disseminate images and information in our societies: they set the context by their commentary.[2] Print and broadcast media prevent pure signals reaching the receiver; internet and mobile phone conversely facilitate them. The challenge for insurgents is to communicate free of interference since they aspire to be mediator and commentator.

This chapter builds on the earlier discussion of how insurgents create memory by manipulating time and investing in patiently constructed narratives. These three components are subsequently brought together in the image of the terrorist act. How it exploits the moment of crisis—the opportunity space—and how it employs rhetorical and dramaturgic techniques, will be examined in detail.

Opportunity Spaces and Images

How does the image affect television viewers, web or mobile phone users? First it is important to reiterate my underlying contention: namely, that states and insurgents dispute time. For insurgents time is critical, being inextricably linked with memory and consequently identity.[3] States own history—that is, they control time via their manufactured, official accounts or memory of events.[4] Citizens internalise them. By contesting control of the past, insurgents legitimise their role in the present, laying claim to the future in the eyes of the populace. The state retaliates. It promulgates a future world where insurgent disruption threatens chaos. Particularly since 2001, we have witnessed a new era where governments consciously manufacture uncertainty and risk. Ulrich Beck goes further:

The concept of risk reverses the relationship of past, present and future. The past loses its power to determine the present. Its place as the cause of present-day experience and action is taken by the future, that is to say, something non-existent, constructed and fictitious. We are discussing and arguing about something that is not the case but could happen if we continue to steer the same course we have been.[5]

POTD creates spaces to be exploited. When POTD strikes there is an immediate response from the onlooker: emotional shock, a brief suspension of understanding or cognition. The moment is short. Insurgents' control is at its optimum when surprising the enemy. Thereupon it recedes. Consequently the key is to maximise each potential opportunity, which may last only hours before traditional media outlets regain control of the information agenda. Implicitly condemning while rationalising the act into familiar journalistic frameworks, these interpretive schema[6] routinely reflect the views of state or media-dominating elites and echo the way such events have previously been previously. The media's critical stance is rarely supportive of the insurgent as state challenger.[7] Hence opportunity spaces are a vital resource in wresting the initiative from the media.

Opportunity spaces invite diverse interpretations. They are often identified with social movements, groups of actors who adopt the same symbols, values, and beliefs creating 'networks of shared meaning'.[8] When new social reforms allow greater freedom to assemble or organise, when liberalised rules increase participation in elections, or even when violent conflict occurs, levels of support and opposition to challengers fluctuate. This causes an ebb and flow in political opportunity and activity, unsettling the status quo.[9] As institutional norms adjust, new spaces appear for rival groups. They are presented with the opportunity to exert their presence within the state hierarchy and cluster their efforts around others with shared values and aims. Yet unless the actual structure of political opportunities changes, what kind of lasting effect can bridge the resource disparity between challenger and power-holder?[10] Political contention is iterative. The process is conceptualised by Ruud Koopman as top-down or bottom-up. In practice it is both. Everyday contested power creates a 'disequilibrium'. This is 'defined by conflict lines, network links, and power relations among actors, both elite and extra-institutional'.[11] Regimes must be weakened or divided if challengers are to seize the advantage. But to their benefit, they are accustomed to neutralising persistent contentious groups. So new tactics, actors, organisations or interpretative frames[12] must emerge to stand any chance of insurgents subverting the status quo.[13]

The opportunity space, however, can be a state of mind, a collective reaction following a brutal interruption to daily equilibrium.[14] It may arise from a hiatus where the state's monopoly of violence is shaken. Chalmers Johnson draws on Parsonian social systems analysis to identify the cause of revolution as a 'disequilibrated social system', a set of social problems which upset the consensus of values in society. And it is 'power deflation', namely 'that during a period of change the integration of a system depends increasingly upon the maintenance and deployment of force by the occupants of the formal authority statuses', which creates the opportunity space.[15] From a different perspective, the philosopher Martin Heidegger conceptualises the moment (*Augenblick*) as a 'moment of vision', where *Augenblick* becomes *Einblick* (insight).[16] However, viewed on a cognitive level, that opportunity space is analogous to society's eruptive 'moment of madness' that Aristide Zolberg identified when trying to make sense of the 'Movement', the countercultural opposition that swept 1960s' college campuses. In moments of shock, he observes, 'all is possible' in the minds of some groups within the population.[17] That same thought is echoed in the words of one antiglobalisation group a couple of generations on. The Free Association prefers to talk of 'moments of excess' where 'everything appears to be up for grabs and time and creativity accelerates' (sic).[18] So moments of madness are moments of shock or excess that can lead to insight and revelation. More broadly, we might see the moment as a terrain where time and space are transected by many timelines of decision-making. These are affected by bureaucratic friction, inter- and intra-institutional competition, and inertia impairing states' ability to formulate a kinetic response to turbulence and thus reinforce their strategic narrative.[19] So a crisis emerges: a 'publicly visible disruption in some institutional space'.[20] A fleeting vacuum waits to be filled with meaning. Those who would transform states to achieve their worldview supply it. Milton Friedman, whose economic theories underpinned the 1980s' monetarist revolution, emphasises the importance of changing the climate of opinion, employing what Naomi Klein subsequently labelled 'shock doctrine'.[21] His aim was to apply it to the conditions necessary for revolutionising a nation's economic thinking:

Only a crisis—actual or perceived—produces real change. When that crisis occurs, the actions taken depend on the ideas that are lying around.[22]

Moreover, actions are contingent upon these ideas being kept alive long enough that 'the politically impossible becomes politically inevitable'.[23] Friedman is somewhat disingenuous in his remark. He is all too aware that those who would transform societies root and branch assiduously work to place those ideas where they can be easily brought to hand. In a crisis ideas are not so much lying around as strategically placed in position. For violent revolutionaries, before they trigger the deed, this is no less true. For shock images to succeed and exploit a crisis suddenly bereft of meaning, the population has to be made receptive in advance. Trotsky called for a 'movement of molecules' where ideas would fuse with 'indignation, bitterness, revolutionary energy'.[24] Thus masses must reach a state of dissatisfaction with a system they consider 'self-defeating, frustrating and hopeless'. Those not persuaded by an alternative must at least restrain from opposing it.[25] The opportunity space is best suited to broad rhetoric, not fine policy print. 'In public discourse, values trump programmes, principles trump programmes, policy directions trump programmes', writes Saul Alinsky, an American activist and inspiration for Obama the candidate.[26] Hence violent deeds attach to broad, emotive, and easily understood ways of describing and redressing grievance. Narrative frames drawing on simplified, constructed explanations of the 'world out there' come into play. Nevertheless, insurgent frames must contest pre-existing frames manufactured and disseminated by states. Significantly these are deep-rooted through the state's privileged position and sustained socialisation of populations. The shock of the moment is transitory, insurgent opportunity space is fleeting. Walter Benjamin saw modern life as increasingly broken down into moments of shock, a 'flash of lightning'[27] undermining the business-as-usual of everyday life.[28] To underscore the enormity of the challenge for POTD, one 'unscientific poll' suggests only 28% of respondents thought 9/11, perhaps the greatest moment of insurgent shock in recent years, had changed America in a decisive way.[29]

Opportunity and Speed

Governments, media and insurgents compete to control the opportunity space. POTD has one asset: speed. Namely, the speed with which insurgents communicate via media is propelled by POTD's inherent drama. In politics '(d)emocracy, consultation, the basis of politics, requires time', argues Paul Virilio.[30] While in war tempo is key in the battlespace: the ratio of "battle speed" to "command-and-control" is critical. When it is too high, 'the system reverts to being self-organising in nature'.[31] Opportunity spaces are traversed by two distinct timelines, and there is a tension between them. First is the kinetic: the time a decision takes to pass through political-military processes aimed at delivering a retaliatory, military strike following an incident. Planning and implementing a response have different timelines. Decision-cycles within advanced armed forces are institutionalised, built on precedent and clear lines of command-and-control. Recently these have accelerated, allowing strategy and operations to piggy-back changing technologies. In World War II, says Jean Seaton, the decision-cycle was seven days; by Desert Storm 1990 it was one to three days; by Iraq 2003 only minutes using data-link. Today a once stop-go process increasingly resembles a continuous decision-making cycle.[32] Manœuvre warfare anchors twenty-first-century Western military orthodoxy, allowing decision-making to gain speed. Independence of mind accentuates battlefield judgment by soldiers and commanders. Decentralised command promotes those in the frontline to out-think the enemy. Psychological confrontation targets the enemy's self-confidence, promoting a 'picture of defeat'.[33] Broadly '(d)ecentralised, informal and flexible' mission command makes operations more fluid for subordinates operating within 'commander's intent'.[34] This simplified picture should be balanced however. Hew Strachan suggests top-level failures at the military-political interface cut across it. An absence of strategy, a frequent 'black hole' in the Iraq War,[35] characterised policy failings underlying the 'War on Terror'. 'Strategy implies that government has a policy and that the strategy flows from the policy'.[36] But this assumption is often groundless. Where there is bureaucratic disjunction, or rival centres of formulating operations become entrenched, friction inevitably delays any down-the-line process.[37]

Second, beyond decision-making timelines another kind crosses the opportunity space: the strategic narrative. This communication operates differently. Here are many parallel communication flows; some travel faster than others. Each competes with a myriad of actors: each occupies its own timeline. In POTD's opportunity space, insurgents command their own communications timeline—self-initiated and self-propelled. So do traditional media reporting insurgent news events. But even in the mediascape new digital media outrun traditional technologies and their information flows. Local populations communicate at different speeds to global social networks. Yet both use a media-spectrum ranging from word-of-mouth to web- or satellite-based connectivity. Each occupies different clock-time. The question is: whose narrative reaches the population first?

The kinetic decision-making timeline impacts the public communications timeline. Smaller, devolved, independent insurgent groups with flatter networked organisations have shorter policy-strategy-operations cycles than state hierarchies. In the late twentieth century groups laid claim to dramatic and 'prestigious' acts of terrorism, with coded phone calls or press tip-offs: the IRA regularly employed the technique.[39] This had the effect of synchronising the media's entry with that of state emergency services in the response process. Contemporary POTD however benefits from intended and opportune events by allowing new media to do its work. It engages different timelines that combat the state's more limited response, frequently introducing the population as the prime source of news ahead of media organisations and the state.

In sum, today's POTD differs significantly from the past. A race to control the opportunity space follows the shock-and-awe of violent deeds. It seeks to shift how populations interpret events and by refram-

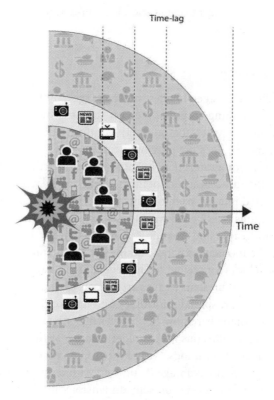

Fig. 4.1: The Opportunity Space[38]

ing the discourse, attach to them a memory of grievance. It creates the opportunity for prepared oppositional frames of contest to be activated. These are easily grasped narratives that legitimise the insurgency while delegitimising the *status quo ante*. The key change is global television's emergence and a renewed primacy of the image. However, the subsequent displacement of analogue by digital technologies moves POTD to a new dimension. It is enhanced by digital technologies' multiplier effect. Consequently, a) messages and images project spontaneously through global networks into virtual and traditional media environments; b) images connect disparate, divergent populations who construct their own identities around fluid points of grievance and oppositional politics; and c) messages circumvent state

113

hierarchies, outpacing bureaucratic decision-making intent on reinforcing the status quo.

Capturing Attention

How does POTD trigger images and messages? POTD is an image-based weapon aiming to guide viewers towards messages, focusing attention amid a welter of competing information. Photographic images fix time. So does the moving picture.

Although '(p)hotographs may be more memorable than moving images, because they are a neat slice of time, not a flow. Television is a stream of underselected images, each of which cancels its predecessor'.[40]

In photographs the outside world loses its dynamics and is rendered 'atomic, manageable and opaque'.[41] Chronologically time appears to stop, while the moment expands, taking on depth and richness. Cameras become 'clocks for seeing'.[42] They encourage awareness of overlapping time past and present. Images create consciousness within a 'new space-time category: spatial immediacy and temporal anteriority' since the image is eternally here/now but forever there/then.[43] By association, new emotions and allusions trigger older memory with its array of incidents and attached meanings. Yet photographs are open-ended, only working to insurgent advantage if suffused with deep meaning.

Barthes identifies two co-present dimensions in photographs: the studium and punctum. The latter, 'that accident which pricks me' intervenes in the frame, interrupting the *studium* which is the observer's familiar, extended field of knowledge and culture.[44] The *punctum* is that detail which fixes our attention in the context of what we already know. It directs where we look and provokes how we think. It locates the centre of gravity of the image. Yet pictures may offer more than one *punctum*. Theoretically for the receiver, meaning could change; observers might impose different perceptions on the viewing experience. Thus the stills-photographer documenting reality only partly constructs the composition to direct the focus of attention. By contrast Hollywood director Alfred Hitchcock could mitigate this weakness in his movies. Famously in *Suspicion* audiences are encouraged to suspect that Cary Grant is carrying a poisoned glass of milk as Joan Fontaine, the bed-bound 'victim', awaits his inexorable advance; his silhouette silently ascends the half-lit staircase bearing the solitary glass of milk on a tray. Says Hitchcock '(t)o make the audience fix their eyes on this glass, I had a little battery and lightbulb put in the milk, which gave it a glow. Then your eye went to it, all the way up the stairs until it came past the camera, very large'.[45] The dramatic effect, both back-story and message, are concentrated in the suspected poisoner's chalice.

Insurgents are rarely blessed with such freedom of control enjoyed by film directors. At best they approximate Hollywood's set designer and floor manager who arrange the *mise-en-scène*. Activists depend on news-cameramen to capture episodes where real-life casts are practically undirected. Formulaic suicide testimonies and IED-strike videos are exceptions that exercise their improvisatory talents. Otherwise expertise rests on triggering high drama moments as news events. As successfully as insurgents judo-throw states, so they use the weight of the media against the media. They have others do their work for them, understanding industry professionals are driven to make 'good television', extracting emotional impact and symbolic meaning from distilled moments. What the cameraman misses, the editor improvises. Where dramatic tension fades from the moving picture, the press-still compensates, immortalising into a single frame. Insurgents are perforce opportunistic. The news event may be deliberately 'story-boarded' in the insurgent's plan but the way the image is framed, captured and disseminated is largely opportune, depending on third parties to complete the project. Occasionally they have the luxury to be strategic and control the production process, creating home-grown video product. These different routes to the population are discussed below.

How do militants emulate Hitchcock's lightbulb? Their stage-management relies on broad and violent brush-strokes that lock into the moment of optimum contact with underlying grievance. The choice between interpretations must be narrowed, foreshortening the distance between insurgent and audience. Their lightbulb scene must be memorable for its drama but also for its ability to condense message meaning visually, graphically. New York's Twin Towers created a perfect backdrop for symbolic but stylised dramaturgy.[46] The image's true force lies not in its violence; nor in its anticipation of a dénouement shortly to be resolved. Rather it is its uncluttered simplicity stripping out extraneous distraction that might complicate the intended message. The more the real is transformed into iconographic representation, the greater chance of prolonging its life and freezing the moment forever. In short, the more likely it is to anchor memory.

No image is unambiguous.[48] War-photographer Nick Ut captured a moment of state-terror in 1972, shortly after South Vietnamese air-

Neda: Reducing the real to the icon. © Press Association/AP/Lefteris Pitarakis.

force (VNAF) Skyraider aircraft dropped napalm bombs on a Vietnamese village. A small girl runs along Route-1 towards camera, naked and screaming from napalm burns. Four children surround her, fleeing, crying. Behind walk four armed soldiers. The distant sky is heavy with oily plumes of napalm smoke and flying debris. This picture might be read otherwise than the iniquity of the US-backed war effort. However the *punctum* of the girl's extreme vulnerability stripped bare of protection, on closer inspection her skin flecked with burns, grips our attention. The secondary focus, an anguished boy is reinforced by advancing South Vietnamese soldiers in the middle distance. They might be liberators or conquerors. But the interplay between soldiers and the distant but all-enveloping sky is irresistible, inextricably linked as force for menace and cause of pain. This perspective rooted in pre-knowledge of war, points us to the polarity of soldier embodying force and child representing innocence. The impact derives from the picture's ability to communicate on three interacting levels: girl; children and soldiers; soldiers and skyline. Attaching blame and triggering grievance is facilitated by the troopers' seeming indifference. They appear complicit in the anguish. The wider awareness of the US-South Vietnamese compact is never far from the frame.

Pakistan's Prime Minister Benazir Bhutto was killed in a terrorist bomb attack on her car at an election rally in Rawalpindi in 2007. The effect on Pakistan's population was 'earth shattering and traumatic'.[49] The organisation behind the fifteen-year old assailant has been attributed to Baitullah Messud and Al-Qaida. Pakistani state intelligence, particularly ISI, and former President Pervez Musharraf were implicated by association or negligence.[50] Several photographs appeared across global media capturing the event.

One photograph shows a car in flames, possibly not even one of the electoral cortege, beneath a poster of Bhutto proclaiming 'Long Live Bhutto'. The unintented irony is overshadowed by the candidate's gaze staring resolutely beyond us. It is haunting and thought-provoking. Associations quickly trigger fixing her as politician rather than woman or mother. An irresistible tension reigns between flames and eyes on the poster. The *punctum* is uncertain. At the foot of the picture lie blood-soaked victims. Yet they appear as bystanders, a visual postscript. The image's strength is its construction on three interacting levels: violence of the flames; stillness of the face; and victims frozen in their shock. The picture is accidental, not stage-managed by assailants. Significantly, to become POTD it need not be planned. Caught in the split-second by a photographer not unaware of simple conventions of photo-journalistic composition, and cropped by a picture editor for maximum impact, it becomes an enduring image. It is neither deliberate insurgent iconograph nor unambiguous, since for Bhutto's supporters those eyes speak defiance from beyond the grave. The poster is enigmatically well-crafted, showing her gentle yet resolute. So why is it subverted by our sneaking suspicion she might not be the innocent martyr? The image suggests an ability to speak to a history of retribution, thus grievance. The wider understanding (*studium*) that Bhutto was identified with misrule and corruption competes with her reputation for espousing democratic politics. Nevertheless a rhetorical question hangs over the incident: is this death-sentence morally too extreme? The point is, in this photograph, the insurgent has the barest chance that audiences might be persuaded the underlying blame for this violence resides with Bhutto. This automatically plays to partisans. While for critics it only confirms their condemnation of the spectacle. But that tension between flames and eyes might just speak to those who straddle the fence. And that is enough for the insurgent objective.

Images as Weapons

Insurgents start from weakness. Violence, killing, and death hold a primal fascination for most viewers. The general response to them is revulsion and fear. As one policeman, eyewitness to an Irish atrocity underlines:

One of the most horrendous moments for me was seeing a head stuck to a wall...we found vertebrae and a ribcage on the roof of a nearby building. The reason we found it was because seagulls were diving on to it. I've tried to put it at the back of my mind for 25 years.[51]

For militants this is the obstacle to clear. There is a further problem. Even if the sensational image replaces reasoned argument as the rhetoric of choice, the volume of rich information it can transmit is limited.[52] Suffering and grievance that perpetrators and their communities experience should merit sympathy from a wider constituency. Somehow all audiences must be persuaded that extreme violent response is legitimate and proportionate. This is a tall order.

Insurgent images rarely go unchallenged for long. News stories speak with the voice of objective authority, framing attacks as moral outrage, and are editorially selective. Soon competing images of popular condemnation challenge any utopian meaning that would attach to the deed. Many incidents are captured not by television but CCTV cameras. Subconsciously audiences are preconditioned to read CCTV footage as capturing something illicit, casting the subject as intruder/criminal/assailant. Yet we all look guilty on CCTV. Grainy, low-lit, top-shot, monochrome and time-coded, CCTV pictures spell subterfuge, guilt, and menace.[53] They come pre-charged with meaning. Caught in the act—Patty Hearst, Columbine School gunmen, '7/7' quartet, or Mumbai bomber Kasab—all are equal before the lens. They are subsumed into the same frame of reference as police photo-IDs we associate with the criminalised and convicted. Therefore to escape criminality and inspire politically, the original image must stand out by force of its drama and invention.

How does violence attach to an idea? Human actors acquire visual syntax through sight. We use it to organise and explain what we look at. Meaning is not inherent in what we see but constructed from cultural convention. Hence the psychologist Daniel Levitin suggests when we are born, our senses are initially interchangeable. The senses are jumbled. So we interpret experiences in a way not yet distinguished according to the criteria we later come to associate with those senses. Consequently, he suggests, cheese may taste D-flat to a baby. As we develop, we acquire shared understandings of how to attribute and tabulate sight, smell, and taste.[54] However, images have fewer and less precise rules than language, so are open to greater ambiguity.[55] Disparate events we witness do not simply talk to each other: audiences participate in joining up the dots. To be meaningful, any schema of associations depends on viewers' previous knowledge. By consistently re-investing in the 'referent system' through a reconstructed insurgent narrative, gradually, imperceptibly viewers' understanding adapts. This process is central to the production of ideology: a 'meaning made necessary by the conditions of society while helping to perpetuate those conditions'.[56] Ideology succeeds when appearing to have no beginning and no end, to be the unquestioning norm of everyday experience. Consequently each event we observe plays into a referent system and viewers are already pre-conditioned to accept its point of origin. Images sit within a broader schema: '(t)here is a cognitive outline in which the product is inserted: we exchange because we know'.[57] Individuals are invited to supply missing information absent from the visual image.

This is simply illustrated by French actress Catherine Deneuve, erstwhile face for Chanel perfume's advertising campaigns in the 1970s.[58] Within a consumerist referent system her face was famously displayed 'in apposition' to a Chanel No. 5 bottle. Blonde hair tightly swept back and discreet diamonds in her ears, the face is cushioned in the marketing photograph by a swathe of purple fabric alongside the geometrical simplicity of the perfume bottle with its sans serif label. The image contains a dissociated face and bottle: no explanation connects the two beyond the word Chanel. The key factor is what Deneuve's face (signifier) means for the viewer: French chic, elegance and sophistication (signified). The bottle has no intrinsic meaning: it is a glass container with amber liquid. What it aspires to is what the face exquisitely portrays. Meaning is not invented for the bottle, so much as transferred from face to bottle. Without pre-knowledge of what that face means to audiences, no connection is possible. Anyone unfamiliar with this referent system will miss the point.[59] Insurgents cannot count on engaging in extended argument. The visual becomes the weapon of impact. And the insurgent attempts to unclutter the image of distracting data when POTD is captured, to produce iconic simplicity and transferred meaning. Not dissimilar from Chanel's subversion.

To illustrate the visual's tendency to greater ambiguity than language (syntactic indeterminacy), Paul Messaris examines 'a New Beginning', a Ronald Reagan campaign advertisement from 1984.[60] Shots were intercut between the President's inauguration, various agricultural and industrial workers, and commuters leaving for work. Were it a Hollywood drama, this might tell the story of a group of people across America leaving for work as the day begins. However in a political campaign context, it implies the hard-working President as 'man of the people', or Reagan the man who revitalised the economy. Or both. Therein lies the ambiguity of vision.[61]

HSBC uses this dichotomy to advertise its sensitivity to a multivalent, multi-cultural world. An airport poster campaign promotes its strapline as the 'world's local bank', demonstrating how the meaning of the same image varies between different countries.[62] In a striking example of visual ambiguity, media owner CBS Outdoor launched a provocative image campaign on the London Underground aimed at driving consumer traffic to a website designed to stimulate audience/user engagement. One of its images shows two tanks ranged against a brooding sky, captioned 'Deterrent or Provocation?'[63] By removing 'Deterrent or Provocation?' we would hopefully still be sufficiently puzzled by the image to raise the question. But what of the caption-free picture of a British soldier fleeing his burning tank in Basra? A symbolic strike, does it connect oppression to the occupying army? Is it redemption or revenge?

'A photograph can't coerce...It won't do the moral work for us. But it can start us on the way'.[64] However, in one research sample of advertisements, 24% of visual metaphors required written text in order to be understood by observers.[65] In a world where 10% remember what they read, 30% by hearing, and 80% by seeing,[66] for insurgents this seems an acceptably high strike rate. Is visual ambiguity such a problem for insurgents? It benefited Reagan the 'great communicator' and other mainstream politicians. Messaris sees two advantages in the weakness and implication of visual syntax. First, audiences work harder when visual arguments are less clearly defined. By investing details from their own life-experience to interpret events, they appropriate new understandings more readily as their own. Second, lack of definition in imagery meets the producer's objective. Visuals suggest rather than specify, without being judged by the same rigorous standards as linguistic argument.[67]

In Chapter One, I defined POTD as a blend of strategic communications and political marketing, suggesting modern advertising has inflected all areas of private and public sector communications, and that insurgents are drawn into this arena of discourse by the hegemony of communications language. As advertising would 'sell something to us',[68] so POTD as a framed event attempts to evoke rather than recount a story. Present attacks echo those past. One triggers the memory of others and activates their meaning too.[69] If POTD is a form of television advertising, its purpose is to convey an idea. And the product it advertises may be a political platform, mood change, or sense of moral concern.[70]

"The only way of communicating an idea is by means of an icon', writes the American logician Charles Peirce.[71] But not all icons are a likeness. Via icons we connect to deeply held, socially constructed myths which may be old or recent. Lakoff and Johnson suggest that his process works because metaphor ('understanding and experiencing one kind of thing in terms of another')[72] and metonymy (using a part to represent the whole) are no mere literary flourishes. Rather metaphor is ontological, a function of how humans interpret the world around them. Our very conceptual system—'human thought processes are largely metaphorical'.[73] What political and commercial marketing understand is the importance of repeating images and associated messages, given 'no metaphor can ever be comprehended or even adequately represented independently of its experiential basis'.[74] They recognise first, people in power impose their metaphors on the way we interpret the world.[75] And second, what counts is 'not the truth or falsity of a metaphor but the perceptions and inferences that follow from it and the actions that are sanctioned by it'.[76] Which chimes with Thomas' Theorem that 'if men define situations as real, they are real in their consequences'.[77] The insurgent rationale absorbs these lessons while acknowledging that products and politicians alike are sold by association and metaphor.[78]

However, there is a difference. A dishwasher's function is clear. But insurgent deeds are no white-good with consumer benefits. Nor can they be interrogated like politicians on the electoral stump. Violent images express negative content and therefore fail to accentuate the positive, or promise the new. Sometimes written or spoken slogans accompany POTD via on-line video or DVD dissemination. Often when the event is fed live, they are absent. Without accompanying

explanation, they remain the essence of pure mood, stimulus and association.[79] The expression of violence is but the initial link within a chain
of mental images leading us back to its underlying cause. An explosion
is read first as the killing of a number of people: a second step is
required to ask the question 'why?'[80] Advertisers are Pavlovians: 'mere
association of a product with a positively evaluated stimulus such as an
attractive picture…may be sufficient to alter attitude toward the product without any "rational" belief change preceding the effect'.[81]

Resonance, Anticipation

This convenient elision of the insurgent and advertising worlds is
achieved through resonance. Resonance and anticipation are bed-fel-
lows: they look backwards and forwards. Together they perform an
important function in the insurgent world. For outgoing messages to
be received with anything resembling original intent, to resonate therefore, requires that two agents 'tune in' to each other, says Alfred
Schütz.[82] This 'sense of cognitive cohesion'[83] occurs when individuals
synchronise, whether or not they are in the same space. Media images
can achieve this. He bases his analysis on music since it too is a 'meaningful context that can be communicated'. Like pictures, tunes produce
a 'quasi-synchronising' effect; listeners are brought into artists' streams
of consciousness 'with quasi simultaneity', even hundreds of years after
the composer's death, in the 'reconstruction of a vivid present'.[84] This
does not of course precondition an audience's response, which may be
active or passive. The group experiences a similar meeting of minds.
What Émile Durkheim calls 'effervescence'—an energy rush—may
surge through a crowd attending a sports match or concert, or watching a live television or online event. A strong sense of collective spirit
and shared identity ensues which across electronic media produces
'socio-mental networks', a virtual meetings of minds.[85]

Anticipation is a keen arrow in the insurgent quiver. Anticipation is
recognised in music and storytelling: it plays into schema.[86] These are
frameworks of memory and understanding that govern how we
think.[87] We think in stories, and storytelling is broadly structured
according to recognisable patterns: 'Summary, Setting, Complication,
Resolution and Coda'.[88] This embraces news reports that follow a
common format: 'Summary (Headline and Lead), Main Events, Backgrounds (Context and History), Consequences (Consequent events or

actions and Verbal Reactions), and Comments (Evaluation and Prediction)'.[89] Similarly music follows formats but operates even more subversively and unconsciously. 'The setting up and then manipulating of expectations is at the heart of music'.[90] What listeners think is about to happen is frequently and consciously dashed. Like music, stills and (perhaps even more) moving pictures lock into viewers' expectations, inviting them to paint in missing data, anticipating what should happen next. In Aristotelian rhetoric this is *enthymeme*.[91] 9/11 fascinates us because paradoxically it conforms to expectations, while nevertheless defying all expectations. There is no precedent other than cinematic disaster movies and computer games.[92] In real life we avoid believing the inevitable will happen. Yet we know it can and will. Such fascination with images does not require sharing political sympathy with their perpetrator. Our desire for the image to resolve itself, like a song which reminds us of other songs we know, is willed on the individual almost despite ourselves. Sean Redmond recalls on seeing 9/11 'being mesmerised, and...darkly excited by the spectacular ruination before us'. This reinforces Jean Baudrillard's rationale: 'we have dreamed of this event, that everybody without exception has dreamed of it, because everybody must dream of the destruction of any power hegemonic to that degree...'[93] So anticipation and resonance coalesce in insurgent acts.

Unseen, Unspoken

What did viewers watching the Mumbai terror strike of November 2008 see in the world of POTD with its 'imprecisely calibrated language of communication and persuasion'?[94] Perhaps the answer lies not in what you see, but what you don't see. Not what you say, but what you don't say.

Two hotels were attacked in Mumbai, the Taj and Oberoi. Hotels are no longer just places for weary travellers. Their boutiques sell expensive merchandise while those with 5-star status boast fine restaurants often catered by celebrity chefs. In their bars guests 'order a bottle of Dom Perignon for one and a half times the average annual income; this in a city where 40 percent of the houses lack safe drinking water'.[95] Mumbai's Taj engulfed in flames during the Black Cats' counterterrorist shoot-out during Operation Black Tornado signalled to global television viewers what Indians were already calling '26/11'.

Its architectural grandeur captured a narrative seeping from many viewers' anterior knowledge. Here was a symbol of 'India Rising': wealth, elegance, success. Frequented by international and Western business people, Bollywood and Hollywood stars, and the cream of India's political establishment, it represented for Indians a 'point[s] of reference in this increasingly interconnected world'.[96] As fires raged, television pictures showed confused Indian security forces surround the building without resolving the crisis. Neither slogan nor banner was on view from the assailants. Something else was missing. Mumbai's is an unenviable reputation, home to sprawling slums of some 12 million poor. Recently many have been displaced, making way for high-rise, up-market real estate.[97] Viewers may have witnessed but one of these economic extremes on their screens. However, both spoke volumes. What Lashkar-e-Taiba terrorists awakened was a referent system.[98] As an image the Taj represented Western values, not just foreign visitors. Reinforcing these was the accumulated knowledge of India's thirty-year neoliberal dash for prosperity, regional hegemony and new-found cultural confidence. The obverse of the coin was a perception of successive governments whose policies had marginalised class, as well as ethnic and religious groups, particularly Muslim.[99] For all that the attack appeared rooted in the political economy of neighbouring Pakistan, home to the assailants, it is not inconceivable that many poor Mumbaikars reacted similarly to the opulence which greeted the terrorists. The Lashkar-e-Taiba fighters' amazement at the Taj's 'Aladdin's cave' was captured on CCTV and intercepted mobile phone-communications back to their Pakistani base.[100] Television news programmes repeatedly described the event as symbolic.[101] Similarly in 2008 Kabul's Serena Hotel had been singled out for Taliban attack. That it hosted the Australian Embassy and foreign aid professionals was perhaps less significant than the fact its basement housed a spa and gym frequented by female aid-workers, which in Kabul was common knowledge. Soon this fact would be known to the rest of the country and international audiences as the assailants, with their traditional Afghan gender proscriptions, targeted the Serena.[102] As evidence of political marketing these bear comparison with Lyndon Johnson's 'Daisy Spot' (1964); in it a little girl pulls the petals from a flower, a military count-down breaches the aura of innocence, before the screen dissolves into an atomic explosion. The missing link, never seen, never mentioned is the presidential challenger Barry Goldwater. The audience however understood the connection. What speaks volumes is what is unseen, and unspoken.

Directing Images

The 'Daisy Spot' was a directed campaign ad. It had three components: the staged, directed innocence of a young girl; a filmed atomic explosion, neither staged nor directed; and the audience's bridging the two via Goldwater's cognitive silhouette. Today global viewers recognise various representations of insurgent conflict. Most are captured by news crews, although the underlying action may be opportune or strategic. Equally, images escape state control and can take on an iconographic status in the public arena. Pictures shot by US security personnel for 'own use' depicted Iraqi prisoners in various positions of humiliation and abuse in Abu Ghraib jail. They added insult to the injury of more state-media sanctioned photographs taken in the Guantanamo Bay detention camp and recordings of collateral civilian deaths from ISAF/NATO aerial and ground bombardment in Afghanistan. Similarly so-called 'collateral murder' video footage shot from a US Apache gunship, captured in graphic detail the killing of unarmed non-combatants in Baghdad. Its effect, reinforced by the soundtrack of the over-zealous crew, was dramatic: 'light 'em all up...keep shootin'...Oh, yeah, look at the dead bastards...Nice!'[103] Here the insurgent's role in the production process is passive. His task remains to position the outcome by conditioning the receiving environment for audiences. Such images serve well and are re-invested in insurrectionist narratives, while speaking to wider humanitarian values within the sponsor states of 'occupying forces'. Insurgent media producers create their own output too. Much is achieved with the adeptness of a generation of consumers fluent in video-production techniques.[104] Recently the web and neutral or sympathetic television stations have aired such programming, although its impact is constrained by region, community and age group.

Insurgent videos are consciously constructed and adopt now familiar formatting templates.[105] Al-Qaeda videos comprise visual sequences; their durations have shortened over the last decade, most recently averaging around 20 minutes.[106] Nicholas O'Shaughnessy describes Phase 1 (01/98–08/01) as 53 minutes; Phase 2 (09/01–06/06) 35 minutes; Phase 3 (07/06–01/08) 32 minutes; latterly (01/08 to 02–03/09) 20 minutes. This trend suggests greater sensitivity to audiences with different tolerance levels for the rhetoric of political causes. It is consistent with written communications addressing audiences inside and outside the fold. And to underscore this point, it is worth recalling from Chapter One Taliban leader Mullah Omar's Eid communiqué

(25/11/2009), when he spoke to nine constituencies simultaneously but saved a different message for each: 1. 'To our Mujahid people';2. 'To the heroic protective mujahideen in the trenches'; 3. 'To those working in the cooperative administration in Kabul'; 4. 'To the Islamic conference and what is referred to as human rights institutions'; 5. 'To the educated, to the writers, and to the literary'; 6. 'To the regional and neighbouring countries'; 7. 'To the rulers of the White House, and the America war supporters'; 8. 'To the supporters of freedom from the people of Europe and the West in general'; 9. 'To the entire Islamic Nation'.[107] O'Shaughnessy extends his analysis, identifying three generic types of video communication: martyr; operations; and talking head. The third has recently become far more prevalent. However where messages in reported news events remain opaque, such ambiguity can be overridden in directed videos. The same research identifies binary oppositional themes, most commonly 'forgiveness/vengeance'; 'heroic/cowardly'; 'honourable/dishonourable'; 'life/death'; 'ours/ theirs'; and 'truth/falsehood'.[108] How producers package this dialectic using political marketing techniques is noteworthy. Emotive appeals to moral goodness conferred on potential signatories to the video's proposition increasingly outstrip fear-mongering and threats. Euphemism, making the negative sound more positive, and dysphemism doing the opposite, have become favoured techniques too.[109]

In sum, for POTD to succeed as a tool of political marketing it must trigger what remains unarticulated, rather than what is made explicit. Metaphor bridges into a sense of grievance. Where violence creates an 'attention space', it momentarily occupies the foreground. The deed can never be a marketing product *per se*. It denies mutual participation, negotiating space between producer and receiver. Beneath the depicted event lurks the ideological message with its myriad layers of political meaning. The event meanwhile remains the memorable soundbite or videobite.

Using Frames to Trigger Action

POTD practitioners, like political marketers and advertising copywriters, exploit symbolic references. Yet they do more than link two objects of meaning through metaphor, such as 'explosion = oppression'. To have any lasting effect, deeds must play into areas of current political discourse and catalyse public opinion. Hence they function within the arena of multi-tiered strategic communications by bridging diverse and disparate target constituencies. Each has its own take on a particular grievance. So how do deeds influence this process?

In short, they anchor discursive frames within social movement organisations (SMOs).[110] Frames are thumb-nail sketches, 'the bumper-sticker version of how issues get interpreted within a certain ideological context'.[111] Individuals link into group attitudes, so 'some set of individual interests, values and beliefs and SMO activities, goals and ideology are congruent and complementary'.[112] Sometimes similar discourses align, creating single platforms for action; sometimes discourses dominate their rivals, mobilising target constituencies in new directions.[113] Albeit academically contested, framing uses symbolic narratives to explain how individuals and groups make sense of the 'world out there' and 'sell' that meaning to others to secure their strategies.[114] 'Big picture' or master frames adapt to host other subsidiary but connected narratives[115]—a regular feature of political marketing and strategic communications.[116] But to inspire collective action, groups embrace a three-step process. First, they diagnose a problem; second, they reach a prognosis and devise appropriate tactics; and third, they underpin a 'call to arms' with compelling arguments.[117] This sounds self-evident. But to maximise effect, frames must resonate with audiences, striking a chord with a society's cultural and political values while locking into deep-seated memory.[118] Consequently 'narrative fidelity'[119] is especially challenging because culture and values are not fixed but dynamic. If society is in constant flux, so too are its defining features. These resemble a '"tool kit" for constructing "strategies of action"'[120] from which individuals create new meaning. Yet the awareness individuals require to shape meaning from situations is neither uniform nor one-dimensional. There are broadly held to be three types of situational awareness: low-level recognition that an idea exists; perception, a medium-level engagement with that idea; and high-level physical or actual effect, a conviction that spurs to action.[121]

POTD would impose its own 'injustice frames', resonating grievance and the attribution of blame, onto rival frames that capture the accepted, dominant wisdom in a community at any particular time. By repeating claims to truth, and placing the blame for insurgent violence on hostile state policies, it walks a fine line between the emotional and rational. There are inherent risks in either option. Psychologists describe emotionally attributing 'undeserved suffering to malicious or selfish acts by clearly identifiable persons or groups' as hot cognition.[122] Identifying an enemy in the shape of state agencies or individual politicians seems simple enough. Once the public feels it has a face on which to pin its grievance, the risk is that the face becomes more important than the problem: so the underlying grievance becomes obscured. The offending face may be punished or removed, yet there may still be no improvement in the state of affairs.[123] Conversely, emphasise the abstract complexity of the problem, then cold cognition comes into play and individuals are let off the hook.[124] So this tension between hot ('misplaced concreteness') and cold cognition ('overdetermined structural analysis') must be resolved for purposeful action to follow.[125]

The Real IRA's (RIRA) bombing 'spectacular' in 1998 illustrates this tension.[126] Detonated in Omagh, it killed twenty-nine and injured hundreds. Most were Catholics, some Republicans. RIRA had scored an 'own goal' and they apologised. Judged by its media impact, it was possibly more significant than a generation of Republican combatant fatalities self-inflicted by their own guns and bombs.[127]

How did RIRA get it so wrong? Poor planning and bungled operational communications led to the car bomb being parked in the wrong place. But the ill-judged action fell foul of public opinion not through operational ineptitude. Rather it misunderstood the communications environment. Misreading shifts in popular mood of nationalist and loyalist constituencies approaching war fatigue, the splinter group undervalued political processes that were being conducted between Sinn Féin and PIRA, Westminster and Dublin. These were beginning to show signs of progress after substantial electoral gains supporting the Good Friday Agreement and the IRA's abandoning 'armed struggle'. The bombing was universally condemned. And that included the Provisionals who unlike the bombers, recognised 'they were operating within a sophisticated set of informal restrictions on their behaviour'.[128] Sinn Féin/PIRA, projected a frame in which they were the authoritative thrust of nationalist and Republican negotiations. Meanwhile they sought to promote themselves as the voice for peace based on 'courage, wisdom, and discipline'.[129] RIRA however remained locked in a different set of narrative frames. Omagh's bomb may have had the Provisionals' 'intellectual fingerprints all over' it; they had after all 'invented' the car-bomb.[130] Nevertheless RIRA's frame broke step with the moment, locked into what James Dingley describes as symbolic acts

Omagh bombing: a failure of framing. © Press Association/Paul McErlane.

not to be analysed according to normal political behaviour. Their aim is to make a statement and to become a focus of people's attention and to affect emotional states, to recall people to their cultural and religious origins, just as acts of sacrifice in religion do.[131]

The political context was one of a redefined relationship between Ireland and Britain, and the two governments' efforts in conjunction with Washington towards negotiating peace.[132] Why RIRA's frame proved so discordant is a question perhaps even RIRA cannot answer. Were they victims of many a revolutionary's fate, to be inward-looking and blinkered as to lose sight of their own constituency? Or were they wrong-footed, in inter-organisational one-upmanship with the dominant PIRA actively preparing the ground in nationalist and wider communities for a constitutional road to peace?[133] RIRA unsuccessfully gauged the mood of the very nationalist population they targeted and relied on for support. Might the effect have been otherwise had no Catholics died? Or were they simply unable to renew the legitimacy of the deed in the light of changing politics and general war-fatigue? Where RIRA failed was in the 'critical discourse moment', one of those 'events that create some perturbation and bring heightened media attention...these moments provide dangers and opportunities in a framing contest—a battle over whose interpretation will prevail'.[134] Sinn Féin/PIRA successfully hijacked the force of the deed turning the public relations potential to their advantage. They engineered a shift in the way communities understood 'what's going on'. RIRA did not.

* * *

Pictures speak louder than words. Rather they speak viscerally and emotively. Therein lies a problem since they are by nature ambiguous, dependent not just on what revelation the image brings to the viewer, but what pre-knowledge the viewer delivers to the image. In a new media environment where multiple forms of dissemination now reach societies at all socio-economic levels, a new problem has emerged: the visual cacophony. In their asymmetric communications struggle with states, insurgents have finally found a way through to mass audiences exerting a degree of autonomy, only to find a morass of conflicting information. So POTD moments become attention-seeking, recognising the need to cut through this fog of war. Their images communicate in brutal ways, locking into frames of discourse where alternative worldviews are diffused to audiences. They resonate with and antici-pate bodies of memory to rival those shaped by the state and media thus driving a wedge between them and the population. They dramat-ically exploit opportunity spaces as crisis moments in the state's con-trol over violence and security, and the media's 'understanding' of the 'world out there'.

Basra 2005: revelation or revenge?
© Reuters/Atef Hassan.

5

TELEVISION MEMORY

Whatever we know about our society, or indeed about the world in which we live, we know through the mass media. This is true not only of our knowledge of society and history but also of our knowledge of nature...

Niklas Luhmann[1]

Traditionally, POTD has formed part of the insurgent arsenal. Today it may be understood in the light of how closely populations are tied to media output. POTD now aims to achieve more than an assault on public attention: it challenges the apparent unity of media hegemony which disseminates its interpretation of world events to audiences.

How is memory shaped across the media landscape? Furthermore, how do insurgents challenge this memory? And why are violent live media events the insurgent's target of choice? Such questions invite the conclusion that states, media, and audiences 'negotiate' frameworks of understanding in an iterative relationship. A continual process of push-and-pull results in consensual memory. Nevertheless media increasingly hold the whip hand. Audiences exercise agency within broadly defined parameters, which the sociologist John Thompson calls 'the mundane character of receptive activity'.[2] Reception is part-and-parcel of every-day routine. Insurgents subvert this process to challenge and shape new memory. However vacuums of understanding occasionally appear (New York 2001, London 2005, Mumbai 2008). Media producers rapidly fill with hegemonic memory those opportunity spaces or gaps that in the shock of the crisis moment seem beyond explanation. Two further dimensions are considered in this context: the event, and LIVE-ness. Both impact audiences. Over decades they acquire 'coded meanings' which audiences internalise. Consequently, both present soft targets for maximum impact when insurgents manipulate audience attention and sympathies. POTD not only uses the judo throw against the state. It challenges the mediaspace which it perceives as dominated by the voice of the state.

The language we use determines how we think about mass media and the mass.[3] Both suggest homogeneity and universality. Yet media are pluralist, comprising multiple organisations whose actions converge and diverge. They are fractured, and compete internally and between each other; their purview is global, their sensibilities parochial, their manner domineering but occasionally compliant. Individuals and groups within the mass behave differently and alike. They demonstrate herd-like instincts and individualism.

Media set agendas for discourse which audiences follow and draw maps by which we steer, telling us what to think about rather than what to think.[4] The global mediaspace is permanently switched 'on'.[5] Viewers are invited to consume content in the form of heightened, hyper-real representation in an electronic, visual world supported by advertising and film-making. Mass media encourage us to convert imagined spaces of exotic people and far-flung places, and the imagined time of diverse life-stories and events, into our own 'mass-mediated reality'.[6] So 'mass media create common reality by shaping the conceptual environment in which humans communicate' in a continual iterative process between producer and receiver. 'The totality of this process constitutes reality'.[7] Nevertheless sceptics reject the direct power of mass media while emphasising its informality.

Insurgents stage events that reach multiple audiences simultaneously but not all broadcast and press systems are uniform in all countries and cultures. Nor is their access to wide-ranging audiences identical. Despite traditional urban-rural divides, advanced 'urban technologies' like cellphones are being adopted in many rural areas, leapfrogging established communications. Meanwhile urban and cosmopolitan elites in most regions, with greater access to television, radio, press, and web, are moving towards Western modes of consumption. These are tempered nationally by local politics and culture.[8]

Mass media are also fraught with paradox and tensions. David Hesmondhalgh highlights their dual role as '"economic" systems of production and "cultural" producers of texts', arguing '(p)roduction is profoundly cultural and texts are determined by economic factors (among others)'.[9] Moreover individually and collectively they act as top-down and bottom-up conduits of power.[10] Traditionally, these are largely hierarchical organisations obeying logics of organisational and market efficiency. But they fall short of implementing them through internal, institutional frictions. What bosses want, bosses don't always get. It is not always employees who resist most: audiences choose what to watch or reject. Mass media are public and private enterprises following market rules, but variously conforming to cultural prescripts and state regulation and intervention. These producers of texts mediate world experience, creating meaning for consumers, yet consumer feedback influences producers' editorial decisions. They are frequently believed but not always trusted. Their content is ephemeral, disposable, nevertheless shapes social relations. And to refine McLuhan's maxim, the global village is both a universalising community and kaleidoscope of localities.[11]

Media are pluralist, allowing cracks to appear which insurgent messages penetrate. Historically distinct, the main cultural industries—press, television, radio, cinema, telephony, internet, advertising, and music—have reached different stages in their evolutionary cycles: press (1840s), fixed-line telephony (1890s), broadcast television (1950s), global satellite television (1980s), internet (1990s), and mobile telephony (2000s). It is now rare in today's fragmented media environment for the overwhelming majority of a country's viewers or readership simultaneously to tune in to the same television show (1970s), huddle around the same radio programme (1930s, 1940s) or browse the same newspaper (1920s).[12] Insurgent acts periodically buck the trend, commanding front-page headlines and the media spotlight. Newspaper business models traditionally rested on 'bundling' and the 'need to make an appointment'. Consequently diverse content was aggregated in a single daily or weekly offering.[13] Using fibre-optic delivery systems, satellite transmission, and digital storage and processing, more flexible media outlets in newly globalised industries offer round-the-clock updating. New technologies contract time-spans and distances; they deliver information faster, more frequently, in a form preferred by dynamic publics with apparently shorter attention spans. The digital revolution impacts producer and consumer variously through 'convergence, mobility, personalisation, on-demand and participation'. Consequently, 'convergence of platforms, services and technical devices is blurring the boundaries between television, radio and print, and creating a single market for video/audio/text'.[14] Once penetrated, this single market means insurgent messages find inter-linked, multiple channels to reach populations.

Part 1: How is Memory Shaped Across the Media Landscape?

Insurgents may or may not analyse their targets explicitly, but as military campaigners they intuitively reconnoitre the landscape. Media are at once their battlefield and enemy. Insurgents have graduated from viewer to message producer.

Ownership and Political Elites

A popular conception persists that political elites and their media 'mouthpieces' impose their ideas and agendas on the general public. This arises from an oversimplified dichotomy in how media are theorised, from the perspectives of producer (communicator, transmitter) versus consumer (audience, receiver). A Marxian lens sees power as a resource arising from unequal ownership and distribution across society and class leading to structured control in social relations. Media occupy positions within the Marxian base and superstructure that comprise the relations of production on society's 'shopfloor'. The superstructure is perpetuated by the base production relations and encompasses the political system and ideology:

The class which has the means of material production at its disposal, has control at the same time over the means of mental production, so that thereby, generally speaking, the ideas of those who lack the means of production are subject to it.[15]

Cultural and communications scholars see it otherwise. They seek more sedimented understanding of audiences, seeing them as active, diverse participants. Communications send out polysemic texts, sets of messages that audiences read in different ways. So individuals become more than passive and uniform. Instead they have minds and wills capable of rejecting messages and producing unintended consequences.[16]

Mass media are a dynamic ecology shot through with complexity and paradox, even viewed through that most muscular prism of political economy.[17] Information has become a byword for late capitalism as economic models in advanced industrial societies have shifted. So this particular discourse should be updated[18] within a broader political economy of Manuel Castells' 'information society', heir to Daniel Bell's 'post-industrial society'.[19] In the 'information society'[20] knowledge and power are two sides of a single coin.[21] They shape 'images and discourses through which people make sense of their world'.[22] Power is exercised through the way informational events are portrayed, a fact not lost on insurgents. Events:

are by definition always open to interpretation, they may be made to serve a variety of political ends. They are an important vector of power. What matters is to control the production and meaning of information in a given context.[23]

The post-1970s neoliberal decades accelerated, expanded and proliferated electronic media through deregulated and liberalised markets and many public information services and national broadcasters were privatised. Abrogated power with potential to shape consumer attitudes, now vested in the hands of private business, raises many concerns. While popular conspiracy theories abound,[24] more considered critics see media owners intervening for corporate self-interest and political gain. Audiences, they argue, are made complicit in their own submission and in a process of 'manufactured consent'. Where self-censorship meets corporate 'propagandising' broadly supportive of government agendas, a consensus emerges among populations that are less than critical.[25] The ideological subtext of mass media becomes to 'amuse, entertain, and inform, and to inculcate individuals with the values, beliefs, and codes of behaviour that will integrate them into institutional structures of the larger society. In a world of concentrated wealth and major conflicts of class interest, to fulfil this role requires systematic propaganda'.[26]

Can so few really dominate so many? Do large shareholders translate boardroom power into control over populations? A snapshot reveals that five men, who could car-pool in one vehicle to get to work, straddle global media ownership. Charismatic market-raiders celebrated for buccaneering exploits[27] at one point reportedly shared 141 joint ventures. In the US market-place they mutually lobbied through the powerful National Association of Broadcasters 'to achieve the laws and regulations that increase their collective power over consumers'.[28] A wave of heated mergers and acquisitions between internet service providers and multi-media conglomerates further fuels this charge. Private and public corporations enjoy enhanced comparative advantage prompting controversial accusations they have 'unparalleled ability to buy off politicians and regulators...they give used car dealers a good name'.[29] This climate of suspicion chimes with broader perceptions of advanced capitalism as 'an economy and a polity which meet and interpenetrate at many levels but remain organised separately; the executives and owners of the cultural apparatus—the press, mass entertainment, sports, and arts—are also interlocked at high levels with the managers of corporate and political sectors'.[30] These sectors may function by different principles, but business and politics are considered too close for the good of the polity.[31] However for Castells power no longer resides in the individual—the local terrain. To enjoy power today is to be included in global networks; to be excluded is to be denied power. In the global domain networks with particular cultures must be overlaid with metaprogrammes. These provide frameworks for recipients to internalise power discourses. He locates new power in 'switchers', individuals who straddle overlapping points in global networks linking key political and communications power-holders and brokers. Entrepreneur Rupert Murdoch is the exemplar.[32]

Especially at moments of national crisis, media find additional airtime to showcase politicians' views, increasing their leeway to set parameters for discursive agendas. Journalists' habitual reliance on government information sources increases. Charges of media quiescence and self-censorship seem reasonably grounded.[33] One year after 9/11, 414 Iraq stories ran on US networks between 9/2002 and 2/2003: 380 had their origins in the White House, Pentagon or State Department.[34] Reporting the popular mood for four weeks following 9/11, networks ran an unusually high number of stories on the 'War' and terrorism: ABC: 86; CBS: 96; NBC: 133; CNN: 316.[35] But it was 'sympathy' for Washington's 'War on Terror', absence of critical distance and muting of dissent that underscored the President's 29 public speeches throughout the four weeks.[36] CBS anchor Dan Rather's patriotism knew few bounds. Sporting a stars-and-stripes lapel-pin during newscasts,[37] he volunteered to stand first in line to fight the war if summoned by the 'Commander-in-Chief'. Meanwhile 'if the terrorists were anything, they were not cowards'[38] ventured commentator Bill Maher. But he was quickly forced to retract publicly to a nation on a 'war-footing', words thought overly supportive of the assailants. Rupert

Murdoch, owner of the conservative Fox News, would take an interest in the language of news scripts: henceforth suicide-bombers should be known as 'homicide-bombers'.[39] For a brief period it was hard to see US media fulfilling their traditional role of independent counterweight to the state's executive. Was this a natural consequence of heightened political crisis? Or did industry bosses' proximity to the political establishment determine the formation of consensus on how events should be interpreted and remembered?[40]

Critical political economists argue that not to understand the make-up of modern conglomerates is to miss the point. Synergistic ownership encourages cross-promotion between various sister outlets in the same conglomerate. Firms can maximise returns on selective content across multiple markets, significantly reducing audience-choice. Companies stand accused too of undermining local, cultural diversity while reinforcing extant class inequalities,[41] which feeds into Orientalist and postcolonial critique.[42] It may be a world of shifting sands and alliances, circumspect observers note,[43] but when under a dozen US-based transnational media conglomerates, and less than forty sizeable North American and Western European firms concentrate ownership across niche and regional markets, there are valid concerns for developing democratic and self-government.[44]

The upshot is a tendency 'to centralise media control in narrow business elites, whose offerings are shaped by advertiser interests; these in turn feature entertainment, the avoidance of controversy, minimal public participation, and the erosion of the public sphere'.[45] Increasing alliances between entertainment content and advertiser-driven finance[46] encourages a market logic antithetical to the public sphere, and according to Robert McChesney, a betrayal of liberal democratic theory.[47] Audiences generally feel only the effect of this process without divining the causes. Insurgents stand outside the system of production but remain fully part of the viewer community, albeit a more critically engaged segment.

Do owners or bosses always get their way? Probably not. Organisations experience friction in many forms.[48] Boardroom power is no guarantee of decisions carried through to the shop-floor or along corridors of middle management. Employees are individuals as much as team-players: unreliable, unpredictable, and occasionally unruly. They resist top-down directives and bottom-up initiatives that sit within longer-term hegemonic tendencies. Actors in the workplace inconsistently separate private (home) and public (workplace) judgments. So media must be understood as discernible environments that are inward-looking even though their industrial rationale is to communicate outwardly.[49] Moreover firms are rarely streamlined decision-making fora, rather 'organised anarchy' and 'garbage cans': 'choices looking for problems, issues and feelings looking for decision situations in which they might be aired, solutions looking for issues to which they might be the answer, and decision makers looking for work'.[50]

If employees in creative industries are so unpredictable, why do so many competitive institutions adopt similar policies and practices? After all, insurgents find few friends to speak up for them in regular newsfare. One answer lies in the bureaucratic organisation of firms, mirroring the bureaucratic state.[51] Organisational fields 'provide(s) a context in which individual efforts to deal rationally with uncertainty and constraint often lead, in the aggregate, to homogeneity in structure, culture and output'. Moreover, power resides in the margins around moments of industrial conflict:

(t)he locus of power has to be sought primarily in the limits which define areas of conflict and restrict the range of alternatives effectively put into dispute. Often indeed, they may be so tightly drawn that there are no alternatives ventilated. There is then no "decision making" because policies appear self-evident.[52]

The point is that decision-making, as a function of problem-solving, is ridden with contest and ambiguity. More broadly, there are unwritten norms and routines which constrain the flexibility of actors, encouraging a process of consensus.

Audiences

POTD is a communications tool. In the theatre of mass media, insurgent ambition aspires to more than societal disruption. Instead violence is a persuasive political technique, however counterintuitive that may appear. For insurgents to challenge media memory successfully will depend on how audiences respond to media output. Do they exercise independent choice?

The idea that audiences are susceptible to imitation, identification, and desensitisation through the power of media—particularly television—endures.[53] This is reinforced by studies of the number of hours people in Western societies watch television.[54] Behaviourists focus on the effects of media messages. Audiences subjected to repeat exposure to television's symbolic field of imagery allegedly see the world through common eyes and shared values. 'Mean World syndrome' was coined to describe this homogenising response: if you view lots of crime programmes, you believe the world is riddled with criminals.[55] One seminal text argues programmes confer status on performers, individuals, organisations, and topics of interest and concern. These not only mould but prioritise attention: they teach audiences not just how to look but where. Furthermore, their claim on substantial audience time reportedly creates a 'narcotising dysfunction' producing passive viewers.[56] However, this is too simplistic according to later impact studies that identify a two-step flow within audiences. Messages are transmitted from media to opinion-leaders positioned throughout society, before they further disseminate them face-to-face to fellow consumers.[57] Audiences bring pre-formed opinions to their viewing habits that are reinforced and inflected by opinion-leaders in the community. They also reflect the views of population sub-groups whose sub-cultures vest their own resistance in challenging the 'myth of consensus'.[58] Add personal taste and programming choice, since not everyone likes to watch or read the same things, and direct influence from broadcasters seems less convincing, certainly less totalising.[59] Hence audiences appear less passive than earlier behaviourists had suggested. More likely, audiences use media to their own ends rather than media-elites employ media to manipulate viewers. Audiences search for what satisfies their needs. In a competitive marketplace someone will supply that need.[60]

Central to POTD as symbolic communicator is the question: are audiences influenced by ideology in the shape of power external to individuals, or of discourse internalised in individuals?[61] Political and economic centres of power are reflected in concentrations of cultural influence, namely media. For Stuart Hall they exert power over key social processes, defining 'which issues will enter the circuit of public communications...the terms in which the issue will be debated...who will speak to the issues and the terms'.[62] Ultimately they control the debate in the media. Authoritative social institutions infiltrate 'truths' into popular discourse. Alongside schools, state agencies and families, media first provide the means for individuals before conditioning them on how to understand the world. All are instrumental in a world of 'biopolitics'.[63] Discourses are framed at the point of production and institutions instrumentally select what to include or exclude. Messaging becomes so internalised in the individual that little room is left for personal negotiation. Thus even 'manufacturing consent' sounds ambitious; this system closes down self-censorship. We become locked into self-perpetuating discursive formations. Once these shape our choices dialectically, where we unconsciously define everything as good versus evil, normal-abnormal, legal-illegal, we are individually propelled and mutually steer fellow members of society to act according to a set of prescriptions. No longer taxi-drivers, we become tram-drivers. Adhere to the chosen discursive formation and we are included, empowered with knowledge and influence. Once excluded, we vanish from the discursive arena.[64] Set that against the Gramscian notion of cultural hegemony. In Marxist theory, ideology imposes control on populations from above via social relations that emerge from economic processes of ownership and production.[65] Distinct from Marxian economism, Gramsci sees dominant classes employ 'common sense' to subordinate others. The chosen method is consent. But since subalterns are constantly reminded of their disadvantage through experiencing the iniquities of everyday life, consent must be continually renewed as subordinated classes naturally resist being controlled. Subordinating elites must negotiate and absorb initiatives from below to modify hegemony. Mass media are one key enabler of this process.[66]

Media employees simultaneously produce and consume. The idea that management and employees be neatly parcelled, allocated roles with contingent attitudes, is simplistic. Similarly the idea that audiences constitute a mass, behaving uniformly invites scrutiny. Some practitioners feel the influence of media on people's lives to be overestimated.[67] They claim audiences/readers and their communicators often run out of step. Previously loyal audiences commonly turn their backs on communicators. Britain's *Observer* newspaper suffered terminal decline following its editorial position on the Suez Crisis.[68] Liverpool residents continued to boycott Britain's *Sun* newspaper twenty years after it pinned responsibility for Hillsborough's football disaster onto Liverpool Football Club's fans rather than police negligence.[69] Events following the death of Princess Diana are salutary.[70] In its immediate aftermath, state machinery moved ponderously to commemorate her death with traditional ceremony and outside broadcast coverage. But journalists quickly registered a popular mood running ahead of the media. A force coursing through society resembled a mediaeval celebration of tragedy—a 'rush of blood to the head all nations occasionally suffer'[71]—searching to beatify the deceased. Prime Minister Tony

Blair regained the initiative, eulogising the 'People's Princess'.[72] Funereal crowds travelled to the capital to capture the moment, to mould its memory. Later those same audiences would restrain the *Daily Express*'s murder conspiracy theories.[73] This time media had run ahead of the audience, only to be hauled back.

Such examples confirm that audiences are active participants, negotiating with symbolic communicators for consensus and memory. Moreover media set frameworks of understanding, maps by which audiences are guided. They constrain and direct debate since they sit at the source of the discursive agenda, after which they influence the course of debate through inclusion or exclusion of topics and speakers. Through repetition, day-to-day practicalities of 'getting the news out' means they reinforce and ritualise ways in which media shape understandings of the world. Audiences are recipients of industrial processes. Nevertheless there is room for audiences to negotiate in an iterative process consistent with Anthony Giddens' concept of 'structuration'.[74] This may be through outright rejection of short-term media consensus or incrementally traded understandings. Earlier I noted recruits to insurgent movements engage in limited exchange between individual and dominant group memories. The latter overshadows that of new arrivals depending on degrees of hierarchical control,[75] before group consensus organically re-asserts itself. Similarly audiences negotiate memory within limited constraints set by dominant media hegemony. However the broader picture is relevant. In media a constant undercurrent reduces depth of content and simplifies meaning. Today's 'soundbite culture' values speed of delivering information and concise expression. Verbal and visual short-hands contribute towards the image being privileged at the expense of the word. We live in the world of the event as image. And this is the entry-point for modern insurgents. Where pictures speak louder than words, an opportunity emerges for insurrectionists to insert themselves between audience and media by staging dramatic visual acts.

Creating Memory

Technology has driven major industrial upheaval in recent decades, and social change has further accelerated technological development. Communications outlets have exploded. Consumers (insurgents are 'consumers among the people') find it easier and cheaper than ever

143

before to access cultural product and buy electronic goods that disseminate media output. iMacs increase deliverability, iPods mobility,
iPhones connectivity: all promise diversity. The blogosphere's infinite
expanse is heralded as the utopia for democratising communication:
everyone gets to speak his or her mind.[76] What if we are only witnessing the 'pretence of diversity'? Why do we assume more communications channels generate more communicators with voices sufficiently
distinct to challenge consensual memory of traditional media? Technological divergence through the web and mobile telephony may only
suggest fragmentation. One newspaper editor argues divergence can
produce convergence in an overcrowded information market-place.[77]
This question is fundamental to the following chapters.

The internet bars access to none since it operates without professional entry-criteria. Its flashes of distinctiveness suggest a generalised
divergence. However most voices replicate what the few already say:
originality is rare. More does not necessarily mean more variety, argues
Peter Stothard.[78] We should resist equating data and information with
argument. Today it remains too early to call. The internet's 'Stage One'
saw an enriching expansion of the digital communications landscape;
'Stage Two' has yet to dawn. What lie ahead are countervailing forces
that may resist wholesale flight from traditional media brands, most of
which have already annexed major swathes of digital territory. Recognised names such as the *New York Times*, the *Guardian*, and BBC have
already gained strong and loyal online followings. Educational conditioning, government regulation, and consumer habits may further con-
found utopian predictions.[79] If so, the web may remain an information
resource for insurgency, but fail to consolidate as a mobilising terrain
of mass memory and collective action on which revolutions can be
built. Social network websites diffuse rumours and fashions virally
across great populations. What insurgents need is sustainable development of memory to challenge state or media hegemony. Viral flows
muster rapid support around particular ideas, but they dissipate as fast
as they appear. How this impacts insurgents is discussed in the following chapters.

Traditional media have a 'herd mentality or consensus' to thank for
divergence turning into convergence. 'Missing the story is a bigger sin
than getting the facts wrong'.[80] That pressure compounds a simple
arithmetic: to be one reporter in three covering a story who disagrees
with the other two is a question of interpretation. On major events, to

be one in fifteen who avers from the other fourteen is to risk getting the sack. So reporters play safe and a consensus emerges.[81] Add to that the many sources of information any reporter must juggle during fast-moving events in conflict zones. The outcome means journalists resort to tried-and-tested frameworks or analytical templates. Under pressure of ever-shortening deadlines, there is a natural tendency to revert to what reporters know works. Gavin Hewitt observes:

you bring with you all kinds of things: your own background, experience, culture. You face the problem of language, culture, the difficulty of understanding, time. It's very complex. Sometimes you'll see a crowd looking on with blank faces. You don't know what they're thinking. They'll often tell you what they think you want to hear. You're aware that you see the facts laid out on the table one way and the population and insurgents see it another way—a different story.[82]

As deadlines loom 'the cardinal sin is the black hole, it is the sackable offence'. The show must go on; no deadline dare be missed.[83] Industrial processes of news production reinforce deep-seated assumptions embedded within tried-and-tested frameworks. In the heightened atmosphere of terrorism there are additional 'conventions which set templates'. The media attempts to 'stay out of trouble'. Government restrictions impact news organisations which are 'conscious of the rules, and want to retain access to all sides'.[84] Ultimately, it is the very representatives of 'official' social institutions that media repeatedly employ as interviewees and experts to transform raw happenings into finished news stories. They become the witnesses for truths mutually constructed within the media.

There is a broader point. Professional codes sit within positivist frameworks of institutional understanding.[85] 'Journalism is the science of progress and change. It assumes an upward trajectory'.[86] In television, structures (programmes) are already in place where viewers expect to find up-to-the-minute reportage and in-depth discussion. The press is already set up to report and analyse unfolding events: newspapers' page-structures reflect expectations that something will happen. Consequently 'papers offer meaning',[87] which plugs into society's 'central value system', itself a consensus.[88] Hence when New York's Twin Towers were struck, initially there were competing frameworks of interpretation. Briefly in some newsrooms, it was perceived as a very big news event, but not the cataclysmic turning-point that very soon it would come to be remembered as. Within hours George Bush had declared the United States to be at war. Very soon conflicting voices were crowded out as consensus emerged. By the following day even France's *Le Monde* would declare 'we're all Americans', further 'giving people permission to be emotional'.[89]

Audiences can revolt. How often do they? Not as much as we think, according to one seasoned reporter. They too are 'locked into journalistic frameworks, especially the iconic image'. They are far removed from events and issues are complex. Ethiopia's Famine is remembered for pictures of starving humanity; Tiananmen Square for a lone protester confronting a line of tanks; Iraq for a British soldier set ablaze scrambling from a Chieftain tank; and Madrid's train-bombing for the contorted serpent of debris. In foreign reporting, memory becomes organised around pictures rather than ideas. Background debates are instantly forgotten, argues Glynn Jones.[90] Hence key images frame the memory of media and public. Journalistic snapshots are recycled repeatedly in a fierce struggle between competitive news outlets to establish memory. 'Most war coverage revolves around incidents in the way that gradually form a narrative. Many heroic deeds are lost because no pictures exist'.[91] So media help us select what is important for us to understand; they then assist our interpreting these events. Furthermore they refine and crystallise our readings around structured images.

In sum, programme-makers and writers subscribe to professional codes of production. Over time in daily practice, these become routinised and internalised in producers and their product. Giving audiences what they want is less science, more professional intuition. The effect is to create a blanket of cohesion.[92] Even this is not uniform. Beneath this cover remains nevertheless sufficient scope for individuals to manœuvre and express choice. Practitioners value too highly their ethos of objectivity, independence and creativity to relinquish them without a struggle.[93] Overall the picture is one of constant pull-and-push. Why is this important for insurgency violence? Because if consensual memory flows uninterrupted from the control of elites, then an apparently cast-iron unified message invites a drastic insurgent response, if it is to be breached. On the other hand, if audiences exercise agency, while addressing fellow audiences, if employees in communications industries freely resist employer diktat, then gentler, more subversive means of persuasion may prove pragmatic. In the end insurgents aim to reach audiences, not control state media outlets. By using

POTD as a 'shock and awe' tactic suggests most insurgents are reconciled to confronting the first scenario.

Part 2: How Event and Spectacle Challenge Media Memory

POTD is a media event. What then is the effect of a dramatic broadcast event when played live to millions of viewers on a national, sometimes global scale? So far we have seen why media are less than cohesive, prone to internal friction. Nevertheless, consensus emerges. Meanwhile audiences are receptive to their messages, although not altogether passive in this relationship. Regardless, through the surfeit of 24-hour production of content, media continue to organise memory. Thus the producer-audience relationship becomes an unbroken feedback-loop weighted in favour of media, which filters and mediates all human experience. However media organisations remain mutually competitive, wherein lies the insurgent opportunity. In the competition for attention, event and spectacular become the strike-weapons of today's insurgencies against media memory.

The high-profile, dramatic event is a more frequent occurrence than the rare spectacular. The two are not the same, although they co-exist in the insurgent canon. We know that life brings tragedies, which we fear, recognising that one day something bad will rupture our security. We hope the worst will not happen today. Events are high drama occurrences that are predictable in their randomness and our unpreparedness. Media put tragedies in context; media hegemony incorporates and manages them. Spectaculars, however, are different. Media struggle to find any explanation, so dumb-struck are they for the briefest hiatus. Spectaculars become acts of dramatic violence producing a moment of moral crisis that would prompt long-term readjustment in the status quo. Violent events are sometimes large-scale, sometimes small. But the event has the latent potential to become elevated to the level of spectacular and escape the clutches of media management. If the media's walls of resistance can be brought down like those of Jericho with a single action, then this is the ideal. Insurgents therefore use POTD against the media, not just the state. They combine 'shock and awe' with the judo throw. Any judo throw looks for the opponent's weak spot. Media's, particularly television's, hunger is for audience attention. Indeed both media and insurgent symbiotically need to be noticed by populations. Therefore LIVE-ness, that

147

is the LIVE broadcast of insurgent strikes, feeds this common craving. So (i) what separates events and spectacles in the media landscape, and (ii) what is LIVE-ness?

Event and Spectacle in the Media Landscape

All symbolic communicators wish to occupy the media landscape. It is the terrain on which they would impose meaning, a universe of mirrored occurrence where the ordinary and extraordinary happen. In the mediascape babies are born, children grow up, couples get married, and one day we all die. These are predictable, the quotidien, the mundane: the heightened but minor dramatic events which form the ups and downs of our lives. Volcanoes erupt, tsunamis engulf, and wars destroy; they become heightened but major dramatic events. These are extraordinary, so predictably unpredictable. They become contingencies against which societies calculate risk, install early-warning systems, and deploy rapid-response forces to limited effect. Man-made or natural, occurrences belong in the normalised flow of the ordinary and extraordinary. The panoply of media organisations shapes its version of events from these. Frameworks of understanding adjust with each passing day. But change remains incremental while continuity is king.[94] A vacuum of meaning must never be allowed to show. Yet so saturated are our lives with information that distilled images, icons stripped bare of extraneous information and meaning[95] are sought to cut through walls of media interpretation. All message producers actively contribute to the media hegemon: commercial advertisers, film-makers, private lobby groups, politicians of all hues, democratic and autocratic. Where today's insurgent wishes to communicate with populations—admittedly not all do—the aim is to create moments that visually shock but communicate meaning. Some will be sufficiently imaginative to shake hegemonic equilibrium to its core, prompting societal crisis of identity and control.[96] These rare cases are spectaculars and are simply unpredictable by design, namely human design. The spectacular should tear a gash in the moral landscape which once repaired, remains nevertheless visible.[97] This is shock and awe politics.

So when is an event an event? When is it a spectacular? Events are predictable in their randomness and our unpreparedness. Yet they still fit established frameworks of understanding. Dialectically they are the extraordinary in a world of the ordinary. This is critical to understanding the challenge facing insurgents, particularly since mass media organise their memory metaphorically around events, not arguments. You remember a war, a famine, a key date in history, but not the debate behind it.[98] POTD is always an event which insurgents are powerless to avoid being gradually subsumed into media memory: media make sense of it. Thus it takes its place in the media landscape and media memory. POTD welcomes the fortuitous, the opportune. Equally it need not be planned as spectacular to shift from the lower to higher state. Nevertheless rarely does it realise its potential to become spectacular and so fracture this orthodoxy, defying media inclusion and annexation.

Whether event or spectacular, POTD submerges violence into one image, where time and space implode. In photographs or images, we are told, 'time is engorged'.[99] Suddenly a moment appears around the event where discourse is possible. Groups claim responsibility, mothers of suicide-bombers are seen to sacrifice willingly the lives of their progeny, crowds gather to celebrate martyrdom, and public grievance is renewed in the full gaze of reporters. Media organisations enthusiastically rearrange time, assisting with the construction of a three-act play from the martyrdom story: first act, news-footage of the aftermath of destruction; second act, last-filmed testimonies of suicide-bombers; and third act, the sorrow of stoic parents left behind. Universal sympathy for the maternal bond volunteers a subtext for the drama: surely no child should pre-decease its parent; surely no mother would give up her child without just cause? In this moment insurgents attempt to create an even playing field to exploit the hiatus and subvert media memory, already straining to impose its own meaning. Such moments are by no means isolated. They exist within an archipelago of POTD moments which resonate with one another (Chapter One).[100] But frequency is both friend and foe. The more they occur, the more their intention becomes visible. The risk is the lessening of shock-impact they generate. Events are intrinsically ambiguous, open to interpretation, thus weak, free to be neutralised. In their immediate aftermath they can be rendered 'typical' so normalised within media memory. But even at their moment of optimum shock, they are vulnerable depending for their existence on media being present at the point of impact to witness and transmit. Consequently POTD + media = event. Alternatively media event – media = non-event.

But what are spectaculars? Spectaculars leave us dumbstruck. Incomprehensible, destabilising, they have no immediate response in language.[101] The spectacular stands outside the landscape, as the philosopher Jean Baudrillard suggests:

against the background of perpetual non-event, another type of event emerges. Ruptures, unexpected events, events that are unclassifiable in terms of history, outside the logic of history—events that are generated against their own image, against their own simulacrum. Events that break the fastidious linkage of the news in the media...They are not events in history, but beyond history, beyond the end of history.[102]

We sometimes talk of 'time standing still'. POTD too thrives by imploding time and space. Creating the effect of time standing still, it cinematographically freeze-frames the action. Life imitates art. It reduces the moving picture to a still photograph, only because it is original and authentic. Rather than create zones of discourse, it momentarily seeks the opposite: to support a vacuum of meaning that cannot be filled with discourse. It is the shock-wave of a shock-and-awe strategy that silences. By shutting out discourse, it seeks to destroy media memory. So spectaculars, altogether different, become an act of dramatic violence that prompts a moment of moral crisis and temporary vacuum aimed at long-term readjustment in the status quo. This is more than a media event. It represents discontinuity played out through cognitive failure of ordinary people and for once experts. It is not so much time stood still, it is time as vacuum.[103] Spectaculars rupture the hegemony. Cognitive dissonance, that less than comfortable psychological tension which allows us to retain two conflicting ideas simultaneously, fails. 'Moral panic' is writ large.[104] For once, the seamless flow of process has been interrupted, made public, and more importantly made personal. The initial response is incredulity, disorientation, and speechlessness. This is what broadcasters fear: 'dead air', the 'black hole'.[105] Spectaculars are a shock to the status quo, which falters. The apotheosis was the Twin Towers attack 2001.[106] Paradoxically spectaculars are 'beyond imagination, but not beyond conception'.[107] They are original. Such 'moral panics' destabilise the status quo momentarily before it can regain its equilibrium. Soon a search for meaning becomes a hunt for the 'other' instigated by political and media elites. It is the rapid response mechanism that tries to fill the momentary vacuum.[108] But what they face is a disjuncture, a shift, irreversible and irreparable. Spectaculars then present a moral crisis. Violence, man-made not natural is its innate component. Catastrophes of nature may be blamed on fate or acts of God: a too easy escape-clause. Yet what defines this POTD is political intention. Moreover it is the all-too-human dimension of the outrage perpetrated by one human on another that singles it out as a unique questioning of the basis of life itself. It explores what Hannah Arendt called revolution's 'twin-edge compulsion of ideology and terror, one compelling men from within and the other compelling them from without'.[109]

This is POTD as spectacular. POTD's aim is twofold: to create an archipelago of violent deeds that trigger associations of grievance and injustice in the target population, and to transcend individual violent events to sublimate in the spectacular. Minor events should resonate with each other, while spectaculars provide focal points that act as beacons within the landscape of revolutionary violence.

Instant, digital, global connectedness is a recent technological development. Instantaneity threatens media and political elites' command-and-control. When thinking time contracts, the ability to make decisions or form strategies suffers; it undermines control of security by the state, and control of meaning by the media. Although we talk of entering a new era of image dominance, the spectacular as hyper-real event may have been with us longer than we think. Oppenheimer's response to Truman's unleashing the atom bomb recognised the darkness of state terror. He lamented: 'we knew the world would not be the same again'.[110] Einstein too expressed dismay at the failure to renounce 'this weapon as too terrible to use'.[111] But although Hiroshima and Nagasaki possessed the scale of a spectacular, they lacked the same instant, global transmission of the image.[112] Holding back that celluloid image muffled and ultimately managed the discourse, rendering the totalising spectacle still-born.[113] Hiroshima/Nagasaki remained Washington's controlled event, recognised for all its tragedy but justified as the least worst, geopolitical option.[114] It nevertheless confounded moral expectations among the informed. But crucially, people around the world were long denied a view of the atrocities. So it remained an act of war rather than outrage against humanity. The tragedy of the Twin Towers, 2001, remains the apogee of the spectacular. Instantaneous and totalising, it was incoherent to the hegemony, although readable by many excluded and disenfranchised populations.[115] For later perpetrators of POTD it was mundanely the biggest bang to date, a kinetic paradigm waiting to be replicated. However Bin Laden gave a more sophisticated reading of the image as message:

this Western civilisation, which is backed by America, has lost its values and appeal. The immense materialistic towers, which preach Freedom, Human Rights, and Equality, were destroyed. These values were revealed as a total mockery, as was made clear when the US government interfered and banned the media outlets from airing our words (which don't exceed a few minutes), because they felt that the truth started to appear to the American people...[116]

More succinctly he observed:

As the Twin Towers of New York collapsed, something even greater and more enormous collapsed with them: the myth of the great America and the myth of democracy.[117]

In sum, events are high drama occurrences that are predictable in their randomness and our unpreparedness. Nevertheless, media hegemony incorporates and manages them. By definition unpredictable, spectaculars are acts of dramatic violence producing moments of moral crisis that create a temporary vacuum and intend long-term readjustment in the status quo. They seek to provoke a Kuhnian paradigm shift.[118]

LIVE-ness

So-called real time, when events unfold before our eyes as they actually occur, is not the only kind of LIVE transmission that audiences witness. Television has expanded the range: each type draws on its own signs and codes. In the process viewers come to recognise different layers of actuality and truth. This reveals possibilities for different memories to resonate, for intertextual meanings to be evoked, and for media-controlled memory to be subverted. Consciously or intuitively insurgents can make use of the LIVE element of the event. Hence LIVE-ness is a rich concept.

Speed is increasingly the unifying factor of all symbolic communication.[119] LIVE-ness is its handmaid. Speed of transmission is certainly a defining component of the event and spectacular. Moreover the image encounters less friction than the word as a primary tool of communication. We are reminded of Goebbels' use of images which 'no matter how he himself manipulated them before they were released, possessed greater credibility than spoken or written words'.[120] For reading is too sedentary and reflective, destroying 'the mass's dynamic efficiency'.[121] The way we perceive technological speed is accelerating with each year, prompting Paul Virilio to revise a McLuhanism:

the limit-speed of the waves which convey messages and images is the information itself, irrespective of its content...'it is not the medium which is the message, but merely the velocity of the medium'.[122]

Speed and LIVE-ness are flows of varying magnitude and force which dissect the media landscape. Today there is a discernible trend towards shorter, more manageable durations of material. Programme and article lengths are increasingly segmented and reduced. Structurally they follow recognisable, tried-and-tested formulae. Soap-operas, sit-coms, gameshows, news, sports, and political discussion look similar, regardless of national or cultural boundaries. Conventions of presentation and performance styles, seating, lighting, music, camera angles, shot-size, and editing techniques are uniform as if by transnational osmosis. These 'globalised' formats shortcut understanding, saving time. Manageability is privileged over intellectual dexterity.[123] When communicators spill onto the web and digital television-channels, they exploit the relative spatial freedom otherwise in short supply in traditional media. But crucially speed and connectivity typify the web. Infinite space and immediate connection blur into one: there is no distance to travel, no time to wait when information is downloaded in split-seconds. Windows 3.0 ushered in instant switching and retention between multiple inputs on the same screen. People and data could be linked immediately. More importantly, contiguous states of consciousness could merge for the user. Yet even in the digital 'badlands' the possibilities are not infinite. Patience is a virtue apparently in short supply. And media organisations are not slow to pander to faltering concentration-spans. Programmes must not only be easily 'read', 'signposted', and comfortingly predictable, they must move with pace, get to the point, rarely over-problematising the proposition. News is now 'low-cal', 'news-lite', and entertainment is even 'liter'. Played out in a climate of acceleration, speed of access, ease of utility ('up-to-the-minute news', '60 second news', 'on the hour, every hour', 'rolling news', 'breaking news'), it is short-term opinion-forming, offering instant emotional gratification.

LIVE-ness is a rich concept. It goes to the heart of how we understand time. It impacts the use of the insurgent deed since it triggers subconscious levels of understanding in the audience. It reminds us we live in multiple flows of time that question daily routine. Celebrations of televised LIVE-ness have historically accompanied technological progress: LIVE-ness once seemed an end to be feted in its own right, now it is a given.[124] Familiar to audiences, it forms part of television culture. We might describe these as: (i) 'LIVE-LIVE' as actuality experienced when unfolding events like news disasters or sports matches are broadcast; (ii) 'interrupted LIVE' breaking into regular transmission schedules, denotes something considered of state importance, rarity and urgency; (iii) 'staged LIVE' is ceremonial, featuring national occasions of celebration or mourning, or inclusive sporting competitions, employing the visual language of pomp and importance;[125] (iv) 'delayed LIVE', shown minutes, even hours after original transmission sees viewers collude with producers in the pretence of LIVE authenticity (radio and television stations employ the convention: "I spoke with the minister earlier…" before replaying the interview in the present tense); (v) but 'playback LIVE' is something else, particularly seen in super-slow-motion. Familiar to viewers of sport, nature programming or feature films, it reprises events in microscopic, atomised detail of time. Thus it loosens its bond with the past, unveils a new lease of present life. By challenging the norm, it reveals a new way of seeing;[126] (vi) similarly fictional 'flashback' really belongs to the present, not the past;[127] (vii) 'pre-recorded LIVE'—New Year's Eve midnight television shows are usually pre-recorded in November but watched and accepted as if genuinely live on December 31st (performers employ in-jokes where studio and television audiences share this 'privileged' knowledge); and (viii) 'recorded and edited LIVE'—the stock of drama where LIVE is completely artificial but demands suspended disbelief to persuade viewers they are participating in a story unfolding before their eyes.

In short, LIVE-ness carries codes which audiences internalise, such awareness enabling them to manipulate different conceptions of time and memory. Immediacy carries symbolic meaning. Sporting events, music performances, journalistic reportage, announcements of state, ceremonial broadcasts, all have their own visual lexicon to communicate symbolic messages. LIVE-ness spells importance, transformative happenings, and turning-points. It can also denote inclusion, celebration, mourning. Most television, radio and even web content is recorded or archival. After all television is not CCTV.[128] Since the earliest years of television when all transmission was LIVE, the recorded programme has increasingly dominated output for reasons of cost-efficiency and reducing risk. In the process the way consumers read what it means for something to be LIVE has been absorbed into the viewing experience. The philosopher Henri Bergson best illustrates this point, understanding the present as multi-dimensional:

The past co-exists with the present that it has been; the past is preserved in itself, as past in general (non-chronological); at each moment time splits itself into present and past, present that passes and past which is preserved.[129]

Few deeds are broadcast LIVE; even fewer unfold over sufficient television time and are accorded sufficient news-significance to interrupt broadcast schedules. Most are captured by journalists following tip-offs, insurgents filming their staged attacks, or the public's random photographing or recording using mobile phones for delayed transmission. POTD's proponents set out to challenge time. Notwithstanding, at the point of transmission even recorded events take on a LIVE quality, triggering associated conventions. They interrupt the flow of continuity and normal life, underpinned by media memory. They manipulate layered time, filling it with meaning through the violent event. Joseph Nye differentiates between command (violent or coercive) and co-optive (soft) power. The latter he divides further into persuasive and attractive power. POTD functions as a rhetorical device, catalysing an alternative case to the state's viewpoint. Antithetically and counter-intuitively it attracts audiences to what in the conventional domain of public diplomacy Nye calls 'shared values and the justness and duty of contributing to the achievement of those values'.[130] So it challenges media interpretations of political events, seeking to displace the hegemony with a revolutionary discourse. But where a vacuum of understanding is revealed by the shock-and-awe spectacular, a zero-point emerges from which a newly inquisitive audience can begin to see the world afresh. The deed transmitted LIVE becomes a primary point of attack. News media are already threatened by shrinking timelines. By focusing on the LIVE event, they further reduce thinking time for actors central to the process of sustaining status quo media memory.

Turning Weakness Into Strength

If audiences and consumers are forced to negotiate with or struggle continuously against the media hegemon for independent memory, this raises an intriguing question about insurgency. Are insurgency and its handmaiden POTD concerned with powerlessness rather than powerfulness? Given that overthrowing the state must usually be considered a long shot, is much insurgency not merely a form of safety-valve, a way of the political status quo letting off steam? The counterinsurgent Frank Kitson surmised that 'insurgents start with nothing but a cause and grow to strength, while the counter-insurgents start with everything but a cause and gradually decline in strength to the point of weakness'. Once 'indoctrinated and organised', the *sine qua non* of success in modern warfare is, according to another counterinsurgent Roger Trinquier, 'the unconditional support of the population'.[131]

The charge that POTD is a tool of the powerless, that far from being active it is reactive, born of unequal resources and means, is a valid claim. Just as state terror is a use of force rooted in and sanctioned by state powerfulness, so the state-challenger's use of terror arises from powerlessness. Until, that is, it enters today's dynamic media ecology, a network of mutually communicating networks. Treated as a kinetic act, POTD's capacity is dramatic but limited whether targeted at hundreds or thousands of potential victims, no matter how many trains, planes, and office blocks are destroyed. By contrast, employed as a communications weapon, it is freed up to draw on the strengths of the insurgent, namely flexibility, speed and imagination. Above all, it aims to command the support of the people; insurgent power resides in the people. It is the solitary counter-weight to state force secured on an alliance between distanced political elites and the military.

For Trotsky, civil confrontation with counterrevolutionary force represented the inevitable, decisive test for the popular struggle: 'an insurrection is, in essence, not so much a struggle against the army as a struggle for the army'.[132] Modern armies by the turn of the twentieth century had introduced universal service, inadvertently opening up a flank to be exploited. Yet as Engels pointed out, industrial militaries had also acquired technical innovations such as rapid-fire weapons, sophisticated artillery and new communications of railways and telegraph that could outmanœuvre and out-gun, if need be, the masses at the barricades.[133] If the kinetic balance of force has further changed a century on with technologically advanced surveillance and remote weaponry, it is only to have disadvantaged the populace even more. Notwithstanding, that trend must be offset by a possibly even greater development in the very nature of conflict. The old paradigm of industrial, continental warfare has shifted, leading Rupert Smith to conclude that contemporary warfare is war fought among the people: it is

the reality in which people in the streets and houses and fields—are the battlefield....Civilians are the targets, objectives to be won, as much as an opposing force.[134]

Fundamentally, he identifies the political will of the people and the emergence of media as a converging force that neutralises state force because it exerts pressure on their political elites.[135] The longer the military fails to insert itself between insurgent and people through persuasion rather than force, the greater the scope for POTD to exert its true effect as a trigger for reconstructed memory. Charles Tilly paints popular will as an almost primordial force within society:

> Deep in every discussion of collective action stirs the lava of a volcanic eruption: collective action is about power and politics; it inevitably raises questions of right and wrong, justice and injustice, hope and hopelessness.[136]

The objective is to release that volcanic eruption. The question, therefore, is: have societies reached the stage where ideas and images functioning as weapons can overcome artillery as weapons? In the information war, played out in global media, has the asymmetric balance of force finally been redressed?

Insurgents employ violence to unseat entrenched interests in society and to eradicate norms that have become internalised in populations. As Philip Windsor points out, guerrillas primarily target the power structures of their enemy and the hegemony of social attitudes.[137] POTD is a child of mixed parentage: communications and political economy. It captures the need for change among the disenfranchised and hopeless, and helps articulate it. Indeed it so often comes to represent the only hope—a sentiment captured in the writings of Frantz Fanon. Societies do replace their governments; some go on to transform their social relations through root-and-branch restructuring of class and power relations. The French, Russian, and Chinese revolutions may be the only examples in the modern era to have created some kind of lasting (albeit short-lived in the last two cases) social transformation.[138] However, smaller acts of state overthrow exist in a variety of contexts brought about by local, regional, and geopolitical circumstance. Unlikely outcomes do not negate ambitious aims. From the comfort of democratic societies it is easy to discount insurgency as hope outrunning expectation. Yet for many marginalised populations watching a civil uprising on their televisions, violence remains the sole political tool of expression. Hence it is both cathartic vent and selective weapon.

Insurgency is more than a safety valve for the disaffected. Rebellions may be a form of violent rejection of governments while revolutions represent a more systematic and organised attempt to realise long-term change. In the twenty-first century societies face a potential watershed in the Digital Revolution. The following chapters will discuss how under certain conditions, violent images can energise and mobilise populations through the unique convergence of internet and mobile telephones interacting within feedback loops with television and press. Whether the digital mediascape can offer a new way of connecting political actors while enabling individuals and groups to mobilise, may be less contentious than whether that energy can be converted into mass organisation and direct action capable of overthrowing governments. The post-WikiLeaks climate testifies to an era when many-to-many communications are finding ways of challenging state controls. In response states, both autocratic and democratic, resort to the force of the judiciary and cyber-strikes against those they define as threats to the status quo. Castells talks of a new conceptualisation of peaceful insurgency when he reviews the accession of 'Obama the insurgent' to the White House. If he is right, then his definition no longer relies on the use of violence in the revolutionary experience.[139] Interestingly that same, erstwhile 'insurgent' now attempts to bring the full force of state power to resist an awakening insurgency in the shape of the non-violent, whistleblower website WikiLeaks as reprisal for its releasing *inter alia* hundreds of thousands of confidential US state documents detailing the wars in Afghanistan and Iraq as well as a plethora of diplomatic cables. Not to mention helicopter video footage of US forces killing unarmed Iraqis in Baghdad, complete with celebratory soundtrack. In retaliation, Obama has revisited the Espionage Act and signed presidential Executive Order 13526 (29/12/2009) to combat whistleblowers and their state-threatening information leaks.[140] In the light of the transformation in the mediascape and technologies that allow consumers direct access to the means of diffusing information into politically charged polities, the conventional view of insurgent weakness demands review. How weakness turns into strength, is discussed further in subsequent chapters.

* * *

In the late twentieth century television became the all-pervasive medium for gathering information and enjoying entertainment, impacting the world's urban populations and increasingly rural communities. But in its terrestrial form, and even in its later digital, satellite guise it retained control of a one-to-many relationship with its viewers. That would begin to change by the millennium, openly restoring a balance which some already acknowledged had always been there but not given its due. Regardless of audiences' weak position within the social relations of the producer-consumer relationship, they have always participated in an iterative communications triangle between state, media, and public. Insurgents attempted to reconfigure the triangle, conflating state and media into one hegemon. This would create a new triangle allowing insurgent and population to engage in a renewed iterative process with state-media. POTD now represents shock and awe politics. Through seismic spectaculars it provokes audiences to fill the moment of incomprehension with new meaning. By freeze-framing time, POTD undermines the continuity of everyday, unquestioned life. It jolts audiences into cognitive dissonance brought about by destabilising time and the way they view LIVE events unfold on television. By staging regular smaller events it triggers resonance between previous acts, connecting like-minded people and iconic places in archipelagos of grievance and cosmology. With the proliferation of global satellite television, the opportunities increased dramatically to link multiple populations and distil anti-state enmity. It would be a slow and uphill road, least of all since many audiences are socialised to reject political violence as a way of resolving even apparently intractable problems. But even this new phase of POTD would soon be supplanted.

Mumbai 2008: Taj Hotel attack.
© Chirodeep Chaudhuri.

6

WHERE THE IMAGINARY MEETS THE VIRTUAL

Online, there are no full stops; the story goes on forever.

Janice Turner[1]

Television as the dominant force in modern communications and insurgency is only part of a wider story. A decade into the new millennium we find ourselves on a technological cusp, facing a digital revolution that has prompted discussion of another 'horse-tank moment' in military affairs.[2] So significant is it, contends the head of Britain's armed forces, that it calls for a complete rethink in the way modern states prepare for future warfare. Hence when he argues 'the screen is our generation's north German plain',[3] the cause of the transformation is not only states' ability to attack other states by engaging in netwarfare.[4] Rather, it is populations' access to cheap, digital technologies which enables informed groups within those populations to mobilise and strike at the state itself.[5]

This chapter examines how migrant diasporas and social networks have been brought closer together by digital technologies in the Information Age, and how social movements, either once 'under the radar' of states or newly emergent, affect slow-moving state bureaucracies. For proponents of insurgency violence, this increases the population of sympathisers and recruits for collective action with the potential to evade the state. i) Digital communications surges; ii) diasporas and social networks; and iii) the consequent dilemma faced by modern states will be discussed.

My argument in this chapter is that recently Propaganda of the Deed has made a radical shift with potentially dramatic consequences. It has become a central operating concept in insurgent strategy. This does not limit POTD to a kinetic, military effect. Nor does it define it simply as symbolic, a communications device that propagates a revolutionary message reliant on repetitive use of violent imagery, and so triggering ideological grievance. Indeed neither precludes the other. However since the 1990s it has become possible for insurgents to move the deed to the centre of their strategic thinking. Such actions may switch quickly between planned operations and serendipitous opportunity: what counts is communicative outcome not purity of intent. This major departure in the way insurgencies are fought takes into account three factors: the increased role of words, ideas, and images in the battle for hearts and minds; the ability to shift vast amounts of data that contain these ideas and images, but in binary form, fast and inexpensively across global populations with relative ease; and the uniquely 'viral' way people use new technologies and engage with this data. This allows population groups to take control of information, and refashion and disseminate it potentially faster than states can respond with official versions of events. Television historically represented a 'one-to-many' medium where investment costs and complexity of technology defined and restricted ownership and control to the few who acted as editorial gatekeepers. We now face a world of 'many-to-many' or peer-to-peer communicators where access is determined only by the price of a mobile phone, computer laptop, and access to the internet. Media-systems and industries meanwhile remain in the ownership of the corporate minority. However despite that ownership the so-called Digital Revolution has increased users' freedom to originate and control the movement of their own ideas and content. Admittedly, the cost of access lies beyond the reach of many marginalised people around the world. Yet even amid relative poverty, mobile phones have had an impact; their take-up leap-frogs other new technologies. Particularly where telephone companies target a business model based on extending high volume use rather than high unit profit.[6] Such reduction in Clausewitzian friction ('the force that makes the apparently easy so difficult')[7] or what Coase calls 'trans-action cost'[8] paves the way for these new, distinctive tools to change the way people communicate. It enables 'action by loosely structured groups, operating without managerial direction and outside the profit motive': namely network communication.[9]

Surges, Flows and Scapes

If we are to declare a revolution in communications, then 'a radical change in both communications and society resulting from the introduction of a new medium' must be apparent.[10] As the internet theorist Clay Shirky indicates, '(r)evolution doesn't happen when society adopts new technologies—it happens when society adopts new behaviours'.[11] What singles out digital and virtual technologies is the speed of transmission, fluidity and self-generating nature of its content. That in turn affects how people behave. Hence Gordon Graham concludes that a revolutionary technology must lay claim to the 'radically new' not merely the 'novel'. Television may foster a passivity among its viewers which is a boon to power-elites. But the internet and web satisfy a key criterion of transforming technologies: they extend power to ordinary citizens with the potential to effect greater control over their social and political well-being.[12] So too do mobile phones. The UN's International Telecommunications Union (ITU) records 45% of inhabitants in the developing world, where mobile phone uptake is globally at its strongest, had a mobile phone by December 2007; even though less than 20% had Internet use.[13]

Such a transformation arises from digital's intrinsic characteristics that offer clear advantages over analogue technology. Digital enables mass compression of information; increases storage capacity almost indefinitely; accelerates dissemination globally and almost instantaneously; enables fast copying and multiplication from the original master; facilitates easy manipulation and re-use by consumers employing standardised software; and increases portability in miniaturised laptops, cameras, memory sticks, mobile phones. Added to the attributes of the internet, this produces a dynamic combination. Since the net is a physical, networked infrastructure with in-built redundancy, originally designed to survive external attack, internet protocols find ways round blockages and damage. Furthermore information is broken down into data packages: small pieces sent across multiple channels of the net, which find their own way willy-nilly to recipients where they are reconstituted, replicating the original information master. This makes for speedy, high volume transmission. Moreover the net is a largely unregulated architecture, an indefinite space with no central control, providing a digital commons which insurgents can share with states.

Digital technologies comprise computer and mobile telephony hardware, audio-visual software, internet infrastructure and airtime that link distant, disparate and divergent populations variously via wireless networks, micro-wave and satellite connections. Individuals thus communicate directly with each other using picture and sound, while cutting out the middle-men—the so-called media gatekeepers. The volume of distribution of these rises as costs fall with mass production efficiencies and consumer market take-up is stimulated by infrastructure investment. Nevertheless penetration varies dramatically between and within countries. Less developed rural economies often provide theatres of insurgent conflict. But even here a mobile phone, as once televisions, may be shared by an entire community or be in widespread use by individuals.[14] Historical barriers between widely distributed urban-dwellers who now form half the world's population, are circumvented by this recent global connectivity. Hence most people's contact with the rest of the world is changing.

The mobile phone's comparative advantage is that it meets the apparent human desire for adaptable and portable technology, and can initiate communication at relatively low cost. It is anticipated that this single consumer good in the form of a smart phone[15] will eventually access the computing power, memory, and multiple functions currently confined to most current household computers and laptops.[16] In short, mobile phones appeal to people's desire for freedom of expression and freedom of movement. Equally 'mobile phone spaces'[17] promise disparate individuals a more fluid sense of togetherness and identification. This may supersede those virtual 'imagined communities' that the reactive process of watching television, listening to radio or reading newspapers or books had hitherto fostered. Computers, laptops and mobile phones inspire users to realise identity communities through regular, active and direct contact. But combine their power by allowing roaming mobile phone-users to access social network sites via low-priced mobile broadband, and population reach expands dramatically.[18]

The Internet meanwhile is an indefinite space, 'a never-ending worldwide conversation'.[19] Cyberspace is not just one space but many, reflecting distinctive characters of diverse communities.[20] The web's attraction is evidenced by its speed of growth, unprecedented in the history of communications.[21] Nevertheless for its detractors it remains unreal, a 'soluble tissue of nothingness'.[22] For devotees, it can be inhabited but neither circumscribed nor regulated by governments.[23] It decouples individuals and communities from their real-world terrain; then it reconnects them in 'virtual communities' that Howard Rheingold describes as 'social aggregations that emerge from the Net when enough people carry on...public discussions long enough, with sufficient human feeling, to form webs of personal relationships in cyberspace'.[24] There they form a new *Gemeinschaft*.[25] To this end users explore the web, connecting to millions of fellow-users with the aid of standardised search engines. It goes further still: it extends choice to these actors. And choice is increasingly being built into the web's business models. While some web companies like Yahoo and AOL offer users portals through which to connect to other users, the most dynamic, like Google, according to its champions, understand 'we are individuals who live in an almost infinite universe of small communities of interest, information, and geography'. Portals with ageing, restrictive business models seek to 'control content and distribution and think they can own customers'. Not so for firms which offer platforms. Acting purely as facilitators, these recognise the freedom of users to choose, to make their own connections *ad infinitum*.[26]

So for insurgents, clear benefits flow from the Digital Revolution. Confronted by the Honda car salesman offering cruise-control as standard with his purchase, Neil Postman poses him a 'Luddite' question: 'What is the problem to which cruise-control is the answer?'[27] We might ask: 'what is the problem to which the computer laptop is the answer?' Problem: insurgents need to send out intricate messages with data-rich, live action images and text. Answer: computer laptops expand data and image capture, and provide processing power. Similarly, 'what is the problem to which the mobile phone is the answer?' Problem: how to communicate with many while staying on the move. Answer: for insurgents, mobile phones offer mobility and connectivity. And smart phones? These combine mobile phones with the facility to take still and moving pictures, receive and send out computer files, and connect users to the net. And what problem does the Internet answer? How can insurgent messages connect the most people with the least effort invested: the net has global, instantaneous reach.

Networks in Real and Virtual Worlds

For insurgents what marks out the internet is its ability to create a 'network effect'. Such an effect is not new. Fixed-line telephone companies like America's Bell and AT&T identified the economic benefits of 'network externality'—exponential growth in connections—nearly a century ago.[28] If two phone-users speak there is one link containing two paths of communication. When three people are connected then six paths, if four then twelve, and so on. Today with the digital internet the process is easier, cheaper, and costs the same no matter how many additional communicants the user connects to. Each new subscriber brings added value to the existing members and network as a whole, whether intended or not. Using web navigation tools, like browser applications (which offer up and retrieve information resources on the web) or search engines (which seek and find web pages), these hyperlinks (multiple connections) can create epidemics or viral loops. Hence the numbers under particular conditions become astronomical, since viral loops are positive feedback loops on a mass scale.

Social networks are collections of individuals or organisations (nodes) that are connected by relationships (links) of friendship, family, interest, business or common values. They are neither new nor dependent on technology. Intersecting all societies, traditional, agricultural, and industrial, they are not contingent on Western notions of economic development.[29] However networked cyber-communities that emerge on the internet do nevertheless represent a different and particular type of social movement: they are self-generating. As each communication invites ever more communications, so shared understandings emerge, creating a common identity and living community.[30] 'Tacit knowledge'[31] or knowledge that arises out of experience characterises these 'communities of practice'. Here individual members engage with the world as social beings developing common practices.[32] According to Michael Polanyi 'we can know more than we can tell'.[33] For some in the business world this thinking has led to a 'Big Shift' in work practice.[34] For other observers its application is even broader, infiltrating all society. Only by understanding how social network communities are structured and social capital (reciprocal relationships) is shaped within them, can we appreciate how violent images and insurgent ideas pass through them.

Social Capital

At the heart of social networks sits social capital. For James Coleman it parallels financial, physical and human forms of capital.[35] It is the glue, 'the stickiness' that binds communities, groups, families or revolutionary cells in reciprocity and trust. At its simplest, according to Robert Putnam, it appears in two forms—bonding and bridging. Bonding is a kind of 'sociological superglue' often identified with grievance-communities, while bridging oils the wheels of community relations like 'sociological WD-40'. Hence it is common to proselytising groups. They are not mutually exclusive. Like financial capital, social capital may be used to good or bad effect. 'Social movements also create social capital, by fostering new identities and extending social networks', says Putnam. He charts how these can be adversely impacted by technological change, with the dilution of community and decline in attendance of America's bowling clubs since the 1950s under television's onslaught. This progressively turned people into 'stay-at-homes', thus loosening their social ties. '(A) dense network of social relations' characterises this concept, not a community of isolated beings, however individually well-intentioned.[36]

In 1960s America, the counter-culture or 'Movement' produced a melting-pot of activism across university campuses and civil society. Luther Gerlach's studies examined Black Power, evangelical, and sexual rights groups among many that flourished. His analysis offers broader context to understanding networks. In it he interrogates traditional bias against what he saw as segmented structures, a bias rooted in the conviction that vertical, hierarchical bureaucracies were inherently efficient. Instead of an amorphous mass, he saw segmented structures acting as loose coalitions between militant and peaceful protesters within a web of affiliation groups. Yet each group continued its own agenda embracing civil rights, racial equality, black separatism, sexual freedom, or ecology. Nevertheless they co-operated. He extrapolated three factors from the 'Movement'. They displayed (i) segmentary organisation where diverse cells grow, coalesce, divide, and proliferate; (ii) polycephalous structure where there are many leaders but no central command-and-control hierarchy; and (iii) networked or reticulate form, meaning linkages extend out from a group into other autonomous cells in society, creating new ties.[37] The advantages of this structure for him are clear. They are 'highly effective and adaptive in innovating and producing social change and in surviving in the face of established order opposition'.[38]

Four decades on, the effect of networked, polycephalous or acephalous, and segmentary organisations can be viewed afresh as they map onto the network of the worldwide web.[39] The internet and its predecessor ARPANET were created as a communications and command-and-control network capable of surviving attack on any one or multiple points.[40] It would achieve this through flat, non-hierarchical structure. Networks broadly appear in three forms: chain, as in a linear smuggling chain where one individual has contact only with his/her neighbour; hub (star or wheel), as in a franchise where decisions must pass through a central but non-hierarchical figure; and complex (full-matrix or all-channel), where all actors are connected to varying degrees to others, as in social movements (this does not preclude certain players from dominating command-and-control processes).[41] All paradigms share common attributes of nodes (key players) and links (their relationships). The existence of organisational hierarchies within all these flat networks varies. But significantly network form is characterised by its fluidity and ability to grow or separate. Consequently velocity of movement and decentralised decision-making differentiate it from more vertically structured hierarchies around which bureaucratic states are built. However the complexity that typifies a bureaucratic hierarchy is different from that of a network. The significant point is that networks have flatter command-and-control structures. Hierarchies have more layers of management through which incoming information must ascend and be analysed, before a policy response or decision is shaped and transmitted downwards. Greater friction arises from human processes of inertia, dissent, or intra- and inter-organisational isolation. It should however be noted that even hierarchies contain networks while networks have varying degrees of hierarchical decision-making.

Self-Generating Communications

When virtual social networks communicate information there is a multiplier effect as new links within the population continually evolve.[42] The defining dimension of this new development is illuminated by exponents of complex, non-linear adaptive systems. As the physicist Fritjof Capra suggests, these are '(l)iving networks' which '...are self-generating'. Hence

(e)ach communication creates thoughts and meanings, which give rise to further communications. In this way, the entire network generates itself, producing a common context of meaning, shared knowledge, rules of conduct, a boundary and a collective identity for its members.[43]

Emergence theories attempt to unravel how decentralised systems cohere as a 'superorganism' in nature[44] and technology. Keller and Segal's slime mould aggregation experiment[45] offers an intriguing insight. By observing how single-celled units behave as individuals and groups depending on changes in climatic conditions, they note such cells move separately searching out nourishment when food supply is short in warmer weather, but coalesce forming a single group, and 'swarm' when temperatures cool and sustenance is more abundant. Earlier theories of 'pacemaker' slime cells acting like generals and releasing compounds as 'instructions' to neighbouring cells were challenged. In effect, this suggested the absence of any hierarchical command-and-control system since no scientific research could identify 'the generals'. Keller's experiments proposed the opposite. That cells were self-organising from below using trails of individually generated pheromones that others would follow. All acted in positive feedback loops, but crucially without requiring a leader.[46] The relevance of this line of inquiry is twofold: first, it is analogous to how networked insurgency groups such as those within the Al-Qaeda cluster of models are believed by some to self-organise;[47] and second, how ideas flow through populations in the new digital information era. Both challenge hierarchical structures familiar to advanced industrial societies. Apparently unpredictable but on closer scrutiny discernible, decentralised movements of bees, ants, fish, and birds are considered alternative ways of conceptualising how networked and large groups function.[48]

'Moreness' (volume) is created by two methods says Kevin Kelly: via linear production which is the basis of the factory assembly-line (sequential); or the swarm model (web), a 'patchwork of parallel operations' where 'action proceeds in a messy cascade of interdependent events'.[49] Ning is a company whose business model capitalises on 'swarming', that is self-generating growth. It provides web-based platforms free for people to create do-it-yourself social networks. Ning boasts: 'Get your Ning Network up and running in less than 30 seconds. Go viral. Exponential growth is in our DNA'. Its site hosts myriad interest-groups whose subscribers join to share common identities, for 'the world's organisers, activists and influencers to create social experiences that inspire action'.[50] Ning set up business in February 2007. Adam Penenberg notes, by month 4 it had 60,000 networks, by month 6 already 80,000. By April 2009 worldwide it counted 1.3 million social networks, 29 million users, having already surpassed 2.7

billion page views per month.[51] In each group every member expands the membership base of the network by signing up new friends or contacts. The process continues as each new friend or contact does the same. It is not the platform provider who does the work, but members themselves driven by the desire to belong to a group. What matters in the numbers game of viral expansion is the viral coefficient which is calculated on the sign-up rate of new members. Anything under 1, the growth curve plotted on a graph slows fairly rapidly (10 members at 0.6 coefficient delivers 25 members; 10 at 0.9 becomes 75). But over 1, an exponential curve develops (the same 10 people at 1.2 increase to 1,271 in the same time-frame).[52] As viral networks expand they create momentum, a multiplier effect: the bigger the network, the faster the growth.[53] Crucially, the more chance there is of the network being hit by a user.[54] It is all about critical mass. So if an idea or an image catches the public imagination, the chances of its rapid and ubiquitous dissemination can be high.

For Malcolm Gladwell, if an idea is to take off and spread through a population, two things are required. First that it be 'sticky', second it be championed by the right kind of person.[55] Stickiness happens when messages make an impact: 'you can't get it out of your head'. There is no preordained formula of what defines a 'sticky' idea, catchy song or lasting image. Nonetheless, once identified, 'relatively simple changes in the presentation and structuring of information…can make a big difference in how much of an impact it makes'.[56] But *per se* a message has no guarantee of sticking. It needs to be helped on its way by key individuals as focal points in a community: what complexity theorists call attractors.[57] This process is otherwise known as the Law of the Few: certain people are able to make an idea cross the 'tipping point' into mass adoption. For Gladwell these comprise three human types: connectors, maven, and salesmen. Each has distinctive characteristics and skills, and exists in all communities. Connectors have a wide circle of contacts and enjoy linking people together: 'they manage to occupy many different worlds and subcultures and niches'.[58] Mavens are knowledge accumulators—the 'go-to-guys' who 'connect(s) people to the marketplace and [have] the inside scoop on the marketplace'.[59] But they are not persuaders. Whereas salesmen are persuaders, influencing others emotionally: what psychologists call 'senders'.[60] The relevance of this discussion to the change in insurgency is that new communities of like-minded individuals can be connected at high speed and in great numbers by new digital technology, and in the process ideas may move through populations aided by certain types of actor common to all societies.

This analysis might be considered too simplistic. A tendency in social sciences to use imprecise metaphors borrowed from pure sciences, like 'contagion' and 'epidemic', obscures the fact that disease travels from one person to the next in a mathematically predictable way: each new contagion-event is independent. If you are sick, your immediate neighbour will either be infected or not. Whereas in social contagion counter intuitively 'the impact of one person's action on another depends critically on what other influences the latter has been exposed to'.[61] Therefore there are greater externalities to be weighed. In social contagion too, whether others are 'infected' by your innovation depends on the number of people in your network. Too many and your voice is diluted, so your message or idea fails to activate others. Too few, and although you are more influential as a fraction of a smaller group, chances are your group will be too small to make sufficient connections necessary for any message to jump externally between groups or networks. Therefore the innovation fails to reach a critical mass or create a 'global cascade'. Cascades continually course through society as ideas, fads, or fashions. But most die out quickly. Few go 'global', acquiring the key dimension of being self-perpetuating. Of these even fewer endure to have a lasting or rarer still, universal effect.[62] Social groups comprise 'vulnerable' and 'stable' nodes or individuals. To be vulnerable means to be more readily influenced, then activated. In retail these are known as early adopters, people who dive first into the marketplace to buy the latest iPod or car. The more numerous and connected the early adopters in a community, the greater chance of innovations catching hold and spreading through the population.[63]

For the last six decades, at the heart of marketing and advertising has reigned the belief that we are all influenced by the opinions of key individuals in our networks of acquaintance. This builds on communications research undertaken using Ohio voter patterns in the 1940 presidential election and refined a decade later, that developed the notion of a two-step flow of communication: namely, that voters were more influenced by their peers than directly by the mass media.[64] One American agency, Roper ASW and its marketing executives would plough the same furrow, talking of 'The Influentials'. Indeed Keller and Berry went on to argue that one in every ten Americans influenced the other nine.[65] More recently, public relations company Burson-Marsteller took their analysis online. They concluded that 'E-fluentials make waves': they pass on positive experiences to 11 others on average and negative views to 17 people, and that it happens 93% of the time in person or by phone, and 87% via e-mail.[66] However, this unusually precise calculation perhaps overestimates the power of a few opinion-leaders. The mathematician Duncan Watts counters that the evidence simply does not support such a view. What is missing is a clearer definition of the processes by which people influence others. Thus by programming a sample of 10,000 contributors, Watts' observations determined that the key criterion was not who started a trend, but how receptive society was to adopting it and when. Hence those who began the process of influence were really 'accidental influentials'. 'Understanding that trends in public opinion are driven not by a few influentials influencing everyone else but by many easily influenced people influencing one another', was closer the mark, he proposed. And '(b)ecause the ultimate impact of any individual—highly influential or not—depends on decisions made by people one, two or more steps away from her or him', too great a chance exists for those further down the line simply to resist or ignore the stimulus, thus hindering the spread of any epidemic. So rather than rely on the few, a wider word-of-mouth base should be sought in the first instance, a 'big-seed' approach to sewing ideas to stimulate cascades.[67] This questioning of the entrenched orthodoxy renders any understanding of how revolutionary ideas spread through actual or virtual crowds even more problematic.

Not all insurgent movements seek similar linkage and nor do they share identical access to media systems and technology. Some prefer relative isolation, focusing on recruitment and targeting objectives locally, such as India's Maoist Naxalites, Peru's Shining Path, Cuba's anti-Castro groups and Malaysia's civil society groups.[68] Others connect to their migratory diasporas for funding like, until recently, Sri Lanka's LTTE (Tamil Tigers)[69] and the Provisional IRA, but their focus remains internal and national. Some like Mexico's EZLN (Zapatistas) centre on local, indigenous issues but campaign internationally seeking solidarity networks via the internet and video distribution. Colombia's Revolutionary Armed Forces (FARC) similarly employ multiple websites in six languages with links for e-mail.[70] So too does Palestine's Hamas reach out online: their international offering includes a comic-strip website targeting young children.[71] Burma's pacifist Aung San Suu

Kyi campaigned for years from outside the country before returning to lead the democracy struggle, thus blending the transnational with the parochial.[72] Others such as Salafi groups aspire to aggregate Muslim communities worldwide into one constituency, unified by faith. Here also there is historical disjuncture between jihadis who favour striking the 'near enemy' and transnationalists who target the 'far enemy'.[73] Overall, such geographical diversity, according to Gabriel Weimann, hides the fact that many are transnational or transregional.[74] However, the technological penetration of urban and increasingly rural communities opens up fresh possibilities for all groups. What raises digital media above instrumental levels of simply connecting people is the ability of these links to support surges of group commitment and enthusiasm. This may yet belie Harold Lasswell's insight that '(p)rofessional revolutionaries can work most effectively in their own culture, even as international war propaganda is most effective when the fellow-national is kept in the foreground'.[75]

So whether ideas progress in cyberspace depends on their being sticky and influenced by key individuals—'salesmen' who move them through networks. But such activity is turbulent. Web surges and cascades rely on freedom to cross national borders and circumnavigate global circuits of communication unrestricted. They are self-organising, digital communications between aggregated individuals transmitted at high speed. An idea that gains traction in one social group can trigger to adjacent groups.[76] Members sympathetically and synchronously[77] propel the same image or message, which may be enhanced or remain unaltered during its passage from one user to the next.[78] 'Weak ties' matter more than 'strong ties' according to sociologist Mark Granovetter: they extend the range of a person's network. Loose acquaintances are likely to offer a wider spread of contacts unknown to oneself than close friends and to be less socially involved with each another. Close friends form dense 'clumps'. So weak ties connect multiple dense 'clumps' in ways individuals could otherwise not access. From a communications perspective they help individuals break out from being 'fragmented and incoherent'.[79] Digital technologies make this process more fluid, instant, and far-reaching: what was once person-to-person or 'word of mouth' now becomes virtual and viral. Indeed as systems become more complex, notes the theoretical physicist Per Bak, 'fluctuations and catastrophes are unavoidable'.[80] Anyone who expects constant, trouble-free equilibrium will be disappointed:

'(t)here has to be a constant flow of energy to maintain the organisation of the system and to ensure its survival. Equilibrium is another word for death'.[81] The exponential capacity of the technology multiplies the message into an epidemic. It spreads to, from and through the workplace, street or home requiring only cellphone or laptop. Its intent may be local, moving from friend to friend or acquaintance. Or it may be global, dispatched into a universe of imagined but unknown receivers. Regardless, the effect is the same. The point is there is neither divide nor barrier. Nor is there a controlling centre in the spiderless web. Information flows proliferate in an *ad hoc*, exponential fashion and crucially may explode in number in brief time-spans, unexpectedly and randomly. So images and ideas can travel within groups who share common identity, and between groups with different defining identities since individuals are members of more than one group at a time,[82] each performing the role of 'gatekeeper'.

Given the porous and multifaceted nature of identity groups, and contiguity of cultural communities that people occupy (professional, recreational, educational, religious, ethnic), traditional divides present fewer obstacles to their progress. This has not gone unnoticed by insurgent groups. The largest social network site Facebook was targeted in December 2008 by pro-jihadi contributors to al-Faloja Islamic Forums. Users were encouraged to 'invade' Facebook and create sympathiser groups that could proselytise the jihadi message. Murad Batal al-Shishani observes a near immediate dividend. Pakistani authorities revealed five American Muslims arrested in Pakistan in December 2009 had been recruited via YouTube and Facebook. They had contacted insurgent groups Lashkar-e-Taiba and Lashkar-e-Jhangvi. A US Department of Homeland Security official told the *Washington Post*: '(o)nline recruiting has exponentially increased with Facebook, YouTube and the increasing sophistication of people online'. However, what militates against real success, says Thomas Hegghammer, is the ease of monitoring by site operators and intelligence services. So although mainstream and radical political parties and groups widely use such sites, Al-Qaeda affiliates' penetration is limited to softer, persuasive campaign material. Anything harder falls prey to speedy removal.[83]

Global cultural flows, says anthropologist Arjun Appadurai, 'occur in and through the growing disjunctures between ethnoscapes, technoscapes, finanscapes, mediascapes and ideoscapes'.[84] His scapes sound quite abstract. However they are like 'discourses', or 'social practices which are produced, re-produced, contested, and transformed only in so far as they are meaningful for specific, situated social actors'.[85] Fluid identities are made possible by people's exposure to media images and migration.[86] Mike Featherstone highlights the 'aestheticisation of everyday life' through media.[87] While for John Urry, increased travel and 'gazing' at the unfamiliar only serve to enhance this tendency.[88] Greater prosperity and faster connectedness encourage more privileged beneficiaries to move cognitively back and forth between different ways of seeing themselves in the world. So for Appadurai mediascapes sit on top of 'image-centred, narrative-based accounts of strips of reality': they shape how we see ourselves. Meanwhile ideoscapes are 'concatenations of images' which capture ideologies: states employ them to retain state power and state-challengers use them to gain it.[89] What this means for those familiar dialectics we use to interpret the world (centre-periphery dynamics, push-and-pull migration, consumer-producer relations) is they fall away to be replaced by more fluid landscapes. These become 'building blocks' of 'imagined worlds'. No longer are many people free to inhabit merely 'imagined communities', but rather 'imagined worlds'.[90] Exploiting the cracks that appear within the complexity of 'disorganised capitalism', means individuals are 'progressively less synchronised within national boundaries'[91] in what Kenichi Ohmae calls a 'borderless world' where nations are now 'fictions'. Thus they become deterritorialised, cut off from familiar ways of defining themselves locally.[92] What now counts is the ability to move through networks, because

(t)he movement, the flows of capital, money, commodities, labour, information and images across time and space are only comprehensible if 'networks' are taken into account because it is through networks that these subjects and objects are able to gain mobility.[93]

Such a view of societies is resisted by the less privileged. However porous weak states may be at their territorial borders, advanced industrial markets are less than welcoming for workers from developing countries seeking employment through migration. Stronger states consistently apply selective constraints at their own borders on the free movement of labour. Whatever life-changes are conjured in the minds of would-be migrants, they are inconsistently evidenced by the 'irresistible forces' and 'immovable ideas' of the global political economy.[94] Notwithstanding, traditional movements of goods and people may not resemble the way information, data and information traffic transect digital infrastructures. While computer access may be restricted in many countries, mobile telephony is advancing apace which may suggest how apparently spontaneous information will eventually diffuse through even marginalised populations.

This contextualises how information flowed virally during the electoral collapse of Spain's Aznar Government following the Madrid train bombing of 2004.[95] One mobile phone SMS (text) message from one Spaniard produced dramatic and unforeseeable consequences.[96] Urging his friends to stage a peaceful protest at the party headquarters of Spain's ruling Conservatives (*Partido Popular*), his brief message quickly brought about mass dissent. Each of ten friends who received it sent it on to a further ten of their friends, until soon after the rendezvous hour a crowd exceeding 5,000 had assembled. They complained Prime Minister Aznar had deliberately suppressed evidence linking Al-Qaeda to the Madrid bombing which had killed 199 people and injured 1,400. He was suspected of personally intervening with press and broadcasters and attempting to divert the blame onto Basque separatists ETA (*Euskadi Ta Askatasuna*). Predictably, so soon before polling-day, an Al-Qaeda strike might be interpreted as terrorist retribution for Aznar's over-enthusiastic support for Bush and Blair and their Iraq incursion. It boded ill for the government's chances of being returned by Spain's electorate. The SMS messaging campaign once activated, spread like a virus. Demonstrators poured onto the streets of Spanish cities, capturing the attention of mainstream media who reported then multiplied the protesters' outrage. Soon King Juan Carlos weighed into the growing controversy setting off renewed feedback loops. Barely three days after the terrorist bombing, Aznar's Conservatives lost the election. The event demonstrated the power of horizontal media networks to trigger feedback loops with traditional mainstream media. Significantly it showed how horizontal, self-generating popular will could transform into collective action.[97] So much so that Castells described it as an act of insurgency using mass self-communication. Although he highlights the unpredictable outcomes of such social movements and insurgent actions, commenting: 'we only know if collective actions were actually subjects of social change in the aftermath of the action'.[98]

SMS is the unintended consequence of the cellphone industry. Lippman sees Spain's mass adoption of SMS as consistent with other forms of viral communication: it 'taught us that synchrony with the culture is more important than technology for some features—it was the populace at large that made it succeed, not the operators themselves'.[99] But using text messaging to create 'flash mobs' enabled spontaneous and leaderless diffusion of information through an emergent network in minimal time. Crucially what it achieves is to substitute many-to-many for one-to-many communication. This reinforces the confrontation between adhocracy (social networks) and bureaucracy (states).[100] There was a precedent for Aznar's demise at the hands of a 'smart mob':[101] Philippines' President Joseph Estrada fell in 2001. Then over a million Manila residents dressed in black, texted, and coalesced over a four-day period to express 'People Power', forcing his political end.[102]

Iran's Islamic Revolution (1978–9) had witnessed nightly scenes of inhabitants of neighbourhoods bashing pots and pans at twilight as a mark of protest. But in 2009 it was Twitter[103] that would help mobilise disaffected voters via hourly message updates on mobile phones. Iran's 'fraudulent' or flawed election result brought an estimated 1.5 to 2 million protesters onto the streets.[104] Linked and prompted *inter alia* by 65,000 members of a Facebook site called 'I Love Iran', angry Iranians read '(t)he march in Tehran is still on.[105] Any rumours that you hear are all propaganda from the government to make you stay away from the rally. Come to the rally at 4 and march for your freedom!'[106]

The volume of mobile and internet traffic surrounding Iran's violence of June 2009 was such that it quickly crashed the servers of Chinese-based Global Internet Freedom Consortium. The organisation was obliged to shut for maintenance before re-opening a restricted service with more manageable capacity. Iranian protesters reportedly demanded normal service be resumed, including YouTube, despite its requirement for greater bandwidth. It prompted the company to conclude: 'we can see that once we have this kind of tools available for the people, then you'll find and use it [sic]. We didn't do any promotion in Iran at all because…we are a Chinese group…But they found our services by themselves and there were millions of users in Iran using this service'.[107]

A dramatic spur to outraged protest in Iran was the killing of Neda Agha-Soltan.[108] More accurately, it was the image of the dying student that was the catalyst, captured on mobile phones by two bystanders. Reproduced in official and unofficial media around the world, it sublimated in the form of a graphic icon. Thus Neda-as-icon served to distil the complexity of the political struggle: 'All struggles are so complex and there are different interpretations of it…I think a story like Neda summarises it, sums it up in a single event', noted one observer.[109] The event fired websites in many countries outside Iran to post messages such as:'(t)hen rise up against your oppressors. It's that simple. There is power in numbers. All it takes is for one to be the first to say, "Enough is enough"'.[110]

Nevertheless it should be stressed to date there has been no reprise of Iran's successful revolution of thirty years ago. In mitigation, defenders of the opposition Green Movement concede successive set-backs lay not in the fact that 'we were few in number', rather 'we were aimless'.[111] Therein may lie a broader lesson.

Similarly in South Korea teenage reaction against importing American beef suspected of mad cow disease precipitated web dissent from television celebrity sites to Agora, an online discussion site in April 2008. 1.3 million signatures collected in a week led to thousands of protesters co-ordinating via text messaging and spilling onto the streets of the capital. 'Citizen journalists' interviewed other teenagers for web-casting to blogs and forums. Numerous websites broadcast a police attack on one girl, and the demonstrations LIVE. The 'mad cow' label was quickly mobilised, extending to generalised anti-government campaigns ('mad cow health care'; 'mad cow education'; 'mad cow labour relations'). Significantly '(i)t was the Net Geners who led the protest. This huge upheaval in Korean society was driven by teenagers'.[112] Conversely for state representatives like Hillary Rodham Clinton this kind of groundswell can undermine state-challengers. Thus a 13-year-old boy organising blood drives through social network sites after the Mumbai attack, an unemployed Colombian engineer who brought 12 million people in 190 cities around the world to demonstrate against FARC activities, and one e-mail resulting in 150,000 protesters marching in Mexico City against drug-related violence underscore this 'freedom to connect' as cyberspace's 'freedom of assembly'.[113] But crucially a force that can subvert the insurgent message can equally undermine state communications: it has no loyalty.

Acephalous, emergent, and speedy forms of communication set contemporary states, both democratic and authoritarian, a new problem: whom or what to attack.[114] It is a common feature between non-violent collective actors and their violent counterparts who utilise POTD. Increasingly various social media, the internet, mobile telephony, Twitter and Facebook, enable the dissemination of information along a spectrum that aims at ideological persuasion, didactic instruction, or shock-and-awe revelation. It becomes what Albert Einstein predicted as the 'information bomb', but in the 'globalisation of the collective imaginary'.[115] Equally where a consumer appliance acts as camera, computer, sound- and picture-communicator, the convergence of technologies through combination and miniaturisation into a single platform is enhanced by two key aspects. Both impact individuals. As producers, people are mobile, emancipated, and unrestricted by place. As recipients, they are constantly contactable without the intervention of any mediator. By the same token, it should be noted, they become trackable by state surveillance. Today's apogee of convergence is the mobile phone.[116] Through the 'instantaneous superimposition of actual and virtual images',[117] time and space contract to expose fresh dimensions for the visual and violent deed and its message. POTD merges real life with the imaginary.

The power of violent images—whether administered by insurgents or states—raises a fundamental question: even given the speed and force of Web 2.0's information surges, can emotional outpourings and mobilising protest translate into collective action? What Henry Jenkins sees as mobilising 'collective intelligence to transform governance', still falls short of insurgent direct action. This goes to the heart of Information Warfare itself.[118] Where is the connection between civil disturbance fed by subversive images, and 'organised' or channelled direct action capable of overthrowing states? If movements are to surmount *Mother Courage's* dilemma ('your anger was short-lived and you need it to be long'),[119] sustaining emotion and directing its force are critical. Any simple equation that assumes newly liberated flows of information lead to popular power, as Twitter executives proclaim, is questionable.[120] Laurie Perry, a researcher on the 'Digital Britain' governmental programme argues, like cyber scholar Evgeny Morozov, that online resistance has so far failed to translate into direct action in the real world. The reason: 'the internet facilitates and accelerates direct action, rather than changing its essential nature'. In fact '(w)hat the internet has achieved is an unprecedented reduction in the cost of entry to the discussion and organisation of protest'.[121] Such sentiments echo tensions between 'technophiles' and 'neo-luddites' underlying a long-running dispute over the political potential of the web.[122] Notwithstanding, David Runciman elevates the discussion to the durability of the modern state:

The web is this fantastic resource for transmitting information and gathering people together around an issue, even in a particular place. But it's very, very short-term. What the web can do is throw up a coalition out of nothing and it can blow them away again. What the state can do over decades, over centuries, is entrench people's identities, organise their fears, organise their hopes.[123]

To summarise, digital technologies change not only how information moves through speed, volume, and reach; they also multiply its dissemination exponentially. Furthermore they transform formerly passive relationships between consumer and traditional 'one-to-many' media-systems, offering an alternative 'many-to-many' communication. Through technological and real world social networks, individuals form identity groups. These interact, developing social capital which as in the real world, bonds solidarity within and builds bridges between communities in the virtual domain.[124] Thus these groups facilitate the instant spread or occasional surge of information in the form of images, text, and voice via video, the web/internet and mobile telephony. Violent images can be 'sticky', lodge in the individual's memory and through the regular process of 'peer-to-peer' traffic become points around which dissent can rapidly coalesce. How this tendency connects to communities in the real world, particularly where identity or diaspora communities share grievances of injustice, will be examined next.

Archipelagos and Diasporas: Defining the Population

'Humans are a migratory species'.[125] So mass international migration and diasporas, new and old, offer recent digital technologies unprecedented opportunity to link dispersed populations. Latterly the location of diaspora communities in Western European societies has invited closer scrutiny from insurgency scholars because of the Islamic faith many of these groups share.[126] Growing politico-religious radicalisation on the part of some community members is therefore read against the geopolitical context of jihadist militancy striking at the West. How ideas helped on their travels by new technologies can unite and mobilise groups, becomes a valid line of inquiry. At the same time Donald Horowitz cautions against the dangers of misreading the 'long reach of ethnic affiliations' and urges we abandon the search for the 'vital essence of ethnicity'. That means affiliations should be seen as varying between communities, ranged along a continuum that grants membership by birth as well as by choice, namely marriage.[127] At the same time Rogers Brubaker observes that when it comes to ethnicity there is a tendency on the part of constructivist writers to talk of 'ethnic groups' and of 'ethnic, racial, and national conflict in groupist terms as the struggles "of" ethnic groups, races, and nations'. Hence we had better not consider ethnicity, race, and nationalism as substantial groups but as 'political, social, cultural and psychological processes...as a contextually fluctuating conceptual variable'.[128]

That said, what Irish nationalist fighters had already absorbed into their insurgent culture in the nineteenth century, Palestinians more from need than choice embraced in the 1970s. Part of globally dispersed communities, forced from their 'homelands' by economic and military events, both Irish and Palestinians learnt the importance of speaking to and winning active support from far-flung cousins. The latter however went a stage further. 'Statelessness and rootlessness'[129] followed these 'victims of a map'[130] wherever they migrated. Their insight would be to recognise a movement engaging in asymmetric warfare in terrain constrained and encircled by the hegemony of neighbouring Israel, needed to shape a new 'battlespace'. So this would become the 'mediaspace' of rapidly growing audiences around the world who enjoyed the fruits of consumer prosperity and pleasures of television as an entertainment and news medium. What they also understood was the power of this medium to lock dispersed groups with families still in Palestine into a sense of common outrage, purpose and identity. Hence the mediaspace became a cognitive space. What recent history had also shown was that Algerian and Vietnamese insurgent strategies had reaped dividends when they focussed on undermining the legitimacy of hostile state forces with those forces' populations back home.[131]

For generations the Irish diaspora and Irish nationalist narrative were connected by the written word. Polemical tracts and romantic literature created common bonds in increasingly literate populations. Later broadcast media would disseminate popular grievance between distant communities. By connecting potentially sympathetic populations via the medium of television, militant factions within the Palestinian Liberation Organisation (PLO), like Fatah and the Popular Front for the Liberation of Palestine (PFLP), could attempt to overcome the weakness of statelessness through the alluring power of cognition.[132] Their focus for communicating messages was not so much the technological medium as the news event itself, the story, which irresistibly appealed to the primordial dynamic of television with its hunger for audience attention.[133] Hence dramatic hijackings of planes and ships, and the Munich Olympics hostage-seizure brought together millions of television viewers across the world, Palestinian and non-Palestinian alike. Black September explained that taking hostages at the Olympics used 'the unprecedented number of media outlets in one city to display the Palestinian struggle—for better or worse'.[134] Palestinian grassroots activists would soon spot that nothing attracted news cameras quite like the prospect of violent pictures. In the 1987 Intifada the Israeli Defense Forces were goaded into the 'ethical dilemmas and operational blunders' of an army of occupation as they faced an asymmetric uprising of street-fighters and stone-throwers.[135] POTD was the victor. However the shift from 'one-to-many' to 'many-to-many' communications made possible by digital technologies would move the story on again.

A generation on, how do 'many-to-many' digital media influence successive waves of mass migration the world has witnessed since? We have seen populations take advantage of technological advances to transform the nature of human communication, expanding volume and means, and rendering individual usage more mobile with fewer editorial controls. People who see themselves as members of identity groups, but also as links to diasporic communities across the globe, may now be reached and unified through low-cost digital media.[136] Meanwhile political elites have finessed techniques of marketing, advertising, and mass persuasion tapping into segmented communities through sophisticated data-mining. But the fragmented audiences they address have grown more self-reflexive and eclectic by origin and profile, consistent with a wider, long-term trend in Western societies in the twentieth century.[137] This growing disjuncture has implications for insurgency.

Migration, permanent or semi-permanent, is nothing new. Successive historical waves[138] have crossed continents and oceans forming close-knit diasporas for various reasons: economic, namely labour and trade, post-colonial and *Gastarbeiter*, and as victims of man-made and natural disaster.[139] So for Lessinger there is 'no single profile of a typical migrant'.[140] In 2006 some 200 million people migrated throughout the world—twice as many as in 1980.[141] By 2008 their remittance flows reached $328 billion compared with $85 billion in 2000.[142] Since the mid-twentieth century and the dismantling of the European powers' nineteenth-century empires, sizeable groups born in newly independent colonies have exercised rights to resettle from peripheries to metropolitan centres. But significantly more answered calls for workforces to fuel economic growth throughout Western countries in successive waves from the 1950s, peaking in the 1970s and tapering in the 1990s.[143] Further migration flows from Eastern Europe into the West followed the fall of the Soviet Union and its satellite states. Such is the apparent 'turbulence' of contemporary migration patterns that they seem 'chaotic', leading some observers to see a threat to international security.[144] On reflection, they represent 'fluid but structured movement, with multidirectional and reversible trajectories'.[145] Where once New York, London and Paris were magnets attracting dispersed populations, these are now eclipsed by China's seabord, the Gulf states, and Latin America's cities.[146]

Today many post-1945 migrant communities in Europe already encompass indigenous second and third generation offspring. Unsurprisingly insurgency scholars have beaten a path to those communities where geographical or ethnic roots map onto religious affiliation. Nevertheless for the young who see themselves 'caught between two cultures', their parents' country of origin can still mark an emotive if ambiguous point of personal identification.[147] Hence both actual and imaginary ties endure and are replenished between far-flung families and their patries, albeit in subtle ways. Continued cultural and religious practices embed them. So too do remittance economies common to most expatriate communities from developing countries.[148] Modern low-cost transportation and televised imagery shorten distances between sending and receiving societies, rendering 'home and host society a single arena of social action'.[149] These reinforce the appeal of the distant and exotic that remains an intrinsic, defining part of individuals' lives. Yet it is more complex still: the simplistic 'caught between two cultures' slogan[150] masks a crisscrossing of multiple cultures and political identities.[151] Individuals are politically implicated in their local environments. But daily life supersedes the nation-state, reaching beyond 'bi-focal' conceptions of community and connecting with broader transnational networks.[152] Identity construction has been variously impacted by governments' policies in receiving societies. Their divergent approaches to multicultural social initiatives, have often favoured delineating rather than obscuring cultural difference.[153] In short, what I suggest here is a constructivist and fluid concept of ethnic identity.[154]

Digital technologies expand opportunities for communication that allow individuals to belong simultaneously to different 'imagined communities'[155] while operating within a 'transnational public sphere'.[156] Hence '(e)ach individual is a member of many groups, and indeed of groups of very different kinds—groups classified by gender, by race, by language, by nationality, etc. Therefore, each person participates in many "cultures"',[157] no matter whether he/she hails from Tamil Hindu, Punjabi Sikh or Pakistani Muslim family origin.[158] Still second and third generation migrants adeptly recognise distinctive markers of international migration, namely 'national identity, global equity, social justice and the universality of human rights'.[159] For these younger European generations,[160] less forgiving of socio-economic inequalities experienced by their parents, grievance has periodically turned into violent protest. Britain's waves of Asian migrant-community unrest have been attributed to various theories, none of which alone satisfactorily answers the root-causes of successive flare-ups of street-rioting. Successive commissions have sought to understand this in Britain. Their conclusions broadly boil down to a failure of government policies of multiculturalism pursued since the 1960s.[161] Political-economy analyses further highlight social dislocation and economic marginalisation experienced through inferior housing and employment, uneven distribution and penetration of educational opportunities, racial segregation at personal and community levels, and institutional discrimination within state agencies like the police and local councils.[162] Recently a more general Islamophobia has elevated anti-Asian discrimination to a new plane in certain communities.[163] A recent British survey suggests that over half the British population equates Islam with extremism.[164] Concurrently, indigenous tensions between cultural heritage and Muslim faith within British-Asian communities are too readily overlooked, argues Shiv Malik.[165] However in European Muslim communities Pew Global Attitudes identifies unemployment as a greater concern than Islamic extremism or decline of religion (although for Britain Pew's relevant data remain ambivalent).[166] Just as analysis of extreme political violence in the shape of terrorism does not conveniently map onto disenfranchised class or low-income groups,[167] equally vexing is a failure to understand the effect of outside stimuli and agents. Namely how and when that intoxicating moment of 'autonomous radicalisation',[168] which is POTD's epiphany, turns the image from a far-flung place into a personal, localised cause, and, later, transforms an individual's grumbling resentment into full-blown militant activism.[169]

However, to suggest these young Britons or fellow Muslim youth across Europe, searching for more authentic identity and meaning, might be immured to exogenous events would be myopic. In recent decades a resurgence of religious fundamentalism including Islam has found expression in extreme political violence in many parts of the world.[170] The politicisation of Islam has been energised by conflicts *inter alia* in Afghanistan (1980s, 2000s), Chechnya (1990s), Bosnia (1990s), Iraq (1990s, 2000s), and Palestine-Israel-Lebanon (1970s–2000s). But a complex interplay between the failure of state modernism and refusal by autocratic political elites to extend the benefits of development to populations throughout the Middle East, compounded by a Western military presence or successive incursions into Muslim countries has fanned the flames of outrage.[171] These historical dimensions of Arab and Muslim lands are too particular and extensive to detail here but they undeniably inflect the local context of diasporic experience in the West.[172]

In today's resurgence of direct action by political groups with Salafi jihadist objectives, a heroic self-assertion allies itself to a compelling strategic narrative emanating from conflict zones. It tells of Muslim peoples under threat from Western cultural values and economic and military force. Thus it offers emotional stimulus to distant communities already sensing dislocation from their immediate surrounds in the West. Events may unfold thousands of miles away in places and battlefields only ever imagined, yet for these young British nationals schooled in the latest techno-products, immersed in the same consumer environment, images of violent conflict are immediate and powerful. Round-the-clock television news programmes disseminate them widely. Website subscribers exchange scenes of violence, directing them at members who share cultural heritage and spiritual antecedence. If anything could vitalise the notion of a global *ummah*, it is perhaps this drip-feed of images drawing sensitised audiences into what is readily perceived as anti-Muslim injustice. This has led some to practice via self-radicalising processes and commitment to insurgent causes what others support emotionally, discursively, and less directly.[173] This remains a complex, multi-dimensional area of inquiry. And it continues to elude conclusive analysis of why such apparent divergence endures within and between Germany's million-plus Turkish Muslims, Britain's Muslim South Asians and France's offspring of Muslim African descent.[174] Or indeed why middle class youth and professionally employed individuals, rather than simply disenfranchised poor, feel driven to direct action.[175]

Recent diasporic generations share this familiarity with media images with their contemporaries across British and European societies. Like them, but perhaps unlike their parents, they have a dual relationship with the image. First, they continue to receive images as traditional viewers or consumers of television or film; second, they capture and send them out into the web's 'digital commons' as producers or peer-to-peer communicators. But the effect of the internet goes further: it questions the very idea that individuals possess a unitary identity, instead offering them a world of 'parallel lives'. '(S)tepping through the looking glass' of the Web, according to psychologist Sherry Turkle, means 'today's life on the screen dramatises and concretises a range of cultural trends that encourage us to think of identity in terms of multiplicity and flexibility'.[176] Such multiplicity is supported by mainstream web-sites which become its new tools. Flickr boasts roughly 6,500 photos that are uploaded free every minute 24 hours a day.[177] And social network sites through which images can cascade, offer access to unprecedented mass communication: Facebook claims 400 million regular users, and in 2009 was signing nearly 1 million new members each day;[178] China's QQ.com advertises 800 million registered users.[179] Moreover employing cheap software programmes users cut up, reconstitute, and invest new life into 'mash-ups', creative re-edits of downloaded videos that now carry their own imprint and point of view, before sending them back into the infinity of the internet towards hosts of like-minded visual commentators. How is this possible? Because '(a)n image stored on a memory disc instead of celluloid film has a plasticity that allows it to be manipulated as if the picture were words rather than a photo'.[180]

In sum, second and third generation offspring of migrants are variously influenced by cultural links of ethnicity, faith, and geography common to global diasporas. Where allied to feelings of disconnect within their countries of birth ('caught between two cultures' aphorism), their sensitivity is heightened to wider, international points of hostility perceived to be directed at their identity communities. These may provide fertile ground for political mobilisation or exploitation. Meanwhile these same offspring are immersed in new consumer and technological environments. Messages now circumvent traditional editorial mediators, instead connecting and enabling individuals to reach mass audiences. This dramatic shift in social contact means images and ideas, from the mundane to radical, gain rapid traction as they surge exponentially through the virtual domain. Emotive images and violent pictures are malleable in their use, attractive in their simplicity and directness, and cathartic if not inspiring as tools for oppositional politics.

Outmanœuvring Bureaucracies

This discussion might suggest violent images have an unrestricted free-flow. This is not always the case. So it is important to question how images reach populations. Insurgents address multiple audiences. As the strategic centre of gravity of the struggle, the people are the prime target constituency for insurgent image-makers. But these message-producers must also engage the state, directing images and information campaigns at state-elite structures and memory-processes that block their way to the people. Thus insurgents involve the state enemy at all levels in a war of ideas, addressing populations with memories of injustice, political elites with tools of influence and persuasion, and state agencies actively deployed in resisting their onslaughts. It is equally important to set the nature of state bureaucracies in the context of the 'complexity' of future war.[181] This is a world that a French Government Defence Review suggests will be 'less predictable, less stable and more contradictory',[182] due in no short measure to technological advances and information flows. Such is their impact already that Gowing observes 'this surge of civilian information is having an asymmetric, negative impact on the traditional structures of power. It is subverting their effectiveness, and calling into question institutional assumptions that as organs of power they will function efficiently and with public confidence'.[183] Two traditional building-blocks of insurgency endure today: the time-space relationship that affects the speed with which combatants make progress, and the ability to adapt to changing circumstances faster than the state.[184] The key point at issue here is whether hierarchical states can respond fast enough to images and ideas campaigns that are produced by 'flat' insurgent organisations and disseminated through technologically enabled social networks within global populations. With digital media we are concerned not just with the velocity of communication, which complicates matters. Rather, it is the self-initiating or non-linear dynamic quality of information in this new environment that opens up a new era of insurgent possibilities. Non-linear dynamics characterise the apparent chaotic nature of flows of information, the seemingly spontaneous way that ideas flicker and catch fire. This requires understanding.[185]

Claims are made in industry for 'widening the span of control' through introducing information and computer technologies. That entails reducing the number of layers in middle management which slow down decision-making, in favour of flatter organisations, through automated procedures and standardised computer programmes.[186] So can the public sector share this optimism? Ponderous, leaden-footed and reactive, Western state organisation is increasingly seen as ill-suited to the Information Age.[187] Modelled on vertical hierarchies, it too easily becomes 'stove-piped', locked into narrow working practices that delay delivering objectives. Command-and-control processes become ridden with friction between departments and agencies thus slowing down decision-making processes. Bureaucratic models vary widely between countries.

The lethargy of state response and performance are commonplace when confronted by horizontally organised networks that would subvert the state. Notwithstanding it is important to note Langdon Winner's cautionary words: '(w)hat one feels about the where's and how's of decision making may have little to do with one's views on administration'.[188] In the twentieth century, hierarchical bureaucracy has proven to be the most effective way of organising complex industrial states with large populations.

Max Weber's three ideal types of imperative authority may be summarised as 'rational-legal', namely efficient, professional bureaucracy; 'traditional' exemplified by sacred precedent of a monarchical or religious order; and 'charismatic', where individual leadership constrains collective action.[189] Yet the Weberian ideal of bureaucracy in many national forms is not strictly borne out in practice.[190] Just as state bureaucracies are challenged by insurgent networks—some complex, ever-mutating organisationally, some simple with their own internal hierarchies—so state bureaucracies are hierarchies that contain formal and informal networks. Deregulation, decentralisation and out-sourcing have enhanced the ability of private sector subcontractors to supply state hierarchies in a series of networks too. Notwithstanding, advanced states overwhelmingly comprise pyramids of vertically structured, hierarchical silos.[191] These in turn sit within fixed networks of agencies and departments, each with its internal family-tree. Cross-departmental networks are perforce dominated by major hubs or crossroads of decision-making. All depend on processes of upward referral ultimately reaching into the highest levels of government. Intersecting these fairly stable structures of operations are informal networks which employees at various tiers share. So people communicate within and across agencies, both in the workplace and outside in social gatherings. Following 1980s public sector reforms driven by market principles, repeated initiatives to 'roll back the state' and decentralise decision-making have yet to show substantive improvements in how information and decisions flow through state bodies.[192] Recently what Nicolas Sarkozy calls the 'return of the state, the end of public powerlessness' following the 2008–9 global economic crisis has seen the state reassert itself. Increased public spending and growing regulation accompany expanded securitisation, surveillance and policing. Equally a rejuvenated state capitalism means companies are encouraged to search abroad for new opportunities as 'governments do not so much reject the market as use it as an instrument of state power'. These characteristics mark out this new hybrid era.[193] Nevertheless what affects administrative efficiency are not simply the grand designs of management restructuring but 'the ineffable forces of human interaction within an organisation's walls'.[194] Similarly it is a fallacy to assume heavy state investment in ICTs undertaken by many countries, simplistically accelerates change and mobility across governments.

Access to digital technologies remains patchy. A few governments are ahead of the game while others lag behind, says Christopher Hood: 'some governments are in effect using horses and carts in an environment where some or all of the population has a state-of-the-art modern vehicle'.[195]

This chimes with broader historical points made by Peter Hennessy's review of British government:

We have inherited a nineteenth century bureaucracy, which for all its modification and refinements, remains ill-suited...to the tasks of translating political wishes into practical reality.[196]

Technology is no cure-all for complex, bureaucratic decision-making. Technological readiness only partly affects workers' day-to-day practices, testing how and whether they are equipped to cope in crises. What counts is the institutional climate for taking decisions under pressure: how quickly information-flows become blocked at key concentrations of information exchange. This is problematised by external political sensitivities and fast-moving timelines influenced by media demands. 'Scale-free', hub-based networks are major traffic intersections in capitalist production and advanced industrial societies. They are supply and distribution points across institutions and organisations where indefinite numbers of links converge. So they represent both strength and weakness. Their technological advantage is they can survive random interruptions; if one area goes down, there is always redundant capacity to skirt any problem.[197] However, in the everyday life of states and public and private services, as Robb identifies, if someone deliberately targets their decision-making capacity, they become organisational weak-spots. These 'systempunkts', he likens to a variation on the Blitzkrieg's *Schwerpunkt*. In short, they are the softest point of vulnerability where attacks set in motion cascades of failure.[198] His insight highlights intentional disruption to vital industries, such as electricity generation and supply, oil and gas refining, and storage and distribution.[199] Dollars and cents lost are potentially astronomical. This analysis speaks to the concept of net- or cyberwars where states attack other states, or non-state actors seek to disable or debilitate seemingly all-powerful modern states with their panoply of technology and financial resources.[200]

However, is there an even higher cost to state credibility? State bureaucracies with their junctions of decision-making face the fog of incoming information. So too do media organisations charged with disseminating analysis. Traditional media corporations broadly underpin the political status quo. They help propagate the state's public information response. Yet they experience similar problems of how to react quickly to breaking news-stories where events outrun the time it takes to verify facts on the ground (Gowing's 'crisis of the timeline'). When states suffer unexpected, deliberate attacks they are tested in ways that exceed humanitarian and economic impact on human life and capital assets. Civil servants' ability to determine the response is critical. Tactically, institutions must process information, analyse source and background, assess continuing risk, and determine responses appropriate in type and scale. Strategically, the policy context into which such measures play is crucial. So too is how governments explain such complexities to their electorates, since confidence and trust are the bedrock of governments' relationship with the populace, the source of authority and legitimacy. Thus, incoming messages of shock-and-awe violence present information-flows that force states to engage with the unexpected at strategic, operational, and tactical levels.

When multiple levels fail to connect, when 'gaps and seams' within administrations are neglected, consequences can be striking. For America's Hart-Rudman Commission, reporting on national security in early 2001, the unimaginable was foreseeable.[201] The picture of a leaderless, disoriented bureaucracy would be highlighted later by the 9/11 Commission Report.[202] Only extreme moral outrage felt by America's population immediately following the attack mitigated the nadir of bureaucratic failure. Instead the tragedy fostered a fertile climate for Washington's administration to recover lost ground through the construction of a war narrative ('Global War on Terror') in the ensuing hours and days.[203] Departmental turf-wars and miscommunications following 9/11 nevertheless persisted in subsequent US governmental responses to Hurricane Katrina in New Orleans and the subprime mortgage crisis.[204] They prompted the view that in some parts the federal bureaucracy was an 'impenetrable forest', beyond implementing reforms.[205] Despite the influential Volcker Commission's muted optimism for change, 'tinkering at the edges' was considered insufficient: '(d)ecisionmaking is too often entangled in knots of conflict, clearance, coordination, and delay. The necessity for coordination and consultation cannot be permitted to overwhelm and needlessly delay decisionmaking'.[206] Such condemnation is far from universal: 'governments and government agencies can change, even in ways that seem far-reaching'.[207]

All organisations experience tension between formal procedures and institutional norms, and informal networks of personnel who conform to but also bend the rules. While social movements are informal, state organisations are formal. Hence 'functions and power relations are more important than people, persisting over the years while people come and go'.[208] Not so informal structures. These are fluid, self-generating and driven by their communications. A complex adaptive system never reaches stability or equilibrium. If it does, 'it's dead'.[209] Reflecting on Luther Gerlach's model of SPIN (segmentary, polycephalous or acephalous, and networked), Rayner argues that it is a social movement's segmentary characteristics that 'allow it to combine multiple strategies that could not be tolerated in a single organisation'.[210] Following London's jihadi POTD—the 7/7 bombings—senior intelligence official David Omand highlighted the need for state agencies to penetrate the enemy's 'OODA Loop', namely its decision-making cycle.[211] But this fails to appreciate two key factors about non-linear dynamic organisations and social movements that proliferate, divide and converge facilitated by modern digital technologies.

First, local cells in a complex insurgency may be identified, tracked, and disabled through human and technical intelligence. While local groups can be removed, the broader movement continues to spawn new offspring. The latter cannot be penetrated and 'controlled' from outside like more traditional insurgencies with delineated boundaries and hierarchical leadership, for example PIRA.[212] Counter-intuitively they must be penetrated from within, organically.[213] Since this is a leaderless movement, individuals and groups have limited direct impact. Second, their actions are unpredictable in conventional terms of linear cause-and-effect. Behaviour is seemingly serendipitous, apparently random. Nevertheless it is attracted as if by gravitational pull.[214] 'Because complex systems have built-in unpredictability, the certainties of the 'command and control' approach to management no longer hold true'.[215] A metaphor might elucidate this. When starlings take flight at dusk in enormous numbers, switching direction time and again, there is no leader, no general in command. Each bird reacts to its neighbour; everyone leads, and no one leads. The notion that an external team can be inserted to divert or subvert spontaneous actions requires a different approach. This may well succeed at the kinetic level. Mission command—devolving initiative and license to unit level so that decisions in theatre can be made without recourse to central command—is built into current army doctrine. The further removed from central political control, the more flexibility comes into play for any platoon negotiating enemy contact. Violent acts in theatre may be anticipated, even pre-empted. But as Miller and Page note, today '(t)errorist acts emerge from, and are perpetuated by, loose networks'.[216] Problems arise when images capturing military-insurgent contact leave the kinetic plane. On-the-ground social networks map onto technological networks in a complex relationship (hitherto under-researched). Their effect requires a different kind of response.

Since we are concerned with insurgent images and ideas flowing through contemporary digital media, what further complicates this picture is at a time of rising insurgencies, terrorists are found in all societies at different states of development, as Hood describes above, from horse-and-cart to state-of-the-art. Furthermore they can project their ambitions long-distance using the latest ICTs. Moreover digital media influence how groups connect to their members. Yet the central issue is how these media-systems offer social networks the speed and flexibility to outwit and outmanoeuvre state bureaucracies in a context Paul

Virilio describes as the 'tyranny' of 'immediacy, ubiquity, instantaneity'.[217] The threat comes from three sources: first, insurgent groups' use of digital technologies *per se*; second, from the proportionate effect of the individual user on his/her target of attack; and third, from flows of communication that flood through these channels. There is a critical difference. First, digital technologies enable insurgent groups to propagate messages to multiple audiences simultaneously: distinct ideological messages ('soft information') cater for different tastes and commitment levels. They also widely disseminate operational materials, manuals, and instructions to fighters and would-be fighters in 'self-starting' cells ('hard information'). Second, proportionate effect is highlighted by the case of a fifteen-year-old Canadian hacker, MafiaBoy, who crippled Yahoo.com with billions of messages sent simultaneously saying 'Yes, I heard you!' before launching a similar attack of 'screaming ghosts' against Amazon.com, eBay, CNN.com, ETrade, and Excite a day later.[218] Third, a flow benefits opportunely from an 'energy' which it may or may not set in motion. Any individual may launch it. But once released, neither insurgent nor initiator can control it. How long it lives or when it dies, is a conundrum engaging complexity theory researchers.[219] Thus if it fires, it resembles a power surge in a mains circuit, following a sudden, unanticipated switch-on that overloads existing wiring, crippling the system to such a degree there can be no immediate bureaucratic resistance. What this calls into question is local capacity to resist when under pressure. Even contingency arrangements in command-and-control processes, as well as organisational imagination and speed of implementation may be found wanting.

Today POTD images represent compelling ideas. So combatting ideas, indeed ideologies or cosmologies of mythical narratives is something quite different from fighting a physical enemy, particularly when states must react to visual acts of violence broadcast indiscriminately with instant global diffusion. This is exacerbated where governments hesitate to intervene in 'opportunity spaces'. The effect is to disorientate an anxious public. Those spaces become the crisis arena for political exploitation when images create an emotional impact within populations, but before collective action erupts.

Government bureaucracies and both public and private media outlets are considered symbiotic by insurgents. They share a common fate; both are vulnerable to changes in the digital mediascape. How? First, the volume and force of communications surges become irresistible, drawing comment and renewed exposure from members of social networks. Governments and media elites cannot be seen not to respond. All too often, as Runciman observes, they respond by 'firefighting'.[220] Anyway, in the failure to capture the 'opportunity space', audiences increasingly find their own explanations via internet open sources. Second, the speed at which they occur wrong-foots the status quo. At least to the degree that regular protocols and standard operating procedures cannot adapt fast enough to make credible responses. Bureaucratic logjams result from a surfeit of decision-making layers common to vertical organisations. And situations risk changing all too frequently and suddenly for government press offices to dominate the story agenda. Meanwhile politicians, sensitive to satisfying their electorates in democracies, remain torn between appearing instantly decisive yet realising the need to be patient and deliberative. Third, surges are unpredictable and spontaneous. Contingency planning for unknown events requires putting in place appropriate resources, manpower, and redundancy. But what captures public attention can often not be planned for, and fighting information is not the same as firefighting. Narratives of events are ephemeral, particularly when driven by emotive imagery. Wars of ideas become long wars. Democratic governments today believe their electorates have patience only for short wars. This lesson does not escape insurgents who increasingly position messaging and imaging at the heart of their strategic operating concept.

Strategic Opportunism

Is POTD active or reactive? Is it simply opportunistic rather than strategic? After all, insurgent control over the image ranges from total to zero. Today's media proliferation not only puts the spotlight on insurgent intent and delivery but problematises how we conceive of what is strategic. When media flows of information and images can move so fast and so far, decision-making cycles not only shrink but grow more fluid. With near immediate ubiquity, the lines between planned and unplanned actions blur. In an ecology of self-generating messages and self-reinforcing feedback loops, web and mobile phone users and television viewers interpret and reinterpret what they see. They determine what they believe to be important. Word of mouth once constrained each individual to be a narrowcaster; now each has the potential to become a broadcaster. Thus peer-to-peer they begin to redress the traditional imbalance between producer and receiver. At the same time, the relationship between population and insurgent grows more touch-sensitive. Societies are entering a new era, the shape of which is yet to be discerned clearly. The implications for the revolutionary movement are not insignificant since message control has always been critical to the cause. Allowing for divergence between groups—some remain hierarchical, others net-worked—all must come to terms increasingly with less tactical control and invest more in greater strategic scene-setting, namely narrative construction. David Rosen's interviews with Palestinian youth suggest how successfully a narrative can function once embedded:

With every suicide bombing the Islamist narrative of empowerment resonates throughout Palestinian society. The bombing conveys a sense of vicarious empowerment where Palestinians have little actual power. No young Palestin-ian whom I have ever spoken to has questioned the justification of suicide bombing or its morality or has showed any concern for its victims. When the issue of victimisation comes up, the bomber is regarded as the victim.[221]

Suicide-video testimonies, IED attacks, and hostage-videos continue to operate within a sphere of production and distribution controlled by the insurgent. In LIVE acts, however, only the scene-setting or stage management is under his direction. Meanwhile accidental image capture of deeds by journalists or passers-by has depended for any insurgent effect on how it plays into the back-story established hitherto in the population. Where states and counterinsurgents commit accidental or collateral atrocities against communities, he has no control, no involvement. Yet when the public becomes an active participant in generating messages and distributing images, they become communications activists by design or default. Not all of them: many will denounce what they see. Alternatively, the hostile user may choose merely to walk away from the image rather than register disgust.

Does this mean the insurgent presses the trigger (where it is relevant) and sits back waiting for sympathisers to do the rest? It is not as simple as to suggest that images once released ricochet around the web universe forever. They have a tendency first to cluster around attractors, beacon brands of recognition, loyalty and trust before further dissemination. In principle, once released into the mediascape, they find sanctuary on some hard drive somewhere, while retaining extraordinary half-lives. They are permanently accessible tools or weapons. What changes this discussion of opportunism versus strategy is speed, and in warfare speed is power. What the fast-moving media ecology now demands of states and state-challengers alike is a closer relationship with information flows. Not through control but influence, hence requiring a more flexible, dynamic approach to messaging. If the media never sleep, neither dares the insurgent. The need to monitor news flows accompanies a merger between strategy and tactics, between the planned and unplanned, the intended and unintended. Whether revolutionaries can come to terms with this trade-off between loss of traditional control and new-found increase in market access will be tested in future decades as the digital universe progresses and states succeed in or fail to manage, legislate and corporatise internet and mobile phone networks. Thus to combine being active and reactive becomes a strategy of fluidity for POTD's sponsors. When near instant communications networks can turn a minor local event into a significant, international news story in an instant, whosoever wraps a framework of interpretation around it, whosoever is first to market, stands to gain most from its fall-out. This might be termed strategic opportunism.

* * *

The insurgent landscape has changed radically in the last two decades, in large part as a consequence of the digital revolution, which has transformed how consumers interact with new communications technologies. Fresh possibilities emerge daily, encouraging populations to engage with ideas and assert old and new identities across the cognitive domain of electronic media. Today we are already passing from the first to the second phase of the internet. What fifteen years ago was hailed as a borderless utopia is already eliding to a fragmented network of networks or more pessimistically a dystopian 'collection of nation-state networks'. The efforts of states and corporations to constrain free access and movement by introducing closed systems is no longer limited to autocratic states like China with its 'Great Firewall'. Democracies like India and Australia are similarly exerting their sovereignty; the United States welcomes freedom of information flows via the web but pursues with the force of law and crime agencies those, such as WikiLeaks, who would promote unrestricted access to sensitive government materials; and Facebook, Google, and Apple are walling off their corporate gardens defying 'net neutrality' while media outlets like the *Times* and *Financial Times* are successfully experimenting with paywalls to annex online space. Nevertheless the broad thrust of change firmly favours insurgents. The digital revolution offers their target populations parallel media-systems. By replacing one-to-many with many-to-many communications, millions of people originate and disseminate content to recipients of their own choosing. Because of the network effect of the internet and mobile telephony, ideas and POTD images can move at exponential speed connecting disparate populations who may be linked by common cause and grievance. Indeed flows of information appear to assume a life of their own when occasionally epidemics of 'infectious ideas' surge through global networks, gaining traction with alarming speed. For states, organised in more rigid administrative structures, this is problematic. Their ability to respond quickly to fast moving emotional and cognitive changes in electorates and subjects is found wanting.

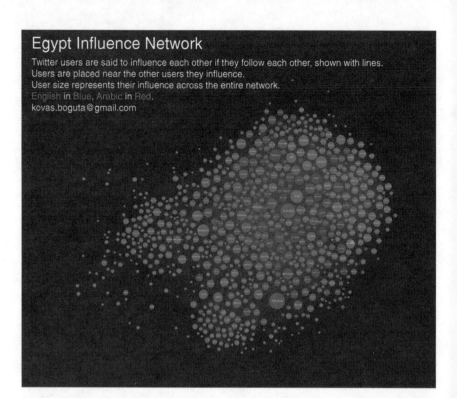

Egypt Influence Network

Twitter users are said to influence each other if they follow each other, shown with lines.
Users are placed near the other users they influence.
User size represents their influence across the entire network.
English in Blue, Arabic in Red.
kovas.boguta@gmail.com

Twitter and Facebook messages surge through networks in Tahrir Square.
© Kovas Boguta and © Demotix/Ahmed Abd El-Fatah.

7

SPONTANEOUS REVOLUTION

De l'audace, de l'audace, encore de l'audace.

Lenin[1]

One moonless night in 2011, Washington got its man. In a bravura display of life emulating art, Black Hawk helicopters skimmed the Pakistani terrain below the range of radar, before hovering above a dusty compound whose unsuspecting occupant was the world's most wanted fugitive. After a near decade of spilled blood and treasure, the killing of Al-Qaeda leader Osama Bin Laden at the hands of US Navy SEALs would be revealing in different ways. Foremost, it would highlight how central the photographic image had become in framing the political debate. 'Seeing is believing' is a knee-jerk response to the drama of history. Viewers, for so long fed a media diet of pillory and revenge, wanted to see the proof—the corpse—with their own eyes. At the same time, that desire betrayed a sense of misgiving, or in plain-speak, lack of trust in politicians felt not just by Western audiences but by many incredulous onlookers in the region. Yet Washington's eventual decision to deny the public sight of Bin Laden's body (in keeping with spiriting it away by helicopter for burial at sea) spoke to a different issue. Grainy footage of a blood-soaked bedroom was all that was offered up. Certainly no sight of that notorious face which had taken a 'kill' shot to the left eye. Fear that the image might join a martyr's pantheon and become the icon of future struggle was understandable. So too that it might just reinforce the stereotype in Arab lands that the imperial West yet again was preaching justice but practising summary execution. On another level it demonstrated that for all the detailed planning that had gone into the military strike, little apparent preparation had been vested in how to tell this long-awaited story beyond a sharp blast of triumphalism. Indeed so long did the deliberations continue—shots of a grave-faced Obama in the White House situation room observing the strike in real time were put out to stop the news gap—that events would prove to dictate the agenda. Subsequent interviews disseminated via television and the web showed local Pakistanis assuring news crews that the man the Americans claimed to be Osama was a mere local nobody, hence a case of mistaken identity. What the delay in effect achieved was to allow speculation to reinforce prejudices on all sides of the credibility gap. The narrative had taken shape on the street, indeed on many streets around the world. For better or worse, the image was now already out there, albeit this time as a photographic negative that filled the gap where the missing photo-positive should have been. American vacillation had missed the opportunity to command the story agenda to Washington's full advantage. Again speed had been underestimated as a key driver in the crisis space that follows the moment of shock and awe.

The same mishandling of the mediaspace would become apparent throughout 2011 during the Arab Uprisings: an unforeseen, complex set of events in which outside actors such as the web-whistleblower WikiLeaks and web-activists Anonymous would play their part. Propaganda of the Deed events across the autocracies of North Africa and the Middle East would take several forms: self-immolation; mass popular protests; brutal attacks on population by security forces; closing down of and strikes against internet services by the state, and counter-strikes by dissidents; indeed even 'heroic acts' during the armed uprising against Libya's Gaddafi regime. The use of IEDs, suicide bombs, and hostage videos would be absent from this theatre. Throughout, organisers and participants were aware of a watching world. Together they offer an insight into the key question of this chapter: can violent images bring down governments? More explicitly, have we reached an age where spontaneity and fluidity are replacing organised mobilisation, dispensing with an insurrectionist vanguard and hierarchical command-and-control?

This chapter looks at the unfolding of the Arab Uprisings; the part played by digital media in those events as contagion spread between neighbouring states; the place for anonymity and spontaneity in insurgencies; and the relationship between spontaneity and political organisation. It concludes, to paraphrase Alvin Toffler, that the future has come too soon. The new revolutionaries are still writing the rules as they go along, exploring the new mediascape. Meanwhile, unprepared states are struggling to counter this historic turbulence.

The Arab Uprisings and Liberation-Technology

While Arab leaders strove to cling to power in the early months of 2011, governments around the world looked on with mixed feelings. Any enthusiasm on the part of outsiders for popular change—an unfamiliar concept in the region—was offset by the discomfort at the lightning speed with which events were unfolding as images of protest and challenge accelerated through the new mediascape. 'We don't have to blow. The winds are blowing. There's no stopping them', declared Hillary Rodham Clinton. For the outside world, the unrest that swept through the Arab states started with a slap.[2] For many on the inside, trouble had been brewing for some time; indeed it had been bubbling to a head throughout the previous year when WikiLeaks also made its uncomfortable entry onto the local political landscape. But an insult administered by a Tunisian female government official across the face of a young market trader over where he could and could not sell his fruit and vegetables, led him to commit self-immolation. Shortly after, he died. Despair at economic and social repression stirred at the heart of this symbolic confrontation. Mohamed Bouazizi's suicide triggered a wave of dissent on the streets of Tunis, elevating him to near mythical, martyr status. The image of the dying trader visited by the nation's President in an act of faux sympathy served only to ignite the animosity of fellow citizens.

Clinton recalls:

what I saw happening was so clear to me that what was going on was just this movement below the surface, that despite the leaders' either refusal or blindness to see what was going on, it was moving...So the leaders might have chosen to be oblivious, but people in the society, not just the young people, but people of all walks of life, they knew that there was this beginning of change.[3]

Earlier events had set the scene for the popular uprising to which Bouazizi's dramatic image provided the spark. In November 2010, WikiLeaks had already released confidential diplomatic cables revealing the condemnation of the US ambassador who accused the presidential family of being mafia-esque. Risks to the long-term stability of the regime were rising, he warned. Immediately Tunisia's government moved to block the WikiLeaks site, only to be countered by mirror websites such as Tunileaks, which sprang up to replicate the same information-leaks.[4] By January 2011, the online action group Anonymous, a shadowy, self-declared revolutionary group that had previously hacked other websites to campaign against inter alia scientology, and the criminalising of WikiLeaks, launched its own manifesto into Tunisia's political space.

It declared:

To the Tunisian government: Attacks on the freedom of speech and information of your citizens will not be tolerated. Any organisation involved in censorship will be targeted. Attacks will not cease until the Tunisian government hears the claim of freedom from its own people. It is in the hands of the Tunisian government to bring this to a resolution.[5]

The tit-for-tat response from the authorities was to deploy force. Yet Anonymous' manifesto was backed by Operation Tunisia, which took the form of repeated 'distributed denial of service' (DDoS) attacks by sympathisers on Tunisian government sites.

POTD took a distinctive turn as similar copy-cat acts to Bouazizi's self-immolation were witnessed in Mauritania, Algeria, Saudi Arabia and Egypt in the following weeks; further uprisings would unfold in Libya, Syria, Yemen, Bahrain as well as Saudi and Algeria but always following different patterns and suggesting divergent outcomes. As December 2010 gave way to January, so the flames of dissent spread from Tunisia to Egypt, the regional centre of power. Here, it took only eighteen days from the first public protest to unseat the thirty-year, pharaonic rule of President Hosni Mubarak. As the military elite sought to regroup, distancing itself in the public mind from the actions of the hated police and secret security agencies, a 'creeping coup' under the guise of nascent parliamentary democracy, was suspected.[6] What would come to be characterised as a Facebook and Twitter revolution, particularly by the world's news outlets, in the end masked a more complex interplay between media, both local and global, and populace. Admittedly, these social media sites proved to be instrumental, but on reflection they were less than causal in changing the course of events. One Middle Eastern analyst commented on Tunisia: 'Social media, from Twitter and Facebook to video upload sites, were crucial in spreading the word about what happened in a country where the press was tightly muzzled. It generated tremendous amounts of solidarity in the Arab world in beyond [sic]. But it's just a means of communication, not a driver in itself'.[7] Nevertheless, at what point momentum can be separated from means of communication, when the medium becomes the message, is questionable. One Syrian would in the coming months tell journalists: 'From the Egyptians we learnt how to mobilise ourselves online. The Bahrainis are the best at appealing to the human rights groups. We looked at how the opposition united in Tunisia and knew we had to do the same'. Flicking between Twitter, Facebook and Skype on his laptop, he would confide: 'Since yesterday I've talked to a guy in Kuwait, a guy in Tunisia, one in Jordan and one in Palestine...I've uploaded a video from Syria and one from Yemen'.[8]

Notwithstanding this regional commonality, each Arab state had its own particular political, social and economic context for rising up against entrenched autocracy; each had its own approach to achieving change. And it is fair to add, at the time of writing, that each faces a different picture of stalled progress towards democracy and a rearrangement of the old order. In Egypt, 28 year-old Khaled Said was beaten up by plainclothes police in June 2010, before dying. Pictures of his severely tortured face, taken in the morgue, generated a surge through social media, spawning the anonymous, solidarity websites 'My Name is Khaled Said'; 'My Name is Khaled Mohamed Said'; and 'We are all Khaled Said'. These would become hubs for disseminating information and organising protest once people took to the streets of Suez, Alexandria and Cairo. Albeit the image that would soon supersede his was one of the mass occupation of Cairo's Tahrir Square—a scene that would be captured day after day in international media. Such public outpourings would rise to a crescendo on Fridays as the day of worship was mobilised to become a 'day of rage'. In widespread Arab capitals a central public space was commandeered both as the optimum location for gathering mass momentum and leverage against the regime, but also as the billboard for revolution writ large on electronic screens across the world. Beijing's Tiananmen Square had acquired the same symbolic force some two decades earlier before being crushed under the tank treads of state repression. Understanding the operational but crucially symbolic significance of these public spaces, Bahrain's monarchy later dispatched bulldozers to its Pearl traffic roundabout in Manama to eradicate the physical location of mass resistance.

In Syria, as foreign journalists were excluded from reporting on confrontations between security forces and protesters, mobile phone camera footage and blogs carrying photographic stills conveyed the story of political violence, showing broad swathes of a population in open revolt. As Arab state appeared to take its lead from neighbouring Arab state, Syria's regime, with its historic reputation for putting down dissent with military brutality, would soon become associated with POTD imagery and pictures of killings and torture.[9] What would come to the forefront of protesters' campaigns there would be the image of children posted on YouTube; in particular, the 13 year-old Hamza al-Khatib who had allegedly died from sustained torture. But other videos also focused on the harrowing accounts and faces of young children, so much so that the region's now familiar 'Fridays of rage' were renamed in Syria as 'Children's Friday' to mark protests on 03/06/2011.[10] Appeals for the United Nations to refer Syria's President Bashar al-Assad to the Security Council and International Criminal Court for having turned the firepower of his 200,000-strong army on its population, paralleled those for Libya's leader Muammar Gaddafi and son Saif al-Islam to be brought to justice following systematic humanitarian outrages in their unsuccessful struggle against rebels in Libya's own revolution. Meanwhile the small oil and gas-rich domain of Bahrain largely quelled its internal dissent by inviting in security forces from neighbouring Saudi Arabia. These responded enthusiastically in support of a fellow Sunni elite seemingly threatened by its majority Shia population. Needless to say, the fiercely authoritarian Saudi police state had successfully suppressed its own internal dissent during this turbulence.

The aim here is not to recount how numerous uprisings unfolded in a manner analogous to Europe's own contagious year of revolution in 1848. While emphasising the Arab states' divergence—some sought peaceful overthrow while others found civil war—[11]their similarity in demanding change that could lead to representative government and better living conditions was pronounced. For foreign analysts picking their way through the fall-out of what the columnist Rami Khouri labelled an 'ever-changing constellation of moving targets in the Middle East', the prospect was daunting.[12] Meanwhile, calls for outside support across the region and the wider world reflected a broad-based understanding among protesters of how ideas and images could mobilise support beyond applying popular pressure in the streets, but instead by exploiting diplomatic avenues within the international community. What part Washington played in bringing down Egypt's Mubarak, despite its apparent reticence to be seen to intervene in sovereign affairs, thus risking further anti-American resentment in the region, remains to be chronicled. Mubarak's response to the digital dissemination of protest images had been to close down the internet in Egypt in late January, aping the pattern already set by Tunisia's leaders before their demise. His own televised address to the nation that month showed a strong-man now visibly weakened yet resistant to Obama's appeal to turn 'a moment of volatility' into 'a moment of promise'.[13] But more interestingly, it showed him to be a man out of step with the speed and nature of change in the new mediaspace. Moreover, according to the *New York Times*, his government's curbing of internet freedom would prove to be the springboard for Washington's stepping up its investment in 'shadow' systems, that is 'stealth wireless networks that would enable activists to communicate outside the reach of governments in countries like Iran, Syria and Libya'.

Later Clinton would argue:

There is an historic opportunity to effect positive change, change America supports…So we're focused on helping them do that, on helping them talk to each other, to their communities, to their governments and to the world.[14]

In 2009 Barack Obama had appealed over the heads of Arab autocrats in his landmark Cairo speech, proclaiming: 'government of the people and by the people sets a single standard for all who hold power: you must maintain your power through consent, not coercion…'.[15] His words had tried to segment his audience, putting clear water between rulers and ruled. Perhaps, however, he had not segmented enough, failing to capture the nuances that marked one nationality from the next and one national group from its neighbour. Moreover, when it came to people expressing their desire for 'change and 'hope' on the streets in the face of these sclerotic regimes (campaign calls resonant with Obama's own ascendancy to the White House), his perceived diplomatic 'flip-flopping' projected an inconsistent policy which often appeared at odds with his administration. Diplomatic conduit Frank

Wisner had pressed Mubarak to remain in office; Hillary Rodham Clinton emphasised the need for time to secure democracy; Obama eventually asserted to his spokesman 'to be clear that I meant what I said when I said it', that Mubarak's time was up.[16] Similar reticence to act was demonstrated in the early days of the Libyan uprising when Colonel Gadaffi turned his guns on his own people. Against a background of UNSC Resolution 1973 in March 2011, one leading newspaper highlighted Obama's loss of nerve:

His Administration is shirking those burdens [of global citizenship], and presiding over a disturbing erosion of American influence. It is a triumph of the lack of will... And when freedom was at stake, the leader of the free world was nowhere to be seen.[17]

What was energising newspapers like *The Times* was an erratic stream of violent imagery escaping the Libyan conflict theatre via mobile phones and social media, as well as a few foreign journalists who had reached the besieged towns of resistance. Its leader column was strident:

Could someone—anyone!—remind Barack Obama that there are lives at stake. It is not just that, when the leader of the free world fails to lead, America debases both its military and its diplomatic currency. It is that by taking only a walk-on part in this drama, the US President is giving Colonel Gaddafi succour.[18]

A consequent sense of urgency was picked up by political elites, particularly in France and the UK, who feared another humanitarian crisis similar to Rwanda's that had publicly drawn a veil over the UN's 'responsibility to protect' ambitions in the early 1990s. Others cautioned against the mission creep that had come to colour history's view of the Afghan incursion. Eventually, Obama acted but within limits, perhaps more with an eye to imminent presidential elections in the United States.

Tahrir Square in Cairo too had earlier become a prime source of opposition rhetoric. But it told its stories through pictures showing the patient swelling of ranks as the mass took up residence in the square. Peaceful opposition and orderly control marked the event. By dramatic contrast, when violence did make an appearance, it was attributed to state secret police, and prisoners who had been released from Cairo's jails acting as *agents provocateurs*, as the regime fought to retain its grip on power. The same tactic failed in Cairo 2011 as it had in France in 1789. Camel-riders also tore through the crowds, allegedly in exchange for payment, to provoke a counter-revolution.

What characterises these uprisings is not just the degree to which Arab entrenched elites were out of step with their populations, as Hillary Rodham Clinton observed. Rather, their conception of speed, both to anticipate and to react to unfolding events, was attuned to the militarised command-and-control structures and predictable processes which for so long had underpinned their regimes and held their subjects in check, often delegated through privileged networks or tribal solidarities, and frequently enforced by extensive, regular and secret police services. After all, these were countries with complex demographies. Libya with its unique *Jamahiriya* (state of the masses), fashioned by Gaddafi to depend on Gaddafi and to deny explicitly political representation to the extent that party creation was a treasonable offence, rested on the permeation of the system by the Gaddafi family, clans and tribes and a web of patronage that included other associated, allied tribes.[19] Egypt, an old and institutionalised state by contrast, embraced a presidential coterie which had been penetrated by military chiefs (Mubarak commanded the air force during the 1973 October War with Israel, later shaping an heroic cult around his role). Nevertheless the military had once been able to maintain its distance from the political regime and carry popular respect as an honest broker during the days of protest. There social and professional advancement was contingent on exploiting the appropriate networks. But for all that, each of these revolts was particular to its domestic context, resulting at worst in civil war. Yet news travels fast: none was safe from the fluidity and velocity of ideas and messages crossing sovereign borders.

While reporting conditions varied—foreign journalists were excluded from Syria; rebel strongholds proved difficult to reach in Libya—the rhetoric in the international community was paralleled by home-produced imagery that reached global attention via television and the web, captured mainly on mobile phones, Twitter and Facebook. This would be reinforced by a constant exchange of messages on social media sites, continually feeding back into traditional media, then looping back into the domestic insurrectionist theatre via whichever outlets remained free from state agency censure. However, this selfsame cycle of mobilising protesters via media nurtured the seeds for undermining the very revolution many sought to achieve. It could be infiltrated by government counter-messaging able to thrive in a climate where third-party verification was minimal. One Syrian dissident wrote: .

Report by the regime of major losses in security officers are simply put bogus. Regime officials have been telling all sorts of fantastical lies especially on Syrian TV and Arab news networks that will make Goebbels blush. One such lie is that Hamzah Al-Khateeb, the child who was tortured to death and had his penis chopped off, was actually a Salafi terrorist who sought to enslave local women. Trying to cover both sides of the story should not be used as an excuse to repeat regime lies to a global audience. Syrian activists are doing their best through their videos, commentaries and interview to compensate for the information embargo imposed by Syrian authorities, and most of what we have conveyed so far was later verified through interviews by eyewitness testimonies provided by refugees in Jordan, Lebanon and Turkey. Meanwhile, the regime continues to spin its tall tales in the hope that repetition will ensnare the hapless journalist, the conspiracy theorist, the anti-imperialist, and occasionally, which is an added bonus, a big network, like say, CNN or BBC, meaning that, eventually, the official lie becomes part of the accepted wisdom. In fact, it has already coloured coverage of the revolution.[20]

Syrian authorities understood the need to hijack and reverse the effects of the Propaganda of the Deed of 13-year old Hamza Al-Khateeb. Like Tunisia's Bouazizi and Iran's Neda Agha-Soltan, the young boy stood to become a symbol of resistance and lightning rod for collective memory. In order to seize the opportunity space, Hamza was claimed by the Assad regime, as his parents were welcomed to the presidential palace in a show of sympathy. Pro-regime cyber activists—the so-called Syrian electronic army—would later set out to 'refute false reports' of government abuse by hacking into and disabling Facebook pages of protesters.[21] Perhaps even more far reaching were the measures taken to exclude foreign journalists from Syria, a strategy previously attempted by Israel in its Gaza campaign of 2009, and the Sri Lankan government's obliteration of the Tamil Tiger sanctuary in the same year: information had nevertheless seeped out of both conflict theatres, albeit belatedly and with little independent verification. When images did emerge from Syria, their reliability was not unsurprisingly judged against the background of rising military attacks on towns which had been centres of dissent, and consistently critical reference to the regime's long-term human rights record.

Taken together the events in the Arab Spring were complex and confusing. Perhaps the only clear dimension was the force of imagery carrying the Propaganda of the Deed as it circulated at high velocity through social media networks and traditional media outlets around the world. The result was that states, regionally and internationally, were repeatedly wrong-footed by the speed of potential change.

Dead Men Do Talk

So can violent images bring down governments? In today's dynamic mediaspace, 2011's Arab uprisings suggest that sometimes even established autocracies may be dislodged with additional pressure exerted by the humanitarian concerns and revised strategic interests of the international community, combining with a popular domestic pressure from below. However, for every fallen dictator (Tunisia, Egypt, Libya, Yemen), there is an autocrat willing to face out rebellion in a do-or-die fight to preserve his grip on power (Syria). For every fallen regime, there remains a reconfiguring of elites who seek to preserve privileges so assiduously earned. Depending on the make-up of each state, therefore, so the factor of time and the staying-power of images and ideas directed at change, as they circulate through populations, become critical factors in determining long-term outcomes. The lessons of Europe's 1848 remain relevant today: oppositions must quickly capitalise on events before revolutionary zeal burns itself out or is snuffed out.

Perhaps we have reached a radical, new age of the digital image which recalibrates the imbalance between state and citizen—where spontaneity and fluidity are replacing organised mobilisation in opposition movements, dispensing with an insurrectionist vanguard and hierarchical command-and-control. If so, can images and ideas alone bring down governments, as regimes give up the ghost and implode? To answer in the affirmative is to place a heavy burden onto the new mediascape. Social media may not have caused the uprisings of 2011 but they surely added a continuous and unprecedented supply of fuel to the fire.

The political scientist Lisa Anderson is one commentator on the Arab Spring who declines to attribute its efflorescence to social media. For her, it is to miss the underlying lessons of political economy and historical legacy. Rather, she sees the critical dimension as:

the revolutions across all these three countries [Tunisia, Egypt, Libya] reflected divergent economic grievances and social dynamics—legacies of their encounters with modern Europe and decades under unique regimes.[22]

Far from being a new phenomenon, Anderson compares contemporary uprisings with those of post-Ottoman 1919 in the same countries, proposing the latter were popular movements that propagated their ideas via broadsheets, just as today's protesters use Facebook. And for Twitter now, read the telegraph then. It was responsible, she says, for delivering the inspiring message of Woodrow Wilson's Fourteen Points speech to the rest of the world that triggered popular outbursts. Consequently,

(t)he important story about the 2011 Arab revolts in Tunisia, Egypt, and Libya is not how the globalisation of the norms of civic engagements shaped the protesters' aspirations. Instead, the critical issue is how and why these ambitions and techniques resonated in these various local contexts.[23]

Notwithstanding, each Arab state may have had its own particular political, social, and economic context for challenging entrenched autocracy, but Anderson's analysis fails to address why neighbouring states rose up so quickly and crucially in a chain-reaction. So it risks overlooking the rousing force of the POTD image that protesters themselves chose to adopt as turning-point events in the revolutionary atmosphere. Such images came to encapsulate the pent up anger of many generations and trigger other sensitised populations. Thus she fails to differentiate between content and delivery mechanism. Furthermore, not to confront the particular, explosive nature of digital (as opposed to analogue) viral dissemination (discussed in my earlier chapters) is to undervalue the pluralist nature of Middle East media; in Egypt, for example, cellphone penetration into rural communities is high, even if internet access is denser in urban centres. Anderson's political economy analysis cannot account for the rapid spread of the spirit of revolution—the contagion—as populations watch other populations spill onto the streets as the only viable means of challenging their political masters.

Similarly, Malcolm Gladwell poses the question from another angle. His reticence *vis-à-vis* social media's ability to reinvent political activism derives from the behaviour of weak versus strong ties. Alluding to Granovetter's theory of weak ties (see above), he argues that Twitter and Facebook are an ideal source for acquiring new ideas, information and indeed acquaintances. However, if those ideas are to be communicated and translated into collective action, then tried-and-tested hierarchical organisation is called for. In short, political movements need leadership, discipline and strategies, not just ideas and passion, if they are to succeed. Citing the sociologist Doug MacAdam, he focuses on 'high risk activism' as being dependent on strong not weak ties, where solid, established relationships between individuals (friends or family members) drive people to expose themselves to danger in the face of state actors exercising violence and sanction. So weak ties work better for disseminating information; strong ties for using that information to drive collective action. Ideology plays a secondary role, he claims.[24]

To what extent this last point proved to be the case in the Arab states in 2011 is questionable. The unifying, liberal message that spread through all the states was one of regime change, backed by calls for greater participation in the political process in order to secure, for most people, cheaper food and increased and more equitable employment opportunities: a freedom plea as ideology. (An Amnesty International report on Egypt broadened the repertoire of discontent to include 'endemic corruption, police brutality, and lack of civil and political rights' as well as 'ostentatious displays of wealth, particularly of the ruling elite').[25] But what animates Gladwell is what he considers to be an overly hopeful and unfounded view of social media's ability to supply the effective infrastructure for successful revolution. In a well-publicised dispute with Gladwell, Clay Shirky, among the most enthusiastic of internet optimists, counters by refining the question: 'Do social media allow insurgents to adopt new strategies? And have those strategies ever been crucial?' His conclusion is in the affirmative: 'Digital networks', he argues, 'have acted as a massive positive supply shock to the cost and spread of information, to the ease and range of public speech by citizens, and to the speed and scale of group co-ordination...these changes do not allow otherwise uncommitted groups to take effective political action. They do, however, allow committed groups to play by new rules'.[26]

And it is these new rules that underpin *The Violent Image* with its new conceptualisation of the Propaganda of the Deed. However, states do not stand still; they constantly learn and adapt. More sophisticated governments have indeed moved increasingly beyond firewalls and denial of service attacks to thwart unwanted messages. Rebecca MacKinnon's study of China's response to internet insurgency is revealing in this regard. China has witnessed two broad kinds of activism on the web: political 'exit' (such as radicals calling for an end to one-party rule), and 'voice' or 'co-operation' (moderates pointing to the rise of online opposition and using government fear of that threat as a tool for negotiating reforms). While the former has been crushed through surveillance and prosecution, the latter sits within a broader framework of managing the flow of information, otherwise known as 'authoritarian deliberation'. It has been likened by the scholar Li Yonggang to a complex system of hydraulic regulation. Far from a complete shut-down of users' access to the web, it represents a flexible calibration of multiple flows of ideas and communication, addressing both routine and crisis events. Again, according to Mian Jiang, China's cyberspace should now be viewed as four deliberative public spaces: government-controlled websites—'central propaganda spaces'; sites operated by private companies within strict rules—'government-regulated commercial spaces'; NGOs' or individuals' websites subject to registration, regulation, and sanction in the case of breach—'emergent civic spaces'; and websites outside China's domain and control, and remedied by the Great Firewall—'international deliberative spaces'. Most public opinion, he argues, is affected by the first two.[27] Following this taxonomy, it would suggest a more nuanced set of distribution channels for insurgent images to negotiate as states choose to shape and influence the communications environment rather than control it directly.[28]

The difficulties faced by groups in authoritarian countries are legion. For all its potential, mobilisation on the ground through digital communication has problems where information flows are concentrated: 'In the run-up to the disputed election [Iran], the Mousavi campaign sought to use Facebook to rally supporters', writes Bruce Etling. 'The government responded by simply blocking access to Facebook. Online communities that congregate at a single URL are easily dismantled; organisations that rely on a centralised node and hierarchical structures are trivial to break up'.[29]

Taken from a different perspective, on an industry level, the very infrastructure of the web, which offers insurgent ideas the chance to proliferate across multiple populations, also harbours the seeds for narrowing the reach of those selfsame ideas. Fears that internet search engines like the market-leader Google, employing hidden algorithms that personalise and thus restrict unwittingly the user's choice of material (the filter bubble), will lead web-users to a mirror-imaging of their existing repertoire of interests, ideas, and attitudes, may mitigate against the spread of the insurgent idea.[30] This parallels the separate notion of how users self-stream. Surveys of blogs reveal an interesting tendency towards balkanisation, that is group polarisation of opinions where self-selecting groups are driven to ever more prejudiced and extreme views through regular exchange. Associated with that is the view that in digital space, individuals edit out what they wish to hear from a cacophony of information (the Babel syndrome). Conversely, the idea that the internet promotes fragmentation and debate via a 'networked public sphere' represents an overly generous view of human communications. At the same time, the rapid success of the social media site Facebook (founded in 2004; boasting nearly 700 million users by May 2011), whose subscriber trajectory was based on an appeal to being different or at least in opposition to the mainstream, may now be reaching a saturation point, having lost its novelty value. Challengers, such as 'A Small World' and niche networks focused on particular interests or markets, are becoming the fashion as Facebook sees a desertion of former users (6 million defectors in the USA; 1.5 million in Canada; 100,000 in each of the UK, Russia and Norway in the month of May 2011), that are only mitigated by newcomers from richly populated Mexico, Indonesia, India and Brazil.[31] The point here is not to assume a regular or friction free environment for the insurgent image. Nor to be conclusive in a dynamic era of change. Shirky treads carefully but goes to the heart of spontaneity, when he proposes that it is apparent that

disciplined non-violence...doesn't come from synchronised turnout...Governments have systematically overestimated access to information....

In effect, they are looking in the wrong direction:

Access to conversations among amateurs is more politically inspiring than access to information. Governments are afraid of synchronised groups, not synchronised individuals.[32]

It is important to point out the reservations expressed by doubters, if only to counter journalistic shorthand that labelled the events in the Arab states of 2010–2011 as a Twitter revolution. What is beyond reproach is the complex impact of popular unrest fired by POTD imagery, a recently transformed digital mediaspace, and consumer access to the tools of communication.

Anonymity and Leaderless Revolution

In the broader discussion we are concerned with how ideas and images mobilise populations, and what limits spontaneity encounters in provoking political change: in the narrower argument how ideas move between individuals and groups, passing through both established and evolving infrastructures, and social networks.[33] The Arab Spring has offered diverse case studies of populations using social media to vent their deep-rooted grievances and to challenge their governments. But so rudimentary have been the formal institutions of opposition following decades of political exclusion that these revolutions are effectively leaderless. More specifically, they offer up few nationally recognised spokespersons around whom to coalesce dissident opinion; at the same time, many actors choose to remain nameless, more accurately faceless while mobilising on the internet. So the very concept of a leaderless revolution can have multiple dimensions: leaderlessness as a normative extension of horizontal, networked communication; leaderlessness as the consequence of marginalised populations now turned to collective action; and leaderlessness as the choice of social actors who prefer to safeguard their identities.

Does anonymity (lack of visibility) of leadership and indeed membership mean that fluid communications obviate the need for political organisation? In November 2008, eleven activists were arrested in France, accused of participating in sabotaging overhead electricity cables on France's railway system. Their alleged 'terrorist manual' or manifesto, accompanied by a statement attributed to the Invisible Committee, discusses new possibilities for waging insurgency, the spirit of which appears to have been inspired by France's 'banlieue' fires of 2005. It bears quoting at length since it raises two central issues, namely visibility and spontaneity:

Visibility must be avoided. But a force that gathers in the shadows can't avoid it forever. Our appearance as a force must be reserved for an opportune moment. The longer we avoid visibility, the stronger we'll be when it catches up with us. And once we become visible our days will be numbered. Either we will be in a position to break its hold in short order, or we'll be crushed in no time.[34]

Such is the dilemma of all traditional terrorist groups: the need to hug the shadows. Compare that with Anonymous, the self-proclaimed, online 'hactivist collective' dedicated to internet freedom, when it echoes this sentiment. On 11 June 2011, a denial of service attack against the website of the Spanish National Police followed the arrest of three alleged members of the collective suspected of having previously struck against the Sony PlayStation Network and government sites. In a letter to the Spanish government, it responded with a different kind of denial:

It has come to our attention that deemed it necessary to arrest three of our fellow anons…which you claim to be the leaders of Anonymous…There are no leaders of Anonymous. Anonymous is not based on personal distinction…You have not detained three participants of Anonymous. We have no members and we are not a group of any kind.[35]

The Invisible Committee and Anonymous: the first group, a seemingly traditional, off-line insurgency; the other, an online magnet for a loose array of contested causes. Both shun the limelight. This goes to the heart of Bruce Etling's point when he argues that civil society organisations and social movements today find sanctuary through anonymity online. Nevertheless, the disadvantage of having no public face is that 'anonymity diminishes the very factors that facilitate effective social and political organising identified by Tilly, Ganz and others: leadership and displays of unity and commitment. It is therefore not surprising', he declares, 'that there are no examples of influential political movements comprised of anonymous participants'.[36] When the porous nature of online activist groups is allied to the fluidity of individuals or sub-groups joining and exiting social movements, long-term message cohesion is threatened. Witness LulzSec, an online hacker group, boasting 260,000 followers to its Twitter feed. Loosely associated with Anonymous, in May 2011 it attacked an FBI affiliated site, having targeted Britain's Serious Organised Crime Agency (SOCA) and the Sony corporation. However, fear of being identified by security agencies provoked one sharp rebuke of a participant who had offered an 'IAmA' (question and answer session) on behalf of LulzSec on the website Reddit:

You guys started an IAmA on reddit?…I will go to your homes and kill you. If you really started an IAmA bro, you really don't understand what we are about here. I thought all this stuff was common knowledge…no more public appearances [sic] without us organising it…If you are not familiar with these hostile environments, don't partake in it.[37]

LulzSec may or may not have exerted any serious influence on activist campaigning on the web before they announced they were ceasing operations after fifty days.[38] But they unwittingly raise the question of the need in the revolutionary theatre for leadership that is both identifiable and in some respect accountable. Continuity and a certain predictability are also key to harnessing and stabilising support. If groups evolve and fracture in short timeframes, the point of identification with a consistency of resolve required by turbulent populations searching for an outlet is threatened.

Spontaneity and Revolution

If spontaneous mass action energised by POTD imagery can bring down governments, must it eventually overcome the state's final defence, namely armed force? Digital mobilisation and organisation rely on diffused messaging through horizontal, networked transmission of ideas, and a fluid coalescence of collective will. What they gain in speed, they sacrifice in command-and-control. What is acquired in unpredictability and flexibility, is surrendered in consistency and perhaps durability.

The Invisible Committee attempts to feel its way through this dilemma. 'Coordinations are unnecessary where coordination exists, organisations aren't needed when people organise themselves', suggests a belief in ad hocracy—a self-generating anarchy and spontaneity that finds a natural equilibrium if people are freed from the organising bureaucracy of emergent coalitions of activists.[39] Recalling the youth uprising of 2001 in Algeria where the occupation of most of the Kabylia region prevented elections taking place, '(t)he movement's strength was', the document underlines, 'in the diffuse complimentarity of its components—only partly represented by the interminable and hopelessly male-dominated village assemblies and other popular committees'.[40] This vein is continued in the accompanying letter to their manifesto: 'There is no need to choose between the fetishism of spontaneity and organisational control: between the "come one, come all" of activist networks and the discipline of hierarchy...'.[41] How such hybrid should be achieved is less clear, particularly when the focus is upon collective action on the ground. Online combining with offline activity, on the other hand, offers potential ways forward through smart mobs (as explored in earlier chapters). Bruce Etling notes '(s)mart mobs, however, particularly where they emerge organically and take governments by surprise, may be possible in all but perhaps the most restrictive authoritarian regimes', recalling successes in the Philippines, Serbia, Kyrgyzstan, as well as the anti-FARC protests, beloved of Hillary Rodham Clinton. Notwithstanding, what flash mobs lack, remains

leadership, discipline, long-term planning and ability to incorporate prior experience...flash mobs do not deliberate; they do not debate the alternatives and select pragmatic and well informed strategic approaches.

Yet he notes:

An interesting prospect is that digital communications will emerge to serve as venues for deliberation and to provide collective leadership for smart mobs. Currently, the closest manifestation to such a decentralised deliberative body is the blogosphere.[42]

The events in the Arab states in 2011 provide a laboratory-in-action. They have also opened a fresh avenue of inquiry in insurgency theory. By no means does this new initiative lend itself to being more transparent or scientifically predictable. However, while the flames of change have guttered where some media and public spaces have been temporarily closed down by repressive leaderships, other polities have won out, at least in the short term, through a blend of popular will and regime implosion, fuelled by hot ideas and even hotter imagery.

Because ideas surge virally through digital technologies releasing pent-up emotions and latent ambitions, does that mean revolution is suddenly within grasp of more opposition groups? A destabilised revolutionary theatre does not of itself deliver revolution. A significant proportion of the people, strategically situated, must coalesce to overthrow the seemingly immovable object of government. Revolution is the exception, not the norm. For revolution to succeed, certain preconditions must be in place:

- a sizeable mass of dissenters must have reached some kind of 'consciousness'—a social movement centred on a grievance;
- the government should have lost legitimacy in the eyes of a sizeable minority or majority of the population;
- coalition unity of political elites must have fractured;
- the international community and neighbouring states should either resist intervening or if they do, commit themselves on behalf of the insurgency; and
- crucially, the army must divide or stand aside.
- States occasionally implode under pressure of popular discontent as leaders' self-confidence drains from political will; the USSR and its satellites give recent substance to this view. Indeed Romania's dictator Nicolae Ceausescu provided one of those rare glimpses when (state) television, broadcasting the leader's fitful speech to a massed crowd, captured on camera the draining of blood from the regime and rapid government débacle. However, traditionally, to challenge disproportionate power and resources enjoyed by controlling elites

in autocracies (even democracies) means bridging the gulf between popular will (consciousness) and direct action. And ultimately, revolutionary action and revolutionary government.

In a pre-digital age, Lenin was all too aware of the dangers of the spontaneous upsurge in the masses outrunning the revolutionary leadership. Without a broader, theoretical understanding on the part of the proletariat of why society needed to change, workers would confine themselves to resolving only iniquities in the workplace, not a root-and-branch transformation of society. So rather than give spontaneity free rein, 'combating spontaneity' for him meant 'the task of social democracy should be to lend the spontaneous movement a consciousness of its own ultimate aims'.[43] For Rosa Luxemburg, spontaneity and vanguardism were not so much in contradiction as moments in a continuum or process. Her Dialectic of Spontaneity and Organisation saw leadership, however, arising from within the movement:

The modern proletariat doesn't carry out its struggle according to a plan set out in some book or theory; the modern worker's struggle is a part of history, a part of social progress, and in the middle of history, in the middle of progress, in the middle of the fight, we learn how we must fight....[44]

By contrast, 'excitative terror', that technique employed by terrorists, was thought to fall short of both consciousness raising and organisation. It failed precisely because, Lenin argued,

the working masses are raised to a high pitch of excitement by the social evils in Russian life, but are unable to gather, if one may put it, and concentrate all these drops and streamlets of popular resentment that are brought forth to a far larger extent than we imagine by the conditions of Russian life and that must be combined into a single gigantic torrent.[45]

So for Lenin the solution to shaping that single gigantic torrent was to demand consciousness-raising and an agitational phase of revolution through the fusion of party and working-class movement. Moreover, it emphasised the need for building discipline and organisation. Yet this was not merely the pre-digital, pre-viral era; it was also a time when the conception of non-violent state overthrow lacked any credible expectation of success. Not only that, it was an era when revolutionaries lacked the mechanism to deliver coordinated delivery of a mass message capable of circumventing elite media ownership. Revolution was therefore inherently violent.[46] For all the initial, quietist progress of the Arab Spring in the Digital Age, particularly Tunisia and Egypt, the path of violence may yet turn out to be the only viable long-term option as counter-revolutionary state elites and hierarchies close ranks to maintain the status quo.

This discussion of the desirability to control mass spontaneity is critical for today's dictatorships and democracies. So also is the question of whether mass mobilisation achieved through such control can afford insurgents a realistic alternative to using violence in overthrowing the state. According to the economist Albert Hirschman, '(t)o qualify as revolutionary, violence must be centralised; it must attack and conquer the central seats of political and administrative power'.[47] That is because state elites are not inclined to cede control willingly. This much was clear to Leon Trotsky, as to Friedrich Engels before him.[48] But changes in modern militaries, Engels would write in 1891, meant:

Contrary to appearance, compulsory military service surpasses general franchise as a democratic agency. The real strength of the German social democracy does not rest in the number of its voters but in its soldiers.[49]

In other words, mass conscription in modernising armies would turn them into a people's army, and as young recruits brought their politics with them, so armed forces would be subject to internal splits. But that was to underestimate the resilience of state institutions. Militaries were rapidly industrialising, so too their weaponry and communications, and streets were being widened in new urban planning. The chances of revolution being attained on the barricades, he would have to cede, was an anachronistic tactic that had probably breathed its last by 1849:

even during the classic period of street battles, the barricade had a moral rather than a material effect...The barricade had lost its charm; the soldier saw behind it no longer the people but rebels...the officer in the course of time had become familiar with the tactical forms of street battles. No longer did he march in direct line and without cover upon improvised breastworks, but out-flanked them through gardens, courts, and houses.[50]

Ultimately an appeal to the democratic awakening of a 'nation in arms', a 'nation motivated by justice', seemed the most realistic way forward. Nevertheless, for Trotsky, the decisive confrontation must be with the army, the counter-revolutionary force that would be mobilised against the people when the survival of the state is threatened. An armed clash becomes inevitable because the army's political mood, that great unknown of every revolution, can be determined only in the process of a clash between the soldiers and the people. The army's crossing over to the camp of the revolution is a moral process; but it cannot be brought about by moral means alone.[51]

He would later refine that position, arguing:

an insurrection is, in essence, not so much a struggle against the army as a struggle for the army. The more stubborn, far-reaching, and successful the insurrection, the more probable—indeed inevitable—is a fundamental change in the attitude of the troops. Guerrilla fighting on the basis of a revolutionary strike cannot in itself, as we saw in Moscow, lead to victory. But it creates the possibility of sounding the mood of the army, and after a first important victory—that is, once a part of the garrison has joined the insurrection—the guerrilla struggle can be transformed into a mass struggle in which a part of the troops, supported by the armed and unarmed population, will fight another part, which will find itself in a ring of universal hatred.[52]

Precisely how guerrilla struggle would transform into mass struggle, Trotsky was less clear about. His assessment fell short of Mao's prescriptive, politico-military strategy of three-phase warfare where there are distinct stages of progression and strategic regression to suit evolving conditions on the ground (indoctrination by cadres; guerrilla warfare; and confrontation between conventional armies of the regime and rebels).[53]

The Bolshevik analysis resonates today in the Arab Uprisings. In a revolutionary theatre, unless the government abandons the reins of power, much rests on the actions of the military—whether it fractures or remains united. The availability of 24-hour news feeds and images diffused by mobile phones and laptops means that throughout 2011 all eyes were trained on the decision of various Arab militaries either to intercede on behalf of popular uprisings or to buttress failing regimes. Insights into their deliberations are rare. Amid a maelstrom of images showing a population in uproar, Egypt's military sought to arrange an orderly post-Mubarak transition, initially through its placeman and former defence minister Field Marshall Mohamed Hussein Tantawi, latterly through parliamentary elections overseen by a military council. Exploiting the close relationship between American and Egyptian militaries, US officials repeated the mantra of social contract: '(d)on't break the bond you have with your own people'. Egypt's armed forces subsequently kept their powder dry.[54] Although paradoxically a revered institution in a land of extreme inequalities, shifting officers from their entrenched positions of power and business interests has proven a greater challenge to the nascent democratic process. Libya's military, meanwhile, initially remained broadly loyal to Colonel Gaddafi barring some high-level defections and desertions from lower ranks, significantly along regional and tribal lines. But that would change as Libya became embroiled in civil war. Syria's army embarked on a brutal clean-up operation of dissident towns around the country, spearheaded by the elite 4th Division (reviving memories of Hafez al-Assad regime's 1982 massacre in Hama), while the Republican Guard remained loyal in defence of the capital.[55] In the Gulf, Bahrain's' Sunni command had forces fire on predominantly Shi'a demonstrators and bulldoze the prime location of protest, Pearl Square. But add to that list Tunisia's military chief's insisting '(t)he army will protect the revolution', having allegedly ordered troops not to fire on protesters,[56] and the picture is far from uniform. In the end, each military reflects national circumstances. So are we now entering an era when people-power expressed through the sheer force of image cascades in digital space will pre-empt such clashes or force regimes to seek resolution by turning on their own populations? The answer is not an easy one; the indications are that insurgents have grasped the initial lesson that the violent image is their chosen strategic operating concept in the war of ideas.

* * *

POTD sits at the heart of the Arab Spring. The Arab Uprisings offer a new, if complex living laboratory for examining how POTD-as-image circulates amid revolutionary turbulence. However, any developments remain work in progress rooted in particular local, regional and geopolitical sets of circumstance. Indeed each affected state will in due course undoubtedly present a different political outcome.

Nevertheless from the Uprisings, a suggestion of some congruent patterns of behaviour is beginning to emerge. The back-story originates in long-standing social or economic grievance as the prerequisite in the pre-revolutionary theatre; then the spark of an emotive, publicised POTD-event ignites the population; the primacy of that symbol-rich, shock-and-awe image disseminated cross-border via electronic circuits and satellites inspires neighbouring polities; protesters erupt onto streets, galvanised by social networks in the community, many of whom are logistically wired-up by social networks in the virtual domain; and it all leads to the massing of dissent captured by the second revolutionary image, namely that of the heaving urban square. Urban spaces, often labelled 'freedom' or 'liberation' (*tahrir*), are less square than circular traffic roundabout or intersection. Crucially, they become the place where temporary stasis arrests the fluidity of all traffic. And the electronic eye does the rest, imposing a new understanding for viewers.

Framed by the television or mobile phone camera, this new picture is as implicitly violent in the way it captures humanity *en masse* as was the initial Propaganda of the Deed image explicit in its eruptive threat to the political *status quo*. And although struggle between protesters and police is frequently played out in side-streets and commercial thoroughfares, it is in the central square, usually in the nation's capital, that security forces' confidence and the resolve of governments are put to the test as the world looks on. Will the government collapse as security forces side with the crowd? Or will government and military remain mutually loyal, turning on the people, risking the escalation of popular violence? This is no simple dichotomy. Yet recent events in these Arab states suggest that even in the first scenario government collapse may not routinely lead to fundamental institutional reform. Hence what may come to be remembered as an Egyptian-style military coup in the maquillage of concession to popular will, may only be accompanied by a cosmetic readjustment of privileged elites. While the second scenario superficially invites a more radical denouement and a truer revolutionary outcome as military excesses, and government indecision and intransigence further inflame the crowd. Thus might events set in train street rioting that bursts out of the image-frame of the square, all the time undermining the stability of state institutions and economic markets.

We have witnessed two POTD images—self immolation or atrocity, and mass dissent. The first speaks to latent grievance; the second, to unshackling of suppression, the emergence of new subjectivities, and crucially, confrontation. Above all, this is performative politics. All media converge to crystallise the popular struggle into this single frame, insouciant of the remainder of the population—bystanders living beyond the electronic *cordon sanitaire*. It is the top-shot locked onto thousands upon thousands of bodies fusing into one vote of rejection that beckons the government to collapse, or the military's patience to snap and intervene. The square within the image, a frame within a frame, simplifies the complexity of revolution for restless viewers of the Information Age.

One main corollary of these events is to question whether the violent image today represents a real prospect of mobilising populations to the extent of achieving governmental overthrow or state transformation. That democracies have grown increasingly sensitive to popular power manifested through imagery has been noted in previous chapters. How authoritarian and militarised regimes respond can now also be weighed. Whatever conclusion we might draw at this early stage nevertheless raises the question of whether spontaneity provides a sufficient force to dispense with on-the-ground leadership and organisation. What adds poignancy to this line of inquiry is the paucity of institutional alternatives that have been observed to entrenched authoritarian systems in this region. It is exemplified by the emergence as Egyptian opposition spokesmen of, on the one hand, Wael Ghonim, a Google marketing executive briefly imprisoned for organising protest through Facebook, and on the other, the established Muslim Brotherhood, a dissident party for decades subjected to state prosecution, if not persecution. Such a discussion walks a familiar path for revolutionaries, albeit one worthy of revisiting with renewed vigour in the digital era. In the meantime, that POTD imagery has moved centre-stage as a strategic operating concept seems less controversial, as we shall now explore.

Finally, for all the pictures and messages that clamour for populations' attention in today's media ecology, powerful images retain the ability to cut through the cacophony and stir individuals emotionally. But they go further. They arouse memories of injustice and grievance, indeed moving communities to such an extent that many rise up to challenge those to whom they attribute blame. The Propaganda of the Deed as image and crystallised message, indeed as a lightning rod for memory, sits within a media universe where events ricochet between different media, traditional and new, where each iteration enhances and multiplies the effect of its original manifestation, and where speed of transmission outpaces governments' ability to muster an adequate response. As populations grow more urbanised and electronically linked, so the capacity for emotive reactions increases in intensity and frequency, and with it the capability for insurgent movements to unsettle regimes. Whether governments falter and fall depends largely on a confluence of factors, both internal and external: are they democratic or autocratic; even so, are they willing to resort to violent suppression of their citizens or do they pull back? This is the legitimacy game. To

223

what extent the accumulation of pressure drives dominant elites to fracture, in search of a new calibration of interests within which they may salvage their privileged position, depends on the degree to which we feel that societies are becoming increasingly in thrall to the influence of pluralist media to shape events. The next chapter reveals an historic shift where insurgents have moved POTD as media image to the centre of their strategic operations, and states have been caught off guard.

Cairo, 2011: Security forces trigger renewed turbulence.
© Reuters/Stringer.

8

THE NEW STRATEGIC OPERATING CONCEPT

The interval between the decay of the old and the formation and establishment
of the new, constitutes a period of transition, which must always necessarily be
one of uncertainty, confusion, error, and wild and fierce fanaticism.

John Calhoun[1]

For over fifty years social observers from Bell to Drucker, Masuda,
Castells, and Urry have described fundamental changes in Western
society fanning out across the world, impacting urban and increasingly
rural dwellers. They share the conviction that information sits at the
heart of an uneven transformation. Driven by various dimensions of
'globalisation', access to information and communications has become
the defining factor dividing rich from poor, and haves from have-nots.
If Castells is right, in the Information Age they determine whether individuals are included or excluded from power-loops.[2] Under certain
conditions particular populations motivated by common identity, occasionally common cause, interact with traditional but particularly digital technologies to unsettle the status quo of states. Where conflicts or
insurgent safe havens invite external intervention, societies at different
stages of development in their use of information technologies are
drawn into the transnational complex of information diffusion. These
then impact populations on the local, but also regional and global levels. Consciously or otherwise individuals find themselves in perpetual
feedback loops.

227

This chapter asks how have insurgent groups embraced changes of the Information Age, and how far have they turned information and communications into a central plank of their strategy? The following analysis is set in the context of recent political economy and strategic developments, before exploring the Al-Qaeda model, widely emulated by other insurgents, as today's most proficient practitioner of the new strategic operating concept. This inquiry centres on two themes: the effects of globalisation and fragmentation, and military reluctance to engage with the transformative influence of information in global conflict. It concludes that neo-liberal economic policies, introduced in the twilight of the Cold War, created new spaces for capitalist expansion, causing massive dislocation in developing and emerging economies. Globalisation revolutionised media and ICT industries, producing fresh cognitive spaces. These beamed into those societies images of the growing gap between rich and poor, and included and excluded. They rejuvenated grievance, fuelling diverse causes for complex insurgencies. In these new spaces insurgents found room to manœuvre, adapting the old relationship between time and space. At the same time Western militaries and their civilian leaders fixed on an overly technological view of future conflict, misreading the nature of change in insurgency. Their enthusiasm for high-tech, high-precision weaponry privileged kinetic engagement as a form of computer-game warfare. Meanwhile insurgents realised that images and messages sent via media networks could become the new cognitive twenty-first century force. This recognition has formed a central platform of the operating strategy of particular groups.

Opening Spaces at the Fin-de-siècle

The late twentieth century saw numerous developments which variously impacted insurgent movements on all continents, the most prominent of which was an opening up of new spaces. What populations could not experience directly in their personal lives, they witnessed via television—and increasingly web-transmitted images. Often these captured existential struggles of minorities that sublimated in violence. But even for those not seduced by violent protest, such images tapped into a recognition that living standards among the world's majority were slipping relative to the few whose rising prosperity was regularly portrayed in television news and fiction. Violent struggles were regularly ascribed to globalisation, a loose concept conflating and revealing an array of social shifts. However complex the causes, how they appeared on television represented a threat to what had gone before. A new international division of labour destabilised established employment patterns. It emerged where increasingly powerful transnational corporations switched manufacturing and distribution centres between regions according to the price of workers' wages, proximity to emerging markets for sales, and favourable tax domains to offshore corporate profits. Meanwhile 1980s structural adjustment policies, prescribed by neo-liberal economic philosophers and espoused by Reagan and Thatcher, crystallised in the Washington Consensus. They had damaging consequences for many states. Imposed by the IMF in return for investment and foreign aid, conditionality required developing countries lower tariff barriers thus allowing cheap imports to undercut local production and consequently drive up unemployment. But while the outsider was 'invited' into impoverished societies, the insider was not so welcome abroad when applying to international labour markets. One further by-product of conditionality was a 'hollowing out of the state', notably in parts of the African continent. As external aid was appropriated by political elites and patronage networks, and malfunctioning bureaucracies grew less capable, in many African states this accelerated or renewed a slide into civil conflict.[3] Porous borders made the problem worse, inviting participation from bad neighbours who exploited cross-border ethnic populations for reasons of security and self-interest. The end of the Cold War left its indelible mark. Erstwhile proxy wars veiled by post-colonial or national liberation struggles, financed and supplied at arm's length by the USA and USSR, took on a different form. When bipolar geopolitics changed almost overnight in 1989–90, external funding for rebel fighters, already on the wane, finally dried up. Massive stocks of small arms flooded out of former Soviet arsenals onto international markets, transported courtesy of ever-falling freight costs as airlines cashed in on deregulation. Weapons and materiel found their way into the hands of opposition groups. Many continued to dominate terrain intent on extracting minerals and natural resources to subsidise their war projects and advance often blatant warlordism (Sierra Leone, Liberia, Angola).[4] This meant hostilities slipped into a state of affairs commonly labelled 'no peace, no war' where proponents had more to gain from sustaining rather than ceasing combat.[5] Elsewhere, civil wars like Guatemala's and El Salvador's that had raged for decades edged towards hard-negotiated peace treaties between exhausted combatants. Nevertheless parallel economies remained in the grip of vested interests within the armed forces. The violence of war merely transmuted into the violence of peace.[6] What resulted displayed some of the hallmarks commentators had already identified in the Balkans conflicts: descent into brutal violence that locked into global networks of organised crime.[7]

Market deregulation that had so dramatically impacted the livelihoods of millions transformed the world of communications too. Broadcasting corporations opened up new spaces into which mass audiences were invited. Satellite television broke state broadcast monopolies as pictures beamed into formerly government-controlled, national footprints. The proliferation of outlets spelled reduced budgets for stations that now shared programme-content to save on the costly business of newsgathering. One by-product was that images and messages were amplified with fewer constraints than hitherto. However what the new television space captured and what would characterise the 1990s was the exploiting of deep-seated ethnic antagonisms by armed groups, undertaken with fresh brutality, inviting commentaries of a 'coming anarchy'.[8] To counter the suffering of civilian populations, the decade saw humanitarian agencies expand their role in failing states. UN peacekeepers and NGOs interceded under the ethos of the UN's 'Responsibility to Protect' initiative and a growing trend towards humanitarian intervention.[9] Regrettably the General Assembly and Security Council repeatedly failed to meet diverse challenges presented by power-sharing, inter-communal strife, insurrection and mass killing in Cambodia (1992–93), Bosnia (1992–95), Somalia (1992–95) and Rwanda (1993–94).[10] Meanwhile the picture was confused. Older insurgents like Ireland's PIRA were preparing to replace the Armalite with the ballot-box, South Africa's ANC was reaching a deal for orderly transition from Apartheid to black majority rule, while recent arrivals like Hamas were injecting renewed militancy into the Middle East following the first Palestinian *intifada*, and Hezbollah secured its hold on terrain and population in Lebanon's refugee camps and Shi'a south. Guerrillas in Nepal fought a traditional Maoist struggle while Mexico's Zapatistas pursued a peasant campaign, deploying a radical internet communications strategy from their forest redoubts. Colombia's FARC fighters graduated to managing their own narcotics economy ostensibly in search of socialist ideals, while Sri Lanka's

Tamil Tigers appealed to an international diaspora for funding, stimulated by the emotional appeal of 'heroic' suicide bombings. Conflict images from around the globe remained consistent: states and rebels exchanged atrocities, populations suffered, and underlying causes disappeared in the melee. The only victor was the media industry.

POTD's terrorist act, widely associated with groups vying for global media attention in what seemed a simpler age (1960s-70s), would become an even more familiar occurrence. Extreme Islamic groups with combat skills honed against the Soviet invader in Afghanistan learned to attract media attention, adapting the experience of earlier Palestinian fighters and Tamil Tiger suicide bombers. Attacks on American embassies in Beirut and Nairobi, the warship *USS Cole*, the foiled attempt to bomb New York's World Trade Center then its ultimately successful destruction in the new century, brought POTD to the fore of public awareness. Repeated reminders would appear in Bali (2002, 2005), Madrid (2004), Moscow (2004, 2010), London (2005), and Mumbai (2008) amid concerted responses from Western and Russian armed forces in Iraq, Afghanistan, and Chechnya. In the following years events—particularly in Pakistan and Afghanistan—turned POTD into a daily feature on global television screens. Those images projected via the Information Revolution announced that many disenfranchised populations would no longer suffer in silence.

Insurgency springs from its political, social and economic context. So it is hardly surprising that its proponents in various guises would be touched by the sweeping transformation heralded in the economic meta-narrative of the late twentieth century. Margaret Thatcher captured the scorched-earth spirit of the times: '(e)conomics are the method; the object is to change the heart and soul'.[11] Neoliberal mantra and one-size-fits-all reforms promised to prise open markets, deregulate banking, and reduce the power of over-regulated states. They heralded in Ohmae's phrase, a 'borderless world'.[12] Politicians and media pundits quickly adopted their language of globalisation. But this was no utopian cosmopolitanism—more Marx than Kant.[13] It represented capitalism's untrammelled progress in the face of a discredited communist alternative, enveloping different cultures while adapting its credo to local circumstance.[14] Meanwhile it wrought its 'creative destruction'. In Harvey's analysis, capital forever searches out fresh markets, new spaces in which to invest its surplus and generate profits anew, making it a remarkable force for innovation. Immense oil surpluses from OPEC price hikes in the 1970s had created a 'crisis of over-accumulation'.[15] An excess of capital could not find sanctuary for profitable reproduction without social and economic change. Hence states pursued neoliberal policies and promoted the search for new spaces to generate opportunity.[16] Developing countries, and following the Soviet breakup, emergent states were keen to reassert national identities. This offered new spaces for investment in natural resources and cheap labour, and rewards that accrue from government and tax incentives that facilitate freely moving capital. Russian communism transformed into 'anarcho-capitalism'.[17] Global markets were invented where non-manufacturing (as some saw it, fictitious) profits were made. Yet when it went wrong, it did so with tragic results. Lightning shifts of funds spread contagion through currency markets, impacting populations from the Far East through Russia to Brazil.[18] A high-tech exchange promised fortunes from the ICT revolution. It proved more alchemy than chemistry, evaporating in the dot.com debacle (1998–9). Like the global banking and housing crisis a decade later, governments had created new spaces for capital, but they had also dramatically affected the lives of many populations.

Space is a key dimension in insurgency and meanwhile insurgents had also learned to exploit space. Not simply the geographical space of old that allows them to cross rivers, mountains, and forests outrunning government forces and buying time, but new arenas shaped by capital's globalised conquests. Katzenbach argues that for Mao time could defeat technology—'unlimited time depends primarily on unlimited space'.[19]—and sees insurgent activities as kinetic force applied in the operations theatre. This soldier's-eye view speaks to the later stages of Mao's doctrine of three-phase warfare. Yet space for Mao's target population was surely enigmatic, even in 1940s China. The 'strategic transfer', or Long March, saw 86,000 Communist troops cross 10,000 kilometres of northern Chinese wilderness.[20] Most of these rural volunteers, we may conjecture, had short cognitive horizons. Like their ancestors they were born into and spent entire lives on peasant plots within groups of villages. Their world was delimited by a central market a couple of hours walk from home.[21] Unclear is the effect such spatial dichotomy had on the average peasant's thinking. How did his/her cognitive map change as he/she left the village network, before crossing old horizons to discover a never-before imagined China? This point is relevant to POTD's recent development which seeks to exploit not just territorial but cognitive space. Cognition and information go hand in hand. Media are their nursemaid.

I have discussed how insurgents seek to control the past to legitimise their role in the present in order to stake a claim to the future (Chapter Three). They are in the memory-making business, hence they construct insurgent views of history to challenge official versions painted by states. POTD is, to borrow Harvey's phrase, an agent of 'time-space compression'.[22] Both geography and history shrink into a common here and now. POTD attempts to seize control of time and history in the minds of the viewing public through 'shock and awe politics'. But it is achievable only if it creates a new *agora* by commanding space traditionally encountered on television networks, via newspaper circulation, more recently on the web. Through dramatic events a crisis must be provoked. In turn, an opportunity space and opportunity spirals must be opened up (Chapter Six).[23] Other spaces have emerged. More broadly the internet has offered new terrain, a borderless world without states, a public space where ideas and images are exchanged.[24] Consumer take-up has increased and widened to include both urban and rural dwellers in industrial societies and numerous urbanites in developing countries. So insurgents' ideological (ideas) as well as operational influence (instruction and tools) have reached new populations. Migrant diaspora communities have shared in the information boom, providing distribution networks and global population spaces. Formerly 'legitimate' insurrectionists, now bereft of 'honest' funding from Cold War patrons foregrounded what perhaps was always a crucial component of uprisings, despite Mao's best exhortations to respect the population:[25] exploiting local people and natural resources. Forced to link explicitly into global networks of criminality, they have developed international space outside the state system to supplement their domestic activities. They operate outside the legality of sovereign states but derive commodities as the basis of their exchange as well as their markets within those states. Yet whether addressing recent migrants or longer established generations, insurgents have also consistently extended their political reach into formal constitutional space. Witness Sinn Féin *vis-à-vis* IRA, and Hezbollah *vis-à-vis* al-Muqawama al-Islamiya.[26] By retaining one foot in legitimate politics and one foot outside, some groups have managed to extend their influence and negotiations, buying more time and space for their projects. Hence finding new space is not just the prerogative of governments. Nor do insurgents merely see terrain as today's operations theatre. Rather the media supplies the cognitive domain as the new battlespace.

Information and the Military

How did militaries read the Information Age? Soft information, the kind that impacts general populations, has become an ever-greater concept of operations with insurgents in recent years. But the same cannot be said for militaries which struggle to prioritise it at the centre of strategic affairs. How important are violent acts that connect populations to information and an appreciation of the causes underlying that violence? This is unclear and much contested. Against a backdrop of unstable populations and growing irregular wars, the success of one conventional war would have clear, adverse consequences. Operation Desert Storm (1991) skewed American military thinkers towards believing continued faith in structuring combat around manœuvre and conventional warfare had been vindicated.[27] Tomahawk cruise missiles fired far out at sea could find their way to Baghdad's streets before penetrating key installations with apparent pinpoint accuracy. A new love for long-distance, precision-guided, high-tech warfare rose phoenix-like from the debris. Expeditionary forces had outwitted Saddam's troops in the desert with rapid movement and manoeuvre. But sophisticated targeting by men poring over screens had moved the story to a new level of efficiency, with the added benefit of minimising friendly casualties. However Martin Van Creveld called for caution:

Weapons do not grow in a vacuum. Even as they help shape ideas concerning the nature of war and the ways it ought to be fought, they themselves are the product of those ideas. The same is even more true of the social organisations—armed forces, general staffs, and defence departments—which produce, field, and use the weapons.[28]

His was a fear of being locked into path dependency. For all the high-level backslapping, Iraq was a one-sided victory. It took the generals' eyes off the ball. They risked remaining hostage to 'big warfare' while overlooking the changing nature of conflict around the globe.[29] One clue lay in Desert Storm itself. Suddenly, war played out live as spectacle in viewers' living rooms, showing precision strikes destroying buildings not people, introduced a new, indeed unexpected consequence into the equation. This was the so-called, albeit soon to be contested, 'CNN effect'. Any advantage scored by the military for technical prowess now provided a setback for politicians. Sensitive to the opinions of their constituents, valuable time to reflect on rapidly unfolding events was lost. Responding to public and media interrogation over the conduct of war changed the game. News now threatened to have the potential to shape foreign policy priorities as and when popular opinion pressured politicians' actions.[30] But politico-military affairs were only a harbinger of trends that would eventually affect all areas of news production and social interest.[31]

In military circles by 2003 it was assumed the Second Gulf War would follow a similar pattern to the first, a 'traditional blitzkrieg' not an 'irregular long, hard slog'.[32] Paul Yingling's searing attack on America's generals (he claimed Iraq like Vietnam had been a failure of leadership) saw them 'checked by a form of war that they did not prepare for and [did] not understand'. They were staring at 'institutional crisis', no less.[33] Furthermore, it implied that 'a marriage of information and communications systems with those that apply military force' was achievable.[34] But these new capabilities would be directed at technological superiority in the three-dimensional battlespace. As such it would deny any shift in patterns of conflict to the civil or political space had occurred, what Mary Kaldor labelled the 'revolution in social relations of warfare'.[35] Information for militaries still meant hard information: intelligence and C2. Not soft information: social, cultural and political knowledge. Unsurprisingly, any newly perceived importance of the political space that prioritised information (and irregular violence) gave rise to a fresh debate.

Much is written on the Revolution in Military Affairs (RMA) and I shall not presume to add to it.[36] Yet the RMA's attraction for some is that following the Cold War the world has witnessed a convergence of factors which impact strategic affairs, such that a new way of looking at conflict and warfare is called for.[37] At its heart are new technologies which change the way armies engage with one another. Information, 'the knowledge we have of the enemy and his country...the foundation of our ideas and actions', Clausewitz saw as fundamental to conducting warfare.[38] The fog of war, argued America's National Defense Panel (NDP) report in 1997 could be dissipated by 'rapid advances in information and information-related technologies'.[39] America could capitalise on its digital edge. Gradually however RMA slipped into the gap between 'rhetoric and the reality of US military policy'.[40] Nevertheless in certain quarters 'information warfare' became a 'synonym for the RMA'.[41] Indeed for TX Hammes information and communications are key dimensions of 'Fourth Generation Warfare' (4GW), the origins of which he unearths in Mao's theory and practice:

Beginning with Mao's concept that political will defeats superior military power and progressing to Intifada 1's total reliance on the mass media and international networks to neutralise Israel's military power, warfare underwent a fundamental change. It shifted from an industrial age focus on the destruction of the enemy's armed forces to an information age focus on changing the minds of the enemy's political decision-makers.[42]

By this analysis, manœuvre warfare has given way to favouring superior political will among populations in the 'long war'.[43] It is the antithesis of the short, sharp shock celebrated in Iraq in 1991. For many who share such conviction, political will further derives strength from a direct link between information and social networks, stretching from sub-national to trans-national levels. It taps into local culture, belief systems, and support. Insurgent strategists are pragmatic. At the same time as making short-term accommodations with shifting power-groups to realise their goals, they recognise a growing fragmentation among audiences. So engineering messages for divergent constituencies becomes a corollary of what William Lind identifies as an ongoing process of media manipulation, especially through nightly television news. There it is all too easy to turn state success into apparent failure. As Lind highlights, 'pictures seen of enemy civilian dead brought into every living room in the country on the evening news can easily turn what may have been a military success (assuming we hit the military target) into a serious defeat'. Overt self-inflicted wounds such as photographs of Iraqi prisoners tortured by US personnel at Abu Ghraib and Guantanamo Bay detainees play unaided into this media strategy. Pushed to its extreme, such a conclusion suggests 'modern insurgency has become essentially a strategic communications campaign supported by military action rather than a military campaign supported by effective strategic communications'.[44] In short, a picture looms of hybrid, asymmetric conflicts which mix-and-match old and new media techniques, high technology, and ideology driven by state and sub-state level participants.[45]

Hybrid conflict chimes with Kaldor's earlier 'new and old wars' model: low-intensity conflicts connected via transnational webs in a globalised world facilitated by information technologies. But far from accepting an RMA, because RMA by definition centres on conventional warfare, for her new wars represent a revolution in social relations rather than technology, even though participants employ these latest technologies.[46] There is more than an echo in Frank Hoffman's notion of 'hybrid wars' which underscores how today's conflict embraces 'conventional capabilities, irregular tactics and formations, terrorist acts, including indiscriminate violence and coercion, and criminal disorder'. These dimensions have been present presumably in wars throughout history, albeit perhaps not simultaneously in the same theatre. What marks the change is the recent blurring of regular and irregular conflicts into a single force.[47] So the charge until recently against military senior command and their political chiefs is one of failing to read the writing on the wall, and more specifically that they remain risk-averse and misconstrue the new information environment.[48] Consequently, high-tech weaponry driven by sophisticated intelligence and information systems was thought capable of penetrating the fog of war. Yet to concentrate on only one type of information emanating from the battlespace ran the risk of turning military engagement into a screen-based computer game. Accordingly, today 'drones' (UAVs) deployed over Afghanistan and tribal areas along Pakistan's border capitalise on state-of-the-art remote surveillance and strike capacity that can be directed fatally at an insurgent enemy.

Here it is important to differentiate between conceptions of information. In traditional military affairs it has two faces: the primacy of incoming battlefield and enemy intelligence, as well as outgoing dissemination of messages through information operations (IO).[49] Confusion arises from various ambiguous interpretations of information warfare. For example, 'netwar' is information warfare by another name, and uses 'network forms of organisation, doctrine, strategy, and technology attuned to the information age'.[50] But 'netwar' manifests itself in what might be viewed as the good and the bad: that is progressive civil society forces, as well as criminals and terrorists.[51] For both to realise netwar's full potential, dense, constantly connected information flows are mandatory. These then move within the same kind of segmented, polycephalous and networked structures in society Gerlach identified in the 1960s' Counterculture (Chapter Six).[52] So netwar is defined not solely by the internet as technology, although it is a critical element, but by social connections and networks. Hence computers and cellphones have opened new horizons not merely for spreading messages but how they diffuse them. Where militaries struggle to adjust is in recognising that 'the media and the public, in War 2.0, are the central battle-ground'. Indeed they have been caught unawares. So suddenly has the era of War 1.0 passed, where public and media were once sidelined in a division of labour separating political from military affairs,[53] that playing catch-up is proving a ponderous business. This leads to accusations that officers above 'major' level are still fighting conventional wars, while junior ranks are tuned into a new state of strategic affairs.[54] Admittedly this is a question of emphasis: will twenty-first century conflict see a return to conventional warfare between states? Or will 'wars among the people' become the dominant paradigm? The likely scenario, conjectures the latest US Capstone Concept, remains war between military powers, albeit not in the short-term. Other forms of war, it concedes, are 'guaranteed' and already 'ongoing' in the shape of low-intensity conflicts.[55] At the highest level this official prognosis nevertheless suggests generals are now more than aware of the underlying threat, even if their actions remain ambivalent:

Potential adversaries have already recognised the strategic importance of the narrative battle and will continue to develop and employ increasingly sophisticated methods in that battle. Influencing public perceptions of battlefield events thus will become both more important and more difficult for joint forces, and commanders even at subordinate levels will find themselves nearly as consumed with shaping the narrative of those events as with planning and conducting the operations that produce them.[56]

One British General felt moved to resign, so strong was his conviction that soft power and information warfare should be shifted as a priority from the 'periphery of the command's thinking to its very epicentre'.[57] Notwithstanding, the divide between Cold Warriors and soldiers who fought in Iraq and Afghanistan endures, appearing to mark a generation gap. And a resistance to root-and-branch change is endemic in a Washington military establishment with so much invested politically in supplying and preparing for industrial warfare. Across the Atlantic, where Europe's threat is perceived as inextricably internal and external in the same breath, a counter-terror response has been adopted on the domestic end of the spectrum while counter-insurgent expeditionary action occupies the other. The UK's CONTEST programme is unambiguous: it believes a form of terrorism unprecedented in scale and type on British soil is being accompanied by an insurgent communications output, both 'relentless' and 'sophisticated'.[58] What nuances the debate for European states is a combination of internal and external factors linked by various immigrant diasporas and digital information technologies. This dyadic linkage leads Britain's government to build its approach on four strategic factors:

- unresolved regional disputes (Palestine, Afghanistan, Bosnia, Chechnya, Lebanon, Kashmir, Iraq) and state failure;
- violent ideological extremism (Al-Qaeda and derivatives) and their strategic narrative of the Western threat to Islam;
- new technologies connecting group operations and communications globally;
- radicalisation and self-starting networks.

In this last, the threat is seen to emanate from four directions:

- Al-Qaida and associated groups primarily on the Afghanistan/Pakistan border;
- their affiliates in Iraq, Maghreb, Saudi peninsular, Yemen and Somalia;
- self-starting networks and lone individuals unconnected to these;
- groups elsewhere, broadly aligned in an ideology shared by these others, yet unconnected, pursuing distinct regional agendas.

They cohere cognitively and emotionally in the same swathe of grievance and faith loosely described as 'global insurgency'.[59] However, the true common denominator remains the media landscape. In its many forms, it links this diverse mix of insurgents. The challenge therefore is the emphasis thrown onto the political terrain, no longer the military sphere.

In sum, a strong case can be made for an emerging threat that increasingly derives from irregular war rather than inter-state conflict. Military concentration on high-technology weaponry and precision-munitions in isolation is misleading. Current deployment of drones over FATA, like mujahideen using Stinger missiles a generation earlier in the Afghan-Soviet conflict, can skew the analysis towards the kinetic.[60] Equally both manœuvre-based and effects-based operations have been found wanting when facing an enemy that neither holds the fixed assets of states, nor organises its forces in anticipated, conventional formations. Thus the centre of gravity is to be found elsewhere, as Maoist theory advocates, in the population. When ICTs allow people to mobilise through 'the software' of ideas,[61] namely information and emotive scenes of violence, the proposition changes. This is not to privilege a cultural approach, nor favour technological determinism. Rather it implies a complex interplay between digital technology and social movements that points to a new way of insurgency wearing down states, particularly democratic ones, in an updated model of popular insurrection.[62]

POTD as Insurgent Concept of Operations

Most wars since 1945 have been fought intra-state[63] and few have been settled through negotiation.[64] Moreover civil wars have come to assume a brutal, sometimes genocidal, some contend primordial character.[65] Like revolution we have come to equate insurgency with violent overthrow. Yet in neither case is violence a prerequisite. Castells points to the election of America's Obama and ejection of Spain's Aznar as exemplars of a new insurgency: popular will swelling from below, toppling established ways when peer-to-peer communication allows sufficient numbers to engage in collective action.[66] To date these are among the exceptions that prove the rule. And crucially they benefited from democratic elections to achieve their ends. Which begs the question raised in previous chapters: can similar outcomes be attained in an election-free environment? The political economy conditions of the 1990s underscored the divide between the world's rich and poor. They persist today. From them springs a 'globalised rancour', where benefits of modernity are denied swathes of societies throughout the developing world.[67] Insurgency has recently become more fractured, more pluralist in form and organisation undermining the uniform image of structured, nationalist groups that until recently challenged colonial rule.[68]

Understanding contemporary insurgency patterns is far from easy. Yet it does not prevent the dissemination of ideas emerging as the central dimension of today's militant groups. Earlier I nuanced existing typologies of insurgency, emphasising new informational objectives and communications technologies that groups adopt. It is apparent that where operational rather than persuasive communications are favoured, feral bands and militias excluded (eastern Democratic Republic of Congo; southern Uganda), information campaigns and technologies vary widely. Very quickly conventional typologies break down. Groups may share similar repertoires of communications technologies. However whom they choose to target with them becomes the defining criterion, simply because a population's access to insurgent output, its receptivity to messages, and its direct engagement with their content are increasingly decisive. Popular insurgencies built around national, state-centric ambitions use their own television and radio stations which may or may not be located on home-soil. Equally they service websites that reach far beyond the immediate operations theatre. These like traditional media net different audiences, whether local (the immediate political movement and population), regional (state and neighbouring states), or global (geopolitically relevant target elites, lobby groups, and diasporas). Witness Hamas and Hezbollah. The former now aims sophisticated animated films at Israel, using computer-generated imagery (CGI).[69] However the new has not simply replaced the old. Hezbollah's internal hardwire telephone line that runs from Beirut to the South is a prized asset, serving as both intelligence and command-and-control line, while offering an alternative to what their leader Hassan Nasrallah sees as more easily intercepted digital communications networks.[70] This reinforces a communications strategy where the movement operates its own television and radio stations, and websites. Meanwhile Colombia's narcotics-financed FARC has re-positioned its historically Marxist foundations embracing a new-look Bolivarism. It stands for a reawakening of South American indigenous identity in the face of American capitalism, spurred by support from Venezuela's President Hugo Chavez. Hence it seeks audiences beyond its peasant safe havens, in more distant Latin American urban centres with internet access. Since the 1980s its leadership has built a more sophisticated public relations expertise underpinned by a dedicated technical infrastructure.[71] Despite the group's overriding negative image as cocaine cultivators and traffickers, this development points to a general trend towards centring information and communications into strategic operating concepts of contemporary insurgent movements. Ownership and use of technology at the source of message production cease to be a matter of haves versus have-nots. All groups mix and match pragmatically. They understand media are no longer discrete entities, that messages quickly amplify and share multiple platforms simultaneously in the global digital space where local, regional, and international become one.

If one type of insurgency exemplifies how electronic or virtual insurrection, employing violent imagery to communicate ideas, has moved centre-stage in strategic operations, it is the amorphous concept of

241

'global insurgency'. For now disparate groups constitute 'global insurgency' in an amorphous jihadi salafi movement. They are not the only movements who wish to communicate with the outside world for funding, recruiting, or diplomatic leverage. Nor should future discussion restrict media-dominated warfare to Islamic movements. Yet Andrew Bacevich singles out a new 'Islamic Way of War' designed to undermine high-tech advantages of conventional forces. It is discernible, he says, in the way groups like Hezbollah, Hamas and Al-Qaeda have blended insurgency, terrorism, information, and economic warfare.[72] Moreover such groups may share a common Muslim faith, but not necessarily the aims of a politicised *ummah*. And because they employ the same tactics does not preclude other ideological movements from adopting a similar approach. Traditional politics of the revolutionary Left may yet re-emerge, just as global environmental coalitions might one day stimulate populations to mass collective violence. So whatever we are looking at, David Kilcullen ventures, 'we have yet to stumble on some kind of unified field theory that fully explains current conflicts'.[73]

Notwithstanding the marriage between Al-Qaeda and Afghan/Pakistani Taliban has proven an unholy alliance founded on faith and finance.[74] Indeed recent research suggests it has been more accommodation than alliance; a complex set of relations with the latter drawn into a mutual struggle in the face of a common invader but all too easily glossed over by Western politicians' efforts to simplify the rhetoric.[75] This relationship invites closer scrutiny for the way different types of information emanate from the conflict theatre to serve different agendas. For the 'alliance' includes multiple insurgencies in what undiscerning eyes all too hastily read as a homogeneous front. Alliances and coalitions constituting Al-Qaeda and Taliban are held to have compatible and overlapping ideologies, yet their ambitions differ. Nor can either be understood in terms of conventional command-and-control. Yet hierarchical command-and-control is significant for any organisation wishing to keep a rein on its public messaging via centralised ideology. Al-Qaeda is widely and repeatedly described as a franchise.[76] But the term is misappropriated from the business world. Theirs is no cookie-cutter version of an overall management plan; instead it distinguishes itself by models of decentralised networks—Silicon Valley and northern Italy might provide more productive commercial metaphors.[77] But even this is interrogated by one study which argues that it is inappropriate to align 'dark networks' with business networks because dispersed, clandestine networks are less cohesive than face-to-face models. So information dissemination based on trust and central co-ordination is weakened where activists do not work side by side, since '(f)ace-to-face interaction is crucial in building a social-support structure for communication'.[78] That said, the British Army in its most recent doctrine highlights an insurgency based on transnational networks and multiethnic society, which it acknowledges to be a complete departure from traditional Maoist paradigms.[79]

Such networks comprise organised but independent groups which adopt the name, spirit and methodology (for example Al-Qaeda in Maghreb, Al-Qaeda in Iraq or Mesopotamia, Al-Qaeda in the Arabian Peninsula) and seek convergence, yet neither full integration of external branding nor unified command-and-control. Al-Qaeda embraces both expeditionary and guerrilla models: New York 2001 saw outside fighters inserted into theatre, while Madrid 2004 and London 2005 witnessed locals active on home soil.[80] Equally it inspires 'self-radicalising' individuals and self-starting grouplets that enjoy divergent degrees of access to Al-Qaeda resources, training and direction. So informal connections enable it to penetrate societies with greater ease, evade immediate detection, and grow spontaneously through recruitment. Its members adopt similar behavioural codes of trust to those found in many societies on the Indian subcontinent or Middle East, which reinforce the network model of growth.[81] Yet its core group, a child born of Western foreign policy and Cold War funding, straddles an internal contradiction. Its modernity clashes with its claims to preserve a traditional worldview rooted in a singular interpretation of faith.[82] Notwithstanding where its structures are formalised, committees for military (operations), politics (inter-jihadi and governmental relations) and information (communications) share strategic prominence.[83] In the sphere of communications they have for several years adopted a strategic rather than tactical marketing approach to their audience; their messages; and their methods. Corman's study of Al-Qaeda documents reveals sophisticated use of segmentation and adaptation, catering messages for different audience demographics, and employing 'the same PR techniques used by large corporations'.[84] One document reflects a lessons-learned debrief from the unsuccessful Syrian campaign. For insiders it attributes failure to '(w)eek [sic] public relations both inside and out...They did not have a planned communicable public relations campaign capable of mobilising their base, backers or supporters. They only issued a few ineffective communiqués'. Meanwhile outsiders are segmented into good guys (backers and supporters still to commit to jihad), and bad guys (both 'fallen' Muslims or the 'near enemy'; and unbelievers or the far enemy'; as well as troublemakers or opposition fighters; and, inevitably, Jews).[85]

A further document is worthy of mention. '*The Battar Media Raid: How to Participate? How to Help? What Is My Role?*' communication from the Global Islamic Media Front (GIMF) sought to promote a media campaign to counter messages by Arab and Western media agencies aimed against the Islamic State in Iraq (ISI) by infiltrating *inter alia* non-Islamic forums:

What we expect from you brothers and sisters is for the [Islamist] forum to be like beehives during the raid... [whereby] one person takes part in distributing [material]... another generates links... one person writes an article... while another writes a poem... People must feel and notice that the forums have changed radically during this blessed raid... beloved [raid participants], the raid is dependent on you... The raid demands of you many things... such as expertise, especially in the following areas: seeking religious knowledge, montage, translation into any language, uploading material onto various types of websites, web design, graphic design, journal and publication design, and hacking and security. If you have expertise in any of these [fields], contact the GIMF representative on any of the forums. If, however, you do not possess this expertise... there are other matters you can [promote]: for example, posting matters related to the raid in most [jihad] forums... posting [material] in non-jihad forums, posting in non-Islamic forums such as music forums, youth forums, sports forums, and others.[86]

The Taliban too has led observers into a conundrum, prompting a tendency to 'overestimate the importance of the Taliban leadership's organisation chart'.[87] So how should we best understand the contradictions of the neo-Taliban (after 2001), originating in Pashtun areas of Afghanistan but extending across the Durand Line into Pakistan where it comprises some forty fighting groups?[88] Networks of autonomous and semi-autonomous groups unite against the 'other', the 'outsider'. Clustered around rival but co-operating charismatic sub-tribe and clan leaders, these are riven by historic, internecine violence. Nonetheless they share *Pashtunwali* cultural codes of honour. Indeed they operate, however 'ineffectively managed', under the approval of Mullah Omar and the Quetta *shura*.[89] Equally they provide evidence of the leaders' aim to 'impose a certain discipline and even a certain structure...even if the outcome is uneven'.[90]

What is revealing is that both are in the communications business: Al-Qaeda (with Arab and Uzbek forces) in a way suggesting strategic offensive, and the Taliban (with predominantly Pashtun and Punjabi contingents)in a nationalist, strategic defensive manner. The Taliban now 'treat propaganda as their main effort, coordinating physical attacks in support of a sophisticated propaganda campaign' writes Kilcullen, summarising what he sees as a five-pronged information strategy: 'Our party, the Taliban'; 'Our people and nation, the Pashtun'; 'Our economy, the poppy'; 'Our constitution, the Shari'a'; 'Our form of government, the emirate'.[91] These form the strategic communications platform that guides more specific policy statements while remaining flexible enough to invite broad-based popular support. Although both movements overlap and support operations in the Afghanistan/Pakistan theatre,[92] the Taliban's excursion into wider, global politics remains rhetorical not military.[93] Nevertheless the desire to influence foreign audiences and intervention forces is of greater import than resourcing strikes abroad. That both Al-Qaeda and the Taliban see communications as central to their projects is surprising if only for the old Taliban's (pre-2001) abhorrence for modern communications technologies, an aversion their successors have abandoned while surviving their first hesitant steps into the art of messaging. POTD strikes in Kabul on the Serena Hotel (01/2008), Afghan National Army parade (04/2008), Justice Ministry (01/2009), diplomatic quarter (10/2009), Presidential Palace (01/2010), NATO's Bagram base (05/2010), and the Kandahar prison-escape (06/2008) have scored memorable publicity coups.[94] So significant indeed that Kabul's state intelligence authorities in 2010 banned journalists from filming and broadcasting Taliban attacks.[95] Formerly contradictory messages coming from different Taliban 'spokesmen' in 2003–4 have now led to a more 'streamlined' process, passing through one official responsible for the south, another the eastern and central areas. Contact with mainstream journalists is via telephone, SMS and email. And popular proselytising appears in colourful print and online magazines, together with now established DVDs circulating in regional bazaars.[96] Traditionally for even the strictest insurgent groups the dilemma of controlling output within an overarching brand-identity and officially sanctioned line continues to haunt their leaders. More widely, command-and-control lines remain diffuse. Spokesman Qari Yousaf optimistically confides:

On fundamental issues, all orders and decrees are coming from the centre, all mujahidin are bound by the stance of the leadership, although in some daily, simple affairs and issues the commander of each area can himself make decisions...as our areas of control expand, the leadership's watch improves and stances become coherent, having control over simple issues becomes possible too.[97]

Nevertheless, cultural strength underpins organisational weakness, argues the Afghanistan analyst Joanna Nathan: 'at their heart Taliban communications have been predicated on understanding of local audiences, amplifying pre-existing perceptions and misperceptions and tapping into popular and deep-rooted narratives and networks created by decades of conflict and conspiracies'.[98] Whether their message projected beyond the Afghanistan and Pakistan theatres is more bravado than strategic is questionable. Three videos (released 05/2010) allegedly feature the voice of assumed deceased Hakimullah Mehsud, leader of Pakistan's Taliban. They claim the intercepted New York attack (Time Square car-bomb 05/2010) was the Taliban *fedayeen's* work. Vehemently denied by Pakistani security authorities as a 'media stunt',[99] it follows a similar announcement, subsequently proven unfounded, that the Binghamton, USA mass-shooting (04/2009) was also their responsibility.[100] Nonetheless their message dissemination inside the operations theatre remains both central and significant. Although in this case it is perhaps easier to gauge insurgent intent than to measure their effect on the population.

Alongside Taliban are Al-Qaeda fighters engaged in local and regional struggles. Their strategists train a firm eye on international politics. Whether via the effect of suicide and IED attacks, or parallel imaging campaigns, a regular stream of video feeds 'vital to al-Qaeda's mission' passes to YouTube and traditional media. Public diplomacy specialist Philip Seib believes Al-Qaeda has become a virtual state, communicating with its "citizens", nurturing ever larger audiences 'through masterful use of the media, with heavy reliance on the internet'.[101] In the wake of the post-2001 removal of Al-Qaeda's core hierarchy in Afghanistan, they set out to target the Islamic masses through a proliferation of web and video communications.[102] The strategy plays to 'an extraordinarily diverse membership, one that is not united by way of any cultic or ideological commonality, to say nothing about that of class, ethnicity or personal background'.[103] This information flow builds on a long-term strategic approach to communications begun by *Maktab-al-Khidamat* (Afghan Services Bureau) and developed by Al-Qaeda at its inception in 1988, employing a media operations department integrated within its organisational structure. Its Advice and Reform Committee was established in London (1991–6) to transmit material supporting clerical opposition to the Saudi regime's acquiescence to US troops being stationed on the Kingdom's 'holy' soil. And since 1996 three key electronic journals—*al-Ansar, al-Neda*, and *Sawt al-Jihad*—have confirmed that communication is at the heart of Al-Qaeda's strategy. These are supported by further production outlets like *al-Sahab* media corporation.[104] Former chief of the CIA's Bin Laden unit, Michael Scheuer notes two aspects to the strategy: first, 'a spectacularly successful online university of strategy, tactics and training for guerrilla warfare and terrorism' which has been likened to a global *madrasa*.[105] Second, and reflecting growing sophistication over the last two decades, a strategic communications rationale that places the Muslim struggle in the context of international relations. It highlights Western foreign policy and the politics of oil, thereby provoking a militant response built around economic and military attrition.[106] So central is the virtual dimension to Al-Qaeda that observers designate them 'the first guerrilla movement in history to migrate from physical space to cyberspace'.[107] The advantages of Iraq, an urban combat zone with more advanced technological connections than Afghanistan, benefited Abu Musab al-Zarqawi's communications campaign in the early 2000s while directing Al-Qaeda in Iraq.[108] His landmark beheading of the American businessman Nicholas Berg has been likened to a '9/11 of jihad on the internet',[109] attracting 15 million downloads from websites.[110] Significantly its shock-and-awe brought images, words and ideas to the centre of the military struggle.[111] Indeed the kinetic and communicative were suddenly intertwined as one. In the process it elicited a younger generation of militant eager to raise electronic messaging to a new aesthetic level;[112] now quality of delivery could match ambition of intent. Ever-growing expectations of digitally literate users living beyond the combat theatre could be satisfied. This only served to underline Bin Laden and Zawahiri's declarations on the primacy of communications in Al-Qaeda strategic operations, that 90% of the battle resides in the media, and that media is the weapon of choice for twentieth-century fighters. Their Washington adversaries would reluctantly have to endorse that conviction.

In sum, what makes Al-Qaeda/Taliban collaboration so potent is that Afghan and more recently Pakistani theatres provide proof-positive of local grievance. Subsequently captured by news content, such resentment angers and radicalises observers beyond the region. Al-Qaeda offers an ideological impetus, structured narrative, and loose networked construction for international diffusion of those images. In fact images and ideas are carried through parallel distribution outlets across all media. What Al-Qaeda strategists divined well in advance of many states was that if a reliable flow of violent images were placed in the public domain, it could be accessed by consumers directly but importantly by traditional media who would multiply the effect by using footage in their own broadcasts. A dependency relationship could be created (witness Al-Jazeera television's consistent output of Al-Qaeda exclusives)[113] favouring the dynamics of a media model based on regular dramatic events and a competitiveness to break stories first. In parallel and in conjunction, digital media would diffuse and amplify messages and images via potentially millions of many-to-many communicators sitting at their computers or plying their cell-phones. Together the two processes would feed off each other, interacting in the global mediaspace, reaching targeted and accidental audiences. The facility of dropping 'shock and awe' political images into this environment to create 'cognitive opportunities' held out a further prospect. One opportunity could compound the next in a succession of opportunity spirals.[114] An image could trigger association with an idea that might cascade through global mediaspace attracting sympathy and converts. Now 'information bombs' could radiate their shrapnel to greater effect than any kinetic explosion. Insurgents might not be able to control the outcome of these ricocheting communications. But they could certainly change the nature of insurgency that states had hitherto had to confront.

IEDs, Suicides and Dirty Bombs

This conclusion will not go unchallenged by its critics. POTD increasingly takes the form of improvised explosive devices (IEDs) and suicide-bombs rather than dirty bombs that indiscriminately target non-combatants. How then can POTD still communicate political messages as a strategic operating concept capable of delivering political, ethical goals? In short, each type of attack, IED, suicide, or chemical, biological, radiological or nuclear weapon (CBRN) exploits a different relationship to the population.

As television cameras followed the shift of geopolitical focus from Iraq to Afghanistan, so too did IEDs cross between theatres as a weapon of choice.[115] Afghan Taliban's IED attacks increased from 2,600 in 2007 to over 8,000 in 2009 when they claimed the lives of 322 Coalition troops, wounding 1,800.[116] Data on population casualties is less easily verified. Suicide bombings continue to haunt Iraq and are prevalent in Pakistan, Afghanistan, Palestine-Israel, Russia, Daghestan and Indonesia. They have accounted for high-profile POTD events in communications hubs including New York, London and Moscow. One data source registers 3,607 fatalities and 9,189 injuries in Pakistan alone in recent years.[117] Both types are regularly read as military attrition when in fact they might be better viewed as political tenacity. Dirty bombs are quite different. They are not just indiscriminate but total in intent and effect. Perhaps it is only a matter of time before another similar to Aum Shinrikiyo's release of sarin nerve gas on Tokyo's subway (1995) occurs. So even though each employs a different rationale, IEDs and suicide-bombs play more comfortably into consequentialist arguments where, however reluctantly or willingly, 'end justifies the means' policies accept collateral death as the price of waging war. IEDs claim local victims, but loss of non-combatant life or limb is accidental rather than deliberate, or at least secondary: the military or state agent is the prime objective. Their location is often skirted by populations with local knowledge of where explosives have been hidden along village paths, mountain tracks and busy highways. Suicide-bombs are even more controversial, shifting from the more demarcated kinetic theatre to a broader engagement, and assuming no prescience on the part of innocent bystanders of when and where violence might strike next. Only recent precedent informs future caution. Hence indiscriminate targeting draws no moral distinction between those who share nationality, ethnicity or faith. Insurgent groups vary in how far they are willing to accommodate collateral damage in effecting their plans. Not all risk alienating the very people who would eventually provide the force to overthrow incumbent governments. Even in cases of non-suicide attacks, namely remote bomb detonations, some militants give advance notice; others do not. Some but not all strike only in the preserves of sectarian rivals. Sheer scale of atrocity does not define whether a terrorist act is kinetic or symbolic. As I have argued above, just as deeds can be strategic or accidental, they can be at once kinetic, symbolic, and/or communicative. Militaries exposed to IEDs may reluctantly but rightly view loss of personnel as the regrettable price of attrition warfare. Indeed even if they acknowledge a symbolic component, they may nevertheless conclude both symbolic and kinetic deaths lead to the same morgue.

Lasswell's aphorism of communication—who says what to whom through which channels to what effect—favours effect over intent. But should insurgents be judged by intent or effect? POTD is problematic because there is room for disjuncture between how acts are intended and actually received. Moreover, the way they are received may vary according to time and circumstance. Violence as the bearer of death may appear unequivocal in its meaning, yet as an act of political spectacle it is open to diverse interpretation.[118] We are reminded that the insurgent environment is fluid, that each act invites a counteract which reshapes the perception of what is politically acceptable. Discourse is not set in stone. Times change, attitudes change; guerrillas become governors. Ireland, Nepal, and South Africa have seen extreme and hostile opponents drawn into post-conflict partnership. But erstwhile guerrilla leaders are feted where once their death-sprees were vilified. And in turn those new regimes condemn the next wave of insurgent.[119] Similarly, even populations at the epicentre of conflict become reconciled to the need for accommodation, ultimately abandoning old enmities. European Jews who post-1945 boycotted German goods, today acquire Volkswagen cars and Bosch washing-machines with equanimity. Hutu and Tutsi, however hesitantly, continue to live side by side despite an inversion in the political order amid the stench of genocide. Distended webs of political elites protect the status quo of advantage: general populations desire the status quo of peace and security. It is not that time is a great healer; rather it allows political narratives to be reshaped. Conflict is dynamic, not static. During open struggle governments and state-challengers adjust their policies, which affects their strategies and the way they validate those compromises to their constituencies.[120] All politics is constructed and media are complicit players in that process. For all that attritional violence is played out on a tactical, military playing field, it makes its appeal to the political process: war is the extension of communication by other means. As Henry Kissinger noted during the Vietnam War:

We fought a military war; our opponents fought a political one. We sought physical attrition; our opponents aimed for our psychological exhaustion. In the process, we lost sight of one of the cardinal maxims of guerrilla warfare:

the guerrilla wins if he does not lose. The conventional army loses if it does not win.[121]

In the third millennium, not only does time favour the patient guerrilla, but digital media expand the spaces in which to perpetuate their struggle. For anyone caught in the vicinity of violent deeds, effects are 'immediate experiences as well as spectacle'. However, the perspective is different when observed long-distance: 'to newspaper readers in Tokyo and television watchers in New York news-stories are pictures in the mind that mean what they need to mean to help them justify their lives'. But '(e)xperienced worlds sometimes change radically and with them the meanings attributed to news accounts'.[122]

Then there is a further type of terrorist act which begs the question whether it threatens to destroy the political process, and thus cease to function as a political tool. If IEDs and suicide bombs can be brought into the fold of persuasive, rational tactics, at what point does the violent image no longer serve the communicative process of the insurrectionist?

Information and 'New Terrorism'

POTD as symbolic violence was all well and good, say some critics, until a few years ago. Following the Cold War, Walter Laqueur's thesis concluded terrorism had ratcheted up several gears. A 'new terrorism', he observed, had arrived displaying many ingredients that made for a toxic brew. And it threatened to transform insurgency, challenging the very notion of POTD as a tool of strategic communications. This is a valid criticism. Traditional 'nuisance terrorism' would potentially be superannuated by millenarian and apocalyptic militants. Unlike their nihilist forebears in Tsarist Russia, these could now lay their hands on disproportionately powerful weapons. Impatient ambitions might therefore be satiated in an endgame, the like of which no sub-state force had hitherto dreamed possible. Now any individual or group could pick-and-mix from religious-sectarian-nationalist convictions and employ chemical, biological, radiological or nuclear weapons (CBRN) to promote them.[123] Whether technical know-how lay beyond their abilities was not really the issue. In time it would come, as would the materials in a world of porous borders, wanton criminality, and loose regulatory controls.[124] However, the tendency for violence to escalate and for weapons of mass destruction (WMD) to leverage a game that might run out of control, was imminent. Whether groups will actually resort to such extremes, and Bruce Hoffmann doubts this, suggesting most are conservative in their practices, is also not the issue.[125] Crucially, so long as bombings, suicide attacks or even plane-strikes against skyscrapers preserve a limited casualty rate, offence against the public sphere remains in check. After all victims are counted in their hundreds, occasionally thousands, but not millions. Yet once activists are able to employ CBRN to attack even part of that sphere and risk destroying the whole, the game changes. The *agora* itself is threatened as a legitimate theatre for political engagement. WMD preclude the need for a politics of persuasion. WMD do not continue insurgent politics by other means: they destroy politics and the public sphere. Otherwise what other message do they send out? Which underlying grievance are they still tapping into? Accordingly, it may once have been possible to argue a case for 'just terrorism' (an echo of 'just war' theory), thus adopting criteria of 'proportionality' or 'last resort'.[126] After all, political violence founded on the rights of the citizen to oust tyrannical, unresponsive governments has its place in Western political thought.[127] Collateral damage within the populace (killing non-combatants and innocent bystanders) might be the high but necessary price to pay to unseat an intransigent, oppressive government. But all mitigation disappears when the people replace the state wholesale as the primary target. And when the threat is to destroy significant swathes of population.

So does 'new terrorism' obviate the need to communicate—does POTD become redundant? Much depends on whether we accept the notion of 'megaterrorism', whether we believe that it is only a matter of time before CBRN becomes a fixture in the insurgent arsenal; and how the insurgent calculation weighs the outcome of mass destruction against the multiplier effect of communication. Which achieves the desired intention? If terrorism aims to appease 'aggressive madness' in the high-technology and WMD era,[128] then the upshot is little more than a nihilist appeal to emotional extremes. Pathology replaces politics. But if the objective is to change a particular state or society for the perceived greater good, whether secular or religious, then WMD are self-defeating. This begs the question at what point insurgents cease to be rational actors. Hoffmann explores this lacuna in terrorism studies asking why 9/11 stands out as a rare 'spectacular' among the panoply militants are capable of delivering. Why are they so short on imagination compared with images even average Hollywood scriptwriters dream up? Indeed why have they been so reluctant to use rocket-propelled grenades against civil aircraft, attack maritime vessels carrying hazardous cargo, or infect agricultural and livestock targets? Instead they opt conservatively for more conventional 'middle range' tactics that fall short of mass destruction.[129] This belies the common assumption that terrorism is a shark that must keep moving forward to stay alive. That adage holds true only if insurgent success is measured by the loudness of bang or the bloodiness of death toll. Not all Hollywood scripts make horror or disaster movies. Lasting memories reside in cameo performances too. Pinned against a wall for 45 minutes, 12 year-old Palestinian Muhammad al-Durrah was shot dead despite his father's best attempts to shield him from Israeli gunfire. So too was an ambulance driver who tried to rescue them. Little wonder the iconic, filmed images were played repeatedly on Palestinian television.[130] POTD's strength resides in the power of the smallest, not just the biggest event to be captured and disseminated thus magnifying its importance across time and space. POTD's attraction is it can be planned or completely accidental beyond the insurgent's control (whichever applied to Muhammad al-Durrah). But POTD's legitimacy derives from terrorist acts being used as tools of insurgent strategic communications, however controversially, thus underscoring insurgency as political process. Destroy political process and you destroy POTD.

* * *

This chapter asked how insurgent groups embraced changes in the Information Age, and whether they have turned information and communications into a central plank of their strategy.

In the third millennium, POTD has become a catalyst in ideological campaigns of grievance and injustice and now stands at the heart of the insurgent operating concept. Three reasons explain this phenomenon: first, the media's appetite and competition for dramatic pictures to drive audience ratings; second, individuals' ability to generate their own messages through newly available interconnected technologies; and third, economic and technological globalisation that have unlocked new spaces which insurgents have moved to occupy and exploit with ideas and images. It is important not to universalise this trend to include all political opposition groups uniformly, nor to suggest they use communications with the same degree of sophistication or fore-sight. What today is commonly referred to as a 'global insurgency' is in fact an amalgam of multiple insurgencies that embrace a spectrum of actors who operate on national, regional and global stages: some have purely local interests but depend on international finance and resource networks; some share local and occasionally transnational ambitions; while others are situated within local lives yet their designs focus primarily on the global. Nevertheless, the degree to which communications have become increasingly important in the strategies of most insurrectionists should not be underestimated. The central operating concept applies where insurgent groups possess both technical means to distribute their message but also networks of diffusion through which messages can spread instantly with minimal friction, either in a controlled or increasingly vicarious fashion. The first circumvents other media players who would come between revolutionary and public. But in the digital age, it does more. It sets in motion a self-generating source of messaging requiring no further insurgent investment of labour or resource. So the public become the foot-soldiers and the image their spear. That image relies on sympathetic constituencies being proprietary towards those messages. Diffusion becomes unpredictable because such constituencies expand as much accidentally as deliberately when connected by ethnic, nationalist, or religious identities within imagined communities. Hence twenty-first century POTD is firmly a tool of communications allowing an ideology or manifesto to be propagated. This competes for support in the public sphere challenging the *status quo*. The point here is POTD has moved beyond being defined as loosely symbolic political violence to become an explicit act of communication. What nineteenth-century practitioners of POTD could barely intuit, today's proponents can effect through a unique conflation of factors. The idea that a new generation of apocalyptic fighter has obviated the need for POTD is premature. Only when WMD pass from rogue or porous states to insurgent, state-sponsored and criminal networks, finally targeting entire populations, is POTD threatened as a rhetorical weapon. Then it is swallowed up like its erstwhile anarchist manifestation a century ago when solitary acts were quickly drowned out by the noise and devastation of industrial World War. For the deed to flourish in its twenty-first century sublimation, the prerequisite is for a participating audience and surviving polity. George Gallup, a figure we identify with the Cold War and the boom-time in political marketing, understood that the world had already entered an era characterised by the 'war of ideas and images'. What he urgently appealed for was a latter-day Clausewitz 'to set out the principles and philosophy of this new kind of warfare', someone also with a 'keen understanding of people and human behaviour'.[131] States and their militaries have been slow to take on the full implications of the upheavals in social relations which emanate from the revolution in digital communications: insurgents have been quicker to do so. Nevertheless, there is still a vacancy for a new Clausewitz.

CONCLUSION

The Violent Image proposes a new way of conceptualising the terrorist act, and speaks to the complexity of contemporary politics. It sets out to fill a gap in the theoretical literature of Propaganda of the Deed, presenting it as the tool of modern revolutionary communications. Thus the insurgent process of employing terrorist acts becomes a way of creating memory through the fragmentation of time and manipulation of grievance narrative. Formerly, violent acts were deployed against state institutions and representatives with the objective of goading states into over-reacting with excessive force; by responding disproportionately, governments would lose legitimacy in the eyes of the population. The revolutionary used the weight of the state against the state. Today, POTD is an act of political violence, a terrorist deed aimed at state targets and sometimes populations with the objective of creating a media event capable of energising audiences to bring about state revolution or social transformation. Recognising that politics is played out in the global mediaspace, revolutionaries now use the weight of the media against the media. It is thus a form of political marketing, as suggested by one French perspective on marketing that talks of 'influencing the behaviour of publics, rather than customers, recognising the wider remit of marketing in modern society', thereby positioning it in terms of wider societal gain.[1]

This development in POTD is no chance occurrence. In capitalist societies Western politics broadly mirror the changes that have taken place in marketing itself. What began with marketing's 'production period' (1890s-1920s) when demand exceeded industrial supply, transitioned to a 'sales period' (1920s-1950s) refined by market research and advertising, then gave way to a 'marketing period' (1950s-1980s) focused on customer needs, before witnessing the current era that increasingly privileges ethical and social concerns. It is widely accepted that marketing is driven by an exchange relationship predicated on customer satisfaction, moreover customer retention and loyalty. The need to segment audiences, to interpret and cater to consumer needs, remains a precept of modern times.[2] Like marketing—itself the articulation of late capitalism—so too has politics changed. Marketing principles and techniques during the twentieth century have moved from the commercial, private sector to inform the public sphere, transforming the way elites frame and conduct politics, and electorates adjust their expectations of their rulers. Unsurprisingly, POTD as a manifestation of extreme opposition politics has also evolved. Insurgents spring from the consuming polity. The same mass media that allowed commercial suppliers to reach populations, particularly television post-World War II and more recently the internet, provide the same distribution channels for insurrectionist producers who need to communicate their own offerings to heterogeneous populations.

As a process of communication POTD functions as political marketing by triggering an iterative, mutual exchange of values, ideas, and associations as insurgents seek to address multiple populations with the intention of awakening and articulating latent or passive desires. Mistakenly, terrorist acts are widely assumed, at best, to be a 'one message fits all' form of address. The means of attracting attention may seem crude, yet the trigger effect plays into a sophisticated process of segmenting and energising distinct audiences. The Afghanistan-Pakistan theatre, for example, is but the epicentre of a mosaic of populations being addressed locally, nationally, regionally, and globally. Such communications target traditional, rural communities in conflict zones, migrant diasporas in the advanced economies of Europe, the Middle East and Asia, and homeland citizens of states whose militaries are engaged in foreign intervention. These various constituencies further segment by ethnicity, religion, gender, nationality, and age when shaping their opinions and beliefs. Belatedly military doctrine and its approach to populations, encapsulated in such thinking as the British Army's 'Influence', recognise that 'adversaries' messages are highly tuned to specific audiences'. Consequently, for the counterinsurgent this requires 'subtle understanding of target audiences that is difficult to achieve'.[3] Although a blunt tool, in this process, POTD segments and speaks to diverse populations in different ways with different effects.

A New Conceptual Framework for POTD

This offers the opportunity for a new conceptualisation of POTD. So dramatically has the role of POTD changed, so significantly has the relationship of audiences to producers altered, that violent images of political terrorism have moved centre-stage in the insurgency strategies of global and some national insurgents. Consequently, POTD has moved beyond the simply kinetic or superficially symbolic to the strategic. Because of the speed of digital technologies, images can move from the tactical level to the strategic in an instant. Lines between the opportune and the planned have become blurred.

The context for this dramatic shift is five-fold:

- Globalisation: in the post-Cold War era, neoliberal economic policies have exacerbated the divide between rich and poor, winners and losers. This amplified grievance fuels low-level conflicts based on identity politics of class, ethnicity and faith.
- Increased mass migration and urbanisation post-1945 expanded the range of traditional social networks. These populations carried with them kith-and-kin structures that often extend to conflict theatres in their homelands.
- Digital Revolution: by the 1980s digital technologies could capture, compress, store and transmit in split seconds unprecedented volumes of data through national and global networks. The impact resembled that of the print revolution that propelled Europe's Protestant Reformation some 500 years before. Its key dimensions are instantaneous interconnectivity, an interconnecting plurality of old and new media, and the emergence of many-to-many communications.
- Virtual social networks map onto traditional social networks: the Digital Revolution means messages and images move exponentially and virally through these networks. Insurgents can now reach audiences with little investment if an idea catches hold.
- Politics has become media politics: the mediascape is the political battleground. The violent image is a form of political marketing

How does this function? *The Violent Image* proposes insurgents use violence by articulating the relationship between revolutionary memory, time, and narrative. '"Who controls the past", ran the Party slogan, "controls the future: who controls the present controls the past".'[4] Such was Orwell's take on the state project presaging a dystopian future. His insight goes to the heart of how states have and continue to build their authority and legitimacy. Time, memory, and narrative are inextricably woven. Why should it be different for insurgents? Political opposition movements would seize the reins of state power since most pursue nationalist ambitions; few aspire to transnational empires or caliphates. The same is true for insurgents: who controls the past legitimises his role in the present and subsequently claims ownership of the future. But in the asymmetric confrontation between state and insurgent, the latter is vilified, criminalised, pathologised as state agencies continually drive a wedge between populations and those who rise from their midst offering alternative models of life and society. The insurgent riposte is to construct its own alternative memory, investing narrative continuity into a string of historical discontinuities, so shaping a coherent story from loose and sometimes incongruous strands (see above, Chapter Three).

Time is malleable. It is constantly shaped for us. However we live in parallel time-spans that blend into the common-sense, state-crafted hegemony of daily life, an harmonious sense of how we understand the present eliding into the past. How we perceive the present and past is critical to the way we see our lives and recognise ourselves as individuals within this trajectory. What the image of the terrorist act achieves through 'shock and awe' is to shatter this cohesion. In the process of fragmentation, a new rival, continuous narrative can be triggered within populations already prepared with appropriate messages, pregnant with the capability of re-imagined grievance. Individuals shape their personal memories through continually rearranging fragments of moments past: insurgents must do the same with political memory (Chapter Two). However, in the 'opportunity space' the crisis moment is short-lived. Because images are ambiguous, insurgents must simplify understandings in an overcrowded information landscape. For this they must constantly invest in constructing narratives of their cause and organisation, of their place in the historical community, and of the wrongs that have been meted on it by the state, of victories won and tragedies suffered. Time, memory and narrative are brought to cohere in crystallised images (Chapter Four). This process must, however, be mediated. In the late twentieth and early twenty-first centuries, the dominant mass medium has been television. Yet while the most remote insurgent act can now gain access to people's homes or communities no matter where, it must also contest media memory—a complex hegemony that emerges from an unruly exchange between producer and audience. The POTD 'spectacular' negotiates this obstacle by first grabbing audience attention through shock and awe, before exploiting television's appetite for LIVE eye-witness news-as-entertainment and its hunger for competition between rival broadcast organisations (Chapter Five).

In the post-1980s Digital Revolution, where technological innovation forces time and space to contract, images and ideas move faster between disparate and formerly disconnected global populations. Yet when a message catches fire, it can spread with dramatic speed spontaneously, virally, and exponentially through networks of interlinked old and new media. In turn, it can surge through real-world social networks which overlap those electronic, virtual networks. Hence societies find themselves in the early phase of a new era in communications (Chapter Six). The Arab Spring or Uprising has spelled out the complex and thus far barely understood nature of these changes as a volatile cocktail of popular sentiment and grievance, and the new digital mediascape has seemingly empowered ordinary people to challenge the grip of political elites in authoritarian countries and indeed democratic states. But how information and ideas attached to images leads to direct action and delivers long-term transformation without traditional revolutionary vanguards is yet to be resolved (Chapter Seven). In the meantime, militaries and their civilian masters, schooled in industrial warfare, have failed to grasp until now that the most significant information is no longer the intelligence that emerges from the conventional, kinetic battlefield. Rather, it is images and ideas—the lifeblood that courses through populations, stimulating and energising them for political change. It is for that same reason that state bureaucracies—for over a century the command-and-control mechanism for complex industrial societies—have become too ponderous, internally fractured and dependent on top-down directives to counter information that self-generates from flat, networked and *ad hoc* electronic communities (Chapter Eight). The implications for insurgency are dramatic.

This new way of conceptualising POTD will have its critics, but those who see the deed merely as a reactive strike, born of the opportunism of the weak, might now consider that we live in times of increased fluidity where speed of transmission elicits a new relationship between the strategic and opportune. Equally, the sheer scale of human suffering, caused in the name of justice for the few or many, will place the act beyond the pale of reasonable politics for the unpersuaded. Perhaps only 'the wretched of the earth' trapped in the depths of oppression can truly understand the complexity of what drives a person to inflict terrorist death on his fellow man. Just as the notion that the powerless might discover a new balance with the powerful in the wars of the Information Age will be rejected by realists who contend that only bullets kill, not information, that only bombs destroy, not images. Yet in 2012, change is in the air.

Broader Reflections

Much is said of states' growing weakness in the face of global markets, transnational institutions, and big business. Following the recent global economic crisis, the Leviathan is fighting back through what Anatole Kaletsky calls capitalism 4.0.[5] Nevertheless in the asymmetric struggle between states and insurrectionists who would subvert their own sovereign states or the international community of states, politicians enjoy unprecedented inter-governmental co-operation and resources. Yet intelligence gathering and data analysis, sophisticated battlefield weaponry, even boots-on-the-ground commitment, however overwhelming, seem often futile to those observers who feel governments are actually fighting a chimera, an idea. The idea may change the closer one gets to the ground, the more it is interrogated in a community context.

Insurgency remains constant in one key respect. Insurrectionists must maximise limited tactical resources: they must imagine what opportunities could arise, and recognise them when they come. Innovation, imagination and opportunity, and the endless production line of sympathisers and fighters that emerge from the population are the insurgent's weapons. Inspiration may be economic or cosmological, political or ethical, as Devji would tell it. Towering above all else must be the idea, the message.

When Propaganda of the Deed was first coined over a century ago, the balance of power and resources between revolutionary and states was no less uneven. However the ability to manufacture and deliver the message was restricted to clandestine printing presses, syndicalist protests, and word-of-mouth dissemination. Insurrectionists operated in a climate of increased pooling of intelligence between states and of judicial pursuit. The market in which they competed was dominated by penny-a-copy, industrially produced newspapers, an attractive blend of entertainment and news offering mass populations a window on the world. But it was not the revolutionary's view that readers saw.

CONCLUSION

In the end, POTD's proponents failed through an inability to control their message dissemination. However POTD itself has subsequently undergone a revolution. Today's new media have introduced a fresh cognitive dimension to time and space where individuals, whether insurrectionist or ordinary citizen, feel they can exercise some personal control over their lives. The old guerrilla terrain of *terra firma* hosted hit-and-run tactics in military engagement. That has not disappeared. Force or the threat of force remains a prerequisite of state overthrow; it is the bedrock of state power. Today time and space compress through instant connections in the virtual, cognitive terrain. In this meeting-place of imaginations individuals and groups share common values and identities with swathes of humanity excluded from mainstream decision-making and fair division of wealth. Our bricks-and-mortar world comprises innovative technologies of web, internet, mobile telephony, and computers which feedback continually into more entrenched means of communication, namely press, radio, cinema, and television. Ideas and identities move effortlessly backwards and forwards across a media landscape which never sleeps. Most of these ideas are shaped by states, then re-shaped by media organisations; many are launched by interest groups. Yet some emerge spontaneously from the daily conversations of millions of people without apparent cause or plan. In turn they pass through networks which are both flesh-and-blood communities and complex, electronic conduits for sending data, information and money. Increasingly traditional bonds of family, friendship, and patronage intersect with newer, more fluid sets of relationships with which they are brought into contact by intrusive, impatient technologies. Whether in dusty villages or decaying ghettoes, many people remain rooted in their local dynamics and traditions, seemingly untouched by change. Incrementally, however, new connectors reach in to join them to a wider world. For the first time ideas move with lightning speed through such networks that transcend sovereign borders, traversing the globe in split seconds. Why certain ideas catch on while others remain still-born is a complex question requiring further inquiry. However some appeal to common understandings of identity, shared values, tastes, and beliefs. They speak to the stories we tell ourselves about ourselves, stories we inherit from our parents, our teachers, our employers, indeed our political leaders; stories we rework as each day we go about our lives alongside the rest of society all engaged in the same continual interaction of working out who we are and what we stand for.

Memory is a neglected aspect of revolutionary struggle. It is socially constructed at all levels, individual, group and society. It serves to inform us where we have come from, who we are in the context of our individual pasts and common presents. It is also integral to our sense of political identity. But when we stop to reflect we recognise time and memory are symbiotic. We live in parallel flows of time: moment-in-time, clock-time, work-time, seasonal time, lifetime, epoch-time. Yet ordinarily we ignore these, submerged in the flow of what is normal and common sense. Insurgents recognise that time and memory legitimise the revolutionary legacy and utopian promise. Past, present and future can be manipulated into a single programme. But states and media organisations have already prescribed the terrain: the battlefield is set. Time and memory are the pillars of political hegemony which insurgents must shock through the violence of POTD if they are to breach the status quo. As it ruptures, time and space coalesce. A shock to the system provokes a crisis: an opportunity space opens up which begs to be explained and filled with meaning as 'official' memory fragments. For a moment insurgents have the chance to offer meaning through public statements that reinforce message campaigns previously disseminated across society. Each event evokes past events; each triggers associations of grievance. Violence strikes the chord, arresting universal attention. But the vehicle is the image, the true lifeblood of electronic networks. Images cross borders whether social, economic, geographic or linguistic, and ricochet between media outlets and their consumers. They make us think as individuals and political actors. But we don't all see images through the same eyes; we may agree on the focus of attention in a picture (*punctum*), yet the pre-knowledge (*studium*) each person brings to it varies. Ambiguity is a finely balanced commodity for any politician in government or opposition. So the key for the rhetorician is to guide audiences to the desired outcome. When the Beatles sang 'will you still need me, will you still feed me, when I'm sixty-four?' the lyric never volunteered an answer. What makes 'of course!' the only possible response is the mood of the accompanying music, its *studium*. Revolutionaries must also appeal to a certain mood music.

Speed is one aspect of time that benefits insurgents. It is a vital component of conventional and irregular warfare. Not just the speed of surprise, but nowadays the velocity of transmitting images as ideas, and their immediate take-up within populations are paramount when digitally connected users and even the less privileged plug into existing technological networks of diffusion. A mobile phone photo communicates to the next user and very quickly finds its way to the web only to be seized by television and press before feeding back onto both web and mobile phones in a perpetual viral cycle. In the war of ideas this is the new WMD. Ideas driven by shocking images can outpace ponderous government hierarchies caught up in second-guessing politicians and their constituents, before further attaching to volatile groups and energised communities. To borrow Robert Hughes' phrase, this is the 'Shock of the New'.

It is not all that is new in these unruly times. Capitalism has created fresh spaces for investment and accumulation. Meanwhile the Cold War paradigm of industrial force has given way to a hybrid form of conflict opening up new opportunities to subvert states. These draw on diverse social, economic, and political factors attracting actors who operate at state, sub- and supra-state levels in a globalised era. At the same time we have come to recognise 'war amongst the people' increasingly as the dominant conflict model for the immediate future. It is a development that is forcing reluctant states to take stock of how to adapt to new conditions and enemies at home and abroad. Meanwhile the very nature of state expeditionary interventions has changed. Amid a growing culture of humanitarianism, their revised objective is to create what Rupert Smith calls 'a condition'. So a decisive battlefield victory that once sought to determine a political result has been replaced by the desire to achieve a 'conceptual space for diplomacy, economic incentives, political pressure, and other measures to create a desired political outcome of stability'.[6] To make matters more complicated, this new conceptual space must be negotiated in a world where media have become a less than welcome fixture in the theatre of operations.[7] And far from being an interloper in the military sphere, the media, that is the 24-hour global mediaspace, now plays host to the theatre of operations, not vice versa. The mediaspace is both enemy and battlefield for insurgents in the war of ideas and images. Populations, rural and urban, may live a world away from each other in distance and privilege but in the media's conceptual space they share a universe as close neighbours. Consequently as information technologies encroach relentlessly on the bricks-and-mortar lives of individuals, so insurgents are shifting their struggles to the emerging cognitive spaces where ideas can energise identities at a moment's notice.

Implications for the Future

The social-psychological relationship between memory (as sedimented beliefs and identity) and speed (fast-moving images) invites further research. In the opportunity space (the moment of shock), the camera is a clock that arrests the flow of time but prompts the recollection of deep-rooted injustice. Moreover that space is the conflict theatre reduced to an image. The first actor to command its cognitive terrain becomes the first to reach the audience with its message. Insurgents are lithe and imaginative: states are ponderous but resourced. Runciman suggested earlier that states invest prodigiously in the long game of shaping the nationalist narrative over decades, indeed centuries. Narratives emanate from policy which derives from strategy. Whether the state is out of touch with the modern populace depends on which constituency is being addressed. However, where the state suffers today is in its delivery mechanism for its narrative. In an era where networks and ad hocracy are rapidly becoming bywords for twenty-first century social change, it begs the question whether governments can create flatter, rapid-reaction communications forces or whether the very complexities of administering mass industrial and post-industrial populations through centralised, bureaucratic control are antithetical to new, societal models and communications.

A further question for revolutionary or insurgency theory remains, namely whether those images and ideas can go that crucial step further and mobilise sufficiently large or influential groups capable of overthrowing states. Because ideas surge virally through digital technologies releasing pent-up emotions and latent ambitions, does that mean revolution is suddenly within the grasp of opposition groups? A destabilised revolutionary theatre does not of itself deliver revolution. A significant proportion of the people, strategically situated, must coalesce to overthrow the seemingly immovable object of government. States occasionally implode under pressure of popular discontent as self-confidence drains from political will; the USSR and its satellites give recent substance to this view. However, to challenge the disproportionate power and resources enjoyed by controlling elites in autocracies or democracies means bridging the gulf between popular will and direct action, and ultimately revolutionary action and revolutionary government. For Trotsky, the crucial confrontation must be with the army, the counter-revolutionary force that would be mobilised against the people when the survival of the state is threatened. Are we now entering an era when violent images and people-power can pre-empt such clashes? Or will use of force always reassert itself?

A third line of inquiry centres on the desirability of revolutionary spontaneity. This naturally arises from any consideration of cascades and surges. Spontaneity is the obverse of the coin of disciplined insurgency and vanguardism. Earlier discussion outlined the ambivalence insurgents like Lenin held towards spontaneous, mass violence in the pre-revolutionary theatre. Violence in the masses was afforded its place since revolutions were held to be *de facto* violent affairs. Yet sporadic acts of violence needed to be rationed and channelled if they were to offer more than a momentary, Promethean spark. That channelling should come from a party vanguard, an appropriately schooled elite that could keep the purity of the ideological message on track and, through organisational control, ensure that the seizure of power remain a realisable project. In the end, Lenin argued, spontaneity was never truly spontaneous: there were always party activists circulating in the crowd, driving on the majority, educating the mass. Despite this, the proletariat's ability to attain consciousness and equip itself for revolutionary victory was dependent on the intervention 'from without' of a revolutionary intelligentsia that could teach it how.

Shakespeare neither disguises nor confines his unease with the volatility and irrationality of the mob to Julius Caesar and Coriolanus; indeed it informs other periods in his political dramaturgy. Similarly, when POTD reached its crescendo in the nineteenth-century, Le Bon typographically betrayed his fear by capitalising the imminent ERA OF CROWDS. 'Little adapted to reasoning', he saw crowds as 'quick to act', and determined 'to utterly destroy society as it now exists'.[8] How ideas spread through digital networks fosters a similar suspicion of the self-generating force of modern online 'smart crowds'. But do physical and online crowds differ in the way ideas pass from member to member? This important question exceeds the scope of this book. But Noelle-Neumann has described the 'spiral of silence', the age-old force of public opinion when tacit observers become active participants and topple governments: her street-laboratory became the events around the collapse of the German Democratic Republic and fall of the Berlin Wall.[9] Others consider how messages converge around 'attractors' and opinion-leaders in the seemingly serendipitous digital universe. Whether violence can be controlled as a revolutionary tool and to what extent it is desirable to do so, is a question that taxed and divided Lenin, Trotsky, Luxemburg and countless revolutionaries who struggled for change in a similarly volatile age. But is an avant-garde elite still vital today to organise and lead the denouement of state overthrow, or does Propaganda of the Deed belong to a new process capable of bridging the divide between the virtual and physical worlds for revolutionaries?

We are living through the early stages of a Digital Revolution that different societies are exploring in different ways. The most dramatic communications revolution the world has experienced for half a millennium is reshaping social relations, and by extension undermining the political *status quo* while promising new processes of representation. However, it is also redefining the way states see themselves inside their physical borders, just as it is redrawing the cognitive boundaries in peoples' minds. Philip Bobbitt captures that spirit when he observes:

National security will cease to be defined in terms of borders alone because both the links among societies as well as attacks on them exist in psychological and infrastructural dimensions, not on an invaded plain marked by the seizure and holding of territory.[10]

What recent releases of WikiLeaks documents have achieved, by directly diffusing via the web and through partnerships with traditional media market-leaders like *The Guardian*, *New York Times*, and *Der Spiegel*, is to undermine states' conviction that today's mediaspace can still be controlled as it was a generation ago. Resort to state force through cyber-attack and judicial prosecution has served to mobilise many anti-state activists. A WikiLeaks, even under cyber-attack, represents a safe haven from which to host and release their 'subversive' archive. What the Al-Qaeda or global insurgency model (flat, networked groups in loose association with a shallow, albeit still hierarchical core) suggests is that insurgencies need no longer mirror-image hierarchical organisational structures and top-down ways of addressing their target populations. As fellow-consumers in those societies, revolutionaries utilise the same technological means. Consequently, with one hand they have gained greater access to populations: unfortunately with the other, they risk losing control over the very messages and traditional machinery of party discipline insurgents have historically propagated. Which raises the question of whether the very nature of insurgent-state balance is changing in a contest where historically revolutionaries have played David to the state Goliath. However dramatic the change, it is premature to gauge how much more has been won than partial redress of the historic imbalance in state-insurgent power relations. What Propaganda of the Deed has achieved is to become the lightning rod for popular discontent and through digital images to impassion and energise populations. In the coming years we shall discover whether it can convert that electric charge into decisive mass action.

NOTES

PREFACE

1. Berwick, Andrew aka Anders Behring Breivik's (2011), 'Communications and Logistics' in *2083: A European Declaration of Independence*, http://www.scribd.com/doc/60849766/Anders-Behring-Breivik-Manifesto-2083—A-European- Declaration-of-Independence-By-Andrew-Berwick, accessed 23 July 2011.
2. James, Clive (1974), p. 223, *The Metropolitan Critic*, London: Faber & Faber.

INTRODUCTION

1. I shall apply two definitions, one from the nineteenth century, the other suited to today. 1) Propaganda of the Deed: an act of political terrorism, thus a technique employed *inter alia* by insurgents with kinetic, symbolic and strategic objectives. Formerly violent acts of terror were deployed against state institutions and representatives with the objective of goading states into over-reacting with excessive force; any disproportionate government response would cost the state legitimacy in the eyes of the population. This was the judo-throw principle: use the weight of the state against itself. 2) Today POTD is a terrorist act of political violence aimed against state targets, sometimes populations, with the objective of creating a media event capable of energising populations to bring about state revolution or social transformation. Today's revolutionary uses the weight of the media against the media.
2. Bell, Daniel (1999), p. liii, *The Coming of Post-Industrial Society*, New York: Best Books. The 'Information Age' is 'founded not on a mechanical technology but on an intellectual technology and (that) the new conceptions of time and space transcend the boundaries of geography... and take place in "real time"'.
3. Strategic Communications: A state-initiated messaging strategy directed at other states aimed at unsettling and/or winning over their populations and political elites. More broadly the harmonising of tiered messages within a hierarchy of communications aimed at changing external and internal audience behaviour. See British Army definition: 'is the articulation of cross-government guidance on influence and supports the synchronisation of the words and deeds of friendly actors to maximise desired effects'. British Army (Nov. 2009), *Security and Stabilisation: The Military Contribution-JDP 3–40*, p. 42, London: Ministry of Defence.

271

4. Strategic operating concept: the positioning and application of kinetic (military) and political (non-military) uses of power to achieve national (strategic) aims. In the insurgent project this means recognising the advantage of employing kinetic, but more significantly and increasingly symbolic, means to contest state-constructed discourses when challenging states for control of the population.

5. Clinton, Hillary (21 July 2010), 'Internet Freedom', speech, Newseum, Washington, DC.

6. Insurgency: a political spectrum that embraces both rebellion and revolution. Its defining aspect is that of a political uprising born of a social movement, namely a community united around a particular value system or set of ideals or grievances aimed at changing the government and sometimes the very structure of society. It can emanate from a majority or minority in the population. To rebel is to strike out violently against the government; revolution is to seek to overthrow it. Insurgency is a political not military process; the mood and attitudes of the population are paramount. Since populations vary, so insurgencies are context specific.

7. Smith, Rupert (2006), *The Utility of Force: The Art of War in the Modern World*, London: Penguin.

8. Mackinlay, John (2009), *The Insurgent Archipelago*, London: Hurst; Galula, David (2006), *Counterinsurgency Warfare: Theory and Practice*, Westport CT: Praeger Security International.

9. Beckett, Ian (2001), pp. 176–8, *Modern Insurgencies and Counterinsurgencies*, Abingdon: Routledge.

10. Ayman al-Zawahiri letter to Abu Musab al-Zarqawi 9 July 2005, in Metz, Thomas, 'Massing Effects in the Information Domain', Military Review, May-June, 2006.

11. Schmid lists 109 definitions including 22 constituent prerequisites of terrorism. Schmid, Alex & Jongman, Albert (1988), *Political Terrorism: a New Guide to Actors, Authors, Concepts, Data Bases. Theories and Literature*, Amsterdam: North Holland Publishing Co. No one volunteers to be called a terrorist. Its connotation is exclusively negative. While guerrilla denotes operational status, insurgent canvasses political validity. Freedom fighter aspires to that highest albeit most nebulous of ideals, freedom. Yet *terrorism* is no absolute condition but a catch-all, a popular shorthand in daily discourse. For Gearty terrorism risks 'linguistic futility'. The 'linguistic anarchy' of Islamic terrorist, narco-terrorist, eco-terrorist, state-sponsored terrorist, international terrorist means the term assumes various mantles, all negative and conveniently subversive: Gearty, Conor (1997), p. 6, *The Future of Terrorism*, London: Phoenix; see also Carlisle, Alex (2007), p. 6, *The Definition of Terrorism: A Report by Lord Carlisle of Berriew QC, Independent Reviewer of Terrorist Legislation*, London: Crown: 'Above the gates of hell is the warning that all that enter should abandon hope. Less dire but to the same effect is the warning given to those who try to define terrorism'; Fisk, Robert (2001), p. 441, *Pity the Nation: Lebanon at War*, Oxford: Oxford University Press: '"Terrorists" are those who use violence against the side that is using the word'; Tiefenbrun, Susan (2003), 'A Semiotic Approach to a Legal Definition of Terrorism', *ILSA Journal of International & Comparative Law*, vol. 9, pp. 357–402; UK Government: *Terrorism Act 2000*, amended, Section 1(c).

12. Mandela, Nelson (2010), p. 336, *Long Walk to Freedom*, London: Abacus; ANC—African National Congress; MK: *Umkhonto we Sizwe* (Spear of the Nation).

13. Social movement: groups of actors who adopt the same symbols, values, and beliefs creating 'networks of shared meaning' with the intention of changing some aspect of the social structure.

14. Wilkinson, Paul (1974), p. 38, *Political Terrorism*, London: Macmillan. Wilkinson defines three types of political terrorism: revolutionary, sub-revolutionary and repressive. He defines POTD as one type of revolutionary terrorism.

15. Skocpol, Theda (1999), *States and Social Revolutions*, Cambridge: Cambridge University Press: focuses on social revolutions as social-structural change and the consequence of class conflict, namely the French, Russian and Chinese revolutions. See her introduction for overview of broad frameworks; Gurr, Ted (1970), *Why Men Rebel*, Princeton NJ: Princeton University Press: analyses increased aggression where individuals see a growing disparity between their opportunities and what they feel they are entitled to; Tilly, Charles (1978), *From Mobilisation to Revolution*, Reading MA & London: Addison-Wesley. Tilly's political conflict approach argues that violence is but an expression of processes of competition between groups in society for power and resources. Johnson, Chalmers (1983), *Revolutionary Change*, Harlow: Longman: revolutions are strategic attempts to use violence to change a social system from the perspective of its underlying values-system, which must first be brought to a crisis. More generally see Kalyvas, Stathis (2006), *The Logic of Violence in Civil War*, New York: Cambridge University Press, ch.1; Cramer, Christopher (2006), *Civil War is Not a Stupid Thing: Accounting for Violence in Developing Countries*, London: Hurst, see 'Violence, Memory and Progress', ch. 1 and 'Categories, Trends and Evidence of Violent Conflict', ch. 2; Whitehead, Neil, (ed.) (2004), *Violence*, Santa Fe: School of American Research Advanced Seminar Series & Oxford: James Currey: see for a more anthropological approach.

16. Held, David & McGrew, Anthony (2007), *Globalization/Anti-globalization: Beyond the Great Divide*, Cambridge: Polity. Note the contest over the intellectual hegemony and normative associations of globalisation. It is variously characterised as increased internationalisation of trade, instant technological and information connectivity, computerised financial delivery systems operating worldwide in real time, international division of labour, the restructuring of social relations in a 'shrinking world', and the collapsing of global and local cultures.

17. Bell (1999), op. cit..

18. Fukuyama, Francis (2006), *The End of History and the Last Man*, New York & London: Free Press; Kaplan, Robert (Feb 1994), 'The Coming Anarchy', *The Atlantic Magazine*; Huntington, Samuel (2002), *The Clash of Civilizations and the Remaking of World Order*, New York: Free Press.

19. Kilcullen, David (2009), p. 28, *The Accidental Guerrilla*, London: Hurst.

20. OCHA (2006), p. 17 '*Humanitarian Negotiations with Armed Groups: A Manual for Practitioners*', http://www.unhcr.org/refworld/docid/46924c322.html, accessed 31 July 2010.

21. (Jan 2010), p. 2-A-4, 'Army Field Manual Countering Insurgency', vol. 1, Part10, London: MOD. This draws on Mackinlay (2009), op. cit.; Contrast Weinstein, Jeremy (2007), '*Inside Rebellion: The Politics of Insurgent Violence*', Cambridge: Cambridge University Press. Weinstein adopts a political economy approach. Initial economic and social endowments shape the strategies of insurgent groups: some prove to be opportunistic, others activist; O'Neil, Bard (2005), *Insurgency & Ter-*

rorism, Washington, DC: Potomac Books. O'Neil identifies nine types: anarchist, egalitarian, traditionalist, apocalyptic-utopian, pluralist, secessionist, reformist, preservationist, and commercialist; Kilcullen, David (2006), p. 2, 'Three Pillars of Counterinsurgency', Presentation to US Government Counterinsurgency Conference, Washington, DC 28 Dec 2006: Kilcullen roots uprisings anthropologically in 'pre-existing social networks (village, tribe, family, neighbourhood, political or religious party) and [that] exist in a complex social, informational and physical environment'.

22. (2009), op. cit., p. 73.

23. Some French analysts employ the term 'nebuleuse', which Jason Burke notes has no direct equivalent in English but alludes to a 'nebulous, floating, dynamically evolving phenomenon that is half-network, half-idea'. See Burke, Jason (26 Aug 2007), '"Islamism" has No Place in Terror's Lexicon', *The Observer*, http://www.guardian.co.uk/commentisfree/2007/aug/26/comment.alqaida, accessed 26 Aug 2010, for a discussion on the inadequacy of counterinsurgency and counter-terror language to express an ideological and simultaneously organisational concept.

24. BBC Television (06 Dec 2006), Richard Dimbleby Lecture.

25. See ch. 2 in *Memory, Myths and Terror* for explanation of the archipelago concept.

26. Memory is a process of constructing historical continuity from discontinuity and where a worldview derives from this process of constructed recollection.

27. Foucault, Michel (1980), *Power/Knowledge*, Harlow: Pearson Education.

28. Debord, Guy (1983), *Society of the Spectacle*, Detroit MI: Black and Red.

29. Political Marketing: an iterative, mutual exchange of values between producers (insurgents) and heterogeneous audiences or consumers (political and social population groups) where divergent messages target segmented groups creating different effects.

30. Propaganda: a devalued currency in the public realm, a linguistic shorthand popularly called 'spin', lies, dark arts and dirty tricks. Usually identified with modern, atomised mass populations and the totalising control of communications. See Glossary for fuller definition and ch. 1 for discussion. Scholars of propaganda offer various definitions. Orwell changed his view of propaganda from writing in *Persuasion* (1944), and after working in the BBC Eastern Service to producing *Nineteen Eighty-Four (1948)*, where he vilifies it and *Newspeak* as a means to totalised domination of the real world.

31. Digital Revolution: the shift from analogue to digital technologies allowing increased miniaturisation, storage, ease of diffusion, and creating changes in the social relations of societies adopting these new technologies.

32. Feyerabend, Paul (1993), *Against Method*, London: Verso

33. Lévi-Strauss, Claude (1966), *The Savage Mind*, Chicago: University of Chicago Press; Derrida describes the bricoleur as one who uses 'the instruments he finds at his disposition around him, those which are already there, which had not been especially conceived with an eye to the operation for which they are to be used and to which one tries by trial and error to adapt them, not hesitating to change them whenever it appears necessary'. Derrida, Jacques (2005), p. 360, *Writing and Difference*, London: Routledge.

34. Danermark, Berth; Ekström, Mats; Jakobsen, Liselotte & Karlsson, July (2002),

p. 150, *Explaining Society: Critical Realism in the Social Sciences*, London: Routledge. See for critical methodological pluralism.

35. Blackmore, Chris, (ed.) (2010), p. 66, *Social Learning Systems and Communities of Practice*, London: Springer.

36. Della Porta, Donatella & Keating, Michael (2008), *Approaches and Methodologies in the Social Sciences. A Pluralist Perspective*, Cambridge: Cambridge University Press.

37. Keating, Michael & Della Porta, Donatella (March-April 2010), p. 10, *In Defence of Pluralism. Combining Approaches in the Social Sciences*, Paper, Political Studies Association, Edinburgh.

38. Ibid., p. 11; see Giddens, Anthony (1982), *Profiles and Critiques in Social Theory*, Berkeley & Los Angeles: University of California Press, ch. 1.

39. Turkle, Sherry & Papert, Seymour (1990), p. 130, 'Epistemological Pluralism: Styles and Voices within the Computer Culture', *Signs*, vol. 16, no. 1, pp. 128–157.

40. Martin, Michael (2000), p. 246, *Verstehen: The Uses of Understanding in Social Science*, New Brunswick NJ: Transaction.

41. Ibid., p. 247.

42. Kirsch, Gesa & Sullivan, Patricia (eds) (1992), p. 254, *Methods and Methodology in Composition Research*, Southern Illinois University Press.

43. Henneberg, Stephan (2004), p. 14, 'Political Marketing Theory: Hendiadyoin or Oxymoron', University of Bath School of Management, Working Paper Series, 2004, 01.

44. Semiotics: a theory of signs and symbols that generate messages and meanings. Metaphor: The means to understand and experience one thing in terms of another, where one element simplifies or elucidates the meaning of the other.

45. Smith, Rogers (2004), p. 43, 'The Politics of Identity and the Tasks of Political Science' in Shapiro, Ian, Smith, Rogers & Masoud, Tarek (eds), *Problems and Methods in the Study of Politics*, Cambridge: Cambridge University Press.

46. Della Porta (2008), op. cit., p. 25.

47. Coolsaet, Rik (2008), p. 31, *Jihadi Terrorism and the Radicalisation Challenge in Europe*, Aldershot: Ashgate.

48. Woodcock tries to summarise the 'libertarian attitude' of anarchism as 'its rejection of dogma, its deliberate avoidance of systematic theory, and, above all, its stress on extreme freedom of choice and on the primacy of the individual judgement'. Cited in Earnshaw, Robert, (ed.) (1994), p. 159, *Postmodern Surroundings*, Amsterdam: Rodopi.

49. Woodcock, George (1963), *Anarchism*, Harmondsworth: Penguin; Rapoport, David (2004), 'Four Waves of Modern Terrorism', in Kurth Cronin, Audrey & Ludes, James M (eds), *Attacking Terrorism: Elements of a Grand Strategy*, Washington, DC: Georgetown University Press: others were the 'Anti-Colonial' (1920s), 'New Left' (late 1960s), and 'Religious' (1979-).

50. Maitron, Jean (1951), *Histoire du Mouvement Anarchiste En France (1880–1914)*, Paris: Société Universitaire d'Editions et de Librairie; Godwin, William (1793, 1992), *Enquiry Concerning Political Justice*.

51. Berlin, Isaiah (1995), *Karl Marx: His Life and Environment*, Oxford: Oxford University Press.

52. Joll, James (1964, 1979), p. 12, *The Anarchists*, London: Methuen.

53. Carlson, Andrew (1972), pp. 58–60, *Anarchism in Germany Vol. 1: The Early Movement*, Metuchen, NJ: Sacrecrow Press.

54. Proudhon, Pierre-Joseph (1851, 1969), *Idée Générale de la Révolution* (Trans), Robinson, John, New York: Haskell House; Although Woodcock recognises his early-career ambiguity: Letter to Marx (17 May 1846), Woodcock, George (1986), p. 138, *Anarchism: A History of Libertarian Ideas and Movements*, Harmondsworth: Penguin.

55. Fleming, Marie (1980), p. 6, 'Propaganda by the Deed: Terrorism and Anarchist Theory in Late Nineteenth-Century Europe', *Studies in Conflict & Terrorism*, vol. 4, no. 1, pp. 1–23.

56. Crenshaw, Martha, (ed.) (1995), p. 42, *Terrorism in Context*, University Park PA: Pennsylvania State University; for Malatesta in the twentieth-century see Marshall, Peter (2010), *Demanding the Impossible: A History of Anarchism*, Oakland CA: PM Press.

57. Avrich, Paul (1988), p. 240, *Anarchist Portraits*, Princeton NJ: Princeton University Press.

58. Kropotkin, Peter (2005), pp. 34–43 *'The Spirit of Revolt'* in Kropotkin's Revolutionary Pamphlets, Whitefish MT: Kessinger.

59. Goldman, Emma (1910), *Anarchism and Other Essays*, New York: Mother Earth.

60. Laqueur, Walter (1999), p. 13, *The New Terrorism: Fanaticism and the Arms of Mass Destruction*, Oxford: Oxford University Press.

61. *Théâtre Bellecour*, Montceau-les-Mines, Roanne cf. Maitron op. cit., p. 137: *Le Révolté*, no. 49, 26/3–1/4/1887; p. 138: no. 4, 30/4–6/5/1887; p. 138: no. 3, 1/4/1882; p. 146: no. 13: 17–30/8/1882; for actions of Charles Gallo, Auguste Vaillant, Emile Henry see Joll, op. cit., pp. 112–118

62. Their internal disagreement centred on spontaneous mass action. Mandel, Ernest (1970), *The Leninist Theory of Organisation*, http://www.ernestmandel.org/en/works/txt/1970/leninist_theory_organisation.htm.

63. Kucherov, Samuel (April 1952), 'The Case of Vera Zasulich', *Russian Review*, vol. 11, no. 2, pp. 86–96.

64. Laqueur, Walter (1987), p. 62, *The Age of Terrorism*, London: Weidenfeld & Nicholson; Jenkins, Gareth (2006), 'Marxism and Terrorism', *International Socialism*, vol. 110; Lutz, James & Lutz, Brenda (2008), p. 134, *Global Terrorism*, Abingdon: Routledge; Gage, Beverly (2009), *The Day Wall Street Exploded: A Story of America in its First Age of Terror*, New York: Oxford University Press.

65. Bakunin, Mikhail (1842), *'La Reaction en Allemagne, Fragment par un Francais'*, http://www.marxists.org/reference/archive/bakunin/works/1842/reaction-germany.htm.

66. Venturi, Franco (2001), p. 597, *Roots of Revolution*, London: Phoenix Press (cf. Dimitri Klemens: *Zemlya I Volya*); Carlson op. cit.; Maitron op. cit..

67. Law, Randall (2009), p. 105, *Terrorism: a History*, Cambridge: Polity.

68. Falk, Candace, (ed.) (2008), *Emma Goldman: A Documentary History of the American Years, vol. 1: Made for America, 1890–1901'*, Champaign, Il: University of Illinois Press; (2008), *'Emma Goldman: A Documentary History of the American Years vol. II: Making Speech Free, 1902–1909'*, Champaign, Il: University of Illinois Press

69. DeNardo, James (1985), p. 242, *Power in Numbers: The Political Strategy of Pro-*

test and Rebellion, Princeton, NJ: Princeton University Press (my italics).However following the Voronezh congress, the party split in two: *Cherny Peredel* (Black Partition) and *Narodnaya Volya* (People's Will) over whether or not to honour the commitment to terrorism and the condemnation of Tsar Alexander II to death. See Chaliand, Gerard & Blin, Arnaud (2007), p. 146, *The History of Terrorism: From Antiquity to Al Qaeda*, University of California Press.

70. Rapoport, David (2004), 'Four Waves of Modern Terrorism', in Kurth Cronin, Audrey & Ludes, James M (eds), *Attacking Terrorism: Elements of a Grand Strategy*, Washington, DC: Georgetown University Press.

71. Barnett, Brooke & Reynolds, Amy (2009), p. 30, *Terrorism and the Press: an Uneasy Relationship*, New York: Peter Lang.

72. Neumann, Peter & Smith, MLR (2008), p. 33, *The Strategy of Terrorism: How it Works and Why it Fails*, Abingdon: Routledge.

73. Richardson, Louise (2005), p. 55, *What Terrorists Want: Understanding the Terrorist Threat*, London: John Murray.

74. Rapoport (2004), op. cit., pp. 47–51.

75. Laqueur (1987), op. cit.; Shatz, Marshall, (ed.) (2002), *Bakunin: Statism and Anarchy*, Cambridge: Cambridge University Press; see introduction.

76. Venturi, op. cit., p. 364; Fishman, WJ (1970), *The Insurrectionists*, London: Methuen, ch. 7;

77. Wilkinson, op. cit., p. 68.

78. Venturi, op. cit.; Tucker, Robert (1969), *The Marxian Revolutionary Idea*, New York: WW Norton; Wilkinson (1974), op. cit.; Laqueur (1987), op. cit..

79. Ibid., pp. 595–6.

80. Wilkinson (1974), op. cit., pp. 55–74.

81. Tucker, op. cit., p. 1.

82. Boym, Svetlana (2010), p. 143, *Another Freedom: The Alternative History of an Idea*, Chicago: University of Chicago Press; Carr, Matthew (2008), *The Infernal Machine: A History of Terrorism*, New York: New Press.

83. Clutterbuck, Lindsay (Spring 2004), p. 154, 'The Progenitors of Terrorism: Russian Revolutionaries or Extreme Irish Republicans?', *Terrorism and Political Violence*, vol. 16, no. 1, pp. 154–181.

84. Hoffman, Bruce (1998), *Inside Terrorism*, New York: Columbia University Press.

85. Ford, Franklin (1985), *'Political Murder'*, Cambridge MA: Harvard University Press.

86. Chaliand, Gerard (1982), p. 30, *'Guerrilla Strategies'*, London: University of California Press; Rapoport (2004), op. cit..

87. Laqueur in Clutterbuck, op. cit., p. 156.

88. Richardson, op. cit., p. 51.

89. Coogan, Tim Pat (2000), p. 4, *The IRA*, London: HarperCollins.

90. Adams, Gerry in English, Richard (2003), p. 5, *Armed Struggle*, Oxford: Oxford University Press.

91. Richardson, op. cit., p. 51.

92. Oppenheimer, Andy (2009), p. 19, *IRA: The Bombs and the Bullets*, Dublin: Irish Academic Press; McConville, Sean(2003), p. 341, *Irish Political Prisoners, 1848–1922: Theatres of War*, Abingdon: Routledge.

93. Hoffman (1998), op. cit., pp. 10–11.

94. Oppenheimer, op. cit., p. 63.

95. Richardson, op. cit., pp. 14, 95.

96. Smelser, Neil (1963), *Theory of Collective Behaviour*, New York: Free Press; Olson, Mancur (1965), *The Logic of Collective Action*, Cambridge, Mass.: Harvard University Press; Granovetter, Mark (1978), 'Threshold Models of Collective Behaviour', *American Journal of Sociology*: vol. 83, no. 6. (May 1978), pp. 420–443.

97. DeNardo (1985), op. cit..

98. Sandler, Todd & Enders, Walter (2007), 'Applying Analytical Methods to Study Terrorism', *International Studies Perspectives*, vol. 8, pp. 287–302.

99. De Mesquita, Ethan Bueno & Dickson, Eric (2007), 'The Propaganda of the Deed: Terrorism, Counterterrorism, and Mobilisation', *American Journal of Political Science*, vol. 5, no. 2, pp. 364–38, see for a good overview of the literature.

100. Ibid., pp. 364–377.

101. Siqueirai in De Mesquita (2007), op. cit..

102. Ferrero, Mario (Dec 2006), 'Martyrdom Contracts', *Journal of Conflict Resolution*, vol. 50, no. 6, pp. 877–855.

103. Laqueur, Walter (2001), 'Left, Right, and Beyond: The Changing Face of Terror', in Hoge, James & Rose, Gideon (eds), *How did this happen? Terrorism and the New War*, pp. 71–82, New York: Public Affairs.

104. Iannaccone, Laurence R. (2003), 'The Market for Martyrs', presented at the 2004 Meetings of the American Economic Association, San Diego, CA.; Berman, Eli & Laitin, David (October 2005), 'Hard Targets: Theory and Evidence on Suicide Attacks', NBER Working Paper 11740; Azam, Jean-Paul (2005), 'Suicide Bombing as Inter-generational Investment', *Public Choice*, vol. 122, pp. 177–98.

105. Wintrobe, Ronald (2006), *Rational extremism: The Political Economy of Radicalism*, Cambridge: Cambridge University Press.

106. Harrison, Mark (2004), 'An Economist Looks at Suicide Terrorism', Unpublished manuscript, University of Warwick, in Ferrero (2006).

107. Ferrero, op. cit., pp. 856–7; 867; 873–4.

108. Pape, Robert (2006), p. 192, *Dying to Win: The Strategic Logic of Suicide Terrorism*, New York: Random House.

109. Ibid., p. 198.

110. Horowitz, Michael (2010), p. 167, *The Diffusion of Military Power*, Princeton NJ: Princeton. University Press. See for the way diffusion processes affect adoption strategies.

111. Bloom, Mia (2005), pp. 23–30, *Dying To Kill: The Allure of Suicide Terror*, New York: Columbia University Press.

112. Fraim, John (2003), p. 34, *Battle of Symbols: Global Dynamics of Advertising, Entertainment and Media*, Einsiedeln: Daimon Verlag.

113. Barnett, op. cit., p. 80.

114. Altheide, David (2009), p. 5, *Terror Post 9/11 and the Media*, New York: Peter Lang.

115. O'Shaughnessy, Nicholas (2004), pp. 29–33, *Politics and Propaganda: Weapons of Mass Seduction*, Manchester: Manchester University Press; Betz, David (2008), 'The Virtual Dimension of Modern Insurgency and Counterinsurgency', *Small Wars & Insurgencies*, vol. 19, no. 4, pp. 510–540; Mackinlay (2009), op. cit..

116. Laqueur, Walter (1999), p. 4, *'The New Terrorism'*, London: Phoenix.

117. Turow, John (1999), *Breaking Up America*, Chicago: University of Chicago Press; see also Weiss, Michael (2000), *The Clustered World*, Boston MA: Little, Brown.

118. (2006), pp. 5, 21–22, 'What is Propaganda, and How Does it Differ from Persuasion', in Jowell, Garth & O'Donnell, Victoria (eds) (2006), *Readings in Propaganda and Persuasion: New and Classic Essays*, Thousand Oaks: Sage.

119. op. cit., p. 111.

120. Pastor, James (2010), pp. 56–7, *Terrorism and Public Safety: Implications for the Obama Presidency*, Boca Raton FL: CRC; Mackinlay (2009), op. cit. see ch. 7; Gowing, Nik (2009), *"Skyful of Lies", and Black Swans: The New Tyranny of Shifting Information Power in Crises*, Oxford: RISJ.

121. Devji, Faisal (2005), p. 92, *Landscapes of the Jihad: Militancy, Morality, Modernity*, London: Hurst.

122. Roy, Olivier (2004), p. 183, *Globalised Islam: The Search for a New Ummah*, London: Hurst.

123. Luttwak, Edward (2009), p. 94, *The Virtual Empire: War, Faith and Power*, New Brunswick NJ: Transaction Publishers.

124. David, GJ & McKeldin, TR (2009), *Ideas as Weapons*, Washington, DC: Potomac Books.

125. Dauber, Cori (2009), *YouTube War: Fighting in a World of Cameras in Every Cell Phone and Photoshop on Every Computer*, Carlisle PA: Strategic Studies Institute.

126. Nacos, Brigitte (2002, 2007), pp. 11, 84, *Mass-mediated Terrorism: The Central Role of the Media in Terrorism and Counterterrorism*, Lanham MD: Rowan & Littlefield.

127. Baines, Paul & O'Shaughnessy, Nicholas (2006), *Muslim Voices: The British Muslim Response to Islamist Video-Polemic: An Exploratory Study*, Cranfield University School of Management.

1. THE TERRORIST ACT AS COMMUNICATOR

1. Performed by Christy Moore; reproduced courtesy of Paul Doran.

2. Op. cit.

3. Lasswell, Harold (1971), p. 84, 'The Structure and Function of Communication in Society' in Schramm, Wilbur & Roberts, Donald, *The Process and Effects of Mass Communication*, Urbana Ill: University of Illinois Press.

4. one-to-many denotes a one-way information flow between publisher and consumer/ reader: many-to-many or peer-to-peer allows consumers to speak directly to each other without mediators.

5. 'messages consist of information in the sense that they are structured experiences... the meaning of a message is the change which it produces in the image' held by receivers. Roberts, Donald (1971), pp. 362–3, 'The Nature of Communication Effects' in Schramm, op. cit., citing Boulding.

6. This idea has been expanded recently, suggesting each epoch spawns an insurgency form which mirrors the particular constitutional model of the state. POTD arose within a state-model trajectory from 1) princely to 2) kingly to 3) territorial to 4) state-nation to 5) nation-state (it occurred at the state-nation/nation-state overlap). Today

it operates within 6) the market-state. See Bobbitt, Philip (2008), *Terror and Consent: The Wars for the Twenty-First Century*, London & New York: Allen Lane.

7. Smith, Neil (2004), p. 9, *American Empire: Roosevelt's Geographer and the Prelude to Globalisation*, Berkeley: University of California Press.

8. Hobsbawm, Eric (1988), pp. 228–9, *The Age of Capital 1848–1875*, London: Cardinal.

9. Stone, Norman (1999), pp. 1–12, *Europe Transformed 1878–1919*, Oxford: Blackwell. Populations exploded as mortality rates fell—Germany 35,000,000 to 60,000,000; Great Britain 25,000,000 to 40,000,000; European Russia 60,000,000 to 140,000,000.

10. Wilson, Edmund (1983), p. 171, *To the Finland Station*, London: Macmillan: depression and mass unemployment—some 50,000—followed the first rapid wave of European rail expansion in 1846–7, contributing to demonstrations, state reaction, and the 1848 revolution in Paris.

11. Hobsbawm (1988), op. cit., p. 362 (table 2). By the mid-1860s 106,886 kilometres of track had been laid; a decade later, more than double. Steamship overall tonnage increased from 1,423,232 to 3,293,072.

12. 'Constant revolutionising of production, uninterrupted disturbance of all social conditions, everlasting uncertainty and agitation distinguish the bourgeois epoch from all earlier ones': (1848), 'Communist Manifesto'http://www.marxists.org/archive/marx/works/1848/communist-manifesto/ch01.htm.

13. Stone, op. cit., p. 13 (sic).

14. Leading to civil disturbance: 'honest poverty knocking at the door of selfish luxury and comfort': Burns, John (1886), p. 16, *The Man with the Red Flag: Speech for the Defence by John Burns in the Trial of the Four Social Democrats for Seditious Conspiracy*, London: The Modern Press (*Socialist Tracts 1883–94*).

15. Engels, Friedrich (1845, 2005), p. 63, *The Condition of the Working Class in England*, London: Penguin. See table p. 57, population increase in Yorkshire's West Riding towns, 1801:564,000—1831:980,000; see Ibid., 'The Industrial Proletariat' for other cities and industrial sector breakdown.

16. Polanyi, Karl (2001), *The Great Transformation*, Boston MA: Beacon Press.

17. Screpanti, Ernesto & Zamagni, Stefano(2005), pp. 163–4, *An Outline of the History of Economic Thought*, Oxford: Oxford University Press; Perry, Peter(1974), *British Farming in the Great Depression 1870–1914*, Newton Abbot: David and Charles; for a re-evaluation of the Depression see Saul, Samuel(1985), *The Myth of the Great Depression 1873–1896*, London: Macmillan; for how American industry was reorganised after the 1893 Panic and its impact on capital-labour relations, race-relations, sectional conflict, Sklar, Martin(1997), *The Corporate Reconstruction of American Capitalism 1890–1916*, Cambridge: Cambridge University Press, ch. 2.

18. Kropotkin, Peter (1887), p. 1, *The Place of Anarchism in Socialistic Evolution*, London: W. Reeves. Argues the fate of revolutions is 'though vanquished they establish the course of the evolution which follows them'. Hence the nineteenth century was viewed as an era attempting to practice ideals lost in the 'failed' revolution of 1789: Parsons, Howard & Somerville, John (1977), *Marxism, Revolution, and Peace: From the Proceedings of the Philosophical Study of Dialectical Materialism*, Amsterdam: BR Grüner.

19. Aristotle (1970), *The Politics*, Harmondsworth: Penguin, Book V, ch. 4; Machiavelli, Niccolo (1963), *The Prince*, Harmondsworth: Penguin. Revolution in the time of Aristotle suggested the inevitable turning of the cycle which replaces one ruler with another. Locke advocated the individual's right to challenge malfunctioning government through self-assertion and popular participation: Locke, John (1728), *Two Treatises on Government*, 5th edn, 2nd Treatise, ch. 19, section 230, London: Bettesworth; Touraine, Alain (1990), *The Idea of Revolution*, Theory, Culture & Society, vol. 7, pp. 121–141; Arendt, Hannah (1990), p. 28, *On Revolution*, London: Penguin: the modern concept of revolution is unknown before the American and French Revolutions. 'European (or indeed world) politics between 1789 and 1917 were largely the struggle for and against the principles of 1789, or even more incendiary ones of 1793': Hobsbawm, Eric (1978), p. 73, *'The Age of Revolution 1789–1848*, London: Abacus.

20. Ideologically and organisationally weak, the 1848 pan-European revolution spread like forest-fire, only to burn itself out within six months. Its failure meant gradual reform would now look for sponsorship beyond the *bourgeoisie*. These had chosen economic prosperity over the vagaries of political change. See Calhoun, Craig (1989), p. 210, 'Classical Social Theory and the French Revolution of 1848', *Sociological Theory*, vol. 7, no. 2, pp. 210–225.

21. 'The world must crack that its equilibrium be restored': Reclus, Elisée (1884), p. 640, 'An Anarchist on Anarchy', *Contemporary Review*, vol. 45, see also Georges Sorel (1908, 2002), *'Reflections on Violence'*, Cambridge: Cambridge University Press

22. Arendt (1990), op. cit..

23. Novak, D (July 1958), p. 307, 'The Place of Anarchism in the History of Political Thought', *The Review of Politics*, vol. 20, no. 3, pp. 307–329.

24. Kropotkin (1887), op. cit., p. 14.

25. Burns, op. cit., p. 20. In his Old Bailey trial for seditious conspiracy Burns describes the *Daily Telegraph* as popularly known for 'making spicy reports, and giving descriptive summaries, sometimes of things that do occur, but very often of things that do not happen'.

26. Graham, Robert, (ed.) (2005), p. 150, *Anarchism: A Documentary History of Libertarian Ideas*, vol. 1, Montreal: Black Rose.

27. Grave, Jean (1899), *Moribund Society and Anarchy*, San Francisco CA: A Isaak.

28. From the first *International* in 1864 through subsequent congresses between 1868 and 1872, this forum became the battle-ground for the manoeuvrings of two ideologues equally committed to revolution but espousing mutually exclusive strategies and doctrines. At stake were fundamental principles: 'Authoritarian versus libertarian, political action versus industrial action, transitional proletarian dictatorship versus immediate abolition of all State power': Woodcock, George (1977, 1986), p. 42, *Anarchism: A History of Libertarian Ideas and Movements*, Harmondsworth: Penguin; See also Maitron, op. cit., pp. 14–15.

29. Lenin, Vladimir (1987), pp. 289–290, *What Is To Be Done? And Other Writings*, New York: Bantam.

30. Lenin, Vladimir (2004), p. 14, *The State and Revolution*, Whitefish MT: Kessinger, citing Engels' *Anti-Dühring*. More precisely Lenin explains Engels' intention that in a two-step transformation the proletarian state eradicates the bourgeois state and it

is the remnants of the former that wither away after the socialist revolution (1992), p. 17, *The State and Revolution*, London: Penguin. Again Lenin underscores the Marxist need for revolutionary violence: 'force plays another role in history [other than as a perpetrator of evil], namely a revolutionary role' (Ibid., p. 19).

31. Lenin (2004), op. cit., p. 63.

32. Kropotkin, Peter (1902, 1987), *Mutual Aid: A Factor of Evolution*, London: Freedom Press.

33. (1793, 1992), op. cit.; Kropotkin (1896, 1911), *The State: Its Historic Role*, http://www.ditext.com/kropotkin/state.html, traces a longer Western lineage to the Commune originating in village community and trade guilds of the Middle Ages. He defines the Commune in opposition to the subjugating will of the state: 'There lies all the difference. There are struggles and conflicts that kill. And there are those that launch humanity forwards' (ch. 5).

34. Joll (1979), op. cit., p. 12; Anarchism's antecedents can be traced to the English Commonwealth and the Levellers, Diggers and Anabaptists.

35. Kucherov, op. cit., p. 91.

36. Barer, Shlomo (2000), *The Doctors of Revolution*, London: Thames and Hudson, ch. 7. Barer sees Bakunin's doctrine as the common denominator to the later Spanish *Anarchists*, Uruguayan *Tupamaros, IRA,* and *Red Brigades,* p. 251 .

37. See Fyodor Dostoyevski's demonological novel *Possessed*: the model for nihilist Verkhovensky is understood to be Nechaev . Also *Crime and Punishment* for his pathological treatment of radicalism.

38. Catechism no. 3, *www.marxists.org/subject/anarchism/nechayev/catechism.htm.*

39. (1842), *'La Réaction en Allemagne, fragment, par un Français'.*

40. Catechism no. 24, op. cit..

41. Catechism no. 12, Ibid.

42. Catechism no. 13, Ibid., (italics sic)

43. Woodcock, op. cit., p. 43; Paul Brousse is widely credited with having introduced the expression 'propaganda of the deed' into print: 'Depuis quelque temps on parle souvent, dans la Fédération jurasienne, d'une chose dont le nom au moins est nouveau: la *Propagandie par le fait'.* Guillaume, James (1905), *'L'International: Documents et Souvenirs'*, Paris, 05 Aug 1877, vol. 4, p. 224, vol. 31.

44. Davies, Norman (1996), p. 840, *Europe: a History*, Oxford & New York: OUP.

45. Hansen, James (1977), p. 101, 'Subjectivism, Terrorism and Political Activism', in Parsons, Howard & Somerville, John (eds), *Marxism, Revolution, and Peace*, Amsterdam: BR Grüner

46. Ibid. (sic).

47. Ibid., p. 109: Marx writes: '*a section of civil society* emancipates itself and attains universal domination; a determinate class undertakes, from its *particular situation,* a general emancipation of society'. (sic)

48. McLuhan, Marshall (1967), *The Gutenberg Galaxy: The Making of Typographical Man*, London: Routledge & Kegan Paul.

49. Raymond, Joad (2003), p. 163, *Pamphlets and Pamphleteering in Early Modern Britain*, Cambridge: Cambridge University Press, see footnote 4; these figures represent surviving titles and are perhaps skewed by the existing collection of George Thomason at the British Library: 22,000 publications in 2,000 volumes. Raymond argues that the 1641 explosion 'amplified an existing trend, and occurred upon a

geographical axis of print and polemic extending between Glasgow, Edinburgh, London, Leiden and Amsterdam'.

50. Ibid., p. 161 citing *Presse Full of Pamphlets* (1642), sig. A2r-v.

51. Darnton, Robert & Roche, Daniel (eds) (1989), p. 145, *Revolution in Print: The Press in France 1775–1800*, Berkeley: University of California Press. 184 periodicals were launched in 1789: 335 in 1790. Most lasted 1–2 issues. By early 1798 Paris had 107 newspapers, and 50–60 provincial papers were published (p. 335, endnote14).

52. Ely, Richard (1886, 2005), p. 265, *The Labor Movement in America*, Boston MA: Adamant Media [my insertion]. ch. 10 for POTD in a survey of anarchist papers.

53. Beniger, James (1986), p. 7, *The Control Revolution: Technological and Economic Origins of the Information Society*, Cambridge MA: Harvard University Press.

54. Ward, Ken (1989), *Mass Communications and the Modern World*, Basingstoke: Macmillan Education; Starr, Paul (2004), *The Creation of the Media: Political Origins of Modern Communications*, New York: Basic Books; Lee, Alfred (1937), *The Daily Newspaper in America*, New York: Macmillan; Chalaby, Jean (1997), 'No Ordinary Press Owners: Press Barons as a Weberian Ideal Type', *Media, Culture & Society*, vol. 19, no. 4, pp. 621–644. Chalaby differentiates between press barons and 'classic' newspaper owners.

55. See http://lincoln.lib.niu.edu/fimage/gildedage/haymarket/results1.php?page=4&ipp=9 for sensationalist images of Chicago's Haymarket Riot 1886 and Western Division Railway workers' strike 1885 from *Frank Leslie's Illustrated Magazine*, and Castaigne's engraving 'Turning Back the Anarchists' at the Board of Trade, in *Century Magazine* 1894: http://www.chicagohistory.org/dramas/act1/theFuseIsLit/atCapitalSCapitol.htm; McLean, George (1972), *The Rise and Fall of Anarchy in America*, New York: Haskell House.

56. Burlingame, Roger (1940), p. 297, *Engines of Democracy*, New York: Charles Scribner's.

57. Schudson, Michael (1981), *Discovering the News: A Social History of American Newspapers*, New York: Basic Books. Argues that literacy and mass circulation were not enough to warrant the growing dominance of news in the press.

58. Op. cit., p. 287.

59. Schudson, op. cit..

60. Beniger, op. cit., p. 433; Starr, op. cit., p. 388.

61. Taylor, Frederick (2003), *Scientific Management*, Abingdon: Routledge.

62. See Hegel's analysis of the objective civil service in Hegel, Georg (2008), *Philosophy of Right*, New York: Cosimo; Marx, Karl (1982), *Critique of Hegel's Philosophy of Right*, Cambridge: Cambridge University Press; (1963), *Eighteenth Brumaire of Louis Bonaparte*, New York: International Publishers; Weber, Max (1964), *The Theory of Social and Economic Organization*, New York: Free Press of Glencoe; (2008), *Economy and Society*, London: Routledge; Bell (1999), op. cit. for a comparative discussion, reflecting on bureaucracy as an independent force above society, and Bakunin's philosophical writings where he argues a strong state depends on military and bureaucratic foundations (p. 85 footnote 58).

63. 'The rise of new social strata to full membership of the nation marked the last three decades of the nineteenth century throughout western and central Europe...National policy was henceforth founded on the support of the masses; and the counterpoint

was the loyalty of the masses to a nation which had become the instrument of their collective interest and ambitions'. E.H. Carr cited in Hutchinson, John & Smith, Anthony (1994), p. 158, *Nationalism*, Oxford: Oxford University Press.

64. Beniger, op. cit., p. 434: 'Inseparable from control are the twin activities of information processing and reciprocal communication. Information processing is essential to all purposive activity, which is by definition goal directed and must therefore involve the continual comparison of current states to future goals. Two-way interaction between controller and controlled must also occur to communicate influence from the former to the latter and to communicate back (as feedback) the results of this action'; Ross, Edward (1901, 2009), *Social Control: A Survey of the Foundations of Order*, New Brunswick NJ: Transaction Publishers.

65. Rauchway, Eric (2004), *The Making of Theodore Roosevelt's America*, New York: Farrar, Strauss and Giroux. See for discussion of America caught between defining POTD causally as assassin's pathology or social deprivation.

66. Oved, Ya'Akov (1992), 'The Future Society According to Kropotkin', *Cahiers du Monde Russe Soviétique, XXXIII*, vol. 33, no. 323, pp. 303–320; Kropotkin (2005), op. cit..

67. Harding, James (2008), *Alpha Dogs: How Political Spin Became a Global Business*, London: Atlantic Books.

68. Collins, Randall (2001), p. 42, 'Social Movements and the Focus of Emotional Attention', in Goodwin, Jeff; Jasper, James & Polletta, Francesca (eds), *Passionate Politics: Emotions in Social Movements*, Chicago & London: Chicago University Press. See Collins broader point that under rare, emotionally charged conditions when insurgents and state engage in 'power show-downs', there is limited 'attention space'. Each side attempts to maximise the opportunity.

69. O'Shaughnessy, John & O'Shaughnessy, Nicholas (2004), *Persuasion in Advertising*, London & New York: Routledge.

70. Creel, George (1920), *How We Advertised America*, New York & London: Harper & Bros.

71. Lippmann, Walter (1922, 1997), *Public Opinion*, New York & London: Free Press Paperbacks.

72. Bernays, Edward (1928), *Propaganda*, New York: Horace Liveright.

73. Lasswell, Harold & Blumenstock, Dorothy (1970), p. 9, *World Revolutionary Propaganda*, Westport CONN: Greenwood Press. Argues that POTD is 'coercion and not propaganda', that it has evolved to refer to 'acts like assassination which are expected to have an influence upon attitudes which is disproportionately greater than usual for an act of the kind' (p. 11).

74. Chomsky, Noam (2004), p. 7, *Hegemony or Survival*, London: Penguin.

75. Jowett, Garth & O'Donnell, Victoria (2006), p. 7, *Propaganda and Persuasion*, Thousand Oaks: Sage.

76. Pratkanis, Anthony & Aronson, Elliot (2001), p. 11, *Age of Propaganda*, New York: WH Freeman.

77. O'Donnell, Victoria & Kable, June (1982), p. 9, *Persuasion: An Interactive Dependency Approach*, New York: Random House.

78. Jowett (2006), op. cit., p. 44; Lasswell, op. cit., p. 5.

79. Doob, Leonard (1950), 'Goebbels' Principles of Propaganda', *Public Opinion Quarterly*, pp. 419–442; also (1949), 'Propaganda and Public Opinion', Cresset Press; See

Stern-Rubarth, Edgar (1933), p. 105, 'The Methods of Political Propaganda' in Wright, Quincy (ed.), *Public Opinion and World-Politics*, Chicago: University of Chicago Press for distinctions between positive, 'advertising one's own advantages' and negative, 'dealing with the weaknesses and disadvantages of one's adversaries', and preventive, anticipating a stand-off between rival propaganda regimes by preparing public opinion for a propaganda campaign. Northcliffe is condemned for mastering negative propaganda. Stuart, Campbell (1920), p. 2, *Secrets of Crewe House*, London: Hodder & Stoughton on creating a 'favourable "atmosphere"'.

80. Lasswell, Harold & Blumenstock, Dorothy (1970), op. cit..

81. Ellul, Jacques (1973), p. 15, *Propaganda: The Formation of Men's Attitudes*, New York: Vintage.

82. O'Shaughnessy, Nicholas (2004), p. 16.

83. Briggs, Asa & Burke, Peter (2005), p. 68, *A Social History of the Media: From Gutenberg to the Internet*, Cambridge: Polity. However Taylor traces propaganda back to the Greek city-states' and Imperial Roman communications through buildings, spectacles, games and coinage in Taylor, Philip (1990), *Munitions of the Mind: War Propaganda from the Ancient World to the Nuclear Age*, Wellingborough: Stephens. Luther's proselytising hymns and printed pamphlets attacking the Church, and Cranach's woodcut images should be added to the list.

84. Starr (2004), op. cit.; Ward (1989), op. cit..

85. L'Etang, Jacquie (2004), *Public Relations in Britain: A History of Professional Practice in the Twentieth Century*, Mahwah NJ &London: Lawrence Erlbaum.

86. Chomsky, op. cit., p. 8.

87. See also Lasswell, Harold (1933), 'The Strategy of Revolutionary and War Propaganda', in Wright, op. cit. for a discussion of Soviet and Communist propaganda.

88. Leiser, Erwin (1974), p. 12, *Nazi Cinema*, London: Secker & Warburg. Hitler and Rosenberg by no means agreed.

89. Doob (1950), op. cit., p. 435.

90. O'Shaughnessy, Nicholas (1989), p. 22, *The Phenomenon of Political Marketing*, Basingstoke: Macmillan.

91. Lenin saw peasants as reactionary, resistant to economic development and capitalism, but revolutionary in their rejection of feudalism. As in Marx's writing, it was thought necessary to distinguish between progressive and conservative elements in the peasantry: Kingston-Mann, Esther (1983), pp. 47–8, *Lenin and the Problem of the Marxist Peasant Revolution*, Oxford: Oxford University Press.

92. Ferdinand Tönnies' concept: Loomis, Charles, (ed.) (2002), *Community and Society*, Mineola NY: Dover Publications.

93. Ellul (1973), op. cit., pp. 90–102. Ellul argues through Russia's enforced migration of ethnic and religious populations, and China's coercive restructuring of society, the way was opened up for the twofold emergence of the individual and mass.

94. *Ejercito Zapatista de Liberacion Nacional* (EZLN); *Fuerzas Armadas Revolucionarios de Colombia* (FARC); *Gerakan Aceh Merdeka* (GAM).

95. Norris, Pippa (2010), p. 360, *Public Sentinel: News Media and Governance Reform*, Washington, DC: World Bank.

95. Drucker, Peter (1969), p. X, *The Age of Discontinuity*, New York: Harper & Row.

96. Freedom House (30 Mar 2009), 'Freedom on the Net: A Global Assessment of Internet and Digital Media', http://www.freedomhouse.org/template.cf.m?page=383&

report=79, accessed 01 July 2010; see my discussion below in Chapter 7 'Sponta-neous Revolution'.

97. Yang, Guobin (2009), *The Power of the Internet in China: Citizen Activism Online*, New York: Columbia University Press. Cf. Bandurski, David (July 2008), 'China's Guerrilla War for the Web', *Far East Economic Review*. On 23 July 2007 China's President Hu appealed to party leaders to 'assert supremacy over online public opinion, raise the level and study the art of online guidance, and actively use new technologies to increase the strength of positive propaganda'.: Norris (2010), op. cit., p. 360.

98. Political marketing is an iterative, mutual exchange of values between producers (insurgents) and heterogeneous audiences or consumers (political and social pop-ulation groups) where divergent messages target segmented groups creating differ-ent effects.

99. (1969), op. cit., p. x.

100. Ibid., pp. 52–3.

101. Van Ham, Peter (2001), 'The Rise of the Brand State: The Postmodern Politics of Image and Reputation', *Foreign Affairs*, vol. 80, no. 5, pp. 2–6: *Vorsprung durch Technik* says Germans stand for progress, technical efficiency and precision: Mer-cedes, BMW, Audi and Porsche are Germany. Slogans like 'I Love New York' and 'Born in the USA' translate as freedom and prosperity in a world acculturated to America's ideals. Bruce Springsteen's musical branding 'Born in the USA', accom-panied Republican Reagan on his successful bid to retain the White House (1984).

102. Searched 07 Aug 2010.

103. Dec 2007, http://www.marketingpower.com/Community/ARC/Pages/Additional/Definition/default.aspx?sq=definition+of+marketing, accessed 09 June 2009.

104. McCarthy, Jerome (1968), pp. 31–3, *Basic Marketing: A Managerial Approach*, Homewood Ill: Richard D, Irwin.

105. Wedel, Michel & Kamakura, Wagner (1999), p. 3, *Market Segmentation: Concep-tual and Methodological Foundations*, Boston MA: Kluwer/ISQM; Turow, John (1999), *Breaking Up America*, Chicago: University of Chicago Press.

106. Lees-Marchment, Jennifer (2004), *The Political Marketing Revolution: Transform-ing the Government of the UK*, London: Manchester University Press; Harvey, David (2005), *A Brief History of Neoliberalism*, Oxford: Oxford University Press.

107. Melder, Keith (1992), *Hail to the Candidate*, Washington: Smithsonian; Walker, Vicki (July 2008), 'All it Takes is Love of History and Five Bucks', *Discover Mid-America*, http://discoverypub.com/feature/2008_01 political.html, accessed 27/06/2009.

108. O'Shaughnessy, Nicholas (Nov. 2003), 'The Symbolic State: A British Experience', *Journal of Public Affairs*, vol. 3, no. 4, pp. 297–312.

109. Kotler, Philip & Zaltman, Gerald (1971), p. 5, 'Social Marketing: An Approach to Planned Social Change', *Journal of Marketing*, vol. 35, no. 3, pp. 3–12.

110. Ibid., p. 7.

111. Harding, op. cit..

112. Lilleker, Darren & Lees-Marshment, Jennifer (eds) (2005), p. 6, *Political Market-ing: A Comparative Perspective*, Manchester & New York: Manchester University Press.

113. Ibid., p. 7–10.

114. O'Shaughnessy, Nicholas (1989), op. cit., p. 25.

115. Lees-Marshment, Jennifer (2008), p. 1, *Political Marketing and British Political Parties*, Manchester & New York: Manchester University Press.

116. Lilleker (2005), op. cit., p. 3, cautions against assuming a universal trend. History, political structures, and traditions are nationally specific. Political organisations are shaped by their pasts and function in the contemporary context (p. 2). However the general advance of consumerism internationally is noted by Baylis, John; Smith, Steve & Owens, Patricia (1999), *The Globalisation of World Politics*, Oxford: Oxford University Press; Barber, Benjamin (1996), *Jihad vs McWorld*, New York: Ballantine. Whilst Belk, Russell (1996), 'On Aura, Illusion, Escape and Hope in Apocalyptic Consumption: The Apotheosis of Las Vegas', in Brown Stephen, Bell Jim, & Carson, David (eds), *Marketing Apocalypse: Eschatology, Escapology and the Illusion of the End*, London: Routledge; Dermody, Janine &Scullion, Richard (2001), 'Delusions of Grandeur? Marketing's Contribution to "Meaningful" Western Political Consumption', *European Journal of Marketing*, vol. 35, no. 9–10, pp. 1085–98, analyse increased power of the individual within consumerism.

117. O'Shaughnessy (1994), p. 2.

118. Lilleker (2005), op. cit., p. 3.

119. Henneberg, Stephan (2004), pp. 6–7, 'Political Marketing Theory: Hendiadyoin or Oxymoron', University of Bath School of Management, Working Paper Series for a discussion of the epistemology.

120. Gould, Philip (1998), p. 328, *The Unfinished Revolution: How the Modernisers Saved the Labour Party*, London: Abacus.

121. Nimmo, Dan (1999), pp. 73–86, 'The Permanent Campaign: Marketing as a Governing Tool', in Newman, Bruce (ed.), *Handbook of Political Marketing*, Thousand Oaks, CA: Sage.

122. Docx, Edward (July 2009), 'Mandy in the Middle', *Prospect*, no. 160, citing Peter Mandelson http://www.prospect-magazine.co.uk/article_details.php?id=10858.

123. Blair, Tony (28 Sept 2004), Speech to Labour Party Conference, full text at http://www.guardian.co.uk/politics/2004/sep/28/labourconference.labour6.

124. O'Shaughnessy (2003), op. cit.; Palmer, Jerry(2002), 'Smoke and Mirrors: Is That the Way It Is? Themes in Political Marketing', *Media, Culture & Society*, vol. 24, no. 3, pp. 345–363 (2002), for critique of the primacy of presentation over policy delivery.

125. Blumenthal, Sidney (1982), *The Permanent Campaign*, New York: Touchstone; Needham, Catherine (2005), 'Brand Leaders: Clinton, Blair and the Limitations of the Permanent Campaign' *Political Studies*, 2005, vol. 53, pp. 343–361, for changes in marketing strategy and terrain between seeking office and office-holding.

126. Boorstin, Daniel (1992), p. 299, *'The Image: A Guide to Pseudo-Events in America'*, New York: Vintage.

127. June 1984 Labour Party Political Broadcast produced by Neville Bolt.

128. Westen, Drew (2007), *The Political Brain: The Role of Emotion in Deciding the Fate of the Nation*, Philadelphia: Public Affairs. Cf. 'Morning in America Again', http://www.youtube.com/watch?v=EU-IBF8nwSY; 'Raine, George (09 June 2004), 'Creating Reagan's Image', *San Francisco Chronicle*, http://www.sfgate.com/cgi-bin/article.cgi?f=/c/a/2004/06/09/BUGBI72U8O1.DTL, accessed 27 July 2009.

129. Manheim, Jarol (1991), *All of the People, All the Time*, Armonk, NY & London: M.E. Sharpe.

130. O'Shaughnessy, John (2004), op. cit., p. 39.

131. Manheim op. cit., p. 5.

132. Packwood, Lane (2009), p. 68, 'Popular Support as the Objective in Counterinsurgency: What Are We Really After?', *Military Review*, May–June pp. 67–77.

133. See Lloyd, Jenny (2005), 'Square Peg, Round Hole? Can Basic Marketing Concepts Such as the "Product" and the "Marketing Mix" Have a Useful Role in the Political Arena?', *Journal of Nonprofit & Public Sector Marketing*, vol. 14, no. 1, pp. 27–46 argues political and commercial markets differ. Loyalties to name, brand and goods are common. Citizens and consumers behave differently. Political parties and goods manufacturers differ. Large parties aim at electoral victory and government: smaller ones may perforce play a strategic game of alliance and blocking. A political product is not an economic good: one evolves, the other is refined. What is a political product: the leadership, representatives, their constitution or policies? Political products are intangible. They may promise one thing in opposition but deliver something else in government.

134. Bob, Clifford (2005), *The Marketing of Rebellion: Insurgents, Media and International Activism*, New York: Cambridge University Press: for marketing strategies affecting Nigerian Ogoni and Mexican Zapatista insurgent appeals to NGOs and external communities.

135. US Government Office of Director of National Intelligence (2005), http://www.globalsecurity.org/security/library/report/2005/zawahiri-zarqawi-letter_9jul2005.htm accessed 1 July 2009. Translation of letter obtained during counterinsurgency operations, 9 July 2005.

136. Crabtree, James (Aug 2009), 'The Real News from Pakistan', *Prospect Magazine*; http://www.youtube.com/watch?v=UzEAQ3Q3BoU, accessed 27/07/2009.

137. Walsh, Declan (02 Apr 2009), 'Video of Girl's Flogging as Taliban Hand Out Justice', *Guardian*, http://www.guardian.co.uk/world/2009/apr/02/taliban-pakistan-justice-women-flogging, accessed 16 Apr 2010.

138. (25 Nov. 2009), 'Mullah Omar: In Celebration of Eid al-Adha', NEFA Foundation http://www.nefafoundation.org/documents-area-afghanistan.html, accessed 13 Apr 2010.

139. 'Implementation of the DOD Strategic Communication Plan for Afghanistan' (2007), p. 2, Washington, DC: US Department of Defense. ISAF: International Security Assistance Force; AQ: A-Qaeda; AQAM: AlQaeda and associated movements; IGO: international governmental organisation; NGO: non-governmental organisation.

140. Cullison, Alan (Sept 2004), 'Inside Al-Qaeda's Hard Drive', *The Atlantic*. Internal language mirrors external communications. When al-Zawahiri wrote of merging *Islamic Jihad* and *Al-Qaeda*, one journalist unveiled his use of the language of international commerce in secret correspondence, warning of 'increased market share for "international monopolies"—the CIA and probably Egyptian intelligence. The merger, he said, could "increase profits"—the publicity that terrorism and support could produce'. The 03 May 2001 email is entirely couched in corporate metaphors.

141. Public diplomacy: a state-initiated messaging strategy where governments speak

publicly to populations of foreign governments with the aim of winning over their sympathy and support.

142. Obama, Barack (2010), p. 2, 'National Framework for Strategic Communication', Washington, DC: White House, http://www.carlisle.army.mil/DIME/documents/NSC%20SCPD%20Report.pdf accessed 30 July 2011.

143. Ibid.

144. (1952, revised 1970), pp. 433–5, 'An Outline for the Study of International Political Communication', in Schramm, Wilbur (ed.), *The Process and the Effects of Mass Communication*, Urbana: University of Illinois Press.

145. Ibid., p. 435; compare with Obama, Barack (2010), p. 13, 'National Framework for Strategic Communication', Washington, DC: White House. 1) target audience perceptions are not readily measured; 2) effects of communications are not easily isolated from those of other policy decisions; 3) communications' effects are long-term, requiring repeat measurement.

146. SC appears in singular and plural forms with little substantive difference. Tatham disagrees, preferring the singular. Tatham, Steve (2008), p. 3, *Strategic Communication: A Primer*, Advanced Research and Assessment Group, Defence Academy of the United Kingdom.

147. O'Hair, Dan; Friedrich, Gustav & Dixon, Lynda (2002), *Strategic Communication in Business and the Professions*, Boston: Houghton Mifflin suggest it is a set of oral and interpersonal skills for the workplace.

148. Murphy, Dennis (July 2008), p. 1, 'The Trouble with Strategic Communication(s)', Issue Paper, Centre for Strategic Leadership, US Army War College, vol. 2.

149. Freedman, Lawrence (2006), p. 85, 'The Transformation of Strategic Affairs', Adelphi Paper 379, Abingdon: Routledge/IISS.

150. Paul, Christopher (2009), p. 2, *Strategic Communication? A Survey of Current Proposals and Recommendations*, Santa Monica CA: RAND; Seib, Philip (2010), 'Public Diplomacy and the Obama Moment', Chatham House lecture, defines public diplomacy as government reaching out to populations, not to other governments.

151. Ibid.

152. Brooks, Rosa (15 Mar 2010), 'Minutes of US Advisory Commission on Public Diplomacy', Washington, DC.

153. Gregory, Bruce (2005), p. 5, 'Public Diplomacy and Strategic Communication: Cultures, Firewalls, and Imported Norms', paper for American Political Science Association Conference on International Communication Conflict.

154. Gates, Robert (2009), p. 2, 9, 'Report on Strategic Communication, Dec. 2009', Washington, DC: Department of Defense.

155. Gramaglia, Charles (Winter 2008), 'Strategic Communication: Distortion and White Noise', *IO Sphere*, p. 10, citing Steve Cambone, US Under Secretary of State for Intelligence.

156. Halloran, Richard (Autumn 2007), 'Strategic Communication', *Parameters*.

157. Nye, Joseph (2004), pp. 5–6, *Soft Power: The Means to Success in World Politics*, New York: Public Affairs/Perseus.

158. Ibid., pp. 107–110. Nye stresses the vulnerability of strategic communication: how long-term relationship building can be undermined by political events. Hence the split with EU partners France and Germany (2003) over support for the US and

Iraqi War, undid Britain's years of investment in the idea of the UK as a loyal EU member.

159. Under the US Marshall Plan net military transactions represented 0.75 percent and total transfers accounted for 1 percent of US national product, and 3 percent of European GDP by mid-1950s: DeLong, Bradford (2004), p. 46, 'Post-World War II Western European Exceptionalism: The Economic Dimension', in Agnew, John & Entrikin, Nicholas, *The Marshall Plan Today: Model and Metaphor*, London: Routledge.

160. Osgood, Kenneth (2006), p. 53, *Total Cold War: Eisenhower's Secret Propaganda Battle at Home and Abroad*, Lawrence: University Press of Kansas; Rawnsley, Gary, (ed.) (1999), *Cold-War Propaganda in the 1950s*, Basingstoke: Macmillan.

161. Nevertheless see United States Smith-Mundt Act 1948 for segregation of domestic and foreign populations.

162. In Bobbitt, Philip (2002), p. xviii, *The Shield of Achilles*, London: Allen Lane.

163. Kolko, Gabriel (1994), *Anatomy of a War: Vietnam, the United States, and the Modern Historical Experience*, New York: The New Press; Nagl, John (2005), *Learning to Eat Soup with a Knife*, Chicago & London: University of Chicago Press; Barber, Noel (2004), *The War of the Running Dogs*, London: Cassell; Mackinlay, John (2002), 'Globalisation and Insurgency': Adelphi Paper 352 London: International Institute for Strategic Studies/Oxford University Press; (2005), 'Defeating Complex Insurgency: Beyond Iraq and Afghanistan', The Royal United Service Institute: Whitehall Paper 64, London: RUSI.

164. Galula (2006), op. cit.; Holman, Valerie & Kelly, Debra (eds) (2000), *France at War in the Twentieth Century: Propaganda, Myth and Metaphor*, New York: Berghahn Books; Alexander, Martin & Keiger, JFV (2002), 'France and the Algerian War: Strategy, Operations and Diplomacy', *Journal of Strategic Studies*, vol. 25, no. 2, 2002.

165. Keane, Jack, General US Army (retired), BBC World Service Radio (30 July 2007).

166. 'Quadrennial Defense Review: Execution Roadmap for Strategic Communication' (2006), 1.2.1 US Department of Defense.

167. Evans, Alex & Steven, David (2009), 'Towards a Theory of Influence for Twenty-First-Century Foreign Policy: Public Diplomacy in a Globalised World', http://www.fco.gov.uk/en/about-the-fco/publications/publications/pd-publication/21c-foreign-policy, accessed 11 June 2009.

168. Obama (2009), op. cit., p. 2.

169. Bird, Conrad (2009), 'Strategic Communication and Behaviour Change: Lessons from Domestic Policy', http://www.fco.gov.uk/en/about-the-fco/publications/publications/pd-publication/behaviour-change, accessed 11 June 2009.

170. Vlahos, Michael (09 May 2006), 'The Long War: A Self-Fulfilling Prophecy of Protracted Conflict and Defeat', *National Interest*, http://www.nationalinterest.org/Article.aspx?id=11982, accessed 27 July 2009.

171. Blair, Tony (2010), *A Journey*, London: Hutchison.

172. Although data-mining and focus group polling significantly aid measurement and prediction in domestic consumer and political marketing.

173. Britain's strategic narrative appears confused. In recent years it read as: Britain's security risk from insurgent use of Afghanistan and building a better future with the Afghan people set the context for policies including strengthening Afghan law-

making and security, introducing democracy through elections, strengthening local government and governance including traditional structures, and promoting economic development. Together they shall overcome the insurgency. Gordon Brown statement to Parliament (29 Apr 2009), 'Why We Are In Afghanistan', http://www.fco.gov.uk/en/fco-in-action/uk-in-afghanistan/why-we're-in-afghanistan/, accessed 26 June 2009. The House of Commons Foreign Relations Committee Report (26 July 2009), criticised the policy for significant 'mission creep' seeing 'the British government being now committed to a wide range of objectives' including counter-insurgency, counter-narcotics, protection of human rights, and state-building: 'Global Security Report: Afghanistan and Pakistan' (p. 9): http://www.publications.parliament.uk/pa/cm200809/cmselect/cmfaff/302/302.pdf: accessed 07 July 2009. Jeremy Greenstock former British Ambassador to UN argues: 'What people don't understand is how what our troops are doing in Helmand, which is to hold off the Taliban, connects with the creation of a stable Afghanistan'. BBC Radio 4 (10 July 2009), *Today Programme*.

174. Jalali, Ali (Spring 2009), p. 8, 'Winning in Afghanistan', *Parameters*, pp. 5–21, for the failure to deliver a unified vision despite the Afghanistan National Development Strategy's June 2008 intention for 'a stable Islamic constitutional democracy at peace with itself and its neighbours'.

175. See Schneider, Mark (20 May 2008), on conflicting messages: 'Strategic Incoherence and Taliban Resurgence in Afghanistan', http://www.crisisgroup.org/home/index.cf.m?id=5447&l=1, accessed 16 June 2009.

176. Corn, David article 27 Mar 2009: 'Holbrooke calls for "Complete Rethink" of Drugs in Afghanistan' http://www.motherjones.com/mojo/2009/03/holbrooke-calls-complete-rethink-drugs-afghanistan, accessed 06 July 2009. See also Buddenberg, Doris & Byrd, William (eds) (2006), 'Afghanistan's Drug Industry', UNODC/World Bank, ch. 4. http://web.worldbank.org/WBSITE/EXTERNAL/COUNTRIES/SOUTHASIAEXT/0, contentMDK:21133060~pagePK:146736~piPK:146830~theSitePK:223547,00.html accessed 06 July 2009. See also UNODC (2009), 'World Drug Report': http://www.unodc.org/, accessed 06 July 2009.

177. (04 June 2009), 'Full Text: Barack Obama's Cairo Speech', *The Guardian*, accessed 01 July 2010

178. Butler, Patrick & Harris, Phil (2009), p. 154, 'Considerations on the Evolution of Political Marketing Theory', *Marketing Theory*, vol. 9, no. 2; 149–164. Psephologists have a narrower definition of segmentation: centre-periphery, state-church, land-industry, owner-worker. Cf. Lipset & Rokkan (eds) (1967), *Party Systems and Voter Alignment: Cross-national Perspectives*, New York: The Free Press; Baines, P; Worcester, R; Jarrett, D & Mortimore, R (2003), 'Market Segmentation and Product Differentiation in Political Campaigns: A Technical Feature Perspective', *Journal of Marketing Management*, vol. 19, no. 2, p. 225.

179. Holmus, Todd, Paul, Christopher & Glenn, Russell (2007), p. 179, 'Enlisting Madison Avenue: The Marketing Approach to Earning Popular Support in Theaters of Operation', Rand/United States Joint Forces Command.

180. Charles, Gemma (06 Apr 2009), 'British Army Uses Doom-Style Online Video Game in Recruitment Drive', *Marketing Magazine*, http://www.marketingmagazine.co.uk/news/issues/896503/British-Army-uses-Doom-style-online-video-game-recruitment-drive/, accessed 25 June 2009; (08 Dec 2005), 'McCann Erickson

Wins \$1.35bn US Army Advertising Account', http://www.brandrepublic.com/News/531992/McCann-Erickson-wins-135bn-US-Army-advertising-account/, accessed 25 June 2009; Trent, Stoney & Doty, James (July-Aug 2005), 'Marketing: An Overlooked Aspect of Information Operations', *Military Review*, pp. 70–74.

181. Fullerton, Jami & Kendrick, Alice (2006), *The Story of the US State Department's Shared Values*, Spokane WA: Marquette, for a nuanced discussion of the controversy.

182. Hoffmann, Frank (summer 2007), 'Neo-Classical Insurgency?', *Parameters*, pp. 71–87; Robb, John (2007), *Brave New War*, Hoboken NJ: John Wiley & Sons.

183. Gregory (2005), op. cit., p. 21.

184. (May 2007), p. 44, 'New Paradigms for Twenty-First Century Conflict', in 'Countering the Terrorist Mentality', *Foreign Policy Agenda*, vol. 12, no. 5, US Department of State.

185. for the British military this is a prerequisite of SC. (Nov. 2009), 'Security and Stabilisation: The Military Contribution-JDP 3–40', Ch. 3, Ministry of Defence.

186. Information war: a contest of ideas, messages and images conducted inter-state, intra-state and between state and state challengers in the global mediaspace.

187. Boyle, Michael (2010), p. 348, 'Do Counterterrorism and Counterinsurgency Go Together', *International Affairs*, vol. 86, no. 2, pp. 333–354.

188. Dorronsoro, Gilles (2009), pp. 8–11 '*The Taliban's Winning Strategy in Afghanistan*', Washington, DC: Carnegie Endowment for Peace. See for conflicting assessments of the organisational unity of Taliban forces and its impact on communications.

189. Giustozzi, Antonio (2008), *Koran, Kalashnikov and Laptop: the Neo-Taliban Insurgency in Afghanistan*, London: Hurst, ch. 4.

190. (Mar 2008), Taliban, *Al Somood* Arabic-language magazine.

191. International Crisis Group: Asia Report no. 158, 24 Jul 2008, 'Taliban Propaganda: Winning the War of Words?', see p. 11 footnote 83 for an extensive breakdown of Taliban media related activities throughout the country. See (17 July 2008), 'The Media Activities of the Taliban Islamic Movement', *Al Somood*, http://worldanalysis.net/postnuke/html/index.php?name=News&file=article&sid=731, accessed 25/06/2009.

192. (19 Sept 2001), 'Mullah Omar's Speech to the Taliban Clerics', *The Guardian*, http://www.guardian.co.uk/world/2001/sep/19/september11.usa15, accessed 25 June 2009.

193. Human Rights Watch (2006), p. 3, 'Lessons in Terror: Attacks on Education in Afghanistan', vol. 18, no. 6(C), citing mother of two girls, Kandahar, 8 Dec 2005.

194. Human Rights Watch (2006), op. cit., p. 34 citing Taliban commander Mohammed Hanif, 23 Mar 2006.

195. (sic).Translated Taliban document from www.toorabora.com: 'The Defeat of the Invaders in Media Field or the Victory of Resistance' (07 Aug 2008). Source: Joanna Nathan, International Crisis Group, Kabul.

196. Castells, Manuel (2004), p. 82, *The Information Age: The Power of Identity*, Malden MA & Oxford: Blackwell.

197. COHA-Council on Hemispheric Affairs(2008), '*The Future of Mexico's EZLN*' http://www.coha.org/2008/11/the-future-of-the-ezln/, accessed 1 July 2009.

198. Hayden, Tom (2001), p. 1, *The Zapatista Reader*, New York: Nation Books.

199. Subcomandante Marcos (2003), *Our Word is our Weapon*, New York: Seven Stories Press; Cf. Clifford, op. cit., ch. 4.

200. For a critique of Zapatista strategy and local divisions among the Maya cf. Collier, George (2005), *'Basta!', Land and the Zapatista Rebellion in Chiapas*, Oakland CA: Food First. 'Pinch of Salt', http://flag.blackened.net/revolt/mexico/comment/andrew_diff_feb01.html accessed 1 Aug 2009.

201. COHA (2008), op. cit..

202. McDonald, Kevin (2006), p. 112, *Global Movements*, Malden MA & Oxford: Blackwell. See also 'Commandante Marcos' interview, http://www.youtube.com/watch?v=jtOX5fOI2co, accessed 1 Jul 2009, 112,976 views.

203. 'Subcomandante Marcos y la Cuarta Guerra Mundial' interview, http://www.youtube.com/watch?v=bA8uWDZdE4o, accessed 1 July 2009–, 113,083 views.

204. Routledge, Paul (1998), p. 248, 'Going Globile', in O'Tuathail, Gearoid & Dolby, Simon *Rethinking Geopolitics*, London: Routledge.

205. Meikle Graham (2004), 'Networks of Influence', in Goggin, Gerard (ed.), *Virtual Nation: The Internet in Australia*, Sydney: University of New South Wales Press.

2. ARCHIPELAGO OF MEMORIES

1. Miller, Arthur (1999), *Timebends, A Life*, London: Methuen.

2. I use narrative in different contexts to mean constructed story-telling; sometimes this is allied to creating identity (an equally contested term) where individuals or groups project a 'story' and 'history' of themselves (cf. French *histoire*).

3. Murphet, Julian (2005), p. 84, 'Narrative Voice', in Fulton, Helen (ed.), *Narrative and Media*, Cambridge: Cambridge University Press details the complex 'breakfast-scene' narrative: 'Orson Welles' directing…Thompson's interview version of… Leland's narrative of…his marriage to Emily Norton'.

4. All illustrations by Angus Margerison and Kevin Woods, www.xyidigital.com.

5. Without tracing memory to Plato and Aristotle, I emphasise how memory becomes detached from fictional imagination, how the present makes the past 'real'. This is important for insurgents. Events they absorb into ideological motivation and feelings of injustice, are often 'imagined', that is 'witnessed' or 'experienced' at arms-length through media. The deed as event or image, and the way it embodies grievance must become as near to a single act of understanding as possible.

6. Sorel, Georges (2005), *Reflections on Violence*, Mineola NY: Dover; Williams (1973), p. 8; Williams, Raymond, 'Bases and Superstructure in Marxist Cultural Theory', *New Left Review*, no. 82, pp. 3–16. For Williams hegemony is not merely manipulation, rather 'a whole body of practices and expectations…It is a set of meanings and values which as they are experienced as practices appear as reciprocally confirming. It thus constitutes a sense of reality for most people in the society' (p. 9).

7. Schwartz, Barry (Dec 1982), 'The Social Context of Commemoration: A Study in Collective Memory', *Social Forces*, vol. 61, no. 2, pp. 374–402.

8. Reid, Elizabeth (1998), 'Variations on the Illusion of One Self', in Gackenbach, Jayne (ed.), *Psychology and the Internet*, San Diego CA: Academic Press; for competing theories on identity formation see Coté, James & Levine, Charles (2006), *Identity Formation, Agency and Culture: A Social Psychological Synthesis*, Mahwah NJ: Lawrence Erlbaum.

9. Eyerman, Ron (2001), p. 7, *Cultural Trauma: Slavery and the Formation of African American Identity*, Cambridge: Cambridge University Press.

10. see Radley, Alan (1990), 'Artefacts, Memory and a Sense of the Past', in Middleton, David & Edwards, Derek (eds), *Collective Remembering*, London: Sage for critique of memory as purely a product of symbolic discourse. For him material objects also influence identity-formation and memory-construction.

11. Ibid., citing Halbwachs

12. Jung, Courtney (2000), *Then I Was Black: South African Political Identities in Transition*, New Haven: Yale University Press. For Jung cultural and political identity are distinct. Political is 'that portion of identity which emerges as salient in the organised struggle for control over the allocation of resources and power residing in the state' (p. 19). However, contemporary insurgency patterns dictate political identity must accommodate transnational actors with non-state ambitions (for example, political Islamists who aim to conjoin diasporas into an historic global caliphate). For Jung, five variables shape political identity: political institutions, mobilising discourse, material conditions, available ideology, and organisation (p. 25). For cultural identity to be politicised some kind of catalyst must transform an 'ascriptive category into an ascriptive group' (p. 20). Taylor's definition addresses contemporary insurgency as 'shared definition of a group that derives from members' common interests, experiences and solidarities' (Ibid.); cf. Taylor, Verta & Whittier, Nancy (1992), p. 105, 'Collective Identity in Social Movement Communities', in Morris, Aldon & Mueller, Carol (eds), *Frontiers in Social Movement Theory*, New Haven: Yale University Press.

13. Cf. Geertz, Clifford (1973), *Interpretation of Cultures*, New York: Basic Books. Culture is framed as an 'historically transmitted pattern of meanings embodied in symbols' born of the nature of man as 'an animal suspended in webs of meaning he himself has spun' (p. 89). Discussing religion, he distinguishes between the *of* and *for* of cultural 'patterns' or models: 'they give meaning, that is, objective conceptual form, to social and psychological reality both by shaping themselves to it and by shaping it to themselves' (p. 93). Similarly I propose insurgent groups act within symbolic systems that inform their existence, and transmit the representation of themselves and their aims to outside communities.

14. Bolt, Neville (Sept. 2008), 'Propaganda of the Deed 2008', RUSI Whitehall Report.

15. See Castells (2009), op. cit. for alternative assemblage model.

16. Rosenfield, Israel & Ziff, Edward (2008), 'How the Mind Works: Revelations', *New York Review of Books*, 26 (June 2008), p. 64, citing Gerald Edelman and his 'Theory of Neural Darwinism'. This argues against the doctrine of localisation of function in the brain; Sejnowski, Terence (1998), Memory and Neural Networks', in Fara, Patricia & Patterson, Karalyn (eds), *Memory*, Cambridge: Cambridge University Press; Rose, Steven (1998), 'How Brains Make Memories', in Fara, op. cit..

17. Rosenfield, Israel (1988), p. 76, *The Invention of Memory: A New View of the Brain*, New York: Basic Books

18. Bartlett, Frederic (1972), p. 312, *Remembering: A Study in Experimental and Social Psychology*, London: Cambridge University Press.

19. Rosenfield (2008), op. cit., p. 8.

20. Michael Oakeshott further differentiates in (1981), 'The Activity of Being a Historian', in *Rationalism in Politics and Other Essays*, London: Methuen, between the

individual making a statement about the world in relation to himself and independent of the self. He sees three ways of perceiving the past: the practical, scientific, and (specious) contemplative. Each demands its own discourse. Notwithstanding, '(t)he past, in whatever manner it appears, is a certain sort of reading of the present' (p. 150). In trying to define the 'historical' past, the practical man reads the past backwards from the present, teleologically. The historian adopts a 'scientific' approach: '(t)his past is without the moral, the political, or the social structure which the practical man transfers from his present to his past' (p. 154).

21. Maines, David, Sugrue, Noreen & Katovich, Michael (April 1983), p. 161, 'The Sociological Import of G.H. Mead's Theory of the Past', *American Sociological Review*, vol. 48, no. 2, pp. 161–173.

22. Mead, GH (1934), p. 176, *Mind, Self, and Society from the Standpoint of a Social Behaviourist*, Chicago: University of Chicago Press.

23. Ibid.

24. Mead, GH (1929, 1970), in Coss, John (ed.), *Essays in Honour of John Dewey*, SI: Octagon.

25. Melucci, Alberto (1989), *Nomads of the Present*, London: Hutchison; Lévi-Strauss, Claude (1977), p. 301, *Structural Anthropology*, Harmondsworth: Penguin.

26. Giddens, Anthony (1984), p. 35, *The Constitution of the Self*, Cambridge: Polity.

27. Bloch, Maurice (1998), p. 82, *How We Think They Think: Anthropological Approaches to Cognition, Memory and Literacy*, Boulder & Oxford: Westview Press.

28. Freud, Sigmund (1999), *The Interpretation of Dreams*, Oxford: Oxford University Press. Freud cites Scholz: 'nothing that is once mentally our own can ever be entirely lost', and explains, citing Delboeuf 'que toute impression même la plus insignifiante, laisse une trace inaltérable, indéfiniment susceptible de reparaître au jour'. (p. 19). He draws on Strümpell to argue: 'the depths of the dream memory also include those images of people, things, places, and experiences from our earliest years which either impressed themselves only slightly on our consciousness, or possessed no psychical value, or have long since lost both, and so, both in the dreams and after we have woken up, they appear quite alien and unfamiliar to us until their origin is discovered' (pp. 15–16). .

29. Freud, Sigmund (1984), 'A Note on the Unconscious in Psychoanalysis', in *On Metapsychology: The Theory of Psychoanalysis*, Harmondsworth: Penguin. Freud suggests the conscious relates to the unconscious through a staged process, like the development of a photograph, where stage 1) represents the 'negative', 2) the 'negative process', and 3) examining and selecting that leads to the 'positive process' (p. 55).

30. Gay, Peter (2006), p. 109 footnote, *Freud: A Life in our Time*, London: MAX.

31. Bergson, Henri (1988), pp. 133–4, *Matter and Memory*, New York: Zone Books. Bergson writes 'whenever we are trying to recover a recollection, to call up some period of our history, we become conscious of an act *sui generis* by which we detach ourselves from the present in order to replace ourselves, first, in the past—a work of adjustment, something like the focusing of a camera. But our recollection still remains virtual; we simply prepare ourselves to receive it by adopting the appropriate attitude…But it remains attached to the past by its deepest roots, and if, when once realised, it did not retain something of its original virtuality, if, being a present

state, it were not also something which stands out distinct from the present, we should never know it for a memory'.

32. Deleuze, Gilles (1988), *Bergsonism*, New York: Zone Books. Deleuze highlights how Bergson signals the fallacy of underlying psychological and physiological theories of memory. Namely, '(t)he past, it is true, seems to be caught between two presents: the old present that it once was and the actual present in relation to which it is now past'.

33. Bergson (1988), op. cit., p. 237.

34. Russell, Bertrand (1969), p. 760, *History of Western Philosophy*, London: George Allen & Unwin.

35. Guerlac, Suzanne (2006), pp. 126–7, *Thinking in Time*, Ithaca: Cornell University Press.

36. Deleuze, op. cit., pp. 58–59.

37. Halbwachs describes 'social frameworks' as the basis for memory. Individual and social memory overlap to the extent that autobiographical memory draws language and experience from a social context. Memory also organises episodes from the past into continuous time. The individual resides within that time. Developing Halbwachs' work, Nora, Pierre (1989), 'Between Memory and History: Les Lieux de Mémoire', *Representations*, no. 26, pp. 7–25; and Yerushalmi, Yosef (1982), '*Zakhor: Jewish History and Jewish Memory*', Seattle: University of Washington Press advanced collective memory theories. However Nora emphasises spatial topography as *loci* of public memory. Cf. Rossington, Michael &Whitehead, Anne (2007), *Theories of Memory*, Edinburgh: Edinburgh University Press for an overview of alternative perspectives, namely External versus Deep Memory; Traumatic; Fake; Historical Accuracy versus Inaccuracy; Postcolonial, Poststructural .

38. Olick, Jeffrey, (ed.) (2002), 'Collective Memory: The Two Cultures', in *Memory and Power in Post-War Europe: Studies in the Presence of the Past*, Cambridge: Cambridge University Press. For critiques of memory studies see Kansteiner Wulf (May 2002), 'Finding Meaning in Memory: A Methodological Critique of Collective Memory Studies', *History and Theory*, no. 41, pp. 179–197; Klein, Kerwin Lee(Winter 2000), 'On the Emergence of Memory in Historical Discourse', *Representations*, no. 69, pp. 127–150

39. Wood, Nancy (1999), p. 2, *Vectors of Memory: Legacies of Trauma in Postwar Europe*, Oxford: Berg.

40. op. cit., p. 180.

41. Giddens, op. cit..

42. 'negotiation certainly seems generic to human relationships and arrangements': Strauss, Anselm (1978), p. 1, *Negotiations: Varieties, Contexts, Processes, and Social Order*, San Francisco: Jossey-Bass. See also (1963), 'The Hospital and its Negotiated Order', in E Freidson (ed.), *The Hospital in Modern Society*, New York: Free Press; (1964), *Psychiatric Ideologies and Institutions*, New York: Free Press.

43. Hodgkin, Katherine & Radstone, Susannah (eds) (2003), p. 8, *Contested Pasts: The Politics of Memory*, London: Routledge. Suggests the self remains distinct: 'The political memory of members of a group is not identical with the personal memories of the individual activist, even though they may share events and concerns in common'. Cf. Carrie Hamilton in Hodgkin, op. cit., see p. 120 on Basque Nationalists.

44. Becker, Howard (1991), *Outsiders: Studies in the Sociology of Deviance*, New York: Free Press; Horowitz L & Liebowitz M (Winter 1968), 'Social Deviance and Political Marginality: Towards a Redefinition between Sociology and Politics', *Social Problems*, no. 15, pp. 280–96.

45. Goffman, Erving (1967), '*Interaction Ritual: Essays on Face-to-Face Behaviour*', London: Allen Lane. Through gestures, glances and exchanged words ('small behaviours') Goffman studies social interaction as ritualised behaviour in 'egocentric forms of territoriality'. The maintenance of face ('face-work') in situations of co-presence, means actors seek to counter-act shame and embarrassment in a reciprocal understanding based on tact.

46. Goffman, Erving (1959), *The Presentation of Self in Everyday Life*, Harmondsworth: Penguin. Compare Da Silva, Filipe Carreira (2007), pp. 3–6, 86–90, *G.H.Mead: A Critical Introduction*, Cambridge: Polity. He explains Mead's approach to 'taking the role of the other' is non-dramaturgical. For him, this 'behavioural disposition' enabling two individuals to respond to the same stimulus in the same way has 'significant effects'. Thinking with the ability to see from the other person's perspective becomes an inner conversation, a 'reflective intelligence' differentiating human thinking. Consequently, thinking is characterised as a social process. Second, 'taking the role of the other' illuminates 'significant symbols'. When a couple parts, one person waves prompting a wave from the other, the meaning of the hand gesture is not intrinsic to the wave, but the product of social interaction. Third, by adopting the role of the 'generalised other' for example in a baseball game, children internalise both rules of the game, and by absorption into their own performance, other participants' understanding of that game. Fourth Mead talks of the 'I' and 'Me'. 'I' represents the self that remembers, and 'Me' is the self-image remembered. Cf. Miller, David, (ed.) (1982), *The Individual and the Social Self: Unpublished Work of George Herbert Mead*, Chicago: University of Chicago Press.

47. Halbwachs, Maurice (1992), p. 49, *Collective Memory*, Chicago: University of Chicago Press. For Halbwachs collective memory precedes personal memory. But Ricoeur highlights Halbwachs' contention that when we attribute memory to ourselves, it is only illusory. So Ricoeur asks: 'Does not the very act of "placing oneself" in a group and of "displacing" oneself or shifting from group to group presuppose a spontaneity capable of establishing a continuation with itself?' If not, how can there be social actors? The question then revolves around the nature and degree of human agency: Ricoeur, Paul (2004), p. 122, *Memory, History, Forgetting*, Chicago: University of Chicago Press. If we extrapolate from Halbwachs' thinking, when an insurgent leaves a group, to drop back into society, or to choose an alternative faction, he or she is not just abandoning an inherited memory and returning to a state of personal or 'non-group' memory. He or she is perforce exchanging one group memory for a new one. Even abandoning insurgency and returning to an apathetic state in a broader hegemony, namely society, he or she adopts the majority memory, thus overriding that of the former insurgency collective.

48. *(sic)* Jedlowski, Paolo (2001), p. 33, 'Memory and Sociology: Themes and Issues', *Time Society*, vol. 10, no. 1, pp. 29–44. However Michel Foucault identifies a deeper process. Memory is transmitted through centres of micro-power in society. *Gouvernementalité* means 'bodies of knowledge, belief and opinion in which we are immersed'. These become internalised by members of society: Dean, Mitchell (2004), p. 16, *Governmentality: Power and Rule in Modern Society*, London: Sage.

49. Connerton, Paul (2007), p. 72, *How Societies Remember*, Cambridge: Cambridge University Press. Argues: '(t)hey are re-enactments of the past, its return in a representational guise which normally includes a simulacrum of the scene or situation recaptured'. But he goes further. These memories need not just be stored in words and images, but bodily practices. Here there are two types of practice: incorporating (a smile, handshake, spoken word) and inscribing (how we employ print or photography). This means '(i)n habitual memory the past is, as it were, sedimented in the body'.

50. Polletta, Francesca & Jasper, James (2001), p. 285, 'Collective Identity and Social Movements', *Annual Review of Sociology*, vol. 27, pp. 283–305.

51. Tilly, Charles cited in Brubaker, Rogers & Cooper, Frederick (2000), p. 12, 'Beyond Identity', *Theory and Society*, vol. 29, pp. 1–47.

52. Brubaker, op. cit..

53. Gleason, Philip (1983), p. 931, 'Identifying Identity: A Semantic History', *The Journal of American History*, vol. 89, no. 4, pp. 910–931.

54. Ibid., p. 918, citing Berger, Peter.

55. (1995), p. 153, *Orlando*, London: Wordsworth.

56. deriving from Freud, and James.

57. Erikson, Erik (1971), *Identity: Youth and Crisis*, London: Faber & Faber.

58. Maslow, Abraham (1973), *On Dominance, Self-Esteem and Self-Actualization*, Monterey CA: Brooks/Cole; Crenshaw (2007), op. cit., p. 604 for discussion of terrorist causation.

59. Arena, Michael & Arrigo, Bruce (2006), p. 20, *The Terrorist Identity: Explaining the Terrorist Threat*, New York: New York University, citing Crenshaw who applies Erikson's theory to Bollinger's research data.

60. Ibid., p. 23, citing Shaw's *Personal Pathway Model*.

61. Post, Jerrold (1998), p. 25, 'Terrorist Psycho-logic: Terrorist Behaviour as a Product of Psychological Forces', in Walter Reich (ed.), *Origins of Terrorism: Psychologies, Ideologies, Theologies, States of Mind*, Washington, DC: Woodrow Wilson Center Press.

62. Sageman, Marc (2004), *Understanding Terror Networks*, Philadelphia: University of Pennsylvania Press. Ch. 3's analysis of global *Salafis* dismisses psychiatric pathology as cause. Similarly, the social psychological rooted in aggression and frustration is considered too vague to substantiate or deny.

63. Post, Jerrold (2007), *The Mind of the Terrorist: The Psychology of Terrorism from the IRA to al-Qaeda*, New York: Palgrave Macmillan.

64. Arena, op. cit., p. 33, citing Worchel.

65. Taylor DM & Louis W (2004), pp. 167–185, 'Terrorism and the Quest for Identity', in Moghaddam F & Marsella, A (eds), *Understanding Terrorism: Psychosocial Roots, Consequences, and Interventions*, Washington, DC: American Psychological Association.

66. Crenshaw, Martha, 'The Logic of Terrorism: Terrorist Behaviour as a Product of Strategic Choice', in Reich (1998), p. 8.

67. Alantine, Gary (1993), 'The Sad Demise, Mysterious Disappearance, and Glorious Triumph of Symbolic Interactionism', *Annual Review of Sociology*, no. 19; Hewitt, Regina (2006), *Symbolic Interactions*, Lewisburg: Bucknell University Press; Da Silva, op. cit..

68. Shalin, Dmitri (1986), p. 10, 'Pragmatism and Social Interactionism', *American Sociological Review*, vol. 51, no. 1: 'pragmatism is a post-Darwinian philosophy in which the principle of subject-object relativity was replaced with that of the relativity of organism and environment, the constitutive activity of Absolute Mind with the instrumental activity of organised individuals, and dialectical logic with the experimental logic of situation'.

69. Thrasher, Frederic (1927), p. 31, *The Gang: A Study of 1,313 Gangs in Chicago*, Chicago: University of Chicago Press.

70. Ibid., p. 194.

71. Zorbaugh, Harvey (1929), *The Gold Coast and a Slum: A Sociological Study of Chicago's Near North Side*, Chicago: University of Chicago Press; Anderson, Nels (1923), *The Hobo: The Sociology of the Homeless Man*, Chicago: University of Chicago Press.

72. Da Silva, op. cit., p. 73.

73. Shalin, op. cit., p. 16.

74. Habermas, Jürgen (1987), *The Theory of Communicative Action: Lifeworld and System, A Critique of Functionalist Reason*, vol. 2, Boston: Beacon Press. This is a process of *Verinnerlichung*, ie 'making objective structures of meaning internal' (p. 13). He argues that authority in Mead's 'generalised other' derives from 'general group will'. This is not the generalised 'will of all' individuals, which may be observed in 'sanctions the group applies to deviations' (p. 38).

75. Durkheim, Emile (1983), p. 88, *Pragmatism and Sociology*, Cambridge University Press. To the pragmatists Durkheim cautioned: 'The social sciences, in particular, express what society is in itself, and not what it is subjectively to the person thinking about it'. cf. Arena op. cit. for a fuller discussion.

76. Parsons, Talcott (1968), *The Structure of Social Action*, New York: Free Press. Parsons, whose structural-functionalism dominated US social science, omitted to acknowledge their contribution to American sociology.

77. Maines, op. cit., p. 168.

78. Connerton, op. cit., p. 19, distinguishes between the memoir-writer or famous individual rooted in political elites and dominant institutions into which he/she intervenes, and subordinate groups. The latter's individual life stories are not inserted into the narrative of the dominant societal group: '(w)hat is lacking in the life histories of those who belong to subordinate groups is precisely those terms of reference that conduce to and reinforce this sense of linear trajectory, a sequential narrative shape: above all, *in relation to the past, the notion of legitimating origins, and in relation to the future, the sense of an accumulation in power and money'*. (my emphasis)

79. Foucault (1980), op. cit..

80. Halbwachs, op. cit., p. 55, citing Durkheim, *Cours Inédits sur la Famille*.

81. Said, Edward (2000), p. 3, *Out of Place: A Memoir*, London: Granta.

82. Halbwachs, op. cit., p. 55.

83. Ibid., p. 60.

84. Fitzduff Mari (2002), 'Beyond Violence: Conflict Resolution Process in Northern Ireland', *UNU Policy Perspectives*, no. 7, United Nations University Press/INCORE. Cf. McDonald, Henry (2008), *Gunsmoke and Mirrors: How Sinn Féin Dressed Up Defeat as Victory*, Dublin: Gill & MacMillan; Myers, Kevin (2006), *Watching the*

Door, Dublin: Lilliput Press; Alonso, Rogelio (2003), *The IRA and Armed Struggle*, London & New York: Routledge.

85. Packer, George (18 Dec 2006), 'Knowing the Enemy', *The New Yorker*, citing McFate, Montgomery; Sageman, op. cit., ch. 4, interrogates the importance of social networks and friendship bonds in facilitating recruitment. Because of the privileged role of ideology in the recruit's perception of why he/she joined the group, the dimension of the personal is obscured. In his sample-study of 150 global *jihadis*, 68 percent demonstrated the importance of friendship, 14 percent family, both kith and kin. Notable figures fall into this last category. Khalid Sheikh Mohammed, his brother, and nephew Ramzi Yousef (who recruited his childhood friends, p. 42) are linked to the Canadian Ahmed Said Khadr. The latter fought alongside Osama Bin Laden at Jaji 1987, and financed the Egyptian Embassy assault, Islamabad 1995. Khadr's three sons were also *jihadis*. Ali Ghufron and three of his brothers participated in the Bali nightclub bombing 2002. (p. 112). Cf. Lofland, John(1977), *Doomsday Cult: A Study of Conversion, Proselytisation, and Maintenance of Faith*, New York: Irvington; Lofland, John & Stark, Rodney(1965), 'Becoming a World-Saver: A Theory of Conversion to a Deviant Perspective', *American Sociological review*, vol. 30, no. 6, pp. 862–75.

86. White, R & Fraser, M (2000), p. 329, 'Personal and Collective Identities and Long-term Social Movement Activism: Republican Sinn Féin', in Stryker, Owens & White (eds), *Self, Identity, and Social Movements*, Minneapolis: University of Minneapolis Press: The 6 were Ruari O'Braidaigh, Des Long, Cathleen Knowles, Joe O'Neill, Frank Graham, and Daithi O'Connell.

87. I include television, internet, mobile telephony, press, radio, and cinema as distribution networks; information, entertainment, and advertising as product. However I privilege audio-visual material and its carriers, for their dominant impact on audiences.

88. Raymond Williams borrows 'flows' from William James: Time is a 'flux rather than a sum of discrete units, that human consciousness was a stream rather than a configuration of separate faculties'. Cf. Mellencamp, Patricia (1990), p. 240–1, 'Television Time and Catastrophe, or Beyond the Pleasure Principle of Television', in Mellencamp, Patricia (ed.), *Logics of Television: essays in Cultural Criticism*, Bloomington, IN: Indiana University Press.

89. Mellencamp, op. cit., p. 241.

90. Lévi-Strauss, Claude (1986), p. 18, *The Raw and the Cooked: Introduction to a Science of Mythology 1*, Harmondsworth: Penguin. For him myths 'are anonymous: from the moment they are seen as myths, and whatever their real origins, they exist only as elements embodied in a tradition. When the myth is repeated, the individual listeners are receiving a message that, properly speaking, is coming from nowhere; that is why it is credited with supernatural origin'.

91. Bhabha, Homi (1994), pp. 306–312, 'Narrating the Nation', in Hutchinson, John & Smith, Anthony (eds), *Nationalism*, Oxford: Oxford University Press.

92. Bell, Duncan(2003), p. 74, 'Mythscapes: Memory, Mythology, and National Identity', *British Journal of Sociology*, vol. 54, no. 1, pp. 63–81.

93. Ibid.

94. Szanto, George (1978), p. 6, *Theater & Propaganda*, Austin and London: University of Texas Press.

95. Ellul (1973), op. cit., p. 40.

96. Barthes, Roland(1957, 1973), *Mythologies*, London: Paladin Grafton.

97. Somers, Margaret (Oct 1994), p. 606, 'The Narrative Constitution of Identity—a Relational and Network Approach', *Theory and Society*, vol. 23, no. 5, pp. 605–649.

98. Ibid., pp. 613–14, 617–19.

99. Carr, David (1986), p. 126, 'Narrative and the Real World: An Argument for Continuity', *History and Theory*, vol. 25, no. 2, pp. 117–131.

100. Science Museum, http://www.sciencemuseum.org.uk/objects/nrm_-_locomotives_ and_rolling_stock/1862–5.aspx, accessed 15 June 2010.

101. Anderson, Benedict (1983, 2006), *Imagined Communities*, London: Verso.

102. Mailer, Norman (1974), p. 18, *Marilyn*, London: Coronet/Hodder.

103. I do not suggest that television and internet consumption are identical. Nor that either is universally consumed throughout the world, thus offering insurgents the same reach to all populations. However where these technologies are prevalent, their impact is manifest. Co-existence and repeat transmission within and between these account for a 'multiplier-effect', affecting both content and audience. During the post-presidential riots in Kenya 2007, one leader of the so-called 'Taliban gang' claimed his Luo group was attacking shopkeepers from the Kikuyu tribe of the incumbent President in order that events be captured by visiting reporters, and shown on global television. Alluding to a 'boomerang effect', he expressed the hope that US President Bush would intervene to evict Kenya's President who had clung to power in a fraudulent election (BBC television, *Newsnight*, July 2008).

104. Kottle, Simon (2006), p. 28, *Mediatised Conflict: Developments in Media and Conflict Studies*, Maidenhead & New York: Open University Press.

105. Herman, Edward & Chomsky, Noam (2002), *Manufacturing Consent: the Political Economy of the Media*, New York: Pantheon.

106. Chandler, Daniel (2000), 'Marxist Media Theory: The Frankfurt School', lecture series Aberystwyth University, citing Herbert Marcuse (1972), 'One-Dimensional Man', http://www.aber.ac.uk/media/Documents/marxism/marxism08.html, accessed 25 Aug 2008.

107. Experiments on television viewing patterns demonstrate it does: '15 min (*sic*) of a relatively mild violent program increases the aggressiveness of a substantial proportion of the viewers, at least one fourth'. Cf. Bushman, Brad & Phillips, Colleen (2001), p. 44, 'If the Television Program Bleeds, Memory for the Advertisement Recedes', *Current Directions in Psychological Science*(April 2001), vol. 10, no. 2, pp. 43–7.

108. de Saussure, Ferdinand (1955), *Cours de Linguistique Générale*, Paris: Payot; Peirce, Charles Sanders (1991), *Peirce on Signs: Writings on Semiotics*, Chapel Hill: University of Carolina Press.

109. Hafner, Katie (2009), p. 203, *A Romance on Three Legs: Glen Gould's Obsessive Quest for the Perfect Piano*, New York: Bloomsbury.

110. Barthes, Roland (1977), *Elements of Semiology*, New York: Hill & Wang.

111. 'The Marlboro Man', National Public Radio 21 Oct 2002, http://www.npr.org/programs/morning/features/patc/marlboroman/, accessed 25 Aug 2008.

112. Eco, Umberto (1977), *A Theory of Semiotics*, London: Macmillan.

113. Barry, Liz (25 Aug 2008), John Donne, 'A Valediction Forbidding Mourning', on

'Fry's English Delight: Metaphors', http://www.bbc.co.uk/radio4/arts/frys_english.
shtml.

114. Sartre, Jean-Paul (1972), p. 127, *The Psychology of Imagination*, London:
Methuen. Sartre suggests that when he hears the word 'Renaissance', he may picture Michelangelo's David. 'This first response of thought naturally takes on the
form of an image'. But this is non-reflective 'unintelligent thought' which strives to
find empirical reassurance. In a museum of Renaissance masterpieces, he says, anyone asked to define the period will immediately scan one of the masterpieces for
'the primary data of experience'. POTD seeks to do the same in reverse: the image
should precede the word or concept.

115. Schwartz, Tony (1972), p. 92, *The Responsive Chord*, New York: Anchor Press/
Doubleday.

116. Cited in Mishra, Pankaj (19 May 2008), 'The End of Innocence', *The Guardian
Review*, p. 4.

117. Sapir, Edward cited by Chandler, Daniel (1994), 'The Sapir-Whorf Hypothesis',
http://www.aber.ac.uk/media/Documents/short/whorf.html, accessed 25 Aug 2008.

118. http://zapatistas.org/, accessed 25 Aug 2008. The Zapatistas Discussion Group
website advertises for sale the 'conspiracy theory' DVD: *The Truth & Lies of
9–11*...The war for oil and drug money.

119. Ortony, Andrew (1975), p. 45, 'Why Metaphors are Necessary and Not Just Nice',
Educational Theory, vol. 25, pp. 45–53.

120. Paivio, Allan (1988), p. 156, 'Psychological Processes in the Comprehension of
Metaphor', in Ortony, Andrew, (ed.) (1988), *Metaphor and Thought*, Cambridge:
Cambridge University Press; citing Susanne Langer (1942).

121. Connerton, op. cit., p. 27, highlights the idea of 'encoding' in cognitive memory.
Three dimensions of mnemonic coding exist, semantic (hierarchical ordering of
logical inter-relationships), verbal (programming for verbal expression), and most
important visual (images) since 'concrete items easily translated into images are
much better retained than abstract items because such concrete items undergo a
double encoding in terms of visual coding as well as verbal expression'.

122. Paivio, op. cit., p. 167.

123. Boroditsky, Lera (1998), p. 3, 'Metaphoric Structuring: Understanding Time
Through Spatial Metaphors', *Cognition*, no. 75 (2000), pp. 1–28.

124. Proust, Marcel, *A La Recherche du Temps Perdu*; Duhamel, Georges, *Chronique
des Pasquier*; Böll, Heinrich, *Das Brot der Frühen Jahre*: for associations of smell
and colour with memory.

125. BBC Radio 4 (29 Aug 2008), 'Has Hollywood Turned its Back on Hit Theme
Tunes?', *World Tonight*.

126. Pinker, Steven (2008), p. 270, *The Stuff of Thought: Language as a Window into
Human Nature*, London: Penguin.

127. Devji (2005), op. cit., pp. 65–74. The virtual parallels the territorial. The contemporary Middle East, he notes, is a 'symbolic constitution' and 'dispersed entity'
linked into the Indian Subcontinent, South East Asia, and East Africa embracing
also the UK, a centre for press and economic ties. But only after the post World
War 1 dismantling of the Ottoman Empire did the region assume a unity. Today
the great mosques of the Holy Land give substance to an idea that underpins an
arena of new social relations. '...the jihad re-constitutes the Middle East or Arab

world by narratives other than those of the nation or region as distinct demographic and geographical entities characterised by collective political or economic cultures'. (p. 74).

128. (2004), op. cit., p. 183.

129. Cole, Michael (1996), p. 4, *Cultural Psychology: A Once and Future Discipline*, Cambridge MA: Belknap Press, citing Richard Shweder.

130. Ricoeur, Paul (2004), p. 326, 'The Hermeneutics of Symbols and Philosophical Reflection: II', in *The Conflict of Interpretations: Essays in Hermeneutics*, London & New York: Continuum.

131. Tugwell, op. cit..

132. Pinker (2008), op. cit., p. 238.

133. Adorno, Theodor & Horkheimer, Max (2008), 'The Culture Industry: Enlightenment as Mass Deception', in During, Simon (ed.), *The Cultural Studies Reader*, London: Routledge.

134. Baudrillard, Jean (1981, 1997), p. 50, *Simulacra and Simulation*, Ann Arbor: University of Michigan Press.

135. We think of television as a continuous image flow. However 35mm film and digital television comprise different numbers of separate frames per second.

136. Sontag, Susan (2002), pp. 17–18, *On Photography*, London: Penguin Books.

137. Ch. 4 examines how far POTD's iconic image can stand alone without accompanying information campaign, and communicate a universal, unequivocal message. This echoes the 30 year dispute over the authenticity and 'quality' of Robert Capa's celebrated war-photo 'Death of a Loyalist Militiaman', Cerro Muriano, Córdoba, 1936. Critic Philip Knightly challenges the image often described as the most famous war photograph. He argues, unlike other iconic photos such as Nick Ut's naked Vietnamese girl running down Route 1, Capra's requires a caption to explain its message (BBC Radio 4, 17 Oct 2008, *Today Programme*).

138. Sontag, op. cit., p. 156.

139. Baudrillard(1981), op. cit., p. 3.

140. Rosa Luxemburg still appealed for spontaneity against overwhelming party discipline, writing shortly before her murder in 1919.

141. Lenin's elder brother Alexander Ulyanov was executed in 1887 for planning POTD, a foiled attempt to kill Tsar Alexander III. His death is considered a prime motivator in Lenin's revolutionary development.

142. Bolt, Neville (2007), *RUSI Journal*, Feb 2008, pp. 98–9, review of Furedi, Frank(2007), *Invitation to Terror*, London: Continuum.

143. Camus, Albert (1968), p. 252, *The Plague*, Harmondsworth: Penguin.

3. INSURGENT MEMORY AND NARRATIVE

1. Proust, Marcel (1970), *The Past Remembered*, New York: Random House.

2. Mali, Joseph (2008), p. 138, 'The Myth of the State Revisited', in Barash, Jeffrey, *The Symbolic Construction of Reality: the Legacy of Ernst Cassirer*, Chicago: University of Chicago Press: today political myths are considered 'foundational' not simply 'fictional' creating 'historical continuity and unity'; Flood, Christopher (2002), p. 105, *Political Myth*, New York: Routledge for a definitional discussion; Tudor, Henry(1972), *Political Myth*, London: Macmillan.

3. Sorel (1908), op. cit., p. 49–50.

4. Rwanda captures both since 1970; former Yugoslavia since 1990; Northern Ireland since 1900.

5. Von Clausewitz, Carl (2008), p. 73, *On War*, Oxford: Oxford University Press.

6. *South China Morning Post*, 26 Feb 2008, p. A4.

7. (3 Sept 2008), 'Exclusif: Nos Journalistes ont Retrouvé les Talibans qui ont Abattu les Dix Soldats Francais', *Paris Match*, http://www.parismatch.com/dans-l-oeil-de-match/reportages, accessed 5 Sept 2008.

8. (5 Sept 2008), 'French Fury at Paris Match Photos of Taliban Fighters with Trophies from Dead Soldiers', Telegraph.co.uk, http://www.telegraph.co.uk/news/worldnews/europe/france/2686114, accessed 5 Sept 2008.

9. 'Milošević's 1989 speech in Gazimestan, the Field of Black Birds (or Kosovo Polje)', trans. BBC, http://www.hirhome.com/bbc_milosevic.htm, accessed 29 June 2010; Brandon, Louise & Doder, Dusko(1999), *'Milosevic: Portrait of a Tyrant'*, New York: Free Press; Mertus, Julie (1999), *Kosovo: How Myths and Truths Started a War*, Berkeley: University of California Press

10. Mertus, Julie (16 March 2006), 'Slobodan Milosevic: Myth and Responsibility', Open Democracy, http://www.opendemocracy.net/conflict-yugoslavia/responsibility_3361.jsp, accessed 29 June 2010.

11. Schwartz, Barry, Zerubavel, Yael & Barnett, Bernice (1986), 'The Recovery of Masada: A Study in Collective Memory', *The Sociological Quarterly*, vol. 27, no. 2, pp. 147–164.

12. Ibid.; Nachman, Ben-Yehuda(1999), 'The Masada Mythical Narrative and the Israeli Army', in Lomsky-Feder, Edna & Ben-Ari, Eyal (eds), *The Military and Militarism in Israeli Society*, Albany NY: State University of New York for a discussion of swearing in of Israeli Defence Force soldiers on Masada since 1956.

13. Schwartz (1986), op. cit..

14. van Blerk, Bok, 'De La Rey', http://www.youtube.com/watch?v=fAhHWpqPz9A, accessed 15 July 2008.

15. Giliomee, Hermann (2003), p. 259, *The Afrikaners: Biography of a People*, Cape Town: Tafelberg

16. McGreal, Chris (26 Feb 2007), 'Afrikaans Singer Stirs up Controversy with War Song', *The Guardian*, citing Max du Preez, http://www.guardian.co.uk/world/2007/feb/26/music.southafrica, accessed 15 Jul 2008.

17. (6 Feb 2007), 'Ministry of Arts and Culture on Bok van Blerks's Supposed Afrikaans "Struggle Song", De La Rey and Its Coded Message to Fermenting Revolutionary Sentiments', http://www.dac.gov.za/media_releases/06Feb07.html, accessed 15 Aug 2008.

18. Hobsbawm, Eric & Ranger, Terence (eds) (2003), p. 13, *The Invention of Tradition*, Cambridge: Cambridge University Press.

19. Trevor-Roper, Hugh (2003), pp. 18–23, in Hobsbawm (2003), op. cit.; Mount, Ferdinand (20 Apr 2008), 'The Welsh Academy Encyclopaedia of Wales', *Sunday Times*, p. 45.

20. Anderson, op. cit.,

21. Many exclude O'Connell arguing his campaign focused on the sectarian with no nationalist ambition.

22. The second IRA ceasefire was declared 20 July 1997; although the Good Friday Agreement was signed 10 Apr 1998.

23. Lyons, FSL (1979), p. 248, *Ireland Since the Famine*, London: Fontana Press.

24. Robert White notes membership of the Wolfe Tone Society did not mean automatically endorsing the IRA's violent methods or Sinn Féin politics, but 'promoted discussion and intellectual debate among a group of people who were interested in social and national issues in Ireland'. (2006), p. 118, *Ruairí Ó Brádaigh: The Life and Politics of an Irish Revolutionary*, Bloomington: Indiana University Press.

25. Smith, MLR (1995), p. 223, *Fighting for Ireland? The Military Strategy of the Irish Republican Movement*, London: Routledge, citing 'Bodenstown 1986' Wolfe Tone Society.

26. Geraghty, Tony (2000), p. 222(opposite), *The Irish War*, Baltimore MD: Johns Hopkins University Press.

27. Ryan, Desmond (1937), p. 4, *The Phoenix Flame: A Study of Fenianism and John Devoy*, London: Arthur Barker

28. Owens, Gary (1990), p. 123, 'Review', *The Canadian Journal of Irish Studies*, vol. 16, no. 2(Dec.1990), pp. 123–5.

29. Tone, Wolfe (1791), p. 8, *An Argument on Behalf of the Catholics of Ireland*, Belfast: Society of United Irishmen of Belfast.

30. Herz, John (1950), 'Idealist Internationalism and the Security Dilemma', *World Politics*, vol. 2, no. 2, pp. 157–180, emphasises the background to 1790s French revolutionary utopianism: '"The Revolution is a universal religion which is France's mission to impose upon humanity"' (p. 165), and 'the famous decree of November 19, 1792, in which the French National Convention declared that France would "come to the aid of all peoples who are seeking to recover their liberty"'.(p. 161). However he proposes by 1793 the Convention declared France '"will not interfere in any way in the government of other powers"' (p. 167). This for Herz was the start of national *Realpolitik*. Tone's invasion should be seen in this light, not purely as an endogenous uprising.

31. McMahon, Sean (2001), p. 78, *Wolfe Tone*, Cork: Mercier Press.

32. Elliott, Marianne (1989), p. 413, *Wolf Tone: Prophet of Irish Independence*, New Haven: Yale University Press.

33. Elliott, op. cit., p. 414.

34. Desmond, op. cit., p. 333; Holt, Edgar (1960), *Protest in Arms: The Irish Troubles 1916–1923*, London: Putnam for Pearse's address citing Tone to the annual Wolfe Tone commemoration.

35. Garvin, Tom (Autumn 1990), p. 20, 'The Return of History: Collective Myths and Modern Nationalisms', *The Irish Review* (1986-), no. 9, pp. 16–30.

36. Cruise O'Brien, Connor (1978), p. 33, *Herod: Reflections on Political Violence*, London: Hutchinson.

37. Elliott. op. cit., p. 418, citing Morrison's article in *An Phoblacht—Republican News* (27 June 1981).

38. Finally Sinn Féin members could participate in Northern Ireland government.

39. Presidential Address by Gerry Adams to Reconvened Sinn Féin Ard Fheis (10 May 1998), http://cain.ulst.ac.uk/events/peace/docs/ga10598.htm, accessed 3 Aug 2008.

40. Lyons, op. cit., p. 110.

41. O'Hegarty, PS (1952), p. 117, *A History of Ireland Under the Union, 1801–1922*,

London: Methuen. 'The extracts...from *The Nation*... were new and intoxicating, they were the voice of a new Ireland...Young men all over Ireland every generation since have listened to it'.

42. Thompson, William (1982), p. 35, *The Imagination of an Insurrection: Dublin Easter 1916*, West Stockbridge VA: Lindisfarne Press. Earlier meetings drew 50–100,000. Clontarf Hill had expected 200,000.

43. However Foster considers Lalor's radicalism a direct reaction to the Famine, and possibly ideas gleaned in France in 1827. Most 'Young Irelanders' were grounded in German romanticism. Foster, Roy (1988), p. 381, *Modern Ireland 1600–1972*, London: Allen Lane.

44. Lalor, James Fintan (1997), p. 22, *Collected Writings 1918*, Poole: Woodstock Books, 'A New Nation' (19 Apr 1847), Letter to the *Nation* newspaper.

45. Mitchel, John (1868), *Jail Journal or Five Years in British Prisons*, New York: PM Haverty.

46. Morash, Christopher (1997), p. 42, 'Making Memories: The Literature of the Irish Famine', in O'Sullivan, Patrick (ed.), *The Meaning of the Famine*, London: Leicester University Press.

47. Mitchel, op. cit., p. 90, [peasants] my insertion.

48. Morash, op. cit., p. 44, citing *The O'Donnells of Glen College: A Tale of the Famine Years in Ireland*.

49. Ibid., pp. 45–6.

50. See the Famine song 'The Fields of Athenry', written in the 1970s, and sung *inter alia* by Irish football supporters, and Republican sympathisers.

51. Dhochartaigh, Michealin & Mc Gorrian, K & Oh Anluian, BG (2008), 'A Brief History of the Irish Republican Army', Real IRA website, via http://irelandsown.net/IRAhistory.htm, accessed 1 Sept 2008.

52. Davis, Graham (1997), pp. 21–2, 'The Historiography of the Irish Famine', in O'Sullivan, Patrick (ed.), *The Meaning of the Famine*, Leicester: Leicester University Press.

53. Ibid., p. 25.

54. http://www.thewildgeese.com/pages/nyfamine.html, accessed 3 Aug 2008. Bob Geldof, Martin McGuinness attended.

55. Mary McAleese (17 July 2002), President of Ireland, Dedication of the Irish Hunger Memorial, Battery Park City, New York. Irish Consulate General, New York, http://www.thewildgeese.com/pages/nyfamine.html accessed 3 Aug 2008.

56. Variously described as 'the Organisation', the Society', the Brotherhood'. In 1873 the 'IRB' settled on Irish Republican rather than Revolutionary Brotherhood. Lyons, op. cit., p. 125.

57. Garvin, Tom (1987), pp. 33–5, *Nationalist Revolutionaries in Ireland 1858–1928*, Oxford: Clarendon.

58. after June 1867.

59. Cf. Ryan (1937), op. cit. for his discussion of James Stephens, John Devoy, Thomas Davis, William Roberts, John O'Mahoney.

60. Cf. Maguire, John Francis (1868), p. 103, *The Irish in America*, London: Longmans, Green & Co: 'The Irish form fully half the population of what still...may be designated as Upper Canada'; Ramon-Garcia, Marta (2010), 'Square-Toed Boots and Felt

Hats: Irish Revolutionaries and the Invasion of Canada (1848–1871)', *Estudios Irlandeses*, no. 5, pp. 81–91.

61. Maguire, op. cit., p. 592, 'an immense body of Fenians, several thousands in number, concentrated in Buffalo, with the intention of crossing the frontier'.

62. Ryan (1937), op. cit., p. 182, citing Devoy's account in *Gaelic American* Aug 1922.

63. Maguire, op. cit., p. 615.

64. Ryan (1937), op. cit., p. 183, citing *The Land of Eire*, p. 33.

65. Paseta, Senia (1998), '1798 in 1898: The Politics of Commemoration', *Irish Review*, no. 22, pp. 46–53.

66. MacLysaght, Edward (1967), pp. 126–8, 'Larkin, Connolly, and the Labour Movement', in Martin, FX, (ed.) (1967), *Leaders and Men of the Easter Rising: Dublin 1916*, London: Methuen.

67. Nevin, Donal (1968), pp. 123–4, 'The Irish Citizen Army', in Edwards, Owen Dudley & Pyle, Fergus (eds), *1916 The Easter Rising*, London: MacGibbon & Kee, citing Larkin's July 1914article in the *Irish Worker*.

68. Ibid., pp. 128–9.

69. Foster, op. cit., p. 478.

70. Nevin, op. cit., p. 130.

71. 'Poblacht Na H Eireann. The Provisional Government of the Irish Republic to the People of Ireland'—IRB proclamation read out on the steps of the Dublin Post Office, 24 Apr 1916.

72. Coogan, op. cit., p. 21.

73. (1916), 'Sinn Féin Rebellion Handbook, Easter 1916', *Weekly Irish Times*, Dublin.

74. Colum, Padraic (1916), p.xxxiii, *The Poems of the Irish Revolutionary Brotherhood*, Boston: Small, Maynard.

75. Mac Lochlainn, Piaras (1971), pp. 28–9, 'Last Words: Letters and Statements of the Leaders Executed after the Rising at Easter 1916', Dublin: Kilmainham Jail Restoration Society, citing Pearse, address to the Court Martial, Kilmainham Jail, 2 May 1916.

76. Bolt, Neville (Feb 2008), 'Propaganda of the Deed and The Irish Republican Brotherhood', *RUSI Journal*, particularly Padraig Pearse, Joseph Plunkett and Thomas MacDonagh.

77. The socialist James Connolly had committed his Irish Citizen Army to the struggle.

78. Thompson, op. cit., p. 89.

79. Ibid., p. 107.

80. Colum (1916), op. cit., p. IX

81. McGhee, Owen (2005), *The IRB: Irish Republican Brotherhood from the Land League to Sinn Féin*, Dublin: Four Courts Press. McGhee argues for the IRB's propagandist over insurrectionary aims.

82. Clohesy, Anthony (2000), p. 76, 'Provisionalism and the (im)possibility of Justice in Northern Ireland', in Howarth, David; Norval, Aletta; Stavrakakis, Yannis (eds), *Discourse Theory and Political Analysis: Identities, Hegemonies and Social Change*, Manchester: Manchester University Press.

83. 'Easter 1916', written May-Sept. 1916 . For an elegiac treatment of the fallen heroes

see 'Sixteen Dead Men', and 'The Rose Tree', Yeats, WB (2000), pp. 152–54, *The Collected Poems of WB Yeats*, Ware: Wordsworth Poetry Library.

84. (1957), pp. 84–5, *The IRB and the 1916 Insurrection*, Cork: Mercier Press.

85. Ibid.

86. Martin, FX (March 1961), p. 238, 'Select documents. XX Eoin MacNeill on the 1916 Rising', *Irish Historical Studies*, vol. XII, no. 47, pp. 226–270 Memorandum 1.

87. Martin, FX (1967), p. 240, '1916—Revolution or Evolution?', in Martin, FX (ed.) (1967), *Leaders and Men of the Easter Rising: Dublin 1916*, London: Methuen.

88. For a comprehensive analysis see Gkotzaridis, Evi (2006*), Trials of Irish History: Genesis and Evolution of a Reappraisal 1938–2000*, London: Routledge.

89. Fitzpatrick, David (1997), 'Militarism in Ireland 1900–1922', in Bartlett, Thomas & Jeffery, Keith (eds), *A Military History of Ireland*, Cambridge: Cambridge University Press. See for a discussion of Irish enlistment to the Boer War and World War One.

90. Jackson, Alvin (1992), p. 164, 'Unionist Myths', *Past and Present*, no. 136, pp. 164–185.

91. Ibid., p. 169.

92. Ibid., p. 171.

93. English, Richard (2004), p. 10, *Armed Struggle; The History of the IRA*, Oxford: Oxford University Press, sees the UVF as direct cause; Martin, FX (ed.) (1963), *The Irish Volunteers 1913–15: Recollections and Documents*, Dublin: James Duffy.

94. Stewart, ATQ (1997), *The Ulster Crisis: Resistance to Home Rule 1912–1914*, Belfast: Blackstaff Press.

95. Foster (1988), op. cit., p. 467.

96. Jackson, Alvin (2002), p. 237, *Ireland 1798–1998: Politics and War*, Oxford: Blackwell.

97. Coogan (2002), op. cit., p. 4, sees the 1916 Rising as an unqualified response to the UVF's formation.

98. For socio-economic versus ideological attitudes to the war effort see Kelly, MJ (2006), p. 242, *The Fenian Ideal and Irish Nationalism*, Woodbridge: Boydell Press.

99. Foster (1988), op. cit.; Garvin (1987), op. cit..

100. Kostick, Conor (2009), *Revolution in Ireland: Popular Militancy 1917 to 1923*, Cork: Cork University Press. See for the rise of working class militancy and its relationship to the politics of violence.

101. Ibid.; Buckley, Mary (1976), 'John Mitchel, Ulster and Irish nationality (1842–1848)', *Studies: An Irish Quarterly Review*, vol. 65, no. 257, pp. 30–44: see for the Mitchel Doctrine 1848.

102. FX Martin (1967), op. cit., p. 251.

103. Foster (1988), op. cit., p. 487 citing Charles Townshend.

104. Garvin (1987), op. cit., p. 11.

105. Bowyer Bell (1972), p. 13, *The Secret Army: A History of the IRA 1915–1970*, London: Sphere Books.

106. Garvin (1987), op. cit., p. 4.

107. Ibid., p. 118.

108. Op. cit., p. 7.

109. Garvin (1987), op. cit., p. 124.

110. MacStiofain, Sean (1975), p. 50, *Revolutionary in Ireland*, Edinburgh: Gordon Cremonesi.

111. O'Malley, Ernie (2002), p. 353, *On Another Man's Wound*, Dublin: Anvil Books.

112. Foster (1988), op. cit., p. 502, citing Gleeson.

113. (4 Jul 1921), 'The Insurrection of 1916 and its Consequences', *Irish Bulletin*, vol. 5, no. 23. The article concludes: 'This brief review shows the sober, uninterrupted progress in recent years of a movement having its roots deep in the past and representing the Irish race. It takes its rise in the collapse, after a generation of fruitless and demoralising intrigues in a foreign parliament of an agitation for Home Rule which never captured the imagination of the Irish people. First actively manifested in a revolt led by a handful of gallant idealists in 1916, it gradually masters the mind and soul of an awakening nation and having once mastered them in the teeth of the most formidable discouragements and under fearful penalties, retains its mastery. There lies the power behind the President'.

114. (1 Jul 1921), *Irish Bulletin*, vol. 5, no. 22: the Nationalist *Enniscorthy Echo, Cork Examiner*, and *Freeman's Journal* are cited as publishing under duress.

115. Coogan, op. cit., p. 22.

116. O'Malley (2002), op. cit., p. 231.

117. O'Malley, Padraig (1990), pp. 4–5, *Biting at the Grave: The Irish Hunger Strikes and the Politics of Despair*, Boston: Beacon Press.

118. Gallagher, Frank (1965), p. 192, *The Anglo-Irish Treaty*, London: Hutchinson.

119. Ibid., p. 189.

120. Moloney, Ed (2002), p. 40, *A Secret History of the IRA*, New York: W.W. Norton.

121. O'Brien, Brendan (1995), p. 120, *The Long War: The IRA & Sinn Féin from Armed Struggle to Peace Talks*, Dublin: O'Brien Press. IRA volunteers were instructed politically from *PIRA's Green Book*. It stated: 'The Irish republican army, its leadership, is the lawful government of the Irish Republic... All other parliaments or assemblies claiming the right to speak for and to pass laws on behalf of the Irish people are illegal assemblies, puppet governments of a foreign power and willing tools of an occupying force'.

122. Neumann, Peter (2005), 'The Bullet and the Ballot Box: The Case of the IRA', *Journal of Strategic Studies*, vol. 28, no. 6, pp. 941–975. Neumann sees two ways electoral participation influenced the transformation of the IRA, namely through exposure to processes of systematic dialogue with other political actors, and to public opinion where aversion to violence undercut the IRA's resolve to armed conflict.

123. McDonald, Henry(14 Sept 2010), 'Real IRA says it will target UK banks', *The Guardian*, http://www.guardian.co.uk/uk/2010/sep/14/real-ira-targets-banks-bankers, accessed 20 Sept 2010. The Real IRA announced a renewed campaign of attacks on targets in England similar to those in the City of London in the 1990s. Furthermore 'they dismissed Sinn Féin's claims that its electoral strategy would ultimately yield a united Ireland...'

124. O'Brien (1995), op. cit., p. 352.

125. Garvin (1987), op. cit., p. 1.

126. See Rodin, David (2007), p. 181, 'Terrorism Without Intention' in Kinsella, David & Carr, Craig (eds), *The Morality of War*, Boulder CO & London: Lynne Rienner. See for discussion of the doctrine of double effect and the moral difference between deliberately targeting (terror bombing) and accidentally striking non-combatants (tactical bombing of military targets).

127. BBC 1 *News at Ten* (15 Nov. 2010), interview with Paul Wood in Kabul; see Guardian/WikiLeaks (26/07/2010), 'A Losing Battle With Taliban's Homemade Weapon', 2004–2009: civilian fatalities by IED: 2,187; civilians injured: 4,811.

128. Framing or frames: Interpretive schemata that allow people to simplify and understand events and problems in their lives, conceptualise the 'world out there' and formulate action-oriented beliefs that underpin collective action.

129. Irish Republican Army, *Green Book*(Volumes I & II), p. 4.

130. O'Brien, Brendan (1999), pp. 23, 212, *The Long War: The IRA and Sinn Féin*, 2nd edn, Syracuse NY: Syracuse University Press.

131. (06 May 1998), South African Press Association, citing Aboobaker Ismail, http://www.justice.gov.za/trc/media/1998/9805/s980506b.htm, accessed 20 Dec 2010.

132. (2010), op. cit., pp. 617–8.

133. Guthrie, Charles & Quinlan, Michael (2007), *The Just War Tradition: Ethics in Modern Warfare*, London: Bloomsbury.

134. (Aug 1996), 'ANC Submission to the Truth and Reconciliation Commission', http://www.justice.gov.za/trc/hrvtrans/submit/anctruth.htm; (12th May 1997), 'ANC Second Submission to the Truth and Reconciliation Commission', http://www.justice.gov.za/trc/hrvtrans/submit/anc2.htm, accessed 30 May 2010.

135. Mandela, op. cit., p. 615.

136. King, Charles (1997), *Ending Civil Wars*, London: IISS Adelphi Paper 308.

4. THE INSURGENT IMAGE

1. Cartier-Bresson, Henri (1952), *The Decisive Moment*, New York: Simon & Schuster.

2. Fourie, Pieter (2001), p. 541, *Media Studies: Institutions, Theories, and Issues*, Lansdowne: Juta Education. Fourie highlights the 'event orientation' of media accounts of the violent deed, a focus on the blood and guts not the underlying issue.

3. Katzenbach's perspective on insurgent time is operational, referring to the Maoist concept of free movement in the countryside. Flexibility across terrain buys insurgents time in the struggle with state forces: 'unlimited time depends primarily on unlimited space' in Mao's protracted war. Katzenbach, Edward & Hanrahan, Gene (1955), p. 325, 'The Revolutionary Strategy of Mao Tse-Tung', *Political Science Quarterly*, vol. 70, no. 3, pp. 321–340.

4. Olick, Jeffrey (2003), p. 2, *States of Memory*, Durham NC: Duke University Press 'Memory and the nation have a peculiar synergy'.

5. Beck, Ulrich (2001), p. 137, *World Risk Society*, Cambridge: Polity.

6. Melucci, Alberto (1989), *Nomads of the Present*, London: Hutchinson Radius.

7. Bin Laden attacks 'the pressures imposed on us by regimes and the media', Kepel, Gilles & Milelli, Jean-Pierre (2008), p. 58, *Al Qaeda in Its Own Words*, Cambridge MA: Belknap. In his 'Message to the American People' he further interprets the past and lays the ground for future opportunity spaces saying 'What I will remember

among their pleas, before the towers fell, is the one regretting having allowed the White House to attack oppressed people in its foreign policy' (p. 76).

8. Yavuz, M Hakan (2003), p. 24, *Islamic Political identity in Turkey*, Oxford: Oxford University Press.

9. McAdam, Doug (1988), p. 128, '*Micromobilization Contexts and Recruitment to Activism*' in Klandermans (1988).

10. Collective action is widely held to depend on resource availability, namely money and time: See Zald (1992); Cress and Snow (1996). But organising capacity is key if individual resources are to be shared and turned into collective action, since resource inequality varies between constituencies and shapes the outcome of events. However see Edwards, Bob & McCarthy, John (2004), pp. 125–128, 'Resources and Social Movement Mobilization', in Snow, David; Soule, Sarah & Kriesi, Hanspeter (eds), *The Blackwell Companion to Social Movements*, Malden MA: Blackwell. Edwards identifies different types of necessary resource: moral embracing solidarity and legitimacy such as in the US Southern civil rights movement; cultural resources such as strategic know-how, or technical knowledge like access to internet and the ability to deploy media production techniques; social-organisational resources such as recruitment and training; human resources like leadership, experience, expertise and labour; and material, namely money, equipment and supplies.

11. Koopman, Ruud (2004), pp. 22–23, 'Protest in Time and Space: The Evolution of Waves of Contention', in Snow (2004), op. cit..

12. See 'Using Frames to Trigger Action', ch. 4: Frames, I argue, are 'thumb-nail sketches' that use symbolic narratives to explain how individuals and groups make sense of the 'world out there' and 'sell' that meaning to others to secure their strategies.

13. Ibid., pp. 24–5.

14. Opportunity spaces are used more loosely: De Bono, Edward (24 June 2002), '*Opportunity Space*', http://www.edwarddebono.com/PassageDetail.php?passage_id=704&, accessed 29 Sept 2009: 'The opportunity space includes all the changes, decisions and choices we can make'. See Wasson, Charles (2006), p. 136, '*System Analysis, Design and, Development: Concepts, Principles and Practices*', Hoboken NJ: John Wiley. 'A *gap* or *vulnerability* in a system, product, or service capability that represents an opportunity for 1) a competitor or adversary to exploit or 2) supplier to offer solutions'.

15. Johnson, Chalmers (1983), p. 91, *Revolutionary Change*, Harlow: Longman, see ch. 2 & 5.

16. This comprises two aspects: *exaiphnes* and *kairos*. See Ward, Koral (2008), Augenblick: the Concept of the "Decisive Moment" in Nineteenth and Twentieth Century Western Philosophy, Aldershot: Ashgate.

17. Zolberg, Aristide (1972), 'Moments of Madness', *Politics and Society*, vol. 2, no. 2, pp. 183–207.

18. The Free Association (2011), pp. 32–3, *Moments of Excess: Movements, Protest and Everyday Life*, Oakland CA: PM Press.

19. 9/11 Commission Report (2004), p. 377, '*Final Report of the National Commission on Terrorist Attacks upon the United States*', Washington, DC: US Government Printing Office illustrates this shock, famously citing Richard Holbrooke speaking

of Bin Laden 'How can a man in a cave outcommunicate the world's leading communications society?' Even more instructive is the bureaucratic timeline in the US administration reported to the Commission, capturing government confusion in the immediate aftermath of the strikes: see p35, 1.3 National Crisis Management. Also Clarke, Richard (2004), *Against All Enemies*, London: Simon & Schuster, ch. 10.

20. Fox Piven, Frances & Cloward, Richard (02 May 1966), 'The Weight of the Poor: A Strategy to End Poverty', *The Nation*, see for generating a crisis through bureaucratic overload.

21. Klein, Melanie (2007), *Shock Doctrine*, London: Allen Lane.

22. Friedman, Milton (2002), p. xiv, 'Preface 1982' to *Capitalism and Freedom*, Chicago: University of Chicago Press.

23. Ibid.

24. Trotsky, Leon (1904), 'The Proletariat and the Revolution', http://www.marxists.org/archive/trotsky/1918/ourrevo/ch02.htm; Mao had conceptualised it as the strategic defensive or political organisational Phase 1 of his 3-phase theory. Mao Tse-Tung (1963), *Selected Military Writings of Mao Tse-Tung*, Peking: Foreign Language Press.

25. Alinsky, Saul (1989), p. xxii, *Rules for Radicals*, New York: Vintage Books.

26. Lakoff, George (2004), p. 89, *Don't Think of an Elephant!*, White River Junction VER: Chelsea Green.

27. Charney, Leo (1995), p. 284, 'In a Moment: Film and the Philosophy of Modernity', in Charney, Leo & Schwartz, Vanessa (eds), *Cinema and the Invention of Modern Life*, Berkeley CA: University of California Press.

28. Lindroos, Kia (2006), p. 115, 'Benjamin's Moment', in Palonen, Kia (ed.), *Redescriptions: Vol. 10*, Piscataway NJ & London: Transaction; Lindroos sees Benjamin emphasising 'revolutionary action as a rupture, a form of action with the potential to intervene in any unquestioned continuum of thinking, action, or political, historical or aesthetic understanding. His aim is to highlight the relevance of various forms of present experiences, for example in understanding revolutionary action as marking the desire to pull 'the emergency break' as opposed to remaining a complacent passenger on the train 'of history'.

29. Dudziak, Mary (2003), p. 212, *September 11 in History: a Watershed Moment?*, Durham: Duke University Press.

30. Virilio, Paul & Lotringer, Sylvère(2008, 1983), p. 42, *Pure War*, Los Angeles CA: Semiotext(e).

31. Moffat, James (2003), p. 58, *Complexity Theory and Network Centric Warfare*, Washington, DC: Department of Defense CCRP.

32. Seaton, Jean (2005), *Carnage and the Media*, London: Penguin/Allen Lane.

33. Cornish, Paul (17 Oct 2002), pp. 18–20, 'Cry Havoc! And Let Slip the Managers of War: The Strategic, Military and Moral Hazards of Micro-managed Warfare', Final Draft, Centre for Defence Studies, International Policy Research Unit, King's College London, http://www.nato.int/acad/fellow/99–01/cornish.pdf, accessed 11 Apr 2007.

34. US Department of the Army (11 Aug 2003), p. 34(1–18), 'Mission Command: Command and Control of Armed Forces', *Field Manual 6–0*, Washington: Headquarters of the Army.

35. Strachan, Hew (2006), p. 59, 'Making Strategy: Civil-Military Relations after Iraq', *Survival*, vol. 48, no. 3, pp. 59–82, citing Colin Grey.

36. Ibid.

37. Ibid., p. 65, for Strachan's analysis of two centres for strategy with no clear connections within the British defence establishment.

38. In the opportunity space POTD takes place within populations increasingly connected by digital communications technologies. News of the event must travel through time-lags, first through connected population (inner circle), then traditional media (middle circle), then state agencies (outer circle).

39. Bell, J Bowyer(1991), p. 161, *The Gun in Politics: an Analysis of Irish Political Conflict, 1916–1986*, New Brunswick NJ: Transaction; Oppenheimer(2008), op. cit.; Shearman, Peter (2004), p. 14, 'Reconceptualizing Security after 9/11', in Sherman, Peter & Sussex, Matthew (eds), *European Security after 9/11*, Aldershot & Burlington VA: Ashgate.

40. Sontag (2002), op. cit., pp. 17–18.

41. Ibid., p. 23.

42. Barthes, Roland (2000), p. 15, *Camera Lucida*, London: Vintage.

43. Barthes, Roland (1977b), p. 44, *Image, Music, Text*, London: Fontana.

44. Barthes, Roland (2000), op. cit., pp. 25–27.

45. Gottlieb, Sidney (ed.) (2003), p. 174, *Alfred Hitchcock: Interviews*, Jackson: University Press of Mississippi. In Hitchcock's 'Rear Window' Miss Lonely Hearts is the only character in the entire film who wears green, 'so that when that green suit went across the street, your eyes never left her' (ibid.).

46. On 11 Sept 2001 four planes were involved, targeting also The Pentagon and White House, symbols of military, and political power. New York epitomised the US as the apotheosis of capitalist-imperialist hegemony. While the White House presented an instantly recognisable, uncluttered image, the Pentagon is for most viewers less familiar. American Airlines flight 11 crashed into the North Tower of the World Trade Center; United Airlines flight 175 crashed into the South Tower; American Airlines flight 77 crashed into the Pentagon; and United Airlines flight 93 came down in the Pennsylvania countryside.

47. Street sign courtesy David Betz.

48. Great disparities govern pre-knowledge such as standard of education, inter-personal exchange, and opinion-leaders. Price, Vincent & Zaller, John (1993), 'Who Gets the News? Alternative Measures of News Reception and their Implications for Research', *Public Opinion Quarterly*, vol. 57, pp. 133–164. See Gunter, Barrie (1997), op. cit., ch. 5. These same disparities affect both cognition and individual memory retention.

49. See (15 Apr 2010) 'Report of UN Commission of Inquiry into the Facts and Circumstances of the Assassination of Former Pakistani Prime Minister Mohtarma Benazir Bhutto', p. 65, par. 266.

50. Ibid., p. 53 for other hypotheses; section B, p. 54, 'Responsibilities'.

51. Oppenheimer, op. cit., p. 65.

52. McLuhan, op. cit. on hot and cool images.

53. Carroll-Mayer, Moira et al (2008), p. 39, 'CCTV Identity Management and Implications for Criminal Justice: some considerations', *Surveillance & Society*, vol. 5, no. 1, pp. 33–50: 'Personal appearances upon publicly located CCTV screens are

unaccompanied by the voice of the actor. They acquire, in the hands of the police however, a "voice-over", it is possible to explain how the superimposition of the voice can lead to the virtual criminalisation of those depicted on CCTV'. Cf. Chong, Philip, et al (2006), 'Reality Based Television and Police Citizen Encounters', *Punishment and Society*, vol. 8, no. 1, pp. 59–85.

54. Levitin, op. cit.; Eco (1977), op. cit..

55. Messaris, Paul (1997), p. xviii, *Visual Persuasion: The Role of Images in Advertising*, Thousand Oaks: Sage; Langer, Susanne (1960), ch. 3, *Philosophy in a New Key*, Cambridge MA: Harvard University Press.

56. Williamson, Judith (2002), p. 13, *Decoding Advertisements: Ideology and Meaning in Advertising*, London: Marion Boyars.

57. Ibid., p. 100.

58. Barthes, Roland (1997a), *Elements of Semiology*, New York: Hill & Wang.

59. Williamson (2002), op. cit., pp. 25–6.See for fuller analysis of the Deneuve ad. See other faces of Chanel no. 5: Marilyn Monroe (1950s); Catherine Deneuve (1970s & 1980s); Carole Bouquet (1990s); Nicole Kidman (2000s); Audrey Tautou (late 2000s).

60. YouTube (1984), '*Reagan: A New Beginning*' (1984), http://www.youtube.com/watch?v=TRI3G-K0P50, accessed 20 Jul 2009.

61. Messaris, Paul (1997), op. cit., pp. xi–xiii.

62. The same message is developed in HSBC television commercials 'The World's Local Bank' http://thefinancialbrand.com/375/hsbc-worldwide-local-bank/, accessed 08 Aug 2011; and 'We recognise how people value things differently' http://www.youtube.com/watch?v=5imDyxNjo-0, accessed 03 Jul 2009. Here onlookers including men, women, old, young and babies anxiously watch as police cars arrive in a forest setting to forcibly remove eco-protesters. One girl is arrested but exchanges words with a lumberjack before she is imprisoned. On release she and the lumberjack encounter each other in the station and both ride off together on his motorbike, her arms folded around him, as the bike disappears down a road that cuts through the forest. Different views? However read the blog which demonstrates viewers' confusion: http://scampblog.blogspot.com/2008/09/hes-lumberjack-and-hes-okay.html, accessed 03 Jul 2009.

63. CBS Outdoor (2009), 'Time to Consider', http://timetoconsider.co.uk/pity_or_pitiful/pitiful/, accessed 03 Jul 2009.

64. Macintyre, Ben (10 Sept 2009), 'The Nature of War Frozen in a Photograph', *The Times*, p. 34, citing Susan Sontag.

65. Kaplan, Stuart (1990), 'Visual Metaphors in the Representation of Communication Technology', *Critical Studies in Mass Communication*, vol. 7, pp. 37–47.

66. Bruner, Jerome cited in Lester, Paul (2006), 'Syntactic Theory of Visual Communication', http://commfaculty.fullerton.edu/lester/writings/viscomtheory.html;(2003), *Visual Communication Images with Messages*, AUS: Wadsworth.

67. Messaris, Paul (1997), op. cit., p. xviii–xix.

68. Williamson (2002), op. cit..

69. Kristeva, Julia (1980), pp. 64–91, 'Word, Dialogue and Novel', in *Desire in Language: A Semiotic Approach to Literature and Art*, New York: Columbia University Press.

70. Pollay cited in Leiss, William; Kline, Stephen & Jihally, Sut (1986), p. 46, *Social*

Communication in Advertising, Toronto: Methuen: advertising has both 'informational' and 'transformational' dimensions. The first transmits information about the product, the second attempts to change the attitudes of the consumer encouraging a 'lifestyle' choice.

71. Peirce, Charles (1932), pp. 158, 'The Icon, Index, and Symbol', in *Collected Papers of Charles Sanders Peirce: vol. 2*, Hartshore, Charles & Weiss, Paul (eds), Cambridge MA: Harvard University Press. He refers to hypoicons that comprise images, diagrams and metaphors. Images possess simple qualities or First Firstnesses. Diagrams are dyadic, employing analogy. Metaphors represent a 'parallelism in something else' (p. 157). But how communicating text transforms into interpreted meaning is culturally specific: (pp. 164–5, footnote1).

72. Lakoff, George & Johnson, Mark (2003), p. 6, *Metaphors We Live By*, Chicago: University of Chicago Press.

73. Ibid., p. 5. But Lakoff diverges from established and objectivist 'comparison theories' on metaphor. These suggest that metaphor is a linguistic phenomenon, describing similarities which already exist (p. 153). Kövecses, Zoltán (2002), p. 6, *Metaphor: A Practical Introduction*, Oxford: Oxford University Press: metaphor is unidirectional flowing from the concrete in the real world to the conceptual and abstract.

74. Ibid., p. 19.

75. See Swidler, Ann (1995), p. 39, 'Cultural Power and Social Movements' in Johnston, Hank & Klandermans, Bert (eds), *Social Movements and Culture*, London: UCL Press who argues from a cultural perspective that power is exercised through semiotic codes which constrain individuals' ability to re-construct meaning.

76. Lakoff (2003), op. cit., p. 157–8.

77. Thomas & Thomas (1928), p. 572, cited in Forsyth, Donelson (2009), p. 11, *Group Dynamics*, Belmont CA: Wadsworth.

78. Leiss, op. cit., p. 241; Pollay, R & Mainprize, S (1984), 'Headlining of Visuals in Print Advertising', in Glover, J (ed.), *Proceedings of the American Academy of Advertising*, Denver: American Academy of Advertising; McQuarrie, Edward & Mick, David (Sept 1992), p. 183, 'On Resonance: A Critical Pluralistic Inquiry into Advertising Rhetoric', *Journal of Consumer Research*, vol. 19, no. 2: 'a metaphor performs a substitution by connecting two things that have some initial similarity in content…resonance performs a substitution by means of a false homology in which the similarity is imposed'; Glucksberg, Sam & Boaz, Keysar (July 1990), 'Understanding Metaphorical Comparisons: Beyond Similarity', *Psychological Review*, vol. 97, pp. 3–18; Durand, Jacques (1987), 'Rhetorical Figures in the Advertising Image', in Umiker-Sebeok, Jean (ed.), *Marketing and Semiotics: New Directions in the Study of the Signs for Sale*, New York: Mouton de Gruyter, pp. 295–318.

79. Goosens, Cees (2003), p. 137, 'Visual Persuasion: Mental Imagery Processing and Emotional Experiences', in Scott, Linda & Batra, Rajeev (eds), *Persuasive Imagery*, Mahwah NJ: Routledge.

80. Various research projects throw light on the subject. A mock-up for a tissue ad designed to suggest its quality of softness presented four options: one with only explanatory text; each of the other three with a single picture, kitten, sunset, abstract-painting respectively. Not unexpectedly the focus-group chose the text, and kitten. The conclusion: the kitten image was equally effective as the text in associ-

ating softness. See Mitchel, A & Olson, J(1981), 'Are Product Attribute Beliefs the only Mediator of Advertising Effects on Brand Attitude?', *Journal of Marketing Research*, vol. 18, pp. 318–332.

81. Rossiter, J & Percy, L (1983), p. 112, 'Visual Communication in Advertising', in Harris, R (ed.), *Information Processing Research in Advertising*, Hillsdale NJ: Lawrence Erlbaum; Messaris, op. cit., ch. 5 for full discussion.

82. Schütz, Alfred (1964.1976), p. 161, 'Making Music Together: A Study in Social Relationship', in Brodersen, Arvid (ed.), *Alfred Schütz Collected Papers II: Studies in Social Theory*, The Hague: Martinus Nijhoff; Schramm, Wilbur (1971), 'How Communication Works', in Schramm, op. cit..

83. Chayko, Mary (2002), p. 67, *Connecting: How We Form Social Bonds and Communities in the Internet Age*, Albany NY: SUNY Press.

84. Schütz, op. cit., pp. 159 & 172; 'Frith, Simon (2004), *Popular Music: Music and Society*, Abingdon: Routledge Section C.

85. Chayko (2002), op. cit., pp. 72–3.

86. Bartlett, Frederic (1967), *Remembering*, London: Cambridge University Press; cf. Levitin, Daniel (2006), *This Is Your Brain On Music*, London: Atlantic, ch. 4 on anticipation in music; ch. 5 for discussion of 'multiple memory models' for high fidelity preservation in long-term memory. These blend 'prototype theory' favoured by constructivists where we store general abstractions of experience and discard detail, with 'exemplar theory' drawing on Gestalt residue theories, where each event is 'encoded as a trace' or act of record-keeping (p. 162). See also Huron, David (2008), *Sweet Anticipation: Music and the Psychology of Expectation*, Cambridge MA: MIT Press.

87. Chiesi, H, Spilich, G & Voss, J (1979), 'Acquisition of Domain-related Information in Relation to High and Low Domain Knowledge', *Journal of Verbal Learning and Verbal Behaviour*, vol. 18, pp. 257–274; Thorndyke, P (1979), 'Knowledge Acquisition from Newspapers', Discourse Processes, vol. 2, pp. 95–112.

88. Van Dijk, Teun (1988), p. 49, *News as Discourse*, Hillsdale NJ: Erlbaum.

89. Ibid., p. 178.

90. Levitin, op. cit., ch. 4.

91. Corman, Steven & Dooley, Kevin (2008), p. 11, 'Strategic Communication on a Rugged Landscape', Consortium for Strategic Communication, Arizona State University, Report no. 0801: 'the unstated premise is in effect supplied by the listener, leading him or her to the "natural" implied conclusion'.

92. Few command the same screen time, similar audience attention or crystallised sequence of events. Unlike the protracted coverage of Black September-Munich 1972, there is a unity of time, place and actors in this deed.

93. Redmond, Sean (2008), p. 33, 'When Planes Fall out of the Sky', in Randell, Karen & Redmond, Sean (eds), *The War Body on Screen*, New York: Continuum; Baudrillard, Jean (2003), *The Spirit of Terrorism*, London: Verso.

94. O'Shaughnessy, Nicholas & Baines, Paul (2009), 'Selling Terror: The Symbolization and Positioning of Jihad', *Marketing Theory*, vol. 9, no. 2, pp. 227–241.

95. Mehta, Suketu (2005), p. 17, *Maximum City: Bombay Lost and Found*, New York: Vintage Departures.

96. Ghosh, Amitav (2009), p. 82, 'Defeat or Victory Isn't Determined by the Success of

the Strike Itself, but by the Response', in *26/11: The Attack on Mumbai*, New Delhi: Penguin/Hindustan Times.

97. Crabtree, James (17 July 2009), 'India's Bloodied Elite', *Prospect*, http://www.prospect-magazine.co.uk/article_details.php?id=10523, accessed15 July 2009; cf. Tripathi, Salil (05 June 2009), 'Indians Deserve Better Governance', *Far East Economic Review*, http://www.feer.com/essays/2009/june/indians-deserve-better-governance, accessed 27 July 2009, for Tripathi's severe critique. Extremes in Mumbai's property market is a central theme of the Oscar-winning feature film 'Slumdog Millionaire' (2008).

98. Williamson, op. cit..

99. Roy, Arundhati (2009), *Listening to Grasshoppers: Field Notes on Democracy*, London: Hamish Hamilton. Roy's polemic is representative of a broader critical literature.

100. Channel 4 television (30 June 2009), 'Terror in Mumbai', *Dispatches*.

101. BBC television (26 & 27 Nov. 2008), *Newsnight*.

102. Davis, Dickie Lt. Col. (July 2008), 'Propaganda of the Deed', King's College London Insurgency Research Group conference presentation.

103. The footage originally recorded on 12 July 2007 was made available through WikiLeaks: 'Op-Ed: The Collateral Damage of the WikiLeaks Video': http://www.digitaljournal.com/article/290280, accessed 01 Mar 2011. see also the interview with Army specialist Ethan McCord in WIRED (20 Apr 2010), http://www.wired.com/dangerroom/2010/04/2007-iraq-apache-attack-as-seen-from-the-ground/, accessed 04 Mar 2011.

104. British troops in Iraq in the mid-2000s observed within a couple of years a sophisticated progression from single camera shoots of stage-managed IED attacks, to using two, and soon three cameras to capture the action in close-up, mid- and wide-shots.

105. Kimmage, Daniel & Ridolfo, Kathleen (2007), p. 35, *Iraqi Insurgent Media: The War of Images and Ideas*, Washington, DC: RFE/RL. Kimmage describes common building blocks used in insurgent video production as freely available on the web: logos, songs, statements outside footage and insurgent footage. Only specific attack footage need be generated.

106. N. Bolt interview with O'Shaughnessy, Nicholas (Nov. 2009): Even so this betrays slow progress in lessons-learned and a failure to acknowledge the value of adapting to a sound-bite culture and short marketing narratives. See Kimmage, Daniel (26 June 2008), 'Fight Terror With YouTube', *New York Times*, http://www.nytimes.com/2008/06/26/opinion/26kimmage.html, accessed 21 Mar 2010: Kimmage depicts *Al-Qaeda* tapes as 'behind the curve' stuck in 'old hat' Web 1.0 levels of production sophistication where Web 1.0 is characterised by 'snazzy' creative resources, and Web 2.0 allows users to self-generate and proliferate messages.

107. Mullah Omar (2009), op. cit..

108. N. Bolt interview with O'Shaughnessy, Nicholas (Nov. 2009), op. cit..

109. Ibid., p. 15.

110. McCarthy, John & Zald, Mayer (May 1977), pp. 1217–1218, 'Resource Mobilization and Social Movements: A Partial Theory', *American Journal of Sociology*, vol. 82, no. 6, pp. 1212–1241. The authors differentiate between social movements (SMs) and social movement organisations (SMOs): A SM is a 'set of opinions and

beliefs in a population which represents preferences for changing some elements of the social structure and/or reward distribution of a society'. After Lowi, they see SMOs as an interest group. Cf. Wilkinson, Paul (1971), *Social Movement*, New York: Praeger

111. Robinson, Glenn (2004), p. 116, 'Hamas as Social Movement', in Wiktorowicz, Quintan, (ed) *Islamic Activism: A Social Movement Theory Approach*, Bloomington IND: Indiana University Press; Cf. Oliver, Pamela & Johnston, Hank (2000), 'What a Good Idea! Frames and ideologies in Social Movement Research', *Mobilization: An International Quarterly*, vol. 5, no. 1, pp. 37–54, for critique of the opacity surrounding conceptualisations of ideology. Frames, they argue, are terms for the marketing and resonating of political ideas. But their shallowness misses the complexity of social construction within ideology.

112. Snow, David; Rochford, Burke; Worden, Steven & Benford, Robert (1986), p. 464, 'Frame Alignment Processes, Micromobilization, and Movement Participation', *American Sociological Review*, vol. 51, no. 4, pp. 464–481,

113. Snow (1986), op. cit., pp. 467–476. Four processes of alignment have been theorised. Frame bridging joins two SMOs within the same movement or loosely associated individuals with common grievances. Amplification clarifies an issue or event, the meaning of which might be obscured by other actors or ambiguity. Extension sees movements expand their membership base by aligning their aims with the values of the would-be member. And transformation fundamentally alters or redefines how issues or events are understood, shifting them into a different framework of interpretation.

114. This analysis is favoured by Snow, Benford and Gamson. For a critical overview, see Fisher, Kimberly (1997), 'Locating Frames in the Discursive Universe', *Sociological Research Online*, vol. 2, no. 3, http://www.socresonline.org.uk/socresonline/2/3/4.html, accessed 02 Jul 2009; For a critical assessment of the literature see Benford, Robert (Nov. 1997), 'An Insider's Critique of the Social Movement Framing Perspective', *Sociological Inquiry*, vol. 67, no. 4, pp. 409–430.

115. Poulson, Stephen (2005), p. 13–15, *Social Movements in Twentieth-Century Iran*, Lanham MD: Lexington. Poulson argues that Iran's master frame is Iranian sovereignty that subsumes both national sovereignty and individual sovereignty frames. The former is shaped in opposition to historic British, US and Russian imperialism and expansionism; the latter tells individuals how leaders expect them to perform if they are to participate in governance. This might entail demonstrating appropriate responses to feelings of national sovereignty. He suggests current Iranian reformers are constrained by narrative frames negotiated during the Iranian Revolution. So piety, gender, age, ethnicity are used by religious leaders in the Guardian Council (electoral supervisors) to exclude potential candidates for office according to its *own* individual sovereignty frame. Opposition groups contest this and use it to reject the legitimacy of the Guardians' frame. He equates their struggle to that for 'free will' and sovereignty in seventeenth-century Europe.

116. Conversely some scholars attribute the existence of frames to individual cognition not inter-party negotiation. So rather than subject to an iterative, malleable process, they are rooted within the individual, providing 'environments' into which fresh information can be inserted. For a social psychology analysis see Moscovici, Serge (1984), 'The Phenomenon of Social Representations', in Farr, Robert &

Moscovici, Serge (eds), *Social Representations*, London: Cambridge University Press; For a linguistic appreciation see van Dijk, Teun (1977), *Text and Context Explorations in the Semantics and Pragmatics of Discourse*, London: Longman; (1980), *Macrostructures: An Interdisciplinary Study of Global Structures in Discourse, Interaction and Cognition*, Hillsdale NJ: Lawrence Erlbaum.

117. Benford, op. cit., pp. 615–617.

118. Ibid., p. 619; cf. Zuo, Jiping & Benford, Robert (June 2008), 'Mobilization Processes and the 1989 Chinese Democracy Movement', *Sociological Quarterly*, vol. 36, no. 1, pp. 131–156. Zuo argues during the 1989 Chinese Democracy Movement, student protesters used collective action frames which resonated with the public's own experience as well as traditional cultural narratives contained within Confucianism, nationalism and communism. The state's counter-strategies and frames failed to arrest the spread of student participation.

119. Fisher, Walter (1998), p. 265, 'Narration as a Human Communication Paradigm: The Case of Public Moral Argument', in Lucaites, John Louis; Condit, Celeste Michelle & Caudill, Sally (eds) (1999), *Contemporary Rhetorical Theory*, New York: Guilford Press.

120. Swidler, Ann (Apr 1986), p. 277, '*Culture in Action: Symbols and Strategies'*, vol. 51, no. 2, pp. 273–286. Cf. Bourdieu, Pierre on *habitus*: 'a system of lasting, transposable dispositions which, integrating past experiences, functions at every moment as a *matrix of perceptions, appreciations, and actions* and makes possible the achievement of infinitely diversified tasks, thanks to analogical transfers of schemes permitting the solution of similarly shaped problems…'(sic) (Ibid.).

121. Endsly, Mica & Garland, Daniel (eds) (2000), *Situational Awareness: Analysis and Measurement*, Mahwah NJ: Lawrence Erlbaum.

122. Gamson, William (1992), p. 32, *Talking Politics*, Cambridge: Cambridge University Press. See McCarthy (1977), op. cit., for their resource mobilisation theory, critique of traditional grievance theory and how revolutionary leaders call upon and mobilise through grievance rhetoric.

123. Media significantly contribute to framing public discourse. A pervading characteristic of its 'metanarrative' is about 'the self-reforming nature of the system' after the removal of the few bad apples (Ibid., p. 35). The 2008–9 world banking crisis remains a salutary example. This is compounded by the 'story-based nature of its coverage, which highlights social movement actors and dramatic acts 'episodically, obscuring the broader issues underlying the collective action'. See Noakes, John & Johnston, Hank (2005), p. 19, 'Frames of Protest: A Road Map to a Perspective', in Johnston, Hank & Noakes, John, *Frames of Protest: Social Movements and Framing Perspectives*, Lanham, MD: Rowman & Littlefield.

124. Bureaucracies regularly adopt this strategy of 'passing the buck' in diverting responsibility and defusing dissent. Alinksy (1989), op. cit..

125. Gamson (1992), op. cit., p. 33.

126. RIRA split from IRA and Sinn Féin, and Sinn Féin expelled RIRA's 32 County Sovereignty Committee in 1997.

127. A third of the IRA's 294 comrades' fatalities were results of 'own goals'. McDonald (2008), p. 11.

128. Dingley, James (2001), p. 461, 'The Bombing of Omagh, 15 Aug. 1998: The

Bombers, Their Tactics, Strategy, and Purpose Behind the Incident', *Studies in Conflict & Terrorism*, vol. 24, pp. 451–465, citing ex-PIRA operative Eamon Collins.

129. Ibid., p. 462.

130. McDonald (2008), op. cit., p. 145, citing ex-IRA prisoner Anthony McIntyre (my italics).

131. Dingley, James & Kirk-Smith, Michael (2000), p. 119, 'How Could They Do It? The Bombing of Omagh, 1998', *Journal of Conflict Studies*, vol. 20, no. 1, pp. 105–126.

132. Ruane, Joseph & Todd, Jennifer (2007), 'Path Dependence in Settlement Processes: Explaining Settlement in Northern Ireland', *Political Studies*, vol. 55, pp. 44–458.

133. Tonge, Jonathan (2010), pp. 60–65, 'From VNSAs to Constitutional Politicians', in Mulaj, Kledja (ed.), *Violent Non-State Actors in World Politics*, London: Hurst. Tonge acknowledges various reasons for the IRA abandoning violence. He dismisses English's claim of ideological change (2003), op. cit. Tonge identifies the climb-down as a 'product of leadership compromise, in order to enter an elite-level consociational government' (p. 61). However he sees PIRA enjoying greater community support than the dissidents, but 'never an electoral mandate for their actions, if measured in terms of majority nationalist support for Sinn Féin' (p. 66).

134. Gamson, William (1990), p. 169, *The Strategy of Social Protest*, Belmont, CA; Wadsworth citing Paul Chilton.

5. TELEVISION MEMORY

1. Luhmann, Niklas (2000), p. 1, *The Reality of the Mass Media*, Cambridge: Polity.

2. Thompson, John (1995), p. 38, *The Media and Modernity*, Cambridge: Polity Press.

3. Orwell, George (1946), p. 1, *Politics and the English Language*, London: News of the World.

4. Cohen, Bernard (1963), *The Press, the Public, and Foreign Policy*, Boston: Little, Brown.

5. There were 66 million blogs worldwide in 2006: 175,000 created daily, BBC (2007), p. 13, *From Seesaw to Wagon Wheel: Safeguarding Impartiality in the 21st Century*, London: BBC Trust; the internet population reach is 1,581 million (http://www.internetworldstats.com/stats.htm accessed 16.03.2009); 1,180 million mobile phones were shipped globally in 2008, http://www.idc.com/getdoc.jsp?containerId=prUS 21659209, accessed 16 Mar 2009; YouTube videos viewed 2008: 5,600 million, Nielsen Video Census/*The Economist*, p. 65, 07 Feb 2009; Castells, Manuel (24 Oct 2008), 'Internet Beyond Myths', lecture, London School of Economics: global internet usage Aug 1995: 10 million; Aug 2008: 1.3 billion. Internet is second only as a social transformation to mobile telephony—1991: 16 million; Aug 2008: 3.6 billion, rendering 50% of the planet linked by wireless. Nevertheless patterns of penetration are uneven. They are largely dominated by urban populations, albeit in an ever-urbanising demographic trend. See UNFPA, 'State of World Population', 2007: urbanites formed 3.3 billion of 6.6 billion globally; 2030: estimated 5 billion (p. 90: indicators), http://www.unfpa.org/swp/2007/english/introduction.html.

6. Nimmo, Dan & Combs, James (1990), *Mediated Political Realities*, New York: Longman; For overview of social constructivism see Johnson-Cartee, Karen (2005), p. 4,

News Narratives and News Framing: Constructing Political Reality, Lanham: Rowan & Littlefield; Lippmann(1922), op. cit.; (1921), 'The World Outside and the Pictures in our Heads', in Schramm (1971), op. cit.; Gergen, Kenneth (1985), 'Social Constructionist Inquiry: Context and Implications', in Gergen, Kenneth & Davis, Keith. *The Social Construction of the Person*, New York: Springer.

7. Johnson-Cartee, op. cit., p. 14, citing Kraus, S.& Davis, D. (1976).

8. Rajagopal, Arvind (2000), p. 295, 'Mediating Modernity: Theorising Reception in a Non-Western Society', in Park, Myung-Jin & Curran, James, *De-Westernising Media Studies*, London: Routledge. He argues that in non-Western societies the hegemonising role of media in securing national unity is overplayed, drawing too readily on Marxist and liberal traditions. Instead 'society is not held together primarily through consensual values. The coercive and constraining power of social institutions, and the sedimented practices operating across these institutions, help reproduce society and are critical in this process'. Cf. Kit-wai Ma, Eric (2000), 'Rethinking Media Studies: the Case of China', in Park, op. cit., p. 21. See also for media reception in the Arab world Fandy, Mamoun (2007)*(Un)civil War of Words*, Westport: Praeger; Rugh, William (2004), *Arab Mass Media: Newspapers, Radio, and Television in Arab Politics*, Westport: Praeger; Lynch, Marc (2006), *Voices of the New Arab Public: Iraq, Al-Jazeera, and Middle East Politics Today*, New York: Columbia University Press.

9. Hesmondhalgh, David (2007), p. 47, *The Cultural Industries*, Los Angeles: Sage.

10. Thompson (1995), op. cit., p. 17 explores 4 types of power—economic, political, coercive and symbolic (table 1.1); Mann, Michael (1986), *The Sources of Social Power: A History of Power from the Beginning to AD 1760*, vol. 1, Cambridge: Cambridge University Press.

11. McLuhan, Marshall (1964), *Understanding Media*, London: Routledge & Kegan Paul.

12. Hall, Peter & Preston, Paschall (1988), p. 265, *The Carrier Wave: New Information Technology and the Geography of Innovation 1846–2003*, part 5, London: Unwin Hyman.

13. Brock, George (8 Apr 2009 & 23 Apr 2009): N Bolt interviews with former Managing Editor, *TheTimes*, London.

14. BBC (2007), op. cit., p. 12; Schiller, Dan (1986), 'Transformation of News in the US Information Market', in Golding Philip (ed.), *Communicating Politics*, Leicester: Leicester University Press.

15. Marx, Karl & Engels, Frederick (1965), *The German Ideology*, London: Lawrence & Wishart.

16. This is no binary schism: overlaps cross-inform each tendency. Further debates embrace *inter alia* power, identity formation, time and speed, texts, moments, technological determinism, rituals, structure/agency, and particularism/universalism.

17. Mosco, Vincent (1996), pp. 70–134, *The Political Economy of Communication: Rethinking and Renewal*, London: Sage. The political economy approach analyses mass consumption and mass media in tandem. Consumption becomes a '*structural* response to the economic crisis of overproduction and as a social response to the *political* crisis' (p. 74) arising from working class development in North America and Western Europe. The concomitant problem was to understand processes centred on families as consumers and audiences, not on institutional producers, the discipline's traditional arena. This tendency was exacerbated by the increased role of

the state throughout the twentieth Century in production, consumption and regulation of communications businesses. Although it should be noted that more recent deregulation of communications markets has moved communications closer to more classically understood models of evaluation. The literature fuels popular conceptions of audience as commodity, see Smythe, Dallas (1977), 'Communications: Blindspot of Western Marxism', *Canadian Journal of Political and Social Theory*, vol. 1 no. 3, pp. 1–27; For cultural imperialism see Schiller, Herbert (1993), 'Not Yet the Post-imperialist Era', in Roach, Colleen (ed.), *Communication and Culture in War and Peace*, Newbury Park CA: Sage; Nordenstreng, Kaarle & Schiller, Herbert (eds) (1993), *Beyond National Sovereignty: International Communication in the 1990s*, Norwood NJ: Ablex; For audience/market manipulation see Ewen, Stuart (1976), *'Captains of Consciousness*, New York: McGraw Hill; (1996), *PR! A Social History of Spin*, New York: Basic Books; Harding (2008), op. cit.; For ownership concentration see Herman (2002), op. cit.; Bagdikian, Ben (2004), *The New Media Monopoly*, Boston MA: Beacon Press; For proximity of corporate media to governmental power see Kellner, Douglas (1990), *Television and the Crisis of Democracy*, Boulder CO: Westview Press; McChesney, Robert(1993), *Telecommunications, Mass Media and Democracy: the Battle for the Control of US Broadcasting*, New York: Oxford University Press.

18. Garnham, Nicholas (2005), 'The Information Society Debate Revisited', in Curran, James (2005), op. cit., p. 288.

19. Bell, Daniel (1976), p. 127: 'what counts is not raw muscle, or energy, but information'. Cf. Webster, Frank (Dec 2005), 'Making Sense of the Information Age', *Information, Communication & Society*, vol. 8, no. 4, pp. 439–458.

20. Castells, Manuel (2004), p. 419, *The Power of Identity*, Oxford: Blackwell. 'At the dawn of the information age, a crisis of legitimacy is voiding of meaning and function the institutions of the industrial era. Bypassed by global networks of wealth, power and information, the modern nation-state has lost much of its sovereignty'.

21. Lyotard, Jean-François (1984), p. 9, *The Postmodern Condition: A Report on Knowledge*, Manchester: Manchester University Press; See Bell, op. cit., pp. lxi–lxiii. He defines data as 'sequences of events or statistics in *an ordered fashion*'; information 'has meaning—news, events, and data—when we can *establish a context* that shows relationships among these items and presents them as organised topics'; knowledge 'derives from verified theory'. See for his critique of Castells who, he says, conflates information and knowledge, and fails to differentiate between 'invention, innovation and diffusion'. For Bell there has been neither knowledge explosion nor revolution (p. xxiv).

22. Murdock, Graham & Golding, Peter (2005), p. 60, 'Culture, Communications and Political Economy', in Curran (2005), op. cit.. This reflects the critical political economy thesis which demarcates itself from mainstream economics. It is holistic, historical, focused on capitalist enterprise and public intervention, and addresses ethically justice, equity and public good. (p. 61)

23. Halliday, Fred (1999), p. 128, 'Manipulation and Limits: Media Coverage of the Gulf War 1990–1', in Allen, Tim & Seaton, Jean, *The Media of Conflict*, London: Zed Books, citing Paul Patton.

24. Aaronovitch, David (2009), *Voodoo Histories: The Role of the Conspiracy Theory in Shaping Modern History*, London: Jonathan Cape. Aaronovitch attributes these

'theories' or 'holes in understanding' to 'hysterias for men' increasingly propagated by web-based social network sites. See Showalter, Elaine (1997), *Hystories: Hysterical Epidemics and Modern Culture*, London: Picador for how mass communications generate mass hysteria in modern culture.

25. Herman (2002), op. cit.. This is achieved through five news filters: 1) scale and cost of media corporations restricts the possibility for new competition in the marketplace. Need for government deregulation and support for media giants invites an undue proximity of interests; 2) Uncontentious programming caters to the interests of advertisers keen to preserve equanimity in the consumer market. Advertisers target affluent, middle class consumers' spending power and seek to avoid controversy; 3) Most news is sourced from government and political elites. The latter are privileged in their access to media outlets and aided by the ease of service from journalists; 4) Governments and big business increasingly use 'flak' (critical response) to attack and correct 'misguided' media content; 5) a worldview dominates media that frames issues in terms of a capitalist-communist dichotomy. This is challenged by McNair, Brian (2006), p. xviii, *Cultural Chaos: Journalism, News and Power in a Globalised World*, London: Routledge. Cultural chaos means '(i)n the context of the globalised news culture, to talk about chaos is to argue that the journalistic environment, far from being an instrument or apparatus of social control by a dominant elite, has become more and more like the weather and the oceans in an age of global warming—turbulent, unpredictable, extreme'.

26. Herman (2002), op. cit., p. 1.

27. Rupert Murdoch (News Corporation), Richard Parson (AOL Time Warner), Michael Eisner (Disney), Sumner Redstone(Viacom), Reinhard Mohn (Bertelsmann). However for Schiller, Herbert (1992), *Mass Communications and American Empire*, Oxford: Westview Press, the global invasion and cultural imperialism by US media corporations began in the economic aftermath of World War II as its commercial firms took advantage of market and state weakness of states disadvantaged by the demands of war and reconstruction.

28. Bagdikian (2004), op. cit., p. 9. The highly controversial 1996 US Telecommunications Act is cited as a prime example. Cf. 'George Orwell Rolls in his Grave', http:// video.google.com/, accessed 21 May 2009. 2 June 2003 Federal Communications Commission Votes 3:2 in favour of loosening media ownership rules. See The Center for Public Integrity, 'Networks of Influence: The Political Power of the Communications Industry', accessed 21 May 2009: 'broadcast, cable and communications companies in the US spent more than $695 million to lobby the federal government from 1998 through 2003. Lobbying expenditures rose 7 percent over the five-year period'.

29. McChesney, Robert (2008), p. 19, *The Political Economy of Media: Enduring Issues, Emerging Dilemmas*, New York: Monthly Review Press.

30. Gitlin, Todd (2003), p. 255, *The Whole World is Watching: Mass Media in the Making and Unmaking of the New Left*, Berkeley: University of California Press.

31. Castells (2009), op. cit..

32. Ibid., pp. 50–3.

33. Jackson, Richard (2005), pp. 64–5, *Writing the War on Terrorism: Language, Politics and Counter-Terrorism*, Manchester & New York: Manchester University Press.

34. Ibid., p. 171.

35. Nacos, Brigitte (2002), p. 146, *Mass-mediated Terrorism*, Lanham MD: Roman & Littlefield

36. Ibid.

37. Gowans, Stephen (22 May 2002), 'Dan Rather's Change of Heart', *Media Monitors Network*, http://www.mediamonitors.net/gowans54.html accessed 13 May 2009. Gowans talks of US media giving the administration 'a free ride'. He speculates had Rather asked tough questions in the immediate aftermath of 9/11, it is doubtful he would have retained his job.

38. Jackson, op. cit., p. 171.

39. Doig, Tommy (June 2007), Fox News Baghdad bureau co-ordinator, interview with N. Bolt, Johannesburg. The Murdoch family holds 40 percent of voting shares and controlling executive positions in the global company News Corp.

40. It is still too early to evaluate to what degree the British press and media will emerge as a body ideologically independent of the executive following the expenses scandal of members of Parliament first publicised in May 2009 by the *Daily Telegraph*. Attempts throughout the media to distance themselves from this political elite and proclaim a 'soft revolution' on behalf of the electorate may not be correctly gauged for some time. What gives this discussion added poignancy within the UK is the globally publicised scandal affecting the media empire of Rupert Murdoch (particularly his *News of the World* newspaper which was forced to close) and its alleged complicity with senior police officers in the Metropolitan Police force, as well as its excessive proximity to British prime ministers and government officials throughout the 1990s and 2000s. At the time of writing, the newspaper's activities are the subject of parliamentary select committee hearings, juridical inquiry and police investigation focused particularly on illegal phone hacking activities. It is suggested other, competitive media outlets might also be implicated in similar corrupt practices.

41. Murdock (2005), op. cit. *Horizontal integration* consolidates sectoral control, offering savings of scale and resource. *Vertical integration* expands reach along the ownership chain of production, from investment to manufacture to distribution. *Diversification* extends ownership between sectors, such as Murdoch's News Corporation with interests in feature film studios, television, newspapers and web social network sites. *Internationalisation* combines integration and diversification through acquisition of regional firms, further extending global reach. Cf. Laughey, Dan (2007), *Key Themes in Media Theory*, Maidenhead: Open University Press/ McGraw-Hill, ch. 7, p. 134.

42. Said, Edward (1978, 2003), *Orientalism*, London: Penguin; Hall, Stuart (ed.) (1997), *Representation: Cultural Representations and Signifying Practices*, London: Sage/Open University; (1995), 'The Whites of their Eyes: Racist Ideologies and the Media', in Dines, G & Humez, JM (eds), *Gender, Race and Class in Media*, London: Sage. Thus race is portrayed by Western, white producers as 'exotic' (Aladdin and his magic lamp); 'dangerous' (Osama Bin Laden); 'humorous' (minstrel performers); 'pitied' (starving refugees in Sudan)': Laughey (2007), op. cit., p. 143, citing Alvarado (1987).

43. Auletta, Ken (1997), p. xiv, *The Highwaymen: Warriors of the Information Superhighway*, New York: Random House.

44. McChesney, Robert (1997), 'The Mythology of Commercial Broadcasting and the Contemporary Crisis of Public Broadcasting', Spry Memorial Lecture. He argues 'So

it was in 1994 that Rupert Murdoch's News Corporation discontinued carrying the BBC World Service television channel in Asia because the Chinese leadership let it be known that doing so would undermine Murdoch's chance at the lucrative Chinese market. And when Disney purchased ESPN in 1995, Disney CEO Michael Eisner acknowledged that ESPN's appeal was that it never antagonised political powers in any nation'.

45. Herman, Edward & McChesney, Robert (1997), p. 189, *The Global Media: The New Missionaries of Corporate Capitalism*, London: Continuum. Bagdikian, op. cit., p. 3, highlights 5 dominant conglomerates: Time Warner, Walt Disney Company, News Corporation, Viacom and Bertelsmann. Note recurring themes in titles: McChesney (1997), *Corporate Media and the Threat to Democracy;* Mazzocco (1994), *Networks of Power: Corporate Television's Threat to Democracy*; Cohen (2005), *'News Incorporated: Corporate Media Ownership and Its Threat to Democracy'*.

46. Post-1980s no Western European state has a television market free of advertising. Cf. Winston, Brian (2005), p. 366, *Messages: Free Expression, Media and the West from Gutenberg to Google*, Abingdon: Routledge.

47. McChesney (2008), op. cit., p. 12.

48. Organisational epistemology is too extensive to reflect. I merely suggest hierarchical processes not be taken at face-value, requiring sensitive inquiry.

49. Schoenberger, Erica (1997), *The Cultural Crisis of the Firm*, Cambridge, MA: Blackwell. For an analysis of senior managements' strategic view of the world and creating corporate self-identity internalised in processes of production and social relations. She analyses how this failed to anticipate the demise of Fordism-Keynesianism and replacement of supply-side just-in-case delivery by demand-driven just-in-time. Schoenberger draws on Kuhn, Thomas (1970), *The Structure of Scientific Revolutions*, Chicago: Chicago University Press. For more on the use of paradigm shifts also see Harvey, David (1990), *The Condition of Postmodernity*, Cambridge, MA: Blackwell for his model of time-space compression.

50. Cohen, Michael; March, James & Olsen, Johan (Mar 1972), p. 1, 'A Garbage Can Model of Organisational Choice', *Administrative Science Quarterly*, vol. 17, no. 1, pp. 1–25. Cf. Starbuck, William (Feb 1983), 'Organisations as Action Generators', *American Sociological Review*, vol. 48, pp. 91–102.

51. DiMaggio, Paul & Powell, Walter (Apr 1983), p. 147, 'The Iron Cage Revisited: Institutional Isomorphism and Collective Rationality in Organisational Fields', *American Sociological Review*, vol. 48, no. 2, pp. 147–160. The authors argue the driving force of Weberian hierarchical organisation is the capitalist market economy where demands of operating business require administration be discharged 'precisely, unambiguously, continuously, and with as much speed as possible'. However trends toward isomorphism continue.

52. Hall (1980), op. cit., p. 65, citing Westergaard.

53. Wertham, Frederic (1954), *Seduction of the Innocent*, London: Museum Press, for early psychological tests on children. These have been largely challenged: see Gunter, Barrie & McAleer, Jill (1997), *Children and Television*, London: Routledge who note the positive benefits and condemn any over-use of media consumption as inevitably detrimental.

54. (11 Apr 2009), p. 66, 'The Not-So-Big Four', *The Economist*, reports in Q4/2008

average television-viewing per American hit a record 151 hours per month. Even in non-Western audiences viewing-response is striking. See BBC television (24 Apr 2009), Newsnight, Johann Hari reviewing the documentary 'Afghan Star' on diverse Afghan responses to Afghanistan's 'Pop Idol/X Factor'-style television talent show. 11 million people, one third of the population, avidly watched the final programme. Later, one of the female finalists feared for her life after dancing and singing contrary to custom. Cf. Fandy, Mamoun (2007) *(Un)Civil War of Words: Media and Politics in the Arab World*, Westport Conn: Praeger. The Arab television market numbers approximately 300million viewers, serviced by 700 satellite stations.

55. For cultivation theory see: Gerbner, G, Gross, L, Morgan, M & Signorelli, N (1986), 'Living with Television: The Dynamics of the Cultivation Process', in Bryant, Jennings & Zillmann, Dolf (eds), *Perspectives on Media Effects*, Hillsdale, NJ: Lawrence Erlbaum; Gerbner, G, Gross, L, Morgan, M & Signorelli, N(1980), 'The Mainstreaming of America: Violence Profile no. 11', *Journal of Communication*, vol. 30, no. 3, pp. 10–29; Barker, Martin & Petley, Julian (eds) (2001), *Ill Effects: The Media/Violence Debate*, London: Routledge.

56. Lazarsfeld, Paul & Merton, Robert (2004), 'Mass Communication, Popular Taste, and Organised Social Action', in *The Communication of Ideas*, Peters, John & Simonson, Peter (eds), *Mass Communication and American Social Thought: Key Texts, 1919–1968*, Lanham, MD: Rowman & Littlefield.

57. Katz, Elihu & Lazarsfeld, Paul (2006), *Personal Influence: The Part Played by People in the Flow of Mass Communications*, London: Eurospan.

58. Hebdige, Dick (1979), *Subculture: The Meaning of Style*, London: Methuen. His theory of subculture proposes that groups create their own internal cohesion and identity, producing language and symbols that marry with their values and experiences. It draws on structuralist precepts advanced by Willis, Paul (1978), *Profane Culture*, London: Routledge (homology) and Lévi-Strauss, Claude (1966), *The Savage Mind*, Chicago: University of Chicago Press *(bricolage)*.

59. For Klapper's phenomenistic approach: Klapper, Joseph (1966), *The Effects of Mass Communication*, New York: Free Press.

60. Katz, Elihu; Blumler, Jay; Gurevitch, Michael (1974), 'Utilisation of Mass Communication by the Individual', in Blumler, Jay & Katz, Elihu (eds), *The Uses of Mass Communications: Current Perspectives on Gratifications Research*, London: Sage.

61. Laughey, op. cit., p. 75.

62. Hall, Stuart (1978), p. 35, *The "Structured Communication" of Events*, University of Birmingham/UNESCO; Mosco, Vincent (1996), op. cit., p. 252; Ang, Ien (1990), 'Culture and Communication: Towards an Ethnographic Critique of Media Consumption in the Transnational Media System', *European Journal of Communication*, vol. 5, pp. 239–260.

63. Foucault, Michel (1972), *The Archaeology of Knowledge*, London: Tavistock.

64. Foucault, Michel (1995), *Discipline and Punish: The Birth of the Prison*, New York: Vintage.

65. Marcuse, Herbert (1991), p. 12, *One-Dimensional Man*, London: Routledge. Communications, consumer commodities and the output of entertainment and information industry contain 'prescribed attitudes and habits…which bind the consumers more or less pleasantly to the producers and, through the latter, to the whole'. It leads to 'happy consciousness', a false consciousness which promotes one-dimen-

sional thought and behaviour. '(I)ndoctrination...ceases to be publicity; it becomes a way of life'. See Lefebvre, Henri (1999), *Everyday Life in the Modern World*, New Brunswick US: Transaction Publishers, particularly pp. 143–193, 'Terrorism and Everyday Life'.

66. Gramsci, Antonio (1991), Buttigieg, Joseph (ed.), *Prison Notebooks*, New York & Oxford: Columbia University Press. Cf. p. 75, Sixth Notebook, no. 88, 'Gendarme Or Night-Watchman State': 'state = political society + civil society, that is, hegemony protected by the armour of coercion'.

67. Brock, op. cit., argues 'the enormous scale and scope of media should not be confused with their increased influence'. Stothard, Peter (Editor of *The Times* 1992–2002) interview with N Bolt 21 Apr 2009, emphasises that people draw on other inputs from outside the media to inform their worldview.

68. Sampson, Anthony (09 Dec 2009), 'Observing David Astor', *The Observer*, http://www.guardian.co.uk/theobserver/2001/dec/09/featuresreview.review2, accessed 29 Apr 2009.

69. 'Reclaim the Kop' campaign: http://www.bebo.com/Profile.jsp?MemberId=3555744631, accessed 29 Apr 2009.

70. McLuhan, op. cit., p. 337. Perhaps for the first time John F Kennedy's funeral 'manifested the power of television to involve an entire population in a ritual process'. The 'cool medium' of television creates, a 'tactual ...depth experience' which changes the behaviour of normally passive detached viewers.

71. Brock, op. cit..

72. 31 Aug 1997 statement from his Sedgefield constituency.

73. 'Operation Paget Inquiry Report into the Allegation of Conspiracy to Murder', Metropolitan Police, http://i.thisislondon.co.uk/i/pix/downloads/OperationPagetFullReport.pdf, accessed 29 Apr 2009.

74. Ibid.; Thompson, op. cit..

75. Weinstein (2007), op. cit., p. 133 discusses the effects of varying hierarchical control between insurgent groups.

76. O'Neil, Mathieu (2009), *Cyberchiefs: Autonomy and Authority in Online Tribes*, London: Pluto Press.

77. Stothard, op. cit..

78. Ibid.

79. Brock, op. cit..

80. Stothard, op. cit..

81. Hewitt, Gavin BBC Television News, Europe Editor, interview with N. Bolt 08 Apr 2009. Hewitt describes a relatively insignificant incident witnessed by a young GMTV reporter in Iraq. An Iraqi civilian knifed an Iraqi soldier. This created a maelstrom which shaped British coverage for 24 hours as the footage was constantly replayed on television. *The Daily Mirror* then led on the story since it played into the culture of the paper and its previous interpretation of events in Iraq. The point is each organisation wants to stamp its own unique perspective on an event. In the process it reinforces the common understanding, turning a minor incident into a true event. Consequently it became important even though knife crime was the least of Iraq's worries. Competition should not be underestimated as a force for driving reporters to the hegemonic centre.

82. Ibid.

83. Jones, Glynn (Apr 2009), Executive Producer, Current Affairs Documentaries, BBC Television, interview with N Bolt.

84. Brock, op. cit..

85. Hall, Stuart (1980), p. 55, *Policing the Crisis: Mugging, the State and Law and Order*, London & Basingstoke: Macmillan, citing Murdock. Repeated use of news frameworks reinforces consensual understandings: '(f)irstly, it recharges and extends the definitions and images in question and keeps them circulating as part of the common stock of taken-for-granted knowledge...Secondly, it "conveys an impression of eternal recurrence, of society as a social order which is made up of movement, but not innovation"'.

86. Stothard, op. cit..

87. Brock, op. cit..

88. Hall (1980), op. cit., p. 55. Hall highlights the process of signification, giving meaning to events, which '*both assumes and helps to construct society as a "consensus"*' (sic). We share 'maps of meaning'. But Hall argues that recently this has been raised to a new ideological level.

89. Brock, op. cit.; Colombani, Jean-Marie (12 Sept 2001), 'We Are All Americans', *World Press Review* online, vol. 48, no. 11, http://www.worldpress.org/1101we_are_all_americans.htm, accessed 20 Apr 2009.

90. Jones, op. cit..

91. Hewitt, op. cit..

92. Decision-making and routinisation of professional codes undermine the prized notion of journalistic objectivity. Gans, Herbert (1979), *Deciding What's News*, New York: Pantheon; Fishman, Mark (1980), *Manufacturing the News*, Austin: University of Texas Press. This seems to contradict my point, but the two are not mutually exclusive.

93. Gitlin (2003), op. cit., ch. 10; Tuchman, Gaye (1972), 'Objectivity as Strategic Ritual: an Examination of Newsmen's Notions of Objectivity', *American Journal of Sociology*, vol. 77, no. 1, pp. 660–679; Tuchman, Gaye (1978), 'Making News by Doing Work: Routinising the Unexpected', *American Journal of Sociology*, vol. 79, no. 1, pp. 110–131.

94. See Alexander, Jeffrey & Jacobs, Ronald (1998), 'Mass Communication, Ritual and Civil Society', in Liebes T & Curran, James (eds), *Media Ritual and Identity*, London: Routledge. They build on Dayan and Katz's theory of media events. My point on the nature of media events is different. Alexander argues 'the narrative elaboration of events and crises—understood as social dramas—is crucial for providing a sense of historical continuity in the crisis-bound, episodic constructions of universalistic solidarity that continually form and reform civil society' (p. 23). Here events are crises woven into the fabric of life. POTD events and spectaculars do not aim to be integrated into the media narrative but stand out and interrupt it. Spectaculars would sever the narrative permanently. See Couldry Nick (2006), pp. 177–194, 'Transvaluing Media Studies', in Curran, James & Morley, David (eds), *Media and Cultural Theory*, London: Routledge, for a critique of this position as over-functionalist and totalising. He cites Michael Schudson's assessment: '(The media's) capacity to publicly include is perhaps their most important feature. (The fact that we each read the same paper as elites) is empowering...the impression it promotes of

equality and commonality, illusion though it is, sustains a hope of democratic life' (*sic*) (p. 181).

95. Virilio, Paul (2005), pp. 111–112, *The Information Bomb*, London: Verso. Resulting from digital convergence the world is on course for an 'image crash'. He argues: 'the competition between icons is currently on the agenda and the competition, in assuming worldwide proportions, is, like everything else in the era of the great planetary market-place, destabilising for the regime of temporality of the whole of iconic information'.

96. Kellner, Douglas (2003), p. 11, *Media Spectacle*, London: Routledge. This should not be confused with Kellner's 'megaspectacles'. These are manifestations of a heightened media culture. They cut across sports, news, entertainment as 'heavily dramatised presentations'. So the race for the White House 2000, is subsumed alongside the Clinton sex scandals, OJ Simpson trial, and 9/11 attack (p. vii). There is an inherent danger in this conflation. I argue most of these constitute events in the media landscape. Kellner defines the OJ Simpson case variously as television spectacle, internet spectacle, race spectacle, multicultural spectacle, Los Angeles spectacle, class spectacle, commodity spectacle, celebrity spectacle, commercial media spectacle, media-mediated spectacle (pp. 97–100). His megaspectacles fall into two categories: 'regularly scheduled'—the Oscars, Super Bowl—and 'other mega-events and media extravaganzas, such as the Gulf War, the OJ Simpson trial, the Clinton sex scandals, or the September 11 terrorist attacks, that come to dominate the media and define an entire era, of politics and culture' (p. 119–120 endnote). See Best, Steve & Kellner, Douglas (2001), *The Postmodern Adventure*, London Routledge. But these are surely dimensions of what I have called extraordinary events. Other than 9/11, they are arresting, attention-grabbing, but not spectacle in the sense of existential moral crisis.

97. Peter Weir's 1998 Hollywood feature film *The Truman Show* echoes this idea. Truman Burbank, the protagonist (played by Jim Carey), has lived since birth within a reality show shot on a studio movie lot. He is unaware that his life is a complete fiction and that he is a television character. His accompanying cast and television audience however are complicit in the lie. One day he uncovers the conceit. He tears a gash through the cyclorama wall of the world's biggest studio (his own fictional world) onto which blue skies, sunrises and sunsets have been continuously projected. The rupture generates an irreversible, cataclysmic break in the suspension of disbelief. Chaos reigns. A new life begins. See Bishop, Ronald (Jan 2000), 'Good Afternoon, Good Evening, and Good Night: The Truman Show as Media Criticism', *Journal Of Communication Inquiry*, vol. 24, no. 1, pp. 6–18.

98. For a discussion on how media impacts audiences' recall of events: Shapiro, Michael & Fox, Julia(Jan. 2002), 'The Role of Typical and Atypical Events in Story Memory', *Human Communication Research*, vol. 28, no. 1, pp. 109–135.

99. Barthes (2000), op. cit..

100. Giduck, John (19 May 2009), lecture, King's College London, offers an alternative four-part typology: (i) 'Decimation Assaults' e.g. suicide-bombings; (ii) 'Mass Hostage' e.g. Beslan siege; (iii) 'Hybrids' e.g. '9/11'; (iv) 'Symphonic Attacks' e.g. Mumbai 11/2008. All media interest in terrorist events, he argues, is governed by time or duration of assault, and numbers of victims threatened or killed. Mumbai is new but not unforeseen. The problem with (i) is that 'shoot and scoot' tactics

offer media insufficient time on camera, whereas (ii) Beslan 3–4 days and (iv) Mumbai 3 days increase the attention potential.

101. Baudrillard (2003), op. cit., p. 74, 'Hypotheses on Terrorism': 'What constitutes an event is that for which there is no equivalent'. Baudrillard moves liberally between the terms 'event' and 'spectacle'. But he notes: 'We try retrospectively to impose some kind of meaning on it, to find some kind of interpretation. But there is none. And it is the radicality of the spectacle, which alone is original and irreducible'(p. 30). Baudrillard's simulacrum resembles my description of spectacular.

102. Baudrillard (2007), p. 121, *In the Shadow of the Silent Majority*, Los Angeles CA: Semiotext(e).

103. Wark, McKenzie (2006), p. 265, 'The Weird Global Media Event and the Tactical Intellectual (version 3.0)', in Chun, Wendy Hui Kyong & Keenan, Thomas (eds), *New Media, Old Media*, New York: Routledge, ch. 18. Wark defines this form of exceptional, momentary threat as a 'weird global media event'. It is characterised by interruptions of routine time. However I argue that routine time has continuity and harmony, but also nuance and depth. Time is not merely binary, ordinary or extraordinary. Yet Wark is defining what I call spectacular: 'The event opens a critical window onto the disjuncture between different kinds of time precisely because it is the moment when times suddenly connect, even if, in connecting, the usual means of making sense of time within the horizon of a specific temporal narrative is obliterated'. This then is a new 'quality of time' (p. 266).

104. I extend Cohen's notion of 'moral panic' beyond its benchmark between social groups. I emphasise the event for its incoherence and momentary unintelligibility. This should not exclude directing the crisis at an internal or external 'enemy'. Cohen, Stanley (2002), p. 9, *Folk Devils and Moral Panics*, London: Routledge For Cohen societies encounter periods of panic. And this extreme reaction is captured by mass media: 'A condition, episode, person or group of persons emerges to become defined as a threat to societal values and interests; its nature is presented in a stylised and stereotypical fashion by the mass media'. Cohen's study of 1960s' mods and rockers informs contemporary portrayals of Muslims and Islamic fundamentalists. However we might argue that panic may supersede the short-term, and become irrevocably part of the way we see life and the world. Thus it transforms an historic worldview. Cf. Erikson, Kai (1966), *Wayward Puritans: A Study in the Sociology of Deviance*, New York: John Wiley. Cohen develops Erikson's concept of 'boundary crisis'. Erikson proposes that periodically a group's uncertainty about itself may be resolved by targeting expressions of behaviour from group members that have been apparent, but not deemed especially threatening hitherto. The response is stereotypical and ritualised. Mass media plays its part: 'a considerable portion of what we call "news" is devoted to reports about deviant behaviour and its consequences' (Cohen 2002, p. 17); cf. Lemert, Edwin (1967), *Human Deviance, Social Problems and Social Control*, Englewood Cliffs NJ: Prentice-Hall; (1951), *Social Pathology: A Systematic Approach to the Study of Sociopathic Behaviour*, New York: McGraw-Hill for theories of primary and secondary deviance.

105. A break in transmission where sound and/or vision disappear.

106. Ulrich Beck suggests this moment signifies the 'silence of language' and the 'com-

plete collapse of language...ever since that moment, we've been living and think-ing and acting using concepts that are incapable of grasping what happened': Furedi, Frank (2007), p. 78, *Invitation to Terror*, London: Continuum. Furedi develops this: 'Other commentators believe that these difficulties are due to the emergence of a radically new and complex global environment, whose features cannot be captured through the language of the twentieth century. They have inter-nalised the narrative of the unknown and the unimaginable and suppose that we simply lack a language with which to represent the incomprehensible character of the threat of global terrorism'.

107. Jones (2009), op. cit..

108. See Badiou, Alain (2005), p. 208, *'Being and Event'*, London: Continuum: 'Every time that a site is the theatre of a real event, the state—in the political sense, for example—recognises that a designation must be found for the couple of the site (the factory, the street, the university) and the singleton of the event (strike, riot, disorder), but it cannot succeed in fixing the rationality of the link. This is why it is a law of the state to detect in the anomaly of this Two—and this is an avowal of the dysfunction of the count—the *hand of a stranger* (the foreign agitator, the ter-rorist, the perverse professor). It is not important whether the agents of the state believe in what they say or not, what counts is the necessity of the statement. For this metaphor is in reality that of the void itself: something unrepresented is *at work*—this is what the state is declaring, in the end, in its designation of an exter-nal cause. The state blocks the apparition of the immanence of the void by the transcendence of the guilty'.

109. Arendt, Hannah (1990), p. 57, *On Revolution*, London: Penguin.

110. http://www.atomicarchive.com/Movies/Movie8.shtml, accessed 28 Apr 2009. I am reminded by Andrea Berger that when Oppenheimer confided to Harry Truman at his first meeting following the Nagasaki tragedy—'Mr President, I feel I have blood on my hands'—Truman called him a 'cry-baby scientist'.

111. Winnaker, Rudolph (Spring 1947), p. 25, 'The Debate about Hiroshima', *Military Affairs*, vol. 11, no. 1, pp. 25–30.

112. The systematic attempt to produce a message beyond the instrumental was clear. US aerial leafleting of the city in Aug 1945 declared 'your city has been listed for destruction by our powerful air force. The bombing will begin in 72 hours. We give the military clique this notification because we know there is nothing they can do to stop our overwhelming power and our iron determination. We want you to see how powerless the military is to protect you. Systematic destruction of city after city will continue as long as you blindly follow your military leaders'. Cf. Chali-and, Gerard & Blin, Arnaud (2007), p. 15, *The History of Terrorism: From Antiq-uity to Al Qaeda*, University of California Press: 'these were acts of violence, committed in the service of political ends, with the intent of spreading fear among the entire Japanese population'.

113. Mitchell, Greg (04 Aug 2005), 'Hiroshima Cover-Up Exposed', *AlterNet*, http://www.alternet.org/mediaculture/23914/, accessed 22 Apr 2009. According to *Edi-tor and Publisher Magazine* the long-hidden footage of the bombing from a Japa-nese cameraman was first aired in 1970 on American television. The first US military colour film was partly aired in the 1980s but much of the 90,000 feet of rushes remains unseen. According to Lt Col (Ret) Daniel McGovern, director of

US military film-makers 1945–6, Japanese footage shot in the aftermath was confiscated and all images were censored. He says: 'I was told by people in the Pentagon that they didn't want those [film] images out because they showed effects on man, woman and child...They didn't want the general public to know what their weapons had done—at a time they were planning on more bomb tests. We didn't want the material out because ... we were sorry for our sins'.

114. Winnaker, op. cit..

115. Furedi (2007), op. cit., p. 3, Furedi notes that 76 percent of West Europeans and 90 percent of Middle Easterners and Latin Americans polled saw 9/11 as an historical turning-point. Yet he argues '(t)he day after a serious disaster is often regarded as the beginning of a new era'.

116. Alluni, Taysir (21 Oct 2001), interview for Al-Jazeera with Osama Bin Laden in Lawrence, Bruce (ed.) (2005), p. 112, *Messages to the World: The Statements of Osama Bin Laden*, London: Verso.

117. Bin Laden's sermon 'Among A Band of Knights' in Lawrence (2005), op. cit., p. 194. This is strikingly reminiscent of Western philosophers' assessments of a hegemony that would characterise the decades from the 1980s: 'The situation was actually quite paradoxical. On one hand, dominating public opinion, one had "democracy"—in its entirely corrupt representative and electoral form—and "freedom" reduced to the freedom to trade and consume. These constituted the abstract universality of our epoch'. See also Badiou (2005), op. cit., p. xi.

118. Kuhn (1970), op. cit..

119. Virilio, Paul (2006), p. 78, *Speed and Politics*, Los Angeles CA: Semiotext(e). See for his analysis of dromology. Acceleration means that implosion replaces explosion as the defining feature of the electronic world. McLuhan (1964), op. cit.; Genosko, Gary (1999), p. 3, *McLuhan and Baudrillard: The Masters of Implosion*, London: Routledge.

120. Doob (1949), op. cit.; (1950), op. cit..

121. Virilio (2006), op. cit., p. 31.

122. (2005), p. 141(italics sic).

123. Dahlgren, Peter & Gurevitch, Michael (2005), p. 387, 'Political Communication in a Changing World', in Curran, James & Gurevitch, Michael (eds), *Mass Media and Society*, London: Hodder Arnold. In journalism, the dominant form of political communication, popularisation, eases and expands entry to the public sphere. Equally it brings the private into the public reinforcing civic awareness and activism. Yet it also 'reflects commodification, and in practice means sensationalism, scandal, personification and excessive dramatisation, derailing *civic-oriented news values*'.

124. Many television landmark moments were self-referential celebrations of technological progress. Witness the transmission of images of Neil Armstrong's first moonwalk. Securing a LIVE signal from the moon into people's homes was as momentous as man stepping onto another planet.

125. FIFA football World Cup tournaments are said to bring the 'football family' together. Sports matches and competitions demand the highest prices for LIVE transmission in the rights-buying marketplace; recorded or highlights come a poor second.

126. The effect of slowing human action to 300 frames per second (10 times slower than

real life transmission) is to present the viewer with the equivalent of 300 still frames conjoined. Nowhere else is such unfolding of human experience matched. Conventions of slow-motion have become accepted in film-making, often depicting moments of high drama or tension. By analogy I attach this hollowing out of the moment to insurgent spectaculars.

127. Ch. 2: contiguous present tenses in *Citizen Kane*.

128. The emergence of Reality Television formats does not denote a CCTV surveillance culture, but a desire by networks to heighten the ordinary to the level of the extraordinary, ie to create events from the mundane. This is the anthropologist's dilemma of 'observer participation' or television producer's 'fly-on-the-wall' filming technique. Awareness of an outside observer changes participant behaviour.

129. Deleuze, Gilles (2008), p. 66, *Cinema 2: The Time-Image*, London: Continuum.

130. (2004), op. cit., p. 7, Nye might deny this application of 'soft power'.

131. (1972), *Low Intensity Operations: Subversion, Insurgency, Peace-keeping*, London: Faber & Faber.

132. Nelson, Harold (1988), pp. 24–5, *Leon Trotsky and the Art of Insurrection*, London: Frank Cass.

133. Ibid., p. 9.

134. Ibid., pp. 3–4.

135. Ibid., p. 278.

136. Tilly, Charles (1978), *From Mobilization to Revolution*, Reading: Addison-Wesley.

137. Windsor, Philip (2002), p. 152, *Strategic Thinking*, London: IISS Studies in International Security.

138. The American Revolution did not so much overthrow the local state as a distant colonial power thus did not experience the same degree of social transformation.

139. (2009), op. cit., p. 300.

140. Bolt (2010), op. cit..

6. WHERE THE IMAGINARY MEETS THE VIRTUAL

1. Turner, Janice (17 July 2010), p. 21, 'We'll soon forget the ballad of Raoul Moat', *The Times*.

2. General Sir David Richards (18 Jan 2010), *Future Conflict and its Prevention: People and the Information Age*, London: IISS speech, referencing Liddell Hart's transition from cavalry to mechanised tank warfare.

3. Ibid.

4. Arquilla, John & Ronfeldt, David (2001), *Networks and Netwars*, Santa Monica, CA: RAND.

5. Richards references the Information Age without adopting the full implications of Fourth Generation Warfare where manpower, firepower and manœuvre are considered predominant paradigms of earlier generations. Information Warfare is itself a broad category, depending on which level it appears, strategic, operational, or tactical.

6. Asia Foundation (2009), pp. 137–145, 'Afghanistan in 2009', http://asiafoundation. org/publications/pdf/627, reports dramatic increase in SMS text messaging as an information source while 1 in 2 Afghans can access a mobile phone. Of urban resi-

dents 81% have mobile phones, 80% have access to television, 77% own a radio, 18% own a computer. Of rural households 44% have mobile phones, 30% can access television, 81% own a functioning radio, 3% own a computer. However 18% in urban, 66% in rural areas say they never watch television. http://www.itu.int/ITU-D/ict/statistics/ict/index.html, accessed 26 Jan 2010.

7. Von Clausewitz (2008), op. cit., p. 68.
8. Coase, Ronald (Nov. 1937), 'The Nature of the Firm', *Economica*, New Series, vol. 4, no. 16, pp. 386–405.
9. Shirky, Clay (2008), p. 47, *Here Comes Everybody: How Change Happens When People Come Together*, London: Penguin.
10. Starr (2004), op. cit., p. 4 (my italics).
11. Op. cit., p. 160.
12. Graham, Gordon (1999), p. 37, *The Internet: a Philosophical Inquiry*, London: Routledge.
13. Asia Foundation (2009), op. cit..
14. Mobile telephony use is sometimes at its highest per head in traditional communities like Somalia and Bangladesh. 7 million Somalis communicate with a 1–3 million diaspora. Winter, Joseph (19 Nov. 2004), 'Telecoms Thriving in Lawless Somalia', *BBC News* online, http://news.bbc.co.uk/1/hi/world/africa/4020259.stm; (03 Nov. 2009), 'Somali Telecoms Thrive Despite Chaos', *Reuters*, http://af.reuters.com/article/investingNews/idAFJOE5A20DB20091103, accessed 10 July 2010. By contrast Human Rights Watch appealed to the Obama administration for an expansion of cellphone network infrastructure in the Democratic Republic of Congo to combat massacres such as the killing of over 300 people in Makombo (Dec 2009) and a further 96 (Jan-Apr 2010) carried out by the Lord's Resistance Army (LRA). Human Rights Watch (21 May 2010), 'DR Congo: New Round of LRA Killing Campaign', http://www.hrw.org/en/news/2010/05/20/dr-congo-new-round-lra-killing-campaign, accessed 26/09/2010.
15. (13 Feb 2010) p. 71, 'Saturated Mobile Networks: Breaking Up', *The Economist*: the advantage of smart phones is their ability to link laptops to mobile networks. Bernstein Research records (end 2008) 189 million mobile-broadband connections and average monthly data-traffic of 175 megabytes, but (end 2009) 312 million averaging 273 megabytes. Network equipment manufacturer Cisco forecasts mobile-data to grow by 3,900 percent by 2015.
16. Zheng, Pei & Ni, Lionel (2006), *Smart Phone and Next Generation Mobile Computing*, San Francisco CA: Morgan Kaufmann.
17. Urry, John (2007), p. 174, *Mobilities*, Cambridge: Polity.
18. Japan's Mixi social network site has 18 million members most of whom favour the cellphone as the device-of-choice for accessing friends compared with a PC: (30 Jan 2010), p. 20, 'Special Report on Social Networking', *The Economist*.
19. Berners-Lee, Tim (Mar 2007), 'The Digital Future of the United States: Part 1 The Future of the World Wide Web', US House of Representatives Committee on Energy and Commerce, http://dig.csail.mit.edu/2007/03/01-ushouse-future-of-the-web.html, accessed 25 Jan 2010. The internet is an open platform which supports many applications *inter alia* the web, email, voice-over protocol.
20. Lessig, Lawrence (2006), pp. 85–6, *Code: Version 2.0*, New York: Basic Books, citing Mark Stefik: '(B)arriers within cyberspace—separate chat rooms, intranet gate-

ways, digital envelopes, and other systems to limit access—resemble the effects of national borders, physical boundaries, and distance. Programming determines which people can access which digital objects and which digital objects can interact with other digital objects'. Thus these spaces have values which are determined by choice.

21. Palfrey, John & Gasser, Urs (2008), p. 3, *Born Digital: Understanding the First Generation of Digital Natives*, New York: Perseus. Note: 2000–2007 internet growth 380.3 percent; global population penetration 25.6 percent of 6,767,805,208—http://www.internetworldstats.com/stats.htm accessed 25 Jan 2010. Internet users Sept 2009: 1.7 billion; 2008–9 increase in users 18 per cent; 2009 90 trillion emails sent—http://royal.pingdom.com/2010/01/22/internet-2009-in-numbers/, accessed 25 Jan 2010.

22. Stoll, Clifford (1996), *Silicon Snake Oil: Second Thoughts on the Information Highway*, London: Pan.

23. Lessig, op. cit., projects a different future: cyberspace anarchy is gradually replaced by cyberspace control. He envisages this developing as a constitution or environment of 'values' which must be broadly built across societies, rather than driven top-down by governments or even corporations. There is no inherent reason for the internet to be unregulated, he argues, given that it is constituted of digits or code.

24. Rheingold, Howard (1994), p. xx, *The Virtual Community: Finding Connection in a Computerised World*, London: Secker & Warburg.

25. Ferdinand Tönnies' definition: a 'truly human and supreme form of community' where 'persons of common faith feel, like members of the same craft, or rank, everywhere united by a spiritual bond...[which] forms a kind of invisible scene or meeting'. Chayko (2002), op. cit., p. 39.

26. Jarvis, Jeff (2008), pp. 5–6, *What Would Google Do?*, New York: Harper Collins. However Google's compliance with the Chinese state in restricting access to certain sites impacted the firm's image predicated on the maxim 'do no evil'.

27. Cited in Graham, op. cit., p. 4.

28. Bell Telephone's (later AT&T's) Theodore Vail promoted the creation of a 'one system', 'one policy', 'universal system'. Bell employee N. Lytkins published a 1917 paper on network externality. See Mueller, Milton (1997), *'Universal Service: Competition, Interconnection, and Monopoly in the Making of the American Telephone System'*, Cambridge MA: MIT Press.

29. DeLanda, Manuel (2006), *A New Philosophy of Society*, London: Continuum, ch. 3&4.

30. Capra, Fritjof (2003), p. 94, *The Hidden Connections*, London: Flamingo.

31. John Hagel and John Seely Brown stress the difference between classical business networks and social networks. The latter foster tacit knowledge. This is intangible knowledge or the kind we have problems identifying and expressing to ourselves and others. Unlike written knowledge, accessing it 'requires long-term trust based relationships and a deep understanding of context'. Hagel III, John & Seely Brown, John & Davison, Lang (04 Jan 2010), 'Networking Reconsidered', *Harvard Business Review*, http://blogs.hbr.org/bigshift/2010/01/networking-reconsidered.html, accessed 04 Feb 2010.

32. Wenger, Etienne (2004), p. 4, *Communities of Practice*, Cambridge: Cambridge University Press; Anderson(2006), op. cit..

33. Polanyi, Michel (1967, 2009), *The Tacit Dimension*, Chicago: University of Chicago Press.

34. Hagel, John (23 June 2009), 'Shift Happens Redux', Hagel develops the concept of the Information Society and Knowledge Economy examining 'flows of knowledge, capital, and talent' as the prime determinant in digital infrastructures. The result for the Big Shift is to create greater uncertainty and volatility in markets thus placing a premium on flows of knowledge. http://edgeperspectives.typepad.com/edge_perspectives/2009/06/shift-happens-redux.html accessed 04 Feb 2010.

35. Coleman, James (1988), p. S118, 'Social Capital in the Creation of Human Capital', *AJS*, vol. 94, Supplement S95-S120. For Coleman social capital is embodied in relations between people and is an instrumental resource. See the role of 'study groups' in radical student activism in South Korea. His analysis highlights three forms of social capital: 'obligations and expectations, which depend on trustworthiness of the social environment, information-flow capability of the social structure'. (p. 119).

36. Putnam, Robert (2000), p. 19–23, *Bowling Alone: The Collapse of and Revival of Community in America*, New York: Simon & Schuster. Putnam differentiates between 'bridging' and 'bonding' capital. The former supports the diffusion of information; the latter is psychologically supportive and suitable for mobilising solidarity. For further typography including inward/outward-looking dichotomy: Putnam, Robert & Goss, Kristin (eds) (2002), *Democracies in Flux*, Oxford: Oxford University Press. See introduction; Bourdieu, Pierre (1977, 2003), *Outline of a Theory of Practice*, Cambridge: Cambridge University Press: Bourdieu views social capital as a resource rooted in class that can be used to improve the fortunes of the individual within a group: 'the habitus, the product of history, produces individual and collective practices, and hence history, in accordance with the schemes engendered by history'.(p. 82)

37. Gerlach, Luther (July-Aug 1971), 'Movements of Revolutionary Change: Some Structural Characteristics', *American Behavioral Scientist*, vol. 14, no. 6, pp. 812–836; Brandt, Lisa Kaye (ed.) (2007), *Cultural Analysis and the Navigation of Complexity*, Lanham MY: University Press of America.

38. Gerlach (1971), op. cit., p. 816.

39. The worldwide web sits on top of the physical infrastructure of the Internet.

40. Leiner, Barry et al (10 Dec 2003, version 3.32), 'A Brief History of the Internet', http://www.isoc.org/internet/history/brief.shtml, accessed 24 Nov. 2009.

41. Arquilla (2001), op. cit., pp. 7–8; Brennan, Rick (2005), 'Future Insurgency Threats' Draft Feb 2005: Office of the Secretary of Defense, Washington, DC: RAND.

42. The fluidity of apparently dense groups raises questions for those suspicious of web communities' ability to endure. See Bell's discussion of waning social capital under the influence of the net. Bell, Robert (25 Nov. 2009), 'Social Capital: Technology's Impact on Society', http://www.govtech.com/dc/articles/734063, accessed 05 Feb 2010. Also Granovetter, Mark (1983), 'The Strength of Weak Ties: A Network Theory Revisited', *Sociological Theory*, vol. 1 (1083), pp. 201–233. Granovetter argues that an individual has a group of close friends (strong ties)—a 'densely knit clump of social structure'. He/she also has acquaintances with weak ties. Each acquaintance has close friends within clumps of social structure. Hence the weak ties are not casual but crucial in linking clumps of distended social structures. Friends serve movements and goal-oriented organisations in recruiting new members. But with-

out weak ties recruitment remains fairly static. Mizuko, Ito et al (2008), *Living and Learning with Digital Media: Summary of Findings from the Digital Youth Project'* Chicago Ill: MacArthur Foundation.

43. (2003), op. cit., p. 94.

44. See for early theories: Wheeler, William (1910, 2005), 'The Ant Colony as an Organism', *Journal of Morphology*, vol. 22, no. 2, pp. 307–325; Lloyd, C Morgan (1923), *Emergent Evolution*, London: Williams and Norgate.

45. Keller, Evelyn & Segal, Lee (Mar 1970), 'Initiation of Slime Mold Aggregation Viewed as an Instability', *Journal of Theoretical Biology*, vol. 26, no. 3, pp. 399–415.

46. See for fuller discussion Johnson, Steven (2001), *Emergence: The Connected Lives of Ants, Brains, Cities, and Software*, London: Penguin; see for his discussion of self-organising systems and how fireflies synchronise oscillating light flashes, Strogatz, Steven (2003), *Sync: The Emerging Science of Spontaneous Order*, London: Penguin.

47. This remains a major point of contention. Sageman, Marc (2008), *Leaderless Jihad: Terror Networks in the Twenty-first Century*, Philadelphia: University of Pennsylvania Press. This draws on Louis Amos's concept of leaderless resistance, defining Al-Qaeda as solely an inspiration for locally self-generating groups, independent from any central organisation and operating within a franchise system. However, for a discussion of the hierarchical committee structure of *Al-Qaeda* including responsibilities for military, religious, media, travel and finance/business see, Stern, Jessica (2003), p. 250, *Terror in the Name of God*, New York: Ecco/Harper Collins. Also Riedel, Bruce (May/June 2007), 'Al Qaeda Strikes Back', *Foreign Affairs*, which sees Al-Qaeda as a 'more dangerous enemy today than it has ever been before', displaying a vertical structure with solid operations base in Pakistan and franchised cadres internationally; Hoffman, Bruce (May/June 2008), 'The Myth of Grass-roots Terrorism: Why Osama Bin Laden Still Matters', *Foreign Policy*, http://www.foreignaffairs.com/articles/63408/bruce-hoffman/the-myth-of-grass-roots-terrorism, accessed 01 Oct 2009: Hoffman disputes Sageman's analysis arguing Al-Qaeda is like a 'shark, which must keep moving forward, no matter how slowly or incrementally, or die'. He cites US National Intelligence Estimate July 2007 and Mike McConnell's assertion that Al-Qaeda 'is and will remain the most serious threat to the Homeland, as its central leadership continues to plan high-impact plots, while pushing others in extremist Sunni communities to mimic its efforts and to supplement its capabilities'. See Berlet, Chip (Fall 2008), 'Leaderless Counterterrorism Strategy', *The Public Eye*, vol. 23, no. 3, http://www.publiceye.org/magazine/v23n3/leaderless_counterterrorism_strategy.html, accessed 27 Aug 2010.

48. Lord points out the differences between insect swarms and human leadership. The latter can see the bigger picture. Nevertheless 'leaders are *not* really in control' (p. xviii). So Lord accepts emergent bottom-up processes where no individual understands the full picture. Lord, Bob (2008), 'Beyond Transactional and Transformational Leadership', in Uhl-Bien, Mary & Marion, Russ, *Complexity Leadership: Part 1 Conceptual Foundations*, Charlotte NC: IAP.

49. Kelly, Kevin (1994), p. 27, *Out of Control*, London: Fourth Estate.

50. http://about.ning.com accessed 26 Aug 2010.

51. Penenberg, Adam (2009), p. 55, *Viral Loop*, London: Sceptre. See http://www.bloomberg.com/news/2010–08–12/andreessen-s-social-networking-startup-ning-

gets-users-to-pay-for-service.html, accessed 26 Aug 2010 for implications of their business model.

52. Ibid., p. 56. I draw on Penenberg's analysis in this section.

53. Anderson, Chris (2006), p. 125, *The Long Tail*, London: Random House, see Pareto's Law or powerlaw curve.

54. Taleb, Nassim Nicholas (2007), p. 178, *Fooled by Randomness: The Hidden Role of Chance in Life and the Markets*, London: Penguin. Taleb cautions against searching for critical points of take-off, favouring unpredictable progressions of non-linear randomness which become apparent after the event.

55. Noelle-Neumann, Elisabeth (1980), p. 114, *The Spiral of Silence: Public Opinion, Our Social Skin*, Chicago: University of Chicago Press. Noelle-Neumann differentiates between concrete and spontaneous crowds, arguing they adhere to different laws. 'They are composed in the one instance of people possessed by, and in the other of people without a fear of isolation'. So overwhelming is the feeling of mutuality in the first that 'individuals no longer need to assure themselves about how to speak or how to act. In such a dense union, even dramatic swings are possible'.

56. Gladwell, Malcolm (2000), p. 25, *The Tipping Point*, London: Abacus. Gladwell cites the cases of Winston's 'ungrammatical' cigarette ad—'Winston tastes like a cigarette should'—and Wendy's Burgers' 'Where's the Beef?'

57. Hunt, Brian; Kennedy, Judy; Li, Tien-Yien & Nusse, Helena (2004), *The Theory of Chaotic Attractors*, New York: Springer.

58. Gladwell, op. cit., p. 48 drawing on the research of Stanley Milgram, and Mark Granovetter's 'weak ties'.

59. Ibid., p. 62, citing Linda Price.

60. Hatfield, Elaine, Cacioppo, John & Rapson, Richard (1994), *Emotional Intelligence*, Cambridge: Cambridge University Press.

61. Watts, op. cit., p. 230.

62. Rogers, Everett (2003), pp. 349–363, *Diffusion of Innovations*, New York: Free Press. Critical mass is defined as 'the point at which enough individuals in a system have adopted an innovation so that the innovation's further rate of adoption becomes self-sustaining'.

63. Watts, op. cit., p. 235.

64. Lazarsfeld, Paul (1948), *The People's Choice*, New York: Columbia University Press; Lazarsfeld, Paul & Katz, Elihu (1955), *Personal Influence*, Glencoe, Ill: Free Press.

65. Keller, Edward & Berry, Jon (2003), *The Influentials*, New York: Free Press.

66. 'E-fluentials: The Power of Online Influence', New York: www.bsm.com.

67. (Feb 2007), 'The Accidental Influentials', *Harvard Business Review*.

68. Bob, Clifford (2005), p. 17, *The Marketing of Rebellion*, New York NY: Cambridge University Press.

69. Cheran, R & Aiken, Sharryn (2005), 'The Impact of International Informal Banking on Canada: A Case Study of Tamil Transnational Money Transfer (Undiyal)', Canada/Sri Lanka, www.apgml.org. The Tamil Tigers were effectively destroyed as a military and territorially based force in 2009 following a government onslaught.

70. Weimann, Gabriel (2006), pp. 75–81, *Terror on the Internet*, Washington, DC: United States Institute of Peace Press.

71. Ibid., p. 83.

72. Clifford, op. cit., p. 48.

73. Gerges, Fawaz (2005), pp. 57–60, *The Far Enemy: Why Jihad Went Global*, Cambridge: Cambridge University Press. See correspondence between Bin Laden in Afghanistan and Ibn al-Khattab (killed 2002) in Chechnya over choice of enemy, strategy, and operating theatre, thus whether to attack America or Russia. Bin Laden wished to target the United States and expel it from Saudi Arabia. Khattab favoured Muslim states in Central Asia such as Daghestan and Chechnya, building on freelance mujahedeen schooled in the Russo-Afghan war in defence of co-religionists in Bosnia-Herzegovina, the Philippines, Kashmir, Eritrea, Somalia, Burma and Tajikistan. See Ulph, Stephen (2005), pp. 31–5, 'The "Management of Barbarism: Lays out Al-Qaeda's Military Strategy"' in Heffelfinger, Christopher (ed.), *Unmasking Terror*, Washington, DC: Jamestown Foundation.

74. Bob, op. cit., p. 50.

75. Lasswell (1933), op. cit., p. 214.

76. Watts (2004), op. cit..

77. Strogatz (2003), op. cit..

78. This adaptability weakens the notion of 'memes' originally advanced by Dworkins. Unlike selfish genes which seek only to replicate themselves, ideas and images gain traction through adaptation and change. Dworkins, Richard (2006), *The Selfish Gene*, Oxford: Oxford University Press, ch. 11.

79. Granovetter, Mark (1983), p. 202, 'The Strength of Weak Ties: A Network Theory Revisited', *Sociological Theory*, vol. 1, pp. 210–233. For weak ties in labour markets and job-hunting see (1973), 'The Strength of Weak Ties', *American Journal of Sociology*, vol. 78, no. 6, pp. 1360–1380; (1974), *Getting a Job: A Study of Contacts and Careers*, Cambridge MA: Harvard University Press.

80. (1996), *How Nature Works: The Science of Self-Organised Criticality*, New York: Copernicus.

81. Cilliers, Paul (1998), p. 4, *Complexity and Post-Modernism*, London: Routledge.

82. Facebook claims 500 million regular subscribers. An average user connects to 80 community pages, groups, events: http://www.facebook.com/press/info.php? statistics, accessed 12/08/2010. It assumes average users 'communicate(s) with a small subset of their entire friend network, they maintain relationships with a group two times the size of this core. This not only affects each user, but also has systemic affects (*sic*) that may explain why things spread so quickly on Facebook', http://www.facebook.com/notes/facebook-data-team/maintained-relationships-on-facebook/55257228858, accessed 27/02/2010. Circa 30 percent of global internet users visit facebook.com; See http://www.alexa.com/siteinfo/facebook.com, accessed 27 Feb 2010. Also http://socialmediastatistics.wikidot.com/start for comparative social media sites data.

83. Al-Shishani, Murad Batal (04 Feb 2010), 'Taking al-Qaeda's Jihad to Facebook', *Terrorism Monitor*, vol. 8, issue 5, Jamestown Foundation, http://www.jamestown.org/programs/gta/single/?tx_ttnews[tt_news]=36002&tx_ttnews[backPid]=457&no_cache=1, accessed 27 Feb 2010.

84. Appadurai (1990), op. cit., p. 301 (sic).

85. Nash, op. cit., p. 91.

86. Appadurai, Arjun (1996), *Modernity at Large: Cultural Dimensions of Globalization*, Minneapolis MINN: University of Minnesota Press.

87. Featherstone, Mike (1991), *Consumer Culture and Postmodernism*, London: Sage.

88. Urry, John (1990), *The Tourist Gaze*, London: Sage.

89. Appadurai (1990), op. cit., p. 299.

90. Ibid.

91. Lash & Urry, op. cit., p. 10.

92. Ohmae, Kenichi (1994), p. 99, *The Borderless World: Power and Strategy in the Global Marketplace*, London: HarperCollins. He argues 'when multiple communication channels develop to put all members in touch with each other, pyramids cannot survive or be built afresh'.

93. Lash & Urry, op. cit., p. 24.

94. Samers, Michael (2010), '*Migration*', Abingdon: Routledge, ch. 4; Pritchett, Lant (2006), *Let Their People Come: Breaking the Gridlock on Global Labor Mobility*, Washington, DC: Center for Global Development; cf. Stiglitz, Joseph & Charlton, Andrew (2004), pp. 15–16, *A Development-Friendly Prioritization of Doha Proposals*, Initiative for Policy Dialogue, New York: Columbia University.

95. Castells (2009), op. cit., pp. 349–361.

96. Short message service.

97. Anheier, Helmut; Kaldor, Mary & Glasius, Marlies (2005), p. 14, *Global Civil Society 2004/5*, London: Sage; Castells (2009), op. cit.; Suarez, Sandra (2006), 'Mobile Democracy: Text Messages, Voter Turnout and the 2004 Spanish General Election', *Representation*, vol. 42, no. 2, 2006.

98. Castells (2009), op. cit., p. 300. Castells defines new insurgency thus: 'I conceptualise social actors aiming for cultural change (a change in values) as social movements, and I characterise the processes aiming at political change (institutional change) in discontinuity with the logic embedded in political institutions as insurgent politics. I posit as a hypothesis that insurgent politics operates the transition between cultural change and political change by incorporating subjects mobilised for political or cultural change into a political system they were not previously a part of'.

99. Lippman, Andrew & Reed, David (2003), *Viral Communications*, Media Laboratory Research.

100. Gloor, Peter (2006), p. 12, *Swarm Creativity: Competitive Advantage through Collaborative Innovation*, Oxford: Oxford University Press. Defines three dimensions of collaborative innovation networks (COIN): innovation 'through massive collaborative creativity; collaboration 'under a strictly ethical code', and communication 'in direct-contact networks' not mediated hierarchies.

101. Mobile ad hoc social network.

102. Rafael, Vicente (2003), 'The Cellphone and the Crowd: Messianic Politics in Contemporary Philippines', *Public Culture*, vol. 15, pp. 399–425; Rheingold, Howard (2002), pp. 157–8, *Smart Mobs: The Next Social Revolution*, Cambridge MA: Basic Books.

103. Twitter: text-based cellphone communication limited to 140 characters; see also Twitpic website for uploading pictures in real time

104. Flaye, Ella (16 June 2009), p. 6, '"It's like a revolution". The million-strong tide of protest too big for thugs to halt', *The Times*.

105. Internet connections can be routed via servers situated beyond the sovereign borders of countries in which opposition groups are active. So they are less prey to interception by the state. Blackberry smartphone emailing, messaging and web-

browsing route directly via a central server in Ontario, Canada. This has prompted the United Arab Emirates and Saudi Arabia to threaten to ban the company's product if they refused to distribute via local servers for example in Riyadh. India and Australia have also expressed concerns over lack of state controls. See Bolt, Neville (Aug/Sept 2010), pp. 47–8, 'The Leak Before the Storm: What Wikileaks Tells Us About Modern Communication', *RUSI Journal*, vol. 155, no. 4, pp. 46–51.

106. Ibid., citing Judith Evans, 'Dissidents use Internet Wiles to Beat Regime's Gag'.

107. Zhou, Chiyu (22 Oct 2009), 'Twitter Against Tyrants: New Media in Authoritarian Regimes', Commission on Security & Co-operation in Europe: US Helsinki Commission, http://www.csce.gov/index.cf.m?FuseAction=ContentRecords.View-Transcript&ContentRecord_id=462&ContentType=H, B&ContentRecordType= B&CF.ID=2373673 &CF.TOKEN=78050836, accessed 21 Nov. 09.

108. The former philosophy student was shot dead by a rooftop marksman during anti-government demonstrations in June 2009. Her death turned her into a national and international symbol of protest, especially among Iranian women. Fathi, Nazila (22 June 2009), 'In a Death Seen Around the World, a Symbol of Iranian Protests', *New York Times*, http://www.nytimes.com/2009/06/23/world/middle-east/23neda.html, accessed 27 Aug 2010.

109. Hassanpour, Amir (22 June 2009), CBC *'An Unintentional Martyr: Neda becomes 'symbol of goodness'*, http://www.cbc.ca/world/story/2009/06/22/f-neda-iran.html, accessed 27 Aug 2010.

110. *'Neda's Photo—June 20 Iran Election Protest in San Francisco'*, http://www.flickr.com/photos/ari/3646312893/, accessed 28 Nov. 2009.

111. Ansari, Ali (13 Feb 2010), 'The Nuking of Iran's Dissent', *The Guardian*.

112. Tapscott, Don (2009), p. 256, *Grown Up Digital: How the Net Generation is Changing Your World*, New York: McGraw-Hill.

113. Clinton (2010), op. cit..

114. States are however developing on-the-ground technological responses. Troops are linked and respond via GPS and wireless communications, adapting military battlefield swarming techniques for use in counter-terrorism. Rheingold (2002), op. cit., pp. 162–3.

115. Virilio (2005), op. cit., p. 112.

116. Ling, Richard Seyler (2004), *The Mobile Connection: the Cell Phone's Impact on Society*, San Francisco CA: Elsevier. Ling asks if mobile phones will lead to 'virtual walled communities' or postmodern, *ad hoc* networks with 'day-in, day-out intensity of other mass actions'.

117. Ibid., p. 119.

118. Jenkins, Henry (2006), p. 208, *Convergence Culture: Where Old and New Media Collide*, New York: New York University Press. However Arquilla (2001), op. cit., notes Chechen rebels and Colombia's FARC guerrillas have already employed swarm techniques:

119. Brecht, Bertolt (1969), p. 57, *Mutter Courage und Ihre Kinder*, Berlin: Suhrkamp Verlag (my translation).

120. Williams, Evan (06 Feb 2010), 'The Virtual Revolution: Enemy of the State', Programme 2, BBC2.

121. Penny, Laurie (16 Dec 2009), 'Three Cheers for the Internet', *Prospect*, Issue 165, http://www.prospectmagazine.co.uk/2009/12/three-cheers-for-the-internet/,

accessed 24 Feb 2009; cf. Morozov, Evgeny (18 Nov. 2009), 'How Dictators Watch Us On The Web', *Prospect*, Issue 165; Shirky, Clay (18 Dec 2009), 'The Net Advantage', *Prospect*, issue 165, http://www.prospectmagazine.co.uk/2009/12/the-net-advantage/, accessed 27 Aug 2010 for discussion on whether the web is a positive force for democracy.

122. Graham (1999), op. cit.; Stoll (1996), op. cit.; Postman, Neil (1993), *Technopoly: The Surrender of Culture to Technology*, New York: Vintage.

123. Runciman, David (06 Feb 2010), 'The Virtual Revolution: Enemy of the State', Programme 2, BBC2.

124. Rheingold (1994), op. cit., p. 57, 'This informal, unwritten social contract is supported by a blend of strong-tie and weak-tie relationships among people who have a mixture of motives and ephemeral affiliations'.

125. Massey, Douglas et al (2002), p. 1 (eds), *Worlds in Motion: Understanding International Migration at the End of the Millennium*, Oxford: Oxford University Press.

126. Mackinlay (2009), op. cit., for a community-level micro-analysis.

127. Horowitz, Donald (1985), p. 55, *Ethnic Groups in Conflict*, Berkeley CA: University of California Press.

128. Brubaker, Rogers (2004), p. 11, *Ethnicity Without Groups*, Boston MA: Harvard University Press.

129. Lindholm Schulz, Helena & Hammer, Juliane (2003), p. 87, *The Palestinian Diaspora: Formations of Identities and Politics of Homeland*, London: Routledge; for the problems of defining Palestinian diaspora as a single identity group see Hanafi, Sari (1999), 'Between Arab and French Agendas: Defining the Palestinian Diaspora and the Image of the Other', in Shamy, Seteney & Herrera, Linda (eds) (1999), *Between Field and Text: Emerging Voices in Egyptian Social Science*, Cairo: AUC.

130. Darwash, Mahmud (1984), *Victims of a Map*, London: Al Saqi.

131. Beckett (2001), op. cit..

132. Kirisci, Kemal (1986), p. 35, *The PLO and World Politics: A Study of the Mobilisation of Support for the Palestinian Cause*, London: Frances Pinter. There were broadly four Palestinian groups: so-called Israeli Arabs; post-1967 residents in the West Bank and Gaza Strip; refugee camp dwellers in Jordan and Lebanon; diaspora in the Arab world, and beyond.

133. Farsoun, Samih & Aruri, Naseer (2006), p. 205 footnote 9, *Palestine and the Palestinians*, Cambridge MA: Westview. Fatah, say the authors, adopted a focoist strategy, seeking to stimulate popularity through revolutionary direct armed attacks, unlike PFLP who employed a Maoist and Leninist approach with political preparation. See Seddon, David (1989), 'Making History: Myths and Realities of the Palestinian Struggle', *Journal of Refugee Studies*, vol. 2, no. 1, 1989, pp. 204–216; Lindholm Schulz (2003), op. cit.; Sayigh, Yezid (1997) *Armed Struggle and the Search for the State*, Oxford: Clarendon; Said, Edward & Hitchens, Christopher (1988), p. 153, *Blaming the Victims: Spurious Scholarship and the Palestinian Question*, London: Verso. See for the use of media in building the Palestinian identity. In 'The Essential Terrorist' Said writes: 'the tragically fixated attitude toward "armed struggle" conducted from exile and the relative neglect of mass political action and organisation inside Palestine exposed the Palestinian movement, by the early 1970s, to a far superior Israeli military and propaganda system, which magnified Palestinian violence out of proportion to the reality'.

134. Beyer, Lisa (04 Dec 2010), 'The Myths and Reality of Munich', *Time*, http://www.time.com/time/magazine/article/0,9171,1137646-1,00.html, accessed 26 Aug 2010.

135. Catignani, Sergio (2010), p. 234, 'The Israeli Defense Forces and the Al-Aqsa Intifada', in Marston, Daniel & Malkasian, Carter (eds), *Counterinsurgency in Modern Warfare*, Oxford: Osprey.

136. Gunaratna, Rohan (Jan 2008), p. 4, 'Strategic Counter-Terrorism: Getting Ahead of Terrorism; Part 3, Mass Media Response to Terrorism', *The Jebsen Center for Counter-Terrorism Studies Research Briefing Series*, vol. 3, no. 1, highlights the funding by radicalised diasporas of groups: Turkish PKK; Basque ETA; Tamil LTTE; also wider Muslim disaporas' funding for militant groups in Algeria, Kashmir, Somalia, Chechnya.

137. Turow (1999), op. cit..

138. Massey (2002), op. cit., pp. 1–8. Massey highlights 4 modern waves: mercantile period 1500–1800; industrial 1800–1925; limited migration 1920s-1950s; post-industrial 1960s-present.

139. Gonzalez, Nancie (1961), 'Family Organisation in Five Types of Migratory Wage Labor', *American Anthropologist*, vol. 62, pp. 1264–1280; (1989), 'Conflict, Migration and the Expression of Ethnicity: Introduction', in Gonzalez, Nancie & McCommon, Carolyn (eds), *Conflict, Migration and the Expression of Ethnicity*, Boulder CO: Westview Press. Gonzalez highlights five causes of migration: seasonal, temporary non-seasonal, continuous, recurrent, permanent, conflict. See Cohen (1997), op. cit.; Lee, Everett (1966), 'A Theory of Migration', *Demography*, vol. 3, no. 1, pp. 47–57.

140. Brettell, Caroline (2000), p. 103, 'Theorising Migration in Anthropology', in Brettell, Caroline & Hollifield, James (eds), 'Migration Theory', New York & London: Routledge

141. Urry, op. cit., p. 168.

142. World Bank (13 July 2009), 'Migration & Development Brief 10'.

143. Messina, Anthony (2002), pp. 1–2, *West European Immigration and Immigrant Policy in the New Century*, Westport Conn: Praeger.

144. Weiner, Myron (1995), *The Global Migration Crisis: Challenge to States and to Human Rights*, New York NY: HarperCollins College.

145. Papastergiadias, Nikos (2000), p. 7, *The Turbulence of Migration: Globalization, Deterritorialization, and Hybridity*, Cambridge: Polity Press.

146. Ibid., pp. 6–7; (2007), *International Migration Outlook, Annual Report 2007*, OECD Publishing; Davis, Mike (2006), p. 5–9, *Planet of Slums*, London: Verso. Such is the nature of urbanisation, rural areas are urbanising *in situ* so that the city is migrating to the countryside, while whole conurbations like West Africa's Gulf of Guinea and Rio/Sao Paolo Metropolitan Region are producing unprecedented urban corridors, 'weaving extraordinary new urban networks, corridors and hierarchies'.

147. Drucker (1969), p. 229. See Drucker's analysis of 'traditional rebellion' against parental background, experienced by second generation immigrants to the US For him post-1945 increase in youth numbers and student populations are key contributors to unrest.

148. Samers, op. cit..

149. Brettell (2000), op. cit., p. 104, citing Margolis and theorists of transnationalism.
150. Taseer, Aatish (28 Aug 2005), 'A British Jihadist', *Prospect*, Issue 113, interview with Hassan Butt.
151. Nagel, Caroline & Staeheli, Lynn (2010), p. 265, 'ICT and Geographies of British Arab and Arab American Activism', *Global Networks*, vol. 10, no. 2, pp. 26–281. Nagel highlights the dangers of excessive concentration on 'homeland' concerns to the exclusion of other issues.
152. Ibid.
153. Lebl, Leslie (winter 2010), 'Radical Islam in Europe', *Orbis*, vol. 54, no. 1, pp. 46–60. Lebl blames this for what he perceives as a European 'civilisational exhaustion'. Phillips, Melanie (2006), *Londonistan*, New York: Encounter Books. Describes the failure of Britain's confidence and its national identity leading to multicultural policies. Gove, Michael (2006), *Celsius 7/7*, London: Weidenfeld & Nicholson analyses Western appeasement in the face of terror threats; also see Ramadan, Tariq, 'Islam is a European Religion', http://www.youtube.com/watch% 3Fv= lxjL3CIs0xw, accessed 04 Feb 2010. Lebl criticises Ramadan for his apparently moderate line but condemns it as a stalking horse for more organised Islamic militancy.
154. Brettell, op. cit., p. 114, defines three conceptual approaches to ethnic identity: primordialist where there is 'deep-rooted attachment to group and culture'; instrumentalist, namely political strategy for pragmatic ends; and situational where ethnic identity is constructed in social and historical contexts, stressing fluidity and contingency. For the last, see Barth, Frederik, (ed.) (1969), *Ethnic Groups and Boundaries: The Social Organisation of Cultural Difference*, London: George Allen & Unwin.
155. Pickerill, Jenny (2007), 'Indymedia and Practices of Alter-Globalisation', *Environment and Planning A*, vol. 39, no. 11, pp. 2668–2684; Zhao, Shanyang (2006), 'The Internet and the Transformation of the Reality of Everyday Life: Toward a New Analytical Stance in Sociology', *Sociological Inquiry*, vol. 76, no. 4, pp. 458–474; Appadurai (1996), op. cit..
156. Calhoun, Craig (2004), 'Information Technology and the International Public Sphere', in Schuler, Douglas & Day, Peter (eds), *Shaping the Network Society*, Cambridge MA: MIT Press.
157. Wallerstein, Immanuel (1991), p. 31, 'Culture as the Ideological Battleground of the Modern World-System', in Featherstone, Mike (ed.), *Global Culture: Nationalism, Globalization and Modernity*, London: Sage.
158. Georgiou, Myria (2005), 'Diasporic and Media Across Europe, Multicultural Societies and the Universalism-Particularism Continuum', *Journal of Ethnic and Migration Studies*, vol. 31, no. 3, pp. 481–498. Georgiou nuances the singularity of transnational migrant discussion: migrants live in local, national and transnational spaces. Somalis in London share particular points of concern through satellite television with Somalis in Paris thus creating an imagined, common identity. But such particularism does not compete with or exclude universal or democratic precepts enshrined within the nation-state or with humanitarian values that safeguard their rights.
159. Global Commission on International Migration Report (2005), p. 10, http://www.

gcim.org/en/; International Crisis Group, 'The Sri Lankan Tamil Diaspora After the LTTE', *Asia Report*, no. 186, 23 Feb 2010.

160. British-Irish, British Afro-Caribbeans, British-Asians, French-Algerians, French Indo-Chinese, Spanish-Moroccans, German-Turks, German Greeks, Dutch-Indonesians.

161. Kepel, Gilles (2004), pp. 244–246, *The War for Muslim Minds*, Cambridge MA: Belknap Press

162. Ritchie, David (2001), 'Oldham Independent Review', http://resources.cohesioninstitute.org.uk/Publications/Documents/Document/Default.aspx?recordId=97; Equality and Human Rights Commission (2009), 'The Equality Implications of being a Migrant in Britain', Research Report 19, www.equalityhumanrights.com; Cantle Report (2001), 'Community Cohesion', Community Cohesion Review Team/ Home Office, http://www.cohesioninstitute.org.uk/Resources/AboutCommunityCohesion; 'Macpherson Inquiry' (1999), http://www.archive.official-documents. co.uk/document/cm42/4262/sli-00.htm.

163. Islam, Yusuf et al (08 Oct 2005), 'Preventing Extremism Together', http://www. communities.gov.uk/archived/general-content/communities/preventingextremismtogether/; see Awan, Akil (2007), 'Transitional Religiosity Experiences: Contextual Disjuncture and Islamic Political Radicalism', in Abbas, T (ed.), *Islamic Political Radicalism: A European Comparative Perspective*, Edinburgh: Edinburgh University Press.

164. BBC Radio 4 (07 June 2010), 'Survey: Brits Associate Muslims with Extremism', *Today*.

165. Malik, Shiv (30 June 2007), 'My Brother the Bomber', *Prospect*, Issue 135. Malik investigates the community institutions surrounding Mohammad Sidique Khan ('7/7 bomber') and draws a carefully nuanced conclusion that membership of a group '(c)onnected by ideas and isolated from the [Pakistani] community as pariahs' was the determinant in the radicalising process. Cf. Emile Durkheim's comparison between 'egotistical suicide' when alienated from society with 'altruistic suicide' when identification with community is excessive: (1970), *Suicide: A Study in Sociology*, London: Routledge & Kegan Paul.

166. (07 June 2006), 'Muslims in Europe: Economic Worries Top Concerns About Religious and Cultural Identity', http://pewglobal.org/reports/display.php?ReportID= 254, accessed 27 Feb 2010.

167. See for statistical comparisons between economic causes of civil wars and political causes of terrorism Sambanis, Nicholas (2008), pp. 188–189, 'Terrorism and Civil War', in Keefer, Philip & Loayza, Norman (eds), *Terrorism, Economic Development, and Political Openness*, Cambridge: Cambridge University Press. See 'Roots of Terrorism?', in Laqueur, Walter (2003), *No End to War: Terrorism in the Twenty-First Century*, New York: Continuum.

168. Ryan, Johnny (2007), pp. 37–8, *Countering Militant Islamist Radicalisation on the Internet*, Dublin: Institute of European Affairs, citing Dutch Security Service, AIVD: In Jan 2007 the service linked popular use of the internet among the young to its role as 'a breeding ground for radicalisation, be it incipient or already internalised'. They later argued 'the most serious threat faced by the Netherlands is from "decentralised networks act[ing] on their own initiative, often spurred on by local circumstances"'.

169. Mackinlay's model of radicalisation—Mackinlay (2009), op. cit., demonstrates phases through which individuals pass before embracing direct action. However this should not assume all potential recruits reach the final stage or that passage is of a uniform pace. The insurgent epiphany still requires extensive research. Sageman (2004), op. cit.: Sageman stresses the primacy of family, kin or friendship relations in his 'bunch of guys' theory. Also Bakker, Edwin (2006) 'Jihadi Terrorists in Europe, their Characteristics and the Circumstances in which they joined the Jihad: an Exploratory Study', *Clingendael Security Paper 2*, The Hague. He rejects many of Sageman's findings, arguing research on motivation and personal circumstances is far from universal, thus inconclusive: 'most of the jihadi terrorists in Europe joined the jihad with very limited or no outside intrusion' (p. 51). See Travis, Alan (20 Aug 2008), 'MI5 Report Challenges Views On Terrorism in Britain', *The Guardian*, http://www.guardian.co.uk/uk/2008/aug/20/uksecurity.terrorism1, accessed 26 Aug 2010, which challenges conventionally held causes and preconditions of radicalisation. Della Porta, Donatella (1988), p. 155, 'Recruitment Processes in Clandestine Political Organisations: Italian Left-Wing Terrorism', in Klandermans, Bert; Kriesi, Hanspeter & Tarrow, Sidney (eds) (1988), *International Social Movement Research* vol. 1, Greenwich Conn: JAI Press. For responses by British television viewers in Muslim communities see Baines (2006), op. cit. This may be read alongside Wike, Richard (2006), 'Where Terrorism finds Support in the Muslim World', Pew Global Attitudes Project, http://pewresearch.org/pubs/26/where-terrorism-finds-support-in-the-muslim-world, accessed 01 Feb 2010.

170. Murawiec, Laurent (2008), *The Mind of Jihad*, Cambridge: Cambridge University Press.

171. Browers, Michaelle (2006), *Democracy and Civil Society in Arab Political Thought*; Syracuse: Syracuse University Press; Heggy, Tarek (2009), *The Arab Cocoon: Progress and Modernity in Arab Societies*, London: Valentine Mitchell; Freedman, Lawrence (2008), *A Choice of Enemies*, London: Phoenix.

172. Malik, op. cit., Reviewing the radicalisation of '7/7 bomber' Mohammad Sidique Khan, he writes '(a)t the heart of this tragedy is a conflict between the first and subsequent generations of British Pakistanis—with many young people using Islamism as a kind of liberation theology to assert their right to choose how to live. It is a conflict between tradition and individuality, culture and religion, tribalism and universalism, passivity and action'.

173. Neumann, Peter (2009), *Old and New Terrorism*, Cambridge: Polity.

174. Appadurai, Arjun (1990), op. cit., p. 301; Roy (2004), pp. 100–107: quantifying the number of Muslims living in the European Union is difficult (estimated 8–12 million) and their distribution extends beyond former colonial associations. What complicates this is how to classify individuals, whether by *jus solis* (place of birth) or *jus sanguinis* (parental blood), by practicing religion or inherited religion, or mixed marriage. See Travis, op. cit. MI5 reports 'British-based terrorists are as ethnically diverse as the UK Muslim population, with individuals from Pakistani, Middle Eastern and Caucasian backgrounds'.

175. 'Glasgow bombers' Bilal Abdulla and Kafeel Ahmed were an NHS doctor and engineering student respectively. http://www.telegraph.co.uk/news/uknews/3689 210/Glasgow-bomb-plot-How-airport-terror-plotters-shared-common-cause-of-Iraq.html, accessed 01 Mar 2010; for UK Home Secretary's statement on student

visas and arrested plotters see (20 Apr 2009) 'Operation Pathway', Commons Hansard, Column 21, http://www.publications.parliament.uk/pa/cm200809/cmhansrd/cm090420/debtext/90420–0004.htm#0904203000002, accessed 01 Mar 2010.

176. Turkle, Sherry (Nov. 1999), pp. 647 & 643, 'Cyberspace and Identity', *Contemporary Sociology*, vol. 28, no. 6, pp. 643–648; (1995), *Life on the Screen: Identity in the Age of the Internet*, New York: Simon & Schuster.

177. http://www.flickr.com/photos/.

178. Stone, Brad (28 Mar 2009), 'Is Facebook Growing Up Too Fast?', *New York Times*, http://www.nytimes.com/2009/03/29/technology/internet/29face.html?_r=1, accessed 12 Oct 2009.

179. http://www.imqq.com/ accessed, 12 Oct 2009.

180. Kelly, Kevin (21 Nov. 2008), 'Becoming Screen Literate', *New York Times Magazine*, http://www.nytimes.com/2008/11/23/magazine/23wwln-future-t.html?pagewanted=1&_r=1.

181. Ainsworth, Bob (15 Sept 2009), former UK Secretary of State for Defence, speech at King's College London.

182. Ibid.

183. (2009), p. 1, *"Skyful of Lies", and Black Swans: The New Tyranny of Shifting Information Power in Crises*, Oxford: RISJ. Gowing focuses on the 'tyranny of the timeline' where media and state responses to crises are no longer in synch. State institutions are unprepared and media organisations hesitate to enter the mediaspace, so new 'information doers' (citizen journalists) who have no professional reservations, can set or dominate the political agenda. He poses the F3 options: 'Should they be first to enter the information space? How fast should they do it? But how flawed might their remarks and first positions turn out to be…'(p. 2).

184. Katzenbach (1955), op. cit.; Nagl (2005), op. cit..

185. See the diagram in Scearce, Diana, Kaper, Gabriel & Grant, Heather McLeod (summer 2010), p. 33, 'Working Wikily', *Stanford Social Innovation Review*, vol. 8, no. 3, pp. 30–37.

186. Klein, Esther (2001), 'Using Information Technology to Eliminate Layers of Bureaucracy', *The National Public Accountant*, vol. 23 (2001), pp. 46–48.

187. Bevir, M & Rhodes, R.A.W (2003), p. 150, *Interpreting British Governance*, London: Routledge; see Burnham, John & Pyper, Robert (2008), *Britain's Modernised Civil Service*, Basingstoke: Palgrave Macmillan. See for alternatives to the Whitehall model e.g. hollowing-out; governance paradigm; network theory; differentiated policy.

188. Winner, Langdon (1986), p. 89, *The Whale and the Reactor*, Chicago: University of Chicago Press.

189. DeLanda (2006), op. cit., pp. 68–69.

190. Picot, Arnold, Reichwald, Ralf & Wigand, Rolf (2008), *Information, Organization and Management*, Berlin & Heidelberg: Springer. See ch. 5; also Lash, Scott & Urry, John (1994), p. 24, *Economies of Signs and Space*, London: Sage.

191. Ibid., p. 192, bureaucracy has a wider meaning than hierarchy, but most critics focus on the dysfunctions of hierarchy. Cf. Bennis, Warren (1993), *Beyond Bureaucracy*, San Francisco: Jossey-Bass; Wilson, James Q (1989), *Bureaucracy: What Government Agencies Do and Why They Do It*, New York: Basic Books.

192. Bolt, Neville (Oct 2009), 'Unsettling Networks', *RUSI Journal*, vol. 154, no. 5, pp. 34–39.

193. (23 Jan 2010), pp. 22–24, 'Leviathan Stirs Again: Briefing—the Growth of the State', *The Economist*.

194. Kleiner, Art (2002), 'Karen Stephenson's Quantum Theory of Trust', *Strategy and Business*, issue 29.

195. Hood, Christopher & Margetts, Helen (2007), p. 193, *The Tools of Government in the Digital Age*, Basingstoke & New York: Palgrave Macmillan.

196. Bevir (2003), op. cit., p. 150.

197. Barabasi, Albert-Laszlo (2002), *Linked: the New Science of Networks*, Cambridge MA: Perseus.

198. Robb (2007), op. cit., pp. 94–110.

199. for effects-based operations see Deptula, David (2001), *Effects-Based Operations: Changes in the Nature of Warfare*, Arlington VA: Aerospace Education Foundation.

200. For discussion of definitions: Cavelty, Myriam Dunn (2010), pp. 123–144, 'Cyberware', in Kassimeris, George & Buckley, John (eds), *The Ashgate Companion to Modern Warfare*, Farnham: Ashgate Publishing; For overview of attacks: Carr, Jeffrey (2010), *Inside Cyber Warfare: Mapping the Cyber Underworld*, Sebastopol CA: see for Schmidt's 'debunking' of cascading failures O'Reilly Media; Ringer, Ryan (04 Mar 2010), 'White House Cyber Czar: There is No Cyberwar', *Wired*, http://www.wired.com/threatlevel/2010/03/schmidt-cyberwar/, accessed 13 July 2010.

201. US Commission on National Security/21st Century (2001), 'Road Map for National Security: Imperative for Change—Phase III Report' had already predicted the real threat of attacks on the US population before the Twin Towers strike, and argued for a review of lethargic and misconnected bureaucracy under threat from a new technological insurgent environment. Cf. Hess, Stephen & Kalb, Marvin (2003), *The Media and the War on Terror*, Washington, DC: Brookings Institute.

202. The 9/11 Commission Report (2004), ch. 1.3, *Final Report of the National Commission on Terrorist Attacks upon the United States*, Washington, DC: US Government Printing Office.

203. Jackson (2005), op. cit.; Croft, Stuart (2006), *Culture, Crisis and America's War on Terror*, Cambridge: Cambridge University Press.

204. Cooper, Christopher & Block, Robert (2006), *Disaster: Hurricane Katrina and the Failure of Homeland Security*, New York: Times Books; Cunningham Bissell, William (2008), 'From Iraq to Katrina and Back: Bureaucratic Planning as Strategic Failure, Fiction and Fantasy', *Sociology Compass*, vol. 2, no. 5, pp. 1431–1461. See for the influence of socio-cultural forms on bureaucratic planning in complex situations. He questions simplistic, single-dimensional understandings of planning. Molotch goes further citing institutional racism in prioritising disaster relief processes rather than idealised expectations of Weberian bureaucracy: Molotch, Harvey (Feb 2006), 'Death on the Roof', *Space and Culture*, vol. 9, no. 1, pp. 31–34.

205. Welch, Susan; Gruhl, John; Comer, John & Rigdon, Susan (2009), pp. 372–3, *Understanding American Government*, Boston MA: Wadsworth. The authors list in mitigation the fragmented nature of America's political system and interference and over-ride by political appointees as compromising neutral execution of duties.

206. (01/2003), p. 14, 'Urgent Business for America: Revitalising the Federal Government for the 21ˢᵗ Century', Report of the National Commission on the Public Service, http://www.docstoc.com/docs/830980/National-Commission-on-the-Public-Service-Releases-Final-Report, accessed 21 Nov. 2009.

207. Dumond, John & Eden, Rick (2005), p. 217, *Improving Government Processes: From Velocity Management to Presidential Appointments*, Santa Monica CA: RAND.

208. Capra (2003), op. cit., p. 96.

209. Battram, Arthur (1998), p. 35, *Navigating Complexity*, London: The Industrial Society.

210. Rayner, Steve (2007), pp. 5–6, 'Creating a Climate for Change', in Brandt, Lisa Kaye (ed.), *Cultural Analysis and the Navigation of Complexity*, Lanham MD: University Press of America.

211. Omand, David (2005), p. 108, 'Countering International Terrorism: The Use of Strategy', *Survival*, vol. 47, no. 4, pp. 107–116; OODA = observe, orient, decide, act.

212. Brock, George (28 Feb 2008), 'Who Really Brought Peace to Belfast', *TLS*, http://entertainment.timesonline.co.uk/tol/arts_and_entertainment/the_tls/article3445728.ece, accessed 13 July 2010. Brock details the lessons for COIN in Ulster: 'Recruit very good spies; then hire some more. Then give it time to work. The murders, the long wait and the compromises of the exit strategy may well grind the moderates to dust. Then wait some more. After that, the politicians can make their entrance'.

213. See Unow, Jaceck (2003/4), 'Modeling the Dynamics of an Information System', *Australasian Journal of Information Systems*, Special Issue; Drazin, Robert, Glynn, Mary Ann & Kazanjian, Robert (2004), 'Dynamics of Structural Change', in Poole, Marshall Scott & Van de Ven, Andrew (eds), *Handbook of Organisational Change and Innovation*, New York: Oxford University Press.

214. Prigogine, Ilya & Stengers, Isabelle (1984), p. 140, *Order out of Chaos: Man's Dialogue with Nature*, London: Heinemann.

215. Battram (1998), op. cit., p. 21.

216. Miller, John & Page, Scott (2007), p. 222, *Complex Adaptive Systems*, Princeton NJ: Princeton University Press.

217. Virilio (2008), op. cit., p. 230.

218. Barabasi (2002), op. cit., pp. 1–2, the strike happened 07 Feb 2002.

219. Rogers, op. cit., p. 351, stresses the inter-relationship between critical mass, logic of collective action, and network externalities.

220. Runciman, David (2010), 'The Virtual Revolution—Rushes Sequences', http://www.bbc.co.uk/blogs/digitalrevolution/2009/10/rushes-sequences-dr-david-runc.shtml, accessed 02 Mar 2010.

221. Rosen, David (2005), p. 129, *Armies of the Young: Child Soldiers in War and Terrorism*, Piscataway NJ: Rutgers University Press.

7. SPONTANEOUS REVOLUTION

1. Lenin's letter citing Georges Danton, sent from Finland to the Bolsheviks in Petrograd 1917: 'act with the greatest determination and on the offensive. The defensive is the

death of every armed rising...Surprise your antagonist...Keep up the moral ascendancy...' Neuman, Sigmund (1971), p. 160, 'Engels and Marx: Military Concepts of the Social Revolutionaries', in Earle, Edward Mead (ed.), *Makers of Modern Strategy: Military Thought from Machiavelli to Hitler*, Princeton: Princeton University Press.

2. Jeffrey Godberg's interview with Hillary Rodham Clinton(10 May 2011), *The Atlantic*, http://www.theatlantic.com/international/archive/2011/05/hillary-clinton-chinese-system-is-doomed-leaders-on-a-fools-errand/238591/1/, accessed 08 June 2011.

3. Godberg, op. cit..

4. http://thenextweb.com/me/2010/12/07/tunisia-blocks-wikileaks-everyone-referencing-it/, accessed 09 Mar 2011.

5. 'Anonymous Press Release 03 Jan 2011', http://www.anonnews.org/index. php?p=press&a=item&i=133, accessed 09 Mar 2011.

6. Taheri, Amir (12 Feb 2011), p. 24, 'Now Showing in Cairo: A Keystone Kops Coup', *The Times*.

7. El Amrani, Issandre (15 Jan 2011), 'Twitter, WikiLeaks and Tunisia' http://www. arabist.net/blog/2011/1/15/twitter-wikileaks-and-tunisia.html, accessed 01 June 2011;

8. Frenkel, Sheera (24 June 2011), p. 42, 'Letter From Ramtha', *The Times*, interview with Muhammad Jamid.

9. Human Rights Watch (01 June 2011), 'We've Never Seen Such Horror: Crimes Against Humanity by Syrian Security Forces', http://www.hrw.org/en/reports/2011/ 06/01/we-ve-never-seen-such-horror, accessed 01 June 2011.

10. Blandford, Nicholas (06 June 2011), p. 25, 'Rebels "Kill 120" as Civil War Looms', *The Times*; http://www.facebook.com/Syrian.Revolution.Eng, accessed 06 June 2011.

11. See Sharp, Gene (2003), *From Dictatorship to Democracy: A Conceptual Framework for Liberation*, Boston MA: Albert Einstein Institution for an influential text which activists in Tunisia and Egypt drew on.

12. (16 May 2011), 'The Magic Key', http://www.middle-east-online.com/ english/?id=46142, accessed 15 June 2011.

13. BBC News (29 Jan 2011), 'Egypt: Mubarak Sacks Cabinet and Defends Security Role', http://www.bbc.co.uk/news/world-middle-east-11777943, accessed 15 June 2011.

14. Glanz, Kames & Markoff, John (12 June 2011), 'US Underwrites Internet Detour Around Censors', http://www.nytimes.com/2011/06/12/world/12internet.html?page wanted=1&_r=1, accessed 13 June 2011. One such project, 'internet in a suitcase', used a 'mesh network' technology capable of transforming cellphones and laptops to fashion a wireless web without requiring a central hub.

15. (04 June 2009), 'Text: Obama's Speech in Cairo', *New York Times* (06 Apr 2009), 'President Obama's Remarks in Turkey', *New York Times*.

16. Hines, Nico (14 Feb 2011), p. 29, 'Obama Furious over Egypt remarks by 'Monster' Clinton', *The Times*.

17. (17 Mar 2011), p. 2, 'Deserted by Obama', *The Times*.

18. (25 Mar 2011), p. 2, 'Obama, Where Art Thou?', *The Times*.

19. International Crisis Group (06 June 2011), 'Popular Protest in North Africa: and

the Middle East (V): Making Sense of Libya', *Middle East/North Africa Report*, no. 107, Executive Summary.

20. Abdulhamid, Ammir (09 June 2011), 'Beware Official Propaganda!', http://syrianrevolutiondigest.blogspot.com/2011/06/beware-official-propaganda.html, accessed 13 June 2011; see also BBC (01 June 2011), 'Syrian Unrest: Inquiry into Hamza Aa-Khatib's Death', http://www.bbc.co.uk/news/world-middle-east-13622959, accessed 13 June 2011.

21. Hashash, Sara (24 July 2011), p. 24, 'Hackers Battle to Silence Syria's Facebook Rebels', *The Sunday Times*. At Damascus University in June, Assad spoke of the group as a 'real army in virtual reality'.

22. (May/June 2011), 'Demystifying the Arab Spring', *Foreign Affairs*, http://www.foreignaffairs.com/articles/67693/lisa-anderson/demystifying-the-arab-spring, accessed 13 June 2011.

23. Ibid.

24. (04 Oct 2010), 'Small Change: Why The Revolution Will Not Be Tweeted', *New Yorker*, http://www.newyorker.com/reporting/2010/10/04/101004fa_fact_gladwell?currentPage=1, accessed 15/06/2011. See also Scott Atran's analysis for a more extreme expression in the closed group of bombers associated with Indonesia's Jemaah Islamiyah: 'The Bali plot and plots after spewed from a tangled web of discipleship, kinship and marriage, social networks of Afghan Alumni and other friends, and not really from any command-and-control organisation…Sixteen of the twenty-six Bali attackers and planners either attended or were associated with one of three JI-linked radical madrassahs'. (2011), pp. 162–3, *Talking to the Enemy*, London: Allen Lane.

25. Amnesty International Report (2010), p. 14, 'Egypt Rises: Killings, Detention and Torture in the 25th Jan Revolution', London: Amnesty International. The report singles out police brutality and emergency legislation, granting new powers of repression to the Ministry of Interior, and by extension to the State Security Investigation services (SSI), 325,000-strong riot police, and the Central Security Forces (CSF).

26. Gladwell, Malcolm & Shirky, Clay (March/April 2011), 'From Innovation to Revolution: Do Social Media Make Protests Possible?', *Foreign Affairs*; Karimjee, Mariya & Kumaraswami, Lakshmi (2011), 'Social Media: Catalyst or Hope?', World Policy Institute, http://www.worldpolicy.org/social-media-catalyst-or-hype, accessed 15 June 2011.

27. MacKinnon, Rebecca (Apr 2011), pp. 35–7, 'Liberation Technology: China's "Networked" Authoritarianism', *Journal of Democracy*, vol. 22, no. 2, pp. 32–46.

28. Deibert, Ronald & Rohozinski, Rafal (2010), p. 7, 'Beyond Denial: Introducing Next-Generation Information Access Controls', in Deibert, Ronald; Palfrey, John; Rohozinski, Rafal & Zittrain, Jonathan (eds), *Access Controlled: Shaping of Power, Rights, and Tule in Cyberspace*, Cambridge MA: MIT Press.

29. Etling, Bruce; Faris, Robert & Palfrey, John (2010), p. 9, *Political Change in the Digital Age: The Fragility and Promise of Online Organizing*, Baltimore MD: John Hopkins University Press; (Dec. 2010), *SAIS Review*, vol. 30, Issue 2, pp. 37–49.

30. Pariser, Eli (2011), *The Filter Bubble: What the Internet Is Hiding From You*, London: Viking.

31. Armstrong, Stephen (19 June 2011), p. 18, 'Dropping Facebook', *The Sunday Times*.

32. Halliday, Josh (12 Mar 2011), 'SXSW 2011: Clay Shirky on Social Media and Revolution', *The Guardian*, http://www.guardian.co.uk/technology/2011/mar/12/sxsw-2011-clay-shirky-social-media, accessed 27 June 2011.

33. It is important to differentiate between flows and infrastructures, particularly on the web, to discern public spheres as spaces circumscribed by connections or nodes from spaces shaped by process or flows of communication. Just because connections exist does not mean all are used equally. That impacts the way we understand networks. Networks have inherent properties that make them suitable for rapid grouping and collective action. Frequently, their advantages are summarised as efficient communication and information processing; scalability; adaptability; resilience; and learning capacity. At the same time, networks should be seen in two ways: as structures and actors. In the first, they exercise influence on their members and produce networked effects; in the latter, they operate as a particular organisational form which differs from the way markets and hierarchies function. Most insurrectionist groups fall within the first category. But increasingly, in an era of sophisticated electronic surveillance and forensic investigation by state agencies, even fluid networks face mounting difficulties of mobilisation and translating the networked effect of POTD into collective action. Eilstrup-Sangiovanni, Mette & Jones, Calvert (Fall 2008), 'Assessing the Dangers of Illicit Networks: Why al-Qaida May Be Less Threatening Than Many Think', *International Security*, vol. 33, no. 2, pp. 7–44; Kahler, Miles (ed.) (2009), *Networked Politics: Agency, Power, and Governance*, Ithaca & London: Cornell University Press.

34. (2009), p. 114, *The Coming Insurrection*, Los Angeles CA: Semiotext(e).

35. (11 June 2011), 'Spain: Anonymous Takes Down National Police Website #OpPolicia', http://www.anonops.blogspot.com/, accessed 20/06/2011.

36. Etling, op. cit., p. 10.

37. Gallagher, Ryan & Arthur, Charles (24 June 2011), 'Inside LulzSec: Chatroom Logs Shine a Light on the Secretive Hackers', *The Guardian*, http://www.guardian.co.uk/technology/2011/June/24/inside-lulzsec-chatroom-logs-hackers, accessed 24 June 2011.

38. Ahmed, Murad & Beaman, Lucinda (27 June 2011), p. 11, 'LulzSec Hackers Shut Down After 50-Day Campaign', *The Times*.

39. 'The Invisible Committee', op. cit., p. 122.

40. Ibid., p. 118. See Werenfels, Isabelle (2007) *Managing Instability in Algeria: Elites and Political Change Since 1995*, Abingdon: Routledge.

41. Ibid., p. 14.

42. Op, cit, pp. 10–11.

43. Ehrenberg, John (1983), p. 295, 'Communists and Proletarians: Lenin on Consciousness and Spontaneity', *Studies in Soviet Thought*, vol. 25, pp. 285–306.

44. Luxemburg, Rosa (1986), pp. 54, 73, *The Mass Strike: The Political Party and the Trade Unions*, London: Bookmarks. 'The revolution, even when the proletariat, with the social democrats at their head, appear in the leading role, is not a manoeuvre of the proletariat in the open field, but a fight in the midst of the incessant crashing, displacing and crumbling of the social foundation. In short, in the mass strike in Russia the element of spontaneity plays such a predominant part, not because the Russian proletariat are "uneducated", but because revolutions do not allow anyone to play the schoolmaster with them'. She continues: 'The mass strike is the first nat-

ural, impulsive form of every great revolutionary struggle of the proletariat and the more highly developed the antagonism is between capital and labour, the more effective and decisive must mass strikes become. The chief form of previous bourgeois revolutions, the fight at the barricades, the open conflict with the armed power of the state, is in the revolution of today only the culminating point, only a moment in the process of the proletarian struggle'. See also Lukács, Georg (1971), p. 41, *History and Class Consciousness*, London: Merlin Press—argues she saw very early that 'the organisation is much more likely to be the effect than the cause of the revolutionary process'.

45. Ibid., citing Lenin's *What Is To Be Done?*.

46. Cf. the use of the general strike, particularly in Russia 1905, against state violence. and conflicting views on the need to resort to co-ordinated violence to challenge the state. Darlington, Ralph (2008) *Syndicalism and the Transition to Communism: an International Comparative Analysis*, Aldershot: Ashgate; see ch. 10.

47. (1963), p. 257, *Journeys Toward Progress*, New York: Twentieth Century Fund.

48. See Engels, Friedrich (1891), Introduction to *The Civil War in France*.

49. Cited in Neuman, Sigmund (1971), p. 169, 'Engels and Marx: Military Concepts of the Social Revolutionaries', in Edward Mead Earle (ed.), *Makers of Modern Strategy*, Princeton: Princeton University Press.

50. Ibid., citing Engels (1895), *Class Struggle in France 1848–1850*; see also Marx, Karl (1871), *Civil War in France*, for his analysis of the Paris Commune 1870–71; (1848) *Civil War Tactics*.

51. Trotsky, Leon, '1905', http://www.marxists.org/archive/trotsky/1907/1905/ch22.htm, accessed 21 June 2011.

52. Nelson, Harold (1988), pp. 24–25, *Leon Trotsky and the Art of Insurrection*, London: Frank Cass.

53. But Mao's is only one of the major strands of theory that would come to dominate twentieth century insurgencies. Mao's rural doctrinal model had emerged from the failure to realise the urban struggle in the industrial centres of China's eastern seabord and cities in the interior on the part of an underdeveloped bourgeoisie and proletariat that had not yet reached the appropriate level of consciousness. Hence the new name of the game was to 'industrialise' the mass peasantry in revolutionary tactics and use the countryside as the shelter, sanctuary and organising terrain for a comprehensive politico-military approach to confronting and defeating government forces. By contrast, the Marxist-Leninist model had located the workers' struggle in the burgeoning factories of European and eventually Russian capitalism. State power resided in the capitals. So certainly since the success of the 1789 French Revolution and through the rapid changes in industrial production that brought waves of migration to cities throughout the nineteenth century, the urban model of initially mobilising barricades, then later as national armies became more tactically aware and better resourced, of appealing to the democratising spirit of the masses, would remain the surviving alternative. Although the question of how far the revolution could be willed on, rather than patiently awaited within the scientific time-scale that Marx had forecast, would test the patience of many insurgents. Hence by the mid-twentieth century, the Cuban revolution would break with the past. Built on the *foquismo* theory of Fidel Castro, Che Guevara and Regis Debray, it rationalised a programme of mobility, ambush and guerrilla fighters as a force independent of the

population. Charismatic revolutionary leadership rising up in arms would be sufficient to attract the wider population by example: spontaneity became a prime asset. But what worked in Cuba, struggled to pay dividends elsewhere, to the extent that Nicaragua's Sandinistas would abandon earlier attempts to apply its lessons in favour of a new prescription under the Tercerista banner.

54. Sanger, David (19 Feb 2011), 'When Armies Decide', *The New York Times*, http://www.nytimes.com/2011/02/20/weekinreview/20military.html?pagewanted=1&_r=1, accessed 21 June 2011.

55. Black, Ian (16 June 2011), p. 25, 'Like Egypt, the Army's Generals Will Be Decisive', *The Guardian*

56. Saleh, Heba & Chaffin, Joshua (24 Jan 2011), 'Tunisian Army Chief Vows To Guard Revolution', http://www.ft.com/cms/s/0/e01ffbc4–27e5–11e0–8abc-00144 feab49a.html#axzz1Pu7BziPL, accessed 21 June 2011.

8. THE NEW STRATEGIC OPERATING CONCEPT

1. Harvey (1990), op. cit., p. 119.

2. (2009), op. cit..

3. Tangri, Roger (1999), *The Politics of Patronage in Africa: Parastatal, Privatisation and Private Enterprise*, Oxford, James Currey; for deeper structural causes see Mamdani, Mahmood (1996), *Citizen and Subject: Contemporary Africa and the Legacy of Late Colonialism*, Princeton: NJ: Princeton University Press.

4. Abdullah, Ibrahim & Muana, Patrick (1998), 'The Revolutionary United Front of Sierra Leone', in Clapham, Christopher (ed.) (1998), pp. 172–193, *African Guerrillas*, Oxford: James Currey; Atkinson, Philippa(1997), *The War Economy in Liberia: a Political Analysis*, London: ODI; Cilliers, Jakkie (2000), 'Resource Wars—a New Type of Insurgency', http://www.iss.co.za/PUBS/BOOKS/Angola/2Cilliers.pdf, accessed 7 Dec 2006; Cilliers, Jakkie & Dietrich, Christian (eds) (2000), *Angola's War Economy: The Role of Diamonds*, Pretoria: Institute for Security Studies; Cramer, Christopher (2006), *Civil War is Not a Stupid Thing: Accounting for Violence in Developing Countries*, London: Hurst; Le Billon, Philippe (2001), 'Angola's Political Economy of War: the Role of Oil and Diamonds-1975–2000', *African Affairs*, vol. 100, Oxford: Oxford University Press; Reno, William (1998), *Warlord Politics and Africa States*, Boulder: Lynne Rienner; Ross, Michael (2003), 'Oil, Drugs and Diamonds: The Varying Roles of Natural Resources in Civil War', in Ballentine, Karen & Sherman, Jake (eds) (2003), pp. 47–72, *The Political Economy of Armed Conflict: Beyond Greed and Grievance*, Boulder: Lynne Rienner.

5. Richards, Paul (2005), *No Peace, No War*, Oxford: James Currey.

6. Keen, David (2003), 'Demobilising Guatemala', Working Paper no. 37, London: Crisis States Programme, DESTIN, London School of Economics.

7. Pugh, Michael & Cooper, Neil (2004), *War Economies in a Regional Context: Challenges of Transformation*, Boulder: Lynne Rienner.

8. Kaplan (1994), op. cit.; Moynihan, Daniel (1993), *Pandaemonium: Ethnicity in International Politics*, Oxford; Oxford University Press.

9. UN (2004), 'A More Secure World: Our Shared Responsibility', Report of the Secretary General's High Level Security Panel on Threats, Challenges and Change, http://

www.un.org/secureworld/report2.pdf; Macrae, Joanna(2001), *Aiding Recovery: The Crisis of AID in Chronic Political Emergencies*, London: Zed Books/ODI.

10. Wheeler, Nicholas (2000), *Saving Strangers: Humanitarian Intervention in International Society*, Oxford: Oxford University Press; Berdal, Mats & Economides, Spyros (2007), *United Nations Interventionism 1991–2004*, Cambridge: Cambridge University Press.

11. Butt, Ronald (03 May 1981), 'Mrs Thatcher: The First Two Years', *The Sunday Times*, http://www.margaretthatcher.org/speeches/displaydocument.asp?docid=104 475, accessed 27 Aug 2010.

12. Ohmae (1990), op. cit..

13. Harvey, David (2000), pp. 25–6, *Spaces of Hope*, Berkeley: University of California Press: see the 'Definition of Globalisation' in Marx and Engels' *Manifesto* ventured by Harvey; Held, David (ed.) (2004), '*A Globalising World? Culture, Economics, Politics*', London: Routledge/Open University.

14. Gray, John (2003), *False Dawn: the Delusions of Global Capitalism*, London: Granta Books, ch. 6.

15. Organization of the Petroleum Exporting Countries.

16. Harvey, David (2010), *The Enigma of Capital and the Crises of Capitalism*, London: Profile.

17. Gray (2003), op. cit., ch. 6.

18. Stiglitz, Joseph (2002), *Globalisation and its Discontents*, London: Penguin.

19. Katzenbach, op. cit., p. 325.

20. Zarrow, Peter (2005), pp. 299–300, *China in War and Revolution 1895–1949*, Abingdon: Routledge.

21. Ibid., p. 96.

22. Harvey (1990), op. cit..

23. Gray recognises states in the twenty first century, where technologies and states provide an 'unprecedented interconnectedness', are 'vulnerable to the ripple effect of strategic surprise', although he questions whether it constitutes an historical change: Gray, Colin (2005), pp. vii-viii, *Transformation and Strategic Surprise*', Carlisle PA: Strategic Studies Institute.

24. Some note a current, cyclical trend towards commercial, closed systems on the web. See Siegler MC (01 May 2010), 'Facebook, The Apps Store, and the Sound of Inevitability', *Tech Crunch*, http://techcrunch.com/2010/05/01/the-internet-is-cyclical/, accessed 03 May 2010. See Goldsmith, Jack & Wu, Tim (2008), 'How Governments Rule the Net', in *Who Controls the Internet: Illusions of a Borderless World*, New York: OUP, ch. 5. Equally states repeatedly try to curtail freedoms on social network websites, exemplified by Pakistan's restrictions on content declared offensive to the prophet Muhammad. These included Facebook, YouTube, and parts of Wikipedia, Twitter and BBC News. See (20 May 2010), p. 62, 'First Facebook, then the World', *The Economist;* see Bolt, Neville (Aug/Sept 2010), 'The Leak Before the Storm', *RUSI Journal*, vol. 155, no. 4, pp. 46–51, for US Government reaction to WikiLeaks and the Afghan Dossier.

25. Mao Tse-Tung (2007), p, p. 92, *On Guerrilla Warfare*, Griffith, Samuel B (trans), Rockford Ill: BN Publishing. See 'Three Rules and Eight Remarks'.

26. Ranstorp in Neumann (2009), op. cit., p. 23, 'Almost all the contemporary terror-

ist groups with a religious imperative are either offshoots or on the fringe of broader movements'.

27. Freedman (2006), op. cit., p. 14; Mahnken, Thomas (2008), p. 157, *Technology and the American Way of War*, New York: Columbia University Press.

28. Van Creveld, Martin (1991), p. 32, *The Transformation of War*, New York: Simon & Schuster.

29. Kaldor, Mary (2006), *New & Old Wars*, Cambridge: Polity.

30. The 'CNN effect' gained initial currency before finding its critics by the mid-1990s who offered more nuanced understanding of how political elites absorb and respond to media information. See Livingston, Steve (1997), 'Clarifying the CNN Effect: An Examination of Media Effects According to Type of Military Intervention', Harvard MA: Joan Shorenstein Center/Research Paper R-18. Livingston cites former Secretary of State James Baker: 'You are in a real-time mode. You don't have time to reflect' (p. 3). Doorey discusses the '*Al Jazeera* effect' where the capability of television, hitherto the 'most policed of all media', was expanded by satellite television and transformed public opinion-making on the Arab Street: Doorey, Timothy (2009), p. 148, 'Waging an Effective Strategic Communications Campaign in the Global War on Terror', in David, GJ & McKeldin, TR, *Ideas as Weapons*, Washington, DC: Potomac Books.

31. Cf. the death of singer Michael Jackson. On the 25 June 2009 Jackson suffered cardiac arrest at 14.26. The 'upskirt' gossip website TMZ broke the story 18 minutes later at 14.44. LA Times newspaper waited until 15.15 to publish. Crowds formed outside the hospital around 16.00. However CNN television news, stable-mate to TMZ at Time Warner awaited coroner's office confirmation before announcing at 16.25. Meanwhile rival global broadcaster BBC 24 had reported the death citing TMZ as source. Twitter throughout was logging 5,000 tweets per second—an 'instant doubling of tweets per second' before crashing. Google's usage 'hotness' index showed access at 'volcanic' before suffering 'error pages'. The timescale was so short, the news agenda and rumours surrounding cause of death were beyond control. Los Angeles Times (26 June 2009), 'Television Misses Out As Gossip Website TMZ Reports Michael Jackson's Death First', http://articles.latimes.com/2009/June/26/local/me-jackson-media26; BBC News (26 June 2009), 'Web Slows After Jackson Death', http://news.bbc.co.uk/1/hi/8120324.stm, accessed 28 May 2010.

32. Krepinevich, Andrew (2009), p. 14, *7 Deadly Scenarios: A Military Futurist Explores War in the Twenty First Century*, New York NY: Bantam Dell. Krepinevich notes the US Defence Department developed two concepts of operations: 'projecting power in the face of anti-access/anti-denial (A2/AD) capabilities, and defeating modern irregular forces' (p. 300). Diffusion of military technology, which cannot remain the preserve of the US indefinitely, risks becoming 'wasted assets' as other powers share and neutralise American superiority. However he identifies a failure of Rapid Defence Operations (RDO), cousin to Effects Based Operations (EBO), that destroys enemy 'centre of gravity'. Israel's 2006 war with Lebanon's *Hezbollah* resulted in defeat when the latter refused to confront Israeli forces, thus undermining effects based operations. The knock-on effect on US Joint Forces Command was demonstrable, he argues (pp. 301–2).

33. Yingling, Paul (May 2007), 'A Failure in Generalship', *Armed Forces Journal*; Bacevich, Andrew (Oct 2008), 'The Petraeus Doctrine', *Atlantic Magazine*, http://

www.theatlantic.com/magazine/archive/2008/10/the-petraeus-doctrine/6964/2/, for discussion of 'crusaders' and 'conservatives'. The former see US military difficulties in Iraq as self-inflicted, resulting from resistance to embracing COIN and fear of being sucked into another Vietnam. The result was a lack of preparation for irregular warfare.

34. Freedman (2006), op. cit., p. 14.

35. Kaldor, op. cit., p. 4.

36. Freedman, Lawrence (Aug 2005), 'War Evolves into the Fourth Generation', *Contemporary Security Policy*, vol. 26, no. 2, pp. 254–263; Terriff, Terry; Karp, Aaron & Karp Regina (eds) (2009), *Global Insurgency and the Future of Armed Conflict: Debating Fourth Generation Warfare*, Abingdon: Routledge.

37. See for the primacy of ICTs (1997), 'Joint Vision 2010', and (2000), 'Joint Vision 2020', Washington: US Joint Chiefs of Staff.

38. Op. cit., Book 1, ch. 6.

39. Mahnken, op. cit., p. 157, citing National Defense Panel Report.

40. Bacevich, Andrew (2002), pp. 135–6, *American Empire: the Realities and Consequences of US Diplomacy*, Cambridge MA: Harvard University Press, see for failures of RMA.

41. Benbow, Tim (2004), p. 104, *The Magic Bullet? Understanding the Revolution in Military Affairs*, London: Brassey's.

42. (Aug 2005), p. 205, 'War Evolves into the Fourth Generation', *Contemporary Security Policy*, vol. 26, no. 2, pp. 189–221; (Nov. 2007), 'The Message is the Insurgency', *Marine Corps Gazette*, pp. 18–30'(2009), 'Information Warfare', in David, op. cit. See also Lind, William; Nightingale, Keith; Sutton, Joseph; Wilson, Gary (1989), 'The Changing Face of War: Into the Fourth Generation', *Marine Corps Gazette*, Oct 1989, pp. 22–26. Terrorism is not hailed as new but in tandem with high technology developments, ideology and media manipulation it threatens a new era.

43. Hammes (2005), op. cit., p. 205.

44. Hammes (2007), p. 20; While Lawrence Freedman acknowledges the changing role of information and how it plays into 'culture' as a strategic factor, he regards 4GW as derived from 'poor history' since the first three generations are concerned with regular battle: Freedman, op. cit., p. 21. Colin Gray is another who dismisses the notion: '(i)nformation itself does not coerce or kill; it has to act on and through weapons systems of all kinds'; Benbow, op. cit., p. 111.

45. Lt Gen David Barno, US Commander Afghanistan 2003–5, sees the neo-Taliban as typical of 4GW: 'Fourth Generation warfare argues that the enemy's target becomes the political establishment and the policymakers of his adversary, not the adversary's armed forces or tactical formations. The enemy achieves victory by putting intense, unremitting pressure on adversary decision makers, causing them to eventually capitulate, independent of military success or failure on the battlefield'; Giustozzi (2008), op. cit., p. 98.

46. Kaldor (2007), op. cit., pp. 2–3.

47. Hoffman, Frank (2007), p. 8, *Conflict in the Twenty-First Century: The Rise of Hybrid Wars*, Arlington VA: Potomac Institute for Policy Studies: crucially for Hoffman hybrid wars do not put paid to conventional wars.

48. (Dec 2006), *US Army Marine Corps Counterinsurgency Field Manual FM 3–24*,

Chicago Ill: University of Chicago Press; British Army (2009), op. cit. Recently these updated doctrines have sought to rectify this, attempting to relate information to culture.

49. US Army FM 3–24 (Dec 2006), op. cit., ch. 5–19, 'IO synchronised with public affairs, can neutralise insurgent propaganda and false claims'.

50. Arquilla (2001), op. cit., p. 6.

51. Ibid., p. 20.

52. By contrast, 'cyber warfare' comprises deliberate attacks via computers and the internet targeting digital systems, processes, data and infrastructure of states (and corporations). Information and information flows may be impeded, disrupted or damaged. Whilst netwars focus on social relationships, cyber warfare emphasises technical processes. The US DoD sees it as 'the art and science of fighting; of defeating an opponent without spilling their blood'. See Carr (2010), op. cit., p. 2; Clarke, Richard & Kane Robert (2010), *Cyber War: The Next Threat to National Security and What To Do About It*, New York NY: HarperCollins.

53. Rid, Thomas & Hacker, Marc (2009), p. 10, *War 2.0: Irregular Warfare in the Information Age*, Westport Conn: Praeger. War 1.0 and 2.0 are separated by the dot. com crash of the late 1990s.

54. Baron, David (10 Sept 2009), 'Testimony Before the House Armed Services Subcommittee on Oversight and Investigations'. 'Officer leadership in this era faces demands that may make the relative intricacy of soldiering during the Cold War simple in comparison' in Burton, Brian & Nagl, John (Feb 2010), p. 13, *Keeping the Edge: Revitalizing America*, Washington, DC: Center for a New American Security.

55. US DoD (Jan 2009), p. 9, 'Capstone Concept for Joint Operations', Version3, http://www.jfcom.mil/newslink/storyarchive/2009/CCJO_2009.pdf, accessed 28 Apr 2010.

56. Ibid., p. 5.

57. Mackay, Andrew & Tatham, Steve (2009), p. 9, 'Behavioral Conflict', Shrivenham Paper, no. 9, UK Defence Academy.

58. CONTEST (Mar 2009), p. 18, *Pursue, Prevent, Protect, Prepare: The United Kingdom's Strategy for International Terrorism*, London: HMG.

59. Ibid., p. 11. A trans-Atlantic consensus endorsing terrorist organisations black-listed by US State Department: 19 Jan 2010 list: http://www.state.gov/s/ct/rls/crt/2009/140900.htm; for UK 'Proscribed Terrorist Groups', http://www.homeoffice.gov.uk/publications/counter-terrorism/proscribed-terror-groups/, accessed 28 Apr 2010.

60. FATA: Federally Administered Tribal Areas.

61. Hoffmann, Frank (2009), p. 101, 'Maneuvering Against the Mind', in David (2009), op. cit..

62. Merom, Gil (2003), *How Democracies Lose Small Wars: State, Society, and the Failures of France in Algeria, Israel in Lebanon, and the United States in Vietnam*, New York: Cambridge. University Press. Democracies says Merom, have a lower threshold for suppression of opposition using prolonged violence. Pressure from the population deters the need for drastic measures.

63. Gurr, Ted (1993), *Minorities at Risk: A Global View of Ethnopolitical Conflicts*, Washington, DC: United States Institute of Peace Press.

64. Walter, Barbara (1997), *'The Critical Barrier to Civil War Settlement'*, International Organisation, vol. 51, pp. 335–364: Walter identifies 8 out of 41 conflicts reached

a negotiated settlement. While Sinno, Abdulkader (2008), p. 2, *Organisations at War in Afghanistan and Beyond*, Ithaca NY: Cornell University Press, notes 2 out of 41; see also Weinstein, op. cit..

65. Moynihan (1993), op. cit.; Kaplan (1994), op. cit..

66. Castells (2009), op. cit., p. 300.

67. Halliday, Fred (21 Apr 2004), 'Terrorism in Historical Perspective', *Open Democracy*, http://www.opendemocracy.net/conflict/article_1865.jsp, accessed 05 May 2010; See Vlahos' assessment that many global insurgencies may have different roots. Vlahos suggests a possible *renovatio* with global implications similar to the Christian Reformation and Counter-Reformations. Vlahos, Michael (2003), *The Mask of Terror*, www.jhuapl.edu/areas/warfare/papaers/TerrorMaskVlahos.pdf; (2004), 'Culture's Mask: War & Change After Iraq', www.jhuapl.edu/areas/warfare/papaers/CultureMaskVlahos.pdf, accessed 03 Aug 2007.

68. Simplified typologies struggle to capture their growing complexity. Even 'ferals', the base of the terrorising food-chain, have become publicity-seekers conscious of their effect on camera. Some groups adhere to Maoist tactics. They supplement their efforts with whatever weapons and communications meagre budgets can stretch to. Few are blessed with funding levels that flow from controlling terrain for narcotics cultivation or taxing other producers and traffickers in return for safe-passage. Some eye the national palace, wanting only to become the alternative government. While others reach out to distant and disparate identity communities propagating a joined-up ideology through conjoined fellow-travellers and vulnerable fellow-believers. It would be ill-advised to single these last out for stocking their armories with the laptop and the Kalashnikov. Since in an image-driven world where television pictures reach the most distant village, basic information and messaging are no longer the preserve of the educated and privileged (ch. 1).

69. The array of output is impressive. There is a tendency only to look at insurgent programming that celebrates martyrdom, recruitment, or proselytising messages. Didactic children's programming is also prolific. The 'Gilid Shalit' adult cartoon centres on Shalit's father's forlorn wait for the return of his captured son. See YouTube with English subtitles: Prospect (04 May 2010), 'Why Is Hamas Making Cartoons?', http://www.prospectmagazine.co.uk/2010/05/hamass-debt-to-the-graphic-Novel/; http://www.youtube.com/watch?v=Sb8UQCimV4c, both accessed 28 May 2010.

70. See the leader of Hezbollah Nasrallah's speech justifying their communications network. Nasrallah, Hassan (08 May 2008), 'Nasrallah Justifies Lebanon Riots', http://yalibnan.com/site/archives/2008/05/nasrallah_justi.php; http://www.youtube.com/watch?v=YrfxnCoPViI, accessed 28 May 2010.

71. Micolta, Patricia (2009), p. 5, 'The Bolivarian Connection: The Fuerzas Armadas Revolucionaras de Colombia (FARC) and Hugo Chavez', paper presented at Midwest Political Science Association, 67th Annual Conference, Palmer House Hilton, Chicago, http://www.allacademic.com//meta/p_mla_apa_research_citation/3/6/1/6/7/pages361678/p361678-7.php, accessed 30 May 2010. Micolta says in the 1990s FARC built 5 clandestine radio stations, maintaining 12 multilingual internet sites. This accompanied an increase in military fronts from 25 to 65 between the 1980s and mid-1990s.

72. Bacevich, Andrew (11 Sept 2006), 'The Islamic Way of War', *The American Conservative*, http://www.amconmag.com/article/2006/sep/11/00007/, accessed 30 May

2010. Bacevich sees a progression that takes in the Afghan Mujahadeen in the 1980s, the 1987 First Intifada and post 2000 Second Intifada, the US 1993 Somali débacle, Twin Towers 2001, and most recently Iraq and Afghan expeditionary experiences.

73. (2009), op. cit., p. 28.

74. Loyd, Anthony (31 May 2010), p. 27, 'Saudi Dollars Flood into Afghan War Zone', *The Sunday Times*. Loyd notes Saudi funds flow from Al-Qaeda in the Arabian Peninsular via Waziristan to Taliban fighters, thus 'illuminate the difficulties in dividing the Taleban from al-Qaeda influence and the continuing involvement of Saudi donors in sponsoring the insurgency'. See US Government Accountability Office (Sept 2009), *Combating Terrorism*, Washington, DC.

75. Strick Van Linschoten, Alex & Kuehn, Felix (2012) *An Enemy We Created: The Myth of the Taliban-Al Qaeda Merger in Afghanistan* London: Hurst, 2012.

76. See Ronfeldt on alternative appropriate corporate design models: 'conglomerates', 'cartels', 'multi-hub networks' (12 Jan 2010), http://al-sahwa.blogspot.com/2010/01/follow-up-to-al-qaeda-franchise-or.html; McLaughlin, Joshua (2009), 'The al Qaeda Franchise Model: An Alternative', www.smallwarsjournal.com, accessed 14 July 2010.

77. Whether it is a network, coalition, or social movement may be enlightened by Tarrow's discussion in Tarrow, Sidney (2005), pp. 163–34, *The New Transnational Activism*, Cambridge: Cambridge University Press. Networks, he argues, are looser, less meaningful than coalitions or movements. Coalitions are 'collaborative, means-oriented arrangements that permit organisational entities to pool resources in order to effect change'. But 'movements are "sustained interactions between challengers and authorities on matters of policy and/or culture"'.

78. Eilstrup-Sangiovanni, Mette & Jones, Calvert (2010), pp. 341 and 358, 'Assessing The Dangers of Illicit Networks', in Brown, Michael et al (eds), *Contending with Terrorism: Roots, Strategies and Responses*, Cambridge MA: MIT Press.

79. British Army (2010), op. cit., p. CS2–1.

80. Kilcullen (2009), op. cit., pp. 32–33.

81. Eilstrup-Sangiovanni, op. cit., for discussion of trust in networks.

82. Halliday (2004), op. cit..

83. Corman, Steven & Schiefelbein, Jill (20 Apr 2006), p. 5, 'Communication and Media Strategy in the Jihadi War of Ideas', Consortium for Strategic Communication, Arizona State University.

84. Ibid., p. 2.

85. Ibid., pp. 10–11.

86. MEMRI (14 June 2007), '*Global Islamic Media Front Instructs Islamists to Infiltrate Popular Non-Islamic Forums to Spread Pro-Islamic State Propaganda*', MEMRI Special Dispatches Series 1621, http://memri.org/bin/articles.cgi?Page=archives&Area=sd&ID=SP162107, accessed 01 Mar 2008; see also Bolt et al (2008b), op. cit., p. 12.

87. Smith, Graeme (2009), p. 193, 'What Kandahar's Taliban Say', in Giustozzi, Antonio (2009) (ed.), *Decoding the New Taliban: Insights from the Afghan Field*, London: Hurst.

88. Ahmed, Samina (17 Mar 2010), International Crisis Group presentation at RUSI, London.

89. Smith, op. cit., p. 204, Smith's field research shows fighters describing him variously

as a 'figurehead', 'commander of the faithful selected by 1,000 mullahs', 'indispensible', 'not necessarily required for their war'.

90. Giustozzi (2009), op. cit., p. 293.

91. (2009), op. cit., p. 58.

92. In 2009–2010 *Al-Qaeda* is reported to have spearheaded some Taliban offensives, co-ordinating Afghan and Pakistani groups. See Marwan, Bishara (02 Feb 2010), 'TangoingwiththeTaliban',http://blogs.aljazeera.net/imperium/2010/02/02/tangoing-taliban.

93. (04–10 Sept 2008), 'La Parade des Talibans Avec Leurs Trophées Francais', *Paris Match*.

94. See (03 May 2009), 'Why the Taliban is Winning the Propaganda War', *Time Magazine*, http://www.time.com/time/world/article/0,8599,18954 96,00.html, accessed 26 May 2010.

95. (01 Mar 2010), 'Afghanistan Bans Coverage of Taliban Attacks', *Reuters*, http://www.reuters.com/article/idUSSGE6200CS20100301.

96. Nathan, Joanna (2009), p. 26, 'Reading the Taliban', in Giustozzi (2009), op. cit..

97. Ibid., p. 29.

98. Ibid., p. 38.

99. AlertNet (03 May 2010), 'US Attacks', http://www.alertnet.org/thenews/newsdesk/SGE64207P.htm, accessed 29 Aug 2010.

100. al-Jazeera (03 May 2010), 'Pakistan Taliban Chief Threatens US', http://english.aljazeera.net/news/americas/2010/05/20105385413857720.html.

101. Seib, Philip (May-June 2008), 'The Al-Qaeda Media Machine', *Military Review*, pp. 74–80.

102. Kurth Cronin, Audrey (2009), p. 170, *How Terrorism Ends*, Princeton: Princeton University Press; Exum, Andrew (May 2008), 'The Spectacle of War: Insurgent Video Propaganda and Western Response, 1990-Present', *Arab Media & Society*.

103. Devji, op. cit., p. 25.

104. Scheuer, Michael (30 May 2007), 'Al-Qaeda's Media Doctrine: Evolution from Cheerleader to Opinion-Shaper', *Terrorism Focus*, vol. 14, Issue 15, Washington, DC: Jamestown Foundation.

105. Paz, Reuven cited in Wohlgelernter, Elli (20 Feb 2003), 'Radical Muslim Groups Targeting Israeli-American "Conspiracy" Expert', *Jerusalem Post*, http://www.religionnewsblog.com/2430/radical-muslim-groups-targeting-israeli-american-conspiracy-expert.

106. Scheuer (2007), op. cit..

107. Glasser, Susan & Coll, Steve (7 Aug 2005), 'Terrorists Move to the Web as Base of Operations', *Washington Post*, http://www.washingtonpost.com/wp-dyn/content/article/2005/08/05/AR2005080501138.html.

108. Initially of 'al-Tawhid wal-Jihad', later known as 'al-Qaida in Iraq'.

109. Glasser, Susan & Coll, Steve (09 Aug 2005), 'The Web as Weapon', *Washington Post*, http://www.washingtonpost.com/wp-dyn/content/article/2005/08/08/AR2005080801018.html, citing Evan Kohlmann.

110. Bolt (2008b), op. cit., p. 16.

111. Weaver, Mary Anne (July 2006), 'The Short, Violent Life of Abu Musab al-Zarqawi', *The Atlantic*. Weaver cites Pentagon papers, implicating the Bush administration in building up al-Zarqawi's prominence in a psyops campaign.

112. Labi, Nadya (July-Aug 2006), 'Jihad 2.0', *The Atlantic*, http://www.theatlantic.com/magazine/archive/2006/07/jihad-20/4980/, accessed 17 July 2010.

113. (29 May 2010), p. 56, 'More Powerful Than Ever', *The Economist*, this despite the channel being denied a bureau presence in Egypt and Saudi for alleged bias favouring the Muslim Brotherhood and Hamas.

114. McAdam, Doug, Tarrow, Sidney & Tilly, Charles (2001), p. 243, *Dynamics of Contention*, Cambridge: Cambridge University Press: 'Opportunity spirals operate through sequences of environmental change, interpretation of that change, action, and counteraction, repeated as one action alters another action's environment'.

115. Duffield, John & Dombrowski, Peter (eds) (2009), p. 26, *Balance Sheet: the Iraq War and US National Security*, Stanford CA: University of California Press.

116. Deutsche Welle (29 Apr 2010), 'German Army Opens IED Research Center for Soldiers', http://www.dw-world.de/dw/article/05516501,00.html, accessed 26 May 2010; BBC TV Panorama (24 May 2010), 'A Very British Hero'.

117. Pakistan Body Count: Between 20 Nov. 1995 and 01 May 2010 representing 255 incidents. http://www.pakistanbodycount.org/bla.php, accessed 26 May 2010.

118. Walzer would disagree. For him 'just terror' like 'just war' principles are constant. Walzer, Michael (2006a), 'Just War and Terror', *Philosophia*, vol. 34, pp. 3–12.

119. BBC (13 July 2010), 'Robinson and McGuinness Condemn NI Rioting', http://www.bbc.co.uk/news/10617267.

120. Gurr (1993), op. cit., p. 69.

121. Mack, Andrew (Jan 1975), p. 184, 'Why Big Nations Lose Small Wars: The Politics of Asymmetric Conflict', *World Politics*, vol. 27, no. 2, pp. 175–200.

122. Edelman, Murray (1988), p. 101, *Constructing the Political Spectacle*, Chicago: University of Chicago Press (my italics).

123. Laqueur, Walter (2002), *The New Terrorism: Fanaticism and the Arms of Mass Destruction*, London: Phoenix Press; Simon, Steven & Benjamin, Daniel (Spring 2000), 'America and the New Terrorism', *Survival*, vol. 42, no. 1, IISS.

124. Andrea Berger of RUSI differentiates between CBR and N. The nuclear option, she argues, remains beyond the probable reach of insurgents without state sponsorship: 'Firstly, material has to be acquired, whether gifted or stolen. Indigenous production is largely inconceivable. Thereafter, fissile material has to be effectively weaponised, something a number of "rogue" nuclear states themselves have struggled with. Weaponisation of fissile material is a vastly different challenge than weaponisation of a CBR source. The technical challenges of weaponisation change depending on your delivery capabilities. You can conduct a chemical attack (a la Aum Shinrikyo, 1995) using plastic bags filled with chemicals and then stabbing them with pens to release the source material. You can't do the same with nuclear, even if it is a "crude" device'. Personal correspondence 19 Sept 2011.

125. Hoffmann, Bruce, http://www.fas.org/irp/congress/2002_hr/100802hill.html. Cf. Ben-Dor, Gabriel & Pedhazur, Ami (2004), p. 9, 'The Uniqueness of Islamic Fundamentalism and the Fourth Wave of International Terrorism', in Weinberg, Leonard & Pedhazur, Ami (eds), *Religious Fundamentalism and Political Extremism*, London: Frank Cass. Argues that Islamic fundamentalism produces greater violence and more indiscriminate killing than that of other political or religious groups. By contrast Barkun (2004), op. cit. sees in 'new religions' an introverted character and not a homogeneous commitment to a campaign of violence.

126. Advocates of 'ends justify the means' consequentialism demand terrorist acts demonstrate three things: 1) the objective must be adequate to the harm inflicted; 2) the act must be capable of delivering the objective; 3) it must be the least costly means of attaining that objective. These are difficult conditions to fulfil, but crucially to measure. But why should the insurgent have to meet conditions of certain delivery implied in 2) when state bombing of targets in or close to non-combatant centres often fails to honour the same? Primoratz, Igor (2006), p. 62–3, 'Terrorism in the Israeli-Palestinian Conflict', in Law, Stephen (ed.) (2008), *Israel, Palestine and Terror*, London: Continuum. Guthrie introduces a degree of subjectivism: '(t) he essence of the doctrine {just war}, however, is disciplined pragmatism, and judgement does have to be used in the application of the criteria in specific situations; they are not tick-box tests that can be used simply or mechanically' Guthrie, Charles & Quinlan, Michael (2007), p. 15, *The Just War Tradition: Ethics in Modern Warfare*, London: Bloomsbury. However for non-consequentialists terrorism undermines values that protect individual freedom, not least the right not to be killed. Some commentators return to the paramount prerequisite of reasonable hope of success in attaining fulfilment of just war. Consequently they conclude terrorism can never satisfy this conceptual link. Walzer, Michael (2006b), *Just and Unjust Wars*, New York: Basic Books, ch. 12.

127. Locke (1728), op. cit..

128. Laqueur, op. cit., p. 282.

129. Hoffmann, Bruce (2002), p. 312, 'Rethinking Terrorism and Counterterrorism Since 9/11', *Studies in Conflict & Terrorism*, vol. 25, pp. 303–316.

130. BBC (02 Oct 2000), 'Boy Becomes Palestinian Martyr', http://news.bbc.co.uk/1/hi/952600.stm. It has been suggested this controversial scene was staged: Camera (13 Oct 2005), 'Anatomy of a French Media Scandal', http://www.camera.org/index.asp?x_article=855&x_context=3, accessed 15 July 2010.

131. Hogan, J Michael (2000), p. 143, 'Science of Cold War Strategy', in Medhurst, Martin & Brands, HW (eds), *Critical Reflections on the Cold War: Linking Rhetoric and History*, College Station Tex: Texas A&M University Press.

CONCLUSION

1. Baines, Paul; Fill, Chris & Kelly, Page (2008), p. 5, *Marketing*, Oxford: Oxford University Press.

2. Ibid., pp. 8–14.

3. British Army (Nov. 2009), op. cit., pp. 36 & 38; US Army (2007), op. cit., pp. 3–6, sections 3–36 & 3–34 to 3–38.

4. Orwell, George (1949, 1989), *Nineteen Eighty-Four*, London: Penguin.

5. Kaletsky, Anatole (2010), *Capitalism 4.0: The Birth of a New Economy*, New York: Public Affairs.

6. op. cit., p. 170.

7. Ibid., p. 287.

8. Le Bon, Gustave (1896, 2007), pp. 14–15, *The Crowd*, Charleston SC: BiblioBazaar.

9. Ibid.

10. (2002), p. 813, *The Shield of Achilles*, New York: Knopf.

BIBLIOGRAPHY

9/11 Commission Report (2004), *Final Report of the National Commission on Terrorist Attacks upon the United States*, Washington, DC: U.S. Government Printing Office.

Aaronovitch, David (2009), *Voodoo Histories: The Role of the Conspiracy Theory in Shaping Modern History*, London: Jonathan Cape.

Abdulhamid, Ammir (09 June 2011), 'Beware Official Propaganda!' http://syrianrevolutiondigest.blogspot.com/2011/06/beware-official-propaganda.html, accessed 13 June 2011.

Abdullah, Ibrahim & Muana, Patrick (1998), 'The Revolutionary United Front of Sierra Leone', in Clapham, Christopher, ed, *African Guerrillas*, pp. 172–193, Oxford: James Currey.

Adams, Gerry (10 May 1998), 'Presidential Address by Gerry Adams to Reconvened Sinn Féin Ard Fheis', http://cain.ulst.ac.uk/events/peace/docs/ga10598.htm, accessed 03 Aug 2008.

Adams, Gerry in English, Richard (2003), *Armed Struggle*, Oxford: Oxford University Press.

Adorno, Theodor & Horkheimer, Max (2008), 'The Culture Industry: Enlightenment as Mass Deception', in During, Simon, ed, *The Cultural Studies Reader*, 3rd edn, London & New York: Routledge.

Ahmed, Samina (17 Mar 2010), International Crisis Group presentation at RUSI, London.

Ahmed, Murad & Beaman, Lucinda (27 June 2011), 'LulzSec Hackers Shut Down After 50-Day Campaign', *The Times*, p. 11.

Ainsworth, Bob (15 Sept 2009), UK Secretary of Defense, speech, King's College London.

Al-Shagra, Ahmad F (07 Dec 2010), 'Tunisia Blocks Wikileaks and Everyone Referencing It', *The Next Web*, http://thenextweb.com/me/2010/12/07/tunisia-blocks-wikileaks-everyone-referencing-it/, accessed 19 Aug 2011.

Alantine, Gary (winter 1993), 'The Sad Demise, Mysterious Disappearance, and Glorious Triumph of Symbolic Interactionism', *Annual Review of Sociology*, no. 19.

Alexander, Jeffrey & Jacobs, Ronald (1998), 'Mass Communication, Ritual and Civil Society', in Liebes T & Curran, James (eds), *Media Ritual and Identity*, London: Routledge.

BIBLIOGRAPHY

Alexander, Martin & Keiger, JFV (2002), 'France and the Algerian War: Strategy, Operations and Diplomacy', *Journal of Strategic Studies*, vol. 25, issue 2.

AlertNet (03 May 2010), 'U.S. Attacks', http://www.alertnet.org/thenews/newsdesk/SGE64207P.htm, accessed 29 Aug 2010.

Alinsky, Saul (1989), *Rules for Radicals*, New York: Vintage Books.

al-Jazeera (03 May 2010), 'Pakistan Taliban Chief Threatens U.S'., http://english.aljazeera.net/news/americas/2010/05/20105385413857720.html, accessed 30 Sept 2010.

Alluni, Taysir (21 Oct 2001), interview for *al-Jazeera* with Osama Bin Laden, in Lawrence, Bruce (2005), p. 112, *Messages to the World: The Statements of Osama Bin Laden*, London & New York: Verso.

Alonso, Rogelio (2003), *The IRA and Armed Struggle*, London & New York: Routledge.

Al-Shishani, Murad Batal (04 Feb 2010), 'Taking al-Qaeda's Jihad to Facebook', Jamestown Foundation, *Monitor*, vol. 8, Issue 5, http://www.jamestown.org/programs/gta/single/?tx_ttnews[tt_news]=36002&tx_ttnews[backPid]=457&no_cache=1, accessed 27 Feb 2010.

Al Somood Magazine (17 Jan 2008), 'The Media Activities of the Taliban Islamic Movement', *Al Somood*, http://worldanalysis.net/postnuke/html/index.php?name=News&file=article&sid=731, accessed 25 June 2009.

Altheide, David (2009), *Terror Post 9/11 and the Media*, New York: Peter Lang.

Alvarado M; Gutch R & Wolle, T (1987), *Learning the Media*, London: Macmillan.

American Marketing Association (Dec 2007), http://www.marketingpower.com/Community/ARC/Pages/Additional/Definition/default.aspx?sq=definition+of+marketing, accessed 09 June 2009.

Amnesty International (2010), *Egypt Rises: Killings, Detention and Torture in the 25th January Revolution*, London: Amnesty International.

'ANC Submission to the Truth and Reconciliation Commission' (Aug 1996), http://www.justice.gov.za/trc/hrvtrans/submit/anctruth.htm; 'ANC Second Submission to the Truth and Reconciliation Commission' (12 May 1997), http://www.justice.gov.za/trc/hrvtrans/submit/anc2.htm, accessed 30 May 2010.

Anderson, Benedict (1983, 2006), *Imagined Communities*, London & New York: Verso.

Anderson, Chris (2006), *The Long Tail*, London: Random House.

Anderson, Lisa (May/June 2011), 'Demystifying the Arab Spring', *Foreign Affairs*, http://www.foreignaffairs.com/articles/67693/lisa-anderson/demystifying-the-arab-spring, accessed 13 June 2011.

Anderson, Nels (1923), *The Hobo: The Sociology of the Homeless Man*, Chicago: University of Chicago Press.

Ang, Ien (1990), 'Culture and Communication: Towards an Ethnographic Critique of Media Consumption in the Transnational Media System', *European Journal of Communication*, vol. 5, pp. 239–260.

Anheier, Helmut; Kaldor, Mary & Glasius, Marlies (2005), *Global Civil Society 2004/5*, London: Sage.

Anonymous Press Release (03 Jan 2011), http://www.anonnews.org/index.php?p=press&a=item&i=133, accessed 09 Mar 2011.

Anonymous (11 June 2011), 'Spain: Anonymous Takes Down National Police Website #OpPolicia', http://www.anonops.blogspot.com/, accessed 20 June 2011.

Ansari, Ali (13 Feb 2010), 'The Nuking of Iran's Dissent', *The Guardian*.

BIBLIOGRAPHY

Appadurai, Arjun (1990), 'Disjuncture and Difference in the Global Cultural Economy', *Theory, Culture & Society*, vol. 7, pp. 295–310.

—— (1996), *Modernity at Large: Cultural Dimensions of Globalisation*, Minneapolis, University of Minneapolis Press.

Arena, Michael & Arrigo, Bruce (2006), *The Terrorist Identity: Explaining the Terrorist Threat*, New York & London: New York University.

Arendt, Hannah (1990), *On Revolution*, London: Penguin.

Armstrong, Stephen (19 June 2011), 'Dropping Facebook', *The Sunday Times*, p. 18.

Arquilla, John & Ronfeldt, David (2001), *Networks and Netwars: The Future of Terror, Crime, and Militancy*, Santa Monica, CA: RAND.

Asia Foundation (2009), 'Afghanistan in 2009', http://asiafoundation.org/publications/pdf/627, accessed 26 Jan 2010.

Atkinson, Philippa (1997), 'The War Economy in Liberia: a Political Analysis', London: ODI Atomic Archive, http://www.atomicarchive.com/Movies/Movie8.shtml, accessed 28 Apr 2009.

Atran, Scott (2011), *Talking to the Enemy*, London: Allen Lane.

Auletta, Ken (1997), *The Highwaymen: Warriors of the Information Superhighway*, New York: Random House.

Avrich, Paul (1988), *Anarchist Portraits*, Princeton NJ: Princeton University Press.

Awan, Akil (2007), 'Transitional Religiosity Experiences: Contextual Disjuncture and Islamic Political Radicalism', in Abbas, T. (ed.), *Islamic Political Radicalism: A European Comparative Perspective*, Edinburgh: Edinburgh University Press.

Ayman al-Zawahiri letter to Abu Musab al-Zarqawi 09 July 2005, in Metz, Thomas (May/June 2006), 'Massing Effects in the Information Domain', *Military Review*.

Azam, Jean-Paul (2005), 'Suicide Bombing as Inter-generational Investment', *Public Choice*, vol. 122, pp. 177–98.

Bacevich, Andrew (2002), *American Empire: the Realities and Consequences of U.S. Diplomacy*, Cambridge MA: Harvard University Press.

—— (11 Sept 2006), 'The Islamic Way of War', *The American Conservative*, http://www.amconmag.com/article/2006/sep/11/00007/, accessed 30 May 2010.

—— (Oct 2008), 'The Petraeus Doctrine', *Atlantic Magazine*, http://www.theatlantic.com/magazine/archive/2008/10/the-petraeus-doctrine/6964/2/, accessed 30 Sept 2010.

Badiou, Alain (2005), *Being and Event*, London & New York: Continuum.

Bagdikian, Ben (2004), *The New Media Monopoly*, Boston MA: Beacon Press.

Baines, Paul; Worcester, Robert; Jarrett, David & Mortimore, Roger (2003), 'Market Segmentation and Product Differentiation in Political Campaigns: A Technical Feature Perspective', *Journal of Marketing Management*, vol. 19, no. 2.

Baines, Paul & O'Shaughnessy, Nicholas (2006), *Muslim Voices: The British Muslim Response to Islamist Video-Polemic: An Exploratory Study*, Cranfield University School of Management.

Baines, Paul; Fill, Chris & Kelly, Page (2008), *Marketing*, Oxford: Oxford University Press.

Bak, Per (1996), *How Nature Works: The Science of Self-Organised Criticality*, New York NY: Copernicus.

Bakker, Edwin (2006), 'Jihadi Terrorists in Europe, their Characteristics and the Circumstances in which they joined the Jihad: an Exploratory Study', Clingendael Security Paper 2, The Hague.

Bakunin, Mikhail (1842), 'La Reaction en Allemagne, Fragment par un Francais', http://www.marxists.org/reference/archive/bakunin/works/1842/reaction-germany.htm, accessed 30 Sept 2010.

Bandurski, David (July 2008), 'China's Guerrilla War for the Web', *Far East Economic Review*.

Barabasi, Albert-Laszlo (2002), *Linked: The New Science of Networks*, Cambridge MA: Perseus.

Barber, Benjamin (1996), *Jihad vs McWorld*, New York: Ballantine.

Barber, Noel (2004), *The War of the Running Dogs*, London: Cassell.

Barer, Shlomo (2000), *The Doctors of Revolution*, London: Thames and Hudson.

Barker, Martin & Petley, Julian (eds) (2001), *Ill Effects: The Media/Violence Debate*, London: Routledge.

Barkun, Michael (2004), 'Religious Violence and the Myth of Fundamentalism', in Weinberg, Leonard & Pedahzur, Ami (eds), *Religious Fundamentalism and Political Extremism*, London: Frank Cass.

Barnett, Brooke & Reynolds, Amy (2009), *'Terrorism and the Press: An Uneasy Relationship'*, New York: Peter Lang.

Barno, David (10 Sept 2009), 'Testimony Before the House Armed Services Subcommittee on Oversight and Investigations', in Burton, Brian & Nagl, John (eds) (Feb 2010), *Keeping the Edge: Revitalising America*, Washington, DC: Center for a New American Security.

Barry, Liz (25 Aug 2008), John Donne's 'A Valediction Forbidding Mourning', on 'Fry's English Delight: Metaphors' http://www.bbc.co.uk/radio4/arts/frys_english.shtml, accessed 25 Aug 2008.

Barth, Frederik (ed.) (1969), *Ethnic Groups and Boundaries: The Social Organisation of Cultural Difference*, London: George Allen & Unwin.

Barthes, Roland (1957, 1973), *Mythologies*, London: Paladin Grafton.

—— (1977a), *Elements of Semiology*, New York: Hill & Wang.

—— (1977b), *Image, Music, Text*, London: Fontana.

—— (2000), *Camera Lucida*, London: Vintage.

Bartlett, Frederic (1967), *Remembering*, London: Cambridge University Press.

—— (1972), *Remembering: A Study in Experimental and Social Psychology*, London & New York: Cambridge University Press.

Battram, Arthur (1998), *Navigating Complexity*, London: The Industrial Society.

Baudrillard, Jean (1981, 1997), *Simulacra and Simulation*, Ann Arbor: University of Michigan Press.

—— (2003), *The Spirit of Terrorism*, London: Verso.

—— (2007), *In the Shadow of the Silent Majority*, Los Angeles CA: Semiotext(e),

Baylis, John; Smith, Steven & Owens, Patricia (1999), *The Globalisation of World Politics*, Oxford: Oxford University Press.

BBC (2007), 'From Seesaw to Wagon Wheel: Safeguarding Impartiality in the 21st Century', Report, London: BBC Trust.

BBC News (02 Oct 2000), 'Boy Becomes Palestinian Martyr', http://news.bbc.co.uk/1/hi/world/middle_east/952600.stm accessed 28 Sept 2010.

—— (26 June 2009), 'Web Slows After Jackson Death', http://news.bbc.co.uk/1/hi/technology/8120324.stm, accessed 28 Sept 2010.

BIBLIOGRAPHY

———— (13 July 2010), 'Robinson and McGuinness Condemn NI Rioting', http://www.bbc.co.uk/news/10617267, accessed 28 Sept 2010.

———— (29 Jan 2011), 'Egypt: Mubarak Sacks Cabinet and Defends Security Role', http://www.bbc.co.uk/news/world-middle-east-11777943, accessed 15 June 2011.

———— (01 June 2011), 'Syrian Unrest: Inquiry into Hamza Aa-Khatib's Death', http://www.bbc.co.uk/news/world-middle-east-13622959, accessed 13 June 2011.

BBC Radio 4, (29 Aug 2008), 'Has Hollywood Turned its Back on Hit Theme Tunes?', *World Tonight*.

———— (07 June 2010), 'Survey: Brits Associate Muslims with Extremism', *Today*.

BBC Television (06 Dec 2006), Richard Dimbleby Lecture: General Sir Mike Jackson.

———— (24 Apr 2009), Johann Hari review of documentary 'Afghan Star', *Newsnight*.

———— (24 May 2010), 'A Very British Hero', *Panorama*.

———— (15 Nov 2010), interview with Paul Wood in Kabul, *News at Ten*.

Beck, Ulrich (2001), *World Risk Society*, Cambridge: Polity.

Becker, Howard (1991), *Outsiders: Studies in the Sociology of Deviance*, New York: Free Press.

Beckett, Ian (2001), *Modern Insurgencies and Counterinsurgencies*, Abingdon: Routledge.

Belk, Russell (1996), 'On Aura, Illusion, Escape and Hope in Apocalyptic Consumption: the Apotheosis of Las Vegas', in Brown Stephen, Bell Jim, & Carson, David (eds), *Marketing Apocalypse: Eschatology, Escapology and the Illusion of the End*, London: Routledge.

Bell, Daniel (1999), *The Coming of Post-Industrial Society*, New York: Best Books.

Bell, Duncan (March 2003), 'Mythscapes: Memory, Mythology, and National Identity', *British Journal of Sociology*, vol. 54, no. 1, pp. 63–81.

Bell, Robert (25 Nov 2009), 'Social Capital: Technology's Impact on Society', http://www.govtech.com/dc/articles/734063, accessed 05 Feb 2010.

Benbow, Tim (2004), *The Magic Bullet? Understanding the Revolution in Military Affairs*, London: Brassey's.

Ben-Dor, Gabriel & Pedhazur, Ami (2004), 'The Uniqueness of Islamic Fundamentalism and the Fourth Wave of International Terrorism', in Weinberg, Leonard & Pedhazur, Ami (eds), *Religious Fundamentalism and Political Extremism*, London: Frank Cass.

Benford, Robert (Nov 1997), 'An Insider's Critique of the Social Movement Framing Perspective', *Sociological Inquiry*, vol. 67, no. 4, pp. 409–430.

Beniger, James (1986), *The Control Revolution: Technological and Economic Origins of the Information Society*, Cambridge MA: Harvard University Press.

Bennis, Warren (1993), *Beyond Bureaucracy*, San Francisco: Jossey-Bass.

Berlin, Isaiah (1995), *Karl Marx: His Life and Environment*, Oxford: Oxford University Press.

Bergson, Henri (1988), *Matter and Memory*, New York: Zone Books.

Berlet, Chip (Fall 2008), 'Leaderless Counterterrorism Strategy', *The Public Eye*, vol. 23, no. 3, http://www.publiceye.org/magazine/v23n3/leaderless_counterterrorism_strategy.html, accessed 27 Aug 2010.

Berdal, Mats & Economides, Spyros (2007), *United Nations Interventionism 1991–2004*, Cambridge: Cambridge University Press.

Berman, Eli & Laitin, David (October 2005), *Hard targets: Theory and Evidence on Suicide Attacks*, NBER Working Paper 11740.

BIBLIOGRAPHY

Bernays, Edward (1928), *Propaganda*, New York: Horace Liveright.

Berners-Lee, Tim (Mar 2007), 'The Digital Future of the United States: Part 1 The Future of the World Wide Web', U.S. House of Representatives Committee on Energy and Commerce, http://dig.csail.mit.edu/2007/03/01-ushouse-future-of-the-web.html, accessed 25 Jan 2010.

Berwick, Andrew (aka Anders Behring Breivik), (2011), *2083: A European Declaration of Independence*, http://www.scribd.com/doc/60849766/Anders-Behring-Breivik-Manifesto-2083—A-European-Declaration-of-Independence-By-Andrew-Berwick, accessed 23 July 2011.

Best, Steve & Kellner, Douglas (2001), *The Postmodern Adventure*, London Routledge.

Betz, David (2008), 'The Virtual Dimension of Modern Insurgency and Counterinsurgency', *Small Wars & Insurgencies*, vol. 19, no. 4, pp. 510–540.

Bevir, M & Rhodes, R.A.W (2003), *Interpreting British Governance*, London: Routledge.

Beyer, Lisa (04 Dec 2010), 'The Myths and Reality of Munich', *Time*, http://www.time.com/time/magazine/article/0,9171,1137646–1,00.html, accessed 26 Aug 2010.

Bhabha, Homi (1994), 'Narrating the Nation', in Hutchinson, John & Smith, Anthony D. (eds), *Nationalism*, Oxford & New York: Oxford University Press pp. 306–312.

Bin Laden, Osama, 'Among A Band of Knights', in Lawrence, Bruce (2005), *Messages to the World: The Statements of Osama Bin Laden*, London: Verso.

Bird, Conrad (2009), 'Strategic Communication and Behaviour Change: Lessons from Domestic Policy', http://www.fco.gov.uk/en/about-the-fco/publications/publications/pd-publication/behaviour-change, accessed 11 June 2009.

Bishop, Ronald (2000), 'Good Afternoon, Good Evening, and Good Night: The Truman Show as Media Criticism', *Journal Of Communication Inquiry*, Jan. 2000, vol. 24, no. 1, pp. 6–18.

Black, Ian (16 June 2011), 'Like Egypt, the Army's Generals Will Be Decisive', *The Guardian*, p. 25.

Blackmore, Chris (ed.) (2010), *Social Learning Systems and Communities of Practice*, London: Springer.

Blair, Tony (28 Sept 2004), speech to Labour Party Conference, 'Full Text: Blair's Conference Speech', *The Guardian*, http://www.guardian.co.uk/politics/2004/sep/28/labourconference.labour6, accessed 30 Sept 2010.

—— (2010), *A Journey*, London: Hutchison.

Blandford, Nicholas (06 June 2011), p. 25, 'Rebels "kill 120" as civil war looms', *The Times*, http://www.facebook.com/Syrian.Revolution.Eng, accessed 06 June 2011.

Bloch, Maurice (1998), *How We Think They Think: Anthropological Approaches to Cognition, Memory and Literacy*, Boulder & Oxford: Westview Press.

Bloom, Mia (2005), *Dying To Kill: The Allure of Suicide Terror*, New York: Columbia University Press.

Blumenthal, Sidney (1982), *The Permanent Campaign*, New York: Touchstone.

Bob, Clifford (2005), *The Marketing of Rebellion: Insurgents, Media and International Activism*, New York: Cambridge University Press.

Bobbitt, Philip (2002), *The Shield of Achilles*, London: Allen Lane.

—— (2008), *Terror and Consent: The Wars for the Twenty-First Century*, London & New York: Allen Lane.

Bolt, Neville (Feb 2008), review in *RUSI Journal*, vol. 152, no. 1, pp. 98–9 of Furedi, Frank (2007), *Invitation to Terror*, London: Continuum.

——— (Feb 2008a), 'Propaganda of the Deed and The Irish Republican Brotherhood', *RUSI Journal*, vol. 152, no. 1, pp. 98–99.

——— (Oct 2009), 'Unsettling Networks', *RUSI Journal*, vol. 154, no. 5, pp. 34–39.

——— (August/September 2010), 'The Leak Before the Storm: What WikiLeaks Tells Us About Modern Communication', *RUSI Journal*, vol. 155, no. 4, pp. 46–51.

Bolt, Neville; Betz, David & Azari, Jaz (September 2008b), 'Propaganda of the Deed 2008', RUSI Whitehall Report, pp. 48–54.

Boorstin, Daniel (1992), *The Image: A Guide to Pseudo-events in America*, New York: Vintage.

Boroditsky, Lera (1998), 'Metaphoric Structuring: Understanding Time Through Spatial Metaphors', *Cognition 75 (2000)*, pp. 1–28.

Bourdieu, Pierre (1977, 2003), *Outline of a Theory of Practice*, Cambridge: Cambridge University Press.

Bowyer Bell, J. (1972), *The Secret Army: A History of the IRA 1915–1970*, London: Sphere Books.

——— (1991), *The Gun in Politics: an Analysis of Irish Political Conflict, 1916–1986*, New Brunswick NJ: Transaction.

Boyle, Michael (Mar 2010), 'Do Counterterrorism and Counterinsurgency Go Together', *International Affairs*, vol. 86, no. 2, pp. 333–354.

Boym, Svetlana (2010), *Another Freedom: The Alternative History of an Idea*, Chicago: University of Chicago Press.

Brand Republic (08 Dec 2005), 'McCann Erickson Wins $1.35 billion U.S. Army Advertising Account', http://www.brandrepublic.com/News/531992/McCann-Erickson-wins-135bn-US-Army-advertising-account/, accessed 25 June 2009.

Brandon, Louise & Doder, Dusko (1999), *Milosevic: Portrait of a Tyrant*, New York: Free Press.

Brandt, Lisa Kaye (ed.) (2007), *Cultural Analysis and the Navigation of Complexity*, Lanham MY: University Press of America.

Brecht, Bertolt (1969), *Mutter Courage und Ihre Kinder*, Berlin: Suhrkamp Verlag.

Brennan, Rick et al (2005), 'Future Insurgency Threats', Draft 02/2005: for the Office of the Secretary of Defense, (RAND, DRR-3443-OSD SOLIC, 2005), Washington, DC: RAND.

Brettell, Caroline (2000), 'Theorising Migration in Anthropology', in Brettell, Caroline & Hollifield, James (eds), *Migration Theory*, New York & London: Routledge.

Briggs, Asa & Burke, Peter (2005), *A Social History of the Media: From Gutenberg to the Internet*, Cambridge: Polity.

Brock, George (28 Feb 2008), 'Who Really Brought Peace to Belfast', *TLS*, http://entertainment.timesonline.co.uk/tol/arts_and_entertainment/the_tls/article3445728.ece, accessed 13 July 2010.

——— (8 Apr 2009 & 23 Apr 2009), N Bolt interviews with former Managing Editor, *The Times*, London.

Browers, Michaelle (2006), *Democracy and Civil Society in Arab Political Thought*, Syracuse: Syracuse University Press.

British Army (Nov 2009), 'Security and Stabilisation: The Military Contribution-JDP 3–40', London: Ministry of Defence.

—— (Jan 2010), 'Army Field Manual Countering Insurgency', London: Ministry of Defence.

Brooks, Rosa (15 Mar 2010), 'Minutes of U.S. Advisory Commission on Public Diplomacy', Washington, DC.

Brown, Gordon (29 Apr 2009), 'Why We Are In Afghanistan', Statement to Parliament, http://www.fco.gov.uk/en/fco-in-action/uk-in-afghanistan/why-we're-in-afghanistan/, accessed 26 June 2009.

Brubaker, Rogers (2004), *'Ethnicity Without Groups'*, Boston MA: Harvard University Press

Brubaker, Rogers & Cooper, Frederick (2000), 'Beyond Identity', *Theory and Society*, vol. 29, pp. 1–47.

Buddenberg, Doris & Byrd, William (eds) (2006), 'Afghanistan's Drug Industry', UNODC/World Bank, http://web.worldbank.org/WBSITE/EXTERNAL/COUN-TRIES/SOUTHASIAEXT/0, contentMDK:21133060~pagePK:146736~piPK:146830 ~theSitePK:223547,00.html, accessed 06 July 2009.

Buckley, Mary (Spring 1976), 'John Mitchel, Ulster and Irish nationality (1842–1848)', *Studies: An Irish Quarterly Review*, vol. 65, no. 257, pp. 30–44.

Burke, Jason (26 Aug 2007), '"Islamism" has No Place in Terror's Lexicon', *The Observer*, http://www.guardian.co.uk/commentisfree/2007/aug/26/comment.alqaida, accessed 26 Aug 2010.

Burlingame, Roger (1940), *Engines of Democracy*, New York: Charles Scribner's.

Burnham, John & Pyper, Robert (2008), *Britain's Modernised Civil Service*, Basingstoke & New York: Palgrave Macmillan.

Burns, John (1886), *The Man with the Red Flag: Speech for the Defence by John Burns in the Trial of the Four Social Democrats for Seditious Conspiracy*, (*Socialist Tracts 1883–94*), London: The Modern Press.

Bushman, Brad & Phillips, Colleen (2001), 'If the Television Program Bleeds, Memory for the Advertisement Recedes', *Current Directions in Psychological Science*, (April 2001), vol. 10, no. 2, pp. 43–7.

Butler, Patrick & Harris, Phil (2009), 'Considerations on the Evolution of Political Marketing Theory', *Marketing Theory*, vol. 9, no. 2, pp. 149–164.

Butt, Ronald (03 May 1981), 'Mrs Thatcher: The First Two Years', *The Sunday Times*, http://www.margaretthatcher.org/speeches/displaydocument.asp?docid=104475, accessed 27 Aug 2010.

Butterworth, Alex (2010), *The World That Never Was: The True Story of Dreamers, Schemers, Anarchists and Secret Agents*, London: Bodley Head.

Calhoun, Craig (1989), 'Classical Social Theory and the French Revolution of 1848', *Sociological Theory*, vol. 7, no. 2, pp. 210–225.

—— (2004), 'Information Technology and the International Public Sphere', in Schuler, Douglas & Day, Peter (eds), *Shaping the Network Society*, Cambridge MA: MIT Press.

Camera (13 Oct 2005), 'Anatomy of a French Media Scandal', http://www.camera.org/index.asp?x_article=855&x_context=3, accessed 15 July 2010.

Cameron, David (15 June 2010), 'Bloody Sunday' Saville Inquiry statement to Parliament.

Camus, Albert (1968), *The Plague*, Harmondsworth: Penguin.

BIBLIOGRAPHY

Cantle Report (2001), 'Community Cohesion', Community Cohesion Review Team/ Home Office, http://www.cohesioninstitute.org.uk/Resources/AboutCommunityCohesion, accessed 30 Sept 2010.

Capra, Fritjof (2003), *The Hidden Connections*, London: Flamingo.

Carlisle, Alex (2007), *The Definition of Terrorism: A Report by Lord Carlisle of Berriew QC, Independent Reviewer of Terrorist Legislation*, London: Crown.

Carlson, Andrew (1972), *'Anarchism in Germany' Vol 1: The Early Movement*, Metuchen, NJ: Sacrecrow Press.

Carr, David (May 1986), 'Narrative and the Real World: An Argument for Continuity', *History and Theory*, vol. 25, no. 2, pp. 117–131.

Carr, Jeffrey (2010), *Inside Cyber Warfare: Mapping the Cyber Underworld*, Sebastopol CA: O'Reilly Media.

Carr, Matthew (2008), *The Infernal Machine: A History of Terrorism*, New York: New Press.

Carroll-Mayer, Moira; Fairweather, Ben & Stahl, Bernd Carsten (2008), 'CCTV Identity Management and Implications for Criminal Justice: some considerations', *Surveillance & Society*, vol. 5, no. 1, pp. 33–50.

Cartier-Bresson, Henri (1952), *'The Decisive Moment'*, New York: Simon & Schuster.

Castells, Manuel (2004), *The Information Age: The Power of Identity*, Malden MA & Oxford: Blackwell.

—— (2004), *The Power of Identity*, 2nd edn, Oxford: Blackwell.

—— (24 Oct 2008), 'Internet Beyond Myths', lecture, London School of Economics.

—— (2009), *Communication Power*, Oxford: Oxford University Press.

Catignani, Sergio (2010), 'The Israeli Defense Forces and the Al-Aqsa Intifada', in Marston, Daniel & Malkasian, Carter (eds), *Counterinsurgency in Modern Warfare*, Oxford: Osprey.

Cavelty, Myriam Dunn (2010), 'Cyberware', in Kassimeris, George & Buckley, John (eds), *The Ashgate Companion to Modern Warfare*, Farnham: Ashgate Publishing.

CBS Outdoor (2009), 'Time to Consider', http://timetoconsider.co.uk/pity_or_pitiful/pitiful/, accessed 03 July 2009.

Century Magazine (1894), http://www.chicagohistory.org/dramas/act1/theFuseIsLit/atCapitalSCapitol.htm, accessed 30 Sept 2010.

Chalaby, Jean (1997), 'No Ordinary Press Owners: Press Barons as a Weberian Ideal Type', *Media, Culture & Society*, vol. 19, no. 4, pp. 621–644.

Chaliand, Gerard (1982), *Guerrilla Strategies*, London: University of California Press.

Chaliand, Gerard & Blin, Arnaud (2007), *The History of Terrorism: From Antiquity to Al Qaeda*, University of California Press.

Chandler, Daniel (1994), 'The Sapir-Whorf Hypothesis', http://www.aber.ac.uk/media/Documents/short/whorf.html, accessed 25 Aug 2008.

Chandler, Daniel (2000), 'Marxist Media Theory: The Frankfurt School', citing Herbert Marcuse (1972), *One-Dimensional Man*, http://www.aber.ac.uk/media/Documents/marxism/marxism08.html, accessed 25 Aug 2008.

Channel 4 Television (30 June 2009), *Dispatches: 'Terror in Mumbai'*.

Charney, Leo (1995), 'In a Moment: Film and the Philosophy of Modernity', in Charney, Leo & Schwartz, Vanessa (eds) *Cinema and the Invention of Modern Life*, Berkeley CA: University of California Press.

Chayko, Mary (2002), *Connecting: How We Form Social Bonds and Communities in the Internet Age*, Albany NY: SUNY Press.

Cheran, R & Aiken, Sharryn (2005), 'The Impact of International Informal Banking on Canada: A Case Study of Tamil Transnational Money Transfer (Undiyal)', Canada/Sri Lanka, www.apgml.org.

Chiesi, H, Spilich, G & Voss, J (1979), 'Acquisition of Domain-related Information in Relation to High and Low Domain Knowledge', *Journal of Verbal Learning and Verbal Behaviour*, vol. 18, pp. 257–274.

Chomsky, Noam (2004), *'Hegemony or Survival'*, London: Penguin.

Chong, Philip; Shon, Ho & Arrigo, Bruce (2006), *'Reality Based Television and Police Citizen Encounters'*, Punishment and Society, vol. 8, no. 1, pp. 59–85.

Cilliers, Jakkie (2000), 'Resource Wars—a New Type of Insurgency', http://www.iss. co.za/PUBS/BOOKS/Angola/2Cilliers.pdf, accessed 7 Dec 2006.

Cilliers, Jackie & Dietrich, Christian (eds) (2000), *Angola's War Economy: The Role of Diamonds*, Pretoria: Institute for Security Studies.

Cilliers, Paul (1998), *Complexity and Post-Modernism*, London: Routledge.

Clarke, Richard (2004), *Against All Enemies*, London: Simon & Schuster.

Clarke, Richard & Knake, Robert (2010), *Cyber War: The Next Threat to National Security and What To Do About It*, New York NY: HarperCollins.

Clinton, Hillary (21 Jan 2010), 'Internet Freedom' speech, Newseum, Washington, DC.

Clohesy, Anthony (2000), 'Provisionalism and the (Im)possibility of Justice in Northern Ireland', in Howarth, David; Norval, Aletta; Stavrakakis, Yannis (eds), *Discourse Theory and Political Analysis: Identities, Hegemonies and Social Change*, Manchester & New York: Manchester University Press.

Clutterbuck, Lindsay (2004), 'The Progenitors of Terrorism: Russian Revolutionaries or Extreme Irish Republicans?' *Terrorism and Political Violence*, vol. 16, no. 1 (Spring 2004), pp. 154–181.

Coase, Ronald (Nov 1937), 'The Nature of the Firm', *Economica*, New Series, vol. 4, no. 16, pp. 386–405.

Cockcroft, Lucy, (05 Sept 2008), 'French Fury at Paris Match Photos of Taliban Fighters with Trophies from Dead Soldiers', *The Telegraph* online, http://www.telegraph. co.uk/news/worldnews/europe/france/2686114, accessed 05 Sept 2008.

COHA-Council on Hemispheric Affairs (2008), 'The Future of Mexico's EZLN', http:// www.coha.org/2008/11/the-future-of-the-ezln/, accessed 1 July 2009.

Cohen, Bernard (1963), *The Press, the Public, and Foreign Policy*, Boston: Little, Brown.

Cohen, Elliot (2005), *News Incorporated: Corporate Media Ownership and Its Threat to Democracy*, Amherst: Prometheus Books.

Cohen, Michael; March, James & Olsen, Johan (1972), 'A Garbage Can Model of Organisational Choice', *Administrative Science Quarterly*, vol. 17, no. 1, Mar. 1972, pp. 1–25.

Cohen, Stanley (2002), *Folk Devils and Moral Panics*, London: Routledge.

Cole, Michael (1996), *Cultural Psychology: A Once and Future Discipline*, Cambridge Mass. & London: Belknap Press of Harvard University Press.

Coleman, James (1988), 'Social Capital in the Creation of Human Capital', *AJS*, vol. 94, Supplement S95-S120.

Collier, George (2005), 'Basta!', Land and the Zapatista Rebellion in Chiapas', *Pinch of*

Salt, Oakland CA: Food First, http://flag.blackened.net/revolt/mexico/comment/andrew_diff_feb01.html, accessed 1 Aug 2009.

Collins, Randall (2001), 'Social Movements and the Focus of Emotional Attention', in Goodwin, Jeff; Jasper, James & Polletta, Francesca (eds), *Passionate Politics: Emotions in Social Movements*, Chicago & London: Chicago University Press.

Colombani, Jean-Marie, http://www.worldpress.org/1101we are all americans.htmll, accessed 20 Apr 2009.

Colum, Padraic (1916), *The Poems of the Irish Revolutionary Brotherhood*, Boston: Small, Maynard and Company.

Condit, Celeste Michelle & Caudill, Sally (eds) (1999), *Contemporary Rhetorical Theory*, New York: Guilford Press.

Connerton, Paul (2007), *How Societies Remember*, Cambridge: Cambridge University Press.

CONTEST (Mar 2009), *Pursue, Prevent, Protect, Prepare: The United Kingdom's Strategy for International Terrorism*, London: HM Government.

Coogan, Tim Pat (2000), *The IRA*, London: HarperCollins.

Coolsaet, Rik (2008), *Jihadi Terrorism and the Radicalisation Challenge in Europe*, Aldershot: Ashgate.

Cooper, Christopher & Block, Robert (2006*), Disaster: Hurricane Katrina and the Failure of Homeland Security*, New York: Times Books.

Corman, Steven & Schiefelbein, Jill (20 Apr 2006), *Communication and Media Strategy in the Jihadi War of Ideas*, Consortium for Strategic Communication, Arizona State University.

Corman, Steven & Dooley, Kevin (2008), 'Strategic Communication on a Rugged Landscape', Consortium for Strategic Communication, Arizona State University, Report no. 0801.

Corn, David (27 Mar 2009), 'Holbrooke calls for "Complete Rethink" of Drugs in Afghanistan', *Mother Jones*, http://www.motherjones.com/mojo/2009/03/holbrooke-calls-complete-rethink-drugs-afghanistan, accessed 06 July 2009.

Cornish, Paul (17 Oct 2002), pp. 18–20, 'Cry Havoc! And Let Slip the Managers of War: The Strategic, Military and Moral Hazards of Micro-managed Warfare', Final Draft, Centre for Defence Studies, International Policy Research Unit, London: King's College London http://www.nato.int/acad/fellow/99–01/cornish.pdf, accessed 11 Apr 2007.

Coté, James & Levine, Charles (2006), *Identity Formation, Agency and Culture: A Social Psychological Synthesis*, Mahwah NJ: Lawrence Erlbaum.

Couldry Nick (2006), 'Transvaluing Media Studies', in Curran, James & Morley, David, *Media and Cultural Theory*, London & New York: Routledge, pp. 177–194.

Crabtree, James (Jan 2009), 'India's Bloodied Elite', *Prospect Magazine*, http://www.prospect-magazine.co.uk/article_details.php?id=10523, accessed 15 July 2009.

——— (Aug 2009), 'The Real News from Pakistan', *Prospect Magazine*, http://www.youtube.com/watch?v=UzEAQ3Q3BoU, accessed 27 July 2009.

Cramer, Christopher (2006), *Civil War is Not a Stupid Thing: Accounting for Violence in Developing Countries*, London: Hurst.

Creel, George (1920), *How We Advertised America*, New York & London: Harper & Bros.

BIBLIOGRAPHY

Crenshaw, Martha (ed.) (1995, 2004), *Terrorism in Context*, University Park, PA: Pennsylvania State University.

—— (1998), 'The Logic of Terrorism: Terrorist Behaviour as a Product of Strategic Choice', in Reich, Walter (ed.), *Origins of Terrorism*, Baltimore MD: John Hopkins University Press.

Croft, Stuart (2006), *Culture, Crisis and America's War on Terror*, Cambridge: Cambridge University Press.

Cruise O'Brien, Connor (1978), *Herod: Reflections on Political Violence*, London: Hutchinson.

Cullison, Alan (Sept 2004), 'Inside Al-Qaeda's Hard Drive', *The Atlantic*.

Cunningham Bissell, William (2008), 'From Iraq to Katrina and Back: Bureaucratic Planning as Strategic Failure, Fiction and Fantasy', *Sociology Compass*, vol. 2, no. 5, pp. 1431–1461.

Dahlgren, Peter & Gurevitch, Michael (2005), 'Political Communication in a Changing World', in Curran, James & Gurevitch, Michael eds, *Mass Media and Society*, 4th edn, London: Hodder Arnold.

Danermark, Berth; Ekström, Mats; Jakobsen, Liselotte & Karlsson, Jan Ch. (2002), *Explaining Society: Critical Realism in the Social Sciences*, London: Routledge.

Darlington, Ralph (2008), *Syndicalism and the Transition to Communism: An International Comparative Analysis*, Aldershot: Ashgate.

Darnton, Robert & Roche, Daniel (eds) (1989), *Revolution in Print: The Press in France 1775–1800*, Berkeley, Los Angeles & London: University of California Press.

Darwash, Mahmud (1984), *Victims of a Map*, London: Al Saqi.

Da Silva, Filipe Carreira (2007), *G.H.Mead: A Critical Introduction*, Cambridge: Polity.

Dauber, Cori (2009), *YouTube War: Fighting in a World of Cameras in Every Cell Phone and Photoshop on Every Computer*, Carlisle PA: Strategic Studies Institute.

David, GJ & McKeldin, TR (2009), *Ideas as Weapons*, Washington, DC: Potomac Books.

Davies, Norman (1996), *Europe: A History*, Oxford & New York: OUP.

Davis, Dickie Lt. Col. (Jan 2008), 'Propaganda of the Deed', King's College London Insurgency Research Group conference presentation

Davis, Graham (1997), 'The Historiography of the Irish Famine', in O'Sullivan (ed.), *The Meaning of the Famine*, London &Washington, DC: Leicester University Press.

Davis, Mike (2006), *Planet of Slums*, London: Verso.

Davison, W Phillips and George, Alexander (1952, revised 1970), pp. 433–5, 'An Outline for the Study of International Political Communication', in Schramm, Wilbur (ed.), *The Process and the Effects of Mass Communication*, Urbana: University of Illinois Press.

Dean, Mitchell (2004), *Governmentality: Power and Rule in Modern Society*, London: Sage.

De Bono, Edward (24 June 2002), 'Opportunity Space', http://www.edwarddebono.com/PassageDetail.php?passage_id=704&, accessed 29 Sept 2009.

De Lillo, Don (19 May 2008), cited in Mishra, Pankaj, 'The End of Innocence', *The Guardian Review*.

De Mesquita, Ethan Bueno & Dickson, Eric (April 2007), 'The Propaganda of the Deed:

Terrorism, Counterterrorism, and Mobilisation', *American Journal of Political Science*, vol. 5, no. 2, pp. 364–38.

Debord, Guy (1983), *Society of the Spectacle*, Detroit MI: Black and Red.

Deibert, Ronald & Rohozinski, Rafal (2010), 'Beyond Denial: Introducing Next-Generation Information Access Controls', in Deibert, Ronald; Palfrey, John; Rohozinski, Rafal & Zittrain, Jonathan (eds), *Access Controlled: Shaping of Power, Rights, and Tule in Cyberspace*, Cambridge MA: MIT Press.

DeLanda, Manuel (2006), *A New Philosophy of Society*, London: Continuum.

Deleuze, Gilles (1988), *Bergsonism*, New York: Zone Books.

—— (2008), *Cinema 2: The Time-Image*, London: Continuum.

DeLong, Bradford (2004), 'Post-World War II Western European Exceptionalism: The Economic Dimension', in Agnew, John & Entrikin, Nicholas, *The Marshall Plan Today: Model and Metaphor*, London: Routledge.

Della Porta, Donatella (1988), 'Recruitment Processes in Clandestine Political Organisations: Italian Left-Wing Terrorism', in Klandermans, Bert; Kriesi, Hanspeter & Tarrow, Sidney, *International Social Movement research*, vol. 1, Greenwich CON: JAI Press.

Della Porta, Donatella & Keating, Michael (2008), *Approaches and Methodologies in the Social Sciences. A Pluralist Perspective*, Cambridge: Cambridge University Press.

DeNardo, James (1985), *Power in Numbers: The Political Strategy of Protest and Rebellion*, Princeton, NJ: Princeton University Press.

Dermody, Janine & Scullion, Richard (2001), 'Delusions of Grandeur? Marketing's Contribution to "Meaningful" Western Political Consumption', *European Journal of Marketing*, vol. 35, no. 9–10, pp. 1085–98.

Derrida, Jacques (2005), *Writing and Difference*, London: Routledge.

De Saussure, Ferdinand (1955), *Cours de Linguistique Générale*, Paris: Payot.

Deptula, David (2001), *Effects-Based Operations: Changes in the Nature of Warfare*, Arlington VA: Aerospace Education Foundation.

Deutsche Welle (29 Apr 2010), 'German Army Opens IED Research Center for Soldiers', http://www.dw-world.de/dw/article/0,5516501,00.html.

Devji, Faisal (2005), *Landscapes of the Jihad: Militancy, Morality, Modernity*, London: Hurst.

Dhochartaigh, Michealin & Mc Gorrian, K & Oh Anluian, BG (2008), 'A Brief History of the Irish Republican Army', Real IRA website, http://irelandsown.net/IRAhistory.htm, accessed 1 Sept 2008.

DiMaggio, Paul & Powell, Walter (Apr 1983), 'The Iron Cage Revisited: Institutional Isomorphism and Collective Rationality in Organisational Fields', *American Sociological Review*, vol. 48, no. 2, pp. 147–160.

Dingley, James & Kirk-Smith, Michael (2000), 'How Could They Do It? The Bombing of Omagh, 1998', *Journal of Conflict Studies*, vol. 20, no. 1, pp. 105–126.

Dingley, James (2001), 'The Bombing of Omagh, 15 August 1998: The Bombers, Their Tactics, Strategy, and Purpose Behind the Incident', *Studies in Conflict & Terrorism* (2001), vol. 24, pp. 451–465.

Discover Mid-America (January 2008), http://discoverypub.com/feature/ 2008_01political.html, accessed 27 June 2009.

Docx, Edward (July 2009), 'Mandy in the Middle', *Prospect*, Issue 160, http://www.prospect-magazine.co.uk/article_details.php?id=10858, accessed 30 Sept 2010.

Doig, Tommy (June 2007), Fox News Baghdad bureau co-ordinator, interview with N Bolt, Johannesburg, RSA.

Doob, Leonard (1949), *Propaganda and Public Opinion*, Cresset Press.

—— (Fall 1950), 'Goebbels' Principles of Propaganda', *Public Opinion Quarterly*, pp. 419–442.

Doorey, Timothy (2009), 'Waging an Effective Strategic Communications Campaign in the Global War on Terror', in David, GJ & McKeldin, TR, *Ideas as Weapons*, Washington, DC: Potomac Books.

Doronsoro, Gilles (2009), *The Taliban's Winning Strategy in Afghanistan*, Washington, DC: Carnegie Endowment for Peace.

Drazin, Robert, Glynn, Mary Ann & Kazanjian, Robert (2004), 'Dynamics of Structural Change', in Poole, Marshall Scott & Van de Ven, Andrew (eds), *Handbook of Organisational Change and Innovation*, New York: Oxford University Press.

Drucker, Peter (1969), *The Age of Discontinuity*, New York: Harper & Row.

Durand, Jacques (1987), 'Rhetorical Figures in the Advertising Image', in Umiker-Sebeok, Jean, ed, *Marketing and Semiotics: New Directions in the Study of the Signs for Sale*, New York: Mouton de Gruyter, pp. 295–318.

Durkheim, Emile (1970), *Suicide: A Study in Sociology*, London: Routledge & Kegan Paul.

—— (1983), *Pragmatism and Sociology*, Cambridge University Press.

Dudziak, Mary (2003), *September 11 in History: A Watershed Moment?*, Durham: Duke University Press.

Duffield, John & Dombrowski, Peter (eds) (2009), p. 26, *Balance Sheet: the Iraq War and U.S. National Security*, Stanford CA: University of California Press.

Dumond, John & Eden, Rick (2005), *Improving Government Processes: From Velocity Management to Presidential Appointments*, Santa Monica CA: RAND.

Dworkins, Richard (2006), *The Selfish Gene*, Oxford: Oxford University Press.

Earle, Edward Mead (ed.) (1944), *Makers of Modern Strategy: Military Thought from Machiavelli to Hitler*, Princeton: Princeton University Press.

Earnshaw, Robert (ed.) (1994), *Postmodern Surroundings*, Amsterdam: Rodopi.

Eco, Umberto (1977), *A Theory of Semiotics*, London: Macmillan.

Edelman, Murray (1988), *Constructing the Political Spectacle*, Chicago: University of Chicago Press.

Edwards, Bob & McCarthy, John (2004), 'Resources and Social Movement Mobilization', in Snow, David; Soule, Sarah & Kriesi, Hanspeter (eds), *The Blackwell Companion to Social Movements*, Malden MA & Oxford: Blackwell Publishing.

Ehrenberg, John (1983), 'Communists and Proletarians: Lenin on Consciousness and Spontaneity', *Studies in Soviet Thought*, vol. 25, pp. 285–306.

Eilstrup-Sangiovanni, Mette & Jones, Calvert (Fall 2008), 'Assessing the Dangers of Illicit Networks: Why al-Qaida May Be Less Threatening Than Many Think', *International Security*, vol. 33, no. 2, pp. 7–44.

—— (2010), 'Assessing The Dangers of Illicit Networks', in Brown, Michael; Cote, Owen; Lynn-Jones, Sean & Miller Steven (eds), *Contending with Terrorism: Roots, Strategies and Responses*, Cambridge MA: MIT Press.

BIBLIOGRAPHY

El Amrani, Issandre (15 Jan 2011), 'Twitter, WikiLeaks and Tunisia', http://www.arabist.net/blog/2011/1/15/twitter-wikileaks-and-tunisia.html, accessed 01 June 2011.

Elliott, Marianne (1989), *Wolf Tone: Prophet of Irish Independence*, New Haven & London: Yale University Press.

Ellul, Jacques (1973), *Propaganda: The Formation of Men's Attitudes*, New York: Vintage.

—— (2006), 'What is Propaganda, and How Does it Differ from Persuasion', in Jowell, Garth & O'Donnell, Victoria (eds), *Readings in Propaganda and Persuasion: New and Classic Essays*, Thousand Oaks: Sage.

Ely, Richard Theodor (1886, 2005), *The Labor Movement in America*, Boston MASS: Adamant Media Corporation.

Endsly, Mica & Garland, Daniel (eds) (2000), *Situational Awareness: Analysis and Measurement*, Mahwah NJ: Lawrence Erlbaum.

Engels, Friedrich (1845, 2005), *The Condition of the Working Class in England*, London: Penguin.

English, Richard (2003), *Armed Struggle; The History of the IRA*, Oxford: Oxford University Press.

Equality and Human Rights Commission (2009), 'The Equality Implications of being a Migrant in Britain', *Research Report*, no. 19, www.equalityhumanrights.com.

Erikson, Erik (1971), *Identity: Youth and Crisis*, London: Faber & Faber.

Erikson, Kai (1966), *Wayward Puritans: A Study in the Sociology of Deviance*, New York: John Wiley.

Etling, Bruce; Faris, Robert & Palfrey, John (Dec 2010), 'Political Change in the Digital Age: The Fragility and Promise of Online Organizing', *SAIS Review*, vol. 30, Issue 2, pp. 37–49, Baltimore MD: John Hopkins University Press.

Evans, Alex &Steven, David (2009), 'Towards a Theory of Influence for Twenty-First-Century Foreign Policy: Public Diplomacy in a Globalised World', http://www.fco.gov.uk/en/about-the-fco/publications/publications/pd-publication/21c-foreign-policy, accessed 11 June 2009.

Evans, Judith (16 June 2009), 'Dissidents Use Internet Wiles to Beat Regime's Gag', *The Times*, p. 6.

Ewen, Stuart (1976), *Captains of Consciousness*, New York: McGraw Hill.

Ewen, Stuart (1996), *PR! A Social History of Spin*, New York: Basic Books.

Exum, Andrew (May 2008), 'The Spectacle of War: Insurgent Video Propaganda and Western Response, 1990-present', *Arab Media & Society*.

Eyerman, Ron (2001), *Cultural Trauma: Slavery and the Formation of African American Identity*, Cambridge: Cambridge University Press.

Falk, Candace (ed.), (2008), *Emma Goldman: A Documentary History of the American Years Vol. 1: Made for America, 1890–1901*, Champaign, Il: University of Illinois Press.

—— (2008), *Emma Goldman: A Documentary History of the American Years Vol.II: Making Speech Free, 1902–1909*, Champaign, Il: University of Illinois Press.

Fandy, Mamoun (2007), *(Un)Civil War of Words: Media and Politics in the Arab World*, Westport & London: Praeger Security International.

Farsoun, Samih K & Aruri, Naseer H (2006), *Palestine and the Palestinians*, 2nd Edn, Cambridge MA: Westview.

Featherstone, Mike (1991), *Consumer Culture and Postmodernism*, London: Sage.

BIBLIOGRAPHY

Ferrero, Mario (Dec 2006), 'Martyrdom Contracts', *Journal of Conflict Resolution*, vol. 50, no. 6, pp. 877–855.

Feyerabend, Paul (1993), *Against Method*, London: Verso.

Fisher, Kimberly (1997), 'Locating frames in the Discursive Universe', *Sociological Research Online*, vol. 2, no. 3, http://www.socresonline.org.uk/socresonline/2/3/4.html.

Fisher, Walter (1998), 'Narration as a Human Communication Paradigm: The Case of Public Moral Argument', in Lucaites, John Louis; Condit, Celeste Michelle & Caudill, Sally (eds), *Contemporary Rhetorical Theory: A Reader*, New York: Guildford Press.

Fishman, Mark (1980), *Manufacturing the News*, Austin: University of Texas Press.

Fishman, William (1970), *The Insurrectionists*, London: Methuen.

Fisk, Robert (2001), *Pity the Nation: Lebanon at War*, Oxford: Oxford University Press.

Fitzduff Mari (2002), 'Beyond Violence: Conflict Resolution Process in Northern Ireland', *UNU Policy Perspectives*, no. 7, United Nations University Press/INCORE, Tokyo, New York, Paris.

Fitzpatrick, David (1997), 'Militarism in Ireland 1900–1922', in Bartlett, Thomas & Jeffery, Keith (eds), *A Military History of Ireland*, Cambridge: Cambridge University Press.

Flaye, Ella (16 June 2009), '"It's Like a Revolution". The Million-Strong Tide of Protest too Big for Thugs to Halt', *The Times*, p. 6.

Fleming, Marie (1980), 'Propaganda by the Deed: Terrorism and Anarchist Theory in Late Nineteenth-Century Europe', *Studies in Conflict & Terrorism*, vol. 4, no. 1, pp. 1–23.

Flood, Christopher (2002), *Political Myth*, New York: Routledge.

Ford, Franklin (1985), *Political Murder*, Cambridge MA: Harvard University Press.

Forsyth, Donelson (2009), *Group Dynamics*, Belmont CA: Wadsworth.

Foster, Roy (1988), *Modern Ireland 1600–1972*, London: Allen Lane.

Foucault, Michel (1972), *The Archaeology of Knowledge*, London: Tavistock Publications.

———— (1980), *Power Knowledge*, Harlow: Pearson Education.

———— (1995), *Discipline and Punish: The Birth of the Prison*, New York: Vintage.

Fourie, Pieter (2001), *Media Studies: Institutions, Theories, and Issues*, Lansdowne: Juta Education.

Fox Piven, Frances & Cloward, Richard (02 May 1966), 'The Weight of the Poor: A Strategy to End Poverty', *The Nation*.

Fraim, John (2003), *Battle of Symbols: Global Dynamics of Advertising, Entertainment and Media*, Einsiedeln: Daimon Verlag.

Frank Leslie's Illustrated Magazine, http://lincoln.lib.niu.edu/fimage/gildedage/haymarket/results1.php?page=4&ipp=9, accessed 30 Sept 2010.

Freedom House (30 Mar 2009), 'Freedom on the Net: A Global Assessment of Internet and Digital Media', http://www.freedomhouse.org/template.cfm?page=383&report=79, accessed 01 July 2010.

Freedman, Lawrence (2005), 'War Evolves into the Fourth Generation', *Contemporary Security Policy*, vol. 26, issue 2, pp. 254–263.

———— (2006), 'The Transformation of Strategic Affairs', Adelphi Paper 379, Abingdon: Routledge/IISS.

―――― (2008), *A Choice of Enemies*, London: Phoenix.

Frenkel, Sheera (24 June 2011), p. 42, 'Letter From Ramtha', *The Times*, interview with Muhammad Jamid.

Freud, Sigmund (1984), 'A Note on the Unconscious in Psychoanalysis', in *On Metapsychology: The Theory of Psychoanalysis*, Harmondsworth: Penguin.

―――― (1999), *The Interpretation of Dreams*, Oxford & New York: Oxford University Press.

Friedman, Milton (2002), 'Preface 1982', to *Capitalism and Freedom*, Chicago: University of Chicago Press.

Frith, Simon (2004), *Popular Music: Music and Society*, Abingdon: Routledge.

Fullerton, Jami & Kendrick, Alice (2006), *The Story of the U.S. State Department's Shared Values*, Spokane WA.

Furedi, Frank (2007), *Invitation to Terror*, London & New York: Continuum.

Fukuyama, Francis (2006), *The End of History and the Last Man*, New York & London: Free Press.

Gage, Beverly (2009), *The Day Wall Street Exploded: A Story of America in its First Age of Terror*, New York: Oxford University Press.

Gallagher, Frank (1965), *The Anglo-Irish Treaty*, London: Hutchinson.

Gallagher, Ryan & Arthur, Charles (24 June 2011), 'Inside LulzSec: Chatroom Logs Shine a Light on the Secretive Hackers', *The Guardian*, http://www.guardian.co.uk/technology/2011/jun/24/inside-lulzsec-chatroom-logs-hackers, accessed 24 June 2011.

Galula, David (2006), *Counterinsurgency Warfare: Theory and Practice*, Westport CT: Praeger Security International.

Gamson, William (1990), *The Strategy of Social Protest*, Belmont CA: Wadsworth.

―――― (1992), *Talking Politics*, Cambridge: Cambridge University Press.

Gans, Herbert (1979), *Deciding What's News*, New York: Pantheon Books.

Garnham, Nicholas (2005), 'The Information Society Debate Revisited', in Curran, James & Gurevitch, Michael (eds), *Mass Media and Society*, London: Hodder Arnold.

Garvin, Tom (1987), *Nationalist Revolutionaries in Ireland 1858–1928*, Oxford: Clarendon.

Garvin, Tom (Autumn 1990), 'The Return of History: Collective Myths and Modern Nationalisms', *The Irish Review* (1986), no. 9, pp. 16–30.

Gates, Robert (2009), 'Report on Strategic Communication, December 2009', Washington, DC: Department of Defense.

Gay, Peter (2006), *Freud: A Life in our Time*, London: MAX.

Gearty, Connor (1997), *The Future of Terrorism*, London: Phoenix.

Geertz, Clifford (1973), *Interpretation of Cultures*, New York: Basic Books.

Genosko, Gary (1999), *McLuhan and Baudrillard: The Masters of Implosion*, London: Routledge.

'George Orwell Rolls in his Grave', http://video.google.com/, accessed 21 May 2009.

Georgiou, Myria (2005), 'Diasporic and Media Across Europe, Multicultural Societies and the Universalism-Particularism Continuum', *Journal of Ethnic and Migration Studies*, vol. 31, no. 3, pp. 481–498.

Geraghty, Tony (2000), *The Irish War*, Baltimore & London: Johns Hopkins University Press.

Gerbner, G; Gross, L, Morgan, M & Signorelli, N (1980), 'The Mainstreaming of America: Violence Profile No. 11', *Journal of Communication*, vol. 30, no. 3, pp. 10–29.

——— (1986), 'Living with Television: The Dynamics of the Cultivation Process', in Bryant, Jennings & Zillmann, Dolf (eds), *Perspectives on Media Effects*, Hillsdale, NJ: Lawrence Erlbaum.

Gergen, Kenneth (1985), 'Social Constructionist Inquiry: Context and Implications', in Gergen, Kenneth & Davis, Keith, *The Social Construction of the Person*, New York: Springer.

Gerges, Fawaz A (2005), *The Far Enemy: Why Jihad Went Global*, Cambridge: Cambridge University Press.

Gerlach, Luther (July-Aug 1971), 'Movements of Revolutionary Change: Some Structural Characteristics', *American Behavioral Scientist*, vol. 14, no. 6, pp. 812–836.

Ghosh, Amitav (2009), 'Defeat or Victory isn't Determined by the Success of the Strike itself, but by the Response', in *26/11: The Attack on Mumbai*, New Delhi: Penguin/Hindustan Times.

Giddens, Anthony (1982), *Profiles and Critiques in Social Theory*, Berkeley & Los Angeles: University of California Press.

Giddens, Anthony (1984), *The Constitution of the Self*, Cambridge: Polity.

Giduck, John (19 May 2009), Lecture, King's College London.

Giliomee, Hermann (2003), *The Afrikaners: Biography of a People*, Cape Town: Tafelberg.

Gitlin, Todd (2003), *The Whole World is Watching: Mass Media in the Making and Unmaking of the New Left*, Berkeley: University of California Press.

Giustozzi, Antonio (2008), *Koran, Kalashnikov and Laptop: The Neo-Taliban Insurgency in Afghanistan*, New York: Columbia University Press.

——— (2009), *Decoding the New Taliban*, London: Hurst.

Gkotzaridis, Evi (2006*), Trials of Irish History: Genesis and Evolution of a Reappraisal 1938–2000*, London: Routledge.

Gladwell, Malcolm (2000), *The Tipping Point*, London: Abacus.

——— (04 Oct 2010), 'Small Change: Why The Revolution Will Not Be Tweeted', *New Yorker*, http://www.newyorker.com/reporting/2010/10/04/101004fa_fact_gladwell?currentPage=1, accessed 15 June 2011.

Gladwell, Malcolm & Shirky, Clay (Mar/Apr 2011), 'From Innovation to Revolution: Do Social Media Make Protests Possible?', *Foreign Affairs*, accessed 15 June 2011.

Glanz, Kames & Markoff, John (12 June 2011), 'U.S. Underwrites Internet Detour Around Censors', *The New York Times*, http://www.nytimes.com/2011/06/12/world/12internet.html?pagewanted=1&_r=1, accessed 13 June 2011.

Glasser, Susan & Coll, Steve (07 Aug 2005), 'Terrorists Turn to the Web as Base of Operations', *Washington Post*, http://www.washingtonpost.com/wp-dyn/content/article/2005/08/05/AR2005080501138.html, accessed 30 Sept 2010.

——— (09 Aug 2005), 'The Web as Weapon', *Washington Post*, http://www.washingtonpost.com/wp-dyn/content/article/2005/08/08/AR2005080801018.html, accessed 30 Sept 2010.

Gleason, Philip (Mar 1983), 'Identifying Identity: A Semantic History', *The Journal of American History*, vol. 89, no. 4, pp. 910–931.

Global Commission on International Migration Report(2005), http://www.gcim.org/en/, accessed 30 Sept 2010.

Gloor, Peter (2006), *Swarm Creativity: Competitive Advantage through Collaborative Innovation*, Oxford: Oxford University Press.

BIBLIOGRAPHY

Glucksberg, Sam & Boaz, Keysar (Jan 1990), 'Understanding Metaphorical Comparisons: Beyond Similarity', *Psychological Review*, vol. 97, pp. 3–18.

Godberg, Jeffrey (10 May 2011), interview with Hillary Rodham Clinton, The Atlantic http://www.theatlantic.com/international/archive/2011/05/hillary-clinton-chinese-system-is-doomed-leaders-on-a-fools-errand/238591/1/, accessed 08 June 2011.

Godwin, William (1793, 1992), *Enquiry Concerning Political Justice*, Oxford: Woodstock.

Goffman, Erving (1959), *The Presentation of Self in Everyday Life*, Harmondsworth: Penguin.

Goffman, Erving (1967), *Interaction Ritual: Essays on Face-to-Face Behaviour*, London: Allen Lane.

Goldman, Emma (1910), *Anarchism and Other Essays*, New York: Mother Earth Publishing Association.

Goldsmith, Jack & Wu, Tim (2008), *Who Controls the Internet: Illusions of a Borderless World*, New York: OUP.

Gonzalez, Nancie (1961), 'Family Organisation in Five Types of Migratory Wage Labor', *American Anthropologist*, vol. 62, pp. 1264–1280.

―――― (1989), 'Conflict, Migration and the Expression of Ethnicity: Introduction', in Gonzalez, Nancie & McCommon, Carolyn (eds), *Conflict, Migration and the Expression of Ethnicity*, Boulder CO: Westview Press.

Goosens, Cees (2003), 'Visual Persuasion: Mental Imagery Processing and Emotional Experiences', in Scott, Linda & Batra, Rajeev (eds), *Persuasive Imagery*, Mahwah NJ: Routledge.

Gottlieb, Sidney (ed.) (2003), *Alfred Hitchcock: Interviews*, Jackson: University Press of Mississippi.

Gould, Philip (1998), *'The Unfinished Revolution: How the Modernisers Saved the Labour Party'*, London: Abacus.

Gove, Michael (2006), *Celsius 7/7*, London: Weidenfeld & Nicholson.

Gowans, Stephen (22 May 2002), 'Dan Rather's Change of Heart', *Media Monitors Network*http://www.mediamonitors.net/gowans54.html, accessed 13 May 2009.

Gowing Nik, (2009), *"Skyful of Lies", and Black Swans: The New Tyranny of Shifting Information Power in Crises*, Oxford: RISJ.

Graham, Gordon (1999), *The Internet: a Philosophical Inquiry*, London & New York: Routledge.

Graham, Robert (ed.) (2005), *Anarchism: A Documentary History of Libertarian Ideas*, vol. 1, Montreal: Black Rose.

Gramaglia, Charles (Winter 2008), 'Strategic Communication: Distortion and White Noise', *IO Sphere*, pp. 10–14.

Gramsci, Antonio (1991), *Prison Notebooks*, Buttigieg, Joseph (ed.), New York & Oxford: Columbia University Press.

Granovetter, Mark (1973), 'The Strength of Weak Ties', *American Journal of Sociology*, vol. 78, no. 6, pp. 1360–1380.

―――― (1974), *Getting a Job: A Study of Contacts and Careers*, Cambridge MA: Harvard University Press.

―――― (May 1978), 'Threshold Models of Collective Behaviour', *American Journal of Sociology*, vol. 83, no. 6, pp. 1420–1443.

—— (1983), 'The Strength of Weak Ties: A Network Theory Revisited', *Sociological Theory*, vol. 1, pp. 201–233.

Grave, Jean (1899), *Moribund Society and Anarchy*, San Francisco CA: A Isaak.

Gray, Colin (2005), *Transformation and Strategic Surprise*, Carlisle PA: Strategic Studies Institute.

Gray, John (2003), *False Dawn: the Delusions of Global Capitalism*, London: Granta Books.

Gregory, Bruce (2005), 'Public Diplomacy and Strategic Communication: Cultures, Firewalls, and Imported Norms', paper for American Political Science Association Conference on International Communication Conflict.

Guerlac, Suzanne (2006), *Thinking in Time*, Ithaca & London: Cornell University Press.

Guillaume, James (1905), 'L'International: Documents et Souvenirs', *Paris*, vol. 4, p. 224 (issue 31, 5 Aug 1877),

Gunaratna, Rohan (Jan 2008), 'Strategic Counter-Terrorism: Getting Ahead of Terrorism; Part 3, Mass Media Response to Terrorism', *The Jebsen Center for Counter-Terrorism Studies Research Briefing Series*, vol. 3, no. 1,

Gunter, Barrie & McAleer, Jill (1997), *Children and Television*, London: Routledge.

Gurr, Ted (1970), *Why Men Rebel*, Princeton NJ: Princeton University Press.

—— (1993), *Minorities at Risk: A Global View of Ethnopolitical Conflicts*, Washington, DC: United States Institute of Peace Press.

Guthrie, Charles & Quinlan, Michael (2007), *The Just War Tradition: Ethics in Modern Warfare*, London: Bloomsbury.

Habermas, Jürgen (1987), *The Theory of Communicative Action: Lifeworld and System, A Critique of Functionalist Reason*, vol. 2, Boston: Beacon Press.

Hafner, Katie (2009), *A Romance on Three Legs: Glenn Gould's Obsessive Quest for the Perfect Piano*, New York: Bloomsbury.

Hagel, John (23 June 2009), 'Shift Happens Redux', http://edgeperspectives.typepad.com/edge_perspectives/2009/06/shift-happens-redux.html, accessed 04 Feb 2010.

Hagel, John & Seely Brown, John (04 Jan 2010), 'Networking Reconsidered', *Harvard Business Review*, http://blogs.hbr.org/bigshift/2010/01/networking-reconsidered.html, accessed 04 Feb 2010.

Halbwachs, Maurice (1992), Coser, Lewis (ed.), *Collective Memory*, Chicago & London: University of Chicago Press.

Hall, Peter & Preston, Paschall (1988), *The Carrier Wave: New Information Technology and the Geography of Innovation 1846–2003*, London: Unwin Hyman.

Hall, Stuart (1978), 'The "Structured Communication" of Events', University of Birmingham: Stenciled Occasional Papers/UNESCO symposium 'Obstacles to Communication Systems'.

—— (1995), 'The Whites of their Eyes: Racist Ideologies and the Media', in Dines, G & Humez, JM (eds), *Gender, Race and Class in Media*, London: Sage.

Hall, Stuart et al (1980), *Policing the Crisis: Mugging, the State and Law and Order*, London & Basingstoke: Macmillan.

Halliday, Fred (1999), 'Manipulation and Limits: Media Coverage of the Gulf War 1990–1', in Allen, Tim & Seaton, Jean, *The Media of Conflict*, London & New York: Zed Books.

—— (21 Apr 2004), 'Terrorism in Historical Perspective', *Open Democracy*, http://www.opendemocracy.net/conflict/article_1865.jsp, accessed 05 May 2010.

BIBLIOGRAPHY

Halliday, Josh (12 Mar 2011), 'SXSW 2011: Clay Shirky on Social Media and Revolution', *The Guardian*, http://www.guardian.co.uk/technology/2011/mar/12/sxsw-2011-clay-shirky-social-media, accessed 27 June 2011.

Halloran, Richard (2007), 'Strategic Communication', *Parameters*, Autumn 2007.

Hammes, TX (Aug 2005), 'War Evolves into the Fourth Generation', *Contemporary Security Policy*, vol. 26, no. 2, pp. 189–221.

—— (Nov 2007), 'The Message is the Insurgency', *Marine Corps Gazette*, pp. 18–30.

—— (2009), 'Information Warfare', in David, GJ & McKeldin, TR, *Ideas as Weapons*, Washington, DC: Potomac Books.

Hanafi, Sari (1999), 'Between Arab and French Agendas: Defining the Palestinian Diaspora and the Image of the Other', in Shamy, Seteney & Herrera, Linda (eds), *Social Between Field and Text; Emerging Voices in Egyptian Social Science*, Cairo: AUC.

Hansen, James (1977), 'Subjectivism, Terrorism and Political Activism', in Parsons, Howard & Somerville, John (eds), *Marxism, Revolution, and Peace*, Amsterdam: BR Grüner BV.

Harding, James (2008), '*Alpha Dogs: How Political Spin Became a Global Business*', London: Atlantic Books.

Harrison, Mark (2004), 'An Economist Looks at Suicide Terrorism', Unpublished manuscript, University of Warwick, in Ferrero, Mario (Dec 2006), 'Martyrdom Contracts', *Journal of Conflict Resolution*, vol. 50, no. 6, pp. 877–855.

Hassanpour, Amir (22 June 2009), cited in 'An Unintentional Martyr: Neda Becomes 'Symbol of Goodness', *CBC News*, http://www.cbc.ca/world/story/2009/06/22/f-neda-iran.html, accessed 27 Aug 2010.

Hatfield, Elaine, Cacioppo, John & Rapson, Richard (1994), *Emotional Intelligence*, Cambridge: Cambridge University Press.

Harvey, David (1990), *The Condition of Postmodernity*, Cambridge MA: Blackwell.

—— (2000), *Spaces of Hope*, Berkeley: University of California Press.

—— (2005), *A Brief History of Neoliberalism*, Oxford: Oxford University Press.

—— (2010), *The Enigma of Capital and the Crises of Capitalism*, London: Profile.

Hashash, Sara (24 July 2011), 'Hackers battle to silence Syria's Facebook rebels', *The Sunday Times*, p. 24.

Hayden, Tom (2001), *The Zapatista Reader*, New York: Nation Books.

Hebdige, Dick (1979), *Subculture: The Meaning of Style*, London: Methuen.

Hegel, Georg (2008), *Philosophy of Right*, New York: Cosimo.

Heggy, Tarek (2009), *The Arab Cocoon: Progress and Modernity in Arab Societies*, London: Valentine Mitchell.

Held, David (ed.) (2004), *A Globalising World? Culture, Economics, Politics*, London: Routledge/ Open University.

Held, David & McGrew, Anthony (2007), *Globalisation/Anti-globalisation: Beyond the Great Divide*, Cambridge: Polity.

Henneberg, Stephan (2004), 'Political Marketing Theory: Hendiadyoin or Oxymoron', University of Bath School of Management, Working Paper Series.

Herman, Edward S & McChesney Robert W (1997), *The Global Media: The New Missionaries of Corporate Capitalism*, London & New York.

Herman, Edward & Chomsky, Noam (2002), *Manufacturing Consent: the Political Economy of the Media*, New York: Pantheon.

Hess, Stephen & Kalb, Marvin (2003), *The Media and the War on Terror*, Washington, DC: The Brookings Institute.

Hewitt, Gavin, BBC Television News, Europe Editor, interview with N Bolt 08 Apr 2009.

Hewitt, Regina (2006), *Symbolic Interactions*, Lewisburg: Bucknell University Press.

Herz, John (Jan 1950), 'Idealist Internationalism and the Security Dilemma', *World Politics*, vol. 2, no. 2, pp. 157–180.

Hesmondhalgh, David (2007), *The Cultural Industries*, Los Angeles & London: Sage.

Hines, Nico (14 Feb 2011), p. 29, 'Obama Furious Over Egypt Remarks by 'Monster' Clinton', *The Times*.

Hirschman, Albert (1963), *Journeys Toward Progress*, New York: Twentieth Century Fund.

Hobsbawm, Eric (1978), *The Age of Revolution 1789–1848*, London: Abacus.

———— (1988), *The Age of Capital 1848–1875*, London: Cardinal.

Hobsbawm, Eric & Ranger, Terence (eds) (2003), *The Invention of Tradition*, Cambridge: Cambridge University Press.

Hodgkin, Katherine & Radstone, Susannah (eds) (2003), *Contested Pasts: The Politics of Memory*, London & New York: Routledge.

Hoffman, Bruce (1998), *Inside Terrorism*, New York: Columbia University Press.

———— (2002), 'Rethinking Terrorism and Counterterrorism Since 9/11', *Studies in Conflict & Terrorism*, vol. 25, pp. 303–316.

———— (2002), 'Joint Inquiry Staff Statement', http://www.fas.org/irp/congress/2002_hr/100802hill.html accessed 30 Sept 2010.

———— (May/June 2008), 'The Myth of Grass-roots Terrorism: Why Osama Bin Laden Still Matters', *Foreign Policy*, http://www.foreignaffairs.com/articles/63408/bruce-hoffman/the-myth-of-grass-roots-terrorism, accessed 01 Oct 2009.

Hoffman, Frank (2007), *Conflict in the 21st Century: The Rise of Hybrid Wars*, Arlington VA: Potomac Institute for Policy Studies.

———— (Summer 2007), 'Neo-Classical Insurgency?', *Parameters*, pp. 71–87.

———— (2009), 'Maneuvering Against the Mind', in David, GJ & McKeldin, TR (eds), *Ideas as Weapons*, Washington, DC: Potomac Books.

Holman, Valerie & Kelly, Debra (eds) (2000), *France at War in the Twentieth Century: Propaganda, Myth and Metaphor*, New York: Berghahn Books.

Holmus, Todd, Paul, Christopher & Glenn, Russell (2007), *Enlisting Madison Avenue: The Marketing Approach to Earning Popular Support in Theaters of Operation*, Santa Monica: Rand/United States Joint Forces Command.

Holt, Edgar (1960), *Protest in Arms: The Irish Troubles 1916–1923*, London: Putnam.

Hood, Christopher & Margetts, Helen (2007), *The Tools of Government in the Digital Age*, Basingstoke & New York: Palgrave Macmillan.

Horowitz, Donald (1985), *Ethnic Groups in Conflict*, Berkeley CA: University of California Press.

Horowitz L & Liebowitz M (Winter 1968), 'Social Deviance and Political Marginality: Towards a Redefinition between Sociology and Politics', *Social Problems*, no. 15, pp. 280–96

Horowitz, Michael (2010), *'The Diffusion of Military Power'*, Princeton NJ: Princeton University Press

HSBC Television, 'The World's Local Bank', http://thefinancialbrand.com/375/hsbc-worldwide-local-bank/, accessed 08 Aug 2011.

——, 'We Recognise How People Value Things Differently', http://www.youtube.com/watch?v=5imDyxNjo-0, accessed 03 July 2009.

Human Rights Watch (2006), *Lessons in Terror: Attacks on Education in Afghanistan*, vol. 18, no. 6 (C),

Human Rights Watch (01 June 2011), 'We've Never Seen Such Horror: Crimes Against Humanity by Syrian Security Forces', http://www.hrw.org/en/reports/2011/06/01/we-ve-never-seen-such-horror, accessed 01 June 2011.

Hunt, Brian; Kennedy, Judy; Li, Tien-Yien & Nusse, Helena (2004), *The Theory of Chaotic Attractors*, New York: Springer.

Huntington, Samuel (2002), *The Clash of Civilizations and the Remaking of World Order*, New York: Free Press.

Huron, David (2008), *Sweet Anticipation: Music and the Psychology of Expectation*, Cambridge MA: MIT Press.

Hutchinson, John & Smith, Anthony (1994), *Nationalism*, Oxford: Oxford University Press.

Iannaccone, Laurence R (2003), 'The Market for Martyrs', presented at the 2004 Meetings of the American Economic Association, San Diego, CA.

International Crisis Group (24 July 2008), 'Taliban Propaganda: Winning the War of Words?', *Asia Report*, no. 158, http://www.crisisgroup.org/.

—— (23 Feb 2010), 'The Sri Lankan Tamil Diaspora After the LTTE', *Asia Report*, no. 186, http://www.crisisgroup.org/.

—— (06 June 2011), 'Popular Protest in North Africa: and the Middle East (V): Making Sense of Libya', *Middle East/North Africa Report*, no. 107, Executive Summary.

Irish Bulletin (01 July 1921), vol. 5, no. 22.—— (04 July 1921), 'The Insurrection of 1916 and its Consequences', vol. 5, no. 23.

Irish Republican Army, *Green Book*, vol. 1 & 2,

Islam, Yusuf et al (Aug-Oct 2005), 'Preventing Extremism Together', http://www.communities.gov.uk/archived/general-content/communities/preventingextremismtogether/, accessed 02 Mar 2010.

Jackson, Alvin (1992), 'Unionist Myths', *Past and Present*, no. 136.

—— (2002), *Ireland 1798–1998: Politics and War*, Oxford: Blackwell.

Jackson, Richard (2005), *Writing the War on Terrorism: Language, Politics and Counter-Terrorism*, Manchester & New York: Manchester University Press.

Jalali, Ali (Spring 2009), 'Winning in Afghanistan', *Parameters*.

James, Clive (1974), *The Metropolitan Critic*, London: Faber & Faber.

Jarvis, Jeff (2008), *What Would Google Do?*, New York: Harper Collins.

Jedlowski, Paolo (2001), 'Memory and Sociology: Themes and Issues', *Time Society*, vol. 10, no. 29.

Jenkins, Henry (2006), *Convergence Culture: Where Old and New Media Collide*, New York & London: New York University Press.

Jenkins, Gareth (06 Apr 2006), 'Marxism and Terrorism', *International Socialism*, issue 110.

Johnson, Chalmers (1983), *Revolutionary Change*, Harlow: Longman.

Johnson, Steven (2001), *Emergence: The Connected Lives of Ants, Brains, Cities, and Software*, London: Penguin.

Johnson-Cartee, Karen (2005), *News Narratives and News Framing: Constructing Political Reality*, Lanham: Rowan & Littlefield.

Joll, James (1964, 1979), *The Anarchists*, London: Methuen.

Jones, Glynn (Apr 2009), Executive Producer, Current Affairs Documentaries, BBC Television, interview with N Bolt.

Jowett, Garth & O'Donnell, Victoria (2006), *Propaganda and Persuasion*, Thousand Oaks: Sage.

Jung, Courtney (2000), *Then I Was Black: South African Political Identities in Transition*, New Haven & London: Yale University Press.

Kahler, Miles (ed.) (2009), *Networked Politics: Agency, Power, and Governance*, Ithaca & London: Cornell University Press.

Kaldor, Mary (2007), *New & Old Wars*, Cambridge: Polity.

Kaletsky, Anatole (2010), *Capitalism 4.0: The Birth of a New Economy*, Philadelphia PA: Public Affairs.

Kalyvas, Stathis (2006), *The Logic of Violence in Civil War*, New York: Cambridge.

Kansteiner Wulf (May 2002*)*, 'Finding Meaning in Memory: A Methodological Critique of Collective Memory Studies', *History and Theory*, no. 41, pp. 179–197.

Kaplan, Robert (Feb 1994), 'The Coming Anarchy', *The Atlantic Magazine*.

Kaplan, Stuart (1990), 'Visual Metaphors in the Representation of Communication Technology', *Critical Studies in Mass Communication*, vol. 7, pp. 37–47.

Karimjee, Mariya & Kumaraswami, Lakshmi (2011), 'Social Media: Catalyst or Hope?', World Policy Institute, http://www.worldpolicy.org/social-media-catalyst-or-hype, accessed 15 June 2011.

Katz, Elihu; Blumler, Jay; Gurevitch, Michael (1974*)*, 'Utilisation of Mass Communication by the Individual', in Blumler, Jay & Katz, Elihu (eds), *The Uses of Mass Communications: Current Perspectives on Gratifications Research*, London: Sage.

Katz, Elihu & Lazarsfeld, Paul (2006), *Personal Influence: The Part Played by People in the Flow of Mass Communications*, London: Eurospan.

Katzenbach, Edward & Hanrahan, Gene (Sept 1955), 'The Revolutionary Strategy of Mao Tse-Tung', *Political science Quarterly*, vol. 70, no. 3, pp. 321–340.

Keane, Jack (30 July 2007), BBC World Service Radio.

Keating, Michael & Della Porta, Donatella (March/April 2010), 'In Defence of Pluralism. Combining Approaches in the Social Sciences', Paper, Political Studies Association, Edinburgh.

Keen, David (2003), 'Demobilising Guatemala', Working Paper, no. 37, London: Crisis States Programme, DESTIN, London School of Economics.

Keller, Evelyn & Segal, Lee (Mar 1970), 'Initiation of Slime Mold Aggregation Viewed as an Instability', *Journal of Theoretical Biology*, vol. 26, no. 3, pp. 399–415.

Kellner, Douglas (1990), *Television and the Crisis of Democracy*, Boulder CO: Westview Press.

Kellner, Douglas (2003), *Media Spectacle*, London: Routledge.

Kelly, Kevin (1994), *Out of Control*, London: Fourth Estate.

——— (21 Nov 2008), 'Becoming Screen Literate', *New York Times Magazine*, http://www.nytimes.com/2008/11/23/magazine/23wwln-future-t.html?pagewanted=1&_r=1, accessed 30 Sept 2010.

Kelly, Matthew (2006), *The Fenian Ideal and Irish Nationalism*, Woodbridge: Boydell Press.

BIBLIOGRAPHY

Kepel, Gilles (2004), *The War for Muslim Minds*, Cambridge MA & London: Belknap Press.

Kepel, Gilles & Milelli, Jean-Pierre (2008), *Al Qaeda in Its Own Words*, Cambridge MA: Belknap Press.

Khouri, Rami (16 May 2011), 'The Magic Key', http://www.middle-east-online.com/english/?id=46142, accessed 15 June 2011.

Kilcullen, David (28 Dec 2006), 'Three Pillars of Counterinsurgency', presentation to U.S. Government Counterinsurgency Conference, Washington, DC.

—— (May 2007), 'New Paradigms for 21st Century Conflict', in 'Countering the Terrorist Mentality', Foreign Policy Agenda, U.S. Department of State, vol. 12, no. 5.

—— (2009), *The Accidental Guerrilla*, London: Hurst.

Kimmage, Daniel & Ridolfo, Kathleen (2007), *Iraqi Insurgent Media: The War of Images and Ideas*, Washington, DC: RFE/RL.

Kimmage, Daniel (26 June 2008), 'Fight Terror With YouTube', *New York Times*, http://www.nytimes.com/2008/06/26/opinion/26kimmage.html, accessed 21 Mar 2010.

King, Charles (1997), *Ending Civil Wars*, London: IISS Adelphi Paper 308.

Kingston-Mann, Esther (1983), *Lenin and the Problem of the Marxist Peasant Revolution*, Oxford: Oxford University Press.

Kirisci, Kemal (1986), *The PLO and World Politics: A Study of the Mobilisation of Support for the Palestinian Cause*, London: Frances Pinter.

Kirsch, Gesa & Sullivan, Patricia (eds) (1992), *Methods and Methodology in Composition Research*, Southern Illinois University.

Kitson, Frank (1972), *Low Intensity Operations: Subversion, Insurgency, Peace-keeping*, London: Faber & Faber.

Kit-wai Ma, Eric (2000), p. 21, 'Rethinking Media Studies: the Case of China', in Park, Myung-Jin & Curran, James, *De-Westernising Media Studies*, London: Routledge.

Klapper, Joseph (1966), *The Effects of Mass Communication*, New York: Free Press.

Klein, Esther (2001), 'Using Information Technology to Eliminate Layers of Bureaucracy', *The National Public Accountant*, vol. 23 (2001), pp. 46–48.

Klein, Kerwin Lee (Winter 2000), 'On the Emergence of Memory in Historical Discourse', *Representations 69*, Special Issue 'Grounds for Remembering', pp. 127–150.

Klein, Melanie (2007), *Shock Doctrine*, London: Allen Lane.

Kleiner, Art (2002), 'Karen Stephenson's Quantum Theory of Trust', *Strategy and Business*, issue 29.

Kolko, Gabriel (1994), *Anatomy of a War: Vietnam, the United States, and the Modern Historical Experience*, New York: The New Press.

Koopman, Ruud (2004), 'Protest in Time and Space: The Evolution of Waves of Contention', in Snow, David; Soule, Sarah & Kriesi, Hanspeter *The Blackwell Companion to Social Movements*, Malden MA: Blackwell.

Kostick, Conor (2009), *Revolution in Ireland: Popular Militancy 1917 to 1923*, Cork: Cork University Press.

Kotler, Philip & Zaltman, Gerald (July 1971), 'Social Marketing: An Approach to Planned Social Change', *Journal of Marketing*, vol. 35, no. 3, pp. 3–12.

Kottle, Simon (2006), *Mediatised Conflict: Developments in Media and Conflict Studies*, Maidenhead & New York: Open University Press.

Kövecses, Zoltán (2002), *Metaphor: A Practical Introduction*, Oxford & New York: Oxford University Press.

Kraus, S & Davis, D (1976), *The Effects of Mass Communication on Political Behaviour*, University Park: Pennsylvania State University Press.

Krepinevich, Andrew (2009), *7 Deadly Scenarios: A Military Futurist Explores War in the Twenty First Century*, New York NY: Bantam Dell.

Kristeva, Julia (1980), 'Word, Dialogue and Novel', in *Desire in Language: A Semiotic Approach to Literature and Art*, New York: Columbia University Press.

Kropotkin, Peter (1887), *The Place of Anarchism in Socialistic Evolution*, London: W. Reeves.

—— (1896, 1911), 'The State: Its Historic Role', http://www.ditext.com/kropotkin/state.html, accessed 30 Sept 2010.

—— (1902, 1987), *Mutual Aid: A Factor of Evolution*, London: Freedom Press.

—— (2005), 'The Spirit of Revolt', in *Kropotkin's Revolutionary Pamphlets*, Whitefish MT: Kessinger.

Kucherov, Samuel (Apr 1952), 'The Case of Vera Zasulich', *Russian Review*, vol. 11, no. 2, pp. 86–96.

Kuhn, Thomas (1970), *The Structure of Scientific Revolutions*, Chicago: Chicago University Press.

Kurth Cronin, Audrey (2009), *How Terrorism Ends*, Princeton: Princeton University Press.

Labi, Nadya (July-Aug 2006), 'Jihad 2.0', *The Atlantic*, http://www.theatlantic.com/magazine/archive/2006/07/jihad-20/4980/, accessed 17 July 2010.

Lakoff, George & Johnson, Mark (2003), *Metaphors We Live By*, Chicago & London: University of Chicago Press.

Lakoff, George (2004), *Don't Think of an Elephant!*, White River Junction VER: Chelsea Green.

Laqueur, Walter (1987), *The Age of Terrorism*, London: Weidenfeld & Nicholson.

Laqueur, Walter (2001), 'Left, Right, and Beyond: The Changing Face of Terror', in Hoge, James & Rose, Gideon (eds), *'How did this happen? Terrorism and the New War*, pp. 71–82, New York: Public Affairs.

Laqueur, Walter (2002), *The New Terrorism: Fanaticism and the Arms of Mass Destruction*, London: Phoenix Press.

—— (2003), *No End to War: Terrorism in the Twenty-First Century*, New York: Continuum.

Lalor, James Fintan (1997), *Collected Writings 1918*, Poole: Woodstock Books.

Langer, Susanne (1960), *'Philosophy in a New Key'*, Cambridge MA: Harvard University Press

Lash, Scott & Urry, John (1994), *'Economies of Signs and Space'*, London: Sage

Lasswell, Harold (1933), 'The Strategy of Revolutionary and War Propaganda', in Wright, Philip Quincy (ed.), *Public Opinion and World Politics*, Chicago: University of Chicago Press.

Lasswell, Harold & Blumenstock, Dorothy (1970), *World Revolutionary Propaganda*, Westport CONN: Greenwood Press.

Lasswell, Harold (1971), 'The Structure and Function of Communication in Society', in Schramm, Wilbur & Roberts, Donald *The Process and Effects of Mass Communication*, Urbana Ill: University of Illinois Press.

Laughey, Dan (2007), *Key Themes in Media Theory*, Maidenhead: Open University Press/McGraw-Hill.

BIBLIOGRAPHY

Law, Randall (2009), *Terrorism: A History*, Cambridge: Polity.

Lazarsfeld, Paul & Merton, Robert (2004), 'Mass Communication, Popular Taste, and Organised Social Action', in 'The Communication of Ideas', in Peters, John & Simonson, Peter (eds), *Mass Communication and American Social Thought: Key Texts, 1919–1968*, Lanham, MD & Oxford: Rowman & Littlefield, pp. 230–241.

Le Billon, Philippe (2001), 'Angola's Political Economy of War: the Role of Oil and Diamonds-1975–2000', *African Affairs*, vol. 100, Oxford: Oxford University Press.

Le Bon, Gustave (1896, 2007), *The Crowd*, Charleston SC: BiblioBazaar.

Lebl, Leslie (Winter 2010), 'Radical Islam in Europe', *Orbis*, vol. 54, no. 1, pp. 46–60.

Lee, Alfred (1937), *The Daily Newspaper in America*, New York: Macmillan.

Lee, Everett (1966), 'A Theory of Migration', *Demography*, vol. 3, no. 1, pp. 47–57.

Lefebvre, Henri (1999), *Everyday Life in the Modern World*, New Brunswick U.S.& London: Transaction.

Lees-Marchment, Jennifer (2004), *The Political Marketing Revolution: Transforming the Government of the UK*, London: Manchester University Press.

——— (2008), *Political Marketing and British Political Parties*, Manchester & New York: Manchester University Press.

Leiner, Barry et al (10 Dec 2003, Version 3.32), 'A Brief History of the Internet', http://www.isoc.org/internet/history/brief.shtml, accessed 24 Nov 2009.

Leiser, Erwin (1974), *Nazi Cinema*, London: Secker & Warburg.

Leiss, William; Kline, Stephen & Jihally, Sut (1986), *Social Communication in Advertising*, Toronto: Methuen.

Lenin, Vladimir (1987), *What Is To Be Done? And Other Writings*, New York: Bantam.

——— (1992), *The State and Revolution*, London: Penguin.

——— (2004), *The State and Revolution*, Whitefish MT: Kessinger.

Lemert, Edwin (1951), *Social Pathology: A Systematic Approach to the Study of Sociopathic Behaviour*, New York: McGraw-Hill.

Lemert, Edwin (1967), *Human Deviance, Social Problems and Social Control*, Englewood Cliffs NJ: Prentice-Hall.

Lessig, Lawrence (2006), *Code: Version 2.0*, New York: Basic Books.

Lester, Paul Martin (2003), *Visual Communication Images with Messages*, AUS: Wadsworth.

——— (2006), 'Syntactic Theory of Visual Communication', http://commfaculty.fullerton.edu/lester/writings/viscomtheory.html, accessed 30 Sept 2010.

L'Etang, Jacquie (2004), *Public Relations in Britain: A History of Professional Practice in the Twentieth Century*, Mahwah NJ & London: Lawrence Erlbaum.

Levi-Strauss, Claude (1966), *The Savage Mind*, Chicago: University of Chicago Press.

——— (1977), *Structural Anthropology*, Harmondsworth: Penguin.

——— (1986), *The Raw and the Cooked: Introduction to a Science of Mythology 1*, Harmondsworth: Penguin.

Levitin, Daniel (2006), *This Is Your Brain On Music*, London: Atlantic Books.

Lindholm Schulz, Helena & Hammer, Juliane (2003), *The Palestinian Diaspora: Formations of Identities and Politics of Homeland*, London: Routledge.

Lindroos, Kia (2006), 'Benjamin's Moment', in Palonen, Kia (ed.), *Redescriptions: Vol. 10*, Piscataway NJ & London: Transaction.

Ling, Richard Seyler (2004), *The Mobile Connection: the Cell Phone's Impact on Society*, San Francisco CA: Elsevier.

Lippman, Andrew & Reed, David (2003), *Viral Communications*, Media Laboratory Research.

Lippmann, Walter (1921), 'The World Outside and the Pictures in our Heads', in Schramm, Wilbur & Roberts, Donald (eds) (1971), *The Processes and Effects of Mass Communication*, Urbana: University of Illinois Press.

Lippmann, Walter (1922, 1997), *Public Opinion*, New York & London: Free Press Paperbacks.

Lipset & Rokkan (eds) (1967), *Party Systems and Voter Alignment: Cross-national Perspectives*, New York: The Free Press.

Lilleker, Darren & Lees-Marshment, Jennifer (eds) (2005), *Political Marketing: A Comparative Perspective*, Manchester & New York: Manchester University Press.

Livingston, Steve (1997), *Clarifying the CNN Effect: An Examination of Media Effects According to Type of Military Intervention*, Harvard MA: Joan Shorenstein Center/ Research Paper R-18.

Lloyd, C Morgan (1923), *Emergent Evolution*, London: Williams and Norgate.

Lloyd, Jenny (2005), 'Square Peg, Round Hole? Can Basic Marketing Concepts Such as the "Product" and the "Marketing Mix" Have a Useful Role in the Political Arena?', *Journal of Nonprofit & Public Sector Marketing*, vol. 14, no. 1, pp. 27–46.

Locke, John (1728), *Two Treatises on Government*, 5th edn, 2nd Treatise, Ch.19, section 230, London: Bettesworth.

Lofland, John & Stark, Rodney (1965), 'Becoming a World-Saver: A Theory of Conversion to a Deviant Perspective', *American Sociological Review*, vol. 30, no. 6, pp. 862–75.

Lofland, John (1977), *Doomsday Cult: A Study of Conversion, Proselytisation, and Maintenance of Faith*, New York: Irvington.

Loomis, Charles (ed.) (2002), *Community and Society*, Mineola NY: Dover Publications.

Lord, Bob (2008), 'Beyond Transactional and Transformational Leadership', in Uhl-Bien, Mary & Marion, Russ, *Complexity Leadership: Part 1 Conceptual Foundations*, Charlotte NC: IAP.

Los Angeles Times (26 June 2009), 'Television Misses Out As Gossip Website TMZ Reports Michael Jackson's Death First', http://articles.latimes.com/2009/jun/26/local/ me-jackson-media26, accessed 28 May 2010.

Loyd, Anthony (31 May 2010), 'Saudi Dollars Flood into Afghan War Zone', *Sunday Times*, p. 27.

Luhmannn, Niklas (2000), *The Reality of the Mass Media*, Cambridge: Polity.

Lukács, Georg (1971), *History and Class Consciousness*, London: Merlin Press.

Luttwak, Edward (2009), *The Virtual Empire: War, Faith and Power*, New Brunswick NJ: Transaction Publishers.

Lutz, James & Lutz, Brenda (2008), *Global Terrorism*, Abingdon: Routledge.

Luxemburg, Rosa (1986), *The Mass Strike: The Political Party and the Trade Unions*, London: Bookmarks.

Lynch, Marc (2006), *Voices of the New Arab Public: Iraq, Al-Jazeera, and Middle East Politics Today*, New York: Columbia University Press.

Lyons, FSL (1979), *Ireland Since the Famine*, London: Fontana Press.

Lyotard, Jean-François (1984), *The Postmodern Condition: A Report on Knowledge'*, Manchester: Manchester University Press.

Machiavelli, Niccolo (1963), *The Prince*, Harmondsworth: Penguin.

Macintyre, Ben (10 Sept 2009), 'The Nature of War Frozen in a Photograph', *The Times*, p. 34.

Mackay, Andrew & Tatham, Steve (2009), 'Behavioural Conflict', Shrivenham Paper, no. 9, UK Defence Academy.

Mackinlay, John (2002), 'Globalisation and Insurgency', Adelphi Paper 352, London: International Institute for Strategic Studies, Oxford University Press.

—— (2005), 'Defeating Complex Insurgency: Beyond Iraq and Afghanistan', The Royal United Service Institute: Whitehall Paper 64, London: RUSI.

—— (2009), *The Insurgent Archipelago*, London: Hurst.

MacKinnon, Rebecca (Apr 2011), 'Liberation Technology: China's "Networked" Authoritarianism', *Journal of Democracy*, vol. 22, no. 2, pp. 32–46.

MacLysaght, Edward (1967), 'Larkin, Connolly, and the Labour Movement', in Martin, FX (ed.), *Leaders and Men of the Easter Rising: Dublin 1916*, London: Methuen.

Mac Lochlainn, Piaras F (1971), *Last Words: Letters and Statements of the Leaders Executed after the Rising at Easter 1916*, Dublin: Kilmainham Jail Restoration Society.

Macpherson Inquiry (1999), http://www.archive.official-documents.co.uk/document/cm42/4262/sli-00.htm, accessed 30 Sept 2010

Macrae, Joanna (2001), *Aiding Recovery: The Crisis of AID in Chronic Political Emergencies*, London: Zed Books/Overseas Development Institute.

Mack, Andrew (Jan 1975), 'Why Big Nations Lose Small Wars: The Politics of Asymmetric Conflict', *World Politics*, vol. 27, no. 2, pp. 175–200.

MacStiofain, Sean (1975), *Revolutionary in Ireland*, Edinburgh: Gordon Cremonesi.

Maguire, John Francis (1868), *The Irish in America*, London: Longmans, Green & Co.

Mahnken, Thomas (2008), *Technology and the American Way of War*, New York: Columbia University Press.

Mamdani, Mahmood (1996), *Citizen and Subject: Contemporary Africa and the Legacy of Late Colonialism'* Princeton: NJ: Princeton University Press.

Mailer, Norman (1974), *Marilyn*, London: Coronet/Hodder.

Maines, David, Sugrue, Noreen & Katovich, Michael (Apr 1983), 'The Sociological Import of G.H. Mead's Theory of the Past', *American Sociological Review*, vol. 48, no. 2, pp. 161–173.

Maitron, Jean (1951), *Histoire du Mouvement Anarchiste En France (1880–1914)*, Paris: Société Universitaire d'Editions et de Librairie.

Mali, Joseph (2008), 'The Myth of the State Revisited', in Barash, Jeffrey, *The Symbolic Construction of Reality: the Legacy of Ernst Cassirer*, Chicago: University of Chicago Press.

Malik, Shiv (30 June 2007), 'My Brother the Bomber', *Prospect*, issue 135.

Mandel, Ernest (1970), 'The Leninist Theory of Organisation', http://www.ernestmandel.org/en/works/txt/1970/leninist_theory_organisation.htm, accessed 30 Sept 2010.

Mandela, Nelson (2010), *Long Walk to Freedom*, London: Abacus.

Manheim, Jarol (1991), *All of the People, All the Time*, Armonk, NY & London: M.E. Sharpe.

Mann, Michael (1986), *The Sources of Social Power: A History of Power from the Beginning to AD 1760*, vol. 1, Cambridge: Cambridge University Press.

Mao Tse-Tung (1963), *Selected Military Writings of Mao Tse-Tung*, Peking: Foreign Language Press.

BIBLIOGRAPHY

Mao Tse-Tung (2007), *On Guerrilla Warfare*, Griffith, Samuel B., trans., Rockford Ill: BN Publishing.

Marcuse, Herbert (1991), *One-Dimensional Man*, London: Routledge.

Marketing Magazine (06 Apr 2009), 'British Army Uses Doom-Style Online Video Game in Recruitment Drive', *Marketing Magazine*, http://www.marketingmagazine.co.uk/news/issues/896503/British-Army-uses-Doom-style-online-video-game-recruitment-drive/, accessed 25 June 2009.

Marshall, Peter (2010), *Demanding the Impossible: A History of Anarchism*, Oakland CA: PM Press.

Martin, FX (Mar 1961), 'Select documents. XX Eoin MacNeill on the 1916 Rising', *Irish Historical Studies*, vol. 12, no. 47, pp. 226–270, Memorandum 1.

—— (1963), *The Irish Volunteers 1913–15: Recollections and Documents*, Dublin: James Duffy.

—— (1967), '1916—Revolution or Evolution?', in Martin, FX (ed.), *Leaders and Men of the Easter Rising: Dublin 1916*, London: Methuen.

Martin, Michael (2000), *Verstehen: The Uses of Understanding in Social Science*, New Brunswick NJ: Transaction.

Marwan, Bishara (02 Feb 2010), 'Tangoing with the Taliban', http://blogs.aljazeera.net/imperium/2010/02/02/tangoing-taliban, accessed 26 May 2010.

Marx, Karl (1848), 'Communist Manifesto', http://www.marxists.org/archive/marx/works/1848/communist-manifesto/ch01.htm, accessed 30 Sept 2010.

—— (1963), *Eighteenth Brumaire of Louis Bonaparte*, New York: International Publishers.

—— (1982), *Critique of Hegel's Philosophy of Right*, Cambridge: Cambridge University Press.

Marx, Karl & Engels, Friedrich (1965), *The German Ideology*, London: Lawrence & Wishart.

Massey, Douglas et al (eds) (2002), *Worlds in Motion: Understanding International Migration at the End of the Millennium*, Oxford: Oxford University Press.

Mazzocco, Dennis & Schiller, Herbert (1994), *Networks of Power: Corporate Television's Threat to Democracy*, Boston MA: South End Press.

McAdam, Doug (1988), 'Micromobilization Contexts and Recruitment to Activism', in Klandermans, Bert; Kriesi, Hanspeter & Tarrow, Sidney (eds), *From Structure to Action: Comparing Social Movement Research Across Cultures*, Greenwich Conn: JAI Press.

McAdam, Doug, Tarrow, Sidney & Tilly, Charles (2001), *Dynamics of Contention*, Cambridge: Cambridge University Press.

McAleese, Mary (17 July 2002), President of Ireland, Dedication of the Irish Hunger Memorial, Battery Park City, New York, Irish Consulate General, New York, accessed 03 Aug 2008.

McCarthy, Jerome (1968), *Basic Marketing: A Managerial Approach*, Homewood Ill: Richard D Irwin.

McCarthy, John & Zald, Mayer (May 1977), 'Resource Mobilization and Social Movements: A Partial Theory', *American Journal of Sociology*, vol. 82, no. 6, pp. 1212–1241.

McChesney, Robert (1993), *Telecommunications, Mass Media and Democracy: the Battle for the Control of U.S. Broadcasting*, New York: Oxford University Press.

McChesney, Robert (1997), 'The Mythology of Commercial Broadcasting and the Contemporary Crisis of Public Broadcasting', Spry Memorial Lecture, Vancouver & Montreal.

—— (1997), *Corporate Media and the Threat to Democracy*, New York: Seven Stories Press.

—— (2008), *The Political Economy of Media: Enduring Issues, Emerging Dilemmas*, New York: Monthly Review Press.

McConville, Sean (2003), *Irish Political Prisoners, 1848–1922: Theatres of War*, Abingdon: Routledge.

McDonald, Henry (2008), *Gunsmoke and Mirrors: How Sinn Féin Dressed Up Defeat as Victory*, Dublin: Gill & MacMillan.

—— (14 Sept 2010), 'Real IRA Says it Will Target UK Banks', *The Guardian*, http://www.guardian.co.uk/uk/2010/sep/14/real-ira-targets-banks-bankers, accessed 20 Sept 2010.

McDonald, Kevin (2006), *Global Movements*, Malden MA & Oxford: Blackwell.

McGhee, Owen (2005), *The IRB: Irish Republican Brotherhood from the Land League to Sinn Féin*, Dublin: Four Courts Press.

McGreal, Chris (2007), 'Afrikaans Singer Stirs up Controversy with War Song', *The Guardian*,

http://www.guardian.co.uk/world/2007/feb/26/music.southafrica, accessed 15 Aug 2008.

McLaughlin, Joshua (2009), 'The al Qaeda Franchise Model: An Alternative', *Small Wars Journal*, www.smallwarsjournal.com.

McLean, George (1972), *The Rise and Fall of Anarchy in America*, New York: Haskell House.

McLuhan, Marshall (1964), *Understanding Media*, London: Routledge & Kegan Paul.

McLuhan, Marshall (1967), *The Gutenberg Galaxy: The Making of Typographical Man*, London: Routledge & Kegan Paul.

McMahon, Sean (2001), *Wolfe Tone*, Cork: Mercier Press.

McQuarrie, Edward & Mick, David (Sept 1992), 'On Resonance: A Critical Pluralistic Inquiry into Advertising Rhetoric', *Journal of Consumer Research*, vol. 19, no. 2.

McNair, Brian (2006), *Cultural Chaos: Journalism, News and Power in a Globalised World*, London & New York: Routledge.

Mead, George Herbert (1934), *Mind, Self, and Society from the Standpoint of a Social Behaviourist*, Chicago: University of Chicago Press.

Mehta, Suketu (2005), *Maximum City: Bombay Lost and Found*, New York: Vintage Departures.

Meikle Graham (2004), 'Networks of Influence', in Goggin, Gerard (ed.), *Virtual Nation: the Internet in Australia*, Sydney: University of New South Wales Press.

Melder, Keith (1992), *Hail to the Candidate*, Washington, DC: Smithsonian.

Mellencamp, Patricia (1990), 'Television Time and Catastrophe, or Beyond the Pleasure Principle of Television', in Mellencamp, Patricia (ed.), *Logics of Television: essays in Cultural Criticism*, Bloomington: Indiana University Press.

Melucci, Alberto (1989), *Nomads of the Present*, London: Hutchinson Radius.

MEMRI (14 June 2007), 'Global Islamic Media Front Instructs Islamists to Infiltrate Popular Non-Islamic Forums to Spread Pro-Islamic State Propaganda', MEMRI Special Dispatches Series 1621, http://memri.org/bin/articles.cgi?Page=archives&Area=sd&ID=SP162107, accessed 01 Mar 2008.

Merom, Gil (2003), *How Democracies Lose Small Wars: State, Society, and the Failures of France in Algeria, Israel in Lebanon, and the United States in Vietnam*, New York: Cambridge University Press.

Mertus, Julie (1999), *Kosovo: How Myths and Truths Started a War*, Berkeley: University of California Press.

Mertus, Julie (16 Mar 2006), 'Slobodan Milosevic: Myth and Responsibility', *Open Democracy*, http://www.opendemocracy.net/conflict-yugoslavia/responsibility_3361.jsp, accessed 29 June 2010.

Messaris, Paul (1997), *Visual Persuasion: The Role of Images in Advertising*, Thousand Oaks: Sage.

Messina, Anthony (2002), *West European Immigration and Immigrant Policy in the New Century*, Westport Conn: Praeger.

Micolta, Patricia (2009), 'The Bolivarian Connection: The Fuerzas Armadas Revolucionaras de Colombia (FARC), and Hugo Chavez', Paper presented at Midwest Political Science Association, 67th Annual Conference, Palmer House Hilton, Chicago: http://www.allacademic.com//meta/p_mla_apa_research_citation/3/6/1/6/7/pages361678/p361678-7.php, accessed 30 May 2010.

Miller, Arthur (1999), *Timebends, A Life*, London: Methuen.

Miller, David (ed.) (1982), *The Individual and the Social Self: Unpublished Work of George Herbert Mead*, Chicago: University of Chicago Press.

Miller, John & Page, Scott (2007), *Complex Adaptive Systems: An Introduction to Computational Models of Social Life*, Princeton NJ: Princeton University Press.

Milošević's 1989 speech in Gazimestan, the Field of Black Birds (or Kosovo Polje), trans. by BBC, http://www.hirhome.com/bbc_milosevic.htm, accessed 29 June 2010.

Mitchel, A & Olson, J (1981), 'Are Product Attribute Beliefs the only Mediator of Advertising Effects on Brand Attitude?', *Journal of Marketing Research*, vol. 18, pp. 318–332.

Mitchel, John (1868), *Jail Journal or Five Years in British Prisons*, New York: PM Haverty.

Mitchell, Greg (04 Aug 2005), 'Hiroshima Cover-Up Exposed', http://www.alternet.org/mediaculture/23914/, accessed 30 Sept 2010.

Mizuko, Ito et al (2008), *Living and Learning with Digital Media: Summary of Findings from the Digital Youth Project*, Chicago Ill: MacArthur Foundation.

Moffat, James (2003), *Complexity Theory and Network Centric Warfare*, Washington, DC: Department of Defense CCRP.

Moloney, Ed (2002), *A Secret History of the IRA*, New York: WW Norton.

Molotch, Harvey (Feb 2006), 'Death on the Roof', *Space and Culture*, vol. 9, no. 1, pp. 31–34.

Morash, Christopher (1997), 'Making Memories: the Literature of the Irish Famine', in O'Sullivan, Patrick (ed), *The Meaning of the Famine*, London & Washington: Leicester University Press, pp. 40–55.

Morozov, Evgeny (18 Nov 2009), 'How Dictators Watch Us On The Web', *Prospect*, issue 165.

Mosco, Vincent (1996), *The Political Economy of Communication: Rethinking and Renewal*, London: Sage.

Moscovici, Serge (1984), 'The Phenomenon of Social Representations', in Farr, Robert & Moscovici, Serge (eds), *Social Representations*, London: Cambridge University Press.

BIBLIOGRAPHY

Motlagh, Jason(03 May 2009), 'Why the Taliban is Winning the Propaganda War', *Time Magazine*, http://www.time.com/time/world/article/0,8599,1895496,00.html.

Mount, Ferdinand (20 Apr 2008), p. 45, 'The Welsh Academy Encyclopaedia of Wales', *The Sunday Times*.

Moynihan, Daniel (1993), *Pandaemonium: Ethnicity in International Politics*, Oxford; Oxford University Press.

Mueller, Milton (1997), *Universal Service: Competition, Interconnection, and Monopoly in the Making of the American Telephone System*, Cambridge MA: MIT Press.

Mullah Omar (2001), 'Mullah Omar's Speech to the Taliban Clerics', *The Guardian*, http://www.guardian.co.uk/world/2001/sep/19/september11.usa15, accessed 30 Sept 2010.

——— (25 Nov 2009), 'Mullah Omar: In Celebration of Eid al-Adha', *Terror Watch*, NEFA Foundation http://www.nefafoundation.org/documents-area-afghanistan.html, accessed 25 June 2009.

Murawiec, Laurent (2008), *The Mind of Jihad*, Cambridge: Cambridge University Press.

Murdock, Graham & Golding, Peter (2005), 'Culture, Communications and Political Economy', in Curran, James & Gurevitch, Michael (eds), *Mass Media and Society*, London: Hodder Arnold.

Murphet, Julian (2005), 'Narrative Voice', in Fulton, Helen, ed, *Narrative and Media*, Cambridge: Cambridge University Press.

Murphy, Dennis (Jan 2008), 'The Trouble with Strategic Communication(s)', Issue Paper, Centre for Strategic Leadership, U.S. Army War College, vols. 2–08.

Myers, Kevin (2006), *Watching the Door*, Dublin: Lilliput Press.

Nachman, Ben-Yehuda (1999), 'The Masada Mythical Narrative and the Israeli Army', in Lomsky-Feder, Edna & Ben-Ari, Eyal (eds), *The Military and Militarism in Israeli Society*, Albany NY: State University of New York.

Nacos, Brigitte (2007), *Mass-mediated Terrorism: The Central Role of the Media in Terrorism and Counterterrorism*, Lanham MD: Rowan & Littlefield.

Nagel, Caroline & Staeheli, Lynn (2010), 'ICT and Geographies of British Arab and Arab American Activism', *Global Networks*, vol. 10, no. 2, pp. 26–281.

Nagl, John (2005), *Learning to Eat Soup with a Knife*, Chicago: & London: University of Chicago Press.

Nasrallah, Hassan (08 May 2008), 'Nasrallah Justifies Lebanon Riots', http://yalibnan.com/site/archives/2008/05/nasrallah_justi.php; http://www.youtube.com/watch?v=YrfxnCoPViI, accessed 28 May 2010.

Nathan, Joanna (2009), 'Reading the Taliban', in Giustozzi, Antonio (2009), *Decoding the New Taliban*, London: Hurst.

National Public Radio (21 Oct 2002), 'The Marlboro Man', http://www.npr.org/programs/morning/features/patc/marlboroman/, accessed 25 Aug 2008.

Nazila, Fathi (22 June 2009), 'In a Death Seen Around the World, a Symbol of Iranian Protests', *The New York Times*, http://www.nytimes.com/2009/06/23/world/middleeast/23neda.html accessed 27 Aug 2010

Nechaev, Sergei (1869), 'The Revolutionary Catechism', www.marxists.org/subject/anarchism/nechayev/catechism.htm, accessed 30 Sept 2010.

Needham, Catherine (2005), 'Brand Leaders: Clinton, Blair and the Limitations of the Permanent Campaign', *Political Studies*, vol. 53, pp. 343–361.

Nelson, Harold (1988), *Leon Trotsky and the Art of Insurrection*, London: Frank Cass.

Neumann, Peter (2005), 'The Bullet and the Ballot Box: The Case of the IRA', *Journal of Strategic Studies*, vol. 28, issue 6, pp. 941–975.

—— (2009), *Old and New Terrorism*, Cambridge: Polity.

Neumann, Peter & Smith, MLR (2008), *The Strategy of Terrorism: How it Works and Why it Fails*, Abingdon: Routledge.

Nevin, Donal (1968), 'The Irish Citizen Army', in Edwards, Owen Dudley & Pyle, Fergus (eds), *1916: The Easter Rising*, London: MacGibbon & Kee.

Neuman, Sigmund (1971), 'Engels and Marx: Military Concepts of the Social Revolutionaries', in Edward Mead Earle (ed.), *Makers of Modern Strategy*, Princeton: Princeton University Press.

New York Times (04 June 2009), 'Text: Obama's Speech in Cairo'.

—— (06 Apr 2009), 'President Obama's Remarks in Turkey'.

Nimmo, Dan (1999), pp. 73–86, 'The Permanent Campaign: Marketing as a Governing Tool', in Newman, Bruce (ed.), *Handbook of Political Marketing*, Thousand Oaks, Cal: Sage.

Nimmo, Dan & Combs, James (1990), *Mediated Political Realities*, New York: Longman.

Noakes, John & Johnston, Hank (2005), 'Frames of Protest: A Road Map to a Perspective', in Johnston, Hank & Noakes, John, *Frames of Protest: Social Movements and Framing Perspectives*, Lanham: Rowman & Littlefield.

Noelle-Neumann, Elisabeth (1980), *The Spiral of Silence: Public Opinion, Our Social Skin*, Chicago: University of Chicago Press.

Nora, Pierre (1989), pp. 7–25, 'Between Memory and History', in 'Les Lieux de Mémoire', *Representations 26*.

Nordenstreng, Kaarle & Schiller, Herbert (eds) (1993), *Beyond National Sovereignty: International Communication in the 1990s*, Norwood NJ: Ablex.

Norris, Pippa (2010), *Public Sentinel: News Media and Governance Reform*, Washington, DC: World Bank.

Novak, D (July 1958), 'The Place of Anarchism in the History of Political Thought', *The Review of Politics*, vol. 20, no. 3, pp. 307–329.

Nye, Joseph (2004), *Soft Power: The Means to Success in World Politics*, New York: Public Affairs/Perseus.

Oakeshott, Michael (1981), 'The Activity of Being a Historian', in *Rationalism in Politics and Other Essays*, London & New York: Methuen.

Obama, Barack (2010), 'National Framework for Strategic Communication', Washington, DC: White House, http://www.carlisle.army.mil/DIME/documents/NSC%20SCPD%20Report.pdf, accessed 05 Sept 2010.

O'Brien, Brendan (1995), *The Long War: The IRA & Sinn Féin from Armed Struggle to Peace Talks*, Dublin: The O'Brien Press.

—— (1999), *The Long War: The IRA and Sinn Féin*, 2nd edn, Syracuse NY: Syracuse University Press.

OCHA (2006), 'Humanitarian Negotiations with Armed Groups: A Manual for Practitioners', http://www.unhcr.org/refworld/docid/46924c322.html, accessed 31 July 2010.

O'Donnell, Victoria & Kable, June (1982), *Persuasion: An Interactive Dependency Approach*, New York: Random House.

O'Hair, Dan; Friedrich, Gustav & Dixon, Lynda (2002), *Strategic Communication in Business and the Professions*, Boston: Houghton Mifflin.

O'Hegarty, PS (1952), *A History of Ireland Under the Union, 1801–1922*, London: Methuen.

Ohmae, Kenichi (1994), *The Borderless World: Power and Strategy in the Global Marketplace*, London: HarperCollins.

Olick, Jeffrey (ed.) (2002), 'Collective Memory: The Two Cultures', in *Memory and Power in Post-War Europe: Studies in the Presence of the Past*, Cambridge: Cambridge University Press

Olick, Jeffrey (ed.) (2003), *States of Memory: Continuities, Conflicts, and Transformations in National Retrospection*, Durham NC: Duke University Press.

Oliver, Pamela & Johnston, Hank (Spring 2000), 'What a Good Idea! Frames and Ideologies in Social Movement Research', *Mobilization: An International Quarterly*, vol. 5, no. 1, pp. 37–54.

Olson, Mancur (1965), *The Logic of Collective Action*, Cambridge, MA.: Harvard University Press.

Omand, David (Winter 2005), 'Countering International Terrorism: The Use of Strategy', *Survival*, vol. 47, no. 4, pp. 107–116.

O'Malley, Ernie (2002), *On Another Man's Wound*, Dublin: Anvil Books.

O'Malley, Padraig (1990), *Biting at the Grave: The Irish Hunger Strikes and the Politics of Despair*, Boston: Beacon Press.

O'Neil, Bard (2005), *Insurgency & Terrorism*, Washington, DC: Potomac Books.

O'Neil, Mathieu (2009), *Cyberchiefs: Autonomy and Authority in Online Tribes*, London: Pluto Press.

'Operation Paget Inquiry report into the allegation of conspiracy to murder', http://i.thisislondon.co.uk/i/pix/downloads/OperationPagetFullReport.pdf, accessed 29 Apr 2009.

Oppenheimer, Andy (2009), *IRA: The Bombs and the Bullets*, Dublin: Irish Academic Press.

Ortony, Andrew (Winter 1975), 'Why Metaphors are Necessary and Not Just Nice', *Educational Theory*, vol. 25, pp. 45–53.

Orwell, George (1946), *Politics and the English Language*, London: News of the World.

—— (1949, 1989), *Nineteen Eighty-Four*, London: Penguin.

O'Shaughnessy, John & O'Shaughnessy, Nicholas (2004), *Persuasion in Advertising*, London & New York: Routledge.

O'Shaughnessy, Nicholas (1994), *The Phenomenon of Political Marketing*, Basingstoke: Macmillan.

—— (Nov 2003), 'The Symbolic State: A British Experience', *Journal of Public Affairs*, vol. 3, no. 4. pp. 297–312.

—— (2004), *Politics and Propaganda: Weapons of Mass Seduction*, Manchester: Manchester University Press.

O'Shaughnessy, Nicholas & Baines, Paul (2009), 'Selling Terror: The Symbolization and Positioning of Jihad', *Marketing Theory*, vol. 9, no. 2, pp. 227–241.

Osgood, Kenneth (2006), *Total Cold War: Eisenhower's Secret Propaganda Battle at Home and Abroad*, Lawrence: University Press of Kansas.

BIBLIOGRAPHY

Oved, Ya'Akov (Apr-Sept 1992), 'The Future Society According to Kropotkin', *Cahiers du Monde Russe Soviétique*, vol. 33, nos 2–3, pp. 303–320.

Owens, Gary (Dec 1990), 'Review', *The Canadian Journal of Irish Studies*, vol. 16, no. 2, pp. 123–5.

Packer, George (18 Dec 2006), 'Knowing the Enemy', *The New Yorker*.

Packwood, Lane (May-June 2009), 'Popular Support as the Objective in Counterinsurgency: What Are We Really After?', *Military Review*, pp. 67–77.

Paivio, Allan (1988), 'Psychological Processes in the Comprehension of Metaphor', in Ortony, Andrew (ed.), *Metaphor and Thought*, Cambridge: Cambridge University Press.

Pakistan Body Count (20 Nov 1995–01 May 2010), http://www.pakistanbodycount.org/bla.php, accessed 26 May 2010.

Palfrey, John & Gasser, Urs (2008), *Born Digital: Understanding the First Generation of Digital Natives*, New York: Perseus.

Palmer, Jerry (2002), 'Smoke and Mirrors: Is That the Way It Is? Themes in Political Marketing', *Media, Culture & Society*, vol. 24, no. 3, pp. 345–363.

Papastergiadias, Nikos (2000), *The Turbulence of Migration: Globalization, Deterritorialization, and Hybridity*, Cambridge: Polity Press.

——— (2007), *International Migration Outlook, Annual Report 2007*, OECD Publishing.

Pape, Robert (2006), *Dying to Win: The Strategic Logic of Suicide Terrorism*, New York: Random House.

Paris Match (03 Sept 2008), 'Exclusif: Nos Journalistes ont Retrouvé les Talibans qui ont Abattu les Dix Soldats Francais', http://www.parismatch.com/dans-l-oeil-de-match/reportages, accessed 05 Sept 2008,

——— (04–10 Sept 2008), 'La Parade des Talibans Avec Leurs Trophées Francais'.

Pariser, Eli (2011), *The Filter Bubble: What the Internet Is Hiding From You*, London: Viking.

Parsons, Howard & Somerville, John (1977), *Marxism, Revolution, and Peace: from the Proceedings of the Philosophical Study of Dialectical Materialism*, Amsterdam: BR Grüner.

Parsons, Talcott (1968), *The Structure of Social Action*, New York: Free Press.

Paseta, Senia (summer 1998), '1798 in 1898: The Politics of Commemoration', *Irish Review*, no. 22, pp. 46–53.

Pastor, James (2010), *Terrorism and Public Safety: Implications for the Obama Presidency*, Boca Raton FL: CRC.

Paul, Christopher (2009), *Strategic Communication? A Survey of Current Proposals and Recommendations*, Santa Monica: RAND.

Peirce, Charles (1932), 'The Icon, Index, and Symbol', in Hartshore, Charles & Weiss, Paul (eds), *Collected Papers of Charles Sanders Peirce*, vol. 2, Cambridge MA: Harvard University Press.

Peirce, Charles Sanders (1991), *Peirce on Signs: Writings on Semiotics*, Chapel Hill: University of Carolina Press.

Penenberg, Adam (2009), *Viral Loop*, London: Sceptre.

Penny, Laurie (16 Dec 2009), 'Three Cheers for the Internet', *Prospect*, issue 165, http://www.prospectmagazine.co.uk/2009/12/three-cheers-for-the-internet/, accessed 24 Feb 2009.

BIBLIOGRAPHY

Perry, Peter (1974), *British Farming in the Great Depression 1870–1914*, Newton Abbot: David and Charles.

Pew Global (07 June 2006), 'Muslims in Europe: Economic Worries Top Concerns About Religious and Cultural Identity', http://pewglobal.org/reports/display.php?ReportID=254, accessed 01 Feb 2010.

Phillips, Melanie (2006), *Londonistan*, New York: Encounter Books.

Pickerill, Jenny (2007), 'Indymedia and Practices of Alter-Globalisation', *Environment and Planning A*, vol. 39, no. 11, pp. 2668–2684.

Picot, Arnold, Reichwald, Ralf & Wigand, Rolf (2008), *Information, Organization and Management*, Berlin & Heidelberg: Springer.

Pinker, Steven (2008), *The Stuff of Thought: Language as a Window into Human Nature*, London & New York: Penguin.

Polanyi, Karl (2001), *The Great Transformation*, Boston MA: Beacon Press.

Polanyi, Michel (1967, 2009), *The Tacit Dimension*, Chicago: University of Chicago Press.

Pollay, R & Mainprize, S (1984), 'Headlining of Visuals in Print Advertising', in Glover, J (ed.), *Proceedings of the American Academy of Advertising*, Denver: American Academy of Advertising.

Polletta, Francesca & Jasper, James (2001), 'Collective Identity and Social Movements', *Annual Review of Sociology*, vol. 27, pp. 283–305.

Post, Jerrold (1998), 'Terrorist Psycho-logic: Terrorist Behaviour as a Product of Psychological Forces', in Walter Reich (ed.), *Origins of Terrorism: Psychologies, Ideologies, Theologies, States of Mind*, Washington, DC: Woodrow Wilson Center Press.

Post, Jerrold (2007), *The Mind of the Terrorist: The Psychology of Terrorism from the IRA to al-Qaeda*, New York: Palgrave Macmillan.

Postman, Neil (1993), *Technopoly: The Surrender of Culture to Technology*, New York: Vintage.

Poulson, Stephen (2005), *Social Movements in Twentieth-Century Iran*, Lanham MD: Lexington.

Pratkanis, Anthony & Aronson, Elliot (2001), *Age of Propaganda*, New York: WH Freeman.

Price, Vincent & Zaller, John (1993), 'Who Gets the News? Alternative Measures of News Reception and their Implications for Research', *Public Opinion Quarterly*, vol. 57, pp. 133–164.

Prigogine, Ilya & Stengers, Isabelle (1984), *Order out of Chaos: Man's Dialogue with Nature*, London: Heinemann.

Primoratz, Igor (2006), 'Terrorism in the Israeli-Palestinian Conflict', in Law, Stephen (ed.) (2008), *Israel, Palestine and Terror*, London & New York: Continuum.

Pritchett, Lant (2006), *Let Their People Come: Breaking the Gridlock on Global Labor Mobility*, Washington, DC: Center for Global Development.

Prospect Magazine (04 May 2010), 'Why Is Hamas Making Cartoons?', http://www.prospectmagazine.co.uk/2010/05/hamass-debt-to-the-graphic-novel/, accessed 28 May 2010.

Proudhon, Pierre-Joseph letter to Marx (17 May 1846), in Woodcock, George (1986), *Anarchism: A History of Libertarian Ideas and Movements*, Harmondsworth: Penguin.

BIBLIOGRAPHY

Proudhon, Pierre-Joseph (1851, 1969), *Idée Générale de la Révolution*, Robinson, John, trans., New York: Haskell House.

Proust, Marcel (1970), *The Past Remembered*, New York: Random House.

Pugh, Michael & Cooper, Neil, with Goodhand, Jonathan (2004), *War Economies in a Regional Context: Challenges of Transformation*, Boulder, London: Lynne Rienner.

Putnam, Robert (2000), *Bowling Alone: The Collapse of and Revival of Community in America*, New York: Simon & Schuster.

Putnam, Robert & Goss, Kristin (eds) (2002), *Democracies in Flux*, Oxford: Oxford University Press.

Radley, Alan (1990), 'Artefacts, Memory and a Sense of the Past', in Middleton, David & Edwards, Derek (eds), *Collective Remembering*, London: Sage.

Rafael, Vicente (2003), 'The Cellphone and the Crowd: Messianic Politics in Contemporary Philippines', *Public Culture*, vol. 15, pp. 399–425.

Raine, George (09 June 2004), 'Creating Reagan's Image', *San Francisco Chronicle*, http://www.sfgate.com/cgi-bin/article.cgi?f=/c/a/2004/06 Sept BUGBI72U8O1.DTL, accessed 27 July 2009.

Rajagopal, Arvind (2000), 'Mediating Modernity: Theorising Reception in a Non-Western Society', in Park, Myung-Jin & Curran, James, *De-Westernising Media Studies*, London: Routledge.

Ramadan, Tariq, *'Islam is a European Religion'*, http://www.youtube.com/watch%3Fv=lxjL3CIs0xw, accessed 04 Feb 2010.

Ramon-Garcia, Marta (2010), 'Square-Toed Boots and Felt Hats: Irish Revolutionaries and the Invasion of Canada (1848–1871)', *Estudios Irlandeses*, no. 5, pp. 81–91.

Rapoport, David (2004), 'Four Waves of Modern Terrorism', in Kurth Cronin, Audrey & Ludes, James M (eds), *Attacking Terrorism: Elements of a Grand Strategy*, Washington, DC: Georgetown University Press.

Rauchway, Eric (2004), *The Making of Theodore Roosevelt's America*, New York: Farrar, Strauss and Giroux.

Rawnsley, Gary (ed.) (1999), *Cold-War Propaganda in the 1950s*, Basingstoke: Macmillan.

Raymond, Joad (2003), *Pamphlets and Pamphleteering in Early Modern Britain*, Cambridge: Cambridge University Press.

Rayner, Steve (2007), 'Creating a Climate for Change', in Brandt, Lisa Kaye (ed.), *Cultural Analysis and the Navigation of Complexity*, Lanham MD: University Press of America.

'Reagan: A New Beginning' (1984), http://www.youtube.com/watch?v=TRI3G-K0P50, accessed 20 July 2009.

'Reclaim the Kop' campaign, http://www.bebo.com/Profile.jsp?MemberId=3555744631, accessed 29 Apr 2009

Reclus, Elisée (Jan-June 1884), 'An Anarchist on Anarchy', *Contemporary Review*, vol. 45.

Redmond, Sean (2008), 'When Planes Fall out of the Sky', in Randell, Karen & Redmond, Seam (eds), *The War Body on Screen*, New York & London: Continuum.

Reich, Walter (ed.) (1998), *Origins of Terrorism*, Baltimore MD: John Hopkins University Press.

Reid, Elizabeth (1998), 'Variations on the Illusion of One Self', in Gackenbach, Jayne (ed.), *Psychology and the Internet*, San Diego CA: Academic Press.

BIBLIOGRAPHY

Regan, Gerry, (2002), 'New York Dedicates Its Famine Memorial', *The Wild GeeseToday*, http://www.thewildgeese.com/pages/nyfamine.html.

Reno, William (1998), *Warlord Politics and Africa States*, Boulder, London: Lynne Rienne.

Reuters (03 Nov 2009), 'Somali Telecoms Thrive Despite Chaos', http://af.reuters.com/article/investingNews/idAFJOE5A20DB20091103, accessed 10 July 2010.

Reuters (01 Mar 2010), 'Afghanistan Bans Coverage of Taliban Attacks', http://www.reuters.com/article/idUSSGE6200CS20100301,06 Apr 2010.

Rheingold, Howard (1994), *The Virtual Community: Finding Connection in a Computerised World*, London: Secker & Warburg.

Rheingold, Howard (2002), *Smart Mobs: The Next Social Revolution*, Cambridge MA: Basic Books.

Richards, General Sir David (18 Jan 2010), 'Future Conflict and its Prevention: People and the Information Age', speech, London: IISS.

Richards, Paul (2005), *No Peace, No War*, Oxford: James Currey.

Richardson, Louise (2005), *What Terrorists Want: Understanding the Terrorist Threat*, London: John Murray.

Ricoeur, Paul (2004), *Memory, History, Forgetting*, Chicago &London: University of Chicago Press.

—— (2004)), 'The Hermeneutics of Symbols and Philosophical Reflection: II', in *The Conflict of Interpretations: Essays in Hermeneutics*, London & New York: Continuum.

Riedel, Bruce (May/June 2007), 'Al Qaeda Strikes Back', *Foreign Policy*.

Rid, Thomas & Hecker, Marc (2009), *War 2.0: Irregular Warfare in the Information Age*, Westport Conn: Praeger Security International.

Ritchie, David (2001), 'Oldham Independent Review', http://image.guardian.co.uk/sys-files/Guardian/documents/2001/12/11/Oldhamindependentreview.pdf.

Ringer, Ryan (04 Mar 2010), 'White House Cyber Czar: There is No Cyberwar', *Wired*, http://www.wired.com/threatlevel/2010/03/schmidt-cyberwar/, accessed 13 July 2010.

Robb, John (2007), '*Brave New War*', Hoboken NJ: John Wiley & Sons.

Roberts, Donald (1971), 'The Nature of Communication Effects', in Schramm, Wilbur & Roberts, Donald, *The Process and Effects of Mass Communication*, Urbana Ill: University of Illinois Press.

Robinson, Glenn (2004), 'Hamas as Social Movement', in Wiktorowicz, Quintan (ed.), *Islamic Activism: A Social Movement Theory Approach*, Bloomington IND: Indiana University Press.

Rodin, David (2007), 'Terrorism Without Intention', in Kinsella, David & Carr, Craig (eds), *The Morality of War*, Boulder CO & London: Lynne Rienner.

Rogers, Everett (2003), *Diffusion of Innovations*, New York: Free Press.

Ronfeldt, David (12 Jan 2010), http://al-sahwa.blogspot.com/2010/01/follow-up-to-al-qaeda-franchise-or.html, accessed 14 July 2010.

Rose, Steven (1998), 'How Brains Make Memories', in Fara, Patricia & Patterson, Karalyn (eds), *Memory*, Cambridge: Cambridge University Press.

Rosen, David (2005), *Armies of the Young: Child Soldiers in War and Terrorism*, Piscataway NJ: Rutgers University Press.

Rosenfield, Israel (1988), '*The Invention of Memory: A New View of the Brain*', New York: Basic Books.

Rosenfield, Israel & Ziff, Edward (26 June 2008), 'How the Mind Works: Revelations', *New York Review of Books*, p. 64.

Ross, Edward (1901, 2009), *Social Control: A Survey of the Foundations of Order*, New Brunswick NJ: Transaction Publishers.

Ross, Michael (2003), pp. 47–72, 'Oil, Drugs and Diamonds: The Varying Roles of Natural Resources in Civil War', in Ballentine, Karen & Sherman, Jake (eds), *The Political Economy of Armed Conflict: Beyond Greed and Grievance*, Boulder, London: Lynne Rienner.

Rossington, Michael & Whitehead, Anne (2007), *Theories of Memory*, Edinburgh: Edinburgh University Press.

Rossiter, J & Percy, L (1983), 'Visual Communication in Advertising', in Harris, R (ed.), *Information Processing Research in Advertising*, Hillsdale NJ: Lawrence Erlbaum.

Routledge, Paul (1998), 'Going Globile', in O'Tuathail, Gearoid & Dolby, Simon, *Rethinking Geopolitics*, London: Routledge.

Roy, Arundhati (2009), *Listening to Grasshoppers: Field Notes on Democracy*, London: Hamish Hamilton.

Roy, Olivier (2004), *Globalised Islam: The Search for a New Ummah*, New York: Columbia University Press.

Ruane, Joseph & Todd, Jennifer (2007), 'Path Dependence in Settlement Processes: Explaining Settlement in Northern Ireland', *Political Studies*, vol. 55, pp. 442–458.

Rugh, William (2004), *Arab Mass Media: Newspapers, Radio, and Television in Arab Politics*, Westport & London: Praeger Security International.

Runciman, David (06 Feb 2010), 'The Virtual Revolution: Enemy of the State', Programme 2, BBC2,

———— (2010), 'The Virtual Revolution—Rushes Sequences', BBC 2, http://www.bbc.co.uk/blogs/digitalrevolution/2009/10/rushes-sequences-dr-david-runc.shtml, accessed 02 Mar 2010.

Russell, Bertrand (1969), *History of Western Philosophy*, London: George Allen & Unwin.

Ryan, Desmond (1937), *The Phoenix Flame: A Study of Fenianism and John Devoy*, London: Arthur Barker.

Ryan, Johnny (2007), *Countering Militant Islamist Radicalisation on the Internet*, Dublin: Institute of European Affairs.

Sageman, Marc (2004), *Understanding Terror Networks*, Philadelphia PA: University of Pennsylvania Press.

———— (2008), *Leaderless Jihad: Terror Networks in the Twenty-first Century*, Philadelphia: University of Pennsylvania Press.

Said, Edward (2000), *Out of Place: A Memoir*, London: Granta.

———— (1978, 2003), *Orientalism*, London: Penguin.

Said, Edward & Hitchens, Christopher (1988), *Blaming the Victims: Spurious Scholarship and the Palestinian Question*, London & New York: Verso.

Saleh, Heba & Chaffin, Joshua (24 Jan 2011), 'Tunisian Army Chief Vows To Guard Revolution', http://www.ft.com/cms/s/0/e01ffbc4–27e5–11e0–8abc-00144feab49a.html#axzz1Pu7BziPL, accessed 21 June 2011.

Sambanis, Nicholas (2008), 'Terrorism and Civil War', in Keefer, Philip & Loayza, Norman (eds), *Terrorism, Economic Development, and Political Openness*, Cambridge: Cambridge University Press.

BIBLIOGRAPHY

Samers, Michael (2010), *Migration*, Abingdon: Routledge.

Sampson, Anthony (09 Dec 2009), 'Observing David Astor', *The Guardian*.

Sandler, Todd & Enders, Walter (2007), 'Applying Analytical Methods to Study Terrorism', *International Studies Perspectives*, vol. 8, pp. 287–302.

Sanger, David (19 Feb 2011), 'When Armies Decide', *The New York Times*, http://www.nytimes.com/2011/02/20/weekinreview/20military.html?pagewanted=1&_r=1, accessed 21 June 2011.

Sartre, Jean-Paul (1972), *The Psychology of Imagination*, London: Methuen.

Saul, Samuel (1985), *The Myth of the Great Depression 1873–1896*, London: Macmillan.

Sayigh, Yezid (1997) Armed Struggle and the Search for the State, Oxford: Clarendon.

Scheuer, Michael (30 May 2007), 'Al-Qaeda's Media Doctrine: Evolution from Cheerleader to Opinion-Shaper', *Terrorism Focus*, vol. 14, issue 15, Washington, DC: Jamestown Foundation.

Schiller, Dan (1986), 'Transformation of News in the U.S. Information Market', in Golding Philip (ed.), *Communicating Politics*, Leicester: Leicester University Press.

Schiller, Herbert (1992), *Mass Communications and American Empire*, Oxford: Westview Press.

——— (1993), 'Not Yet the Postimperialist Era', in Roach, Colleen (ed.), *Communication and Culture in War and Peace*, Newbury Park CA: Sage.

Schmid, Alex & Jongman, Albert (1988), *Political Terrorism: A New Guide to Actors, Authors, Concepts, Data Bases, Theories and Literature*, Amsterdam: North Holland Publishing Co.

Schneider, Mark (20 May 2008), 'Strategic Incoherence and Taliban Resurgence in Afghanistan', http://www.crisisgroup.org/home/index.cfm?id=5447&l=1, accessed 16 June 2009.

Schoenberger, Erica (1997), *The Cultural Crisis of the Firm*, Cambridge MA & Oxford: Blackwell.

Schramm, Wilbur (1971), 'How Communication Works', in Schramm, Wilbur & Roberts, Donald (eds), *The Process and Effects of Mass Communication*, Urbana ILL: University of Illinois Press.

Schudson, Michael (1981), *Discovering the News: A Social History of American Newspapers*, New York: Basic Books.

Schütz, Alfred (1964, 1976), 'Making Music Together: A Study in Social Relationship', in Brodersen, Arvid (ed.), *Alfred Schütz Collected Papers II: Studies in Social Theory*, The Hague: Martinus Nijhoff.

Schwartz, Barry (Dec 1982), 'The Social Context of Commemoration: A Study in Collective Memory', *Social Forces*, vol. 61, no. 2, pp. 374–402.

Schwartz, Barry, Zerubavel, Yael & Barnett, Bernice M. (1986), 'The Recovery of Masada: A Study in Collective Memory', *The Sociological Quarterly*, vol. 27, no. 2, pp. 147–164.

Schwartz, Tony (1972), *The Responsive Chord*, New York: Anchor Press/Doubleday.

Science Museum, http://www.sciencemuseum.org.uk/objects/nrm_-_locomotives_and_rolling_stock/1862–5.aspx, accessed 15 June 2010.

Seaton, Jean (2005), *Carnage and the Media*, London: Penguin/Allen Lane.

Seddon, David (1989), 'Making History: Myths and Realities of the Palestinian Struggle', *Journal of Refugee Studies*, vol. 2, no. 1, pp. 204–216.

Shalin, Dmitri (1986), 'Pragmatism and Social Interactionism', *American Sociological Review*, vol. 51, no. 1.

Siegler MC (01 May 2010), 'Facebook, The Apps Store, and the Sound of Inevitability', *TechCrunch*, http://techcrunch.com/2010/05/01/the-internet-is-cyclical/, accessed 03 May 2010.

(1916), 'Sinn Féin Rebellion Handbook, Easter 1916', *Weekly Irish Times*, Dublin.

Screpanti, Ernesto & Zamagni, Stefano (2005), *An Outline of the History of Economic Thought*, Oxford: Oxford University Press.

Seib, Philip (May-June 2008), 'The Al-Qaeda Media Machine', *Military Review*.

—— (2010), 'Public Diplomacy and the Obama Moment', lecture, Chatham House, London.

Sejnowski, Terence (1998), 'Memory and Neural Networks', in Fara, Patricia & Patterson, Karalyn (eds), *Memory*, Cambridge: Cambridge University Press.

Shapiro, Michael & Fox, Julia (Jan 2002), 'The Role of Typical and Atypical Events in Story Memory', *Human Communication Research*, vol. 28, no. 1, pp. 109–135.

Sharp, Gene (2003), *From Dictatorship to Democracy: A Conceptual Framework for Liberation*, Boston MA: Albert Einstein Institution.

Shatz, Marshall (ed.) (2002), *Bakunin: Statism and Anarchy*, Cambridge: Cambridge University Press.

Shearman, Peter (2004), 'Reconceptualizing Security after 9/11', in Sherman, Peter & Sussex, Matthew (eds), *European Security after 9/11*, Aldershot & Burlington VA: Ashgate.

Shirky, Clay (2008), *Here Comes Everybody: How Change Happens When People Come Together*, London: Penguin.

—— (18 Dec 2009), 'The Net Advantage', *Prospect*, issue 165, http://www.prospect-magazine.co.uk/2009/12/the-net-advantage/, accessed 27 Aug 2010.

Showalter, Elaine (1997), *Hystories: Hysterical Epidemics and Modern Culture*, London: Picador.

Simon, Steven & Benjamin, Daniel (2000), 'America and the New Terrorism', *Survival*, vol. 42, no. 1, IISS.

Sinno, Abdulkader (2008), *Organisations at War in Afghanistan and Beyond*, Ithaca NY & London: Cornell University Press.

Siqueira, Kevin & Sandler, Todd, 'Terrorist Versus the Government: Strategic Interaction, Support and Sponsorship', *Journal of Conflict Resolution*, forthcoming, cited in De Mesquita, Ethan Bueno & Dickson, Eric (April 2007), 'The Propaganda of the Deed: Terrorism, Counterterrorism, and Mobilisation', *American Journal of Political Science*, vol. 5, no. 2, pp. 364–38.

Sklar, Martin (1997), *The Corporate Reconstruction of American Capitalism 1890–1916*, Cambridge: Cambridge University Press.

Skocpol, Theda (1999), *States and Social Revolutions*, Cambridge: Cambridge University Press.

Smelser, Neil (1963*), Theory of Collective Behaviour*, New York: Free Press.

Smith, Graeme (2009), 'What Kandahar's Taliban Say', in Giustozzi, Antonio, *Decoding the New Taliban*, London: Hurst.

Smith, MLR (1995), *Fighting for Ireland? The Military Strategy of the Irish Republican Movement*, London & New York: Routledge.

Smith, Neil (2004), *American Empire: Roosevelt's Geographer and the Prelude to Globalisation*, Berkeley CA: University of California Press.

Smith, Rogers (2004), 'The Politics of Identity and the Tasks of Political Science', in Shapiro, Ian, Smith, Rogers & Masoud, Tarek (eds), *Problems and Methods in the Study of Politics*, Cambridge: Cambridge University Press.

Smith, Rupert (2006), *The Utility of Force: The Art of War in the Modern World*, London: Penguin.

Smythe, Dallas (1977), 'Communications: Blindspot of Western Marxism', *Canadian Journal of Political and Social Theory*, vol. 1, no. 3, pp. 1–27.

Snow, David; Rochford, Burke; Worden, Steven & Benford, Robert (Aug 1986), 'Frame Alignment Processes, Micromobilization, and Movement Participation', *American Sociological Review*, vol. 51, no. 4, pp. 464–481.

Somers, Margaret (Oct. 1994), 'The Narrative Constitution of Identity—a Relational and Network Approach', *Theory and Society*, vol. 23, no. 5, pp. 605–649.

Sontag, Susan (2002), *On Photography*, London: Penguin Books.

Sorel, Georges (1908, 2002), *Reflections on Violence*, Cambridge: Cambridge University Press.

——— (2005), *Reflections on Violence*, Hulme TE & Roth, J, trans., Mineola NY: Dover.

South African Ministry of Culture (6 Feb 2007), 'Ministry of Arts and Culture on Bok van Blerks's Supposed Afrikaans "Struggle Song", De La Rey and Its Coded Message to Fermenting Revolutionary Sentiments', http://www.dac.gov.za/media_releases/06Feb07.html, accessed 15/8/2008.

South African Press Association (06 May 1998), http://www.justice.gov.za/trc/media/1998/9805/s980506b.htm, accessed 20 Dec 2010.

Starbuck, William (Feb 1983), 'Organisations as Action Generators', *American Sociological Review*, vol. 48, pp. 91–102.

Starr, Paul (2004), *The Creation of the Media: Political Origins of Modern Communications*, New York: Basic Books.

Stern, Jessica (2003), *Terror in the Name of God*, New York: Ecco/Harper Collins.

Stern-Rubarth, Edgar (1933), 'The Methods of Political Propaganda', in Wright, Quincy (ed.), *Public Opinion and World-Politics*, Chicago: University of Chicago Press.

Stewart, ATQ (1997), *The Ulster Crisis: Resistance to Home Rule 1912–1914*, Belfast: Blackstaff Press.

Stiglitz, Joseph (2002), *Globalisation and its Discontents*, London: Penguin.

Stiglitz, Joseph & Charlton, Andrew (2004), 'A Development-Friendly Prioritization of Doha Proposals', Initiative for Policy Dialogue, New York: Columbia University.

Stirner, Max (1844, 2009), *Der Einzige und Sein Eigentum*, Charleston SC: Bibliolife.

Stoll, Clifford (1996), *Silicon Snake Oil: Second Thoughts on the Information Highway*, London: Pan.

Stone, Brad (28 Mar 2009), 'Is Facebook Growing Up Too Fast?', *New York Times*, http://www.nytimes.com/2009/03/29/technology/internet/29face.html?_r=1, accessed 30 Sept 2010.

Stone, Norman (1999), *Europe Transformed 1878–1919*, Oxford: Blackwell.

Stothard, Peter, Editor of *The Times*, 1992–2002, interview with N Bolt 21 Apr 2009.

Strachan, Huw (2006), 'Making Civil-Military Relations after Iraq', *Survival*, vol. 48, no. 3, pp. 59–82.

Strauss, Anselm (1963), 'The Hospital and its Negotiated Order', in E Freidson (ed.), *The Hospital in Modern Society*, New York: Free Press.

―――― (1964), *Psychiatric Ideologies and Institutions*, New York: Free Press.

―――― (1978), *Negotiations: Varieties, Contexts, Processes, and Social Order*, San Francisco CA: Jossey-Bass.

Strick Van Linschoten, Alex & Kuehn, Felix (2012), *An Enemy We Created: The Myth of the Taliban-Al Qaeda Merger in Afghanistan*, London: Hurst, 2012.

Strogatz, Steven (2003), *Sync: The Emerging Science of Spontaneous Order*, London: Penguin.

Stuart, Campbell (1920), *Secrets of Crewe House*, London: Hodder & Stoughton.

Suarez, Sandra (2006), 'Mobile Democracy: Text Messages, Voter Turnout and the 2004 Spanish General Election', *Representation*, vol. 42, no. 2.

Subcomandante Marcos (2003), *Our Word is Our Weapon*, New York: Seven Stories Press.

―――― 'Commandante Marcos' interview, http://www.youtube.com/watch?v=jtOX 5fOI2co, accessed 1 July 2009.

―――― 'Subcomandante Marcos y la Cuarta Guerra Mundial' interviewhttp://www.youtube.com/watch?v=bA8uWDZdE4o, accessed 1 July 2009.

Swidler, Ann (Apr 1986), *Culture in Action: Symbols and Strategies*, vol. 51, no. 2, pp. 273–286.

―――― (1995), 'Cultural Power and Social Movements', in Johnston, Hank & Klandermans, Bert (eds), *Social Movements and Culture*, London: UCL Press.

Szanto, George (1978), *Theater & Propaganda*, Austin and London: University of Texas Press.

Taheri, Amir, (12 Feb 2011), p. 24, 'Now Showing in Cairo: A Keystone Kops Coup', *The Times*.

Taleb, Nassim Nicholas (2007), *Fooled by Randomness: The Hidden Role of Chance in Life and the Markets*, London: Penguin.

Taliban (07 Aug 2008), 'The Defeat of the Invaders in Media Field or the Victory of Resistance', www.toorabora.com.

Tangri, Roger (1999), *The Politics of Patronage in Africa: Parastatal, Privatisation and Private Enterprise*, Oxford, James Currey.

Tapscott, Don (2009), *Grown Up Digital: How the Net Generation is Changing Your World*, New York: McGraw-Hill.

Tarrow, Sidney (2005), *The New Transnational Activism*, Cambridge: Cambridge University Press.

Taseer, Aatish (28 Aug 2005), 'A British Jihadist', *Prospect*, issue 113, interview with Hassan Butt.

Tatham, Steve (2008), 'Strategic Communication: A Primer', Advanced Research and Assessment Group, Defence Academy of the United Kingdom.

Taylor, DM & Louis, W (2004), pp. 167–185, 'Terrorism and the Quest for Identity', in Moghaddam F & Marsella, A (eds), *Understanding Terrorism: Psychosocial Roots, Consequences, and Interventions*, Washington, DC: American Psychological Association.

BIBLIOGRAPHY

Taylor, Frederick (2003), *Scientific Management*, Abingdon: Routledge.

Taylor, Philip (1990), *Munitions of the Mind: War Propaganda from the Ancient World to the Nuclear Age*, Wellingborough: Stephens.

Taylor, Verta & Whittier, Nancy (1992), 'Collective Identity in Social Movement Communities', in Morris, Aldon & Mueller, Carol (eds), *Frontiers in Social Movement Theory*, New Haven: Yale University Press.

Terriff, Terry; Karp, Aaron & Karp Regina (eds) (2009), *Global Insurgency and the Future of Armed Conflict: Debating Fourth Generation Warfare*, Abingdon: Routledge.

The Center for Public Integrity, 'Networks of Influence: The Political Power of the Communications Industry', http://projects.publicintegrity.org/telecom/report.aspx?aid=405, accessed 30 Sept 2010.

The Economist (11 Apr 2009), p. 66, 'The Not-So-Big Four'.

—— (23 Jan 2010), pp. 22–24, 'Leviathan Stirs Again: Briefing—the Growth of the State'.

—— (30 Jan 2010), p. 20, 'Special Report on Social Networking'.

—— (13 Feb 2010), p. 71, 'Saturated Mobile Networks: Breaking Up'.

—— (20 May 2010), p. 62, 'First Facebook, Then the World'.

—— (29 May 2010), p. 56, 'More Powerful Than Ever'.

The Free Association (2011), *Moments of Excess: Movements, Protest and Everyday Life*, Oakland CA: PM Press.

The Guardian (04 June 2009), 'Full Text: Barack Obama's Cairo Speech' .

The Guardian/WikiLeaks (26 July 2010), 'A Losing Battle With Taliban's Homemade Weapon'.

The Invisible Committee (2009), *The Coming Insurrection*, Los Angeles CA: Semiotext(e).

The Times (6 Aug 2008), 'The New New World Order', leader.

—— (17 Mar 2011), p. 2, 'Deserted by Obama'.

—— (25 Mar 2011), p. 2, 'Obama, Where Art Thou?'

Thorndyke, P (1979), 'Knowledge Acquisition from Newspapers', *Discourse Processes*, vol. 2, pp. 95–112.

Thompson, John (1995), *The Media and Modernity*, Cambridge: Polity Press.

Thompson, William Irwin (1982), *The Imagination of an Insurrection: Dublin Easter 1916*, West Stockbridge, VA: The Lindisfarne Press.

Thrasher, Frederic (1927), *The Gang: A Study of 1,313 Gangs in Chicago*, Chicago: University of Chicago Press.

Tiefenbrun, Susan (2003), 'A Semiotic Approach to a Legal Definition of Terrorism', *ILSA Journal of International & Comparative Law*, vol. 9, pp. 357–402.

Tilly, Charles (1978), *From Mobilisation to Revolution*, Reading MA & London: Addison-Wesley.

Tone, Wolfe (1791), *An Argument on Behalf of the Catholics of Ireland*, Belfast: The Society of United Irishmen of Belfast.

Tonge, Jonathan (2010), 'From VNSAs to Constitutional Politicians', in Mulaj, Kledja (ed.), *Violent Non-State Actors in World Politics*, London: Hurst.

Touraine, Alain (1990), 'The Idea of Revolution', *Theory, Culture & Society*, vol. 7, pp. 121–141.

BIBLIOGRAPHY

Travis, Alan (20 Aug 2008), 'MI5 Report Challenges Views On Terrorism in Britain', *The Guardian*, http://www.guardian.co.uk/uk/2008/aug/20/uksecurity.terrorism1, accessed 26 Aug 2010.

Trent, Stoney & Doty, James (July-Aug 2005), 'Marketing: An Overlooked Aspect of Information Operations', *Military Review*, pp. 70–74.

Tripathi, Salil (05 June 2009), 'Indians Deserve Better Governance', *Far East Economic Review*, http://www.feer.com/essays/2009/june/indians-deserve-better-governance, accessed 27 July 2009.

Trotsky, Leon (1904), 'The Proletariat and the Revolution', http://www.marxists.org/archive/trotsky/1918/ourrevo/ch02.htm, accessed 30 Sept 2010.

―――― '1905', http://www.marxists.org/archive/trotsky/1907/1905/ch22.htm, accessed 21 June 2011.

Tuchman, Gaye (1972), 'Objectivity as Strategic Ritual: An Examination of Newsmen's Notions of Objectivity', *American Journal of Sociology*, vol. 77, no. 1, pp. 660–679.

Tuchman, Gaye (1978), 'Making News by Doing Work: Routinising the Unexpected', *American Journal of Sociology*, vol. 79, no. 1, pp. 110–131.

Tucker, Robert (1969), *The Marxian Revolutionary Idea*, New York: WW Norton.

Tudor, Henry (1972), *Political Myth*, London: Macmillan.

Tugwell, Maurice (1979), 'Revolutionary Propaganda and Possible Counter-Measures', PhD Thesis, London: Kings College London.

Turkle, Sherry (1995), *Life on the Screen: Identity in the Age of the Internet*, New York: Simon & Schuster.

―――― (Nov 1999), 'Cyberspace and Identity', *Contemporary Sociology*, vol. 28, no. 6, pp. 643–648.

Turkle, Sherry & Papert, Seymour (Autumn 1990), 'Epistemological Pluralism: Styles and Voices within the Computer Culture', *Signs*, vol. 16, no. 1, pp. 128–157.

Turner, Janice (17 July 2010), 'We'll Soon Forget the Ballad of Raoul Moat', *The Times*, p. 21.

Turow, John (1999), *Breaking Up America*, Chicago: University of Chicago Press.

UK Government (2000), 'Terrorism Act 2000', amended, Section 1 (c),

―――― (2010), 'Proscribed Terrorist Groups', http://www.homeoffice.gov.uk/publications/counter-terrorism/proscribed-terror-groups/, accessed 28 Apr 2010.

Ulph, Stephen (2005), 'The "Management of Barbarism: Lays out Al-Qaeda's Military Strategy"', in Heffelfinger, Christopher (ed.), *Unmasking Terror*, Washington, DC: Jamestown Foundation.

UN (2004), 'A More Secure World: Our Shared Responsibility', Report of the Secretary General's High Level Security Panel on Threats, Challenges and Change, http://www.un.org/secureworld/report2.pdf, accessed 30 Sept 2010.

UN Commission of Inquiry (15 Apr 2010), 'Report into the Facts and Circumstances of the Assassination of Former Pakistani Prime Minister Mohtarma Benazir Bhutto'.

UNFPA (2007), 'State of World Population', http://www.unfpa.org/swp/2007/english/introduction.html, accessed 16 Mar 2009.

UN International Telecommunications Union (Dec. 2007), 'Developed Versus Developing Economies: Trends Over Time', http://www.itu.int/ITU-D/ict/statistics/ict/index.html, accessed 26 Jan 2010.

BIBLIOGRAPHY

UNODC (2009), 'World Drug Report', http://www.unodc.org/, accessed 06 July 2009.

Unow, Jaceck (2003/4), 'Modeling the Dynamics of an Information System', *Australasian Journal of Information Systems*, Special Issue.

Urry, John (1990), *The Tourist Gaze*, London: Sage.

—— (2007), *Mobilities*, Cambridge: Polity.

U.S. Army (2007), *U.S. Army Marine Corps Counterinsurgency Field Manual FM 3–24*, Chicago Ill: University of Chicago Press.

U.S. Commission on National Security/21st Century (2001), 'Road Map for National Security: Imperative for Change—Phase III Report'.

U.S. Department of the Army (11 Aug 2003), 'Mission Command: Command and Control of Armed Forces', Field Manual 6–0, Washington, DC: Headquarters of the Army.

U.S. Department of Defense (2006), 'Quadrennial Defense Review: Execution Roadmap for Strategic Communication', Washington, DC.

—— (2007), 'Implementation of the DOD Strategic Communication Plan for Afghanistan', Washington, DC.

—— (15 Jan 2009), 'Capstone Concept for Joint Operations', Version 3, Washington, DC, http://www.jfcom.mil/newslink/storyarchive/2009/CCJO_2009.pdf, accessed 28 Apr 2010.

—— (2010), 'Report on Strategic Communication, December 2009', Washington, DC, http://www.carlisle.army.mil/dime/documents/DoD%20report%20on%20Strategic%20Communication%20Dec%2009.pdf.

U.S. Department of State: (19 Jan 2010), 'Terrorist Organizations', http://www.state.gov/s/ct/rls/other/des/123085.htm, accessed 28 Apr 2010.

U.S. Government Accountability Office (Sept 2009), 'Combating Terrorism', Washington, DC.

U.S. Government Office of Director of National Intelligence (2005), http://www.globalsecurity.org/security/library/report/2005/zawahiri-zarqawi-letter_9jul2005.htm, accessed 1 July 2009.

U.S. Joint Chiefs of Staff (1997), 'Joint Vision 2010', Washington, DC: US Joint Chiefs of Staff.

—— (2000), 'Joint Vision 2020', Washington, DC: US Joint Chiefs of Staff.

Van Blerk, Bok, 'De La Rey', YouTube, http://www.youtube.com/watch?v= fAhH-WpqPz9A, accessed 15 July 2008.

Van Creveld, Martin (1991), *The Transformation of War*, New York: Simon & Schuster.

Van Dijk, Teun (1977), *Text and Context Explorations in the Semantics and Pragmatics of Discourse*, London: Longman.

—— (1980), *Macrostructures: An Interdisciplinary Study of Global Structures in Discourse, Interaction and Cognition*, Hillsdale NJ: Lawrence Erlbaum.

—— (1988), *News as Discourse*, Hillsdale NJ: Erlbaum;

Van Ham, Peter (Sep-Oct.2001), 'The Rise of the Brand State: The Postmodern Politics of Image and Reputation', *Foreign Affairs*, vol. 80, no. 5, pp. 2–6.

Venturi, Franco (2001), *Roots of Revolution: A History of the Populist and Socialist Movements in Nineteenth Century Russia*, London: Phoenix Press.

BIBLIOGRAPHY

Virilio, Paul (2005), *The Information Bomb*, London & New York: Verso.

——— (2006), *Speed and Politics*, Los Angeles CA: Semiotext(e).

Virilio, Paul & Lotringer, Sylvère (1983, 2008), *Pure War*, Los Angeles CA: Semiotext(e).

Vlahos, Michael (2003), 'The Mask of Terror', www.jhuapl.edu/areas/warfare/papaers/TerrorMaskVlahos.pdf, accessed 3 Aug 2007.

——— (2004), 'Culture's Mask: War & Change After Iraq', www.jhuapl.edu/areas/warfare/papaers/CultureMaskVlahos.pdf, accessed 3 Aug 2007.

——— (09 May 2006), '*The Long War: A Self-Fulfilling Prophecy of Protracted Conflict and Defeat*', National Interest online http://www.nationalinterest.org/Article.aspx?id=11982, accessed 27 July 2009

Von Clausewitz, Carl (2008), *On War*, Oxford: Oxford University Press.

Walker, Vicki (Jan 2008), 'All it Takes is Love of History and Five Bucks', *Discover Mid-America*, http://discoverypub.com/feature/2008_01political.html, accessed 27 June 2009.

Wallerstein, Immanuel (1991), 'Culture as the Ideological Battleground of the Modern World-System', in Featherstone, Mike (ed.), *Global Culture: Nationalism, Globalization and Modernity*, London: Sage.

Walsh, Declan (02 Apr 2009), 'Video of Girl's Flogging as Taliban Hand Out Justice', *The Guardian*, http://www.guardian.co.uk/world/2009/apr/02/taliban-pakistan-justice-women-flogging, accessed 16 Apr 2010.

Walter, Barbara (1997), 'The Critical Barrier to Civil War Settlement', *International Organisation*, vol. 51, pp. 335–364.

Walzer, Michael (2006a), 'Just War and Terror', *Philosophia*, vol. 34, pp. 3–12.

——— (2006b), *Just and Unjust Wars*, New York: Basic Books.

Ward, Ken (1989), *Mass Communications and the Modern World*, Basingstoke: Macmillan Education.

Ward, Koral (2008), *Augenblick: The Concept of the "Decisive Moment" in Nineteenth and Twentieth Century Western Philosophy'*, Aldershot: Ashgate.

Wark, McKenzie (2006), 'The Weird Global Media Event and the Tactical Intellectual (version 3.0)', in Chun, Wendy Hui Kyong & Keenan, Thomas (eds), *New Media, Old Media*, New York & London: Routledge.

Wasson, Charles (2006), *System Analysis, Design and, Development: Concepts, Principles and Practices*, Hoboken NJ: John Wiley & Sons.

Watts, Duncan (2004), *Six Degrees: The Science of a Connected Age*, London: Vintage Books.

Weaver, Mary Anne (July/Aug 2006), 'The Short, Violent Life of Abu Musab al-Zarqawi', *Atlantic Magazine*.

Weber, Max (1964), *The Theory of Social and Economic Organization*, New York: Free Press of Glencoe.

Weber, Max (2008), *Economy and Society*, London: Routledge.

Webster, Frank (Dec 2005), 'Making Sense of the Information Age', *Information, Communication & Society*, vol. 8, no. 4, pp. 439–458.

Wedel, Michel & Kamakura, Wagner (1999), *Market Segmentation: Conceptual and Methodological Foundations*, Boston MASS: Kluwer/ISQM.

Weimann, Gabriel (2006), *Terror on the Internet*, Washington, DC: United States Institute of Peace Press.

Weiner, Myron (1995), *The Global Migration Crisis: Challenge to States and to Human Rights*, New York NY: HarperCollins College.

Weinstein, Jeremy (2007), *Inside Rebellion: The Politics of Insurgent Violence*, Cambridge: Cambridge University Press.

Weiss, Michael (2000), *The Clustered World*, Boston MA: Little, Brown.

Welch, Susan; Gruhl, John; Comer, John & Rigdon, Susan (2009), *Understanding American Government*, Boston MA: Wadsworth.

Wenger, Etienne (2004), *Communities of Practice*, Cambridge: Cambridge University Press.

Werenfels, Isabelle (2007), *Managing Instability in Algeria: Elites and Political Change Since 1995*, Abingdon: Routledge.

Wertham, Frederic (1954), *Seduction of the Innocent*, London: Museum Press.

Westen, Drew (2007), *The Political Brain: The Role of Emotion in Deciding the Fate of the Nation*, Philadelphia PA: Public Affairs.

Wheeler, Nicholas (2000), *Saving Strangers: Humanitarian Intervention in International Society*, Oxford: Oxford University Press.

Wheeler, William (1910, 2005), 'The Ant Colony as an Organism', *Journal of Morphology*, vol. 22, no. 2, pp. 307–325.

Wheen, Francis (03 Apr 2010), 'Paradise Postponed', *Financial Times*.

White, R & Fraser, M (2000), 'Personal and Collective Identities and Long-term Social Movement Activism: Republican Sinn Féin', in Stryker, Owens & White (eds), *Self, Identity, and Social Movements*, Minneapolis & London: University of Minneapolis Press.

White, Robert (2006), *Ruairí Ó Brádaigh: The Life and Politics of an Irish Revolutionary*, Bloomington: Indiana University Press.

Whitehead, Neil (ed.) (2004), *Violence*, Santa Fe: School of American Research Advanced Seminar Series & Oxford: James Currey.

Wike, Richard (2006), 'Where Terrorism finds Support in the Muslim World', *Pew Global Attitudes Project*, http://pewresearch.org/pubs/26/where-terrorism-finds-support-in-the-muslim-world, accessed 01 Feb 2010.

WikiLeaks, 'Op-Ed: The Collateral Damage of the WikiLeaks Video', http://www.digitaljournal.com/article/290280, accessed 01 Mar 2011.

Wiktorowicz, Quintan (ed.) (2004), *Islamic Activism: A Social Movement Theory Approach*, Bloomington IND: Indiana University Press.

Wilkinson, Paul (1971), *Social Movement*, New York: Praeger.

——— (1974), *Political Terrorism*, London: Macmillan.

Williams, Evan (06 Feb 2010), *The Virtual Revolution: Enemy of the State*, Programme 2, BBC2.

Williams, Raymond (Nov-Dec 1973), 'Bases and Superstructure in Marxist Cultural Theory', *New Left Review*, no. 82, pp. 3–16.

Williamson, Judith (2002), *Decoding Advertisements: Ideology and Meaning in Advertising*, London & New York: Marion Boyars.

Willis, Paul (1978), *Profane Culture*, London: Routledge.

Wilson, Edmund (1983), *To the Finland Station*, London: Macmillan.

Wilson, James Q (1989), *Bureaucracy: What Government Agencies Do and Why They Do It*, New York: Basic Books.

Windsor, Philip (2002), *Strategic Thinking*, London: IISS Studies in International Security.

Winnaker, Rudolph (Spring 1947), 'The Debate about Hiroshima', *Military Affairs*, vol. 11, no. 1, pp. 25–30.

Winner, Langdon (1986), *The Whale and the Reactor*, Chicago: University of Chicago Press.

Winston, Brian (2005), *Messages: Free Expression, Media and the West from Gutenberg to Google*, Abingdon & New York: Routledge.

Winter, Joseph (19 Nov 2004), 'Telecoms Thriving in Lawless Somalia', *BBC News*, http://news.bbc.co.uk/1/hi/world/africa/4020259.stm, accessed 30 Sept 2010.

Wintrobe, Ronald (2006), *Rational extremism: The Political Economy of Radicalism*, Cambridge: Cambridge University Press.

WIRED (20 Apr 2010), http://www.wired.com/dangerroom/2010/04/2007-iraq-apache-attack-as-seen-from-the-ground/, accessed 04 Mar 2011.

Wohlgelernter, Elli (20 Feb 2003), 'Radical Muslim Groups Targeting Israeli-American "Conspiracy" Expert', *Jerusalem Post*, http://www.religionnewsblog.com/2430/radical-muslim-groups-targeting-israeli-american-conspiracy-expert, accessed 30 Sept 2010.

Wood, Nancy (1999), *Vectors of Memory: Legacies of Trauma in Postwar Europe*, Oxford: Berg.

Woodcock, George (1963), *Anarchism*, Harmondsworth: Penguin.

—— (1986), *Anarchism: A History of Libertarian Ideas and Movements*, Harmondsworth: Penguin.

Woolf, Virginia (1995), *Orlando*, London: Wordsworth.

World Bank (13 July 2009), 'Migration & Development Brief 10'.

Yang, Guobin (2009), *The Power of the Internet in China: Citizen Activism Online*, New York: Columbia University Press.

Yavuz, M Hakan (2003), *Islamic Political Identity in Turkey*, Oxford: Oxford University Press.

Yeats, WB (2000), *The Collected Poems of WB Yeats*, Ware: Wordsworth Poetry Library.

Yerushalmi, Yosef (1982), *Zakhor: Jewish History and Jewish Memory*, Seattle: University of Washington Press.

Yingling, Paul (May 2007), 'A Failure in Generalship', *Armed Forces Journal*.

YouTube HSBC television commercial, 'We recognise how people value things differently', http://www.youtube.com/watch?v=5imDyxNjo-0, accessed 03 July 2009.

——, 'Morning in America Again', http://www.youtube.com/watch?v=EU-IBF8nwSY, accessed 27 July 2009.

——, 'Reagan: A New Beginning' (1984), http://www.youtube.com/watch?v=TRI3G-K0P50, accessed 30 Sept 2010.

——, 'Hamas Releases Gilad Shalit Cartoon in English Version 25 April 2010', http://www.youtube.com/watch?v=Sb8UQCimV4c, accessed 28 May 2010.

Zarrow, Peter (2005), *China in War and Revolution 1895–1949*, Abingdon: Routledge.

Zheng, Pei & Ni, Lionel M (2006), *Smart Phone and Next Generation Mobile Computing*, San Francisco CA: Morgan Kaufmann

Zhao, Shanyang (2006), 'The Internet and the Transformation of the Reality of Everyday Life: Toward a New Analytical Stance in Sociology', *Sociological Inquiry*, vol. 76, no. 4, pp. 458–474.

Zhou, Chiyu (22 Oct 2009), 'Twitter Against Tyrants: New Media in Authoritarian Regimes', Commission on Security & Co-operation in Europe: U.S. Helsinki Commission, http://www.csce.gov/index.cfm?FuseAction=Content Records. ViewTranscript& ContentRecord_id=462&ContentType=H, B&ContentRecordType=B&CFID=2373 6173&CFTOKEN=78050836, accessed 21 Nov 09.

Zolberg, Aristide (1972), 'Moments of Madness', *Politics and Society*, vol. 2, no. 2, pp. 183–207.

Zorbaugh, Harvey Warren (1929), *The Gold Coast and a Slum: A Sociological Study of Chicago's Near North Side*, Chicago: University of Chicago Press.

Zuo, Jiping & Benford, Robert (June 2008), 'Mobilization Processes and the 1989 Chinese Democracy Movement', *Sociological Quarterly*, vol. 36, no. 1. pp. 131–156.

INDEX

9/11 Commission: Report (2004), 191

Abu Sayyaf: ideology of, 35

Adams, Gerry: 101, 103; address to Sinn Féin party conference (1988), 87–8; President of Sinn Féin, 87

Advanced Research Projects Agency Network (ARPANET): origins of, 167–8

Afghanistan: 8, 46, 82, 231, 238–9, 249, 258; Bagram Air Base, 245; Durand Line, 244; ISAF/NATO presence in, 46, 125, 245; Kabul, 41, 124, 126, 245; Kandahar, 245; Operation Enduring Freedom, 158, 185; Pashtun areas of, 244; Soviet Invasion of (1979–89), 9, 185, 231

African National Congress (ANC): 45, 230; Church Street bombing (1983), 103–4; electoral performance of (2004), 84; Maseru outpost killing (1982), 104; Special Operations Units, 103; submission to TRC (1996–7), 104; Umkhonto we Sizwe (MK), 3

Agha-Soltan, Neda: killing of (2009), 177–8, 208

Agora: 178

Aitken, Max (Lord Beaverbrook): Minister of Information, 34

al-Ansar: 247

Al-Jazeera: media output of, 248

al-Neda: 247

Al-Qaeda: 169, 174, 199, 239, 242, 247; affiliates of, 48, 117, 174, 243; brand, 36; insurgency videos, 125; members of, 40, 245; model of, 228, 268; propaganda used by, 47; strategists of, 248

Al-Qaeda in the Arabian Peninsula: 243

Al-Qaeda in Iraq: 243

Al-Qaeda in Maghreb: 243

al-Sahab: 247

al-Sawt al-Jihad: 247

Alexander II, Tsar: assassination of (1881), 31

Algeria: 202; Civil War (1991–2002), 216

Alinsky, Saul: influence of, 110

Amazon.com: MafiaBoy hacking incident (2000), 193

America Online Inc. (AOL): internet services, 165

American Broadcasting Company (ABC): News coverage in aftermath of 9/11, 138

American Fenian Society: founding of (1858), 91